THE FACTS ON FILE
DICTIONARY OF
EDUCATION

Jay M. Shafritz
University of Pittsburgh

Richard P. Koeppe
University of Colorado at Denver

Elizabeth W. Soper
Colorado Department of Education

Facts On File®
New York • Oxford

The Facts On File Dictionary of Education

Library of Congress Cataloging-in-Publication Data

Shafritz, Jay M.
    The Facts On File dictionary of education / Jay M. Shafritz,
Richard P. Koeppe, Elizabeth W. Soper.
        p.   cm.
    ISBN 0-8160-1636-4
    1. Education—Dictionaries.   I. Koeppe, Richard P. II. Soper,
Elizabeth W. III. Title. IV. Title: Dictionary of education.
LB15.S43 1988
370'.321—dc19   88-24554
                                                          CIP

British CIP data available on request

Printed in the United States of America

10 9 8 7 6 5 4 3 2

FOREWORD

In the jargon-filled world of "educationese," the wonder is that a comprehensive school person's dictionary, such as the FACTS ON FILE DICTIONARY OF EDUCATION, has never truly become part of the professional literature. In the other classic professions—law, medicine, the military, and the clergy—an authoritative dictionary focusing solely on the language peculiar to the profession has been an integral part of any respectable professional library for generations. And that's one reason why the FACTS ON FILE DICTIONARY OF EDUCATION is a welcome and long overdue addition to the lore of education.

Its principal strength is that it was written by an experienced and highly successful school practitioner—Dr. Richard P. Koeppe, a longtime local school district superintendent in Colorado—in concert with a team of several well-respected educational scholars, headed by Dr. Jay Shafritz of the University of Pittsburgh. This melding of the practical and academic dimensions ensures that the dictionary is both readily understandable and accurate to a fault.

Moreover, the original draft of the FACTS ON FILE DICTIONARY OF EDUCATION was reviewed by a wide cross section of educators and lay citizens concerned about schooling from diverse perspectives. These professional and lay people serve education in the individual elementary and secondary schools, at the school district level, in intermediate educational units, state departments of education, the state government, in colleges and universities that prepare teachers and school administrators and provide con-tinuing in-service education to them, and in professional associations.

Representatives from all these groups—professional and lay people alike—reviewed the draft and commented on the substance of the dictionary. These are the people who daily make the lexicon of education evolve as a dynamic part of our ever-developing, living English language. They provide counsel and advice on its comprehensiveness, accuracy, clarity of explanation, conciseness of expression, and general format. The result: a book that is a real contribution toward improved communication in and about education.

The comments received were taken seriously by the authors, who incorporated the substance wherever feasible into the final text. This fact, in tandem with the superior quality of the understanding of the subject matter, scholarly research, and plain writing of the authors, makes the FACTS ON FILE DICTIONARY OF EDUCATION a reference book that deserves to be on the desk—or readily available on a nearby shelf—of every person who works in public or private education as a professional, a volunteer, as part of its governance, or as the wordsmiths of the educational media who tell the world, rightly or wrongly, what is happening in the schools.

The FACTS ON FILE DICTIONARY OF EDUCATION is a book whose time has truly come.

Thomas A. Shannon
Executive Director
National School Boards Association
Alexandria, Virginia

AUTHORS' PREFACE

Writing a dictionary of any kind is always an interesting proposition. Where does one start? And an even more difficult question . . . where does one stop? This last question is especially relevant for a dictionary in an ever-changing and extraordinarily diverse field of study such as education.

The media are constantly reporting new concepts and trends in education which would make valuable entries. The professional literature offers a continuous flow of new concepts and references. Furthermore, there are an inordinate number of "experts" in this field. Since practically everybody has gone to school (and had children who went or go to school), all of these legitimate "experts" have strong opinions about the nature of schools and education. This makes for very critical readers.

Consequently, the authors have sought to anticipate a potential audience of knowledgeable critics who will be looking for the most recent educational concepts, references and discoveries. We have also continued to seek out that last elusive entry or reference of substantial historical significance.

This dictionary is designed to be a tool and a reference source for all who wish to have access to knowledge about the theory, practices, terms, concepts, laws, institutions, literature, people and resources concerned with education from the preschool to high school levels. Any dictionary is at best a work in progress. Unless a subject is a dead language or an expired technology, its terminology is constantly changing. This is certainly true of education. Each year, for example, new court decisions, new legislation, new theories and new research findings come into being. This

dictionary seeks to capture and codify the language of education, fully aware that when finished, it will be incomplete. A living language does not wait on publishers' deadlines.

While this effort may be incomplete by its nature, it is nevertheless comprehensive by design. Contained herein are virtually all of the words, terms, phrases, processes, names, laws, and court cases with which those concerned with education would be familiar. The criteria for including entries had to be rather loosely defined because the subject—education—is so broad and overlaps so many other fields such as law, accounting, personnel, psychology, statistics, economics, and medicine. As a rule of thumb, if a term was found in more than one other standard reference or text of the many dozens reviewed, it was included here.

In general, those items which are more central to current concerns of education tend to be given more detailed coverage than those more peripheral to the subject. There are basically two types of definition: (1) those that are given brief glossary descriptions, and (2) those that are given more comprehensive coverage, occasionally in the form of author's comments and interpretations. The references at the end of some of the entries serve as an example of the usage of the term as well as to provide sources for further exploration for the reader.

In addition to the entries that the reader might expect to find in a dictionary concerned with education, there are some special kinds of entries that warrant a word of explanation:

Biographical entries. There are a great many identifications of individuals, both living and dead, who have been significant in the history, writing, research, and practice of education. Such entries are designed to merely identify an individual, that being the purpose of a dictionary. The authors readily concede that some notable individuals may have been excluded or that other individuals may have been described in words too brief to do them justice.

Court cases. Numerous legal decisions that are especially significant to education, mostly those of the U.S. Supreme Court, are included here. Such judicial decisions in their original format are many pages long, and are so for good reason. A brief review of a case, as summarized here, will not have all of the information on which the formal action was based. These entries are intended to give the reader only a cursory understanding of the legal issues. The full legal citation is given with each entry of this type so that the reader may locate the full text of any of these court cases.

Publications. A list of all of the journals and magazines dealing with education would be almost as large as this entire dictionary. Included are only those periodicals that most consistently address the core issues and concerns of educators. Each periodical entry contains a statement of purpose as well as an appropriate address.

Laws. Many laws that directly impact broad educational policy are summarized. The reader should be aware that these entries are necessarily brief summaries of complicated laws that are constantly subject to amendment.

Organizations. Major organizations and professional associations that bear on education have been included though the inclusions certainly do not exhaust the breadth of relevant organizations, particularly those that operate at a more local level. As with publications, an exhaustive list might encompass an entire book of this magnitude.

Tests. Included are descriptions of those commercially available tests and inventories that are most commonly used in education. The test publishers and their addresses are noted.

No one writes a dictionary alone, especially when the work has three authors. The authors are extremely grateful to those individuals who reviewed the initial manuscript and who made valuable comments and suggestions. The reviewers were Gail F. Farwell, professor of guidance and counseling at the University of Wisconsin-Madison; Gerald Kaplan, an attorney specializing in school law; Thomas Shannon, executive director of the National School Boards Association; Robert D. Gilberts, dean of the school of education at the University of Oregon; Calvin M. Frazier, recently retired commissioner of education for the State of Colorado and former president of the National Council of Chief State School Officers; and Alice Kaiser of the University of Pittsburgh. We made extensive use of public domain materials published by a variety of federal government agencies, especially the U.S. Department of Education, and we wish to acknowledge the legions of anonymous public servants who produced the various manuals, glossaries, analyses, directories, and guidelines that we found so useful.

A special acknowledgement must go to Pamela Kramer for her many hours of typing and retyping the manuscript in preparation for submission to the publisher. Melanie Hardaway and Tim Tieperman, our student researchers, are also thanked. Special thanks are due to our various family members who lived through the intensity of this project, including "Cool Colin" who kept his cool while his mom made herself unavailable for more weekends and evenings than we care to acknowledge.

While the authors had considerable assistance in producing this dictionary, all mistakes, omissions or other flaws to be found herein are solely our responsibility.

Jay M. Shafritz
Richard P. Koeppe
Elizabeth W. Soper

A

A-95 review *See* OFFICE OF MANAGEMENT AND BUDGET (OMB) CIRCULAR A-95.

AAA *See* AMERICAN ARBITRATION ASSOCIATION; AUTOMATIC ATTENDANCE ACCOUNTING.

AACD *See* AMERICAN ASSOCIATION FOR COUNSELING AND DEVELOPMENT.

AAO *See* AFFIRMATIVE ACTION OFFICER.

AASA *See* AMERICAN ASSOCIATION OF SCHOOL ADMINISTRATORS.

AB Abbreviation for the Latin "Artium Baccalaureus," meaning bachelor of arts.

AB in Ed (or Education) Bachelor of arts in education.

AB in SecEd (or Secondary Education) Bachelor of arts in secondary education.

abandonment 1. Quitting a job without formally resigning. 2. Deserting a child for whom one is legally responsible; a parent or caretaker leaving a child without adequate supervision or provision for his/her needs for an excessive period of time. State laws vary in defining adequacy of supervision and the length of time a child may be left alone or in the care of another before abandonment is determined. The age of the child also is an important factor. In legal terminology, "abandonment cases" are suits calling for the termination of parental rights. *See also* ABUSE and NEGLECT. 3. Giving up property rights with no intention of reclaiming them. Thus books or equipment can be abandoned if put in the trash or given away. 4. Turning over damaged property to an insurer in order to claim its insured value. 5. Taking a fixed asset off the books after it is no longer serviceable.

abatement 1. Any reduction, decrease, alleviation, or mitigation. 2. An amount subtracted from a full tax. 3. A reduction in a tax assessment. 4. A reduction of a previously recorded expenditure or receipt item by such things as refunds, rebates, and collections for loss or damages to school property.

ABD All but dissertation; a doctoral candidate who has completed all the requirements for a doctorate except a dissertation.

abdication The giving up of an office or responsibility by ceasing to perform its function rather than by formally resigning or relinquishing.

ABE *See* ADULT BASIC EDUCATION.

ability 1. The present power to perform a physical or mental function. 2. An individual's potential to perform. 3. A natural talent. 4. An acquired skill. *See also* APTITUDE.
See Stephen Dakin and A. John Arrowood, "The Social Comparison of Ability," *Human Relations* (February 1981).

ability, academic 1. A facility with those verbal and mathematical skills that are most useful in formal education. 2. Abstract as opposed to mechanical or social skills.

ability, educative A measure of an individual's ability to benefit from, and advance in, traditional schooling.

1

This is expressed as a grade of schooling that can be reached; thus one person's educative ability may be high school graduation while another may have the ability to progress on to a doctorate.

ability, financial 1. A term that refers to the availability of resources of an institution, individual or other entity. 2. A student's ability to pay educational costs. 3. The ability of a public school district to raise revenue by its own resources.

ability grouping 1. Placing pupils in differing learning sections or tracks according to test scores or the subjective judgment of their teachers. This creates a group that can all be taught at the same level. 2. Providing specially designed enrichment programs for gifted and talented pupils for all or part of the school day. 3. Any grouping of children according to a preset criterion such as reading level or intelligence test scores.

See Aage Sorenson and Maureen Hallinan, "Effects of Ability Grouping on Growth in Academic Achievement," *American Educational Research Journal* (Winter 1986).

For a discussion of the efficacy of this practice, *see*: Helen Abadzi, "Ability Grouping Effects on Academic Achievement and Self-Esteem: Who Performs in the Long Run as Expected," *Journal of Educational Research* (September/October 1985).

ability test 1. A performance test designed to reveal a measure of present ability (e.g., a typing test). 2. Any test used to measure intelligence or aptitude. *See* Alexandra K. Wigdoor and Wendell R. Garner, Eds., *Ability Testing: Uses, Consequences, and Controversies* (Washington, D.C.: National Academy Press, 1982).

ability to pay 1. The principle of taxation which holds that the tax burden should be distributed according to a person's wealth. It is based on the assumption that as a person's income increases, the person (whether an individual or a corporation) can and should contribute a larger percentage of income to support government activities. The progressive income tax is based on the ability to pay principle. For the first major analysis of this, *see* "Of Taxes," from Book V, Chapter II, Part II, of Adam Smith's *The Wealth of Nations* (1776). 2. A concept from labor relations and collective bargaining that refers to an employer's ability to assume the costs of requested wage and benefit increases. 3. A financial aid concept referring to a student's (or the student's family's) ability to pay tuition and other educational fees.

Abington School District v. Schempp *See* SCHOOL DISTRICT OF ABINGTON TOWNSHIP V. SCHEMPP.

able 1. A descriptive term for any student whose intellectual abilities are significantly greater than that of other children of the same age. 2. Any student with a high learning capacity in a given field.

Abood v. Detroit Board of Education 431 U.S. 209 The Supreme Court case which in 1977 upheld the constitutionality of an agency shop. *See also* AGENCY SHOP.

abrogation of agreement The formal cancellation of a collective bargaining agreement or any agreement or portion thereof.

absence 1. Nonattendance of a student on a day or half day when school is in session. This frequently is counted to the nearest half day or half session. There are two basic kinds of student absences: excused and unexcused. *See also* DAY OF ABSENCE and SESSION. 2. The nonperformance of assigned duties by a staff member during the hours of the day when such duties are to be performed; short-term unavailability for work, lasting at least one day or normal tour of duty. If an employee is absent from the job for a lesser period, it is usually considered a lateness. Staff absences are often classified as either for personal or professional reasons.

See Nigel Nicholson, Colin A. Brow, and J.K. Chadwick-Jones, "Absence From Work and Job Satisfaction," *Journal of Applied Psychology* (December 1976); and Carol Boyd Leon, "Employed But Not At work: A Review of Unpaid Absences," *Monthly Labor Review* (November 1981).

absence without leave   Absence without prior approval.

absentee   Any worker not present for one or more scheduled days of work.

See John Scherba and Lyle Smith, "Computerization of Absentee Control Programs," *Personnel Journal* (May 1973); and Steve Markham and Dow Scott, "Controlling Absenteeism: Union and Nonunion Differences," *Personnel Administrator* (February 1985).

absenteeism   As defined by the U.S. Bureau of Labor Statistics:

the failure of workers to appear on the job when they are scheduled to work. It is a broad term which is applied to time lost because sickness or accident prevents a worker from being on the job, as well as unauthorized time away from the job for other reasons. Workers who quit without notice are also counted as absentees until they are officially removed from the payroll.

Generally, absenteeism is associated with unnecessary, unexcused, or habitual absences from work.

See Donald R. Winkler, "The Effects of Sick-Leave Policy on Teacher Absenteeism," *Industrial and Labor Relations Review* (January 1980).

absolute standards   Judgments which use standard, nationally recognized criteria to evaluate students or teachers as opposed to merely comparing them to their peers who may not be representative of the population at large.

abstract   1. Intellectual or theoretical; something that does not exist in reality but only in the mind; principles or representatives that reflect reality. 2. A summary of the major aspects of a much larger written or oral presentation as in *Child Development Abstracts* or *Dissertation Abstracts*.

ABT   Bachelor of arts in teaching.

abuse   1. The furnishing of excessive services to beneficiaries, violating regulations, or performing improper practices. 2. Child abuse. 3. Taking unfair or illegal advantage of a privileged position. See also CHILD ABUSE.

abuse and neglect   1. A legal concept involving demonstrable damage or exposure to potential damage of children of minority age who are assumed to be in need of the protection and guardianship of adults. 2. Any evidence of physical or emotional damage to a child or a failure to attend to a child's basic needs. 3. State statutes which typically require that instances of suspected child abuse and neglect be reported to the appropriate authorities. School personnel can be legally charged with failure to report suspected child abuse or neglect in a timely manner.

See Norman S. Ellerstein, Ed., *Child Abuse & Neglect: A Medical Reference* (New York: Wiley, 1981). Janet Mason and L. Poindexter Watts, "The Duty of School Personnel to Report Suspected Abuse and Neglect," *School Law Bulletin* (Spring 1986).

abused parent   A parent who has been abused as a child.

INDICATORS OF CHILD ABUSE AND NEGLECT

Category	Child's Appearance	Child's Behavior	Caretaker's Behavior
Physical Abuse	• bruises, welts, burns, fractures, lacerations, abrasions • blood on clothing or underwear	• wary of physical contact • apprehensive • extreme agression or withdrawal • poor peer relations	• uses harsh discipline • seems unconcerned about child or is overly protective • offers poor explanation for injuries to child • substance abuser
Neglect	• consistently dirty, hungry or inappropriately dressed • tired or listless • without supervision • lacks routine medical care	• delinquent • begs or steals food or material objects • misses school	• chaotic home life • apathetic or depressed • chronic illness or mental disorder • substance abuser
Emotional Abuse	• little tangible evidence	• overly compliant or passive • extremely aggressive or demanding • engages in inappropriately adult or infantile behavior • lags in development	• belittles or blames child • cold and rejecting • treats siblings unequally • seems unconcerned about child • substance abuser

academic 1. A course of study in high school which meets minimum requirements for college admission. 2. A professor or researcher who deals with an academic subject area in a higher education establishment. 3. The liberal arts in general. 4. Having to do with ideas; theoretical. 5. Any system of formal education.

academic achievement A measure of knowledge gained in formal education usually indicated by test scores, grade point averages, and degrees.

academic aptitude 1. The ability to deal with intellectual abstractions. 2. Those inherent and learned capabilities needed for success in traditional formal schooling; scholastic aptitude. Thus, the leading academic aptitude test is the Scholastic Aptitude Test (SAT). 3. A projection of performance capability usually measured by a test. Sometimes, a projected judgment based on cumulative data.

academic dress 1. The gowns, mortarboard caps and hoods that students earn the right to wear upon graduation. 2. Things worn to indicate an office in a university; for example, a university president might wear academic insignia, a chain and medallion of office.

academic enrichment Adding additional material to a course of study to increase the depth of knowledge potential. This can be done for an entire class or limited to those students capable of dealing with the subject in a more sophisticated manner.

academic freedom 1. Intellectual freedom in an educational setting at any level. 2. Freedom of expression within an academic community. 3. The right claimed by teachers, especially those in higher education, to teach and publish without political interference or institutional censorship.

See Richard Hofstadter and Walter P. Metzger, *The Development of Academic Freedom in The United States* (New York: Columbia University Press, 1952); Russell Kirk, *Academic Freedom: An Essay in Definition* (Chicago: Henry Regnery Co., 1955); Sidney Hook, *Academic Freedom and Academic Anarchy* (New York: Cowles, 1970); and Edmund L. Pingoffs, ed., *The Concept of Academic Freedom* (Austin: University of Texas Press, 1975).

See PERRY V. SINDERMANN.

academic standing 1. The relative position of a student vis-à-vis all other students; thus a student may be first, fifteenth, or one-hundredth in a class. 2. A student's performance expressed in terms of grade point average.

academic year *See* REGULAR SCHOOL TERM.

academically gifted *See* GIFTED.

academician 1. A scholar. 2. A professor in a higher education institution who teaches in a field of academic substance.

academy 1. A private high school. *See* Theodore R. Sizer, *The Age of Academies* (New York: Teachers College Press, Columbia University, 1964). 2. A four-year post-secondary school or junior college; for example, a military academy. 3. The world of higher education in general. 4. A professional society or institute for the advancement of an art or science. 5. A building or institution for the study, practice or advancement of the fine arts. 6. Plato's school in Ancient Greece.

Accelerated College Enrollment Program (ACE) A program for high school students whereby they can enroll in regular courses on a university campus and receive regular university credit prior to their graduation from high school and their formal university matriculation. The program is administered by the College Board.

accelerated college entrance The admission to college of students who have demonstrated exceptional academic aptitudes before they have completed the normal four years of high school. Some colleges allow this if a student has completed all of the minimum requirements for high school graduation by the end of the junior year.

accelerated promotion A promotion in school indicating progress that is more rapid than the usual practice; this may involve a "double promotion" (two grades' progress in one year) or some other arrangement for promoting a child at a rate more rapid than one grade per year.

acceleration 1. The completion of a predetermined amount of schoolwork in less time than is required normally. 2. Programs that allow gifted and talented pupils to complete minimally required schoolwork in less than the normal period. *See* J. A. Kulik and C.C. Kulik, "Synthesis of Research on Effects of Accelerated Instruction," *Educational Leadership*, 42:2 (1984).

acceleration program One approach to education for gifted children, which involves student progress through an educational program at a rate faster than conventional. There are two types of acceleration: subject matter acceleration, where a student is allowed to take a given course earlier than would typically be the case; and grade acceleration, where a student is allowed to skip an entire grade and take a complete program of courses more advanced than usual. *See* ACCELERATED PROMOTION. Contrast with ENRICHMENT PROGRAM. *See* GIFTED CHILDREN.

acceptance 1. A teacher or any other individual's dealing with a student by not making value judgments on his or her behavior; such "acceptance" is designed to improve the student's self-image. 2. Being admitted to an educational institution.

acceptance fee A sum of money required by colleges of a student who has just been accepted for admission to hold a place in the next entering class. This fee, which amount varies greatly, is generally not refundable but is usually applicable to normal tuition and fees.

accession rate Also called hiring rate. The number of employees added to a payroll during a given time period, usually expressed as a percentage of total employment.

accident frequency rate As computed by the Bureau of Labor Statistics, the total number of disabling injuries per million hours worked.

accident prevention The total planned effort to eliminate the causes and severity of injuries and accidents in an organization, an industry or a building.

accident severity rate Generally computed as the number of work days lost because of accidents per thousand hours worked.

accident and sickness benefits Any of a variety of regular payments made to employees who lose time from work due to off-the-job disabilities occasioned by unfortunate events or illness.

accidental death benefit A feature found in some life insurance policies that provides for payment of additional amounts to the beneficiary if the insured party dies as a result of an accident. When such provisions allow for an accidental death benefit that is twice the normal value of the policy, they are known as "double-indemnity" provisions.

accident-proneness The concept implies that certain kinds of personalities are more likely to have accidents than others. However, psychological research supports the assertion that accident-proneness is more related to situational factors than to personality factors. For the classic analysis on the subject, *see* A.G. Arbous and J.E. Kerrich, "The Phenomenon of Accident-Proneness," *Industrial Medicine and Surgery* (April 1953).

Nevertheless, Joseph T. Kunce established a relationship between "Vocational Interest and Accident Proneness," in the *Journal of Applied Psychology* (June 1967).

accommodation Under Piaget's theory of learning, refers to the modification of an individual's behavior and cognitive understanding of the world in response to a changing environment and the introduction of new phenomena. The basic conceptual structure shifts, i.e. the old "accommodates" to the new (contrast with ASSIMILATION).

account A self-contained financial record-keeping system for one particular subject or type of transaction.

account, controlling See CONTROLLING ACCOUNT.

account, property See PROPERTY ACCOUNT.

account, summary See SUMMARY ACCOUNT.

accountability 1. The extent to which one is responsible to a higher authority—legal or organizational—for one's actions in society at large or within one's particular organizational position; to be answerable for how authority has been exercised and responsibilities discharged. 2. The capability and the responsibility to account for the expenditure of money and the commitment of other resources in terms of the results achieved. This involves both the stewardship of money and other resources and the evaluation of achievement in relation to specified goals. 3. The provision of evidence that a program or process is achieving its stated goals. In education, accountability by the system (or individual classroom, building or district) may be required by students, parents, administrators, school boards, or public funding agencies, including taxpayers. Various approaches or models can be used to evaluate programs or systems for the purpose of accountability, such as the Planning, Programming, Budget System or Management by Objectives. COMPETENCY-BASED TESTING is an approach that can be utilized to measure minimum student achievement. Professional reaction to accountability measures is often negative due to a perceived infringement upon professional autonomy.

See Frank J. Sicard and Richard K. Jantz, eds., *Accountability in American Education* (Boston: Allyn and Bacon, 1972); Sidney P. Marland, "Accountability in Education," *Teachers College Record* (February 1972); and T. Martin, George E. Overholt, et al., *Accountability in American Education: A Critique* (Princeton, N.J.: Princeton Book Co., 1976); Maurice Kogan, *Education Accountability: An Analytic Overview* (Dover, N.H.: Hutchinson Education, 1986).

accountant A person who, by virtue of education and experience, is assumed to be competent to (1) design accounting systems, and (2) record, classify, and summarize financial transactions and interpret and report on the results of financial operations and on the financial status of a school district.

accounting   Generally speaking, the procedure for maintaining systematic records of happenings, occurrences, and events relating to persons, objects, or money and summarizing, analyzing, and interpreting the results of such records.

Cash accounting is the recording of transactions at the time payments are actually made and received. *Accrual accounting* means that revenues are recorded when they are earned, and expenses are recorded as they are incurred.

accounting, financial   *See* FINANCIAL ACCOUNTING.

accounting, memorandum   *See* MEMORANDUM ACCOUNTING.

accounting, noncyclic   A financial record-keeping approach in which books are not closed at the end of fiscal periods (for example, the end of a month or a year). Instead, information cycles through the system continuously, and current financial reports are "pulled" at (and for) any point in time they are desired by management. Noncyclic accounting is assisted by a computerized accounting system.

accounting, single fund   *See* SINGLE FUND ACCOUNTING.

accounting cycle   The repetitive processing of financial transactions during a specified time—typically one month. The basic steps in the accounting cycle are: (1) enter transactions in journals, (2) balance the journals, (3a) post information from the journals to the general ledger, (3b) post information from the journals to the subsidiary ledger accounts, (4) reconcile and balance the ledger accounts, (5) prepare financial statements, and (6) use the information to improve operations. *See also:*
   BALANCE SHEET
   FINANCIAL STATEMENTS

GENERAL LEDGER
JOURNAL
JOURNALIZING
OPERATING STATEMENT
SUBSIDIARY LEDGER

accounting equation   The mathematical representation of the basic relationships between parts of a financial statement. For example, the accounting equation for the relationship among assets, liabilities and fund balances (on a balance sheet) is:
   A = L (+) FB
   Assets = Liabilities (+) Fund
   Balances

accounting ledgers   *See* LEDGER.

accounting period   A period at the end of which and for which financial statements are prepared; for example, July 1 to June 30.

accounting principles   *See* GENERALLY ACCEPTED ACCOUNTING PRINCIPLES.

Accounting Principles Board   The body within the American Institute of Certified Public Accountants (AICPA) that establishes and revises generally accepted accounting principles. *See also* FINANCIAL ACCOUNTING STANDARDS BOARD and GENERALLY ACCEPTED ACCOUNTING PRINCIPLES.

accounting system, double entry   *See* DEBITS AND CREDITS.

accounts payable   Amounts owed to others for goods and services received and assets acquired.

accounts receivable   Amounts due from others for goods furnished and services rendered.

accreditation   1. The process by which an organization evaluates and recognizes a program of study or services or an institution as meeting certain predetermined standards. The recognition is also called accreditation. Similar assessment of individuals is called "certification." 2. An official decision by a state Department of Education, or another recognized agency having official authority, that, in its judgment, the unit under review has met the established standards of quality (which may or may not have legal status).

accreditation status   That status held by an institution on the basis of evaluation by state, regional, national, or professional accrediting agencies. The accreditation status of an institution often bears upon the validity of the credits earned from it by an individual for his or her certification purposes.

accrediting agency   An organization which has the formal authority to promulgate standards for educational institutions or programs and to sanction those institutions or programs that meet the established criteria for educational effectiveness.

accrual   *See* ACCOUNTING.

accrue   To record revenues when earned or when levies are made, and to record expenditures as soon as they result in liabilities, regardless of when the revenue is actually received or the payment is actually made. Sometimes, the term is used in a restricted sense to denote the recording of revenues earned but not yet due, such as accrued interest on investments and the recording of expenditures that result in liabilities that are payable in another accounting period, such as accrued interest on bonds.

accrued   Due and payable but not yet paid; accrued expenses are those that have been incurred and have not been paid as of a given date.

accrued interest   Earned monies accumulated between interest dates but not yet due.

accrued interest on investments purchased   Earned monies on investments between the last payment date and date of purchase.

accrued interest payable   Earned monies which are due and payable and have been earned and have been recorded as revenue but which have not been collected.

accrued interest receivable   Earned monies which have been recorded as revenue but which have not been collected.

accrued liabilities   Amounts owed but not yet due; for example, accrued interest on bonds or notes.

accrued revenue   Levies made or other revenue earned and not collected regardless of whether due or not.

acculturation   1. Learning, understanding, assimilating and/or absorbing aspects of another culture through extensive contact with that culture. 2. The process of adjusting to the demands of a particular culture or organization. 3. A primary phenomenon that happens to children in school.

ACE   *See* ACCELERATED COLLEGE ENROLLMENT PROGRAM.

achievement   1. Accomplishment of specified objectives. 2. Past performance. 3. What an individual or organization has accomplished in the past, in contrast with "ability," which refers to what an individual or organization can do now (in the present) or in the future. *See also* ABILITY and APTITUDE.

achievement age   The performance on a test stated in terms of the chronological age for which such performance is expected or average.

achievement battery   *See* ACHIEVEMENT TEST.

achievement drive   Also called achievement need. The motivation to strive for high standards of performance in a given area of endeavor. For the classic work on achievement motivation, *see* David C. McClelland, *The Achieving Society* (Princeton: Van Nostrand Reinhold Co., 1961).

Also see David C. McClelland, "Achievement Motivation Can be Developed," *Harvard Business Review* (November-December 1965); Perry Pascarella, *The New Achievers* (New York: The Free Press, 1984); David O. Levine, *The American College and the Culture of Aspiration* (Ithaca: Cornell University Press, 1986).

achievement quotient   A ratio of expected and actual performance, usually on a standardized test.

achievement test   An examination that measures the extent to which a person has acquired certain information or mastered certain skills, usually as a result of specific instruction.

A collection of achievement tests designed to measure levels of skill or knowledge in a variety of areas is called an achievement battery.

See Norman E. Gronlund, *Constructing Achievement Tests*, 2nd ed. (Englewood Cliffs, N.J.: Prentice-Hall, 1977).

acquired ability   Any skill that is gained by individual effort as opposed to those innate skills that are inherited.

across-the-board increase   An upward adjustment in wages, whether expressed in dollars or percentage of salary, given to an entire workforce.

ACT   *See* AMERICAN COLLEGE TESTING PROGRAM.

acting out   1. Aggressive or sexual behavior explained by some psychoanalytic theorists as carrying out fantasies or expressing unconscious feelings and conflicts. 2. Children's play or play therapy activities used as a means of expressing hitherto repressed feelings. 3. The behavior of an abusive parent who may be unconsciously and indirectly expressing anger toward his or her own parents or other significant person. 4. Any misbehavior in school that calls attention to itself.

action organization   A nonprofit organization which devotes a substantial amount of effort to seeking to influence legislation or participating in a political campaign to aid or oppose a candidate for public office or to support or defend a ballot proposition.

action plan   A description of the specific steps and responsibilities involved in achieving an objective or goal.

action research   In its broadest context, the application of the scientific method to practical problems. As the basic model underlying organization development, action research is the process of collecting data about an ongoing organizational system to feed back into the system, then altering a variable within the organizational system in response to this data or testing a hypothesis and evaluating the results by collecting more data. The process is repeated as needed. Compare to ORGANIZATION DEVELOPMENT.

See Gerald I. Susman and Roger D. Evered, "An Assessment of the Scientific Merits of Action Research," *Administrative Science Quarterly* (December 1978); and Michael Peters and Viviane Robinson, "The Origins and Status of Action Research," *The Journal of Applied Behavioral Science* 20:2 (1984).

actionable   An act or occurrence that provides adequate reason for a grievance or lawsuit.

active listening   A counseling technique in which the counselor listens to both the facts and the feelings of the speaker. Such listening is called "active" because the counselor has the specific responsibilities of showing interest, of not passing judgment, and of helping the speaker to work out his or her problems. When the other person gives a positive or expanded response, those are indicators of success in the active listening processes. For a discussion, *see* Carl R. Rogers and Richard E. Farson, "Active listening," *Readings in Management: An Organizational Perspective*, edited by C.R. Anderson and M.J. Gannon (Boston: Little, Brown, 1977).

active membership status   The membership status of students who have attended classes during a given school term and have not withdrawn or been assigned to inactive status because of being absent for a given number of consecutive days.

active response   1. Participation in the learning process that involves doing, making, moving, solving, or any activity relevant to the idea or concept being taught. 2. An important component of programmed instruction. 3. Anything other than simply looking and listening that will enhance the learner's acquisition of new skills or knowledge.

active vocabulary   The words that a person can readily use in speaking and writing. This is in contrast to the larger passive vocabulary of words that can be recognized when used by another source.

activity   1. A learning situation. 2. A detailed step in a work plan; for example, for a project, a subtask. The most detailed and shortest duration statement of effort in a work plan. 3. A specific and distinguishable line of work performed by one or more individuals or organizational components for the purpose of discharging a function or sub-function for which the unit or individual is responsible. For example, food inspection is an activity performed in the discharge of the public health function. *See also* BUDGET ACTIVITY and FUNCTIONAL CLASSIFICATION.

activity fund   An account created to record the income and expenses for student activities; for example, football and baseball games, concerts, plays, etc.

activity learning   Any learning process in which a student must do something other than sit and listen; for example, conduct an experiment, make a model or research facts.

activity ratio   Any measure of how well an organization manages its resources that uses ratios or rates. *See also* RATIO and RATIO ACCOUNTING.

activity statement   *See* OPERATING STATEMENT.

activity therapy   Using leisure activities (art, drama, music, athletics, etc.) for the purposes of behavioral change, growth or modification of some type.

actuarial projections   Mathematical and statistical calculations involving the rate of mortality for a given group of people.

actuary   A specialist in the mathematics and statistics of insurance.

ACYF   *See* ADMINISTRATION FOR CHILDREN, YOUTH, AND FAMILIES.

ad hoc   A Latin phrase meaning "for this special purpose" or "for this one time." In education, frequently applied to committees that are assembled for a particular function.

ad hoc arbitrator   An arbitrator selected by the parties involved to serve on one case. Nothing prevents the arbitrator from being used again if both parties agree. *Ad hoc* or temporary, single-case arbitration is distinguished from "permanent" arbitration, where arbitrators are named in an agreement to help resolve disputes about an agreement that may arise any time during the life of the agreement. *See also* ARBITRATION.

ad hoc committee   A committee created for a specific task or purpose whose existence ceases with the attainment of its goal.

ad-hocracy   Alvin Toffler's term, in *Future Shock* (New York: Random House, 1970) for "the fast-moving, information-rich, kinetic organization of the future, filled with transient cells and extremely mobile individuals." Adhocracy is a contraction of ad hoc (Latin for "to this" or temporary) and bureaucracy.
  See George A. Miller, "Beyond Adhocracy," *Pacific Sociological Review* (January 1977); and Henry Mintzberg and Alexandra McHugh, "Strategy Formation in an Adhocracy," *Administrative Science Quarterly* (June 1985).

ad valorem taxes levied   Taxes levied on the assessed valuation of real and personal property located within the legal limits of a school district. Separate accounts may be maintained for real property and for personal property.

ad valorem taxes levied by another governmental unit   Taxes levied for school purposes by a governmental unit other than a school district. In such cases the school district may not be the final authority, within legal limits, in determining the amount to be raised. After a district has determined that a certain amount of revenue is necessary, another governmental unit may exercise discretionary power in reducing or increasing the amount. Separate accounts may be maintained for real property and for personal property.

ADA   Average daily attendance. *See* AVERAGE DAILY ATTENDANCE.

adaptation   1. Under Piaget's theory of learning, an underlying function of a human being's interaction with the environment; the ability to experience the external environment and adjust internally in response. 2. An individualization in scope or sequence of instruction or the introduction of a mechanical aid of any kind to accommodate to individual differences that interfere with instruction. Examples of adaptations include enlarged print for a partially sighted student, a picture recipe for a non-reader, and a head-worn pointer for a physically handicapped student.

adapted education   1. In general, changes in instruction that are intended to address individual needs. 2. May refer to substantial modifications in curriculum and academic expectations for students who cannot reasonably be expected to achieve typical grade level requirements and whose educational programs may deviate significantly from the regular school program.

adapted physical education (APE)   Programs in physical education that have been modified to accommodate the needs of students who are physically or mentally handicapped.
  See H. Harrison Clarke and David H. Clarke, *Developmental and Adapted Physical Education*, 2nd ed. (Englewood Cliffs, N.J.: Prentice-Hall, 1978).

adaptive acceleration   Informally allowing, indeed encouraging, an able child to work at a higher grade level than the rest of a class.

adaptive behavior   A psychosocial term that refers to learned skills that are situation-specific and that reflect a person's ability to accommodate to his or her environment.

Adaptive Behavior Scales   An interview-based instrument that is designed to measure functional skill development in individuals who have developmental disabilities. The scale assesses adaptive behavior in several areas such as independent functioning, physical development, communication, economic activity, and socialization and is used for ages three to adult. It is published by:

American Association on Mental Deficiency
5210 Connecticut Avenue, NW
Washington, DC 20015

adaptive education   A general term referring to modifications or changes in instructional strategies, techniques, materials, or expectations to address individual differences. For a research analysis estimating the effects, see Hersholt Waxman et al., "Adaptive Education and Student Outcomes: A Quantitative Synthesis," *Journal of Educational Research* (March/April 1985).

See also D. Rothrock, "The Rise and Decline of Individualized Instruction," *Educational Leadership*, 39:(1982).

adaptive program   A type of programmed or computer assisted instruction that changes the presentation of the teaching material according to the pattern of learner responses. The speed, sequence, level of difficulty or other aspects of the presentation can all be adjusted to increase the likelihood of correct responses. *See also* ATTENTION DEFICIT DISORDER.

addiction   *See* DRUG ADDICTION.

adjunctive program   A term that is sometimes used to refer to a self-teaching approach that utilizes the presentation of a series of questions at the end of a text, or a portion of a text, so that the reader can monitor his or her level of acquisition of the material.

adjustable rate mortgage   Also flexible rate loan. A mortgage which can vary in any of its terms during its life, as agreed on in the mortgage contract. Typically, the initial year(s) interest rate is lower than the rate offered on a standard fixed rate mortgage, and subsequent years' interest rates change with an annually accepted index (for example, the U.S. Treasury bill rate.) *See also* MORTGAGE.

adjusted case   According to the National Labor Relations Board, labor disputes in which an informal settlement agreement is executed and compliance with its terms is secured. The central element in an "adjusted" case is the agreement of the parties to settle differences without recourse to litigation.

adjusted routing patterns   An adaptation of the established school bus routings. One use is to return to their homes those students involved in school activities in after-school hours.

adjustment entries   Also adjusting journal entries. An accounting procedure used at the close of a fiscal period (for example, a school year) to record income and expenses in the proper period, to make the operating statement reflect the correct income, to adjust the balance sheet account balances to actual balances, and to correct errors. *See also:*

ACCOUNTING CYCLE
DEPRECIATION
FINANCIAL STATEMENTS
FISCAL YEAR
OPERATING STATEMENT

Adler, Mortimer J. (1902-) A 20th-century philosopher, educator, and author of numerous books including *The Revolution in Education* (1958) and *Reforming Education* (1977). Adler was one of the early proponents of the educational reform movement in the United States during the 1970s and 1980s. In 1982 he wrote the first of his "Paideia Trilogy," *The Paideia Proposal*, which was followed in 1983 by *Paideia Problems and Possibilities* and in 1984 by *The Paideia Program*. These books, which suggested substantial educational reforms, have sparked much response in the literature. *See* PAIDEIA PROPOSAL.

Adler v. Board of Education 342 U.S. 485 (1952) The Supreme Court ruling that allowed for individuals to be disqualified for employment in the public schools because of membership in proscribed organizations. This ruling has been severely restricted by subsequent rulings.

ADM *See* AVERAGE DAILY MEMBERSHIP.

administration 1. The management and direction of the affairs of governments and institutions. 2. The execution and implementation of public policy. 3. The time in office of a chief executive such as a president, governor, or superintendent. 4. In schools, administration refers specifically to the superintendent and his or her coadministrators, including building principals, who are responsible for implementing school district policy as established by the school board.

administration areas Building areas devoted to school business activities, pupil personnel management, or public relations where such areas are not designated for other purposes.

administration, central The administrative authority of an entire school system.

administration, educational *See* EDUCATIONAL ADMINISTRATION.

administration building A building used primarily for housing personnel and equipment engaged in activities which have as their purpose the general regulation, direction, and control of the affairs of the school district that are systemwide and not confined to one school, subject, or narrow phase of school activity.

Administration for Children Youth and Families (ACYF) The federal agency of the Department of Health and Human Services that administers HeadStart and other programs.
ACYF
Department of HHS
200 Independence Avenue, S.W.
Washington, DC 20201
(202) 245-6296

administrative accountability That aspect of administrative responsibility by which officials are held answerable for general notions of democracy and morality as well as for specific management responsibilities.

administrative action Any step taken by an administrator in the general regulation, direction, or control of the affairs of the organizational unit.

administrative advocacy The presentation of alternative policies to an administrative agency. This practice recognizes that public administration is a highly political process involving significant differences of judgment. The most feasible course of action often emerges from the competition produced when each interested group pleads for the cause that it represents, whether that cause be more funds to carry out agency policies, the survival of a particular program, or the desire for a more efficient system of administrative decision making.

See Paul Davidoff, "Advocacy and Pluralism in Planning," *Journal of the American Institute of Planners* (December 1965); William W. Vosburgh and Drew Hyman, "Advocacy and Bureaucracy: The Life and Times of a Decentralized Citizen's Advocacy Program," *Administrative Science Quarterly* (December 1973); and Jeffrey M. Berry, "Beyond Citizen Participation: Effective Advocacy Before Administrative Agencies," *Journal of Applied Behavioral Science* (October-December 1981).

administrative agency   1. A unit of an executive branch of government set up to implement a law. 2. Any civilian governmental body (whether it be a board, bureau, department or individual), other than a court or legislature, which deals with the rights of private parties by adjudication, rulemaking, investigation, prosecuting, etc. 3. In the context of labor relations, any impartial private or governmental organization that oversees or facilitates the labor relations process.

administrative analysis   Totality of the approaches and techniques that allow an organization to assess its present condition in order to make adjustments that further enhance the organization's ability to achieve its goals. See also SYSTEMS ANALYSIS.

administrative assistant   One who aids an executive officer in performing his or her assigned activities in an education agency.

administrative board   A body of an organization which is mandated directly to govern the day-to-day administrative affairs of the organiza-

tion. The administrative board operates in contrast to a policy-making board that is not necessarily involved in day-to-day administrative affairs. See also BOARD OF DIRECTORS and GOVERNANCE.

administrative cost rate   The percent of total expenses budgeted (as in a grant) or expended for administrative costs.

administrative costs   Also administrative expenses. Costs incurred to administer or manage an organization or program. Often, a grantor will stipulate or negotiate maximum allowable administrative costs or an administrative cost rate.

administrative intern   One who performs activities that are aimed at learning and that are a part of an educational or training plan. The intern, whose work may be teaching or administration, is closely supervised and his or her performance is periodically evaluated.

administrative jurisdiction   A geographic area used as the basis for performing one or more administrative functions. Examples: county, town, sewer district, water district, school district, police precinct.

administrative monitoring   A type of supervision and evaluation which involves the educational administrator in investigating the degree to which teachers and other staff are carrying out their responsibilities and seeing to it that program objectives are being met.

administrative morality   The use of ethical, political, or social precepts to create standards by which the quality of public administration may be judged.

See Paul H. Appleby, *Morality and Administration in American Govern-*

ment (Baton Rouge: Louisiana State University Press, 1952); and Joel L. Fleishman, Lance Liebman and Mark H. Moore, eds., *Public Duties: The Moral Obligations of Government Officials* (Cambridge: Harvard University Press, 1981).

administrative objective   *See* OBJECTIVE, ADMINISTRATIVE.

administrative order   A directive carrying the force of law, issued by an administrative agency or executive officer. An executive may issue an executive or administrative order in lieu of a specific or directive by acting under his or her "general powers."

administrative personnel School staff members who are primarily engaged in activities which have as their purpose the general regulation, direction, and control of affairs as opposed to classroom teaching.

administrative remedy   A means of resolving a difference between parties by going to an administrative agency rather than the courts for a decision. People may be required to "exhaust all administrative remedies" by submitting their problems to the proper agency before taking their case to court. In civil rights cases this is often not required due to the lack of respect for administrative actions or commitment to remedies.

administrative staff members per 1,000 students in average daily membership   The number representing the total full-time equivalency of principal assignments, assistant principal assignments, central administrative staff assignments (including area administrators and their staffs), and assignments for supervising, managing, and directing academic departments in the schools during a given period of time, multiplied by

1,000 and divided by the average daily membership of students during this period.

administrative team   1. In large school districts, the superintendent of schools and his or her immediate deputies, associates, and assistants. 2. In smaller school districts, all of the above plus individual school principals.

administrative unit   1. A management entity for a geographic area, which for specified public school purposes is under the control of a board of education and the supervision of one or more administrative officers. 2. A subsection within a larger organization that handles specific administrative functions for the organization (e.g., personnel services).

administrator   1. Any manager. 2. The head of a government agency, such as a superintendent of schools. 3. A staff member who has been given the responsibility to manage or direct the activities of a school district or portion of these activities.

admission test   An examination that may be used as a part of the selection procedure for acceptance to an educational institution or, as in some public colleges, as a device for validating work of doubtful quality.

admissions   Money received for a school-sponsored activity such as a dance or football game. Admissions may be recorded in separate accounts according to the type of activity.

ADO   *See* ALLEGED DISCRIMINATORY OFFICIAL.

adolescence   A stage of human development that individuals generally go through during their teenage years. This period includes growth toward sexual maturity, independence, and an orientation of identification focused on peers. It is also the time in life when probably the greatest conflict exists between the drive for individuality and the desire for conformity. Adolescence is a time of obvious physical changes as well as emotional upheavals.

See Ronald W. Tyrell et al., *Growing Pains in the Classroom: A Guide for Teachers of Adolescents* (Englewood Cliffs, N.J.: Prentice-Hall, 1977); Arthur Jersild et al., *The Psychology of Adolescence* (New York: Macmillan, 1978); Boyd McCandless and Richard Coop, *Adolescents: Behavior and Development*, 2nd ed. (New York: Holt, Rinehart and Winston, 1979); James F. Adams, ed., *Understanding Adolescence: Current Developments in Adolescent Psychology*, 4th ed. (Boston: Allyn and Bacon, 1980); Joseph Adelson, ed., *Handbook of Adolescent Psychology* (New York: John Wiley and Sons, 1980); and Franklin E. Zimring, *The Changing Legal World of Adolescence* (New York: Free Press, 1982).

adolescence, early   The time between the ages of approximately 12 to 16 (later for boys than girls) when the onset of adult sexuality (puberty) occurs. Primary changes include menstruation for girls and sexual potency for boys. Secondary sex characteristics that appear are pubic and facial hair and subcutaneous fat for girls. The individual can experience intense emotional swings during this time, which is why many educators choose not to work in junior high schools.

See Jerome Kagan and Robert Coles, eds., *Twelve to Sixteen: Early Adolescence* (New York: W.W. Norton, 1972).

adult   An individual who has reached a specified minimum legal age of adulthood, usually 18 years. *See also* LEGAL ADULT.

adult basic education   Learning experiences concerned with the fundamental tools of learning for adults who have never attended school or who have interrupted formal schooling and need this knowledge and these skills to raise their level of education, to increase self-confidence and/or self-determination, to prepare for an occupation, and to function more responsibly as citizens.

See Angelica Cass and Arthur P. Crabtree, *Adult Elementary Education* (New York: Noble and Noble, 1956).

adult education program   A program of instruction primarily for adults and youth beyond the age of compulsory school attendance.

See Malcolm S. Knowles, *The Adult Education Movement in the United States* (New York: Holt, Rinehart and Winston, 1962); and Alan Boyd Knox, *Helping Adults Learn* (San Francisco; Jossey-Bass, 1986).

adult learner   An adult who is enrolled in any course of study, whether special or regular, to develop new skills or qualifications, or improve existing skills and qualifications.

adult school   A separately organized school providing instruction for adults and youth beyond the age of compulsory school attendance.

adult/continuing education   Instruction designed to meet the unique needs of adults and youth—beyond the age of compulsory school attendance—who have either completed or interrupted their formal education. This may be provided by a school system, college, or other agency or institution (including a technical institute or area vocational school) through activities and media such as formal classes, correspondence study, radio, television, lectures, concerts, demonstrations, and counseling.

See Jack W. Fuller, *Continuing Education and the Community College*

(Chicago: Nelson-Hall, 1979); Peter Jarvis, *Adult and Continuing Education: Theory and Practice* (New York: Nichols, 1983).

advance funding   The authority to obligate and disburse funds during a fiscal year from a succeeding year's budget or appropriation. The funds so obligated increase the budget authority for the fiscal year in which obligated, and reduce the budget authority of the succeeding fiscal year.

advance organizers   Ideas introduced by teachers to help students understand new concepts or facts; a general organization which helps to put new learning into a comprehensible context.
   See Joseph T. Lawton and Susan K. Wanska, "The Effects of Different Types of Advance Organizers on Classification Learning." *American Educational Research Journal*, 16:3(1979).

advanced adult education programs   Learning experiences designed to develop the knowledge, skills, appreciations, attitudes, and behavioral characteristics considered to be needed by adults who, having completed or interrupted formal schooling, have accepted adult roles and responsibilities and are preparing for postsecondary careers and/or postsecondary education programs.

advanced (or honors) courses   Special accelerated courses for students who have achieved a high standard of performance in a special subject area or who have generally high scholarship.

advanced placement program (APP)   A nationwide program established by the College Entrance Examination Board in 1955 whereby students can take specially designed courses in high school that will qualify for subsequent college credit if the student is able to meet criteria, as determined by the college of his or her choice, on a national examination in the subject area. While the courses are individually designed by the high school faculty, the nature and content of APP courses are strongly influenced by the examinations.

advanced placement   1. Any means by which a high school student can gain formal college course credits. 2. The advanced standing accorded a student upon admission to college. 3. Any program, whether high school or college level, that allows students to demonstrate a proficiency in a subject in order to have specific formal courses waived.

advanced placement test   An examination to measure the achievement of a student in a subject-matter area which may qualify him or her to bypass the usual initial college course in this area and begin college work with a more advanced course and possibly with some college credit.

advanced standing   Academic credit granted by an institution of higher education for work done in college-level high school courses, for work completed at another college, for military service, or on the basis of examination.

advances   Amounts of money prepaid in contemplation of the later receipt of goods, services, or other assets. Advances are ordinarily made only to payees to whom an organization has an obligation. A common example is travel advances, which are amounts made available to employees prior to the beginning of a trip for costs to be incurred.

adventure playground   Any play area equipped with materials with which children can build something as part of inventive play. Typical "adventure" materials include ropes, pipes, blocks, and other non-adorned items.

adversary evaluation *See* EVALUATION, ADVERSARY.

adversary proceeding Any formal hearing, trial, or legal contest in which both sides are appropriately represented and challenge each other's view of fact and/or law before an impartial decisionmaker and/or jury.

adversary system The Anglo-American system of law where a judge (or jury) acts as an impartial decision-maker between opposite sides, each of which has an opportunity to prove its assertion of guilt or innocence. This is in contrast to an inquisitional system in which accused parties must exonerate themselves before a judge (or judges) who functions both as a judge and as a public prosecutor.

See Anne Strick, "What's Wrong with the Adversary System: Paranoia, Hatred, and Suspicion," *Washington Monthly* (January 1977); and Arthur R. Miller, "The Adversary System: Dinosaur or Phoenix," *Minnesota Law Review* (October 1984).

adverse action 1. An act that is against someone else's interests. 2. A personnel action considered unfavorable to an employee, such as discharge, suspension, or demotion. 3. A use of land that harms local property values, such as a gas station or prison on land zoned for and occupied by single family homes.

adverse effect A differential rate of selection (for hire or promotion) that works to the disadvantage of an applicant subgroup, particularly subgroups classified by race, sex, and other characteristics on the basis of which discrimination is prohibited by law.

adverse impact The term for a selection process for a particular job or group of jobs that results in the selection of members of any racial, ethnic, or sex group at a lower rate than members of other groups. Federal EEO enforcement agencies generally regard a selection rate for any group that is less than four-fifths (4/5) or 80 percent of the rate for other groups as constituting evidence of adverse impact.

adverse-inference rule An analytical tool used by the Equal Employment Opportunity Commission (EEOC) in its investigations. The EEOC holds that when relevant evidence is withheld by an organization and the EEOC feels that there is no valid reason for such a withholding, the EEOC may presume that the evidence in question is adverse to the organization being investigated. The EEOC Compliance Manual permits use of the adverse-inference rule only if "the requested evidence is relevant," the evidence was requested "with ample time to produce it and with notice that failure to produce it would result in an adverse inference," and the "respondent produced neither the evidence nor an acceptable explanation."

adviser 1. A staff person who is assigned to help students make choices about what courses to take or other educational or personal matters. 2. A faculty member who is assigned to work with a student group or organization in carrying out specific programs or activities. Sometimes spelled "advisor."

advisory board An elected or appointed body of an organization or program that provides advice and expertise on administrative and/or program matters to the senior staff and/or the governing board of the organization.

advisory council A group of persons appointed under legislative or regulatory authority, to provide advice, consultation, or counsel in one or more areas of concern. Such a council may be temporary—to accomplish a specific, preconceived purpose—or it may be of a standing or permanent nature.

advocacy   An intervention strategy in which a person assumes an active role in assisting or supporting a specific child and/or family or a cause on behalf of children and/or families. This could involve finding and facilitating services for specific cases or developing new services or promoting program coordination. The advocate uses his or her power to meet client needs or to promote causes.

advocacy, administrative   See ADMINISTRATIVE ADVOCACY.

advocacy organization   Or advocacy group. A nonprofit organization that takes an active role in supporting or promoting social or personal causes. The term includes cause- and issue-oriented organizations and groups including, for example, those involved in the environmental, consumer, civil rights, right-to-life, right-to-die, and women's choice movements. There are a number of organizations that are devoted exclusively to advocating for groups or individuals who are in need of help regarding educational and other services required because of handicapping conditions. Many of these organizations developed out of a recognition that there are groups of people who exist with similar needs and with an inability to speak effectively for themselves. These organizations are independent of the educational system, or other service systems, and can both intercede and educate on behalf of students with handicaps and their families. While not an exhaustive list, the following organizations are some that were specifically established to serve this advocacy purpose and have also played an important role in influencing national policy:

Center for Law and Education
Guttman Library
6 Appian Way
Cambridge, MA 02138

Center on Human Policy
Syracuse University
Syracuse, NY 13210

Children's Defense Fund
1520 New Hampshire Ave., N.W.
Washington, DC 20036

Closer Look Information Center for
the Handicapped
P.O. Box 1492
Washington, DC 20013

Mental Health Law Project
1220 19th Street, N.W.
Washington, DC 20036

National Center for Law and the
Handicapped
1235 North Eddy Street
South Bend, IN 46617

aesthetics (or aesthetic education)   1. The study of various art forms (visual arts, music, dance, etc.), including art appreciation, artistic expression, and understanding different geographic and historical cultures through their arts. 2. Developing taste and judgment with regard to art. 3. Developing creative expression as a recreational/leisure skill.

AFDC   See AID TO FAMILIES WITH DEPENDENT CHILDREN.

affected class   According to the U.S. Department of Labor's Office of Federal Contract Compliance:
persons who continue to suffer the present effects of past discrimination. An employee or group of employees may be members of an affected class when, because of discrimination based on race, religion, sex, or na-

tional origin, such employees, for example, were assigned initially to less desirable or lower paying jobs, were denied equal opportunities to advance to better paying or more desirable jobs, or were subject to layoff or displacement from their jobs.

affective development   The growing integration of an individual's emotions, feelings, beliefs, and attitudes into a value structure. According to BLOOM'S TAXONOMY this development takes place in five consecutive stages: receiving, responding, valuing, organizing, and characterizing.

affective domain   One of the three critical learning areas described by Benjamin Bloom in BLOOM'S TAXONOMY. The affective domain refers to emotions, feelings, values and attitudes. Contrast with COGNITIVE DOMAIN and PSYCHOMOTOR DOMAIN.
See Thomas A. Ringness, *The Affective Domain in Education* (Boston: Little, Brown, 1975).

affective education   Educational programs or curricula that address the emotions, attitudes, and values of students. The objectives of such a program may be to teach students to recognize, express, and manage feelings, to make choices, or to examine their belief systems. Affective education, which gained popularity in the 1970s, has experienced a "Moral Majority" backlash in the 1980s in some localities where it is believed that values should be taught at home and the purpose of school is to teach "academics."
See James Wiggins and Dori English, *Affective Education: A Methods and Techniques Manual for Growth* (Washington, D.C.: University Press of America, 1977); and John P. Miller, *Humanizing The Classroom: Models of Teaching in Affective Education* (New York: Praeger, 1976).

affidavit   A written statement made under oath before a person permitted by law to administer such an oath (a notary public, for example). Such statements are frequently used in legal proceedings, labor arbitrations, and other formal hearings.

affiliated   1. Related organizations. For example, the IRS often views organizations as affiliated if they have interlocking directorates and if one (or more) of the organizations is committed to the actions of another by its governing instruments. 2. An affiliated school is associated with a teacher-training college and offers that college's students opportunities for student teaching.

affirmative action   A term that first gained currency in the 1960s, meaning the removal of "artificial barriers" to the employment of women and minority group members. Toward the end of that decade, however, the term got lost in a fog of semantics and came out meaning the provision of compensatory opportunities for hitherto disadvantaged groups. In a formal, legal sense, affirmative action now refers to specific efforts to recruit, hire, and promote disadvantaged groups for the purpose of eliminating the present effects of past discrimination.
See Paul J. Mishkin, "The Uses of Ambivalence: Reflections on the Supreme Court and the Constitutionality of Affirmative Action," *University of Pennsylvania Law Review* (March 1983); Nelson C. Dometrius and Lee Sigelman, "Assessing Progress Toward Affirmative Action Goals in State and Local Government: A New Benchmark," *Public Administration Review* (May-June 1984); and Cardell K. Jacobson, "Resistance to Affirmative Action: Self-Interest or Racism?" *Journal of Conflict Resolution* (June 1985).
See also:
EQUAL EMPLOYMENT OPPORTUNITY

REGENTS OF THE UNIVERSITY OF
  CALIFORNIA V. ALLAN BAKKE
  REVERSE DISCRIMINATION
  RIGHTFUL PLACE
  TITLE VII
  United Steelworkers of America v. Weber et al
  Wygant v. Jackson Board of Education

affirmative action groups   Also
called protected groups. Those segments of the population that have been
identified by federal, state, or local laws
to be specifically protected from
employment discrimination. Such
groups include women, identified
minorities, the elderly, and the handicapped.

affirmative action officer   An individual within an organization who has
the primary responsibility for the
development, installation and
maintenance of the organization's
affirmative action program.

affirmative action plan   An
organization's written plan to remedy
past discrimination against, or under-
utilization of, women and minorities.
The plan itself usually consists of a
statement of goals, timetables for
achieving milestones, and specific
program efforts.

affirmative action program   A
formal course of action undertaken by
employers to hire and promote women
and minorities in order to remedy past
abuses or maintain present equity. The
most basic tool of an affirmative action
program is the affirmative action plan.

affirmative order   An order
issued by the National Labor Relations
Board (NLRB) or similar state agency
demanding that an employer or union
take specific action to cease performing
and/or undo the effects of an unfair
labor practice. For example, a state
administrative agency might issue an
affirmative order to a school district to

"make whole" a wrongfully discharged
employee by reinstating the employee
with full back pay and reestablishing the
employee's seniority and other rights.

affirmative   recruitment
Recruiting efforts undertaken to assure
that adequate numbers of women and
minorities are represented in applicant
pools for positions in which they have
been historically underutilized.

AFL-CIO   *See* AMERICAN FEDERA-
TION OF LABOR-CONGRESS OF INDUSTRIAL
ORGANIZATIONS.

AFSA   *See* AMERICAN FEDERATION
OF SCHOOL ADMINISTRATORS.

AFSCME   *See* AMERICAN FEDERA-
TION OF STATE, COUNTY AND MUNICIPAL
EMPLOYEES.

AFT   See AMERICAN FEDERATION
OF TEACHERS.

age, basal   *See* BASAL AGE.

age as of September 1   As used
in student records, age at last birthday
on or prior to September 1. Age may be
recorded and reported by years, i.e., an
official school age reported as eight
years means that the child has reached
his or her eighth birthday on or prior to
September 1, but has not reached his or
her ninth birthday. Age may also be
recorded and reported by years and
months, as of September 1, or by birth
date. Age may be verified by a document such as a birth certificate, parent's
affidavit, hospital certificate, age certificate, entry in family Bible, baptismal
certificate, passport, and previously
verified school record.

age certificate   A legal statement
from a bureau of vital statistics or similar
agency certifying the date of birth of an
individual. *See also* BIRTH CERTIFICATE.

Age Discrimination Act of 1975
Structurally unrelated to the Age Discrimination in Employment Act of 1967, the Age Discrimination Act of 1975 bars discrimination because of age in all federally assisted programs. Not limited to employment, the 1975 act covers any type of enterprise or activity provided only that it is the recipient of federal monies.

Age Discrimination in Employment Act of 1967   As amended, this prohibits employment discrimination on the basis of age and prohibits (with certain exceptions) mandatory retirement. The law applies to all public employers, private employers of 20 or more employees, employment agencies serving covered employers, and labor unions of more than 25 members. The ADEA prohibits help wanted advertisements that indicate preference, limitation, specification, or discrimination based on age. For example, terms such as "girl" and "35-55" may not be used because they indicate the exclusion of qualified applicants based on age.

In addition to the federal law, many states have age discrimination laws or provisions in their fair employment practices laws that prohibit discrimination based on age. Some of these laws parallel the federal law and have no upper limit in protections against age discrimination in employment; others protect workers until they reach 60, 65, or 70 years of age.

See Cynthia E. Gitt, "The 1978 Amendments to the Age Discrimination in Employment Act—A Legal Overview," *Marquette Law Review* (Summer 1981); Michael H. Schuster and Christopher S. Miller, "Performance Appraisal and the Age Discrimination in Employment Act," *Personnel Administrator* (March 1984); and Michael H. Schuster and Christopher S. Miller, "An Empirical Assessment of the Age Discrimination in Employment

Act," *Industrial and Labor Relations Review* (October 1984).
See also
   EQUAL EMPLOYMENT OPPORTUNITY
     COMMISSION V. WYOMING
   OSCAR MAYER & CO. V. EVANS
   UNITED AIRLINES V. MCMANN

age equivalent   A measure of achievement or development expressed in terms of age.

age norm   The average test performance of a large group of students of a given age.

age of onset   The age at which a condition first occurs or becomes apparent; usually used in the context of a disease or handicap.

age-grade distribution   The number or percentage of students of each age in each grade, usually presented in an age-grade distribution table.

ageism   Also called age discrimination. In the tradition of racism and sexism, discrimination against those who are considered old.

agency   1. Any department, office, commission, authority, administration, board, government-owned corporation, or other independent establishment of any branch of government in the United States. 2. A formal relationship whereby one person is authorized to act for another.

agency shop   A union security provision, found in some collective bargaining agreements, that requires that nonunion employees of the bargaining unit must pay for the union's representational services as a condition of continuing employment. The agency shop was designed as a compromise between the union's desire to eliminate "free riders" by means of compulsory membership (the union shop) and management's wish that union membership be voluntary. Its constitutionality was upheld by the U.S. Supreme Court in *Abood v. Detroit Board of Education*, 431 U.S. 209 (1977). Later, in *Chicago Teachers Union v. Hudson*, 89 L. Ed. 2d 232 (1986), the Court prohibited a requirement making nonmembers of the union pay for union activities other than representation. For legal analyses, *see* Raymond N. Palombo, "The Agency Shop in a Public Service Merit System," *Labor Law Journal* (July 1975); and Charles M. Rehmus and Benjamin A. Kerner, "The Agency Shop After *Abood*: No Free Ride, But What's the Fare?" *Industrial and Labor Relations Review* (October 1980).

agenda   An order of business; a sequential listing of items to be addressed during a meeting. Preferably, a meeting's agenda should be prepared and distributed to participants in advance so that they may be prepared and better able to participate in deliberations and decisions. Compare to hidden agenda. A typical agenda for a board meeting and more formal committee meetings includes:
  Call to order
  Call and record attendance
  Establish a quorum
  Read and/or act to approve the minutes of the previous meeting
  Announcements
  Additions or changes to the agenda
  Reports (for example, staff, committees, and/or officers)
  Appointments (for example, to committees)
  Old business (that is, business remaining from previous meetings)
  New business
  Announce or establish next meeting time and place
  Adjournment

aggregate cost method   Also called aggregate method. A projected funding technique that computes pension benefits and costs for an entire plan rather than for its individual participants.

aggregate days absence   The sum of the days of absence of all students when school is in session during a given reporting period. Only days on which the students are under the guidance and direction of teachers are generally considered as days in session. *See also* DAY IN SESSION.

aggregate days attendance The sum of the days present (actually attended) of all students when school is in session during a given reporting period. Only days on which the students are under the guidance and direction of teachers are generally considered as days in session. *See also* DAY IN SESSION and DAY OF ATTENDANCE.

aggregate days membership The sum of the days present and absent of all students when school is in session during a given reporting period. Only days on which the students are under the guidance and direction of teachers are generally considered as days in session. *See also* DAY IN SESSION and MEMBERSHIP.

aggregate liability   The total amount that an insurer will pay for liabilities assumed under a policy.

aging schedule   A report showing how long accounts receivable have been owed and which ones are overdue. *See also* ACCOUNTS RECEIVABLE and COLLECTION RATE.

agraphia   The inability to write or print or to remember writing patterns. *See* D. Frank Benson, *Aphasia, Alexia and Agraphia* (New York: Churchill Livingstone, 1979).

algorithm 25

agreement   A contract; an intention of two or more parties to enter into a contract with one another, combined with an attempt to form a valid contract. *See also*:

INDEX OF AGREEMENT
MASTER AGREEMENT
MODEL AGREEMENT
OPEN-END AGREEMENT

AICPA   *See* AMERICAN INSTITUTE OF CERTIFIED PUBLIC ACCOUNTANTS.

Aid to Families with Dependent Children (AFDC)   The largest federal welfare program after the Food Stamp Program. Part of the Social Security Act of 1935, the Aid to Dependent Children program was expanded by 1962 amendments to the Social Security Act and renamed. AFDC provides federal funds, administered by the states, for children living with a parent or a relative who meets state standards of need. The program has been controversial because of charges that it promotes illegitimacy and encourages fathers to abandon their families so their children can become eligible for AFDC. In 1987 about 3.8 million families were receiving AFDC. *See* Russell L. Hanson, "The 'Content' of Welfare Policy: The States and Aid to Families with Dependent Children," *Journal of Politics* (August 1983).

Air Force Reserve Officer's Training Corps (AFROTC)   A combined program of regular academic study and specific military study, which may include financial assistance, that culminates in both a bachelor's degree and a commission in the U.S. Air Force. Graduates are required to complete four to six years of active service.

Albemarle Paper Co. v. Moody   422 U.S. 405 (1975) U.S. Supreme Court case that established the principle that once discrimination has been proven in a Title VII (of the Civil Rights Act of 1964) case, the trial judge ordinarily does not have discretion to deny back pay. For analyses, *see* William H. Warren, "Albemarle v. Moody: Where It All Began," *Labor Law Journal* (October 1976); Thaddeus Holt, "A View from Albemarle," *Personnel Psychology* (Spring 1977); and James Ledvinka and Lyle F. Schoenfeldt, "Legal Developments in Employment Testing: Albemarle and Beyond," *Personnel Psychology* (Spring 1978).

alcoholism   A detrimental dependency on alcoholic beverages. It was only in 1956 that the American Medical Association first recognized alcoholism as a disease. However, it is still not universally recognized as such. Almost all large organizations have programs to deal with alcoholic employees.
See Tia Schneider Denenberg and R.V. Denenberg, *Alcohol and Drugs: Issues in the Workplace* (Washington, D.C.: The Bureau of National Affairs, 1983); Joseph Madonia, "Managerial Responses to Alcohol and Drug Abuse Among Employees," *Personnel Administrator* (June 1984); and Tim Bornstein, "Drug and Alcohol Issues in the Workplace: An Arbitrator's Perspective," *Arbitration Journal* (September 1984).

aleatory contract   A legal agreement with effects and results that depend on an uncertain event; for example, insurance agreements are aleatory.

algorithm   1. A repeatable, step-by-step procedure to solve a problem or to accomplish a task. Algorithms for computerized applications (and, in recent years, in general usage) make each step a yes-or-no decision with only two choices. *See* L.N. Landa, *Algorithmization in Learning and Instruc-*

tion, ed., Relix F. Kopstein; trans. from the Russian by Virginia Bennett (Englewood Cliffs, N.J.: Educational Technology Publications, 1974). 2. A procedure for performing mathematical computations that uses a formula to determine each term of a mathematical expression.

alien   A foreign-born resident of the United States who does not possess the privileges of a citizen of the United States.

alien student (F-1 Classification)   A person admitted to the United States solely for the purpose of study.

alienation   A concept originally from Marxism which held that industrial workers would experience feelings of disassociation because they lacked control of their work (and thus be ripe for revolution). The word has lost its Marxist taint and now refers to any feelings of estrangement from one's work, family, society, etc.
   See John F. Witte, *Democracy, Authority, and Alienation in Work* (University of Chicago Press, 1980); Abraham K. Korman, Ursula Wittig-Berman, and Dorothy Lang, "Career Success and Personal Failure: Alienation in Professionals and Managers," *Academy of Management Journal* (June 1981); and Beverly H. Burris, *No Room at the Top: Underemployment and Alienation in the Corporation* (New York: Praeger, 1983).

alleged discriminatory official (ADO)   An individual charged in a formal equal employment opportunity complaint with having caused or tolerated discriminatory actions. For an analysis of the due process procedures to which ADOs are entitled, *see* Glenn E. Schweitzer, "The Rights of Federal Employees Named as Alleged Discriminatory Officials," *Public*

Administration Review (January-February 1977).

allegiance, pledge of   The affirmation of allegiance recited when the American flag is presented on ceremonial occasions. It reads: "I pledge allegiance to the flag of the United States of America and to the republic for which it stands, one nation under God, indivisible, with liberty and justice for all." It was first written by Francis Bellamy in 1892 and published in the September 8th issue of *Youth's Companion*, a weekly magazine. In 1942 Congress made the pledge officially part of the U.S. Code. In 1954 Congress added "under God."

allocate   1. A financial reporting term indicating the distribution of funds by a funding source. 2. The assignment of revenues or costs to a cost center, a program, or an organizational unit. 3. The assignment of a position or class of positions to a particular salary grade in the salary schedule based on an evaluation of its relative worth.

allotment   The amount allotted for a certain period and/or purpose.

allotment ledger   A subsidiary ledger which contains an account for each allotment showing the amount allotted, expenditures, encumbrances, the net balance, and other related information.

allowable charge   A generic term referring to the maximum fee that a third party payor will use in reimbursing a provider for a given service. An allowable charge may be different from either a reasonable, customary, or prevailing charge.

allowable costs   *See* COSTS, ALLOWABLE.

allowances   Amounts included in a budget request or projection to cover possible additional proposals, such as anticipated pay increases and contingencies for relatively uncontrollable programs and other requirements. Allowances remain undistributed until they occur or become firm, then they are distributed to the appropriate functional classification(s).

alma mater   1. Latin meaning "benign mother"; a reference to any school that one attended or from which one graduated. 2. The official song of a school.

Alpha Delta Kappa   An honorary fraternal organization in education, over 100,000 members.
Alpha Delta Kappa
1615 W. 92nd Street
Kansas City, MO 64114
(816) 363-5525

alternative schools (or alternative education)   A facility or program that differs from a traditional, conventional school in both curriculum and methodology. Usually designed to meet the unique needs of a specific population (e.g., gifted students, potential drop-outs, etc.), alternative schools are generally smaller, more personal, and more flexible than a conventional school. Examples of alternative models include schools-within-schools, schools-without-walls, basic skills or vocational schools, and performing arts schools. Alternative education is offered by public schools in some localities as well as by private enterprises. See Sue-Ann Rosch, Stephen Shapiro and Mary Bolinger, "Alternative Schools Work," *The Advocate* (Winter 1984); Dean Banks, "An Alternative to Alternative Education," *The American School Board Journal* (July 1987).

alumni   The former students of a school; usually those who graduated. An alumnus is a single former student.

AM   Abbreviation for the Latin "Artium Magister," meaning master of arts.

Ambach v. Norwick 441 U. S. 68 (1979)   The Supreme Court decision which held that barring aliens from permanent certification as public school teachers did not violate the 14th Amendment's equal protection clause. The ruling upheld the New York education law's citizenship requirement for public (but not private) school teachers.

American Arbitration Association (AAA)   A public service, nonprofit organization, formed in 1926, dedicated to the resolution of disputes of all kinds through the use of arbitration, mediation, democratic election, and other voluntary methods. The AAA does not act as an arbitrator. Its function is to submit to parties selected lists from which disputants may make their own choices and to provide impartial administration of arbitration. The AAA's library serves other educational institutions as a clearinghouse of information and answers the research inquiries of AAA members and of students. Although headquartered in New York, the AAA has regional offices throughout the United States.
American Arbitration Association
140 W. 51st Street
New York, NY 10020
(212) 484-4000

American Assembly of Collegiate Schools of Business (AACSB)   An organization of institutions devoted to higher education for business and administration, formally established in 1916. Its membership has grown to encompass not only educational institutions but also business, government, and professional organizations as well, all seeking to improve and promote higher education for business and working to solve problems of mutual concern. Through its accrediting function, the AACSB provides guidelines to educational institutions in program, resource, and faculty planning. The Accreditation Council of AACSB is recognized by the Council on Postsecondary Accreditation and by the U.S. Department of Education as the sole accrediting agency for bachelors and masters programs in business administration.

AACSB
605 Old Ballas Road
Suite 220
St. Louis, MO 63141
(314) 872-8481

1755 Massachusetts Avenue, N.W.
Suite 320
Washington, DC 20036
(202) 483-0400

American Association for Counseling and Development (AACD)

A professional association of 40,000 members that is concerned with personnel and guidance work at all educational levels, in community agencies, rehabilitation programs, government, business/industry, and research facilities. Formerly (until 1983) the American Personnel and Guidance Association.

American Association for
Counseling and Development
5999 Stevenson Avenue
Alexandria, VA 22304
(703) 823-9800

American Association of Colleges for Teacher Education (AACTE)

An organization of professionals in higher education concerned with the preparation of teachers.

AACTE
One Dupont Circle, N.W., Room 610
Washington, DC 20036
(202) 293-2450

American Association of School Administrators (AASA)   The

major professional association for administrators and executives of school systems and educational service agencies. Its primary functions are communication and professional development activities for the membership, which numbers 18,000. Training activities are sponsored by the association's National Academy for School Executives. The association publishes *The School Administrator*, a magazine distributed 11 times a year. The annual membership meeting is typically held in February or March.

American Association of School
Administrators
1801 N. Moore Street
Arlington, VA 22209
(703) 528-0700

American Education Research Association (AERA)   The major

professional organization for researchers in education. The organization has eight subdivisions: administration, curriculum and objectives, instruction and learning, measurement and research methodology, counseling and human development, history and historiography, social context of education and school evaluation and program development. AERA has three major publications: *American Education Research Journal, Review of Education Research,* and *Educational Researcher.*

AERA
1230 Seventeenth St., N.W.
Washington, DC 20036
(202) 223-9485

American Educational Research Journal   A quarterly journal

published by the American Educational Research Association and carrying original reports of empirical and theoretical studies in education.

Subscription Address:
AERA, Subscriptions
1230 17th St., N.W.
Washington, DC 20036
Editorial Address:
Virginia R. Koehler, Editor

American Educational Research Journal
College of Education
University of Arizona
Tucson, AZ 85721

American Educator   A quarterly journal for teachers that is published by the American Federation of Teachers.

American Federation of Labor-Congress of Industrial Organizations (AFL-CIO)

A voluntary federation of over 100 national and international unions operating in the United States and representing in total over 13,000,000 workers. The AFL-CIO is not itself a union; it does no bargaining. It is perhaps best thought of as a union of unions. The affiliated unions created the AFL-CIO to represent them in the creation and execution of broad national and international policies and in coordinating a wide range of joint activities.

Initially organized in 1881 as a federation of craft unions (the Federation of Organized Trade and Labor Unions), the AFL changed its name to the American Federation of Labor in 1886 after merging with those craft unions that had become disenchanted with the Knights of Labor. In 1955, the AFL merged with the Congress of Industrial Organizations to become the AFL-CIO.

Each member union of the AFL-CIO remains autonomous, conducting its own affairs in the manner determined by its own members. Each has its own headquarters, officers, and staff. Each decides its own economic policies, carries on its own contract negotiations, sets its own dues, and provides its own membership services. Each of the affiliated unions is free to withdraw at any time. But through its voluntary participation, it plays a role in establishing overall policies for the U. S. labor movement, which in turn advances the interests of every union.

AFL-CIO
815 16th Street, N.W.
Washington, DC 20036
(202) 637-5000

American Federation of School Administrators (AFSA)

An affiliate of the AFL-CIO for school principals, vice-principals, supervisors, and other educational administrators that is specifically concerned with the concerns and rights of these personnel. A newsletter called *News* is published seven times a year.

American Federation of School Administrators
853 Broadway, Room 2109
New York, NY 10003
(212) 477-2580

American Federation of State, County and Municipal Employees (AFSCME)

The largest union of state and local government employees. Founded in 1936 it has grown to 1,200,000 members in 3,000 locals.

AFSCME
1625 L Street, N.W.
Washington, DC 20036
(202) 452-4800

American Federation of Teachers (AFT)

The major labor union for teachers. The AFT was established in 1916 and is currently affiliated nationwide with the American Federation of Labor-Congress of Industrial Organizations (AFL-CIO). The organization publishes both a monthly newspaper, *American Teacher*, and a quarterly journal, *American Educator*. While the AFT is the primary labor union for teachers, the National Education Association (NEA) is by far the largest organization of teachers and in many ways functions as a union on behalf of its membership.

AFT
555 New Jersey Ave., N.W.
Washington, DC 20001
(202) 879-4400

See Robert J. Brown, *Teachers and Power: The Story of the American*

Federation of Teachers (New York: Simon and Schuster, 1972); and Marshall O. Donley, *Power to the Teacher: How America's Educators Became Militant* (Bloomington: Indiana University Press, 1976).

American Field Service   An educational exchange program developed shortly after World War I that allows individual students from all over the world the experience of living with a family in another country and attending school, usually for an entire year (although summer programs are also available). Nearly 70 countries participate in this program.

> American Field Service
> 313 E. 43rd St.
> New York, NY 10017

American Group Psychotherapy Association (AGPA)   Professional association organized in 1942 to provide a forum for the exchange of ideas among qualified professional persons interested in group psychotherapy; to publish and to make publication available on all subjects relating to group psychotherapy; to encourage the development of sound training programs in group psychotherapy for qualified mental health professionals; to establish and maintain high standards of ethical, professional group psychotherapy practice; and to encourage and promote research in group psychotherapy.

> American Group Psychotherapy
> Association
> 1995 Broadway
> New York, NY 10023
> (212) 787-2618

American Institute of Certified Public Accountants (AICPA) The national standards-setting and educational organization of the Certified Public Accounting (CPA) profession. The AICPA periodically issues accounting and audit guides for different types of organizations and industries.

> American Institute of Certified Public
> Accountants
> 1211 Avenue of the Americas
> New York, NY 10032
> (212) 575-6200

American Occupational Therapy Association (AOTA)   The major professional organization for occupational therapists and certified occupational therapy assistants, with 40,000 members. The organization conducts research and supports professional training in research. A monthly journal, *American Journal of Occupational Therapy*, a newsletter, and other special reports and monographs are published.

> AOTA
> 1383 Piccard Drive, Suite 301
> Rockville, MD 20850
> (301) 948-9626

American Personnel and Guidance Association   *See* AMERICAN ASSOCIATION FOR COUNSELING AND DEVELOPMENT.

American Physical Therapy Association (APTA)   The major professional organization for physical therapists, with 43,000 members. The association acts as an accrediting body for training programs in physical therapy, establishes standards, and offers advisory services to both training and service programs. A monthly magazine (*Physical Therapy*), monthly newsletter, and quarterly journal (*Clinical Management in Physical Therapy*) are published.

> APTA
> 1111 North Fairfax Street
> Alexandria, VA 22314
> (703) 684-2782

American Psychological Association   Founded in 1892 and incorporated in 1925, the APA is the major psychological organization in the United States. With more than 58,000 members, it includes most of the qualified psychologists in the country. The purpose of the APA is to advance psychology as a science and a profession and as a means of promoting human welfare by the encouragement of psychology in all its branches in the broadest and most liberal manner. Publications include the *Journal of Educational Psychology* and *Educational Psychologist.*

American Psychological Association
1200 Seventeenth Street, N.W.
Washington, DC 20036
(202) 955-7600

The American School Board Journal A monthly publication of the National School Board Association that includes articles and reports of general interest to school administrators and school board members.

Editorial and subscription address:
The American School Board Journal
1680 Duke Street
Alexandria, VA 22314

American Sign Language (AMESLAN) A signing system used by many persons with hearing handicaps. The system has its own grammatical rules and does not follow typical English structure. It is considered by many to be a true language of its own. Ameslan is not typically taught in schools because it does not follow the rules of English.

American Society for Personnel Administration (ASPA) A nonprofit professional association of personnel and industrial relations managers. Founded in 1948, ASPA today serves over 33,000 members with 380 chapters in the United States and 37 other countries. It is the largest professional association devoted exclusively to human resource management.

American Society for Personnel Administration
606 North Washington Street
Alexandria, VA 22314
(703) 548-3440

American Society for Training and Development (ASTD) A national professional society of 22,000 members for persons with training and development responsibilities in business, industry, government, public service organizations, and educational institutions. Founded in 1944, ASTD is the only organization devoted exclusively to the comprehensive education, development, and expansion of the skills and standards of professionals in training and human resource development. Formerly (until 1964), the American Society of Training Directors.

American Society for Training and Development
P.O. Box 5307
Madison, WI 53705
(608) 274-3440

American Speech-Language-Hearing Association (ASHA) The major professional organization for speech-language pathologists and audiologists, with over 45,000 members. The Association acts as an accrediting agency for university training programs, clinics, and hospital programs and as a certifying body for qualified professionals. A monthly magazine (*ASHA*) and three quarterly journals are published, including *Language, Speech and Hearing Services in the Schools.*

ASHA
10801 Rockville Pike
Rockville, MD 20852
(301) 897-5700

American Teacher The monthly newspaper published by the American Federation of Teachers.

amortization 1. The paying off of a debt in regular and equal payments. A gradual reduction of the principal of a loan, together with payment of interest, according to a known schedule of payments at regular intervals. By the end of the life of a loan, its principal balance will be fully paid off, in contrast with a loan involving a balloon payment. 2. Breaking down the value and costs of an intangible asset year by year over its estimated useful life. 3. Any dividing up of benefits or costs by time periods, primarily for tax purposes.

analogy training Specific instruction in analogical reasoning or the solution of analogy problems (i.e., man is to woman as boy is to _____); any one of a number of strategies to help students improve reasoning skills.
See Patricia Alexander et al., "Analogy Training: A Study of The Effects on Verbal Reasoning," *Journal of Educational Research* (November/December 1986); and R.J. Sternberg, *Intelligence, Information Processing and Analogical Reasoning: The Componential Analysis of Human Abilities* (Hillsdale, N.J.: Erlbaum, 1977).

analysis, sensitivity *See* SENSITIVITY ANALYSIS.

analysis-level thinking From Bloom's taxonomy, a thinking or learning process that involves the ability to develop conclusions through the study of components of a phenomenon or event. Contrast with KNOWLEDGE LEVEL, COMPREHENSION LEVEL, APPLICATION LEVEL, SYNTHESIS LEVEL, EVALUATION LEVEL. *See* BLOOM'S TAXONOMY.

ancillary services The supportive activities and resources necessary for the efficient achievement of the objectives of an organization or institution.

andragogy The art and science of teaching adults and of adult learning in a climate where the adult is given primary consideration. Andragogy refers specifically to teaching adults as contrasted with pedagogy which is the art/science of teaching in general. *See* Malcolm S. Knowles and Associates, *Andragogy in Action: Applying Modern Principles of Adult Learning* (San Francisco: Jossey-Bass, 1984).

anecdotal record Notes describing exactly what a student said or did in specific situations. When accumulated, anecdotal records may yield a picture of the student's developing behavior patterns, interests, attitudes, strengths, and problems.

Angell, James Burrill (1829-1916) The president of the University of Michigan (1871-1909) who was a leading advocate for making higher education accessible to all qualified students. *See* Shirley W. Smith, *James Burrill Angell: An American Influence* (Ann Arbor: University of Michigan Press, 1954).

annual current expenditures per student in ADA The annual current expenditures divided by the average daily attendance for the year. *See also* CURRENT EXPENDITURES PER STUDENT.

annual current expenditures per student in ADM The annual current expenditures divided by the average daily membership for the year. *See also* CURRENT EXPENDITURES PER STUDENT.

annual leave Leave that may be taken by the staff member during the school year through authorization without loss of pay or personnel benefits. Annual leave is exclusive of sick leave. Some or all accumulated annual leave may or may not be carried forward from one school year to the next, depending upon local system regulation.

annual meeting   The yearly meeting of the members or governing board of an organization. Annual meetings typically are specified in the articles of organization or bylaws.

annual report   1. A financial and programmatic report which summarizes the past year's activities. 2. Any formal report describing the past year's activities of a program or organizational unit.

annual review   A meeting scheduled either at the end of the academic year or on the anniversary of a student's initial staffing and placement into special education services. The Education for All Handicapped Children Act of 1975 (P.L. 94-142) requires that each handicapped student's special education placement and program be reviewed at least once a year. Generally the annual review is attended by the special education teacher, the parents, the student, if appropriate, and other educational staff who may be providing services to the student, such as a regular education teacher or related service staff. The primary purpose of the review, under the law, is to determine whether instructional objectives have been achieved.

annual withdrawal rate   The total number of times students withdraw from school during a given regular school term, divided by the number of different students in active membership status during the term, expressed as a percentage. *See also* ACTIVE MEMBERSHIP STATUS.

annuitant   One who is the recipient of annuity benefit payments.

annuity   An agreement or contract by which a person purchases a claim to a future series of payments made at fixed intervals over a specified time period, often in the form of payments made by an insurance company during the remainder of a lifetime.

anomie   A social condition in which previously established norms of behavior have been dissipated or rejected; consequently there is no effective social control of individual behavior. A state of anomie is characterized by attitudes of aimlessness, futility, and lack of motivation. The concept was "discovered" and named by the French sociologist Emile Durkheim (1858-1917). Compare to ALIENATION.
See Stephen R. Marks, "Durkheim's Theory of Anomie," *American Journal of Sociology* (September 1974).

anorexia nervosa   A medical condition especially found in teenage girls in which there is a severe, sometimes fatal, loss of appetite caused by an unreasonable fear of gaining weight. *See* Felicia F. Romeo, *Understanding Anorexia Nervosa* (Springfield, Ill.: Charles C. Thomas, 1986).

AOTA   *See* AMERICAN OCCUPATIONAL THERAPY ASSOCIATION.

APA   *See* AMERICAN PSYCHOLOGICAL ASSOCIATION.

apathy-futility syndrome   The aspect of an immature personality that is often associated with child neglect and characterized by an inability to feel and to find any significant meaning in life. Often arising from early deprivations in childhood, this syndrome is frequently perpetuated from generation to generation within a family system.

APB   *See* ACCOUNTING PRINCIPLES BOARD.

APE   *See* ADAPTED PHYSICAL EDUCATION.

APGA   *See* AMERICAN PERSONNEL AND GUIDANCE ASSOCIATION.

aphasia A language disorder that is assumed to be related to neurological dysfunctions of the brain. Aphasia can affect both the ability to understand words (receptive aphasia) or the ability to speak (expressive aphasia). Aphasia was first identified as an adult acquired disorder that usually resulted from a cardiovascular accident (stroke) that damaged the brain. Congenital or developmental aphasia was first described when language symptoms were observed in children that resembled those of adult stroke victims. *See* Frederic L. Darley, *Aphasia* (Philadelphia: W.B. Saunders, 1982); Ivar Revvang, *Aphasia and Brain Organization* (New York: Plenum Press, 1985).

appeal 1. Any proceeding or request to a higher authority that a lower authority's decision be reviewed. 2. A formal request to a higher court that it review the actions of a lower court. Compare to CERTIORARI. 3. A challenge to a ruling made by a presiding officer of a legislature. If the challenge is supported by a majority vote of the legislators, the initial ruling is overridden.

appellant One who appeals a case to a higher authority.

appellate Any court which considers appeals concerning a lower court's actions.
See Harold Leventhal, "Appellate Procedures: Design, Patchwork, and Managed Flexibility," *UCLA Law Review* (February 1976); and Dickson Philips, Jr., "The Appellate Review Function: Scope of Review," *Law and Contemporary Problems* (Spring 1984).

appellate jurisdiction The power of a court, board or commission to review cases that have previously been decided by a lower authority.

appellee The party who is a defendant in an appeal. This is usually the victor in a lower court case.

apple-polisher 1. A student who acts in an extremely sycophantic way toward teachers. 2. An employee who acts in an unduly ingratiating manner toward his or her employer.

applicant tally A tally system by which the equal employment opportunity (EEO) status of applicants for positions is recorded at the time of application or interview. By periodically comparing applicant tally rates with rates of appointment and/or rejection, the progress of affirmative action recruitment efforts can be measured.

application-level thinking From Bloom's taxonomy, a thinking or learning process that involves the ability to use in an unfamiliar context information that has been previously learned. Contrast with KNOWLEDGE-LEVEL THINKING, COMPREHENSION LEVEL, SYNTHESIS LEVEL THINKING, EVALUATION LEVEL. *See* BLOOM'S TAXONOMY.

applied costs The financial measure of resources consumed or applied within a given period of time to accomplish a specific purpose, such as performing a service, carrying out an activity, or completing a unit of work or a specific project, regardless of when ordered, received, or paid for.

applied research Research activity concerned with specific problems for which immediately applicable findings are sought. This activity may represent the application of knowledge derived from basic research or may involve testing alternative practices in the school system, school, or classroom. When brought to bear on problems of curriculum and instruction, this type of research is conducted to solve immediate practical problems related to the content, resources, and/or processes of instruction and learning. For administration and management, applied research might be used to help solve problems such as those associated with coordinated purchasing and warehousing, space utilization, maintenance schedules, transportation routes, and useful life of equipment.

appointing officer Also appointing authority. The individual who has the formal power to make appointments to positions in an organization.

appointment A nonelective government job. Most jurisdictions offer several different kinds of appointments. For example, the federal government offers the following four varieties in its merit system:

1. *temporary appointment*—does not ordinarily last more than one year.
2. *term appointment*—made for work on a specific project that will last more than one year but less than four years.
3. *career-conditional appointment*—leads after three years' continuous service to a career appointment.
4. *career appointment*—employee serves a probationary period and then has promotion, reinstatement, and transfer privileges. After completion of probation, this type of employee is in the last group to be affected in layoffs.

apportionment See ALLOTMENT.

appraisal 1. The act of making an estimate of value, particularly of the value of property, by systematic procedures that include physical examination, pricing, and often engineering estimates. This is often done for tax or insurance purposes. 2. An assess-

ment of the effectiveness of one's work. *See* PERFORMANCE APPRAISAL.

appraised value The value established by an assessment.

appreciation 1. An increase in the value of property; the excess of the present value of a given piece of property over its original cost. 2. Perception and acknowledgement of the quality of an individual's work or efforts.

apprentice A worker who is developing in a recognized occupation in accordance with a written training contract between the worker and the employer or employers that provides for a given period of planned work experience through employment on the job, supplemented by appropriate related instruction, and with other specified provisions of the arrangement.

apprenticeship The training through which a staff member has learned or is learning a recognized trade by means of on-the-job work experience and concurrent related instruction on the basis of contractual agreement or the laws of the state for registering apprenticeship programs. Compare to INTERN.

For an evaluation of current practices, *see* Norman Parkin, "Apprenticeships: Outmoded or Undervalued?" *Personnel Management* (May 1978); and Vernon M. Briggs, Jr. and Felician F. Foltman, eds., *Apprenticeship Research: Emerging Findings and Future Trends* (Ithaca, N.Y.: Cornell University, New York State School of Industrial and Labor Relations, 1981).

appropriate education A term used in special education; derived from the language of the Education for All Handicapped Children Act of 1975 (P.L. 94-142) to mean an education that addresses the unique, individual needs of a student.

appropriate unit　Also known as BARGAINING UNIT and appropriate bargaining unit. A group of employees that a labor organization seeks to represent for the purpose of negotiating agreements; an aggregation of employees that has a clear and identifiable community of interest and that promotes effective dealings and efficiency of operations. It may be established on a locational, craft, functional, or other basis.

appropriation　1. A legislature's setting aside funds to pay for something authorized by law. 2. An act of a legislature that permits agencies to incur obligations and to make payments out of the treasury for specified purposes. An appropriation usually follows the enactment of authorizing legislation and is the most common form of budget authority, but in some cases the authorizing legislation also provides the budget authority.

Appropriations are categorized in a variety of ways such as by their period of availability (one-year, multiple-year, no-year), the time of legislative action (current, permanent), and the manner of determining the amount of the appropriation (definite, indefinite).

appropriation, advance　An appropriation provided by a legislature for use in a fiscal year or more, beyond the fiscal year for which the appropriation act is passed. Compare to ADVANCE FUNDING.

appropriation, supplemental An appropriation enacted as an addition to a regular annual appropriation act. It provides additional budget authority beyond original estimates for programs or activities (including new programs authorized after the date of the original appropriation act) for which the need for

funds is too urgent to be postponed until the next regular appropriation.

appropriation ledger　A ledger containing an account with each appropriation. Each account usually shows the amount originally appropriated, transfers to or from the appropriation, amount charged against the appropriation, the encumbrances, the net balance, and other related information. If allotments are made and a separate ledger is maintained for them, each account usually shows the amount appropriated, transfers to or from the appropriation, the amount allotted, and the unallotted balance. *See also* ALLOTMENT LEDGER.

appropriation limitation　A statutory restriction (or "limitation amendment") in appropriation acts that establishes the maximum or minimum amount that may be obligated or expended for specified purposes.

appropriations received from other local governmental units Money received from the appropriations of another local governmental unit. For example, federal forest funds may be allocated to local school districts through the county commissioner who decides the share of funds that the school district will receive.

approval　The official act of a state's Department of Education, or another recognized agency having official authority, certifying that a unit of organization complies with the legal requirements or prescribed standards for the operation of such units.

APTA　*See* AMERICAN PHYSICAL THERAPY ASSOCIATION.

aptitude　1. The capacity to acquire knowledge, skill, or ability with experience and/or a given amount of formal or informal education or training.

2. Learning readiness; the mix of personal and behavioral characteristics that allows an individual to do well in learning situations.

aptitude test   1. Any test designed to predict level of success in formal instruction. 2. A battery of separate tests designed to measure an individual's overall ability to learn.

Aquilar v. Felton 473 U.S. 402 (1985)   Supreme Court decision that invalidated a New York City public school practice of providing Title I remedial programs to students in parochial schools and reaffirmed that it was not constitutionally permissible to use public funds to pay for teaching in religious schools, regardless of the nature of the instruction.

arbiter/arbitrator   One chosen to decide a disagreement. In a formal sense an arbiter is one who has the power to decide while an arbitrator is one who is chosen to decide by the parties to the dispute; but the words tend to be used interchangeably.

arbitrability   Whether or not an issue is covered by a collective bargaining agreement and can be heard and resolved in arbitration. The U.S. Supreme Court held, in *United Steelworkers v. Warrior & Gulf Navigation Co.*, 363 U.S. 574 (1960), that any grievance is arbitrable unless there is an express contract provision excluding the issue from arbitration; doubts "should be resolved in favor of coverage."

See Mark M. Grossman, *The Question of Arbitrability: Challenges to the Arbitrator's Jurisdiction and Authority* (Ithaca, N.Y.: Cornell University, New York State School of Industrial and Labor Relations, 1984).

arbitration   The means of settling a dispute by having an impartial third party (the arbitrator) hold a formal hear-ing and render a decision that may or may not be binding on both sides. The arbitrator may be a single individual or a board of three, five, or more. When boards are used, they may include, in addition to impartial members, repre-sentatives from both of the disputants. In the context of labor relations arbitrators are selected jointly by labor and management, recommended by the Federal Mediation and Conciliation Service, by a state or local agency offer-ing similar referrals, or by the private American Arbitration Association.

See Henry S. Farber, "Role of Arbitration in Dispute Settlement," *Monthly Labor Review* (May 1981); Harry Graham, "Arbitration Results in the Public Sector," *Public Personnel Management* (Summer 1982); and Frank Elkouri and Edna Asper Elkouri, *How Arbitration Works*, 4th ed. (Washington, D.C.: Bureau of National Affairs, 1985).

For a review of a number of cases of arbitrated grievances in schools, most involving teacher discipline, see Robert Coulson, *Arbitration in the Schools* (New York: American Arbitration Association, 1986).

arbitration, compulsory   A negotiating process whereby the parties are required by law or by collective bargaining contract to arbitrate their dis-pute. Some state statutes concerning collective bargaining impasses in the public sector mandate that parties who have exhausted all other means of achieving a settlement must submit their dispute to an arbitrator. The intent of such requirements for compulsory, and by definition binding, arbitration is to in-duce the parties to reach agreement by presenting them with an alternative that is certain even though it may be un-pleasant in some respects to everyone involved.

See Carl M. Stevens, "Is Compulsory Arbitration Compatible with Bargain-ing?" *Industrial Relations* (February

1966); and Mollie H. Bowers, "Legislated Arbitration: Legality, Enforceability, and Face-Saving," *Public Personnel Management* (July-August 1974).

arbitration, binding   *See* BINDING ARBITRATION.

arbitration acts   Laws that help (and sometimes require) the submission of certain types of problems (often labor disputes) to an *arbitrator.*

arbitration clause   A provision in a collective bargaining agreement or contract stipulating that disputes arising during the life of the contract over its interpretation are subject to arbitration.

arbitration standards   The four fundamental criteria that arbitrators must be concerned with in making their judgments: acceptability, equity, the public interest, and ability to pay. The mix of these factors that will be applied in any particular case of arbitration will depend upon the arbitrator's proclivities, the nature of the dispute, and, if it is in the public sector, the standards, if any, set forth in the pertinent legislation.

arbitrator   *See* ARBITER.

architectural barriers   Physical aspects of a building that might hinder or prevent access by people with physical handicaps. The lack of a ramp, for example, may prevent a person in a wheelchair from entering a building having only stairways for access. The Architectural Barriers Act of 1968 (Public Law 90-480) as amended, requires that buildings constructed with federal funds be accessible to and usable by the physically handicapped.

area labor-management committees   Groups of local labor and management leaders who seek to solve problems affecting the economic well-being of an entire community, rather than just a particular worksite or industry.

area school   A public school that has been approved to provide instruction in a specific instructional area to residents of a state, a county, a major city, or another designated geographic area usually larger than one local basic administrative unit.

area standards picketing Picketing to demand that the primary employer pay "area standards" wages; that is, wages that are paid to union labor by other employers in the same geographic area.

area superintendent   An administrator responsible for all of the schools in a specified geographical area of a larger school district.

area vocational center   A shared-time facility that provides instruction only in vocational education to students from throughout a school system or region. Students attending an area vocational center receive the academic portion of their education program in regular secondary schools or other institutions.

area vocational school   A public school which has been approved by the state board for vocational education to provide instruction in the occupations (other than professional occupations) to residents of the state, a county, a major city, or another designated geographic area usually larger than one local basic administrative unit.

Army Alpha and Beta Tests   In 1917 a special committee of the American Psychological Association was convened to develop tests that would help the U.S. Army classify the abilities of its recruits. The committee developed the Army Alpha Intelligence Test (a verbal test for literate recruits) and the Army Beta Intelligence Test (a nonverbal test suited for illiterate and foreign-born recruits). After World War I, the tests were released for civilian use and became the progenitors of modern industrial and educational group intelligence/aptitude testing.

Army Junior ROTC   A high school ROTC (Reserve Officer Training Corps) military training program that can be made available to secondary school students as a part of the regular school curriculum. Instruction covers topics such as leadership, map reading, first aid, military history, and weapon safety. Participation is without cost and does not obligate the student to subsequent military service.

Army Reserve Officers Training Corps (ROTC)   A college-based military training program that prepares students to be officers in the U.S. Army, Army Reserve, or National Guard. From either a two-year or four-year training program students can be commissioned at the time of their college graduation and then are obligated to serve either three or four (if a college scholarship was granted) years of active duty. The training program provides course work in national defense, military history, leadership skills, and military tactics.

array of services   A model for describing different options for the delivery of special education services that is based strictly on the needs of the student and not on the physical location or availability of the services. This is in contrast to the more typical "continuum of services" model. Under the array of services model the nature, scope, and intensity of specialized services can be varied according to the needs of the student within any physical location and, presumably, within, or as close as possible to, the mainstream of educa-

tion. In other models it is assumed that the student "goes" to where the required service is available and the student usually progresses linearly (if at all) through each successive step in the model as less intense services may be required.

art therapy   1. The use of art as a means of communication between a patient and a trained therapist. 2. Using art to facilitate the expression of emotions, thoughts, or creativity. *See* Kathleen Mileski Hanes, *Art Therapy and Group Work: An Annotated Bibliography* (Westport, Conn.: Greenwood, 1982); and Judith Aron Rubin, *Child Art Therapy*, 2nd ed. (New York: Van Nostrand Reinhold, 1984).

Arthur Adaptation of the Leiter International Performance Scale   *See* LEITER INTERNATIONAL PERFORMANCE SCALE. The Arthur Adaptation is published by:
C.H. Stoelting Company
1350 S. Kostner Avenue
Chicago, IL 60623

articles of association   Also charter; the articles of organization which are filed with the appropriate office of state government by some nonprofit associations. Articles of association serve the same purpose for a nonprofit organization as do articles of incorporation for a for-profit company.

articles of incorporation   The creating document for a corporation. *See also* GOVERNING INSTRUMENT.

articles of organization   The creating document for an organization. For example, articles of incorporation are the articles of organization for a corporation; for an unincorporated entity, the articles of organization may be, for example, a constitution or articles of association. Bylaws are not articles of organization. *See also* BYLAWS and GOVERNING INSTRUMENT.

articulation 1. The coordination of programs and course contents among the various educational levels. This allows for progressively more demanding work on the part of students as they continue through the system. Articulation can be from grade to grade, from middle school to high school, from department to department, etc. 2. The process of speaking.

artificial barriers to employment Limitations (such as age, sex, race, national origin, parental status, credential requirements, criminal record, lack of child care, and absence of part-time or alternative working patterns/schedules) in hiring, firing, promotion, licensing, and conditions of employment that are not directly related to an individual's fitness or ability to perform the tasks required by the job.

artificial intelligence A descriptive term for the capacity of computers to "think" and solve problems. For an analysis of this aspect of modern computer technology, *see* Avron Burr and Edward Feigenbaum, ed., *The Handbook of Artificial Intelligence* (Stanford, Calif.: HeurisTech Press, 1981).

Also see The Editors of Time-Life Books, *Artificial Intelligence* (Alexandria, Va.: Time-Life Books, 1986).

artificial language Any language created for a specific purpose as opposed to one that spontaneously arose within a culture. Computer languages such as BASIC and FORTRAN are artificial languages used to communicate with computers. ESPERANTO is an artificial "world language."

artificial person An entity to which the law gives some of the legal rights and duties of a person; for example, a corporation.

arts and crafts A typical part of the art curriculum in elementary schools and adult education programs (also sometimes offered in secondary schools) that includes the production of articles such as woodwork, handicrafts, metalwork, weaving, needlework, pottery, basketry, prints, and jewelry. Arts and crafts can range from simple hobbies as a leisure-time activity to high level artistic production as a career.

ASBO *See* ASSOCIATION OF SCHOOL BUSINESS OFFICIALS.

ASCD *See* ASSOCIATION FOR SUPERVISION AND CURRICULUM DEVELOPMENT.

ASHA *See* AMERICAN SPEECH-LANGUAGE-HEARING ASSOCIATION.

ASPA *See* AMERICAN SOCIETY FOR PERSONNEL ADMINISTRATION.

assembly An official meeting of more than a single class of students scheduled on school premises, usually in an auditorium, during the school day. Assemblies are used for communicating with students, for cultural programs, to supplement classroom teaching, and to create a sense of school spirit. *See* Addyse Lane-Palagyi, *Successful School Assembly Programs* (West Nyack, N.Y.: Parker Publishing Co., 1971).

assertiveness training Training program designed to help reticent people communicate and express their ideas and feelings more effectively. The ideal level of assertiveness lies between passivity and aggressiveness. The concept was pioneered by J. Wolpe in his *Psychotherapy by Reciprocal Inhibition* (Stanford, Calif.: Stanford University Press, 1958).

For a general discussion, *see* Harold H. Dawley, Jr. and W.W. Wenrich, *Achieving Assertive Behavior: A Guide to Assertive Training* (Belmont, Calif.: Wadsworth, 1976); Michael D. Ames, "Non-Assertion Training Has Value

Too," *Personnel Journal* (July 1977); Madelyn Burley-Allen, *Managing Assertively: How to Improve Your People Skills* (New York: John Wiley, 1983); and Elaira Zuker, *Mastering Assertiveness* (New York: American Management Associates, 1983).

assessment   1. Evaluating the value of property for the purposes of taxation. Assessment criteria vary from state to state, but commonly are based on the full (estimated or presumed) market value or on a percentage of market value. 2. Contributions to political parties that are determined according to a schedule of rates and made in order to retain a civil service patronage appointment. Prior to World War II this was a common practice in the United States, even for positions in education. 3. An extra payment required by law such as an assessment to pay additional taxes. 4. The financial damages charged to the loser of a lawsuit. 5. Amounts paid by union members in addition to their regular dues when a union needs funds urgently in order to support a strike or some other union-endorsed cause. The amount of these assessments is usually limited by a union's constitution and/or bylaws. 6. Any technique or instrument used to evaluate students, teachers, or programs; a process for determining a student's level of functioning, both strengths and weaknesses, in a variety of areas, such as communication, cognition, social-emotional, physical, prior to determining need and eligibility for specialized educational services. 7. The determination of the validity of a reported case of suspected child abuse or neglect through investigatory interviews with persons involved. This could include interviews with the family, the child, school, and neighbors, as well as with other professionals and paraprofessionals having direct contact with the child. Compare to EVALUATION.

See Jerome M. Sattler, *Assessment of Children's Intelligence and Special Abilities*, 2nd ed. (Boston: Allyn and

Bacon, 1982); Richard M. Wolf, *Evaluation In Education: Foundations of Competency Assessment and Program Review*, 2nd ed. (New York: Praeger, 1984); Duncan Harris and Chris Bell, *Evaluating and Assessing for Learning* (New York: Nichols, 1986).

assessment area   A particular aspect of behavior or ability that is evaluated or appraised by means of a test or other measurement instrument.

assessment center   1. A term typically used for the process of intense observation of a subject undergoing any of a variety of tests, simulations, and stress situations over a period of several days. Assessment centers have proven to be an increasingly popular way of identifying individuals with future executive potential so that they may be given the appropriate training and development assignments. 2. An organization offering career counseling services. 3. A school facility that is used primarily, or totally, as a place for administering tests or other forms of evaluation to students.

assessment ratio   A property tax computation; the ratio between the market value and assessed value. Assessment ratios vary tremendously because some jurisdictions value property at or close to actual market value and others use formulas calling for assessed values to be various fractions of market value.

asset-linked annuity   *See* VARIABLE ANNUITY.

assets   Also current assets and fixed assets. 1. The book value of items owned by an enterprise or jurisdiction as reflected on a balance sheet. 2. All of the property of a person, association, corporation, or estate that may be applied to or subject to paying his, her, or its liabilities and other obligations. *Current assets* are cash or those highly liquid items that are convertible to a known amount of cash usually within a year (e.g., accounts receivable, securities, inventory, and amounts due from other organizations). *Fixed assets* are those items that normally are not convertible into cash within a year (e.g., buildings, equipment, and machinery).

assigned risk   A risk that an insurance company does not care to insure but that, because of state law or other reasons, must be insured. Insuring assigned risks usually is handled through a group of insurers. The individual assigned risks are assigned to the companies in turn or in proportion to their share of the total insurance business in the state. Assignment of risk is quite common in casualty insurance.

assignment   1. A learning experience required of a student or class. 2. A specific group of activities for which a staff member has been given responsibility. 3. The transfer of property, rights in property, or money to another person or organization.

assignment of wages   Also called attachment of wages; a procedure whereby an employer, upon the authorization of the employee, automatically deducts a portion of the employee's wages and pays it to a third party, usually a creditor. When this is ordered by a court, the process is known as garnishment.

assimilation   Under Piaget's theory of learning, this occurs when new information is taken in and integrated within the framework of already existing knowledge. The basic conceptual structure remains unchanged, i.e., the old "assimilates" the new. Contrast with ACCOMMODATION.

assistant principal   A staff member (usually called an assistant, deputy, or associate principal) who performs high-level executive management functions in an individual school, group of schools, or unit(s) of a school district. The assistant principal often performs disciplinary functions as well.

assistant/associate or deputy superintendent   A staff member performing assigned professional and administrative activities that assist the chief executive officer of the school administrative unit in the development of general administrative policies and in conducting the general administration of the school administrative unit. The usual ranking of hierarchical authority is the deputy superintendent (who may serve as the acting superintendent in the absence of the superintendent), the associate superintendent, and the assistant superintendent.

associate degree   A degree commonly conferred upon the successful completion of a two-year program of studies at a junior college or technical institute.

Associate in Applied Science (AAS)   A degree commonly conferred upon the successful completion of a two-year postsecondary program of studies composed of general education, electives, and a major concentration in a chosen technical, semiprofessional, or professional area of study.

Associate in Arts (AA)   A degree commonly conferred upon the successful completion of a two-year postsecondary program of studies composed essentially of courses in the liberal arts.

Associate in Science Degree (AS)   A degree commonly conferred upon the successful completion of a two-year postsecondary program of studies composed of courses in the liberal arts and sciences.

association, unincorporated   Although it is often a legal requirement, many smaller nonprofit organizations and associations do not bother incorporating—that is, filing articles of association or organization with the appropriate office of state government. These are referred to as unincorporated associations.

Association for Persons with Severe Handicaps, The (TASH)

A professional organization of approximately 6,000 members who are involved in education and other areas of service for persons with severe handicaps. The Association strongly advocates quality education and community participation for persons with disabilities and publishes a monthly newsletter and quarterly journal.

TASH
7010 Roosevelt Way, N.E.
Seattle, WA 98115
(206) 523-8446

Association for Supervision and Curriculum Development (ASCD)

A professional organization of school district supervisors, curriculum coordinators, consultants, university professors, administrators, and other educational personnel that provides professional training experiences, disseminates information and encourages research and policy development regarding curriculum. The association conducts National Curriculum Study Institutes across the country and publishes a magazine, *Educational Leadership*, eight times a year; a journal, *Journal of Curriculum Supervision*, quarterly; a newsletter, *Update*, and an annual yearbook.

ASCD
225 N. Washington Street
Alexandria, VA 22314
(703) 549-9110

Association of School Business Officials (ASBO)

An organization for school business managers and other school administrators performing business management functions for the school district. The association publishes a monthly magazine, *School Business Affairs*, a bimonthly newsletter, an annual membership directory, and books relevant to the membership's interests.

ASBO
1760 Reston Avenue, Suite 411
Reston, VA 22090
(703) 478-0405

associative learning A process of acquiring, comprehending, and retaining information by relating it to prior knowledge. Associative learning involves a number of cognitive processes: information storage, abstraction, transfer and retrieval. *See* James G. Greeno et al., *Associative Learning: A Cognitive Analysis* (Englewood Cliffs, N.J.: Prentice-Hall, 1978).

assumption-of-risk doctrine 1. The common-law concept that an employer should not be held responsible for an accident to an employee if the employer can show that the injured employee had voluntarily accepted the hazards associated with a given job. 2. A common defense for tort actions concerning athletic injuries. In this case, rather than employer/employee as in the above definition, the concept refers to school district and student.

ASTD *See* AMERICAN SOCIETY FOR TRAINING AND DEVELOPMENT.

at risk 1. The special risk of injury or disease of certain groups; for example, teachers or students who are pregnant are "at risk" if a school has an outbreak of German measles because this disease is known to cause birth defects. 2. Increased probability for school failure or learning problems because of factors associated with socioeconomic status, other family variables, physical/neurological abnormalities, potential suicide, or substance abuse. 3. In infancy and early childhood years the increased probability for developing physical or mental handicaps due to factors such as low birth weight, complications at birth or before, exposure to disease, and age or nutritional status of mother.

athletic conference An organization of schools for the purpose of regulating and scheduling sports competitions among teams representing the membership. The conference will frequently arrange for tournaments or other championship events.

athletic director The employee who schedules all interscholastic athletic activities for a school or school district. This is sometimes used as an informal title for the chair of a physical education department.

athletic scholarship 1. A grant-in-aid that is offered in recognition of outstanding athletic ability in one or more competitive sports. 2. A financial incentive to attract an athelete of unusually high ability to enhance the potential of an educational institution's competitive sports program. 3. Financial assistance that is typically accompanied by requirements imposed by an intercollegiate sports league or association. *See* Alan Green, *The Directory of Athletic Scholarships* (New York: Facts On File, 1987).

athletics Organized competitive sports that are beyond the scope of the typical physical education offerings of the school. Athletic programs are usually, though not always, of an interscholastic nature, that is, taking place between individuals or teams representing two or more schools.

at-large An election where one or more candidates for a legislature or school board are chosen by all of the voters of a jurisdiction. This is in contrast to an election by district where voters are limited to selecting one candidate to represent their legislative district. At-large elections have often been criticized because they make it more difficult (compared to district elections) for members of a minority group to gain office.

attachment of wages *See* ASSIGNMENT OF WAGES.

attendance The presence of a student on days when school is in session. A student may be counted present only when he or she is actually at school or is present at another place at a school activity that is sponsored by the school, is a part of the program of the school, and is personally supervised by a member or members of the school staff. This may include authorized independent study, work-study programs, field trips, community-based training, athletic contests, music festivals, student conventions, instruction for homebound students, and similar activities when officially authorized under policies of the local school board. It does not include "making up" schoolwork at home or activities supervised or sponsored by private individuals or groups. *See also* DAY OF ATTENDANCE.

attendance, aggregate days *See* AGGREGATE DAYS ATTENDANCE.

attendance, average daily (ADA) *See* AVERAGE DAILY ATTENDANCE (ADA).

attendance, day of *See* DAY OF ATTENDANCE.

attendance, percentage of *See* PERCENTAGE OF ATTENDANCE.

attendance area The geographic area wherein reside the students normally served by a particular school.

attendance law A state law which governs compulsory school attendance, the number of days or hours a year school must be in session, the minimum age to drop out of school, and other matters related to school attendance.

attendance officer   A staff member performing assigned activities having as their purpose the early identification of nonattendance of students, the analysis of causes of non-attendance, the enforcement of compulsory attendance laws, and the improvement of school attendance. Traditionally called a truant officer, this person sometimes has the legal authority to arrest parents who refuse to send their children to school.

attendance personnel   Staff members assigned activities for promoting and improving school attendance of students.

attendance register   A record containing information such as (a) the names of students who have entered or are expected to enter a class or school; (b) identification information about each student, such as sex, date of birth, and address; and (c) information concerning his or her entry or reentry, membership, attendance, absence, tardiness, and withdrawal.

attendance services   Activities that promote the identification of patterns of nonattendance, the promotion of positive attitudes toward attendance, the analysis of causes of nonattendance, early action on problems of nonattendance, and the enforcement of compulsory attendance laws.

attendance and social work services   Activities that are designed to improve student attendance at school or that attempt to prevent or solve student problems involving the home, the school, and the community. *See also* SCHOOL SOCIAL WORK.

attendance unit   The school to which all students of a particular age range from a given geographical area are assigned.

attendant   A general term designating a staff member performing assigned activities to watch over and provide a degree of physical care for school property or pupils.

attending behavior   1. Behavior in which one individual pays close attention to another, watching and listening, in anticipation of forthcoming communication. 2. Behavior that is highly desired on the part of students by teachers. 3. The behavior that occurs prior to a discriminative stimulus.

attention deficit disorder (ADD)   A condition in children that creates learning and behavioral difficulties in school. Specifically, these children have problems with attending to tasks and with impulse control. *See* HYPER-ACTIVITY.

attention span   The length of time an individual can continuously concentrate on a particular task or educational activity. Generally speaking, one's attention span increases with age. *See* Paula J. Caplan, *Children: Learning and Attention Problems* (Boston: Little, Brown, 1979).

attitude   A learned predisposition to act in a consistent way toward particular persons, objects, or conditions. Educational institutions seek to encourage in students those attitudes that will give them the desire to learn.

attitude scale   Any series of attitude indices that have given quantitative values relative to each other. *See* Allen L. Edwards, *Techniques of Attitude Scale Construction* (New York: Irvington Press, 1979).

attitude survey   A questionnaire, usually anonymous, that elicits the opinion of people (such as employees, students, neighbors, or consumers).

attitudinal test An examination to measure the mental and emotional set or pattern of likes and dislikes held by an individual or group, often in relation to such considerations as controversial issues and personal adjustments.

attribution A procedure for allocating costs, employee time, or property use among several functions, programs, organizational units, or other dimensions, on the basis of the best possible estimate; may be used when objective data are not available for proration.

attrition A reduction in the size of a work force through normal processes, such as voluntary resignations, retirements, discharges for cause, transfers, and deaths.

atypical behavior Behavior of an individual that is markedly different from that of others in the same chronological age group. Frequently used in reference to the peculiar behaviors of children who are seriously emotionally disturbed or who have autism.

atypical characteristic A characteristic of an individual in a given chronological age group that is markedly different from that of the mean. *See also* EXCEPTIONAL CHILDREN.

atypical condition A condition of an individual in a given chronological age group that is markedly different from that of the main. An individual having an atypical condition may reveal one or more atypical characteristics that enable an identification of the condition. *See also* ATYPICAL CHARACTERISTIC.

atypical pupil A pupil revealing a physical, mental, or behavioral characteristic that is markedly different from that of the mean of his or her chronological age group. *See also* ATYPICAL CHARACTERISTIC; EXCEPTIONAL CHILDREN; and EXCEPTIONAL PUPILS.

audiogram A graph depicting the weakest sound, expressed in decibels, that a person can hear at various frequency or pitch levels.

audiolingual approach An approach to language instruction emphasizing that element of language (sound) that is spoken in normal, everyday, conversational interchange as differentiated from language as gesture or as writing. This is sometimes referred to as the "aural-oral" approach.

audiologist A staff member who is a specialist in communicative disorders, including the scientific study and management of speech, hearing, and language disabilities. Primary responsibilities are of a clinical nature, which involves diagnostic, evaluative, and therapeutic activities in the area of hearing disabilities.

audiology services Activities organized for the identification of pupils with hearing loss; determination of the range, nature, and degree of hearing dysfunction; referral for medical or other professional attention as appropriate to the habilitation of hearing; language habilitation; auditory training, speech reading (lip reading), and speech conservation as necessary; creation and administration of programs of hearing conservation; and counseling and guidance of pupils, parents, and teachers as appropriate.

audiometer A piece of equipment used to test hearing.

audiometrist A staff member performing assigned activities of testing the auditory perception of individuals by means of specifically designed electrical or mechanical testing equipment.

audiovisual aids   Optical, electronic, and other devices—and related supplies—that are designed to enhance learning through the combined senses of hearing and sight, e.g., sound, motion pictures, printed materials, and television. Frequently two or more of these components are combined into electronic distribution systems, some of which incorporate remote or dial access capabilities.
See Edgar Dale, *Audiovisual Methods in Teaching*, 3rd ed. (New York: Holt, Dryden, 1969). *See also* EDUCATIONAL MEDIA.

audiovisual room   An instruction area designed, or provided with special built-in equipment, for audiovisual material storage, screening, and listening, which is separate from the school library and does not serve as an adjunct to other rooms or areas.

audiovisual services   Activities such as selecting, preparing, caring for, and making available to members of the instructional staff equipment, films, filmstrips, transparencies, tapes, television programs, and other similar materials, whether maintained separately or as a part of an instructional materials center. Included are activities in the audiovisual center, television studio, and related work-study areas, and the services provided by audiovisual personnel.

audiovisual technician   A staff member performing assigned skilled activities in the use and care of audiovisual equipment and with the techniques of instructional presentation through the use of machines, charts, and other audiovisual equipment and materials.

audit   1. To attend a course of instruction, which is normally "for credit," without seeking credit or taking examinations. 2. A review of the operations of an organization, especially its financial transactions, to determine whether it has spent monies in accordance with the law, in the most efficient manner, and with desired results.
See also:
COMPLIANCE
CONTRACT AUDIT
DESK AUDIT
FINANCIAL AUDIT
GENERALLY ACCEPTED ACCOUNTING PRINCIPLES
PROGRAM EVALUATION
PROGRAM RESULTS AUDITS

audit program   The detailed steps and procedures to be followed in conducting an audit and preparing an audit report. A written audit program should be prepared for each audit, and it should include such information as the purpose and scope, background information needed to understand the audit objectives and the entity's mission, definitions of unique terms, objectives, and reporting procedures.

audit report   The document prepared by an auditor following a completed financial review; it should include: (1) scope of the audit; (2) summary of findings; (3) recommendations; (4) certificate; and (5) financial statements.

audit services   Activities pertaining to independent audit services provided to a board of education.

audit standards   General measures of the quality and adequacy of the audit work performed. They also relate to the auditor's professional qualities.

audit trail   A systematic cross-referencing from an accounting record (a record of a transaction) to its source (for example, receipts) to properly explain it, document it, and/or check its accuracy—in other words, so that an auditor can "follow its trail."

auditor   1. A staff member performing the assigned technical activities of verifying the accuracy and appropriateness of receipts, expenditures, accounts, and accounting statements in accordance with the laws and regulations that are applicable. 2. An outside organization conducting an audit.

auditorium   An instructional space designed and constructed with a built-in stage, sloping floor, and/or fixed seating for use as an assembly center. *See also* INSTRUCTION AREA.

auditor's opinion   The expression in an auditor's report as to whether the information in the financial statement is presented fairly in accordance with generally accepted accounting principles (or with other specified accounting principles applicable to the auditee) applied on a basis consistent with that of the preceding reporting period.

auditory handicap   An impairment in hearing that adversely affects the performance of an individual. A person identified as having an auditory handicap may be referred to as "hard of hearing" or "deaf," according to the nature and severity of the handicap.

aural-oral approach   A system for teaching language, often to students with hearing impairments, which emphasizes listening and speaking. *See* AUDIOLINGUAL APPROACH.

authoring system   Software designed to help writers, such as teachers, develop instructional materials for computers. BASIC and FORTRAN are the most generally used authoring languages because they can accommodate a number of instructional techniques.

authoritarian teaching   A style of teaching wherein the teacher makes all of the decisions, allows for little discussion in the classroom, teaches largely by lecture, and grades students primarily on their ability to reproduce the information that has been given by the teacher.

authority   1. The feature of a leader or institution that compels others to grant it obedience, usually because of some ascribed legitimacy. 2. A government corporation such as the Tennessee Valley Authority or the Port of New York Authority. 3. The power inherent in a specific position or function that allows an incumbent to perform assigned duties and assume delegated responsibilities.

authority, backdoor   Legislation enacted outside the normal appropriation process that permits the obligation of funds. The most common forms of backdoor authority are borrowing authority (authority to spend debt receipts) and contract authority. Entitlement programs may sometimes take the form of backdoor authority, since the enactment of the basic benefit legislation may, in effect, mandate the subsequent enactment of the appropriations to pay the statutory benefits.

authorization card   A form signed by a worker to authorize a union to represent the worker for purposes of collective bargaining. The U.S. Supreme Court held, in *National Labor Relations Board v. Gissel Packing Co.*, 395 U.S. 575 (1969), that the National Labor Relations Board had the power to require an employer to bargain with a union that had obtained signed authorization cards from a majority of the employees. In such circumstances a secret ballot election is considered unnecessary.

See Daniel F. Gruender and Philip M. Prince, "Union Authorization Cards: Why Not Laboratory Conditions?" *Labor Law Journal* (January 1981).

authorization election   Poll conducted by the National Labor Relations Board (or other administrative agency) to determine if a particular group of employees will be represented by a particular union or not. Authorization election is used interchangeably with certification election (because if the union wins, it is certified as the representative of the workers by the administrative agency) or representative election (because a winning union becomes just that, the representative of the workers).

See Julius G. Getman, Stephen B. Goldberg, and Jeanne B. Herman, *Union Representation Elections: Law and Reality* (New York: Russell Sage Foundation, 1976); John J. Lawler, "The Influence of Management Consultants on the Outcome of Union Certification Elections," *Industrial and Labor Relations Review* (October 1984); and James E. Martin, "Employee Characteristics and Representation Election Outcomes," *Industrial and Labor Relations Review* (April 1985).

autism   A handicapping condition that manifests itself at an early age and typically involves a variety of disorders in learning, communication, and socialization. Because of some of the atypical behaviors associated with the condition, autism has been previously thought to be an emotional disorder. Therefore, in the initial regulations relating to the Education for All Handicapped Children Act of 1975 (P.L. 94-142) autism was included under the category of "emotionally disturbed." More recently autism has been acknowledged to be a developmental disorder of organic origin (though the exact etiology of the disorder is still unknown). In 1981 an amendment to existing federal regulations for P.L. 94-142 was established to move autism to the category of "other health impaired" under the definition of handicapped children.

See Michael Rutter and Eric Schopler, *Autism: A Reappraisal of Concepts and Treatment* (New York: Plenum Press, 1978).

automatic attendance accounting (AAA)   The recording of student attendance using computer terminals in each classroom.

automatic data processing   The use of machines and devices in the storing of individual items of information in a form by which they may be rapidly and accurately retrieved, processed, and reproduced as single line items, as lists of items, or in desired combinations with other items.

automatic promotion   Advancing students from one grade to the next regardless of educational attainment. Such a policy sometimes leads to the graduation from high school of adults who are functionally illiterate.

automatic renewal   A collective bargaining contract clause that extends the agreement automatically in the absence of notice by either party to negotiate a new contract.

automatic wage adjustment   The raising or lowering of wage rates in direct response to such previously determined factors as an increase or decrease in the Consumer Price Index.

automatic wage progression   The increasing of wages premised on length of service.

auxiliary agency   An administrative unit whose prime responsibility is to service other agencies of the greater organization. Personnel units are often considered to be auxiliary agencies.

auxiliary services   Programs and activities that serve to support the basic educational mission. Examples include a school bus system, food services, and health services.

average   1. The arithmetic mean of a group; a measure of central tendency. Compare to MEAN, MEDIAN, MODE. 2. A summary of students' grades in a class or in total. 3. In the middle, neither very high nor very low in a ranking. 4. Ordinary, mediocre, not outstanding in any way.

average age of students   The total of the ages (expressed in years and months) of the students of a given group divided by the number of students in the group.

average class size   The total membership of classes of a given type, as of a given date, divided by the number of such classes.

average daily absence   1. The number of students generally absent from a school or school district in any given day. 2. The aggregate of days of absence of a given school during a given reporting period divided by the number of days school is in session during this period. Only days on which the students are under the guidance and direction of teachers are considered as days in session. The average daily absence for groups or schools having varying lengths of terms is the sum of the average daily absences obtained for the individual schools. *See also* AGGREGATE DAYS ABSENCE; DAY IN SESSION; and DAY OF ABSENCE.

average daily attendance (ADA)   1. The number of students generally in attendance (i.e, students present at school) at a school or in a school district on any given day. 2. The aggregate of days of attendance of a given school during a given reporting period divided by the number of days school is in session during this period. Only days on which the students are under the guidance and direction of teachers are considered as days in session. The reporting period is generally a given regular school term. The average daily attendance for groups of schools having

varying lengths of terms is the sum of the average daily attendances obtained for the individual schools.

Average Daily Attendance in Public Schools, 1984-85

1.	California	4,142,050
2.	Texas	2,888,727
3.	New York	2,335,100
4.	Ohio	1,674,200
5.	Michigan	1,603,560
6.	Illinois	1,603,118
7.	Pennsylvania	1,550,800
8.	Florida	1,399,779
9.	New Jersey	1,042,049
10.	North Carolina	1,016,580
11.	Georgia	978,300
12.	Virginia	899,052
13.	Indiana	898,480
14.	Massachusetts	795,955
15.	Tennessee	766,598
16.	Louisiana	719,100
17.	Missouri	707,030
18.	Wisconsin	700,498
19.	Washington	689,506
20.	Alabama	684,773
21.	Minnesota	658,404
22.	Maryland	612,000
23.	Kentucky	583,000
24.	South Carolina	569,330
25.	Oklahoma	551,500
26.	Colorado	505,724
27.	Arizona	484,575
28.	Iowa	459,729
29.	Connecticut	446,000
30.	Mississippi	435,678
31.	Oregon	413,662
32.	Arkansas	403,679
33.	Utah	367,305
34.	Kansas	364,105
35.	West Virginia	335,635
36.	Nebraska	250,986
37.	New Mexico	247,830
38.	Idaho	199,111
39.	Maine	194,400
40.	Hawaii	151,553
41.	New Hampshire	144,530
42.	Nevada	140,100
43.	Montana	138,900
44.	Rhode Island	120,622
45.	South Dakota	116,675
46.	North Dakota	112,370
47.	Wyoming	95,660
48.	Alaska	87,230
49.	Delaware	84,228
50.	Vermont	83,000
51.	Dist. of Col.	76,064
	United States total	36,528,840

SOURCE: National Education Association Research, *Estimates* data bank.

average daily membership (ADM)   The number of students enrolled in a school or district. The aggregate of days of membership (i.e., students enrolled) of a given school during a given reporting period divided by the number of days school is in session during this period. Only days on which the students are under the guidance and direction of teachers are considered as days in session. The reporting period is generally a given regular school term. The average daily membership for groups of schools having varying lengths of terms is the sum of the average daily memberships obtained for the individual schools. For purposes of obtaining statistical comparability only, student-staff ratios involving kindergarten and prekindergarten students attending a half-day session are computed as though these students are in membership for a half day.

average daily membership of students transported The aggregate days' membership during a given reporting period of students transported to and from school divided by the number of days school is in session during this period.

average daily number of students participating in national school lunch and/or breakfast programs The total number of servings per month for elementary and secondary school students in national lunch and/or breakfast programs, divided by the number of days the meal is served.

average deviation Also called mean deviation. Measure of dispersion that provides information on the extent of scatter, or the degree of clustering, in a set of data.

average length of term in days For the state as a whole, the aggregate days' attendance for the state divided by the average daily attendance for the state.

average membership per school The total membership of schools in a reporting unit, as of a given date, divided by the number of schools in the unit.

average number of children per school district The total number of children of school age in a given state (or intermediate unit) divided by the number of local basic administrative units within the state (or intermediate unit).

average number of children per attendance area The total number of children of school age in an administrative unit divided by the number of attendance areas within the administrative unit.

average number of students served lunch per day The total number of students served lunch during a given reporting period divided by the number of days on which lunch was served.

average number of students transported The aggregate number of days individual students are transported between home and school during a given reporting period divided by the number of days transportation is provided.

average transportation cost per student transported The annual current expenditures for student transportation divided by the average daily membership.

average unit cost of equipment At any given time, the total cost of an equipment group being accounted for under group control divided by the number of individual equipment items in the group. *See also* GROUP CONTROL.

aversive 1. Any consequence for a student's actions or behavior which is experienced as objectionable or painful. 2. A stimulus that inflicts discomfort or pain.

avocation A subordinate activity or hobby practiced by the staff member in which the staff member has an enduring interest.

award 1. At the end of the arbitration process, the final decision of the arbitrator(s) when such arbitration is binding on both parties. 2. The giving of a contract to the winner in a competitive bidding situation. 3. Formal recognition for academic, athletic, or other achievement.

B

BA   See BACHELOR'S DEGREE.

B Mod   See BEHAVIOR MODIFICATION.

baby boom   That age cohort born in the two decades after World War II. This group of almost 74 million people makes up about 30 percent of the U.S. population. The boom came about because population growth was suppressed, first by the depression of the 1930s and then by the prolonged absence of men for the World War II effort. With the return of prosperity and of men in the postwar period, a "baby boom" commenced. As the babies in the boom grew older, their sheer numbers had significant impact on educational institutions at all levels.

See Louise B. Russell, *The Baby Boom Generation and the Economy* (Washington, D.C.: The Brookings Institution, 1982); and Frank D. Bean, "The Baby Boom and Its Explanations," *Sociological Quarterly* (Summer 1983).

bachelor's degree   A degree usually conferred upon the successful completion of a four-year college program of studies.

back loaded   A labor agreement providing for a greater wage increase in its later years; for example, a three-year contract that provides for a two percent increase in the first year and six percent in each of the remaining two years. *See also* FRONT LOADED.

back to basics   A movement within education which advocates the development of basic skills at the expense of other educational elements. A back to basics approach would emphasize the three Rs: "reading, 'riting, and 'rithmetic" and deemphasize music, art, social studies, etc. For a critical analysis of the back to basics movement *see* Henry M. Levin, "Back to Basics and the Economy," *Radical Trends* (1984); special issue from Stanford University, Institute for Research on Educational Finance and Goverment.

backlash   1. Any counterreaction by one group (sexual, ethnic, national, etc.) against preference shown toward another group. 2. A negative reaction by whites to the civil rights efforts of blacks and other protected classes when the whites feel threatened. Busing to achieve school integration and compensatory hiring practices are two situations that often create a backlash.

See Lillian B. Rubin, *Busing and Backlash: White Against White in a California School District* (Berkeley: University of California Press, 1972).

back-to-work   movement   Striking employees returning to their jobs before their union has formally ended a strike.

backward   A child whose educational attainment or development in general is noticeably less than that of an average child. This is an antiquated usage.

backward chaining   An instructional paradigm based on operant conditioning theory to teach a complex task or activity that consists of a "chain" of discrete steps. The student is first taught to complete the last step of the sequence after the instructor has completed all steps up to that point. The student then learns the second to last step and the last step together after the steps up to that point have been done. The student is taught each new step in the sequence in reverse order and in combination with the steps already learned until the entire sequence can be accomplished. *See also* CHAINING.

BAEd   Bachelor of arts in education.

BAEIEd   Bachelor of arts in elementary education.

BAGEd   Bachelor of arts in general education.

Bagley, William Chandler (1874-1946)   An educational philosopher who was a leading critic of progressive education and a founder of the essentialist movement which called for a disciplined mastery of teacher prescribed core subjects.
    See Isaac L. Kandel, *William Chandler Bagley, Stalwart Educator* (New York: Teachers College, Columbia University, 1961).

Bakke decision   *See* REGENTS OF THE UNIVERSITY OF CALIFORNIA V. ALLAN BAKKE.

balance sheet   An itemized accounting statement that reflects total assets, total liabilities, and residual balances or retained earnings as of a given date.

balanced curriculum   An institutional program with a variety of aims and objectives for pupils, supported by an overall plan of instruction having flexibility in required and optional areas of content to be studied and diversity in types of learning experiences.

balanced budget   A budget in which receipts are equal to outlays.

balances, budget   The residual amounts remaining in budgeted accounts at the close of a fiscal period.

An *obligated balance* is the amount of obligations incurred (formal commitments made) but for which payments have not been made. An *unobligated balance* is the portion of the budget which has not been obligated. An *unexpended balance* is the sum of the obligated and unobligated balances.

balloon payment   Also balloon loan and balloon mortgage. A loan or mortgage in which the last payment (or a limited number of intermediate payments) is much larger than any of the other regular payments.

Balwin Identification Matrix   A system for identifying gifted and talented students.

band curve chart   Or cumulative band chart. Chart on which the bands of a graph are plotted one above the other.

banding   *See* ABILITY GROUPING.

bank credit   A written promise by a bank that an organization or person may borrow up to a specified amount.

BANs   *See* BOND ANTICIPATION NOTES.

baptismal or church certificate   A form issued by a church certifying the baptism of a child. This form records the date of birth and often is acceptable as verification for this date.

bar graph or histogram   Any graphic presentation that uses bars of various length to symbolize differences in quantity, size, or amount.

bargaining   *See* COLLECTIVE BARGAINING.

bargaining agent   The union organization (not an individual) that is the exclusive representative of all the workers, union as well as nonunion, in a bargaining unit.

bargaining agreement   *See* LABOR AGREEMENT.

bargaining rights   The legal rights that all workers have to bargain collectively with their employers.

bargaining strength   The relative power that each of the parties holds during negotiations. The final settlement often reflects the bargaining power of each side. *See* Samuel B. Bacharach and Edward J. Lawler, "Power and Tactics in Bargaining," *Industrial and Labor Relations Review* (January 1981); and Samuel B. Bacharach and Edward J. Lawler, *Bargaining: Power, Tactics, and Outcomes* (San Francisco, Jossey-Bass, 1981).

bargaining unit   A group of employees, union members as well as others, that an employer has recognized and/or an administrative agency has certified as appropriate for representation by a union for purposes of collective bargaining. All of the employees in a bargaining unit are subsequently covered in the labor contract that the union negotiates on their behalf. The size of a bargaining unit is important in that it significantly affects the relative bargaining strength of both labor and management.

Barnard, Henry (1811-1900) The first U.S. Commissioner of Education, from 1867 to 1870. As an early advocate of universal public education, he helped foster the development of common school districts. *See* Robert B. Downs, *Henry Barnard* (Boston: Twayne, 1977).

Barr v. Matteo 360 U. S. 564 (1959)   Supreme Court case concerning the immunity of public administrators from civil suits for damages in connection with their official duties. The Court, without majority opinion, held that the acting director of the Office of Rent Stabilization had such an immunity. By implication, other public employees would be immune from civil suits depending upon the nature of their responsibilities and duties.
See also:
BUTZ V. ECONOMOU
SPALDING V. VILAS
WOOD V. STRICKLAND

basal age   1. A level of achievement on a test expressed in terms of age. 2. The age used as a base in psychological testing representing the age equivalency level of the test items that the subject can consistently answer correctly; thus a child of 10 could have a basal age on a particular test of eight, or vice versa.

basal reader   1. A text or programs on a teaching machine designed to develop elementary reading skills in a progressive manner. 2. Any elementary text.

base period   The time that an employee must work before becoming eligible for certain employment benefits.

BASecEd   Bachelor of arts in secondary education.

baseline data   1. Information on a subject or group of subjects before change is introduced. This baseline data allows a researcher to measure the rate or effect of change. 2. Information that a teacher records on student behavior or level of achievement prior to initiating a new instructional program in order to measure progress.

basic education   A term frequently used in referring to education emphasizing literacy in language, mathematics, natural sciences, and history and related social sciences. *See also* ADULT BASIC EDUCATION.
See Carl F. Hansen, *The Amidon Elementary School: A Successful*

Demonstration in Basic Education (Englewood Cliffs, N.J.: Prentice Hall, 1962); Eugene M. Boyce, *The Coming Revolution in Education: Basic Education and the New Theory of Schooling* (Lanham, Md.: University Press of America, 1983).

Basic Educational Opportunity Grant Program (BEOG)   A federal program of financial scholarships established in the early 1970s for post-secondary students who are enrolled at least half-time in undergraduate institutions or vocational/technical schools. Grants are made on the basis of need rather than scholastic ability and the range of award amounts is established annually by Congress. Since 1981 the program has been called the Pell Grant Program after Senator Claiborne Pell of Rhode Island. This grant program is administered at the federal level and applications are made directly to the federal government, Department of Education.

basic research   Research activity that is primarily directed at the development and evaluation of theory, in which immediate applicability of findings is not a major concern. This type of research is primarily concerned with the discovery of new knowledge. Compare to APPLIED RESEARCH.

basic school unit   A school system; a single school district.

Basic Skills and Educational Proficiency Program   A federal program established by the Educational Amendments of 1978 (P.L. 95-561) to assist both public and private agencies to improve basic academic skills—including mathematics, reading, and oral and written communication—for children, youth, and adults. It was actually an expansion of the previous federal RIGHT TO READ program.

basic skills test   An examination measuring the ability of a person to use fundamental reading and computational skills that are the basis of later learning and achievement. See IOWA TESTS OF BASIC SKILLS.

basic workday   The number of hours in a normal workday. Premium payments or compensatory time off may be made for time worked in excess of the basic workday. The eight-hour day is widely accepted as the standard basic workday.

basic workweek   The number of hours in a normal workweek. Premium payments or compensatory time off must usually be made for time worked in excess of the basic workweek. The 40-hour week is widely accepted as the standard basic workweek. See also FAIR LABOR STANDARDS ACT and *GARCIA V. SAN ANTONIO METROPOLITAN TRANSIT AUTHORITY.*

battered child syndrome   A phrase which describes a combination of physical and other signs indicating that a child's internal and/or external injuries result from acts committed by a parent or caretaker. In some states, the battered child syndrome has been judicially recognized as an accepted medical diagnosis. Frequently this term is misused or misunderstood as the only type of child abuse and neglect. Compare to CHILD ABUSE.

See Henry C. Kempe and Ray Helfer, *Helping the Battered Child and His Family* (Philadelphia: J.B. Lippincott, 1972).

battery   1. Two or more tests administered together and standardized on the same population so that the results on the various tests are comparable. The term battery is also used to refer to any tests administered as a group. 2. Offensive contact or physical violence with a person without his/her consent, and which may or may not be preceded by a threat of assault. Because a minor cannot legally give consent, any such contact or violence against a child is considered battery. The action may be aggravated, meaning intentional, or it may be simple, meaning that the action was not intentional or did not cause severe harm. Assault is occasionally used to mean attempted battery.

Bayley Scales of Infant Development   A commonly used developmental test of both mental and psychomotor development for infants and young children below the age of 2 1/2. It is published by:
    The Psychological Corporation
    555 Academic Court
    San Antonio, TX 78204

BBEd   Bachelor of business education.

BEd   Bachelor of education.

behavior   1. Any response made by an organism, such as a student, to a stimulus, such as an internal thought or impulse or an external intrusion. 2. In the context of classroom discipline, a student's responses to his or her environment may be evaluated as good or bad, positive or negative, or otherwise from a judgmental perspective.

behavior management   A general term referring to strategies or approaches used to eliminate or reduce the occurrence of undesirable behaviors on the part of a student. Such approaches generally involve the application of either positive or negative consequences contingent on the behavior of the student. Compare to DISCIPLINE.

behavior modification (B Mod) The use of controlled consequences to change the behavior of individuals or groups.

See Roger D. Klein et al., eds., *Behavior Modification in Educational Settings* (Springfield, Ill.: Charles C. Thomas, 1973); Abraham Givner and Paul S. Graubard, *A Handbook of Behavior Modification for the Classroom* (New York: Holt, Rinehart and Winston, 1974); and Robert J. Presbie and Paul L. Brown, *Behavior Modification*, 2nd ed. (Washington, D.C.: Education Association, 1985).

behavior pattern   A special grouping or mosaic of responses of a student that, in the judgment of a trained observer, possesses some intrinsic unity. The responses obtained are considered to result from inner psychological needs; as such they are more or less automatic, with the student having little control over them.

behavioral assessment   A measure obtained by observing a student over a period of time, either continuously or at predetermined intervals, and recording particular behaviors.

behavioral counseling   1. A counseling approach in which specific behavioral objectives are agreed upon and reinforcement techniques are used to achieve them. 2. One of the major counseling theory classifications that utilize a variety of specific intervention strategies, such as operant conditioning, social learning, or reciprocal inhibition.

behavioral norms   1. Socially reinforced patterns of behavior. 2. Representative averages of behavior. Compare to NORM.

behavioral objectives   Instructional goals stated in terms that can be measured; what is expected of a child (or adult) after instruction in a specific subject.
    See Morris Lewenstein, "In Defense of Behavior Objectives," *Social Education* (November-December 1976); and

---

EXAMPLE OF A BEHAVIORALLY ANCHORED NUMERICAL RATING SCALE

Rating	Behavioral Anchor
1	Knows rules of racquetball, can bounce ball and hit it with racquet
2	Hits forehand strokes with consistency, backhand is weak
3	Hits both forehand and backhand strokes with consistency
4	Can place ball accurately, including serves
5	All strokes are accurate, firm and consistent; topspin and under-spin strokes can be employed as required

---

Anita J. Harrow, *A Taxonomy of the Psychomotor Domain; A Guide for Developing Behavioral Objectives* (New York: David McKay Co., and Longman, 1977).

behavioral problem   A loose term for a child who is consistently disruptive during class.

behavioral sciences   A general term for all of the academic disciplines that study human and animal behavior by means of experimental research. The phrase was first put into wide use in the early 1950s by the Ford Foundation to describe its funding for interdisciplinary research in the social sciences; and by faculty at the University of Chicago who were seeking federal funding for research and were concerned in an era of McCarthyism that their social science research might be confused with socialism.

behavioral technology   1. A general term that refers to any systematic program of instruction aimed at achieving acceptable classroom behavior on the part of a student (i.e., eliminating undesirable behaviors) and/or teaching the student to exert internal control over impulsive behavior while imposing external control through the use of artificial reinforcement or punishment. *See* STIMULUS. 2. The use of behavior modification techniques in instruction.

behavioralism   1. A philosophic disposition toward the study of the behavior of people in society as opposed to studying the institutional structures of their society. Thus, for example, one should not emphasize study of the structure of the U.S. Department of Education because what is really important is the behavior of its employees. 2. The scientific study of social phenomena that emphasizes the use of the scientific method for empirical investigations and the use of quantitative techniques.

behaviorally anchored rating scale   A performance evaluation technique that is premised upon the scaling of critical incidents of performance. *See* Michael Loar, Susan Mohrman and John R. Stock, "Development of a Behaviorally Based Performance Appraisal System," *Personnel Psychology* (Spring 1982).

behaviorism   That school of psychology which holds that only overt behavior is the proper subject matter for the entire discipline. Behaviorists suggest that psychology should avoid introspection but rather concentrate on analyzing human behavior in the same manner that animals are objectively studied. John Broadus Watson (1878-1958) is generally considered the originator of the behaviorism movement in psychology. According to the foremost exponent of behaviorism, B.F.

Skinner, in *About Behaviorism* (New York: Knopf, 1974), "Behaviorism is not the science of human behavior; it is the philosophy of that science."

See Walter Bernard Kolesnik, *Humanism and/or Behaviorism in Education* (Boston: Allyn and Bacon, 1975); Gerald A. Teller, "Is Behaviorism a Form of Humanism?" *Educational Leadership* (May 1977); and Thomas M. Alonzo et al., "Behaviorism vs. Humanism: Two Contrasting Approaches to Learning Theory," *Southern Journal of Educational Research* (Summer 1977).

Bell, Alexander Graham (1847-1922)   The inventor of the telephone who was also a pioneer in the education of the deaf. *See* Robert V. Bruce, *Bell: Alexander Graham Bell and The Conquest of Solitude* (Boston: Little, Brown, 1973).

Bell, Terrel H. (1921-)   The secretary of education from 1981 to 1985. For his account of how he stopped the Reagan administration from keeping its 1980 campaign promise to abolish the department, *see* Terrel H. Bell, *The Thirteenth Man: A Reagan Cabinet Memoir* (New York: Free Press, 1988).

bell curve   A representation of the normal distribution in statistics. *See* NORMAL DISTRIBUTION.

Bender Visual Motor Gestalt Test (Bender-Gestalt)   An instrument used primarily to measure visual-perceptual functioning but also commonly used to assess emotional adjustment, brain damage, and cognitive functioning. The test consists of nine increasingly complex geometric designs that the individual is asked to copy or reproduce from memory. It may be used with individuals from the ages of four years through adult. It is published by:
Western Psychological Services
12031 Wilshire Boulevard
Los Angeles, CA 90025

Bender-Gestalt Test   *See* BENDER VISUAL MOTOR GESTALT TEST.

beneficiary   A person, group, or organization to whom an insurance policy is payable.

benefit   1. A sum of money provided in an insurance policy payable for certain types of loss, or for covered services, under the terms of the policy. The benefits may be paid to the insured or, on his or her behalf, to others. 2. A measurable, monetary return realized from a program or service rendered. 3. Intangible rewards, perhaps from learning or from teaching.

benefit, death   *See* DEATH BENEFIT.

benefit, direct   A result attained that is related closely to a project or program in a cause-and-effect relationship; for example, an increase in body tone as a result of an exercise program.

benefit, indirect   A result that is achieved circuitously; for example, a decrease in absenteeism due to increased exercise arising from a school district wellness program. *See also* SPILLOVER EFFECT.

benefit, net   *See* NET BENEFIT.

benefit period   The period of time for which payments for benefits covered by an insurance policy are available. The availability of certain benefits may be limited over a specified time period; for example, two well-baby visits during a one-year period. While the benefit period is usually defined by a set unit of time, such as a year, benefits may also be tied to a spell of illness.

benefit theory   The belief that those who are to gain from a government action should to the extent possible pay for the benefits received. Thus, for example, gasoline taxes paid by drivers help pay for highway repair and construction and fees for fishing licenses help pay for restocking lakes. The use of property taxes to support public school expenses is thought by some property owners to be in conflict with benefit theory, especially when said property owners do not have children in public schools.

benefit-cost analysis   *See* COST-BENEFIT ANALYSIS.

benefits, fringe   *See* FRINGE BENEFITS.

benevolent organization   An organization such as a nonprofit organization that attempts to do good to, or for, others. The organization is for benefit rather than for profit. Also, a specific category of organizations that includes, for example, benevolent life insurance associations that may qualify for tax-exempt status under IRS Code 501(c)(12).

Bennett, William J. (1943-) The secretary of the U.S. Department of Education from 1985 to 1988.

bequest, also legacy   Instructions in a will to distribute personal property to an individual or organization.

Berne, Eric (1910-1970)   The psychoanalyst who founded the field of transactional analysis. Major works include: *Games People Play: The Psychology of Human Relationships* (New York: Grove Press, 1964); *Principles of Group Treatment* (New York: Oxford University Press, 1966); *What Do You Say After You Say Hello?* (N.Y.: Grove Press, 1972); *Intuition & Ego States: The Origins of Transactional Analysis* (New York: Harper & Row, 1977).

For a biography, *see* Warren D. Cheney, "Eric Berne: Biographical Sketch," in Eric Berne, *Beyond Games and Scripts* (New York: Grove Press, 1976).

Bertalanffy, Ludwig von (1901-1972)   Austrian-Canadian biologist considered to be the "father of general systems theory." His basic statement on the subject is: *General System Theory: Foundations, Development, Applications,* rev. ed. (New York: George Braziller, 1968). For a biography, *see* Mark Davidson, *Uncommon Sense: The Life and Thought of Ludwig von Bertalanffy (1901-1972), Father of General Systems Theory* (Boston: Houghton Mifflin, 1963).

Beth Israel Hospital v. National Labor Relations Board 437 U.S. 483 (1978)   The Supreme Court case that upheld a National Labor Relations Board determination that employees seeking to organize a bargaining unit of hospital employees could not be prohibited from distributing leaflets in a hospital cafeteria patronized predominantly by hospital employees. To a limited extent, the Court gave its approval to the NLRB's attempt to permit a substantial range for union communication to actual and potential members, provided such communication does not disrupt employer's business activities.

Bethel School District No. 403 v. Fraser 474 U.S. 814, 1046 (1986) The 1986 U.S. Supreme Court decision that held that First Amendment rights to freedom of speech did not prevent school officials from disciplining a student for using offensively lewd language during a speech at a school assembly. The Court ruled that "it is a highly appropriate function of public school education to prohibit the use of vulgar and offensive terms in public discourse."

BFAEd   Bachelor of fine arts education.

BFOQ   *See* BONA FIDE OCCUPATIONAL QUALIFICATION.

bias   1. The tendency of a statistical sample to err in a particular direction. 2. Said of tests when particular subgroups of the population consistently score lower than the general population. *See also* CULTURALLY BIASED. 3. Any predisposition on a matter. 4. The exercise of discrimination toward protected classes (minorities and women).

biased sample   Sample that does not truly represent the total population from which it was selected.

Bible School   1. Religious instruction designed as a summer or vacation school. 2.A private elementary and/or secondary school that is usually run by a Protestant Church with a fundamentalist orientation and which emphasizes bible study. *See also* CHRISTIAN SCHOOL.

bibliotherapy   The use of books or other reading materials to help an individual deal with identified anxieties or emotional problems.

bid   A formal offer to do something, such as build a building or provide trash collection, at a set price. Public school systems are often required by law to receive competitive bids for major contracts.

bid shopping   Disclosing low bids received for contract work in order to get lower bids from other vendors.

big brother   1. A special form of familial protection, as in the charitable Big Brother Association, artificially created in order to offer a substitute for a missing paternalistic influence. While the term is often used sincerely, there can be a sense of a false benevolence about it. 2. George Orwell's (1903-1950) symbolization from his novel, *1984* (London, 1949), of government so big and intrusive that it literally oversaw and regulated every aspect of life. Now "big brother" has evolved to mean any potentially menacing power constantly looking over one's shoulder in judgment.

Big Brothers/Big Sisters of America   A network of local agencies that provide children from a single parent home with an adult friend who can provide regular guidance, understanding, and acceptance. Matches between child and adult are made with the assistance of a professionally trained worker who supervises and supports the relationship.

> Big Brothers/Big Sisters National Office
> 117 South 17th Street
> Suite 1200
> Philadelphia, PA 19103
> (215) 567-2748

bilingual education   1. An educational program in which two languages are used, the primary language of the society and the primary language of individuals being instructed. The general goals are to facilitate learning, to acknowledge the native language of the students and foster a positive self-concept, and to help students understand differences among cultures that different languages reflect. 2. A form of instruction, emphasizing language teaching, that involves the use of the learner's native language concurrent with the society's language as an interim mode until the student has gained sufficient knowledge of the language of the society so that it can be used as the sole mode for instruction. Contrast with ESL, English as a second language.

Prior to the mid-1960s, monolingual education in American schools was consistent with the "melting-pot" theory of our nation's founding, i.e., all citizens should become assimilated into our culture, including our language. The passage of the Bilingual Education Act in 1968 recognized the fact that the United States is a multicultural, multilanguage society, that a significant proportion of schoolchildren in the

United States speak languages other than English, and that these children tended to do poorly in monolingual schools. A trend backward started in California in 1986 with the passage of a state statute to formally establish English as the primary state language and this trend has continued in other states.

See Francesco Cordasco with George Bernstein, comps., *Bilingual Education in American Schools: A Guide to Information Sources*, Education Guide Series, Vol. 3 (Detroit: Gale Research Co., 1979). For a collection of a variety of approaches to bilingual education in the early years of school, see Theresa Escobedo, ed., *Early Childhood Bilingual Education: A Hispanic Perspective* (New York: Teachers College Press, Columbia University, 1983).

See also Ricardo Otheguy, "Thinking about Bilingual Education: A Critical Appraisal," *Harvard Educational Review* (August 1982); Eugene E. Garcia and Raymond V. Padilla, eds., *Advances in Bilingual Education Research* (Tucson: University of Arizona Press, 1985); and Kenji Hakuta, *Mirror of Language: The Debate on Bilingualism* (New York: Basic Books, 1986).

billing journal   An accounting journal used to record all billings (invoiced sales) for services provided to clients or other organizations. A billing journal should contain information on the date of each billing, the person or organization billed, the amount due, when payment is due, and which subsidiary or general ledger accounts are affected (are debited or credited.)

After the billing journal is totaled and balanced at the end of each fiscal period (for example, a month or a year), it is posted to the general ledger and to the accounts receivable subsidiary ledger. *See also:*

ACCOUNTING CYCLE
DEBITS AND CREDITS
GENERAL LEDGER
JOURNAL
POSTING
SUBSIDIARY LEDGER
TRIAL BALANCE

bimodal distribution   Frequency distribution in which there are two modes—two most frequently occurring scores. A graphic presentation would show two peaks.

binder   A temporary, preliminary insurance contract.

binding arbitration   Actually a redundancy! Arbitration, unless it is advisory, is by its nature binding upon the parties. *See also* ARBITRATION.

Binet, Alfred (1857-1911) French psychologist who originated the first modern intelligence test. For a biography, see Theta Holmes Wolf, *Alfred Binet* (Chicago: University of Chicago Press, 1973).

biofeedback   A process for learning voluntary control over autonomic body functions by "feeding back" physiological data to the person who creates it. Physiologic activities—often ones that are associated with stress, such as heart rate, blood pressure, or muscle tension—are monitored with instruments and displayed (or signaled) to the person being monitored. If the biofeedback learning process is effective, the individual learns to recognize the physiologic activities without the use of monitoring equipment and, therefore, is able to voluntarily control them. Biofeedback often is one element in a wellness program. *See also* STRESS.

bipartite board   A labor-management committee established as a part of a grievance process in order to resolve a dispute short of arbitration.

Birmingham Business College, Inc. v. Commissioner   A landmark 1960 decision by the U.S. Court of Appeals for the Fifth Circuit (276 F. 2d 476 5th Cir. 1960) in which the Birmingham Business College was denied tax-exempt status because some of its net earnings inured to the college's shareholders.

birth certificate   A written statement or form issued by an office of vital statistics verifying the name and date of birth of the child as reported by the physician attending at the birth; or a statement in written form issued by the physician attending the child's birth, recording the child's name and date of birth, and acceptable as a birth certificate by the political subdivision where issued.

birth leave   Paid time off upon the birth of a child. This phrase is generally associated with men; women take maternity leave. *See* Nancy Norman and James T. Tedeschi, "Paternity Leave: The Unpopular Benefit Option," *Personnel Administrator* (February 1984).

biserial correlation   Correlation between the score on a particular item and the total test score.

Bivens v. Six Unknown Named Federal Narcotics Agents 403 U.S. 388 (1971)   The Supreme Court case establishing the principle that individuals could sue public officials for damages in connection with the violation of their constitutional rights, especially those covered by the 4th Amendment.

black colleges   Institutions of higher education that were originally established to provide opportunities for post-secondary education for black Americans. Most of these colleges and universities are located in the southern part of the United States and most continue to have, and may seek to maintain, a predominantly black student popula-

tion even though they cannot deny admission to whites on the basis of race.

See Charles V. Willie and Ronald R. Edmonds, eds., *Black Colleges in America* (New York: Teachers College Press, 1978).

black education   1. The study of black history and culture; often called "black studies." 2. The education that blacks (as opposed to other groups) tend to receive in the United States.

Black English   A recognized dialect of standard American English that has its roots in the linguistic and cultural African heritage of black Americans. Black English has its own linguistic structure as well as differences in vocabulary and pronunciation. One characteristic of the dialect is the tendency to contract sentences so that it takes fewer words to express the same meaning.

For a discussion of potential school-related influences, *see* Bruce Cronnell, "Black-English Influences in the Writing of Third- and Sixth-grade Black Students," *Journal of Educational Research*, (March/April 1984). *See also* J. Dillard, ed., *Perspectives on Black English* (The Hague: Mouton, 1975).

Blacky Pictures   A modified projective test designed for use with children age five and above. The technique involves a series of cartoon drawings of a dog, Blacky, and his family about which the child is asked to "tell a story." It is published by:

Psychodynamic Instruments
P.O. Box 1221
Ann Arbor, MI 48106

blind   Individuals who are sightless or who have such limited vision that they must rely on hearing and touch as their chief means of learning.

blind trust   The placement of assets in a trust designed to prevent the owner from influencing or even knowing about its management. This is done when the owner wants to avoid the reality or perception of private inurement or conflict of interest or, for example, by a private foundation to avoid having a controlling interest in another organization.

block grant   A grant that is distributed in accordance with a statutory formula for use in a variety of activities within a broad functional area largely at the recipient's discretion. For a perspective on the use of block grants in education, see Mary E. Vogel, "Education Grant Consolidation: Its Potential Fiscal and Distribution Effects," *Harvard Educational Review*, (May 1982).

block groups   Collective representation from a small area of a school district, often a square block or a linear block area, used to gather information from or to give information to that area of the community.

block parent   A parent or parents in the community designated as the person from whom children or adults can receive assistance. They may be identified by signs in the window or on the house.

block plan   1. A system of dividing a school community into blocks for ease of communication. Each block is an area capable of being contacted by a designated person living in the block. 2. In higher education, a system used in some colleges whereby a student studies only one course at a time in depth.

Bloom, Benjamin (1911-)   The American psychologist known for his study of mastery learning and his development of a systematic classification scheme for educational objectives. *See* BLOOM'S TAXONOMY. For a description of his theories, *see* Benjamin Bloom, *Mastery Learning: Theory and Practice*, (New York: Holt, Rinehart and Winston, 1971); and more recently, Benjamin Bloom, *All Our Children Learning* (New York: McGraw-Hill, 1981).

Bloom's   Taxonomy   A systematic classification of educational objectives developed by Benjamin Bloom and others in the 1950s. The classification divides learning into three domain areas: cognitive, affective, and psychomotor. Each domain is then divided into categories and subcategories representing hierarchical levels of learning. *See* AFFECTIVE DOMAIN, COGNITIVE DOMAIN, PSYCHOMOTOR DOMAIN. For Bloom's original description of his classification system *see* Benjamin S. Bloom et. al., eds., *Taxonomy of Educational Objectives: Handbook I* (New York: David McKay, 1956).

BLS   *See* BUREAU OF LABOR STATISTICS.

Blue Cross and Blue Shield   Nonprofit group health insurance plans for, respectively, hospital and physician fees.

blue sky bargaining   Unreasonable and unrealistic negotiating demands by either side, made usually at the beginning of a negotiating process. The only "useful" purposes of such bargaining are to (1) satisfy an outside audience that their concerns are being attended to, (2) delay the "real" negotiations because such a delay is thought to hold tactical advantage, and (3) provide a basis for compromise as the negotiations progress.

blue collar worker   A manual worker, one whose work is primarily physical (i.e., dealing with things) rather than mental or social. The category includes skilled, semiskilled, and unskilled workers, and includes farm workers as well as factory workers, miners, and construction workers. The term is used to differentiate the manual worker from the "white collar worker."

BMEd   Bachelor of music education.

board of directors   The body of people that, under the authority of the organization's constitution and bylaws, controls and governs the affairs of the organization. *See also:*
ADMINISTRATIVE BOARD
ADVISORY BOARD
DIRECTOR
GOVERNANCE

board of education   The elected or, in less than five percent of the approximately 15,000 boards of education in the U.S., appointed body that has been vested with the general governance of a public school district or system as part of the United States institution of representative government. The governance responsibilities include authorizing, financing, and evaluating the educational activities in a given school system, school, or geographic area as well as employing the superintendent of schools. Such bodies sometimes are known by terms such as school boards, governing boards, boards of directors, school committees, and school trustees. In some cases, this term is also used loosely by private schools. *see also* PUBLIC BOARD OF EDUCATION; and, for a number of articles on America's School Boards, both state and local, *See Phi Delta Kappan* (September 1987).

Board of Education v. Allen 392 U.S. 236 (1968)   Supreme Court case that allowed tax dollars to be used for nonreligious textbooks for parochial school students because the books benefited the students rather than the religion.

board of trustees   The equivalent of a board of directors for some charitable or educational organizations. *See also:*
DIRECTOR
GOVERNANCE
TRUSTEE

board or commission   A group charged with the policy direction of a governmental function. Boards or commissions are used when it is desirable to have bipartisan leadership or when their functions are of a quasi-judicial nature. *See* Paul D. Blanchard and Robert L. Kline, "Decision-Making: School Boards from a Political Perspective," *Journal of Political Science* (Fall 1977).

board profile   An inventory of existing individual board (of directors) members' skills and experiences, areas of community contact and influence, important socio-demographic characteristics and date of (board) term expiration. The profile is analyzed by, for example, a nominating committee to identify needed skills, contacts, and socio-demographic representation to be met by nominees. For example, the expiration of three board members' terms might deplete a board of (1) skills and experience in public relations and strategic planning, (2) contacts with state legislative leaders and the print media, and (3) representation from minorities. The nominating committee thereby establishes its priorities in seeking candidates. *See also:*
BOARD OF DIRECTORS
BOARD ROTATION
DIRECTOR
NOMINATING COMMITTEE

board responsibility   The area of responsibility consisting of those activities that are not delegated by the governing board of the school system to the chief executive officer and his or her staff but are retained by the board. This typically includes all policy-making functions.

board rotation   A schedule for regular replacement of directors on a staggered basis (for example, one third of the members' terms expire every two years). Board rotation provides the organization with continuity of leadership and regular infusions of new ideas and talents. It provides directors with a finite board term and, therefore, a known period of obligation.

boarding school   Almost always a private elementary or secondary school at which the students live (in dormitories or residence halls) during the school term. Secondary level boarding schools are often called prep schools. See James McLachlan, *American Boarding Schools: A Historical Study* (New York: Scribner, 1970).

Bob Jones University v. Simon 416 U.S. 725 (1974)   A landmark U.S. Supreme Court case that affirmed federal public policy against support for racial segregation (and, presumably, other forms of racial discrimination) in nonprofit educational institutions. See also GREEN V. CONNALLY and WRIGHT V. REGAN.

Bob Jones University v. United States   See FREE EXERCISE CLAUSE.

Boehm Tests of Basic Concepts A group-administered norm-referenced test for preschool and primary level students that measures their understanding of 50 frequently used abstract concepts. It is published by:

The Psychological Corporation
555 Academic Court
San Antonio, TX 78204

bona fide occupational qualification (BFOQ or BOQ)   Bona fide is Latin for "good faith." A necessary occupational qualification; a job requirement that would be discriminatory and illegal were it not for its necessity for the performance of a particular job. Title VII of the Civil Rights Act of 1964 allows employers to discriminate against applicants on the basis of religion, sex, or national origin when being considered for certain jobs if they lack a BFOQ. However, what constitutes a BFOQ has been interpreted very narrowly by the EEOC and the federal courts.

See Jeffery M. Shaman, "Toward Defining and Abolishing the Bona Fide Occupational Qualification Based on Class Status," *Labor Law Journal* (June 1971); and Thomas Stephen Neuberger, "Sex as a Bona Fide Occupational Qualification Under Title VII," *Labor Law Journal* (July 1978).

bona fide union   A union that is freely chosen by employees and that is not unreasonably or illegally influenced by their employer.

bond   A certificate of indebtedness issued by a borrower to a lender that constitutes a legal obligation to repay the principal of the loan plus accrued interest.

bond, fidelity   See FIDELITY BOND.

Bond, Horace Mann (1904-)   A black American scholar and educator and one of the best-known authorities on black educational history. He wrote several books and articles, including *The Education of the Negro in the American Social Order* (New York: Octagon Press, 1966) and *Black American Scholars* (Detroit: Belamp, 1972).

For an analysis of his early career, see Michael Fultz, "A Quintessential American: Horace Mann Bond, 1924-1939," *Harvard Educational Review* (November 1985).

bond anticipation notes (BANs)
A form of short-term borrowing used to accelerate progress on approved capital projects. Once the revenues for a project have been realized from the sale of long-term bonds, the BANs are repaid. BANs may also be used to allow a borrower to wait until the bond market becomes more favorable for the sale of long-term securities.

bond attorney   The attorney who approves the legality of a bond issue.

bond bank   An arrangement whereby small units of government within a state are able to pool their long-term debt in order to create a larger bond issue at more advantageous rates.
See Martin T. Katzman, "Measuring the Savings from State Municipal Bond Banking," *Governmental Finance* (March 1980); and David S. Kidwell and Robert J. Rogowski, "Bond Banks: A State Assistance Program that Helps Reduce New Issue Borrowing Costs," *Public Administration Review* (March-April 1983).

bond discount   The excess of the face value of a bond over the price for which it is acquired or sold. The price does not include accrued interest at the date of acquisition or sale.

bond funds   Funds established to account for the proceeds of bond issues pending their disbursement.

bond issue   The offering for sale at a specific time of a set of bonds to provide capital construction funds for a school district.

bond premium   The excess of the price at which a bond is acquired or sold over its face value. The price does not include accrued interest at the date of acquisition or sale.

bond proceeds receivable   An account used to designate the amount receivable upon sale of bonds.

bond rating   The appraisal of the soundness and value assigned to a bond by one of several bond rating companies, such as Standard and Poor or Moody. Rating systems differ, but the highest rating given usually is "Aaa," and the lowest rating of an "investment quality bond" usually is "Baa."

bond register   A record in which the number of the bonds issued and redeemed, dates of issue and redemption, and principal and interest payments are recorded.

bonded debt   The part of a school district's debt which is covered by its outstanding bonds. Sometimes called "funded debt," the total amount of the debt may be limited by state law.

bonding   1. The psychological attachment of mother (and, more recently acknowledged, father) to child that develops during and immediately following childbirth. Bonding is typically a natural occurrence but it may be disrupted by separation of mother and baby or by situational or psychological factors causing the mother to reject the baby at birth. 2. Any close personal and psychological attachment between an adult and a child, between two adults, between any person and a member of his or her peer group, etc. 3. A contract involving three parties: an insurance company, the beneficiary (who often pays the bond premium), and the principal (against whose acts the beneficiary is indemnified). The insurance company promises to pay the beneficiary for damages due to the failure of performance or dishonesty of the principal. *See also* BENEFICIARY and FIDELITY BOND.

bonding limit   A maximum amount that a school district may become liable for through bond issues. A bonding limit may be established by state law or by the voters of the district.

bonds, callable   So designated because the issuing jurisdiction may repay part or all of the obligation prior to the maturity date. For this reason "callable" bonds ordinarily carry higher interest rates. Noncallable bonds, on the other hand, may not be repurchased until the date of maturation.

bonds, moral obligation   State or local government bonds that are backed only by the jurisdiction's promise to repay; they are specifically not backed by a jurisdiction's "full faith and credit." Such bonds will often carry a higher interest rate than other municipal bonds because "full faith and credit" bonds will always be paid first.

See Richard M. Jones, "The Future of Moral Obligation Bonds as a Method of Government Finance in Texas," *Texas Law Review* (January 1976)

bonds, municipal/tax exempt municipal bonds   The debt instruments of sub-national governments; terms used interchangeably with public borrowing and debt financing. This causes some confusion because they appear to refer only to bonds issued by local government. Yet bonds issued by states, territories, or possessions of the United States, or by any municipality, political subdivision (including cities, counties, school districts, and special districts for fire prevention, water, sewer, irrigation, and other purposes), or public agency, or instrumentality (such as an authority or commission) are subsumed under the rubric "municipal bonds." While the interest on municipal bonds is exempt from federal taxes, state and local exemptions may vary.

Tax-exempt bonds allow jurisdictions to borrow money at lower than commercial market interest rates. The buyers of the bonds find them an attractive investment because their high marginal tax rates make a tax-free investment more advantageous than a taxable one paying even higher interest.

See Michael D. Joehnk and David S. Kidwell, "A Look at Competitive and Negotiated Underwriting Costs in the Municipal Bond Market," *Public Administration Review*, (May-June 1980); Jay H. Abrams, "Financing Capital Expenditures: A Look at the Municipal Bond Market," *Public Administration Review* (July-August 1983); Robert B. Inzer and Walter J. Reinhart, "Rethinking Traditional Municipal Bond Sales," *Governmental Finance* (June 1984); and Robert L. Bland, "The Interest Cost Savings from Experience in the Municipal Bond Market, " *Public Administration Review* (January-February 1985).

bonds, revenue   Municipal bonds whose repayment and dividends are guaranteed by revenues derived from the facility constructed from the proceeds of the sale of the bonds (e.g., stadium bonds or dormitory bonds). As revenue bonds are not pledged against the tax base of the issuing jurisdiction, they are usually not regulated by the same debt limitations imposed by most states on the sale of general obligation bonds. Additionally, revenue bond questions usually do not have to be submitted to the voters for approval as they do not commit the full-faith-and-credit of the jurisdiction.

See Philip J. Fischer, Ronald W. Forbes, and John E. Petersen, "Risk and Return in the Choice of Revenue Bond Financing," *Governmental Finance* (September 1980).

bonds, serial   Bonds that are sold in such a way that a certain number of them are retired each year.

bonds, term   Bonds that all mature on the same date.

bonds authorized-unissued   Bonds that a school district can issue without further proceedings other than to direct their sale.

bonds payable   The face value of bonds issued and outstanding.

bonus points   Additional grade points awarded students in secondary schools and junior colleges for performance in schoolwork of unusual difficulty, e.g., for advanced courses. This does not refer to a system of rewards or "tokens" sometimes used as a teaching technique.

book learning   A mildly pejorative term for theoretical knowledge gained from books as opposed to practical experience in a given subject.

book talks   Oral presentations by librarians to groups of students in order to stimulate an interest in reading.

book value   1. The worth of something as recorded on an organization's balance sheet, rather than its worth as established by the market. 2. An organization's net worth, or its clearly proven assets minus its liabilities.

bookkeeping   Collecting, compiling, and retaining an organization's financial information in an organized fashion. Bookkeeping precedes the preparation of financial statements. A subset of accounting. *See also* ACCOUNTANT and ACCOUNTING.

bookmobile   A library on a truck or van that travels an established route to service individuals or groups who would not otherwise have easy access to library services.

books of original entry   Journals in which transactions are recorded initially for subsequent posting in the organization's ledgers. *See also:*
ACCOUNTING CYCLE
JOURNAL
LEDGER

BOQ   *See* BONA FIDE OCCUPATIONAL QUALIFICATION.

Boston English Classical School   The first publicly supported high school in the United States, established in 1821.

Boston Public Latin Grammar School   The first recorded secondary school in North America, established in 1635. It was designed to prepare elite young males for positions of political and/or religious leadership. The term "public" did not connote public support but implied that the school was open to anyone who could afford the fees necessary for enrollment.

Boulwareism   An approach to collective bargaining in which management makes a final "take-it-or-leave-it" offer that it believes is both fair and is the best it can do. The concept is named for Lemuel R. Boulware, a vice president of the General Electric Company, who pioneered the tactic in the 1950s. If the final offer is rejected by the union, management grants the benefits of the offer to all nonunion workers and assures the union that there will be no retroactive benefits when the union finally accepts the "final" offer. Because this tactic called for management to communicate directly to the workers, circumventing the union, it was challenged as an unfair practice. Boulwareism, as used by General Electric, was found in violation of the National Labor Relations Act in a 1969 ruling of the U.S. Circuit Court of Appeals in New York. The company's appeal to the U.S. Supreme Court was denied. The major defense of Boulwareism is Lemuel R. Boulware, *The Truth About Boulwareism: Trying to Do Right Voluntarily* (Washington, D.C.: Bureau of National Affairs, 1969).

bowdlerize   To edit a play or novel so that "offensive" portions (usually those dealing with sexual matters) are removed in order to spare students such exposure and prevent certain parents from being upset about what their children read in school. The word comes from Thomas Bowdler (1754-1825) who published a famous expurgated edition of Shakespeare's plays.

boycott   1. In general usage, to ostracize. During the mid-19th century, Charles C. Boycott, a retired English army captain, managed the Irish estate of an absentee owner. His methods were so severe and oppressive that the local citizens as a group refused to deal with him in any manner. When Captain Boycott was forced to flee home to England, the first *boycott* or nonviolent intimidation through ostracism was a success. *See* Joyce Marlow, *Captain Boycott and The Irish* (New York: Saturday Review Press, 1973). 2. In the context of labor relations, a boycott is any refusal to deal with or buy the products of a business as a means of asserting pressure in a labor dispute.

Boyer, Ernest L. (1928-)   A well-known contemporary educator and educational administrator who, as the president of the Carnegie Foundation for the Advancement of Teaching, has been a significant supporter of research and policy development in education. He is the author of a widely influential analysis of secondary education in America, *High School: A Report on Secondary Education in America* (New York: Harper and Row, 1983). Boyer has also authored numerous articles, including "Improving Urban Schools," *State Education Leader* (December 1986).
See CARNEGIE FOUNDATION FOR THE ADVANCEMENT OF TEACHING.

Boys Market v. Retail Clerks' Local 770 398 U.S. 235 (1970) The U.S. Supreme Court case that held that when a labor contract has a no-strike provision and provides an arbitration procedure, a federal court may, upon the request of an employer, issue an injunction to terminate a strike by employees covered by such a contract. *See also* ARBITRATION and STRIKE.

Boys Town   A private multiservice program (including residential and educational services) for maladjusted youth that was founded by Father Edward Flanagan (1886-1948) as an orphanage for homeless boys. The program currently serves approximately 400 boys in its residential facility alone and is supported primarily through private donations. It is located in Omaha, Nebraska.

BPhEd   Bachelor of physical education.

Bradford, Leland P. (1905-) Director of the National Training Laboratories from 1947 to 1967, who pioneered the development of "sensitivity" training. Major works include *T-Group Theory and Laboratory Method: Innovation in Re-Education*, co-editor (New York: John Wiley, 1964); *Making Meetings Work: A Guide for Leaders & Group Members* (San Diego: University Associates, 1976).

braille   The tactile means by which persons who are blind are enabled to read and write using a system of raised dots (the patterns of which represent letters and numbers). The system was first developed by Louise Braille (1809-1852) in France. The raised dots are arranged in different configurations for each letter of the alphabet and for other symbols, such as numbers and punctuation marks. Each configuration contains from one to six dots arranged in a quadrangular cell. Learning to read braille is much more difficult than learning to read print because it relies on the use of memory to a great extent, and, because the perceptual unit of braille is the single cell, the reader is not able to perceive a number of words at one time as one can when reading print. Reading materials in braille can be obtained from the American Printing House for the Blind and from the Library of Congress. *See* Randall K. Harley et al., *The Teaching of Braille Reading* (Springfield, Ill.: Charles C. Thomas, 1979).

brain drain   A pejorative term referring to the unfortunate flow of human capital—talent—from a country, an area, or an organization. While historically used to describe the exodus of doctors, scientists, and other professionals from a particular country, it is colloquially used to refer to the departure of any valued employee or group of employees.

brainstorming   Frequently used to describe any group effort to generate ideas. It has a more formal definition—a creative conference for the sole purpose of producing suggestions or ideas that can serve as leads to problem-solving. The concept has been most developed by Alex Osborn. *Applied Imagination* (New York: Scribner, 1963).

For a how-to-do-it account, *see* Ronald H. Gorman and H. Kent Baker, "Brainstorming Your Way to Problem-Solving Ideas," *Personnel Journal* (August 1978). *Also see* Toby Katz, "Brainstorming Updated," *Training and Development Journal* (February 1984).

branch campus   A campus of an educational institution (usually an institution of higher education) that is located in a community different from that of its parent institution and beyond a reasonable commuting distance from the main campus of the parent institution.

branching program   1. A format for programmed instruction where the sequence for the presentation of material is dependent on the learner's response to multiple-choice questions. Contrast with LINEAR PROGRAMMING where the sequence of presentation is predetermined and static. 2. A type of ADAPTIVE PROGRAM.

breach of contract   1. The violation by either party of any contract negotiated between two parties and entered into in good faith, including learning contracts, counseling contracts, or administrative contracts. 2. The violation of a collective bargaining agreement by either party. If established grievance machinery is not adequate to deal with the dispute, traditional lawsuits remain as a remedy.

break-even point   The sales volume at which income (or revenues) equals total costs; for example, the number of tickets that must be sold to a fundraising event before a profit is realized.

BREd   Bachelor of religious education.

bridge loan   Temporary, short-term financing; for example, to build or buy a new building before the old one is sold.

brief   A written statement prepared by each side in a formal lawsuit or hearing that summarizes the facts of the situation and makes arguments about how the law should be applied.

brief, Brandeis   A legal brief that takes into account not only the law, but also the technical data from social or scientific research that have economic and sociological implications for the law as well as society. This kind of legal argument was pioneered by Louis D. Brandeis (1856-1941) who later served on the Supreme Court (1916-1939). It was a "Brandeis" brief that helped win the *Brown v. Board of Education* case when the lawyers for Brown proved that separate educational facilities were inherently unequal by testimony from psychologists about the effects segregation had on black children.

Brigance Inventory of Early Development   An individually-administered scale that assesses developmental functioning in the areas of psychomotor, self-help, communication, and general knowledge in children with a developmental level below seven years. It is published by:

Curriculum Associates, Inc.
8 Henshaw Street
Woburn, MA 01801

Brookhart v. Illinois State Board of Education 534 F. Supp. 725 (C.D. Ill. 1982)   One of a number of court cases that ruled that handicapped students are entitled to receive diplomas for completion of school even when they fail to pass minimum competency tests.

brother-sister arrangement   A relationship between a sponsoring organization and an auxiliary charitable organization in which the two are operated as independent organizations rather than the latter being operated as a subsidiary of the former.

Brown v. Board of Education 347 U.S. 483 (1954)   The first Supreme Court case (known as "Brown I") to rule that public schools violated the U.S. Constitution by discriminating in their admission practices on the basis of race. The decision denies the doctrine of "separate but equal" that had been established in 1896 in *Plessy v. Ferguson*. This case was the consolidation of cases from four separate states (Kansas, South Carolina, Virginia, and Delaware) where blacks were seeking admission to public schools on a non-segregated basis. Because of all of the complexities involved in the issue the Court ruled the next year in *Brown v. Board of Education* 349 U.S. 294 (1955) (known as "Brown II"), that local school authorities would be responsible for implementing the Brown I decision, that they should make a "prompt and reasonable start" toward compliance, and that federal courts would monitor the action of local boards.

brown-nosing   A scatological reference to apple polishing behavior; acting in an unduly sycophantic manner toward one's teachers.

brownie points   A pejorative term for presumed marks of approval for acts done by students for teachers that other students consider to be demeaning or servile.

Bruner, J.S. (1915-)   An American psychologist who has been widely influential in the area of instruction and curriculum development. Bruner identified three modes of expression that characterize, in a hierarchical manner, the intellectual development of children: enactive (motor responses), iconic (pictorial images), and symbolic (language). He is the author of *The Process of Education* (Cambridge: Harvard University Press, 1960).

BSAEd   Bachelor of science in art education.

BSBEd   Bachelor of science in business education.

BSEd   Bachelor of science in education.

BSElEd   Bachelor of science in elementary education.

BSHEc   Bachelor of science in home economics.

BSHEd   Bachelor of science in health education.

BSHPhEd   Bachelor of science in health and physical education.

BSMEd   Bachelor of science in music education.

BSOE   Bachelor of science in occupational education.

BSPhEd   Bachelor of science in physical education.

BSPhT   Bachelor of science in physical therapy.

BSR   Bachelor of science in recreation.

BSSecEd   Bachelor of science in secondary education.

BSTIEd   Bachelor of science in trade and industrial education.

BSVHEc   Bachelor of science in vocational home economics.

BSVTEd   Bachelor of science in vocational-trade education.

Buckley Amendment   Popular name for the Family Educational Rights and Privacy Act of 1974 that provides that federal funds are to be denied to any school that refuses to reveal student records to parents prior to the time that a student reaches the age of 18 or to students who are over 18 and who then have the right to access their own records and to decide if parents may have access. Senator James Buckley of New York sponsored the law.

budget   A plan of financial operation embodying an estimate of proposed expenditures for a given period or purpose and the proposed means of financing them. The budget usually consists of three parts. The first part contains a message from the budget-making authority together with a summary of the proposed expenditures and the means of financing them. The second part consists of schedules supporting the summary. The schedules show in detail the proposed expenditures and means of financing them together with information as to past years' actual revenues and expenditures and other data used in mak-

ing the estimates. The third part is composed of drafts of the appropriation, revenue, and borrowing measures necessary to put the budget into effect.

budget, executive   The process by which agency requests for appropriations are prepared and submitted to a budget bureau under a chief executive for review, alteration, and consolidation into a single budget document that can be compared to expected revenues and executive priorities before submission to a legislature or board.

budget, line-item   The classification of budgetary accounts according to narrow, detailed objects of expenditure (such as motor vehicles, clerical workers, or reams of paper) used within each particular agency or organization, generally without reference to the ultimate purpose or objective served by the expenditure.

budget, operating   Short-term plan for managing the resources necessary to carry out a program. "Short-term" can mean anything from a few weeks to a few years. Usually an operating budget is developed for each fiscal year with changes made as necessary.

budget activity   Categories within most accounts that identify the purposes, projects, or types of activities financed.

budget cycle   The timed steps of the budget process, which includes preparation, approval, execution, and audit. *See* Jerry Banks and Robert F. Clark, "Evaluation Research and the Budget Cycle," *Policy Studies Journal* (Special Issue No. 3, 1980).

budget deficit   The amount by which budget outlays exceed budget receipts for any given period.

budget document The instrument used by the budget-making authority to present a comprehensive financial program to the appropriating body.

budget estimates Estimates of budget authority, outlays, receipts, or other budget measures that cover current and future years.

budget period The length of time for which a budget is effective. The budget period for most operating budgets is one year.

budget surplus The amount by which a government or school district's budget receipts exceed its budget outlays for any given period.

budget update A statement summarizing amendments to or revisions in the budget requested, estimated outlays, and estimated receipts for a fiscal year that has not been completed.

budget year The fiscal year for which the budget is being considered; the fiscal year following the current fiscal year.

budgetary accounts Those accounts necessary to reflect budget operations and conditions, such as estimated revenues, appropriations, and encumbrances, as distinguished from proprietary accounts. *See also* PROPRIETARY ACCOUNTS.

budgetary control The control or management of the business affairs of a school district in accordance with an approved budget with a view toward keeping expenditures within the authorized amounts.

budgeting No less than the single most important decision-making process in United States public institutions today. The budget itself is also a jurisdiction's most important reference document. In their increasingly voluminous formats, budgets simultaneously record policy decision outcomes, cite policy priorities as well as program objectives, and delineate a government's total service effort.

A public budget has four basic dimensions. First, it is a political instrument that allocates scarce public resources among the social and economic needs of the jurisdiction. Second, a budget is a managerial and/or administrative instrument. It specifies the ways and means of providing public programs and services; it establishes the costs and/or criteria by which activities are evaluated for their efficiency and effectiveness. It is the budgeting process that ensures that all of the programs and activities of a jurisdiction will be reviewed or evaluated at least once during each year (or cycle). Third, a budget is an economic instrument that can direct a nation's or a state's economic growth and development. Certainly at the national level—and to a lesser extent at the state and regional levels—government budgets are primary instruments for redistributing income, stimulating economic growth, promoting full employment, combating inflation, and maintaining economic stability. Fourth, a budget is an accounting instrument that holds government officials responsible for the expenditure of the funds with which they have been entrusted. Budgets also hold governments accountable in the aggregate. The very concept of a budget implies that there is a ceiling or a spending limitation, which literally (but theoretically) requires governments to live within their means.

For texts, see Robert D. Lee and Ronald W. Johnson, *Public Budgeting Systems*, 2nd ed. (Baltimore: University Park Press, 1977); Albert C. Hyde and Jay M. Shafritz, ed., *Government Budgeting Theory, Process, Politics* (Oak Park, Ill.: Moore, 1978); Aaron Wildavsky, *The Politics of the Budgetary*

Process, 4th ed. (Boston: Little, Brown, 1984); and John Greenhalgh, *School Site Budgeting* (Lanham, Md.: University Press of America, 1984).

See also:
AUDIT
BALANCED BUDGET
BUDGETING, PERFORMANCE
DEBT FINANCING
DISBURSEMENTS
PLANNING, PROGRAMMING, BUDGETING
   SYSTEMS
RECONCILIATION
UNCONTROLLABLE EXPENSES

budgeting, capital   A budget process that deals with planning for large expenditures for capital items. Capital expenditures should be for long-term investments (such as bridges and buildings) that yield returns for years after they are completed. Capital budgets typically cover five- to 10-year periods and are updated yearly. Items included in capital budgets may be financed through borrowing (including tax-exempt municipal bonds), savings, grants, revenue sharing, special assessments, etc.

A capital budget provides for separating the financing of capital or investment expenditures from current or operating expenditures. The federal government has never had a capital budget in the sense of financing capital or investment type programs separately from current expenditures.

See John Matzer, Jr., ed., *Capital Financing Strategies for Local Governments* (Washington, D.C.: International City Management Association, 1983); Ronald W. Chapman, "Capital Financing: An Old Approach Reapplied," *Public Productivity Review* (December 1983); and Raymond J. Staffeldt and Kenneth Unger, "Pennsylvania's Capital Budgeting System," *State Government* (Fall 1985).

budgeting, cost-based   Also obligation-based budgeting. Budgeting in terms of costs to be incurred; that is, the resources to be consumed in carrying out a program, regardless of when the funds to acquire the resources were obligated or paid, and without regard to the source of funds. For example, inventory items become costs when they are withdrawn from inventory, and the cost of buildings is distributed over time, through periodic depreciation charges, rather than in a lump sum when the buildings are acquired.

budgeting, incremental   A method of budget review that focuses on the increments of increase or decrease in the budget of existing programs. Incremental budgeting, which is often called "traditional budgeting," is a school of thought counter to more rational, systems-oriented approaches such as zero-base budgeting. But this old approach nicely takes into account the inherently political nature of the budget process and so will continue to be favored by legislative appropriations committees, if not by budget theorists.

See John Wanat, "Bases of Budgetary Incrementalism," *American Political Science Review* (September 1974); Harvey J. Tucker, "Incremental Budgeting: Myth or Model?" *Western Political Quarterly* (September 1982); and Allen Schick, "Incremental Budgeting in a Decremental Age," *Policy Sciences* (September 1983).

budgeting, performance   A type of budgeting that is concerned with performance work assessment and efficiency. Performance budgeting presents purposes and objectives for which funds are allocated, examines costs of programs and activities established to meet these objectives, and identifies and analyzes quantitative data measuring work performed and accomplishments. Performance budgeting tends to be retrospective, focusing on previous performance and work accomplishment.

The terms *performance budgeting* and *program budgeting* tend to be used interchangeably, but they are not synonymous. In performance budgeting, programs are generally linked to the various higher levels of an organization and serve as labels that encompass and structure the subordinate performance units. These units—the central element of performance budgeting—are geared to an organization's operational levels, and information about them is concrete and meaningful to managers at all levels. Program budgeting, on the other hand, might or might not incorporate performance measurement, yet still might be useful for delineating broad functional categories of expenditure for review at higher levels. Overall, performance budgeting tends to be retrospective—focusing on previous performance and work accomplishments—while program budgeting tends to be forward-looking, policy planning, and forecasts.

budgeting, planning programming *See* PLANNING, PROGRAMMING, BUDGETING SYSTEMS.

budgeting, program *See* BUDGETING, PERFORMANCE.

budgeting, zero-base A budgeting process that is first and foremost a rejection of the incremental decision-making model of budgeting. It demands a rejustification of the entire budget submission (from ground zero), whereas incremental budgeting essentially respects the outcomes of previous budgetary decisions (collectively referred to as the budget base) and focuses examination on the margin of change from year to year.

See Peter A. Phyrr, "The Zero-Base Approach to Government Budgeting," *Public Administration Review* (January-February 1977); Allen Schick, "The

Road from ZBB," *Public Administration Review* (March-April 1978); and Charles E. Hill, "Zero-Based Budgeting: A Practical Application," *Governmental Finance* (March 1983).

budgeting services Activities concerned with supervising budget planning, formulation, control, and analysis.

building level teams 1. A broad term for a group of staff representing an individual school building who meet together for some particular purpose. 2. In some systems the term refers to a group of building staff who meet specifically to address special needs of students in the building, such as failure to achieve satisfactory progress or behavioral problems. Typically the building team consists of the principal, a counselor, and special education personnel who will assist the classroom teacher in planning accommodations or modifications for a student in question. This process is favored in many schools as an effective means of using special education teachers in a consultative capacity and thus reducing the number of referrals of students for direct special education services.

bump, or bumping A layoff procedure that gives an employee with greater seniority the right to displace or "bump" another employee. Sometimes bumping rights are restricted to one office or department. Because of bumping rights, the laying off of a single worker can lead to the sequential transfers of a dozen others.

bureau Government department, agency, or subdivision of same.

Bureau of the Education of the Handicapped (BEH) Previous designation for the Office of Special Education Programs, U.S. Department of Education. During the years following the passage of the Education for All Handicapped Children Act of 1975 the personnel, structure, and name of the agency responsible for the administration of the act changed frequently. BEH is recalled by many professionals in the special education field because it was the designation for the agency when first implementing the Act and is credited for many of the early innovative programs as well as blamed for the early errors.

Bureau of Labor Statistics (BLS)   The agency responsible for the economic and statistical research activities of the Department of Labor. The BLS is the government's principal fact-finding agency in the field of labor economics, particularly with respect to the collection and analysis of data on human resource and labor requirements, living conditions, labor-management relations, productivity and technological developments, occupational safety and health, structure and growth of the economy, urban conditions and related socioeconomic issues, and international aspects of certain of these subjects.

bureaucracy   1. The public officials of a government. 2. A general invective to apply to any inefficient organization encumbered by "red tape." 3. A specific set of structural arrangements. The dominant structural definition of bureaucracy, indeed the point of departure for all further analyses on the subject, is that of the German sociologist Max Weber (1864-1920), who used an "ideal type" approach to extrapolate from the real world the central core of features that would characterize the most fully developed bureaucratic form of organization. This "ideal type" is neither a description of reality nor a statement of normative preference. It is merely an identification of the major variables or features that characterize bureaucracy. The fact that such features might not be

fully present in a given organization does not necessarily imply that the organization is "non-bureaucratic." It may be an immature rather than a fully developed bureaucracy. At some point, however, it may be necessary to conclude that the characteristics of bureaucracy are so lacking in an organization that it could neither reasonably be termed bureaucratic nor be expected to produce patterns of bureaucratic behavior.

Weber's "ideal type" bureaucracy possesses the following characteristics:

1. The bureaucrats must be personally free and subject to authority only with respect to the impersonal duties of their offices.
2. They are arranged in a clearly defined hierarchy of offices.
3. The functions of each office are clearly specified.
4. Officials accept and maintain their appointments freely—without duress.
5. Appointments are made on the basis of technical qualifications that ideally are substantiated by examinations—administered by the appointing authority, a university, or both.
6. Officials should have a money salary as well as pension rights. Such salaries must reflect the varying levels of positions in the hierarchy. While officials are always free to leave the organization, they can be removed from their offices only under previously stated specific circumstances.
7. An incumbent's post must be his sole or at least his major occupation.
8. A career system is essential. While promotion may be the result of either seniority or merit, it must be premised on the judgment of hierarchical superiors.

9. The official may not have a property right to his position nor any personal claim to the resources that go with it.
10. An official's conduct must be subject to systematic control and strict discipline.

While Weber's structural identification of bureaucratic organization (first published in 1922) is perhaps the most comprehensive statement on the subject in the literature of the social sciences, it is not always considered satisfactory as an intellectual construct. For example, Anthony Downs, in *Inside Bureaucracy* (Boston: Little, Brown, 1967), argues that at least two elements should be added to Weber's definition. First, the organization must be large. According to Downs, "any organization in which the highest ranking members know less than half of the other members can be considered large." Second, most of the organization's output cannot be "directly or indirectly evaluated in any markets external to the organization by means of voluntary quid pro quo transactions."

See also RED TAPE and REPRESENTATIVE BUREAUCRACY.

bureaucrat   An employee of a bureaucracy.

bureaucrats, street level   Those public officials who are literally closest to the people by being in almost constant contact with the public; for example police officers, welfare case workers, or teachers.

See Michael Lipsky, "Toward a Theory of Street-Level Bureaucracy," in Willis D. Hawley et al., *Theoretical Perspectives in Urban Politics* (Englewood Cliffs, New Jersey: Prentice-Hall, 1976); and Nicholas P. Lovrich, Jr., Brent S. Steel, and Mahdun Majed, "The Street-Level Bureaucrat—A Useful Category or a Distinction Without a Difference? *Review of Public*

Personnel Administration (Spring 1986).

burnout   1. A worker's feeling of mental and physical fatigue that causes indifference and emotional disengagement from his or her job. Compare to STRESS.

See Whiton Stewart Paine, ed., *Job Stress and Burnout: Research, Theory, and Intervention Perspectives* (Beverly Hills, Calif.: Sage Publications, Inc., 1982); and Morley D. Glicken and Katherine Janka, "Executives Under Fire: The Burnout Syndrome," *California Management Review* (Spring 1982). 2. The effect of prolonged and heavy marijuana use characterized by slow movements and a blank zombie-like appearance.

bus driver   A staff member performing the assigned activities of operating a pupil transportation vehicle for the purpose of transporting pupils to and from school or on trips involved in school activities.

business administration responsibility   The area of responsibility for managing and conducting the business operations of the school system. It consists of the business management activities for any of the following areas: financial accounting, buildings and grounds administration, purchasing and stores, personnel administration, food services, and pupil transportation.

business agent   A full-time officer of a local union, elected or appointed, who handles grievances, helps enforce agreements, and otherwise deals with the union's financial, administrative, or labor-management problems.

business judgment rule   The general principle of law that holds that if people running an organization make honest, careful decisions within their legal powers, no court will interfere with those decisions—even if the results of a decision are bad.

business manager   A staff member performing assigned activities that have as their purpose the management of the organization of the school system for carrying out its business administration functions.

business necessity   The major legal defense for using an employment practice that effectively excludes women and/or minorities. The leading court case, *Robinson v. Lorrilard Corp.* (444 F.2d 791 [4th Cir. 1971]; *cert. denied*, 404 U.S. 1006 [1971]), holds that the test of the business necessity defense "is whether there exists an overriding legitimate business purpose such that the practice is necessary to the safe and efficient operation of the business."

business school   1. A nonpublic educational institution offering courses in preparation for business occupations such as stenography, bookkeeping, and data processing. Such an institution frequently is referred to as a "Private Business School" or "Business College." 2. A professional school within an institution of higher education.

business support services   Activities concerned with purchasing, paying for, transporting, exchanging, and maintaining goods and services for a school district. Included are the fiscal, acquisition of facilities, operation and maintenance, and internal services for operating all schools.

busing   1. Transporting children to school when they live too far away to walk in a reasonable time. 2. The transporting of children by bus to schools at a greater distance than those that the children would otherwise attend in order to achieve racial desegregation. Busing has often been mandated by the federal courts as a remedy for past practices of discrimination. It has been heartily objected to by parents who want their children to attend neighborhood schools and has in consequence been a major factor in WHITE FLIGHT from central cities. Busing is often used as an example of government by the judiciary because busing, one of the most controversial domestic policies in the history of the United States, has never been specifically sanctioned by the Congress. Compare to *Swann v. Charlotte-Mecklenburg Board of Education*.

See David O. Sears, Carl P. Hensler, and Leslie K. Speer, "Whites' Opposition to Busing: Self-Interest or Symbolic Politics?" *American Political Science Review* (June 1979); John B. McConahay, "Self-Interest versus Racial Attitudes as Correlates of Anti-Busing Attitudes in Louisville: Is It the Buses or the Blacks?" *Journal of Politics* (August 1982); and Gerald W. Heaney, "Busing, Timetables, Goals, and Ratios: Touchstones of Equal Opportunity," *Minnesota Law Review* (April 1985).

busywork   1. Any meaningless assignment given by a teacher. 2. Activities assigned mainly to keep a group occupied rather than as a learning experience. 3. Activities assigned to one group by a teacher so that the teacher will be free to attend to a second group.

Butler, Nicholas Murray (1862-1947)   The president of Columbia University (from 1901-1945), who was a major influence on higher education for teachers, who helped create the College Entrance Examination Board, and who had a major role in establishing the modern high school curriculum. He won the Noble Peace Prize in 1931. *See* Richard F.W. Whittemore, *Nicholas Murray Butler and Public Education* (New York: Teachers College Press, 1971).

Butz v. Economou 438 U.S. 478 (1978)   The Supreme Court case that provided an immunity from suit for civil damages to federal administrative officials exercising adjudicatory functions.

See Gail M. Burgess, "Official Immunity and Civil Liability for Constitutional Torts Committed by Military Commanders After *Butz v. Economou*," *Military Law Review* (Summer 1980); Robert G. Vaughn, "The Personal Accountability of Civil Servants," *The Bureaucrat* (Fall 1980); and Gerald J. Miller, "Administrative Malpractice Before and After *Butz v Economou*," *The Bureaucrat* (Winter 1980-81).

buy American acts   Various state and national laws that require government agencies to give a preference to American-made goods when making purchases. Similar "buy national" practices are also being used by all the major trading partners of the United States. *See* Captain Charles W. Trainor, "The Buy American Act: Examination, Analysis and Comparison," *Military Law Review* (Spring 1974).

buyer   A staff member performing assigned activities such as preparing bids, interviewing sales representatives, and recommending bid awards in connection with the procurement of school supplies, equipment, and other school property.

buzz group   1. Any informal meeting to discuss specific issues. 2. A device that seeks to give all the individuals at a large meeting an equal opportunity to participate by breaking the larger meeting into small groups of from six to eight persons each. These "buzz groups" then designate one person each to report on their consensus (and dissents, if any) when the total group reconvenes.

buzz word   1. A word that specifically designates a particularly popular and up-to-date theory or practice. 2. The currently most acceptable terminology to use in reference to any phenomenon, group, or idea.

BVEd   Bachelor of vocational education.

bylaws   1. The regulations adopted by a corporation's stockholders for its internal governance. 2. The rules on regulations adopted by an organization such as a social club or voluntary association. 3. The laws enacted by subordinate legislative bodies such as municipalities.

C

cabinet   A group of individuals appointed by an institution's president to serve as advisers on policy decisions. Cabinets usually include selected heads of the executive departments of the institution.

cafeteria benefits plan   Also called smorgasbord benefits plan. Any program that allows employees to choose their fringe benefits within the limits of the total benefit dollars for which they are eligible. This allows each employee to have, in effect, his or her own individualized benefit program. Because such programs cost more to administer, they tend to exist mainly as part of high-level, managerial compensation packages. However, increasing computer capabilities will make it likely that such plans will be more widely offered.

See David J. Thomsen, "Introducing Cafeteria Compensation in Your Company," *Compensation Review* (First Quarter, 1978); and Peter W. Stonebraker, "A Three-Tier Plan for Cafeteria Benefits," *Personnel Journal* (December 1984).

cafetorium   An instructional space designed, or adapted, specifically for the combined functions that might normally be served by a separate cafeteria and a separate auditorium.

CAI   *See* COMPUTER ASSISTED INSTRUCTION.

California Achievement Tests

A group-administered norm-referenced test of skill development in reading, math, and language. Its five levels cover grades 1.5 to 12. It is published by:
> CTB/McGraw-Hill
> DelMonte Research Park
> Monterey, CA 93940

California Occupational Preference Survey

Also called Copsystem. A self-report inventory of job activity interest that can be used in vocational guidance and counseling. Areas of interest that are measured include science, technology, business, outdoors, clerical, arts, communication, and service-oriented professions.
> Educational and Industrial Testing Service
> P.O. Box 7243
> San Diego, CA 92107

California Psychological Inventory (CPI)

A true/false questionnaire that is intended to measure the personality characteristics of non-psychiatrically disturbed individuals.
> Consulting Psychologists Press, Inc.
> 577 College Avenue
> Palo Alto, CA 93904

California Short Form Test of Mental Maturity (CTMM/SF)

A test of academic aptitude that measures functional capacities basic to learning, problem-solving, and responding to new situations. It is a shortened version of the California Test of Mental Maturity (CTMM) and omits the measure of spatial relationships.
> California Test Bureau/McGraw-Hill
> Del Monte Research Park
> Monterey, CA 94306

California Test of Mental Maturity (CTMM)

A test of academic aptitude that measures functional capacities basic to learning, problem-solving, and responding to new situations (i.e., logical reasoning, spatial relationships, numerical reasoning, verbal concepts, and memory).
> California Test Bureau/McGraw-Hill
> Del Monte Research Park
> Monterey, CA 94306

callable bond   A security instrument that allows the issuer to repay part or all of the obligation prior to the maturity date. Callable bonds ordinarily carry higher interest rates. *Noncallable bonds*, in contrast, may not be repaid until the date of maturation.

Callier-Azusa Scale   A scale designed to measure developmental skills in areas such as communication, self-help, and psychomotor functioning in children who are multihandicapped. It is published by:

Callier Center for Communication Disorders
University of Texas/Dallas
1966 Inwood Road
Dallas, TX 75235

Cambridge Plan   An elementary school curriculum installed in 1893 in the Cambridge, Massachusetts, schools that allowed brighter students to complete the program of instruction in two years less than others by means of a parallel track curriculum.

candidate   1. One who seeks elective office. The word came from Latin; *candida* was the color of the white togas worn by *candidatus* or candidates for elective office in the ancient Roman republic. 2. An applicant for a civil service position. 3. An applicant for admission to a school or college. 4. An applicant for a scholarship. 5. A registrant for a standardized test such as the SAT. 6. A student matriculated in a course of study at an institution of higher education, i.e., a degree candidate.

Candidates Reply Date Agreement   A concurrence among participating colleges that is sponsored by the College Entrance Examination Board, which stipulates that the participating colleges will not require students to accept or reject an offer of admission prior to May 1. This agreement allows the student an awareness of all opportunities prior to making a decision.

capital budgeting   *See* BUDGETING, CAPITAL.

capital depreciation   The calculated decline in value of capital assets over the usable life of the asset. There are a variety of techniques for calculating the rate and amount of depreciation that often give quite different results.

capital fund campaign   Also called capital program and capital fund drive. Fundraising activities intended to attract major gifts, which typically require more than one year to complete and will be used for the purchase or construction of capital assets, rather than for operating expenses. Capital fund campaigns are commonly conducted simultaneously with regular fundraising activities and, ideally, should not reduce funds raised through the regular fundraising program.

See J.P. Smith, "Rethinking the Traditional Capital Campaign," in F.C. Pray, ed., *Handbook for Educational Fundraising* (San Francisco: Jossey-Bass, 1981).

capital improvement   Any improvement (e.g., modification, addition, or restoration) that has the effect of increasing the usefulness or serviceable life of an existing capital asset, such as a building. Capital improvements increase the recorded worth of the asset by the cost of the improvements. *See* DEPRECIATION.

capital outlay   An expenditure that results in the acquisition of fixed assets or additions to fixed assets that are presumed to have benefits for more than one year. It is an expenditure for land or existing buildings, improvements of grounds, construction of buildings, additions to buildings, remodeling of buildings, or initial purchase, additional purchase, and replacement of equipment.

capitation grant   A grant whose amount is determined on the basis of student population; that is, a head count.

Cardinal Principles of Secondary Education   A statement prepared in 1918 by a National Education Association commission that has strongly influenced high school curricula. The seven principles identified were: (1) health, (2) command of fundamental processes, (3) worthy home membership, (4) vocation, (5) citizenship, (6) worthy use of leisure, and (7) ethical character. *See* Commission on the Reorganization of Secondary Education, NEA, *Cardinal Principles of Secondary Education* (Washington, D.C.: Government Printing Office Bulletin No. 35, 1918).

career counseling   1. A counseling process in which the pupil is assisted in utilizing his or her aptitudes and abilities to develop realistic career plans. 2. Guidance provided to employees in order to assist them in achieving occupational training, education, and career goals.

See Andre G. Beaumont, Alva C. Cooper, and Raymond H. Stockard, *A Model Career Counseling and Placement Program*, 3rd ed. (Bethlehem, Pa.: College Placement Services, Inc., 1980); Russell B. Flanders and Neale Baxter, "The Sweat of Their Brows: A Look Back Over Occupational Information and Career Counseling," *Occupational Outlook Quarterly* (Fall 1981); and Karen Raskin-Young, "Career Counseling in a Large Organization," *Training and Development Journal* (August 1984).

career day   A school-sponsored day on which prospective employers (or

colleges) are all invited to make presentations to students.

career education   1. A vague term for any education that prepares an individual for the world of work. While it includes vocational education, it also encompasses all academic subjects so long as they are part of career preparation. 2. To career/vocational education specialists a specific concept, as differentiated from vocational or job training, which implies long-term future planning and which includes the acquisition of competencies necessary for job retention and advancement in addition to discrete job skill training.

See Jack W. Fuller and Terry O. Whealon, eds., *Career Education: A Life-Long Process* (Chicago: Nelson-Hall, 1979).

career ladder   Series of classifications in which an employee may advance through training, on-the-job experience and/or evaluation reviews into successively higher levels of responsibility and salary. *See* Russ Smith and Margret Waldie, "Multi-Track Career Ladders: Maximizing Opportunities," *Review of Public Personnel Administration* (Spring 1984); and Paul R. Borden, ed., *Establishing Career Ladders In Teaching: A Guide for Policy Makers* (Springfield, Ill.: Charles C. Thomas, 1987).

career lattice   A term that identifies horizontal and/or diagonal paths of occupational mobility leading from the entry level. Most often these paths link parallel paths of vertical or upward occupational mobility. A horizontal path of occupational mobility is often called a job transfer while a diagonal path is often referred to as a transfer-promotional path. This "lateral" mobility usually occurs within an occupational field (i.e., engineering, accounting) but usually not within the same specific occupational classification.

career management   Aspect of personnel management that is concerned with the occupational growth of individuals within an organization.

See Marion S. Kellogg, *Career Management* (New York: American Management Association, Inc., 1972); Douglas T. Hall and Francine S. Hall, "What's New in Career Management," *Organizational Dynamics* (Summer 1976); and Edwin O. Joslin, "Career Management: How to Make it Work," *Personnel* (July-August 1977).

career promotion   Promotion made on the basis of merit, but without competition with other employees. An example is the promotion of an employee who, as he or she learns more about the job, can do more difficult kinds of work and assume greater responsibility, so that he or she is preforming duties classified at a higher grade level.

career system   Sequence of progressively more responsible positions in the same general occupation that an organization makes available to qualified individuals.

caretaker   Also caregiver. 1. A person responsible for a child's health or welfare, including the child's parent, guardian, or other person within the child's own home; or a person responsible for a child's health or welfare in a relative's home, foster care home, or residential institution. A caretaker is responsible for meeting a child's basic physical and psychological needs and for providing protection and supervision. 2. A school janitor.

Carl D. Perkins Vocational Education Act (P.L. 98-524)   Amendments to the Vocational Education Act of 1963, enacted in 1984, that con-

tained a number of provisions for increasing the ability of persons who are handicapped to access vocational education programs.

Carnegie Foundation for the Advancement of Teaching   A well-endowed private, operating foundation established by Andrew Carnegie in 1905 to provide retirement allowances for university teachers and to encourage the profession of teaching and the cause of higher education in the United States and Canada. While it still provides some pension benefits, its primary function is to conduct and to support research and policy studies in education.

Carnegie Foundation
Five Ivy Lane
Princeton, NJ 08540
(609) 452-1780

Carnegie Report   The popular name for *A Nation Prepared: Teachers for the 21st Century*, a report prepared by the Carnegie Forum on Education and the Economy in 1986 that included recommendations for massive reforms in teacher education and for the restructuring of schools. For an analysis of the report, *see* Mark Tucker and David Mandel, "The Carnegie Report—A Call for Re-designing the Schools," *Phi Delta Kappan* (September 1986). For a full report, *see* Carnegie Task Force on Teaching as a Profession, *A Nation Prepared: Teachers for the 21st Century* (New York: Carnegie Forum on Education and the Economy, 1986).

Carnegie unit   A standard of measurement that represents one credit for the completion of a one-year course.

carrel   1. A booth or individually isolated area located in a library or school resource center in which a student can work independently using the books and other resources immediately available. 2. A desk or booth that provides a visual barrier and physical isolation between a student and the rest of a class that is sometimes used in classrooms for students who have behavioral and/or learning problems and who may otherwise either distract or be distracted by other students.

Carroll, John B. (1916-)   A
psychologist and educator who has written much in the areas of lanugage and language learning and who is credited with developing the theoretical basis for mastery learning. Among his publications are *The Study of Language* (1953), *Language and Thought* (1964), and *Perspective on School Learning: Selected Writings* (1985). *See* MASTERY LEARNING.

Carroll's Model of School Learning
A learning model proposed by John B. Carroll in 1963 and credited by Benjamin Bloom as providing the theoretical basis for mastery learning theory. The model suggests that degree of learning is a function of the ratio of the amount of time a learner spends on a task and the amount of time required to learn the task. Therefore, learning mastery will increase if time on a task increases and instructional conditions are such that time needed to learn the task is decreased.

$$\text{degree of learning} = \frac{\text{amount of time needed to learn}}{\text{amount of time spent on task}}$$

For Carroll's original treatise, *see* John B. Carroll, "A Model of School Learning," *Teachers College Record* (1963). For a more recent application, *see* Jason Millman et al., "Relation Between Perseverance and Rate of Learning: A Test of Carroll's Model of School Learning," *American Educational Research Journal* (Fall 1983).

CASE   *See* COUNCIL OF ADMINISTRATORS OF SPECIAL EDUCATION.

case conference   A formal meeting where two or more school professionals get together to discuss an individual student and to develop strategies to help the student reach specified objectives.

case history   1. A confidential file on a student containing notes by school counselors, school psychologists, and others which records a "problem" student's behavior over time. 2. A report that may be prepared by the school nurse or social worker or other appropriate staff that contains information about a student's health and social and family history. Generally completed when a child is referred for special school services, such as special education.

case study   1. A research design that focuses upon the in-depth analysis of a single subject. It is particularly useful when the researcher seeks an understanding of dynamic processes over time. A case study is usually more qualitative than quantitative in methodological approach and is more appropriate for generating hypotheses than for testing hypotheses. In a case study the researcher usually collects data through the review of records, interviews, questionnaires, and observations. It is particularly appropriate for generating insights into new areas of research. 2. An extensive examination of one subject over a long period of time.

caseload   The number of students for whom a professional staff member is responsible for providing services.

casework   A method of social work intervention that helps an individual or family improve their functioning in society by changing both internal attitudes and feelings and external circumstances directly affecting the individual or family. This contrasts with community organization and other methods of social work intervention that focus on changing institutions or society. Social casework relies on a relationship between the worker and client as the primary tool for effecting change.

cash accounting The oldest and simplest form of accounting, cash accounting (or cash basis accounting) records transactions when cash flows into or out of the institution or organizational unit. Thus transactions are recorded when funds are received from various sources and disbursements are recorded either when checks are issued or when they clear the bank.

See M.J. Gross, Jr. and S.F. Jablonsky, *Principles of Accounting and Financial Reporting for Nonprofit Organizations* (New York: Wiley-Interscience, 1979).

cash flow analysis The systematic review and assessment of the movement of money in and out of an institution. Where a *cash accounting* system is used rather than *accrual accounting*, a cash flow analysis is essentially equivalent to an operating statement. Compare to OPERATING STATEMENT.

cash management A series of techniques intended to assure maximum use of temporarily available cash for short-term investments. More specifically, an effective cash management program has several basic purposes:
1. Developing accurate cash projections
2. Managing cash receipts
3. Controlling cash disbursements
4. Establishing sound banking relationships
5. Investing funds

CAT *See* CHILDREN'S APPERCEPTION TEST.

cataloging Activities involved in classifying educational media according to an established classification system and building a catalog to facilitate information retrieval, which includes listings according to such information as subject, author, title, and producer.

categorical aid Educational support funds provided from a higher governmental level and specifically limited to (earmarked for) a given purpose, e.g., special education, transportation, or vocational education.

Catholic schools The largest group of private schools in the United States. They are operated either by local parishes, by a diocese, or by private religious communities. Trends over the past several years suggest that both total enrollment and number of schools are decreasing. *See Catholic Schools in America* (Englewood, Colo.: Fisher Publishing Company, in cooperation with the National Catholic Educational Association, 1980).

Cattell Culture Fair Intelligence Test A basic general intelligence test in which scores are relatively free of educational and cultural influences. This test is particularly desirable where environmental factors may unduly influence conventional test scores. Published by:
Bobbs-Merrill Company, Inc.
4300 W. 62nd Street
Indianapolis, IN 46206

Cattell Infant Intelligence Scale A predictive test that is used to measure the developmental behaviors of infants and young children below the age of 2 1/2. It is administered individually and is published by:
The Psychological Corporation
555 Academic Court
San Antonio, TX 78204

CATV Community antenna television system.

cause A shortened form of "just cause"; an ill-defined legal concept that is used to describe a legitimate reason for taking an administrative action. For example, employees may be terminated from a position for "just cause," or for cause.

cause-effect 1. A term referring to the relationship between one event and another that assumes that the second event is the direct result of the first. 2. A significant learning milestone in Piaget's theory of cognitive development.

CCSSO *See* COUNCIL OF CHIEF STATE SCHOOL OFFICERS.

CEC *See* COUNCIL FOR EXCEPTIONAL CHILDREN.

CEEB *See* COLLEGE ENTRANCE EXAMINATION BOARD.

ceiling Upper limit of ability measured by a test. A test has a low ceiling for a given population if many examinees obtained perfect scores; it has a high ceiling if there are few or no perfect scores.

census *See* SCHOOL CENSUS and CONTINUOUS SCHOOL CENSUS.

census age *See* SCHOOL CENSUS AGE.

census taker A staff member performing assigned activities concerned with the systematic counting of resident persons in a school district and with the recording of such related information about the persons as the school district requires.

central administrative office An office or building used primarily for housing personnel and equipment engaged in activities that have as their purpose the general regulation, direction, and control of the affairs of a local educational agency that are systemwide and not confined to one school, subject, or narrow phase of school activity.

central tendency 1. Any of various statistical measures used to obtain a single number that is considered the most representative value of a series of data. 2. Series of statistical measures that provide a representative value for a distribution, or, more simply, refer to how scores tend to cluster in a distribution. The most common measures of central tendency are the mean, median, and the mode.

certificate 1. A legal document giving authorization from the state, an agency, or an organization for an individual to perform certain services. 2. In the context of education certificates are generally awarded by the state and/or professional organizations for teachers, administrators, and related professional staff. Certificates may be specifically designated by subject, grade level, and/or area of professional expertise such as special education. 3. "Licenses" that meet these criteria would be regarded as certificates.

certificate endorsement The information included in or added to an issued certificate specifically indicating the services that the certificate holder is authorized to perform.

certificate issuing agency The state department, office, or other state agency (or an agency or organization authorized by the state) that issues certificates, licenses, permits, or other credentials to perform school services.

certificate of attendance A document certifying the presence of the student at school during given years or on given days. This document sometimes is awarded in lieu of a diploma or certificate of completion.

certificate of completion A document certifying the satisfactory completion of a course or a program of studies. This document frequently is awarded for courses for which credit toward graduation is not granted. This document sometimes is referred to as a "certificate of training."

certificate of high school equivalency A formal document issued by a state department of education or other authorized agency certifying that an individual has met the state requirements for high school graduation by attaining satisfactory scores on the Tests of General Educational Development or another state-specified examination. Certificates of high school equivalency are official documents that frequently are accepted by employers, post-secondary educational institutions, and others, in the same manner as high school diplomas. *See also* HIGH SCHOOL EQUIVALENCY EXAMINATION and TESTS OF GENERAL EDUCATIONAL DEVELOPMENT (GED).

certificate of training *See* CERTIFICATE OF COMPLETION.

certificate renewal The reissuance of a given certificate held by an individual upon expiration of the term specified on the old certificate and upon evidence submitted by the person that specified conditions for renewal (e.g., experience, additional preparation, or both) have been met.

certificate revocation The annulment of a credential (such as certificate, license, or permit) by the agency which issued it.

certificated Authorized by the state to perform services for which a legal credential is necessary.

certification 1. The general process by which a state (or agency or organization authorized by a state or government) provides a credential to an individual. In the context of education a 1986 report from the Carnegie Foundation recommended a national certification process for teachers based on the establishment of a National Board for Professional Teaching Standards that would determine what teachers need to know and need to be able to do. (*See A Nation Prepared: Teachers for the 21st Century,* a report by the Carnegie Task Force on Teaching as a Profession, May 1986.) A similar recommendation was made regarding school administrators as reported in March 1987 by the National Commission on Excellence in Educational Administration that proposed the establishment of a National Policy Board on Educational Administration. *See* George F. Madaus and Diana Pollin, "Teacher Certification Tests: Do They Really Measure What We Need to Know," *Phi Delta Kappan* (September 1987). 2. In the employer-employee context, a process by which the National Labor Relations Board or other administrative agency determines whether a particular labor union is the majority choice, and thus the exclusive bargaining agent for a group of employees in a given bargaining unit. Decertification is the opposite process.

See Richard Block and Myron Roomkin, "Determinants of Voter Participation in Union Certification Elections," *Monthly Labor Review* (April 1982); William N. Cook, "Determinants of the Outcomes of Union Certification Elections," *Industrial and Labor Relations Review* (April 1983); and James P. Swann, Jr., "The Decertification of a Union," *Personnel Administrator* (January 1983).

certification of birth *See* AGE CERTIFICATE.

certification of eligibles Procedure whereby those who have passed competitive civil service examinations have their names ranked in

STATES REQUIRING TESTS FOR
INITIAL TEACHER CERTIFICATION

State	Year of Implementation	Test Used
Alabama	1981	State
Alaska	–	
Arizona	1980	State
Arkansas	1983	NTE
California	1982	State
Colorado	1983	State
Connecticut	1985	State
Delaware	1983	Other
District of Columbia	–	
Florida	1980	State
Georgia	1980	State
Hawaii	–	
Idaho	–	
Illinois	1988	State
Indiana	1985	NTE
Iowa	–	
Kansas	1986	Other
Kentucky	1985	NTE
Louisiana	1978	NTE
Maine	1988	NTE
Maryland	–	NTE
Massachusetts[1]	–	
Michigan	–	
Minnesota	–	
Mississippi	1977	NTE
Missouri	–	
Montana	–	
Nebraska	1986	Other
Nevada	–	
New Hampshire	1985	NTE
New Jersey	1985	NTE
New Mexico	1983	NTE
New York	1984	NTE
North Carolina	1964	NTE
North Dakota	–	
Ohio	–	
Oklahoma	1982	State
Oregon	–	

Pennsylvania	–	
Rhode Island	–	
South Carolina	1982	NTE
South Dakota	1986	NTE
Tennessee	1981	NTE
Texas	1986	State
Utah	–	
Vermont	–	
Virginia	1980	NTE
Washington	1985	State
West Virginia	1985	State
Wisconsin	–	
Wyoming	–	

State: A state-developed exam; NTE: National Teacher's Exam; Other: Other national or regional exam.
(1) Massachusetts requires competency testing for initial certification for teachers in certain fields only.
SOURCE: Department of Education, Office of Planning, Budget, and Evaluation.

order of score and placed on a list of those eligible for appointment. When a government agency has a vacancy, it requests its personnel arm to provide a list of eligibles for the class to which the vacant position has been allocated. The personnel agency then "certifies" the names of the highest ranking eligibles to the appointing authority for possible selection. Usually only a limited number of the qualified eligibles are certified. When a jurisdiction requires that three eligibles be certified to the appointing authority, this is referred to as the "rule of three."

For an overview, see Carmen D. Saso and Earl P. Tanis, *Selection and Certification of Eligibles: A Survey of Policies and Practices* (Chicago: International Personnel Management Association, 1974).

certified employee organization
Union that an administrative agency has certified as the official representative of the employees in a bargaining unit for the purpose of collective negotiations. Such certification is usually the direct result of a representation election.

certified financial statement   A financial statement or report that has been examined by a certified public accountant and reported upon with an opinion expressed by the accountant.

certiorari   An order or writ from a higher court demanding that a lower court send up the record of a case for review. Except for a few instances of original jurisdiction, most cases that reach the U.S. Supreme Court do so because the Supreme Court itself has issued such a writ or "granted certiorari." If certiorari is denied by the Supreme Court, it means that the justices are content to let the lower court's decision stand. Frequently a U.S. Court of Appeals case citation will include "cert. denied," meaning that certiorari has been denied by the Supreme Court, which has reviewed the case to the extent that it has made a judgment not to review the case further. It takes the votes of four justices in order to grant certiorari. However, at least five votes are normally needed for a majority opinion on the substance of a case.

See Peter Linzer, "The Meaning of Certiorari Denials," *Columbia Law Review* (November 1979); Jan Palmer, "An Econometric Analysis of the U.S. Supreme Court's Certiorari Decisions," *Public Choice* (1982); and S. Sidney Ulmer, "The Supreme Court's Certiorari Decisions: Conflict as a Predictive Variable," *American Political Science Review* (December 1984).

CETA   *See* COMPREHENSIVE EMPLOYMENT AND TRAINING ACT OF 1973.

CFR   *See* CODE OF FEDERAL REGULATIONS.

chaining   A type of learning or instructional paradigm based on operant conditioning theory whereby an individual learns a total task or activity as a sequence of discrete steps and the "response" aspect of each step (in behavioral terminology) becomes the "stimulus" for the next step. The total task, therefore, is a "chain" of interrelated and interdependent parts. Compare to BACKWARD CHAINING.

An example of chaining: Washing hands. S = Stimulus; R = Response; 1 = First; 2 = Second; 3 = Third; etc.

S1   Teacher instruction "wash your hands"
R1   Pick up soap S2
R2   turn on water S3
R3   put hands in water S4
R4   rub hands together S5
R5   Put soap down S6
R6   rinse hands S7
R7   turn off water S8
R8   dry hands

chair   1. One who is chosen by a group to conduct a meeting by serving as a presiding officer. 2. In secondary and higher education the chief administrative officer of a faculty department. 3. A named professorship. To be the John Smith Professor of Education is a higher honor (usually) than to merely be a professor of education.

change agent   1. A descriptive way of referring to organization development consultants or facilitators. 2. An administrator who is oriented toward change and growth in his or her organization.

See Ronald G. Havelock, *The Change Agent's Guide to Innovation in Education* (Englewood Cliffs, N.J.: Educational Technology Publications, 1973); and Stephen R. Michael, "Organizational Change Techniques: Their Present, Their Future," *Organizational Dynamics* (Summer 1982).

Chapter 1   An abbreviated reference to Chapter 1 of the Education Consolidation and Improvement Act of 1981 (previously Title 1 of the Elementary and Secondary Education Act of 1965), which provides federal aid for educational programs for low-income children. These programs are typically translated into elementary school remedial reading and/or math. For a critical discussion, and historical overview, *see* David G. Savage, "Why Chapter 1 Hasn't Made Much Difference," *Phi Delta Kappan* (April 1987). For a contrasting viewpoint *see* Robert E. Slavin; "Making Chapter 1 Make a Difference," *Phi Delta Kappan* (October 1987).

Chapter 2   An abbreviated reference to the second portion of the Education Consolidation and Improvement Act of 1981 which was a block grant initiative to consolidate about 28 previously separate programs including the Emergency School Aid Act, the major federal desegregation effort. For an analysis of the implementation of this federal program, *see* Anne T. Henderson, "Chapter 2: For Better or Worse?," *Phi Delta Kappan* (April 1986). *See also* Richard N. Apling and Christine Padilla, "Distribution and Spending of Chapter 2 Funds," *Educational Analysis* (Winter 1986).

charge-off Also write off; an adjustment made in an institution's financial statements lowering the worth of an asset. Uncollectible student debts, for example, may be charged-off.

charismatic leadership Leadership that is based on the compelling personality of the leader rather than upon formal position. *See* Robert J. House, "A 1976 Theory of Charismatic Leadership," in James G. Hunt and Lars L. Larson, eds. *Leadership: The Cutting edge* (Carbondale: Southern Illinois University Press, 1977).

charitable solicitation permit A legal document issued by a local government agency permitting a charitable organization (including some schools or affiliated organizations) to solicit funds within the jurisdiction of the agency or governmental unit for a specified period of time.

chart of accounts A list of all accounts generally used in an individual accounting system. In addition to account title, the chart includes an account number that has been assigned to each account. Accounts in the chart are arranged with accounts of a similar nature, for example, assets and liabilities.

Chautauqua A movement to provide adult education that started in Chautauqua, New York, in 1874 and rapidly spread throughout the country. The height of its popularity was prior to World War I. *See* Theodore Morrison, *Chautauqua: A Center for Education, Religion, and the Arts of America* (University of Chicago Press, 1974).

The Chautauqua Movement

Chautauqua pleads for a universal education; for plans of reading and study; for all legitimate enticements and incitements to ambition; for all necessary adaptations as to time and topics; for ideal associations which shall at once excite the imagination and set the heart aglow. Chautauqua stretches over the land a magnificent temple, broad as the continent, lofty as the heavens, into which homes, churches, schools, and shops may build themselves as parts of a splendid university in which people of all ages and conditions may be enrolled as students. It says: Unify such eager and various multitudes. Let them read the same books, think along the same lines, sing the same songs, observe the same sacred days—days consecrated to the delights of a lofty intellectual and spiritual life. Let the course of prescribed reading be broad and comprehensive; limited in its first general survey of the wide world of knowledge; opening out into special courses, according to the reader's development, taste, and opportunity. Show people out of school what wonders people out of school may accomplish. Show people no longer young that the mind reaches its maturity long after the school days end, and that some of the best intellectual and literary labor is performed in and beyond middle life.

Source: John H. Vincent, *The Chautauqua Movement* (Boston, 1886).

---

check A bill of exchange drawn on a bank payable on demand; a written order on a bank to pay on demand a specified sum of money to a named person, to his or her order, or to bearer out of money on deposit to the credit of the maker. A check differs from a warrant in that the latter is not necessarily payable on demand and may not be negotiable; and it differs from a voucher in that the latter is not an order to pay. A voucher-check combines the distinguishing marks of a voucher and a check; it shows the propriety of a payment and is an order to pay.

checkoff   Union security provision, commonly provided for in the collective bargaining agreement, that allows the employer to deduct union dues, assessments, and initiation fees from the pay of all union members. The deducted amounts are delivered to the union on a prearranged schedule.

chief elected officer   A person, such as the school board president, who is designated as the leader of an elected body.

chief executive officer (CEO) The individual who is personally accountable to the governing board or the electorate for the activities of an institution or jurisdiction. Typically, the superintendent of schools is a CEO.

chief state school officer   The chief executive officer of the state department of education, commonly referred to as the State Commissioner of Education or the State Superintendent of Schools.

child   A person, known as a minor from birth to legal age of maturity, for whom a parent and/or caretaker, foster parent, public or private home, institution, or agency is legally responsible. The 1974 Child Abuse Prevention and Treatment Act defines a child as a person under 18. In some states, a person of any age with a developmental disability for whom a guardian has been appointed by a court is defined as a child.

child abuse   An act of commission by a parent or caretaker that is not accidental and harms or threatens to harm a child's physical or mental health or welfare. All 50 states have a child abuse reporting law with varying definitions of child abuse and varying provisions as to who must and may report, penalties for not reporting, and required agency action following the report.

See Harold P. Martin, *The Abused Child: A Multidisciplinary Approach to Developmental Issues and Treatment* (Cambridge, Mass.: Ballinger, 1976); and Ray E. Helfer, *Abuse and Neglect: The Family and the Community* (Cambridge, Mass.: Ballinger, 1976); Robert L. Emans, "Abuse in the Name of Protecting Children," *Phi Delta Kappan* (June 1987); Susan Contratto, "Child Abuse and the Politics of Care," *Journal of Education* (Fall 1986).

child benefit theory   A legal concept upheld by the Supreme Court in many cases that holds that public expenditures can be utilized for services and materials for students in parochial schools as long as it can be demonstrated that the benefit is to the child and not to the religious institution. *See* COCHRAN V. LOUISIANA BOARD OF EDUCATION.

child care   *See* DAY CARE.

child development   A pattern of sequential stages of interrelated physical, psychological, and social development in the process of maturation from infancy and total dependence to adulthood and relative independence.

Child Find   1. The identification and location of children who may be handicapped and in need of special education services. P.L. 94-142, the Education for All Handicapped Children Act of 1975, requires that states identify, locate, and evaluate all children, ages from birth to 21, residing in the state who are handicapped. Most states have implemented this provision of the law through Child Find programs that include public awareness campaigns and screening programs that are operated at both a state and local level.

2. Also refers to the search for (and location of) children who are missing from home and who are believed to have run away from home or been abducted.

child labor   This originally meant employing children in a manner that was detrimental to their health and social development; but now that the law contains strong child labor prohibitions, the term refers to the employment of children below the legal age limit.

Efforts by the labor movement and social reformers to prevent the exploitation of children in the workplace date back well into the 19th century. As early as 1842, some states (Connecticut and Massachusetts) legislated a maximum 10-hour work day for children. In 1848, Pennsylvania established a minimum working age of 12 for factory jobs. But it would be 20 years more before any state had inspectors to enforce child labor laws. And it would not be until the late 1930s that federal laws would outlaw child labor (mainly through the Fair Labor Standards Act of 1938). The practice was so entrenched that earlier federal attempts to outlaw child labor were construed by the Supreme Court as being unconstitutional infringements on the power of the states to regulate conditions in the workplace.

For histories of the horrendous conditions that led to the passage of federal and state child labor prohibitions, see Jeremy P. Felt, *Hostages of Fortune: Child Labor Reform in New York State* (Syracuse, New York: Syracuse University Press, 1965); and Walter I. Trattner, *Crusade for the Children: A History of the National Child Labor Committee and Child Labor Reform in America* (Chicago: Quadrangle Books, 1970).

For present-day impact, see Daniel J. B. Mitchell and John Clapp, "The Impact of Child-Labor Laws on the Kinds of Jobs Held by Young School-Leavers," *Journal of Human Resources* (Summer 1980); Lee Swepston, "Child Labor: Its Regulation by ILO Standards and National Legislation," *International Labor Review* (September-October 1982); and Thomas A. Coens, "Child Labor Laws: A Viable Legacy for the 1980s," *Labor Law Journal* (October 1982).

See also FAIR LABOR STANDARDS ACT.

child neglect   An act of omission; specifically, the failure of a parent or other person legally responsible for a child's welfare to provide for the child's basic needs and proper level of care with respect to food, clothing, shelter, hygiene, medical attention, or supervision. Most states have neglect and/or dependency statutes; however, not all states require the reporting of neglect. While there is agreement that some parental care and supervision is essential, there is disagreement as to how much is necessary for a minimally acceptable environment. Severe neglect sometimes occurs because a parent is apathetic, impulse-ridden, mentally retarded, depressed, or psychotic.

See Beatrice J. Kalisch, *Child Abuse and Neglect: An Annotated Bibliography* (Westport, Conn.: Greenwood Press, 1978).

child prodigy   A child who exhibits extraordinary talent at a very young age. Most typically thought of in music or other artistic fields.

child psychology   The study of human growth and development from prenatal stages to adolescence. The broad field focuses primarily on behavior patterns, personality, social relations, learning theories, and psychosexual issues of children.

See Wallace A. Kennedy, *Child Psychology*, 2nd ed. (Englewood Cliffs, New Jersey: Prentice-Hall, 1975); and Terry Faw, *Schaum's Outline of Theory and Problems of Child Psychology* (New York: McGraw-Hill, 1980).

child-centered education   1. An educational system where the primary focus is on the learner and that allows for flexibility based on the child's needs and interests. 2. Education that tends to have a more affective orientation. Contrast with CONTENT-CENTERED and PROCESS-CENTERED EDUCATION.

children with specific learning disabilities   Children who have a disorder in one or more of the basic psychological processes involved in understanding or in using language, spoken or written, which may manifest itself in an imperfect ability to listen, think, speak, read, write, spell, or do mathematical calculations. Learning disabilities include such conditions as perceptual handicaps, brain injury, minimal brain dysfunction, dyslexia, and developmental aphasia. The term does not include children who have learning problems that are primarily the result of visual, hearing, or motor handicaps; of mental retardation; of emotional disturbance; or of environmental disadvantage.

Children's Apperception Test (CAT)   A projective test used to assess a child's personal feelings and conflicts through the use of pictures of animals in various situations about which the child is asked to "tell a story." It is modeled after the adult version, the Thematic Apperception Test (TAT). It is published by:

The Psychological Corporation
555 Academic Court
San Antonio, TX 78204

chilling   1. Any policies or practices that would tend to inhibit others from exercising legal rights. 2. The effects of employment practices, government regulations, court decisions, or legislation (or the threat of these) that may create an inhibiting atmosphere that prevents the free exercise of individual employment rights. A chilling effect tends to keep minorities and women from seeking employment and advancement in an organization, even in the absence of formal bars. Other chilling effects may be positive or negative, depending upon the "chillee's" perspective. For example, even discussion of proposed regulations could "chill" employers or unions into compliance.

chi-square   Statistical procedure that estimates whether the observed values in a distribution differ from the expected distribution and thus may be attributed to the operation of factors other than chance. Particular values of chi-square are usually identified by the symbol "x^2."

Christian schools   Private schools that are generally operated by non-catholic Protestant churches and which emphasize study of the Bible along with basic academics, good study habits, and art appreciation. Proponents claim that their programs are superior to public school education while critics attribute the markedly increased enrollment over the past several years as primarily an attempt to escape federally mandated racial integration. Historically Christian schools developed in response to the constraints imposed upon public schools by the court's interpretations of the U.S. Constitution as prohibiting the teaching of religion in the public schools. Sometimes referred to as Bible schools.

church-related school   1. A private school associated with a religious or church organization that offers religion-oriented instruction at the elementary and/or secondary levels. 2. Sunday school; any part-time religious instruction in a formal setting. Compare to BIBLE SCHOOL, CATHOLIC SCHOOL, PAROCHIAL SCHOOLS, CHRISTIAN SCHOOLS.
See James C. Carper and Thomas C. Hunt, ed., *Religious Schooling in America* (Birmingham, Ala.: Religious Education Press, 1984).

CIPP evaluation model   An educational evaluation model that is designated by the acronym for the four types of educational evaluation included in the model: context evaluation, input evaluation, process evaluation, and product evaluation. The model was first described by David L. Stufflebeam et al. in *Educational Evaluation and Decision Making* (Itasca, Ill.: F.E. Peacock, 1971).

circular processes   A description for a sequence of events that leads to another sequence of events that inevitably terminates in a recapitulation of the initial sequence.

circulation area   A building area used for general traffic, omitting such areas as unit-contained corridors and stairs located within, and serving parts of, a unit or suite.

citizen   1. An individual who owes allegiance to and, in turn, receives protection from, a state. 2. A person born or naturalized in the United States. All U. S. citizens are also citizens of the state in which they have a permanent residence; corporations, which are artificial persons, are citizens of the state in which they were legally created. A citizen may take an active or passive role in the governmental process. The right to vote gives the citizen the opportunity to help select those who will determine public policy. Beyond simply voting, citizens can assist in electoral campaigns, lobby their representatives, or join with others to form interest groups—all in order to advance their personal interests or further their conception of the public interest.

citizen participation   A means of empowering individuals or groups with bargaining power to represent their own interests and to plan and implement their own programs with a view toward social, economic, and political power and control. Some government programs have enabling legislation that specifically requires that citizens affected by the program be involved in its administrative decisions. Presumably the greater the level of citizen participation in a program, the more responsive the program will be to the needs of the community, and, vice versa, the more responsive the community will be to the needs of the program.

See Mary Grisez Kweit and Robert W. Kweit, *Implementing Citizen Participation in a Bureaucratic Society: A Contingency Approach* (New York: Praeger, 1982); Marcus E. Ethridge, "The Policy Impact of Citizen Participation Procedures," *American Politics Quarterly* (October 1982); and Curtis Ventriss, "Emerging Perspectives on Citizen Participation," *Public Administration Review* (May-June 1985).

citizens' councils   A term coined to refer euphemistically to groups of whites who created private schools, private swimming pools, and other private facilities in order to avoid racial integration in the 1950s and 1960s. *See* Neil R. McMillen, *The Citizens' Council: Organized Resistance to the Second Reconstruction, 1954-64* (Urbana: University of Illinois Press, 1971).

citizenship   1. The dynamic relationship between a citizen and the state. The concept of citizenship involves rules of what a citizen might do (such as vote), must do (pay taxes), and can refuse to do (pledge allegiance). Increasingly, the concept involves benefits or entitlements that a citizen has a right to demand from government.

See Lawrence M. Mead, *Beyond Entitlement: The Social Obligations of Citizenship* (New York: The Free Press, 1986).

2. A requirement for public employment in some jurisdictions. For a discussion of recent court rulings, *see* Arnold L. Steigman, "Public Administration by Litigation: The Impact of Court Deci-

sions Concerning Citizenship on Public Personnel Management," *Public Personnel Management* (March-April 1979); and Charles O. Agege, "Employment Discrimination Against Aliens: The Constitutional Implications," *Labor Law Journal* (February 1985).

City of Los Angeles, Department of Water & Power v. Manhart 435 U.S. 703 (1978)

The Supreme Court case that held that a pension plan requiring female employees to contribute more from their wages to gain the same pension benefits as male employees was in violation of Title VII of the Civil Rights Act of 1964. While the actual statistics were undisputed (women live longer than men), the Court reasoned that Title VII prohibits treating individuals "as simply components of a racial, religious, sexual or national class."

See Michael Evan Gold, "Of Giving and Taking Applications and Implications of *City of Los Angeles, Department of Water and Power v. Manhart*," *Virginia Law Review* (May 1979); and Linda H. Kistler and Richard C. Healy, "Sex Discrimination in Pension Plans since *Manhart*," *Labor Law Journal* (April 1981).

City of Newport v. Fact Concerts, Inc. 69 L.Ed. 2d 616 (1981)

The Supreme Court case that held that municipalities are not subject to punitive damages in civil suits.

city-wide school   A specialized public school attended by students from any part of the city who meet entrance criteria. Compare to MAGNET SCHOOL.

civic activities   School-related activities such as parent-teacher association meetings and non-school-related civic activities such as public forums, lectures, and civil defense planning, usually connected with school services.

civic organization   Any group of local citizens who formally associate to further their concept of the public interest. Such groups may be purely local, such as a Parent-Teachers Association, or a chapter of a national association such as the Rotarians or the League of Women Voters.

civil   Pertaining to a community of citizens, their government or their interrelations.

civil defense   A program designed to provide adequate defense for a community of citizens against loss of life or property due to war or natural disaster.

civil rights   1. The protections and privileges given to all citizens by the U.S. Constitution; for example, freedom of assembly or freedom of religion. 2. Those positive acts of government that seek to make constitutional guarantees a reality for all citizens; for example, the Civil Rights Act of 1964. 3. Whatever rights a citizen possesses in any state even if those rights are slight.

Civil Rights Act of 1964   With the possible exception of the Voting Rights Act of 1965, this is by far the most significant civil rights legislation in American history. Forged during the civil rights movement of the early 1960s, the act consists of 11 titles of which the most consequential are Titles II, VI, and VII.

Title II bars discrimination in all places of "public accommodation," if their operations affect commerce (including hotels and other places of lodging of more than five rooms, restaurants and other eating places, gasoline stations, theaters, motion picture houses, stadiums, and other places of exhibition or entertainment).

In Title VI, Congress made broad use of its spending power to prohibit racial discrimination in any program or activity receiving federal financial assistance.

More important, Title VI goes on to provide that compliance with the nondiscrimination requirement is to be effected by the termination or refusal to grant federal funds to any recipient who has been found guilty of racial discrimination.

Finally, Title VII makes it an unfair employment practice for any employer or labor organization engaged in commerce to refuse to hire, fire, or otherwise discriminate against any individual because of race, religion, sex, or national origin. Title VII is enforced by the Equal Employment Opportunity Commission which was also created by the Act. Compare to AFFIRMATIVE ACTION, EQUAL EMPLOYMENT OPPORTUNITY.

See Clifford M. Lytle, "The History of the Civil Rights Bill of 1964," *Journal of Negro History* (1966); Gary Orfield, *The Reconstruction of Southern Education; The Schools and the Civil Rights Act of 1964* (New York: Wiley-Interscience, 1969); Richard J. Hardy and Donald J. McCrone, "The Impact of the Civil Rights Act of 1964 on Women," *Policy Studies Journal* (Winter 1978); Augustus J. Jones, Jr., *Law, Bureaucracy, and Politics: The Implementation of Title VI of the Civil Rights Act of 1964* (Washington, D.C.: University Press of America, 1982); and Charles and Barbara Whalen, *The Longest Debate: A Legislative History of the 1964 Civil Rights Act* (Cabin John, Md.: Seven Locks Press, 1985).

Civil Rights Commission   *See* COMMISSION ON CIVIL RIGHTS.

civil rights movement   The continuing effort of minorities and women to gain the enforcement of the rights guaranteed by the Constitution to all citizens. The modern civil rights movement is often dated from 1955 when Rosa Parks, a black seamstress, refused to sit in the back of a bus (where blacks were required by local law to sit) and was arrested. Dr. Martin Luther King, Jr. then led the Montgomery, Alabama, bus boycott, the first of a long series of nonviolent demonstrations that eventually led to the passage of the Civil Rights Acts of 1957, 1960, and 1964.

See James Button and Richard Scher, "Impact of the Civil Rights Movement: Perceptions of Black Municipal Service Changes," *Social Science Quarterly* (December 1979); Bruce Miroff, "Presidential Leverage over Social Movements: The Johnson White House and Civil Rights," *Journal of Politics* (February 1981); and Lewis M. Killian, "Organization, Rationality, and Spontaneity in the Civil Rights Movement," *American Sociological Review* (December 1984).

civil service   A collective term for all of the employees of a government who are not part of the armed forces. Paramilitary organizations such as police and firefighters are always included in civil service counts in the United States. In other countries where there is less of a distinction between the police and the military, this may be confusing.

Civil service employment is not the same as merit system employment because all patronage positions (those not covered by merit systems) are included in civil service totals. Compare to MERIT SYSTEMS.

civil service commission   A government agency charged with the responsibility of promulgating the rules and regulations of the civilian personnel management system. Depending upon its legal mandate, a civil service commission may hear employee appeals and take a more active (or passive) role in the personnel management process.

See Winston Crouch, *A Guide for Modern Personnel Commissions* (Chicago: International Personnel Management Association, 1973); William M. Timmins, "Conflicting Roles in Personnel Boards: Adjudication versus Policy Making," *Public Personnel Management* (Summer 1985).

class   1. A group of students assigned to one or more teachers or other staff members for a given period of time for instruction or other activity in a situation where the teacher(s) and the students are in the presence of each other. 2. All students in the same grade level such as the fifth grade class or the tenth grade class. 3. The group of students who graduate at the same time, such as the class of 1989. 4. Any scheduled instructional session. 5. Social grouping such as lower class or lower middle class. 6. Character, as in "he has no class" or "he is a class act."

class action   A search for a judicial remedy that one or more individuals may undertake on behalf of themselves and all others in similar situations. Class action suits are common against manufacturers who have sold defective products that have later harmed significant numbers of people who were unaware that there was any danger.

See James W. Loewen, *Social Science in the Courtroom: Statistical Techniques and Research Methods for Winning Class Action Suits* (Lexington, Mass.: Lexington Books, 1982); and Deborah L. Rhode, "Class Conflicts in Class Actions," *Stanford Law Review* (July 1982).

class mother   A mother of an elementary school student who helps with social events, trips, or classroom activities. This could be either a temporary ad hoc assignment or year-long in nature. Also called a room mother.

class period   The portion of the daily session set aside for instruction in classes, when most classes meet for a single such unit of time.

class rank   1. The scholastic ranking of a student in a graduating class (first, 10th, 203rd, etc.). This is usually determined purely by grade-point average. Class rank can be stated as an absolute number or as a part of a statistical percentile. 2. One of several criteria used by colleges and universities for consideration of admission.

class size   1. The membership of a particular class as of a given date; as in the junior class or the graduating class. 2. The number of students in a single class grouping under the direction of a particular teacher. There is little consistent evidence that class size affects student performance other than when the class size is very low (fewer than 20 students). Nevertheless class size has become a common bargaining issue in teacher contracts.

For a discussion of the relationship between class size and instructional outcomes of education, *see* Gene Glass et al., *School Class Size: Research and Policy* (Beverly Hills: Sage Publications, 1982).

See also Larry Hedges and William Stock, "The Effects of Class Size: An Examination of Rival Hypotheses," *American Educational Research Journal* (Spring 1983); Peter F.W. Preece, "Class Size and Learning: A Theoretical Model," *Journal of Educational Research* (July/August 1987).

class time per week   The average number of minutes the staff member is assigned to each class each week, including laboratory periods. *See also* WORKLOAD and UNIT OF WORK.

classical conditioning   1. A process by which two stimuli are frequently paired until the unconditioned (reflex) response to one of the stimuli occurs when the other stimulus is presented alone—a conditioned or learned response. The example of classical conditioning that most beginning students of psychology are introduced to is the dog ("Pavlov's dog") who learns to salivate in response to the sound of a bell after the bell has been paired with the presentation of food many times. The food is the unconditioned stimulus that causes an unconditioned response, salivation. The bell is the conditioned stimulus and salivation is a conditioned response when it occurs in the presence of the bell alone. Contrast with OPERANT CONDITIONING. 2. A school of behavioral psychology that is generally associated with Ivan Petrovich Pavlov (1849-1936).

classical curriculum (or classical education)   A liberal arts curriculum that includes literature, art, philosophy, history, music, and foreign languages (especially Greek and Latin) and that emphasizes the contributions of the great writers of ancient Greek and Rome.

classical languages   Languages that are no longer spoken in everyday use. Refers specifically to ancient Greek and Latin.

classics   1. A body of literature that is generally recognized as enduring over time. 2. Often refers specifically to works created in ancient Greece and Rome.

classification level   A level of concept development where the individual is able to classify two or more given entities according to some like attribute.

classification standards   Descriptions of classes of positions that distinguish one class from another in a series. They are, in effect, the yardstick or benchmark against which positions are measured to determine the proper level within a series of titles to which a position should be assigned.

classified service   All those positions in a governmental jurisdiction that are included in a formal merit system. Excluded from the classified service are all exempt appointments. Classified service is a term that predates the concept of position classification and has no immediate bearing on position classification concepts or practices.

classify   Group positions according to their duties and responsibilities and assign a class title. To reclassify is to reassign a position to a different class, based on a re-examination of the duties and responsibilities of the position.

classroom   A space designed or adapted for regularly scheduled group instruction. This includes the so-called regular classrooms and special use classrooms such as laboratories and shops but excludes such rooms as auditoriums, lunch rooms, libraries, and gymnasiums.

classroom climate   1. The general physical and interpersonal atmosphere in the classroom that is related to the material resources, the emotional attitude of the teacher and students, and the established parameters of classroom behavior. 2. One aspect of education that can either help or hinder learning. *See* Catherine E. Loughlin and Mavis D. Martin, *Supporting Literacy: Developiong Effective Learning Environments* (New York: Teachers College Press, 1987).

classroom management   Organization and procedures used by a teacher to create a classroom environment that is conducive to effective learning by students. Classroom management is not synonymous with classroom discipline. On the contrary it is a proactive, preventative strategy to establish the classroom as an effective learning environment.

For a broad overview of the topic, *see* D. Duke, ed., *Helping Teachers Manage Classrooms* (Alexandria, Va.: ASCD,

1982). *See also* Carolyn M. Everston, "Training Teachers in Classroom Management: An Experimental Study in Secondary School Classrooms," *Journal of Educational Research* (September/October 1985).

classroom teacher   A staff member assigned the professional activities of instructing pupils—in self-contained classes or courses—in classroom situations for which daily pupil attendance figures for the school system are kept. *See* James Michael Cooper and John Hansen, *Classroom Teaching Skills: A Handbook* (Lexington, Mass.: D.C. Heath, 1977).

classroom teachers per 1,000 pupils in average daily membership   The number representing the total full-time equivalency of classroom teaching assignments in a school system during a given period of time, multiplied by 1,000 and divided by the average daily membership (ADM) of pupils during this period.

classroom without walls   *See* SCHOOLS WITHOUT WALLS.

clearinghouse   An association, center, or organization that collects and disseminates information and publications on topics of interest to specific groups and/or organizations.

Cleveland Board of Education v. Lafleur 414 U.S. 632 (1974)   A landmark U.S. Supreme Court case regarding maternity leave. The Court held that arbitrary mandatory maternity leaves were unconstitutional. Requiring pregnant teachers to take unpaid maternity leave five months before expected childbirth was found to be in violation of the due process clause of the 14th Amendment.

clinic   A medical facility or part of a facility used for the diagnosis and treat-ment of outpatients. "Clinic" is irregularly defined, either including or excluding physicians' offices, sometimes being limited to facilities that serve poor or public patients, and occasionally being limited to facilities in which graduate or undergraduate medical education is provided. More broadly, a clinic may include complete inpatient and outpatient facilities and resources. In such cases, the term describes a group practice of specialty and general health care practitioners who have banded together to share resources and increase the marketability of their services. 2. May refer to a facility that provides allied health (i.e., therapy) or educationally-related (i.e., tutoring) services to individuals on a one-to-one or small-group basis. 3. A facility used in professional training programs, such as a counseling clinic or reading clinic.

clinical psychologist   A health professional specializing in the evaluation and treatment of mental and behavioral disorders. A clinical psychologist does not have a degree in medicine, as does a psychiatrist. Most clinical psychologists have doctoral degrees in psychology, plus clinical training in treating psychological disorders. Clinical psychologists are licensed by most states for independent professional practice. They do not treat physical causes of mental illness with drugs or other medical or surgical measures, since they are not licensed to practice medicine. *See* C. Eugene Walker, *Clinical Practice of Psychology: A Guide for Mental Health Professionals* (New York: Pergamon Press, 1981).

clinical supervision model   A model for the supervision of professional education staff that involves collaboration as opposed to coercion on the part of the supervisor and seeks to respect the professionalism of the staff person being supervised. The process as initially described by Morris Cogan in

Clinical Supervision (Houghton Mifflin, 1973) includes eight steps:
1. establishing a supervisory relationship
2. planning lessons with the staff person
3. jointly planning an observation strategy
4. observing the lesson
5. analyzing the observational data
6. planning a conference strategy
7. conferencing to discuss the observation analysis
8. recycling the process and planning opportunities for growth.

See Robert J. Krajewski, "Clinical Supervision: A Conceptual Framework," *Journal of Research and Development in Education* (Winter 1982); Keith Acheson, *Techniques in the Clinical Supervision of Teachers: Pre-Service and In-service Application* (New York: Longman, 1986).

clock-hour   About 60 minutes of classwork or instruction. This may include time for passing from one class to another.

closed shop   A union security provision that would require an employer to hire and retain only union members in good standing. The Labor-Management Relations (Taft-Hartley) Act of 1947 made closed shops illegal. Compare to AGENCY SHOPS. *See* Charles G. Goring and others, *The Closed Shop: A Comparative Study of Public Policy and Trade Union Security in Britain, the USA and West Germany* (New York: St. Martin's Press, 1981).

closing entries   Entries which are made at the end of the accounting period to transfer balances in general ledger receipt, expenditure, appropriation, and estimated revenue accounts to the fund balance account.

closure, psychological   A basic human need to achieve completion of an activity, experience, need, or relationship.

Cloze procedure   A test of reading and language ability. Reading selections are given that omit every 5th, 7th, or 10th word, and the student is expected to fill in the missing words from the context of the selection. *See* Michael C. McKenna, "Cloze Procedure as a Memory-Search Process," *Journal of Educational Psychology* (December 1986).

coaching   1. Directing school sports. *See* William E. Warren, *Coaching and Motivation: A Practical Guide to Maximum Athletic Performance* (Englewood Cliffs, N.J.: Prentice-Hall, 1983). 2. Helping a student outside of regularly scheduled classes. 3. Face-to-face discussions with an organizational subordinate, such as a student teacher, in order to help them improve their on-the-job performance.

Coalition for Essential Schools
An informal network of high schools, organized in 1984 through a project at Brown University and as an outgrowth of the effective schools movement. The goal of the coalition is to support each member's development of a program appropriate to its own setting and constituency that includes some core principles such as an intellectual focus, simple and universal goals, and personalization.

Three significant books that exemplify the goals of the organization are: Theodore R. Sizer, *Horaces' Compromise* (Boston: Houghton Mifflin, 1984); Arthur G. Powell, et al., *The Shopping Mall High School* (Boston: Houghton Mifflin, 1985); and Robert L. Hampel, *The Last Little Citadel: American High Schools Since 1940* (Boston: Houghton Mifflin, 1986).

For a description of the coalition, *see* Theodore R. Sizer, "Rebuilding: First Steps by the Coalition of Essential

Schools," *Phi Delta Kappan* (September 1986). *See also* Linda Chion-Kenney, "A Look at the Coalition for Essential Schools," *American Educator* (Winter 1987).

Cochran v. Louisiana State Board of Education 281 U.W. 370 (1930) The Supreme Court case that established the CHILD BENEFIT THEORY. A school district was making textbooks available to students at a local parochial school and the plaintiffs argued that tax money could not be utilized for religious institutions (church-state separation). The Court ruled that since the beneficiaries were the students and not the parochial schools, the practice was not unconstitutional as charged.

cocurricular activities   Activities, under the sponsorship or direction of the school, of the type for which participation generally is not required and credit generally is not awarded.

code   A comprehensive collection of statutory laws. For example, the U.S. Code is the official compilation of federal laws. A code differs from a collection of statutes in that codes are organized by topics for easy reference rather than in the chronological order that the various laws were passed.

code of ethics   A formal statement of professional standards of conduct to which the practitioners of many professions say they subscribe. Codes of ethics are usually not legally binding so they may not be taken as serious constraints on behavior. *See* James P. Clarre, "Code of Ethics: Waste of Time or Important Control?" *Public Management* (August 1967); and Kenneth Kernaghan, "Codes of Ethics and Administrative Responsibility," *Canadian Public Administration* (Winter 1974);
    For a compilation of the codes of professional ethics of the major professions in the United States, *see* Rena Gorlin,

ed., *Codes of Professional Responsibility* (Washington, D.C.: Bureau of National Affairs, Inc., 1986).

Code of Federal Regulations (CFR)   The annual summary of regulations issued by federal executive agencies that is published in the *Federal Register*, plus regulations issued previously that are still in effect. The *CFR* is divided into 50 titles representing broad subject areas. Individual volumes of the *CFR* are revised at least once each year.

coed   1. Slang for coeducational. 2. A dated reference to a female college student.

coeducational   A school or class that includes both sexes.

coefficient of correlation   *See* CORRELATION COEFFICIENT.

cognition   1. Generally refers to higher level mental processes such as thinking, remembering, problem solving, analyzing, and reasoning. 2. Gaining of knowledge. 3. Intelligence. Compare to THINKING. *See* Elliot W. Eisner, *Cognition and Curriculum: A Basis for Deciding What to Teach* (New York: Longman, 1982).

cognitive behavior modification   An approach to behavior change that integrates behavioral theory with knowledge of cognition and emphasizes the student's role in facilitating his or her own behavior changes utilizing inner speech as an intrinsic guide to behavior. A theory introduced by Donald Meichenbaum in *Cognitive Behavior Modification* (New York: Plenum Press, 1977).

cognitive development   The acquisition through maturation and environmental experiences of the complex skills that comprise thinking and intelligence. According to JEAN PIAGET cognitive development occurs in a natural sequence through successive stages of increasingly complex conceptual abilities. The stages he defined were: sensory-motor, pre-operational, concrete operational, and formal operational (see entries).

See Ruth L. Ault, *Children's Cognitive Development: Piaget's Theories and the Process Approach* (New York: Oxford University Press, 1977); John A. Keats et al., eds., *Cognitive Development: Researches Based on a Neo-Piagetian Approach* (New York: John Wiley and Sons, 1978); and Herbert Klausmeier and Patricia Allen, *Cognitive Development of Children and Youth: A Longitudinal Study* (New York: Academic Press, 1978).

cognitive development model Based on the learning theory of Jean Piaget, the perspective that learning is an interactive process based on both the internal characteristics of the individual and the environment.

cognitive dissonance   Theory first postulated by Leon Festinger, in *A Theory of Cognitive Dissonance* (Evanston, Ill.: Row, Peterson Co., 1957), which holds that when an individual finds himself in a situation where he is expected to believe two mutually exclusive things, the subsequent tension and discomfort generates activity designed to reduce the dissonance or disharmony. For example, a teacher who sees him or herself in an inequitable wage situation could experience cognitive dissonance. The theory of cognitive dissonance assumes that a teacher performing the same work as another but being paid significantly less will do something to relieve the dissonance. Among the options are asking for a raise, restricting output, or seeking another job. For further studies in cognitive dissonance, *see* J.W. Brehm and A.R. Cohn,

Explorations in Cognitive Dissonance (New York: John Wiley, 1962).

cognitive domain   One of the major behavioral areas described by BENJAMIN BLOOM in his taxonomy of learning objectives; the cognitive domain deals primarily with intellectual skills such as problem solving, memory, reasoning, comprehension, recall, and judgment. Compare to AFFECTIVE DOMAIN and PSYCHOMOTOR DOMAIN.

cognitive mapping   Learning through a planned series of behaviors rather than by basic involuntary conditioning. Cues, knowledge, and stimuli are organized by the brain into patterns (cognitive maps) that lead to a preestablished learning goal.

cognitive and perceptual skills test   An examination measuring components of a person's mental ability, such as visual memory, figure-ground differentiation, auditory memory, reasoning ability, and sequential processing.

cognitive process   The process by which one gathers, organizes, analyzes, and interprets information from the environment.

cognitive psychology   A school of psychology that emphasizes the complex processes involved in learning and intellectual functioning. It contrasts with behavioral psychology that essentially views most learning as a basic process of stimulus-response conditioning.

cognitive set or style   One's individual approach to perceiving and responding to experiences based on a predetermined tendency, usually of an intellectual, concrete nature.

cognitive theory in language acquisition   The theory that learning a first, native language is a complex mental process that is not achieved simply by imitation and practice. Contrast with NATIVISTIC THEORY.

cognitively oriented curriculum
Generally refers to a set of educational methods and objectives that are based on the learning theory of Jean Piaget.

COGS *See* COUNCIL OF GOVERN-MENTS.

cohort 1. One-tenth of a Roman legion. 2. In the social sciences a cohort is a group identified as having common characteristics for the purposes of study, usually over time. Cohorts can be identified by age of the year they first had a common experience such as graduating college, entering the military, or winning election to Congress.

COLA *See* COST-OF-LIVING ADJUST-MENT.

Cole v. Richardson 405 U. S. 676 (1971) The Supreme Court case that upheld the right of Massachusetts to exact from its employees a promise to "oppose the overthrow of the government of the United States of America or of this Commonwealth by force, violence or by any illegal or unconstitutional method." A public employer may legitimately require employees to swear or affirm their allegiance to the Constitution of the United States and of a particular state. Beyond that, the limits of constitutional loyalty oaths are unclear. *See also* LOYALTY OATH.

Coleman Report A study published by James S. Coleman of Johns Hopkins University in 1966 under a federal legislative mandate to obtain information about equality in education. Though the study has received much scholarly criticism with regard to its methodology, the results have been widely circulated. Significant findings included evidence that factors

external to school itself were highly correlated with student achievement and that students from disadvantaged families learned more when they attended school with children from more advantaged backgrounds.

See James S. Coleman et al., *Equality of Educational Opportunity* (Washington, D.C.: U.S. Government Printing Office, 1966).

collaboration A generic term that refers to cooperative planning, developing, and implementation of activities between or among various entities. In education collaboration generally refers to either inter-organizational coalitions or cooperation between school and community. For a number of examples of collaboration in education, *see Educational Leadership*, (February 1986).

collaborative school A generic term for several models that encourage cooperation among professionals and administrators in their efforts toward instructional effectiveness. The collaborative model typically emphasizes the role of the individual school and the individual teacher in determining the quality of education; it involves the teachers in decisions about school goals and in planning; and it fosters a climate of collegiality and continuous improvement. *See* Stuart C. Smith, "What the Collaborative School Really Means," *Educational Leadership* (November 1987).

collection rate Also called collection ratio. Computed as collected revenue divided by billed revenue (or invoiced revenue).

collections The process of attempting to collect billed but unpaid (delinquent) monies due from students or other individuals or organizations for services performed or loans made.

Institutions generally have three options open to them at the collection stage:

1. Institutional follow-up, with legal action as a last resort.
2. Institutional follow-up supplemented by action by a collection agency prior to legal action.
3. Immediate referral to a collection agency followed, if necessary, by legal action.

collective bargaining   A comprehensive term that encompasses the negotiating process that leads to a contract between labor and management on wages, hours, and other conditions of employment as well as the subsequent administration and interpretation of the signed contract. Collective bargaining is, in effect, the continuous relationship that exists between union representatives and employers. The four basic stages of collective bargaining are: (a) the establishment of organizations for bargaining, (b) the formulation of demands, (c) the negotiation of demands, and (d) the administration of the labor agreement.

See John Bangs, *Collective Bargaining* (New York: Alexander Hamilton Institute, 1986). *See also* Joseph W. Gabarino, *Faculty Bargaining: Change and Conflict* (New York: McGraw-Hill, 1975); Joyce M. Najita and Helene S. Tanimoto, *Guide to Statutory Provisions in Public Sector Collective Bargaining: Characteristics, Functions and Powers of Administrative Agencies* (Honolulu: Industrial Relations Center, University of Hawaii, 1981); and Charles R. Perry, "Teacher Bargaining: The Experience in Nine Systems," *Industrial and Labor Relations Review* (October 1979).

See also SUNSHINE BARGAINING.

collective bargaining agent   An organization such as the local affiliate of either the National Education Association or the American Federation of Teachers, that is recognized by the institution, either voluntarily or through agent elections, as representing the interests of faculty in collective bargaining.

collective negotiations   An alternate term for "collective bargaining," which, in the public sector, may sometimes be legally and/or semantically unacceptable. *See* Robert T. Woodworth and Richard B. Peterson, *Collective Negotiations for Public and Professional Employees* (Glenview, Ill.: Scott, Foresman & Co., 1969).

college   1. A postsecondary school that offers general or liberal arts education, usually leading to a first degree. While some colleges are independent of other institutions, many are part of larger universities. 2. A graduate school within a university such as a college of medicine. 3. A loose term for any institution offering postsecondary education. 4. A professional or religious organization of those who meet preset high qualifications. For an annotated listing of college guidebooks published in the United States, *see* "A Guide to the College and University Handbooks," *Harvard Educational Review*, (February 1984).

College Board, The   *See* COLLEGE ENTRANCE EXAMINATION BOARD.

"college boards"   A common, colloquial reference to the admissions tests sponsored by the College Entrance Examination Board or to any college entrance tests.

college catalog   A formal statement of degree programs, course offerings, admission requirements, student regulations, and other basic information about a college or university. Catalogs, which are also called bulletins, are usually published anew each year. Most large libraries have microfiche collections of all U.S. college catalogs.

College Entrance Examination Board (College Board or CEEB)

A nonprofit organization founded in 1900 to assist students in moving from secondary education to higher education. The board has a membership of over 2,400 colleges, universities, and other agencies and associations providing services to secondary and post-secondary students. Commonly known programs administered by the College Board include: 1. the Scholastic Aptitude Test (SAT), which is a nationwide college admissions examination; 2. the National Merit Scholarship Qualifying Test, which assists high school students in applying for National Merit Scholarships; 3. the Advanced Placement Program (APP), which allows high school students to earn college credits; 4. the College Level Examination Program (CLEP), which is used to determine eligibility for advanced placement at the college level; 5. the College Scholarship Service, which helps students apply for financial assistance. The Board's offices are in New York City and it periodically publishes a guide to its programs and services.

For a history of the College Board's influence on the substance and standards of American education, *see* John Valentine, *The College Board and the School Curriculum* (Princeton, N.J.: The College Board, 1987).

The College Board
45 Columbus Avenue
New York, NY 10023
(212) 713-8000

College Level Examination Program (CLEP)

A program of the College Entrance Examination Board that allows students to earn college credit by examination. Both "general examinations" in five liberal arts areas (English composition, mathematics, natural sciences, social sciences, and humanities) and specific "subject examinations" in 47 different subjects are offered. Students meeting established criteria on the examinations can "place out" of courses while earning credit for a more advanced college standing.

College Scholarship Service (CSS)

A program of the College Entrance Examination Board (College Board) that provides a standardized format for determining student financial need. The CSS helps the student in applying for financial aid and helps higher education institutions and other scholarship programs in the equitable distribution of resources.

Columbia Mental Maturity Scale

An individually administered test of intelligence that measures classification and discrimination skills in children ages 3 1/2 to 10. It may be appropriately used with individuals who have difficulty responding verbally. It is published by:

The Psychological Corporation
555 Academic Court
San Antonio, TX 78204

commercial education   Vocational education that prepares high school students for relatively low-level careers in business.

commission   A group charged with directing a governmental function whether on an ad hoc or permanent basis. Commissions tend to be used (a) when it is desirable to have bipartisan leadership, (b) when their functions are of a quasi-judicial nature, or (c) when it is deemed important to have wide representation of ethnic groups, regions of the country, differing skills, or special interest groups.

Commission on Civil Rights

The federal agency whose role is to encourage constructive steps toward equal opportunity for all. The commission investigates complaints, holds public hearings, and collects and studies information on denials of equal protection of the laws because of race, color, religion, sex, or national origin. Voting rights, administration of justice, and equality of opportunity in education, employment, and housing are among the many topics of specific commission interest.

The commission, created by the Civil Rights Act of 1957, makes findings of fact but has no enforcement authority. Findings and recommendations are submitted to both the President and the Congress. Many of the commission's recommendations have been enacted by statute, executive order, or regulation. The commission evaluates federal laws and the effectiveness of government equal opportunity programs. It also serves as a national clearinghouse for civil rights information.

See Foster Rhea Dulles, *The Civil Rights Commission: 1957-1965* (East Lansing, Mich.: Michigan State University Press, 1968).

Commission on Civil Rights
1121 Vermont Avenue, N. W.
Washington, DC 20425
(202) 376-8177

Commission on the Reorganization of Secondary Education   A study group of the NATIONAL EDUCATION ASSOCIATION whose 1918 report substantially influenced the evolution of American secondary education. *See* CARDINAL PRINCIPLES OF SECONDARY EDUCATION.

Commissioner of Education   1. The title of the chief education officer in some U.S. states. 2. The former title of the chief education officer in the federal government. When the department of education was created in 1979, the secretary of education became the "new" chief of federal education programs.

committee   1. A part of a larger group appointed to perform a

specialized service on a one-time or continuous basis. 2. A subdivision of a legislature that prepares legislation for action by the respective house, or makes investigations as directed by the respective house. Most standing committees are divided into subcommittees that study legislation, hold hearings, and report their recommendations to the full committee. Only the full committee can report legislation for action by the entire legislature.

committee, ad hoc   *See* AD HOC COMMITTEE.

Committee of Fifteen   A committee on elementary studies appointed by the NATIONAL EDUCATION ASSOCIATION in 1893 which set direction for elementary school education and curricula that has been maintained to the present. The committee supported the concept of an eight-year elementary education that primarily emphasized grammar (hence the designation "grammar school") and secondarily emphasized literature, arithmetic, geography, and history. *See* William T. Harris et al., *Report of the Committee of Fifteen on Elementary Education* (New York: Arno Press, 1969; reprint of the 1895 edition).

Committee of Nine   A committee of the NATIONAL EDUCATION ASSOCIATION formed in 1910 that broadened the definition of high school purpose from that promoted by the Committee of Ten of 1891. The Committee of Nine was the first to suggest that high schools had a responsibility for making students "socially efficient," i.e., committed to fundamental American values and capable of making a contribution to the social development of the country. *See* COMMITTEE OF TEN.

Committee of Ten   A committee on secondary school studies appointed by the NATIONAL EDUCATION ASSOCIATION in 1891 that gave direction for a standardized secondary school curriculum in the United States. The nine subjects included in the curriculum were: 1) Latin, 2) Greek, 3) English, 4) other modern languages, 5) mathematics, 6) physics, astronomy, and chemistry, 7) natural history (biology, zoology and physiology), 8) history, civil government and political economy, and 9) geography. The committee did not acknowledge art or music as important subjects nor did it recognize the potential desirability of differential requirements for students who may not be college bound.

See National Education Association, *Report of the Committee of Ten on Secondary School Studies* (New York: Arno Press, 1969; reprint of the 1893 edition).

common schools   The pre-Civil War public schools that, starting in the 1830s, offered free basic education to all children who attended. This designation was first applied to the public school concept by Horace Mann (see entry). He sought common schools in which the children of all classes and representing all segments of a society would be educated together and thus acquire the mutual respect essential to the functioning of a democracy.

See Lawrence A. Cremin, *The American Common School: An Historic Conception* (New York: Teacher's College, Columbia University, 1951); and Frederick M. Binder, *The Age of the Common School, 1830-1865* (New York: John Wiley, 1974). For a more modern view of the concept, *see* Charles L. Glenn, "The New Common School," *Phi Delta Kappan* (December 1987).

common school district   A small town or rural school district that typically operates only an elementary school program, though it may also have a secondary program.

common school revival   The late 19th-century educational reform movement which called for a common, state-wide curriculum and the expansion of free public education.

communication   Process of exchanging information, ideas, and feelings between two or more individuals or groups. Horizontal communication refers to such an exchange among peers or people at the same organizational level. Vertical communication refers to such an exchange between individuals at differing levels of the organization. *See* William V. Haney, *Communications and Interpersonal Relations*, 4th ed. (Homewood, Ill.: Richard D. Irwin, 1979).

communication disorder   An impairment in speech and/or language (including impaired articulation, stuttering, voice impairment, and a receptive or expressive verbal language handicap) that is sufficiently severe to adversely affect the performance of an individual in the usual school program.

community   1. A group who live in an identifiable area. This can range from the "community of man," which occupies the planet called earth to the Hispanic community of San Antonio, Texas, or the Jewish community of Miami, Florida. 2. A group who have common interests such as the medical community, the Catholic community, or the educational community. 3. All of the people living in a particular locality. 4. A housing development. 5. Shared goods such as a community swimming pool in a city or community property in a marriage.

community college   A junior college usually operated by the board of education of a local basic administrative unit (including the independent local board for one or more community colleges). Instruction is adapted in content, level, and schedule to the needs of the local community. It begins with grade 13, offers at least one but less than four years of work, and does not grant the baccalaureate degree.

See Charles R. Monroe, *Profile of the Community College* (San Francisco: Jossey-Bass, 1972); and Robert Palinchak, *The Evolution of the Community College* (Metuchen, N.J.: Scarecrow Press, 1973).

community control An extreme form of citizen participation in which democratically selected representatives of a neighborhood-sized governmental jurisdiction are given administrative and financial control over such local programs as education, land use, and police protection.

See Mario Fantini, *Community Control and the Urban School* (New York: Praeger, 1970); Norman I. Fainstein and Susan S. Fainstein, "The Future of Community Control," *American Political Science Review* (September 1976).

community council An advisory council to the local school that might be composed of all the block leaders in the area served by the school. Such councils are used in the community education movement to assist the community school director in getting and using information from the community. Sometimes the council members are elected by residents of the community.

community counselor 1. A school employee sometimes called a home counselor. 2. A citizen from the community who is trained in working with families to help them meet family problems and to introduce them to ways of upgrading the quality of home and family life.

community education 1. The concept of the community as a whole, being the primary educative influence upon the members of the community.

This concept recognizes that all people in a community, regardless of age, have educational needs and that resources to meet those needs are largely available in the community. It recognizes that schools can coordinate the efforts of agencies and resources. 2. Developed for public audiences, this is a type of local education that provides understanding about a problem or issue of community and/or societal relevance, and information about appropriate community resources and services available to deal with the problem or issue. Sponsored by a professional agency or citizens' group, community education is usually provided through an ongoing speaker's bureau, through periodic lecture and discussion meetings open to the general public or offered to special groups, and/or through the local media and other publicity devices. See Maurice L. Say, *Community Education: A Developing Concept* (Midland, Mich.: Pendall, 1974).

community foundation A public, charitable corporation or trust organized and operated to benefit charitable organizations in a particular region, community, or area. Community foundations generally offer donors the advantage of (a) freedom to designate areas of giving, (b) central administration, and (c) continuity of leadership.

community of interest Criterion used to determine if a group of employees make up an appropriate bargaining unit.

community relations A school district's efforts to maintain liaison with local civic groups and to serve as the central point for all requests for public speaking engagements, responses to public inquiry, and arranging for tours of, and visits to, schools.

community relations program The totality of efforts by public organizations (such as schools and local police) to create better understanding and acceptance of their missions in their local communities. Compare to PUBLIC RELATIONS.

community school   1. An elementary, secondary, and/or adult/ continuing education organizational arrangement (or institution), operated by a local board of public education, in which instruction and other activities are intended to be relevant and applicable to the needs of all or most segments of the total population of the community served. 2. A community school concept was developed and piloted in the Lansing, Michigan, public schools by the Mott Foundation.

Community Schools and Comprehensive Education Act of 1978   Title VIII of P.L. 95-561, the Educational Amendments of 1978; a federal act to expand community education programs and services for all age groups through the provision of funds to local education agencies, state agencies, and institutions of higher education. *See* COMMUNITY EDUCATION.

community service education A term frequently used synonymously with the term "Adult/Continuing Education." This term reflects the efforts of community colleges and other institutions or agencies to extend their resources (e.g., facilities, personnel, and expertise) into the community through programs of noncredit educational, avocational, or recreational courses, seminars, conferences, workshops, and other events utilizing any applicable facility or locale. *See also* ADULT/ CONTINUING EDUCATION.

community services   Services, other than public school and adult education functions, provided by a school for purposes relating to the community as a whole or some segment

of the community. These include such services as community recreation programs, civic activities, public libraries, programs of custody and care of children, community welfare activities, and services for nonpublic school pupils provided by the public schools on a continuing basis.

community team   Refers to a team of professionals who are responsive to community needs in the area of child abuse and neglect. Often used incorrectly to refer to a multi-disciplinary professional group that only diagnoses and plans treatment for specific cases of child abuse and neglect. More accurately, a community team separates the diagnosis and treatment functions and provides a third component for education, training, and public relations. The community team also includes a community task force or council, comprised of citizens as well as professionals from various disciplines, which coordinates the three community team components and advocates for resources and legislation. Citizens on the community team also monitor the professionals and agency participants.

community wage survey   Any survey whose purpose is to ascertain the structure and level of wages among employees in a local area.

community-based training or community-referenced training A totally adapted curriculum for students who are handicapped based on the premise that school should teach those skills that are necessary for handicapped learners to be able to function effectively in natural community environments both currently and in their future adult lives. Teaching generally takes place in typical community environments and the basic skills taught (e.g., reading, math, communication, motor skills, and social skills) are those that are specifically required in those environments. *See also* FUNCTIONAL CURRICULUM. Contrast with FIELD TRIP, in that the community excursions are for specific skill instruction and not for the purpose of simple exposure to the broader community. *See* Mary A. Falvey, *Community-Based Curriculum* (Baltimore: Paul H. Brooks, 1986).

community/junior college   An institution of higher education that usually offers the first two years of college instruction and career education, grants an associate's degree, and does not grant a bachelor's degree. It is either a separately organized institution (public or nonpublic) or an institution that is a part of a public school system or system of junior colleges. Offerings include transfer, occupational, and/or general studies programs at the postsecondary instructional level and may also include adult/continuing education programs. *See also* COMMUNITY COLLEGE and JUNIOR COLLEGE.

comp time   *See* COMPENSATORY TIME.

comparable worth   Providing equitable compensation for performing work of a comparable value as determined by the relative worth of a given job to an organization. The basic issue of comparable worth is whether Title VII of the Civil Rights Act of 1964 makes it unlawful for an employer to pay one sex at a lesser rate than the other when job performance is of comparable worth or value. For example, should graduate nurses be paid less than gardeners? Or should beginning librarians with a master's degree be paid less than beginning managers with a master's degree? Historically, nurses and librarians have been paid less than occupations of "comparable worth" because they were considered "female" jobs. Comparable worth as a legal concept and as a social issue directly challenges traditional and market assumptions about the worth of a job.

See Elaine Johansen, "Managing the Revolution: The Case for Comparable Worth," *Review of Public Personnel Administration* (Spring 1984); Helen Remick, ed., *Comparable Worth and Wage Discrimination: Technical Possibilities and Political Realities* (Philadelphia: Temple University Press, 1984); Bruce Powell Majors, "Comparable Worth: The New Feminist Demand," *Journal of Social, Political and Economic Studies* (Spring 1985); and D. Pawelek, "Your Constitution: Equal Pay for Similar Work," *Scholastic Update* (May 1987).

comparative analysis   The comparison of data and ratios from the financial statement of an institution with either the same institution's financial statement for a different time period or corresponding ratios of other, similar (peer) institutions.

compensatory damages   Payments for an actual loss that was suffered by a plaintiff. Such payments are intended to compensate the plaintiff for losses, not to punish the defendant, as opposed to punitive damages. *See CITY OF NEWPORT V. FACT CONCERTS, INC.*

compensatory education   An education program that seeks to remedy deficiencies in a disadvantaged student's background by providing specific experiences to make up for what is lacking.

compensatory methodology   Any means to accomplish instructional objectives by bypassing obstacles to normal learning through the use of alternative channels of learning or adaptive devices or materials. Commonly used in reference to the education of deaf, blind, or learning disabled students where it is assumed that the student possesses at least average intellectual capacity and is pursuing typical scholastic objectives. Examples of compensatory methodologies are the use of braille or auditory instruction, with blind students, and the use of sign language with deaf students.

compensatory time   Time off from work offered by an institution in lieu of overtime pay. Compensatory time policy must be in conformance with the FAIR LABOR STANDARDS ACT.

competency test   A test that measures the acquisition of particular skills, generally related to basic academics taught at school (e.g., reading levels, application of computation skills) but might also be related to real-life skills (e.g., preparing a meal, driving a car, making a purchase). *See* TEACHER COMPETENCY TESTING and MINIMUM COMPETENCY TEST. For an interesting side-perspective, *see* Martha M. McCarthy, "The Application of Competency Testing Mandates to Handicapped Children," *Harvard Educational Review* (May 1983).

See also Peter W. Airasian et al., *Minimal Competency Testing* (Englewood Cliffs, N.J.: Educational Technology Publications, 1979).

competency-based certification A specific approach by which a state (or agency or organization authorized by a state) determines individual eligibility for a credential. The process may require individuals to demonstrate a mastery of minimum essential generic and specialization competencies and other related criteria adopted by the board through a comprehensive written examination or through other procedures, rather than granting certification on the basis of the completion of an institutional program.

competency-based education 1. An educational approach based on a predetermined set of knowledge, skills, and abilities that the student is expected to accomplish. This approach became popular in the 1970s in relation to concerns about school accountability. 2. An educational curriculum or program closely related to "survival skill" training where the academic focus is based on functional outcomes, i.e. What does a student need to learn to function in adult life?

See Steck-Vaughn's *Guide to Competency-Based Education*, (Austin, Texas: Steck-Vaugh Company Publishers, 1986); Gene H. Hall and Howard L. Jones, *Competency-Based Education: A Process for the Improvement of Education* (Englewood Cliffs, N.J.: Prentice-Hall, 1976).

competency-based teacher education   A program of study for teacher preparation that is designed on the basis of a predetermined set of outcomes that is usually related to particular skills, knowledge, and attitudes. The program requires the demonstration of specific competencies for completion. *See* Benjamin Rosner, *The Power of Competency-Based Teacher Education* (Boston: Allyn and Bacon, 1972).

competitive admissions   A college or other institution's admissions policy that forces applicants to compete against each other for placement as opposed to admitting all those who meet minimum criteria.

competitive level   All positions of the same grade within a competitive area that are sufficiently alike in duties, responsibilities, pay systems, terms of appointment, requirements for experience, training, skills, and aptitudes that the incumbent of any of them could readily be shifted to any of the other positions without significant training or undue interruption to the work program. In the federal government, the job to which an employee is officially assigned determines his or her competitive level.

competitive promotion   Selection for promotion made from the employees rated best qualified in competition with others, all of whom have the minimum qualifications required by the position.

competitive seniority   Use of seniority in determining an employee's access, relative to other employees, to job related "rights" that cannot be supplied equally to any two employees.

competitive service   A general term for those civilian positions in a governmental jurisdiction that are not specifically excepted from merit system regulations.

competitive wages   Rates of pay that an employer, in competition with other employers, must offer if he or she is to recruit and retain employees.

completion of schoolwork Completing a program of studies and withdrawing from school. This includes graduation from high school (grade 12) or college, or otherwise fulfilling the requirements for a prescribed program of studies. Midyear or year-end transfer to a higher grade within the same school is not considered as completion of schoolwork.

compliance   1. To yield to the demands of significant others, such as those in authority, those with power or peers in the case of group peer pressure. 2. Acting in accordance with the law. Voluntary compliance is the basis of a civil society. No government has the resources to force all of its citizens to comply with all of the criminal and civil laws. Consequently all governments are dependent upon compliance. 3. A technical term used by funding agencies as a criterion to judge whether a grantee is

acting (that is, spending their grant funds) in accordance with the granter's policies or preset guidelines. 4. The behavior of children who readily yield to demands in an attempt to please.

compliance agency   Generally, any government agency that administers and monitors contractual and programmatic adherence to laws and/or regulations. For example, a federal agency is delegated enforcement responsibilities by the U.S. Department of Labor's Office of Federal Contract Compliance Programs (OFCCP) to ensure that federal contractors adhere to EEO regulations and policies. *See* Kenneth C. Marino, "Conducting an Internal Compliance Review of Affirmative Action," *Personnel* (March-April 1980).

composite score   An overall test score derived by combining scores obtained on two or more tests or other measures.

compound entry   A balanced entry that contains two or more debits or two or more credits.

comprehension-level thinking From Bloom's taxonomy, a thinking or learning process involving an understanding of relationships between more than one piece of previously learned information and/or a simple interpretation of new information. Contrast with KNOWLEDGE-LEVEL, APPLICATION-LEVEL, ANALYSIS-LEVEL, SYNTHESIS-LEVEL, EVALUATION-LEVEL. *See* BLOOM'S TAXONOMY.

Comprehensive Employment and Training Act of 1973 (CETA) The law that, as amended, established a program of financial assistance to state and local governments to provide job training and employment opportunities for economically disadvantaged, unemployed, and underemployed persons. CETA provided funds for state and local jurisdictions to hire unemployed and underemployed persons in public service jobs. The CETA reauthorization legislation expired in September 1982. It was replaced by the Job Training Partnership Act of 1982, which provides for job training programs to be planned and implemented under the joint control of local elected officials and private industry councils in service delivery areas designated by the governor of each state.

For analyses of CETA, *see* Pawan K. Sawhney, Robert H. Jantzen, and Irwin L. Herrnstadt, "The Differential Impact of CETA Training," *Industrial and Labor Relations Review* (January 1982); Grace A. Franklin and Randall B. Ripley, *CETA: Politics and Policy 1973-1982* (Knoxville: University of Tennessee Press, 1984).

For the Job Training Partnership Act, *see* Royal S. Dellinger, "Implementing the Job Training Partnership Act," *Labor Law Journal* (April 1984); Susan A. MacManus, "Playing a New Game: Governors and the Job Training Partnership Act," *American Politics Quarterly* (July 1986).

comprehensive high school   A secondary school with a number of departments (e.g., academic, industrial, business, and vocational) offering a diversified program to meet the needs of students with varying interests and abilities.

Comprehensive Tests of Basic Skills (CTBS)   A group-administered test of skill achievement that is required for academic learning. Items are classified by a taxonomy of intellectual skills across the content areas of reading, math, language, reference skills, science, and social studies. Its seven levels cover grades K to 12. It is published by:

CTB/McGraw-Hill
DelMonte Research Park
Monterey, CA 93940

comptroller   *See* CONTROLLER.

compulsory arbitration   Negotiating process whereby the parties are required by law to arbitrate their dispute. Some state statutes concerning collective bargaining impasses in the public sector mandate that parties who have exhausted all other means of achieving a settlement must submit their dispute to an arbitrator. The intent of such requirements for compulsory arbitration is to induce the parties to reach agreement by presenting them with an alternative that is both certain and unpleasant.

See Carl M. Stevens, "Is Compulsory Arbitration Compatible with Bargaining," *Industrial Relations* (February 1966); and Mollie H. Bowers, "Legislated Arbitration Legality, Enforceability, and Face-Saving," *Public Personnel Management* (July-August 1974).

compulsory school attendance   The practice of requiring school attendance by state law.

compulsory school attendance age   The age span during which a child is required by law to attend school.

computer curriculum   An educational plan for how computers will be taught and used in schools. For example, computer awareness at the elementary level, computer literacy at the middle school level, and computer programming at the high school level. *See* Bobbie K. Hentel and Linda Harper, *Computers in Education* (Ann Arbor: University of Michigan Press, 1985).

computer literacy   The ability to control and program a computer for academic, professional, and personal uses; to assess the technical qualities and substantive strengths and weaknesses of hardware, software, and courseware; and to understand the im-

AGES FOR COMPULSORY SCHOOL ATTENDANCE AND ADMISSION

Date	Compulsory attendance[1]	Attendance permitted[2]	Admission to First Grade Age	By What Date
Alabama	7-16	—	—	—
Alaska	7-16	—	6	Nov. 2
Arizona	8-16	6-21	6	Jan. 1
Arkansas	7-15	6-21	6	Oct. 1
California	6-16	—	6	—
Colorado	7-16	6-21	6	—
Connecticut	7-16	5-21	6	Jan. 1
Delaware	5-16	6-21	—	—
District of Columbia	7-17	—	6	Dec. 31
Florida	6-16	—	6	Jan. 1
Georgia	7-16	—	6	Dec. 1
Hawaii	6-18	—	6	Dec. 1
Idaho	7-16	5-21	6	Oct. 16
Illinois	7-16	—	6	Dec. 1
Indiana	7-16	—	6	—
Iowa	7-16	5-21	6	Sept. 1
Kansas	7-16	5-21	6	—
Kentucky	6-18	—	6	Jan. 1
Louisiana	7-16	—	6	Jan. 1
Maine	7-17	5-20	6	Oct. 15
Maryland	6-16	5-20	6	Dec. 31
Massachusetts	6-16	—	6	Sept. 1
Michigan	7-16	5-20	6	Dec. 1
Minnesota	7-16	5-21	6	Sept. 1

Date	Compulsory attendance[1]	Attendance permitted[2]	Admission to First Grade Age	Admission to First Grade By What Date
Mississippi	6-14	6-20	6	Sept. 1
Missouri	7-16	5-20	6	Oct. 1
Montana	7-16	6-21	6	—
Nebraska	7-16	—	6	Oct. 15
Nevada	7-17	6-17	6	Sept. 30
New Hampshire	6-16	—	6	Sept. 30
New Jersey	6-16	5-20	6	—
New Mexico	6-18	—	6	Sept. 1
New York	6-16	5-21	—	—
North Carolina	7-16	—	6	Oct. 1
North Dakota	7-16	6-21	6	Oct. 1
Ohio	6-18	—	6	Sept. 13
Oklahoma	7-18	5-21	6	Nov. 1
Oregon	7-18	6-21	6	Nov. 15
Pennsylvania	8-17	6-18	5 yrs. 7 mos.	Sept. 1
Rhode Island	7-16	—	6	Dec. 31
South Carolina	5-17	6-21	6	Nov. 1
South Dakota	7-16	5-21	6	Nov. 1
Tennessee	7-17	6-21	6	Oct. 31
Texas	7-16	5-21	6	Sept 1
Utah	6-18	—	6	—
Vermont	7-16	—	6	—
Virginia	5-17	5-20	6	Dec. 31
Washington	8-18	6-21	6	Nov. 1
West Virginia	6-16	—	6	Nov. 1
Wisconsin	6-18	6-20	6	Dec. 1
Wyoming	7-16	6-21	6	Sept. 15

(1) During these years (inclusive) a child must attend school unless some approved basis for exemption exists.
(2) During these years (inclusive) a child may attend school on a tuition-free basis.
SOURCE: National Center for Education Statistics, *Digest of Education Statistics, 1985-86*

pact of computers on society, work, and education.

computer-assisted instruction (CAI)
Programmed instruction utilizing an electronic computer as the principal medium of instruction. Instructional material is presented on a terminal under computer control and student responses are processed by the computer. Also called Computer Based Education. See Marcella L. Kysilka, "How Effective is CAI? A Review of Research," *Educational Leadership* (November 1975).

See also Harry M. Levin and Gail Meister, "Is CAI Cost-Effective," *Phi Delta Kappan* (June 1986); and Julie Vargus, "Instructional Design Flaws in Computer-Assisted Instruction," *Phi Delta Kappan*, (June 1986).

computer-assisted instruction services
Activities concerned with planning, programming, writing, and presenting educational programs or segments of programs which have been especially programmed for a computer to be used as the principle medium of instruction.

computer-managed instruction
Use of the computer to select materials, schedule, test, prescribe, and maintain student records.

Conant Report
A study of the American comprehensive high school prepared in 1959 by James B. Conant (1893-1978), former long-term president of Harvard University (1933-1953). The report highlighted the following recommendations: 1) high schools should offer a general education for all students as well as elective alternatives for vocationally-bound and college-bound students; 2) high schools graduating fewer than 100 students should consolidate with other schools; 3) high schools should improve school-community relations; 4) high schools should address individual needs of students, especially the slow learners and the academically gifted. See James B. Conant, *The American High School Today: A First Report to Interested Citizens* (New York: McGraw-Hill, 1959).

Conant also wrote *The Education of American Teachers* (1963) and *The Comprehensive High School* (1967).

concept
1. A general idea or understanding. 2. A thought or a notion. 3. An abstraction of observed events that represents the similarities or common aspects of the objects or events.

concept analysis
Clarification of a concept through definition, identification of attributes, examples, and comparison with other concepts.

Concept Mastery Test (CMT)
A test that measures an individual's ability to deal with ideas or concepts by sampling two kinds of verbal problem: synonyms-antonyms and the completion of analogies. Questions draw on concepts from physical and biological sciences, mathematics, history, geography, literature, and music. The test purportedly measures power or capacity rather than speed.

The Psychological Corporation
555 Academic Court
San Antonio, TX 78701

concept six
A model for year-round schooling that divides the year into six two-month blocks with students attending for four blocks and vacationing for two.

conciliator
An individual who has been agreed upon by disputing parties and who assumes the responsibility for maintaining disputing parties in negotiations until they reach a voluntary settlement. The Federal Mediation and Conciliation Services (FMCS), for example, has commissioners of concilia-

tion at its regional offices who are available to assist parties to settle disputes. *See* ARBITER and MEDIATOR.

concrete operational   One of the stages of cognitive development in children postulated by Jean Piaget. This stage occurs between the ages of seven and eleven years, when rational logic appears and children are able to use systematic reasoning to find the solutions to certain kinds of problem (i.e., concrete rather than abstract).

condemnation proceedings The process by which property of a private owner is taken through right of eminent domain for public use.

conditioned response   A basic component of CLASSICAL CONDITIONING, the response that occurs in the presence of a new stimulus after that stimulus has been paired many times with another stimulus that innately produces the response.

C1 and C2   Symbols used to identify pupils who have completed their schoolwork, as follows: C1—graduated from high school or junior college; C2—completed other schoolwork. *See also* COMPLETION OF SCHOOLWORK.

confidence testing   Testing approach that allows the subject to express his or her attraction to or confidence in possible answers in percentage terms. *See* Ernest S. Selig, "Confidence Testing Comes of Age," *Training and Development Journal* (July 1972).

confidential reports from outside agencies (student record)   Confidential information from the records of cooperating agencies and individuals such as hospitals, child welfare agencies, and the juvenile court; or from correction officers and private

practitioners. Such reports are often provided with the mutual understanding that they will not be incorporated into cumulative records or special student services records, they will be under the direct supervision of qualified school personnel and they will be made available on request to students or their parents. *See also* CUMULATIVE STUDENT RECORD and SPECIAL STUDENT SERVICES RECORD.

confidentiality   A concept in education that involves certain procedures to ensure the protection and privacy of information about an individual student. Confidentiality procedures include provisions such as the maintenance of student school records in secured files, controlling access to records, and eliminating names from data that are publicly recorded for research or documentation purposes. For a comprehensive reference on confidentiality, *see* Robert F. Boruch and Joe S. Cecil, *Assuring the Confidentiality of Social Research Data* (Philadelphia: University of Pennsylvania Press, 1979).

conflict management   Also called conflict resolution. Refers to any activity aimed at keeping interpersonal and interorganizational conflicts constructive rather than allowing them to become destructive. Conflict management is often seen as a fundamental skill for administrators since conflict in organizations is inevitable and even useful up to some point. The important issue is to permit and control conflict for beneficial purposes. Conflict resolution refers more specifically to a conscious effort to solve or otherwise eliminate conflicts.
See R.E. Hill, "Managing Interpersonal Conflict in Project Teams," *Sloan Management Review*, 18:2 (1977), 17-25. For a comprehensive review of recent developments in various fields of conflict management,

resolution, and mediation, *see* Keith Kressel and Dean Pruitt, eds., "The Mediation of Social Conflict," *Journal of Social Issues* (Summer 1985).

conflict of interest   Any situation where a decision that may be made (or influenced) by an officeholder may be (or may appear to be) to that officeholder's personal benefit. Officeholders usually try to avoid both actual conflicts and the appearance of a conflict. A common means of avoiding conflicts is to abstain from voting or acting on an issue in which an interest exists. Thus a judge or an administrator may withdraw from a case or the making of a decision in a situation where his or her ownership of stock or other financial interest might be perceived as being benefitted. The most common means of avoiding a conflict (that is, by abstaining) is not practical for many elected officeholders. A political campaign today may involve so many diverse contributors and supporters that a legislator (or school board member) would be severely restricted in voting if the "automatic" criteria for abstaining was the fact that a campaign contributor would be affected.

See Lloyd N. Cutler, "Conflicts of Interest," *Emory Law Journal* (Fall 1981).

confrontation meeting   Organization development technique that has an organizational group (usually the management corps) meet for a one-day effort to assess their organizational health. *See* Richard Beckhard, "The Confrontation Meeting," *Harvard Business Review* (March-April 1967).

Connick v. Meyers 461 U.S. 138 (1983)   Supreme Court case that applied and expanded the holding of *PICKERING V. BOARD OF EDUCATION* (1968), regarding a public employee's rights to freedom of speech as balanced with the interests of the public employer (the state) in promoting public service.

consent order   Regulatory agency procedure to induce voluntary compliance with its policies. A consent order usually takes the form of a formal agreement whereby an industry or company agrees to stop a practice in exchange for the agency's cessation of legal action against it.

conservatory   1. A school that specializes in teaching music. 2. A school that specializes in teaching both music and theater.

consolidation (or consolidated school)   1. The merging of two or more schools or school districts into a single organizational unit. 2. A mechanism by which state legislatures, other policy makers, or local school districts themselves may make efforts to improve the quality of education in general by reducing the number of widely scattered, small systems that may be fiscally and programmatically inefficient.

consortium   A combination of people, groups, associations, or organizations that have joined for a particular purpose. A consortium may be assembled to accomplish a single, short-term purpose, or as a semipermanent alliance to pursue a number of ongoing purposes. Schools at all levels frequently utilize consortia arrangements for a variety of purposes.

constant dollar   A dollar value adjusted for changes in prices. Constant dollars are derived by dividing current dollar amounts by an appropriate price index, a process generally known as deflating. The result is a constant dollar series as it would presumably exist if prices and transactions were the same in all subsequent years as in the base year. Any changes in such a series would reflect only changes in the real volume of goods and services. Compare to CURRENT DOLLAR.

construct   An idea or concept created or synthesized ("constructed") from available information and refined through scientific investigation. In psychological testing, a construct is usually dimensional, an attribute of people that varies in degree from one person to another. Tests are usually intended to be measures of intellectual, perceptual, psychomotor, or personality constructs (e.g., a clerical test may measure the construct known as "perceptual speed and accuracy" or the performance of invoice clerks may be measured in terms of "ability to recognize errors").

construct validity   Measure of how adequate a test is for assessing the possession of particular psychological traits or qualities.

consultant   1. A person who gives professional or technical advice and assistance. A consultant may perform his or her services under contract (purchased services) or may be an employee on the payroll of a state agency. 2. Individual or organization temporarily employed by other individuals or organizations because of some presumed expertise. Internal consultants are often employed by large organizations to provide consulting services to their various units.

See Arthur N. Turner, "Consulting Is More Than Giving Advice," *Harvard Business Review* (September-October 1982); and Danielle B. Nees and Larry E. Greiner, "Seeing Behind the Look-Alike Management Consultants," *Organizational Dynamics* (Winter 1985).

consultation   1. The provision of consultative services. 2. In education a model of delivering special services (for example, special education or related services such as speech/language therapy) to a student indirectly by providing the classroom teacher with in-formation regarding alternative instructional strategies, adaptation of materials and specialized technologies.

See Duane Brown et al., *Consultation: Strategy for Improving Education* (Boston: Allyn and Bacon, 1979). For a broad-based perspective on consultation, see June Gallessich, *The Profession and Practice of Consultation* (San Francisco: Jossey-Bass, 1982).

consultative services   Advice, assistance, information and counsel available from a state education agency or other entity. Consultative services may be performed under contract (purchased services) or by an employee on the payroll of the agency or organization.

Consumer Price Index (CPI)

The Bureau of Labor Statistics' cost-of-living index, the monthly statistical measure of the average change in prices over time in a fixed "market basket" of goods and services. The CPI is one of the nation's most important measures of inflation. Many employment and union contracts relate wage increases directly to increases in the CPI.

See Richard W. Wahl, "Is the Consumer Price Index a Fair Measure of Inflation? *Journal of Policy Analysis and Management* (Summer 1982); and John L. Marcout, "Revisions of the Consumer Price Index Now Under Way," *Monthly Labor Review* (April 1985).

consumerism   A social and political movement that seeks to extend greater protections to consumers of goods and services. More specifically in education, the trend began in the 1960s to view education as simply another service provided to consumers (students) by producers (schools). This tendency has promoted a greater market orientation among institutions and students (e.g. curriculum is perceived as a "product line" to be modified and advertised in response to market conditions).

content-centered education   1. Education where the primary focus is on the subject matter and not on the student or the learning process. 2. A traditional approach to education. Contrast with CHILD-CENTERED and PROCESS-CENTERED EDUCATION.

context evaluation   A type of evaluation that involves an analysis of problems and needs in a specific educational setting with "need" being defined as the discrepancy between an existing condition and a desired condition.

contingency reserve   Also called contingency fund. A budgetary account put aside (or budgeted) by the institution to cover unanticipated future expenses.

contingent liabilities   Items that may become liabilities as a result of conditions undetermined at a given date, such as guarantees, pending law suits, judgments under appeal, and unsettled, disputed claims.

continuation   A ceremony, like graduation, marking the passage from one school level to the next. Usually used in reference to passage from elementary school to secondary school.

continuing contract   A contract that continues automatically from year to year without action on the part of governing authority, but which may be terminated through appropriate action on the part of the parties involved.

continuing education   See ADULT/CONTINUING EDUCATION.

Continuing Education Unit (CEU)   A measure that is used to document and quantify the completion of a particular amount of non-credit

course work or other educational experiences. CEUs are widely used by professional associations and by employers to document participation in workshops, conferences, seminars, and other in-service training programs. In some areas they may be required for the renewal of licenses or certification and in some systems they can be applied toward salary adjustments. It is generally accepted that one CEU is granted for every 10 contact hours.

See Council on the Continuing Education Unit, *The Continuing Education Unit: Criteria And Guidelines* (Silver Spring, Md.: The Council, 1979).

continuity   The orderly, planned sequence of educational experiences, as from one grade, school level, state of development, or aspect of subject-matter content to another.

continuous assessment   Assessing a student's performance at ongoing, periodic intervals for the purpose of monitoring the student's progress and adjusting the teaching strategies or expectations accordingly.

continuous negotiating committee   Labor-management committee established to review a collective bargaining agreement on a continuous basis.

continuous promotion   The practice of promoting pupils on the basis of chronological age.

continuous school census   An individual record of every resident child from birth to 21 years of age, or within some other age limits, which is checked regularly with all sources of information available to the school so as to provide an accurate current list of all children residing in a given administrative unit.

continuous student accounting   A concept involving the acceptance of responsibility to account positively for a student once he or she has enrolled in the school or school system. The name of the student remains on the membership rolls—even though he or she does not appear for classes at the beginning of a new term—until it is determined that his or her name should be withdrawn from the rolls.

continuum of services   The model that describes the varying levels of intensity in the special services required by students who have special education needs, and breaks down the dichotomous distinction between regular education and special education as two completely separate educational systems within the schools. The continuum model emphasizes the physical location of the services as a key component of the intensity of specialized services required so that the more intense service needs tend to be asso-

---

CONTINUUM OF SERVICES

Regular classroom with consultative assistance	Indirect services by psychologists, resource teachers, supervisor/consultants; no direct service to child
Regular classroom with assistance by itinerant specialists	Limited direct service to child, by specialists (e.g., speech therapists, mobility instructors)
Regular classroom plus resource room help	Part-time, small-group direct service in special station; categorical (e.g., blind) or generic
Regular classroom plus part-time special class	Part-time attendance in full-time special class to meet prescribed needs
Full-time special class	Direct service as part of self-contained group with similar needs
Full-time special day school	Direct service as part of large group with similar needs
Full-time residential school	Direct service encompassing more than school day instruction
Homebound, hospital instructors	Instruction provided in settings having other primary purposes
Special treatment and detention centers	Total environment control, for primary purposes in addition to instruction

Maynard C. Reynolds and Jack W. Birch, *Teaching Exceptional Children in All American Schools* (Reston, Va.: The Council for Exceptional Children, 1982), p. 39.

ciated with facilities farther removed from the mainstream of education. (*See* ARRAY OF SERVICES for contrast.)

contract audit   An examination and assessment associated with government contracts to assure that the terms of the contract have been honored.

contract learning   An independent study alternative that allows students at the secondary or college level to develop an agreement with a teacher regarding specific learning objectives that the student is responsible for achieving and the teacher is responsible for monitoring and grading.

contracted services   Services rendered by personnel who are not on the payroll of a school district, including all related expense covered by the contract. *See also* PURCHASED SERVICES.

contracting-out   Having work performed outside an organization's own work force. Contracting-out is often an area of union-management disagreement, especially in the public sector. While many unions recognize management's right to occasionally subcontract a job requiring specialized skills and equipment not possessed by the organization or its employees, they oppose the letting of work that could be done by the organization's own work force. In particular, unions are concerned if work normally performed by its members is contracted to firms having inferior wages or working conditions or if such action may result in reduced earnings or layoffs of regular employees. Contracting-out is one of the major means of privatizing and thus reducing the size of the public sector.

See Charles Hoch, "Municipal Contracting in California: Privatizing with Class," *Urban Affairs Quarterly* (March 1985); and James Ferris and Elizabeth Graddy, "Contracting Out: For What? With Whom?" *Public Administration Review* (July-August 1986).

contributed services   Also called in-kind contributions; contributions in the form of time and effort—often professional—donated to an institution. Contributed services are often used as a match (frequently called in-kind match) for other grant funds.

control, managerial   A central notion in management regarding the process by which an organization produces the outcomes that management intended. The level of managerial control is determined by the comparison of actual versus planned performance as well as the development and implementation of procedures to correct substandard performance.

control group   In a research design this is a group of similar characteristics to the experimental or subject group that is not exposed to the experimental treatment and that is used for comparative purposes.

control theory   An approach to school discipline and classroom management that focuses on effective instruction, student satisfaction, and attention to five basic human needs: to survive, to belong and love, to gain power, to be free, and to have fun. A construct described by William Glasser in *Control Theory in the Classroom* (New York: Harper and Row, 1986).

controlled reading   Pacing the speed, level, and content of reading instruction to enhance the student's learning of the mechanics of reading.

controller   Also called comptroller. The primary financial officer of an institution or organization.

controlling account   An account usually kept in the general ledger in which the postings to a number of identical, similar, or related accounts are summarized so that the balance in the controlling account equals the sum of the balances of the detailed accounts. The controlling account serves as a check on the accuracy of the detailed account postings and summarizes the expenditures in relation to the budget estimates.

convenient commuting range Distance that can be traversed easily from home to school or work in about one hour's time by public or private transportation.

conventional instruction Instruction characterized by minimal use of technology and maximal involvement of the teacher, chalkboard, and text.

conventional schedule A traditional secondary school schedule that consists of a number of fixed class periods, essentially of the same length, that do not vary from day to day.

conventional school year The traditional nine-month academic year that typically begins in early September, ends in early June, and includes a three-month summer vacation, a two-week winter vacation, and a one-week spring vacation.

conventional wisdom What is generally believed to be true. However, any writer who uses the phrase is setting something up to be knocked down; so, conventional wisdom really means "that which most people believe to be true, but really isn't." The phrase first gained currency after John Kenneth Galbraith used it in his *The Affluent Society* (Boston: Houghton Mifflin, 1958). Galbraith observed: "Only posterity is unkind to the man of conventional wisdom, and all posterity does is bury him in a blanket of neglect."

convergent thinking 1. A mode of intellectual processing that focuses on a single answer or response to any situation. 2. A conventional, safe, and noncreative approach to reasoning and problem-solving. 3. The process of taking a large number of facts and putting them together into one answer. Contrast with divergent thinking.

converted score General term referring to any of a variety of "transformed" scores, by which raw scores on a test may be expressed for such reasons as facilitating interpretation and permitting comparison with scores on other tests' forms. For example, the raw scores obtained by candidates on the various College Board tests are converted to scores on a common scale that ranges from 200 to 800.

cooling-off period Any legal provision that postpones a strike or lockout for a specific period of time in order to give the parties an additional opportunity to mediate their differences. While the device has great popular appeal, it has proven to be of doubtful value because "more time" will not necessarily resolve a labor dispute. The first federal requirements for a cooling-off period were set forth in the War Labor Disputes Act of 1943. This was superseded by the national emergency provisions of the National Labor-Management Relations (Taft-Hartley) Act of 1947, which called for an 80-day cooling-off period in the event of a "national emergency."

cooperating administrator An educational leader (building principal, superintendent, director, or other central office or university administrator) who agrees to supervise and guide the field experience for an administrative intern.

cooperating teacher (or critic teacher) A practicing teacher who supervises the field placement experience of a student teacher.

cooperative education   1. A combination program of study and practice—conducted on an alternating schedule of half days, weeks, or other periods of time—providing employment for students, with organized on-the-job training and correlated school instruction. 2. An educational process wherein students alternate formal studies with actual work experiences. It is distinguished from other part-time employment in that successful completion of the off-campus experiences becomes a prerequisite for graduation.

See Asa Knowles et al., *Handbook of Cooperative Education* (San Francisco: Jossey-Bass, 1972); Jack J. Phillips, "Is Cooperative Education Worth It? One Company's Answer," *Personnel Journal* (October 1977); Ronald W. Stadt and Bill G. Gooch, *Cooperative Education* (Indianapolis: Bobbs-Merrill, Inc., 1977).

cooperative extension education or cooperative extension programs   A unique cooperative venture among federal, state, and county governments, with the state land-grant colleges serving as administrative centers. Heavy emphasis is on agriculture and home economics, but the program has expanded to include health, community development, conservation, and public affairs. It relies mostly on nonclassroom methods of instruction.

cooperative learning   An instructional method by which students cooperate in small teams to learn material that is initially presented by the teacher. The students take responsibility for their own learning, their teammates' learning and for classroom management by checking and monitoring, helping one another with problems and encouraging one another to achieve. *See* Robert E. Slavin, "Cooperative Learning and Individualized Instruction," *Arithmetic Teacher* (November 1987).

cooperative on-the-job training   An educational approach in which pupils in occupational programs of study spend a portion of their time in supervised employment (i.e., in on-the-job training) in business or industry. This activity frequently is referred to as "cooperative work experience."

cooperative part-time employment   Part-time employment combined with schoolwork through cooperation between the school and business or industry.

Cooperative School and College Ability Test (SCAT)   A test designed to measure basic verbal and mathematical abilities. Though most commonly used to yield an estimate of academic potential in college, this test is also used by manager assessment centers.

Cooperative Tests and Services,
   Educational Testing Service
Rosedale Road
Princeton, NJ 08541

cooperative venture   An activity or set of activities performed by a consortium of organizations established to advance the purposes of its member organizations (e.g., a cooperative venture in the establishment, management, and maintenance of a research facility by a consortium of schools and/or government agencies).

cooperative work experience
See COOPERATIVE ON-THE-JOB TRAINING.

cooptation   The efforts of an organization to bring and subsume new elements into its policymaking process in order to prevent such elements from being a threat to the organization or its mission. The classic analysis of cooptation is found in Philip Selznick's *TVA and the Grass Roots* (Berkeley: University of California Press, 1949). *Also see* Frederic J. Fleron, Jr., "Cooptation As a

Mechanism of Adaptation to Change," *Polity* (Winter 1969); and Susan Rose-Ackerman, "Cooperative Federalism and Co-optation," *Yale Law Journal* 72:7(1983).

coordination   In the context of state bureaucracy, those activities of a state education agency (for example) that have the purpose of unifying programs for the accomplishment of common objectives. The coordination of programs may be within the state department of education or between programs within the department and programs outside the department, such as those conducted by other state agencies or by local or regional entities. Coordination can also be defined between local agencies with no involvement from the state-level agencies.

coordinator   A staff member performing assigned activities that have the purpose of unifying programs for the accomplishment of common objectives. The coordination of programs may be within the school system or between programs within the school and programs outside the school.

copayment   A type of cost-sharing whereby insured or covered persons pay a specified flat amount per unit of service or unit of time (for example, $2 per visit or $10 per inpatient hospital day), their insurer paying the rest of the cost. The copayment is incurred at the time the service is used. The amount paid does not vary with the actual cost of the service (unlike coinsurance, which is payment of some percentage of the actual cost).
    See Terry M. Kinney, "Medicaid Copayments: A Bitter Pill for the Poor," *Journal of Legislation*, (Winter 1983).

copyright   An author's exclusive right to control the copying of books, articles, movies, or other originally produced material. Article I, Section 8, of the U.S. Constitution provides that the Congress shall "promote the progress of science and useful arts, by securing for limited times to authors and inventors the exclusive right to their respective writings and discoveries." According to the Copyright Act of 1976 the legal life of a copyright is the author's life plus 50 years or a flat 75 years for one held by a company. The symbol for copyright is ©. Copyrights are registered in the Copyright Office of the Library of Congress.
    See Nicholas Henry, *Copyright, Information Technology, Public Policy* (New York: Marcel Dekker, 1975); and Melville B. Nimmer, *A Preliminary View of the Copyright Act of 1976: Analysis and Text* (New York: M. Bender, 1977).

core course   A required course that is fundamental to a program of study. Introductory courses are often part of the core of a general education while advanced courses may be part of the core of a concentration area.

core current expenditures Measure of total expenditures excluding transportation and food service costs, used in interstate comparisons of educational programs.

core curriculum   Common course requirements for all students in a particular area of study.

corporal punishment   Physical punishment inflicted directly upon the body. Some parents (who may be considered abusive) believe that corporal punishment is the only way to discipline children, and some child development specialists believe that almost all parents must occasionally resort to corporal punishment to discipline or train children. Other professionals believe that corporal punishment is never advisable. In a Supreme Court ruling (*Ingraham v. Wright*, April 19, 1977), corporal punishment in the school was upheld. The Supreme Court ruled that the cruel and unusual punishment clause of the Eighth Amendment does not apply to corporal punishment in the schools. Compare with DISCIPLINE. *See* Irwin A. Hyman and James H. Wise, eds., *Corporal Punishment in American Education* (Philadelphia: Temple University Press, 1979); and Terry L. Rose, "Current Uses of Corporal Punishment in Public Schools," *Journal of Educational Psychology* (June 1984).

corporate contribution   Also called corporate support. A contribution to an institution or an affiliated organization made by a private corporation. Such contributions are not generally made through a corporate foundation, but come directly from the corporation. Obtaining corporate support for institutions usually requires special fund raising techniques. *See* H. Hillman and M. Chamberlain, *The Art of Winning Corporate Grants* (New York: Vanguard, 1980).

corporate foundation   A private foundation created and supported by a single corporation. Corporate foundations support a variety of activities and causes, including education. Frequently, they target their grant funds on programs with high public visibility and in geographical areas where the company operates. *See* F. Koch, *The New Corporate Philanthropy* (New York: Plenum, 1979).

correction for guessing   Reduction in a test score for wrong answers—sometimes applied in scoring multiple-choice questions—that is intended to discourage guessing and to yield more accurate ranking of examinees in terms of their true knowledge.

correctional education   Formal classes, whether elementary, second-ary, or college level, vocational or academic, that are offered in prisons to inmates.

correctional schools   Schools for those pupils who, because of severe antisocial behavior, are not allowed to participate in the regular school program.

corrective institution   An institution in which children and/or youths may be placed because of (and in order to "correct") severely inappropriate patterns of social behavior.

correlation   1. In the context of curricular planning, an endeavor by teachers of courses in two or more subject-matter areas to relate the work of a given group of pupils in these areas to common large problems. 2. Relationship or "going-togetherness" between two sets of scores or measures; the tendency of one score to vary concomitantly with the other.

correlation, biserial   *See* BISERIAL CORRELATION.

correlation coefficient   A number expressing the degree to which two measures tend to vary together. A correlation coefficient can range from -1.00 (a perfect negative relationship to +1.00 (a perfect positive relationship). When there is no correlation between two measures, the coefficient is 0. A correlation coefficient only indicates concomitance; it does not indicate causation. That is, it can show that two variables change in the same or different directions but does not imply that one causes the other's change.

The values of the correlation coefficient are easily misinterpreted since they do not fall along an ordinary, absolute scale. For example, a correlation coefficient of .20 does not signify twice as much relationship as does one of .10, nor can a correlation coefficient be interpreted as a percentage statement. A correlation coefficient is a mathematical index number, which requires for its interpretation some knowledge of that branch of mathematical statistics known as correlation theory. As a very rough guide to interpretation, however, a correlation between a single employment test and a measure of job performance of approximately .20 often is high enough to be useful (such correlations rarely exceed .50), a correlation of .40 is ordinarily considered very good, and most personnel research workers are usually pleased with a correlation of .30. The mathematical symbol for the correlation coefficient is: *r*.

correspondence school   An educational institution that confers credit or degrees for achievements that are completed essentially independently on the basis of course work and assignments that are exchanged by mail between the institution and its students. While this method of instruction has value and validity for many students, particularly those who do not live in close proximity to more traditional educational facilities, correspondence schools in general occupy a less favorable rank on the hierarchy of educational options.

correspondent instruction   *See* INSTRUCTION BY CORRESPONDENCE.

cost, direct   A cost or expense incurred for the direct operation or support of a program, project, or specific activity, as opposed to *indirect costs*. Direct costs, for example, in a research project would include expenses for personnel, equipment, travel, expendable supplies, and activities specific to the completion of project objectives.

cost, fixed   A cost or expense that remains constant as the number of units

of output changes over time. Such costs are easily predicted.

cost, indirect   Costs associated with the conduct of a sponsored project, but which cannot be clearly identified and cannot be directly accounted for on an individual project basis. The Office of Management and Budget has specified which costs are allowable as indirect costs in federal grants. These costs are determined by establishing percentage rates of indirect cost that are then applied to *direct costs* associated with a particular project. Indirect cost rates come in two types, agency-fixed rates and institution-negotiated rates. Agency-fixed rates are determined by the funding agency or legislation. For example, an agency may establish a fixed indirect cost rate of eight percent for specific kinds of grants. Institution-negotiated indirect cost rates, on the other hand, are an agreed-upon rate that is negotiated between the funding agency and the institution and varies greatly.

Typical indirect costs include payroll expenses for organizational supervision, utilities, and general legal expenses—services provided for the entire organization and which indirectly are associated with a specific project. Calculation of indirect costs is very complicated and controversial. Formulas for the distribution of indirect costs often are based on space or personnel allocations, and exist in order to achieve a more accurate reflection of (and, therefore, receive reimbursement for) true program costs. *See OMB Circular A-21. Also see* L.A. Redecke and B. Darling, "The Indirect Cost Predicament" *Journal of The Society of Research Administrators* (1977).

cost, marginal   The cost to produce one additional unit of output. For example, program planners would need to determine the marginal costs of adding one additional student to a course in order to understand the costs of expanding a program.

cost, opportunity The "cost" associated with losing an opportunity to engage in one activity because of resources and time expended pursuing another; the cost of pursuing one goal or implementing one program that consumes resources that are then unavailable for different goals or other programs.

cost, sunk An irrevocable past cost, particularly related to an ongoing project or activity. Costs associated with the planning stage of a construction project, for example, are sunk costs that cannot be recovered regardless of whether or not the building is actually constructed. Sunk costs often influence decisions regarding program or project continuance since there may be resistance to abandoning significant previous investments.

cost accounting That method of accounting which provides for the assembling and recording of all the elements of cost incurred to accomplish a purpose, to carry on an activity or operation, or to complete a unit of work or a specific job.

cost center The smallest segment of a program that is separately recognized in an agency's fiscal records, accounts, and reports. Program-oriented budgeting, accounting, and reporting aspects of an information system are usually built upon the identification and use of a set of cost centers.

cost effectiveness A measure of the extent to which resources (usually financial) that have been allocated to a specific objective actually contribute to accomplishing that objective. Cost effectiveness analyses are often con-

ducted so that alternative means of gaining the objective may be compared.

cost ledger A subsidiary record wherein each project, job, production center, process, operation, product, or service is given a separate account under which all items of its costs are posted in the required detail.

cost per student Current expenditures for a given period of time and/or for given programs, divided by an appropriate student unit of measure such as average daily attendance, or students in average daily membership. *See also:*
CURRENT EXPENDITURES
ANNUAL CURRENT EXPENDITURES PER STUDENT IN ADA
ANNUAL CURRENT EXPENDITURES PER STUDENT IN ADM
CURRENT EXPENDITURES PER STUDENT
CURRENT EXPENDITURES PER STUDENT PER DAY (ADA)
CURRENT EXPENDITURES PER STUDENT PER DAY (ADM).

cost sharing The basic notion that institutions should share a portion of the burden associated with a project or program that is supported by an external organization (e.g., a federal agency). Many federal grant arrangements include cost sharing provisions. More typically, however, institutions establish their own level of cost sharing support since there are no federal requirements regarding level of support.

cost unit The unit of product or service whose cost is computed.

cost-benefit analysis Also called benefit-cost analysis and cost-benefit ratio. A set of techniques used to determine the efficiency and effectiveness of policy and program expenditures in meeting objectives. Cost-benefit analysis involves the quantitative measurement of expenses and benefits associated with specific program alternatives and determining the ratio of costs to benefits. It is most useful for narrowing the range of choices that can yield desirable gains for acceptable costs.

cost-of-living adjustment (COLA)
An increase in compensation in response to increasing inflation. Some union contracts and entitlement programs (such as social security) provide for automatic COLAs if inflation reaches predetermined levels.

Cost-of-Living Index   *See* CONSUMER PRICE INDEX.

costs, allowable   Costs that are permitted under the stipulations of a grant according to the sponsor. FMC (Federal Management Circular) 74-4 indicates that the following are among allowable costs: accounting, advertising, advisory councils, bonding, compensation for personal services, legal expenses, materials and supplies, payroll preparation, printing and reproduction, transportation and travel. Allowable costs may be directed to a particular project receiving sole benefit or to several projects receiving mutual benefits. *See* COSTS UNALLOWABLE.

costs, overhead   *See* OVERHEAD COSTS.

costs, unallowable   Expenses that are not permitted under the stipulations of a grant sponsor. Specifically, the FMC (Federal Management Circular) 74-4 lists among unallowable costs for federal grant accounts: bad debts, contingencies, contributions and donations, entertainment, interest and other financial costs. *See also* COSTS, ALLOWABLE.

Council for Educational Development and Research   A nationwide organization whose membership consists of the nation's REGIONAL

LABORATORIES and RESEARCH AND DEVELOPMENT CENTERS.
Headquarters are at:
CEDaR
1518 K Street, N.W.
Suite 206
Washington, DC 20005
(202) 638-3193

Council for Exceptional Children (CEC)   The first and currently the primary professional association devoted to special education. It was founded in 1922 originally under the name of the International Council for Exceptional Children. From 1941 to 1974 CEC was affiliated with the National Education Association, but it is now an independent organization that has developed a private, nonprofit foundation (the Foundation for Exceptional Children) which promotes research. There are more than 800 state CEC organizations and local chapters and over 46,000 members. CEC has 12 divisions that are either disability-related (e.g., the Division for the Physically Handicapped) or functionally related (e.g., the Teacher Education Division). These divisions are:

CASE   Council of Administrators of Special Education. Comprised of administrators, supervisors, and coordinators of special education programs and college faculty in the area of special education administration and designed to deal with administrative and supervisory problems (organized 1952).

DVH   Division for the Visually Handicapped, Partially Seeing and Blind. Concerned with the education of children who are blind or partially sighted (organized 1952).

TED   Teacher Education Division. Designed to assist professionals who are involved in the education and training of teachers, such as the instructors of college courses and the supervisors of field experiences or student teaching, in all areas of special education (organized 1953).

DOPHHH Division on the Physically Handicapped, Homebound, and Hospitalized. Concerned primarily with the education of crippled and health-impaired children (organized 1957).

TAG The Association for the Gifted. Devoted to the education of gifted and talented children (organized 1958).

CED-MR Division on Mental Retardation. The division for educators of the mentally retarded (organized 1963).

CCBD Council for Children with Behavioral Disorders. Deals with the problems of teaching emotionally disturbed and delinquent children and youth (organized 1964).

DCCD Division for Children with Communication Disorders. Focuses on children with disorders of speech and language (organized 1968).

DCLD Division for Children with Learning Disabilities. Designed to deal with the problems of teaching children who have learning disabilities (organized 1968).

DEC Division for Early Childhood. Deals with the special concerns of those who are involved in the education of young handicapped children (organized 1973).

CEDS Council for Educational Diagnostic Services. Concerned with problems and issues in testing and diagnosing exceptional children (organized 1974).

DCD Division on Career Development. Founded to serve teachers who are involved in vocational training and job placement for exceptional children and youth (organized 1976).

The Council for Exceptional Children
1920 Association Drive
Reston, VA 22091
(703) 620-3660

Council for Learning Disabilities (CLD)

A professional organization for teachers and others interested in the study of learning disabilities. The council, with a membership of 4,000, promotes quality education through teacher training programs and local educational services and publishes a quarterly journal and magazine.

Council for Learning Disabilities
P.O. Box 40303
Overland Park, KS 66204
(913) 492-3840

Council of Administrators of Special Education (CASE)

A functionally related division of the national Council for Exceptional Children (CEC), the membership of which is primarily comprised of administrators from local educational agencies who are responsible for special education services within their school districts. While the membership strongly supports better services and programs for handicapped students and is professionally affiliated with other special education professionals, the membership is also aligned with the American Association of School Administrators, a fact which exerts a significant influence on the official stances of the organization.

CASE
902 W. New York St.
Indianapolis, IN 46223
(317) 264-3403

Council of Chief State School Officers (CCSSO)

The organization for all of the heads (superintendents

and commissioners) of the state education agencies of each of the 50 states, the District of Columbia, and territories receiving U.S. education aid.

Council of Chief State School Officers
379 Hall of States
400 N. Capitol St., N.W.
Washington, DC 20001
(202) 393-8161

council of governments (COGs)
A multi-jurisdictional cooperative arrangement to permit a regional approach to planning, development, transportation, environment, and similar issues that affect a region as a whole. COGs are comprised of designated policymaking representatives from each participating government within the region. COGs are substate regional planning agencies established by states and are responsible for areawide review of projects applying for federal funds and for development of regional plans and other areawide special purpose arrangements. Some COGs have assumed a more enterprising role in the 1980s by acting as contractors for and service providers to their local governments.

See William J. Pitstick, "COGs/Strategies for Legislative Lobbying," *Public Management* (November 1974); Charles W. Harris, "COGs: A Regional Response to Metro-Urban Problems," *Growth and Change*, (July 1975); Harry West, "The Unique Role of the Regional Council Administrator, *"Municipal Year Book, 1981* (Washington, D.C.: International City Management Association, 1981); George Scarborough, "A Council of Governments Approach," *National Civic Review* (July-August 1982); and Nelson Wikstrom, *Councils of Governments: A Study of Political Incrementalism* (Chicago: Nelson-Hall Publishers, 1985).

counselor A staff member performing assigned professional services having the purpose of assisting pupils in making plans and choices in relation to education, vocation, or personal development. For a series of articles about school counseling, *see NASSP Bulletin*, 69:485(December 1985).

counselors per 1,000 students in average daily attendance The number representing the total full-time equivalency of counselor assignments in a school or school system during a given period of time, multiplied by 1,000 and divided by the average daily attendance of students during this period.

counselors per 1,000 students in average daily membership The number representing the total full-time equivalency of counselor assignments in a school or school system during a given period of time, multiplied by 1,000 and divided by the average daily membership of students during this period.

county district A school district which has the same geographical boundaries as the county within which it is located.

County of Washington v. Gunther
68 L.Ed. 2d 751 (1981) A landmark U.S. Supreme Court case, related to pay equity and COMPARABLE WORTH, which held that a charge of sex-based wage discrimination was not precluded by a failure to allege performance of work equal to that performed by male counterparts.

See Laura N. Gasaway, "Comparable Worth: A Post Gunther Overview," *The Georgetown Law Journal* (June 1981); and Barbara N. McLennan, "Sex Discrimination in Employment and Possible Liabilities of Labor Unions: Implications of *County of Washington v. Gunther*," *Labor Law Journal* (January 1982).

course   An organization of subject matter and related learning experiences provided for the instruction of students on a regular or systematic basis, usually for a predetermined period of time (e.g., a semester, a regular school term, or a two + -week workshop). Credit toward graduation or completion of a program of studies generally is given students for the successful completion of a course.

course, noncredit   *See* NON-CREDIT COURSE.

course, vocational   *See* VOCATIONAL COURSE.

course of study   A guide to a series of courses and/or activities that are relevant and appropriate to some specified educational outcome.

courseware   Originally designating instructional materials for computer-assisted instruction only; now includes instructional materials for any medium.

CPM   *See* CRITICAL PATH METHOD.

creationism   1. A theory of the development of human beings and other forms of life that interprets Biblical accounts literally in contrast to the Darwinian theory of evolution. 2. A theory typically supported by fundamentalist, evangelical religious sects who have attempted to lobby for the inclusion of this belief into the teaching of evolution in the schools. For the leading Supreme Court case on this, *see* ED-WARDS V. AGUILLARD.

creative thinking   1. Mental processes involving flexibility, originality, and a broad range of approaches to solving problems with novel solutions. 2. Thinking that goes beyond what is already known and results in original thoughts for the thinker. 3. The mental processes that result in an original product of recognizable quality. *See* E. Paul Torrence, *Creativity in the Classroom* (Washington, D.C.: National Education Association, 1977).

creativity test   Any test that stresses divergent thinking or the ability to create new or original answers; considered useful for examining the culturally disadvantaged and certain ethnic groups whose command of English is not highly developed. Such tests utilize common and familiar objects in order to sample the testee's originality, flexibility, and fluency of thinking. Tasks include suggesting improvements in familiar devices such as telephones or listing many possible uses for a broom handle. The tests are scored simply on the number of acceptable answers given by the subject. *See* John A. Hattie, "Conditions for Administering Creativity Tests," *Psychological Bulletin* (November 1977).

credential   The document issued to an individual by any authorized entity authorizing the holder to perform certain services. "Certificate," "license," "degree," or "permit" are examples of terms frequently used interchangeably with "credential."

credentialism   An emphasis on paper manifestations, such as college degrees, instead of an actual ability to accomplish the tasks of a job. For two attacks on the value of the credentials offered by higher education, *see* John Keats, *The Sheepskin Psychosis* (Philadelphia: J.B. Lippincott, 1965); and Caroline Bird, *The Case Against College* (New York: David McKay, 1975).

For how to avoid the problem, *see* H. Dudley Dewhirst, "It's Time to Put the Brakes on Credentialism," *Personnel Journal* (October 1973). For a history, *see* Randall Collins, *The Credential Society: An Historical Sociology of*

Education and Stratification (New York: Academic Press, 1979).

See also RESTRICTIVE CREDENTIALISM.

credit 1. The unit of value awarded for the successful completion of certain courses, intended to indicate the quantity of course instruction in relation to the total requirements for a diploma, certificate, or degree. Credits are frequently expressed in terms such as "Carnegie units," "credits," "semester credit hours," and "quarter credit hours." 2. A bookkeeping term for funds that are owed to you or payments you have made.

credit by examination 1. Credit earned through the applicant's successful completion of a proficiency test in place of performing activities ordinarily associated with formal course work. 2. The process of certifying achievement by systematic observation of desired behavior.

credit course A course for which students receive credit applicable toward graduation or completion of a program of studies.

credit rating *See* BOND RATING.

creditable service In reference to membership in a retirement system, the number of years of service provided by the staff member that can be counted toward a determination of the date of the staff member's earliest allowable retirement, and usually a determination of the amount of income the staff member will receive upon retirement.

credits (accounting) *See* DEBITS AND CREDITS.

CREF *See* TEACHERS INSURANCE AND ANNUITY ASSOCIATION (TIAA) and COLLEGE RETIREMENT EQUITIES FUND (CREF).

crisis bargaining Collective bargaining negotiations conducted under the pressure of a strike deadline.

crisis intervention 1. A formal effort to help an individual who is experiencing a crisis to reestablish equilibrium. A crisis is a turning point in a person's life. It can be the death of a child, spouse, or parent. It can be a heart attack. It can be anything that tests the limits of an individual's ability to cope. 2. Action to relieve a specific stressful situation or series of problems that are immediately threatening to a child's health and/or welfare. This involves alleviation of parental stress through provision of emergency services in the home and/or removal of the child from the home. 3. Introducing safety into a situation when an individual's behavior threatens harm to others.

See William Getz et al., *Fundamentals of Crisis Counseling: A Handbook* (Lexington, Mass.: Lexington Books, 1974); Romaine V. Edwards, *Crisis Intervention and How it Works* (Springfield, Ill.: Charles C. Thomas, 1977); and Morley D. Glicken, "Managing a Crisis Intervention Program," *Personnel Journal* (April 1982).

crisis teacher A teacher specially trained both in remedial education and in helping pupils overcome emotional problems, who can serve to provide immediate help to individual pupils at times when they are unable to cope with their usual classroom situations. This periodic assistance is intended to enable pupils with behavioral difficulties (which may or may not be accompanied by academic difficulties) to return to their usual classrooms. Close liaison is maintained with classroom teachers and supporting services, and referrals are made as required for diagnosis and intensive help.

criterion An established guideline or rule, used for decision-making, assessment, or evaluation, which is predetermined (e.g. admission criterion). Plural form is criteria.

criterion referenced test   An examination for which an individual's score indicates the relationship of the individual's performance to a specified criterion, e.g., a specified score on a licensure test, a given number of words to be typed per minute with a specified degree of accuracy, ability to operate a given piece of equipment, or ability to perform examples of a type of arithmetic computation with a specified accuracy within a given time limit.

See Peter W. Airasian and George F. Madaus, "Criterion-Referenced Testing in the Classroom," in *Crucial Issues in Testing*, ed. by Ralph W. Tyler and Richard M. Wolf (Berkeley, Calif.: McCutchan Publishing Corp., 1974); and Judith M. Smith et al., *Criterion-Referenced Tests for Reading and Writing* (New York: Academic Press, 1977).

critical path method (CPM)   A project management technique that uses diagrams (e.g., flow chart) to identify and display the path, or sequence, of essential activities, which, if delayed, will delay completion of the total project. The diagram thus outlines the project's "critical path" and can serve as a guide to key events and their interactions.

critical thinking   The mental process of acquiring and evaluating information and coming to a logical, objective conclusion; a skill that is vital to successful performance in traditional educational environments. *See* Rainer H. Kluwe and Hans Spada, *Developmental Models of Thinking* (New York: Academic Press, 1980).

See also Robert Sternberg, "Teaching Critical Thinking: Eight Easy Ways to Fail Before You Begin," *Phi Delta Kappan* (February 1987); Selma Wasserman, "Teaching for Thinking:

Louis E. Raths Revisited," *Phi Delta Kappan* (February 1987); and Paul Chance, *Thinking in the Classroom: A Survey of Programs* (New York: Teachers College Press, 1986).

critical-incident method   A personnel performance appraisal technique that identifies, classifies, and records significant examples—critical incidents—of an employee's behavior. Once incidents are collected, they are ranked in order of frequency and importance, assigned numerical scores, and then used for employee development and counseling.

C-SPAN   The Cable-Satellite Public Affairs Network, the cable television channel that broadcasts live sessions of the House and Senate, press conferences of the National Press Club, and a wide variety of other political presentations such as panels at the annual meetings of the American Political Science Association.

CTBS   *See* COMPREHENSIVE TEST OF BASIC SKILLS.

Cuisenaire Number-In-Color Plan   A multisensory system for teaching basic number concepts to elementary school children utilizing a set of colored rods of differing lengths. *See* Cuisenaire Company of America, Inc., *An Introduction to Cuisenaire Rods* (New Rochelle, N.Y.: Cuisenaire Company of America, Inc., 1980).

cultural electives and cultural imperatives   Two elementary curriculum tracks included in George D. Stoddard's Dual Progress Plan, a model that was developed for academic departmentalization in elementary schools. The cultural imperatives assumed by this plan are language arts and social studies, which were determined to be the two core subject areas that all students must master to be able to function effectively in our culture. The cultural electives in this plan are mathematics, science, art, and music.

See George D. Stoddard, *The Dual Progress Plan* (New York: Harper and Row, 1961).

cultural handicap   A deviation or deficiency in cultural or environmental background that adversely affects the school performance or learning of an individual. Individuals with cultural handicaps may be classified into groups such as: migrant children, the functionally illiterate, the non-English speaking, and members of disadvantaged cultural groups. *See also*

CULTURALLY DIFFERENT
DISADVANTAGED PERSONS
EDUCATIONALLY DEPRIVED CHILDREN.

cultural literacy   As defined by E.B. Hirsch in his popular 1987 book of the same name, "the network of information that all competent readers possess." Hirsch postulates that there is a common set of knowledge about a culture that members of that culture should learn either in or out of school in order to be able to function competently in contemporary society. *See* E.B. Hirsch, Jr., *Cultural Literacy* (Boston: Houghton Mifflin, 1987).

culturally biased   Tests or procedures that discriminate unfairly against minority groups in a culture because of their content, vocabulary, or other culturally determined expectations.

culturally deprived   A term that is typically applied to children who come from families that have a relatively low socio-economic status and that have incomes near or below what is considered to be poverty level. It is assumed, often inaccurately, that children who come from economically poor families also come to school with poor health, poor dietary habits, poor social skills, and poor readiness for learning.

culturally different   Students whose background and family culture (economic and social) depart significantly from the norm of the school, community, or nation. These differences may in some circumstances or in some localities require differentiated educational opportunities if they are to be educated to the level of their ability. *See also* CULTURAL HANDICAP and DISADVANTAGED PERSONS.

culturally disadvantaged   *See*:

CULTURALLY DIFFERENT
DISADVANTAGED PERSONS
EDUCATIONALLY DEPRIVED CHILDREN.

culture, organizational   *See* ORGANIZATIONAL CULTURE.

culture-fair test   Also called culture-free test; a test yielding results that are not CULTURALLY BIASED. For an analysis, *see* R.L. Thorndike, "Concepts of Culture-Fairness," *Journal of Educational Measurement* (Summer 1971).

cum laude   Latin meaning "with distinction"; a phrase used to denote high academic attainment. The next higher level is "magna cum laude" (with great distinction). The highest level is "summa cum laude" (with greatest distinction).

cumulative average   A student's grade point average from the beginning of a high school or college program until graduation (or an interim period).

cumulative frequency   Sum of successively added frequencies (usually) of test scores.

cumulative frequency chart   Graphic presentation of a cumulative frequency distribution, which has the frequencies expressed in terms of the number of cases or as a percentage of all cases.

cumulative percentage   Cumulative frequency expressed as a percentage.

cumulative student record   A continuous and current record of significant, factual information regarding the progress and growth of an individual student as he or she goes through school, generally including personal identifying data; selected family data; selected physical, health, and sensory data; standardized test data; membership and attendance data; and school performance data. (The cumulative student record should be maintained separately from special student services records and confidential reports from outside agencies.)

current dollar   The dollar value of goods or services expressed in terms of prices current at the time the good or service was delivered. Current dollars thus change over time with the impact of inflation. *See also* CONSTANT DOLLAR.

current expenditures per student   Current expenditures for a particular period of time divided by a student unit of measure. The term includes all charges, except for capital outlay and debt service, for specified school systems, schools, and/or program areas divided by the average daily membership or average daily attendance for the school systems, schools, and program areas involved.

current expenditures per student per day (ADA)   The current expenditures per student in average daily attendance during a given school term, divided by the number of days school was in session during this term. *See also* AVERAGE DAILY ATTENDANCE.

current expenditures per student per day (ADM)   The current expenditures per student in average daily attendance during a given school term, divided by the number of days school was in session during this term. *See also* AVERAGE DAILY MEMBERSHIP.

current expenditures per pupil in ADA (Regular School Term)   Current expenditures for the regular school term divided by the average daily attendance of full-time pupils (or full-time equivalency of pupils) during the term. *See also* AVERAGE DAILY ATTENDANCE.

current expenditures per pupil in ADM (Regular School Term)   Current expenditures for the regular school term divided by the average daily membership or full-time pupils (or full time equivalency of pupils) during the term. *See also* AVERAGE DAILY MEMBERSHIP.

current expenditures per student per hour course meets (adult/ continuing education)   Current expenditures for adult education (for a given period of time) divided by aggregated student hours. The term aggregated student hours refers to the total hours, for all courses, or to the enrollment for each course times the number of hours the course meets. (This item may be used in a situation where there is a significant proportion of part-time students.)

current expense   Any expenditure except for capital outlay and debt service. Current expense includes total charges incurred, whether paid or unpaid.

current fund   *See* GENERAL FUND.

current funds   Money received during the current fiscal year from revenue that can be used to pay obligations currently due, and surpluses reappropriated for the current fiscal year.

current liabilities   Debts that are payable within a relatively short period of time, usually no longer than a year. *See also* FLOATING DEBT.

current loans   A loan payable in the same fiscal year in which the money was borrowed. *See also* TAX ANTICIPATION NOTES.

current year's tax levy   Taxes levied for the current fiscal period.

curriculum   1. The planned interaction of students with instructional content, instructional resources, and instructional processes for the attainment of educational objectives. 2. The program of courses in a particular area such as academic, vocational, general, or functional.

See John D. McNeil, *Curriculum: A Comprehensive Introduction* (Boston: Little, Brown, 1972); Ronald Doll, *Curriculum Improvement: Decision Making and Process*, 4th ed. (Boston: Allyn and Bacon, 1978); Decker F. Walker and Jonas F. Soltis, *Curriculum And Aims* (New York: Teachers College Press, 1988).

curriculum coordinator   A school district staff person assigned responsibility for curriculum development and improvement including working with faculty and building principals to improve particular programs, monitoring research activities, and supervising program specialists. Also called "assistant superintendant for instruction," "curriculum director," or "curriculum supervisor."

curriculum council   A group of individuals representing both professional and nonprofessional interests that serves in an advisory capacity to school administrators regarding general matters of curriculum change and improvement or specific curricular areas.

curriculum development   A deliberate process of establishing and prioritizing educational goals, designing the content, methods, and materials necessary to address the goals, implementing a broad range of activities and experiences that comprise the total educational program, and adjusting the plan based on evaluative data. *See* Daniel Tanner and Laurel Tanner, *Curriculum Development: Theory Into Practice* (New York: Macmillan, 1980).

curriculum enrichment   Selectively enhancing a program of study with special events, trips, guest speakers, audiovisual aids, and other special activities or materials.

curriculum guide   A written plan including one or more aspects of curriculum and instruction such as philosophy, policies, aims, objectives, subject matter, resources, and processes. Such a plan may be as narrow in scope as a unit or topic of instruction, or as broad as the entire curriculum of a school system or level of instruction within a state. *See also* COURSE OF STUDY.

cursive writing   The traditional form of handwriting used in our society in which individual letters of words are connected to each other and are usually placed on a slant. Contrast with MANUSCRIPT WRITING.

curtailed session   A school session with less than the number of hours of instruction recommended by a state education agency.

custodial service room   Custodial quarters, custodial service closets, and similar areas designed or adapted for use by the custodial staff.

custodial services responsibility   The area of responsibility for cleaning the buildings of school plants or supporting services facilities; operating such equipment as heating and ventilating systems; preserving the security of school property; and keeping the school plant safe for occupancy and use. It consists of such activities as cleaning, sweeping, disinfecting, heating, lighting, moving furniture, keeping school entrances appropriately locked or unlocked, keeping such facilities as fire escapes and panic bars in working order, and watchman duties.

custodian   A staff member performing assigned activities in school plant housekeeping, servicing school plant equipment, and maintaining the security of the school plant. Such staff members as janitor, assistant custodian, janitress, maid, matron, sweeper, cleaner, attendant, watchman, guard, boiler fireman, and heating and ventilating equipment operator are included in this definition.

custody and care of children The custodial care of children in residential day schools, or child care centers, which are not part of, or directly related to, the instructional program.

cutting score   Also called critical score, passing score, or passing point. Test score used as an employment requirement. Those at or above such a score are eligible for selection or promotion, whereas those below the score are not.

There are many approaches to establishing the cutting score. Perhaps the most defensible is one of the job-related approaches (e.g., using data from a criterion-related validity study). A common and practical approach is the flexible passing score, which is established for each test on the basis of a number of factors (some of which, such as the number of positions to be filled, may not be job-related). Arbitrarily establishing a cutting score of 70 percent in an attempt to be certain all eligibles possess the traits desired for a job (the 70-percent syndrome) is not defensible from a psychometric point of view and has resulted in the costly situation where no applicants are eligible after taking a difficult test.

See Glenn G. McClung, *Considerations in Developing Test Passing Points* (Chicago: International Personnel Management Association, 1974).

cycle scheduling   A scheduling plan, usually in junior high schools, wherein courses that might be taught one or two periods each week throughout the term are taught every day for a succession of weeks. For example, art, music, and industrial arts might be "cycled" in a 36-week term for 12 weeks each.

D

Dalcroze method   A method for teaching music that involves rhythmic body movements (eurythmics), sight reading (solfege) and the creation of new musical compositions (improvisation). Developed by Emile Jacques-Dalcroze.

Dalton plan   The use of individualized assignments and student contracts as the main basis of instruction. Initially developed by Helen Pankhurst for the Dalton High School in Dalton, Massachusetts, in 1920. Today any teaching process based upon the contract concept can be considered a variant of the Dalton Plan. *See* Helen H. Parkhurst, *Education on the Dalton Plan* (New York: E.P. Dutton, 1922).

dame school   Colonial New England elementary schools operated by women in their homes.

DAT   *See* DIFFERENTIAL APTITUDE TEST.

data processing   A broad term for manipulation of data, for example classifying, sorting, putting in, or taking out of a computer, preparing reports, or calculating answers.

database   Also data bank. 1. Information stored in a computer system so that any particular item or set of items can be extracted or organized as needed. Databases typically are structured for query-type use as well as for generating repetitive reports. 2. Computer-accessible information files that contain wide arrays of information such as computer application software packages; and bibliographic citations and abstracts that provide rapid subject access to journal articles, conference papers, dissertations, and other original source documents. Most academic libraries and some large public libraries provide access to such data bases, and many can be accessed with personal computers on a subscription basis.

database management system   A computer software package that manages, updates, secures, and gains computer access to databases. For example, DBase3, DBase4, or Dataflex.

date of construction   1. The date that a construction contract is signed with a contractor. 2. The date construction is completed and accepted.

date of issue   The day a document is formally put out or takes effect. For example, the date of issue of an insurance policy is the first day the policy says it will take effect.

date of organization   The date on which an organization is legally recognized. For example, a corporation is organized on the date on which its articles of incorporation are filed with the appropriate office of state government. The date of organization is important to nonprofit organizations because filing for tax-exemption must be accomplished less than 16 months after the end of the month in which the date of organization occurred.

date of withdrawal from membership   The first day after the date of last school attendance, if known; otherwise, the date of withdrawal is considered to be the date on which it becomes known officially that the student left.

day (or child) care   A newly emerging employee fringe benefit. More than half of all mothers with children under six years of age are now in the labor force.

day care center   A center under professional guidance designed to provide care for prekindergarten children of working parents while providing, at the same time, educational experiences for the children.

day in session   A day on which school is open and the students are under the guidance and direction of teachers. On some days in session the school plant may be closed and the student body as a whole engaged in school activities outside the school plant under the guidance and direction of teachers. Days on which the teaching facility is closed for such reasons as holidays, teachers' institutes, and inclement weather are not considered as days in session.

day of absence   A school day during which a student is in membership but not in attendance (i.e., non-attendance of a student on a day when school is in session). *See also* ABSENCE.

day of attendance   A school day during which a student is present for an entire school session under the guidance and direction of teachers. When a student is present for only part of the session, attendance is generally counted according to the nearest half day. If overcrowded conditions make it necessary for a school to hold two separate sessions per day, a student attending for all of either session is considered as having completed a full day of attendance. An excused absence during examination periods or because of sickness or for any other reason is not counted as a day of attendance. *See also* ATTENDANCE.

day of membership   For a given pupil, any day that school is in session from the date the pupil is placed on the current roll until withdrawn from membership in the class or school. *See also* MEMBERSHIP.

day school   A school attended by students during a part of the day, as distinguished from a residential school where students are boarded and lodged as well as taught.

day student   1. A student who attends the majority of classes during the daytime hours, as defined by the institution. 2. A student who attends a boarding school during the day but does not live there.

DDST   *See* DENVER DEVELOPMENTAL SCREENING TEST.

de facto   Latin, meaning "in fact," "actual." For example, de facto segregation has often occurred without the formal assistance of government; it evolved from social and economic conditions. In contrast, de jure (by law) segregation in schools was once a legal requirement in many states. While segregation practices are no longer sanctioned by government (are no longer de jure), they often remain de facto. According to Shirley Chisholm, *Unbought and Unbossed* (Boston: Houghton Mifflin, 1970), "The difference between *de jure* and *de facto* segregation is the difference between open, forthright bigotry and the shamefaced kind that works through unwritten agreements between real estate dealers, school officials, and local politicians."

de jure   Latin, meaning "by right," "by law." *See* DE FACTO.

deaf-blind   Individuals who have both visual impairments and hearing impairments that cause severe problems in communication, development, and education. Deaf-blind students generally cannot benefit from educational programs designed solely for either deaf students or blind students. Because of the unique educational needs of this population, special federally-funded programs, services, and centers have been made available since the early 1970s.

deafness   1. A degree of hearing impairment sufficient to preclude the learning of language through the auditory channel. 2. Functionally, an inability to hear. 3. One of the categories of handicapping condition mentioned in P.L. 94-142, the Education for All Handicapped Children Act, which makes a student eligible for publicly supported special education services. *See* Donald F. Moores, *Educating the Deaf*, 2nd ed. (Boston: Houghton Mifflin, 1982); Eugene D. Mindel and McCay Vernon, eds., *They Grow in Silence: Understanding Deaf Children and Adults*, 2nd ed. (San Diego: College-Hill Press, 1987).

dean   1. An academic office in a college, usually in charge of a major instructional unit or professional school. 2. A counselor or administrator in a high school or college responsible for discipline, student counseling, student personnel services, or public relations activities. These responsibilities are often divided by sex; thus a "dean of women" has parallel duties with a "dean of men."

death benefit   The money from a pension plan that is paid to an employee's survivors or estate. Payments may be made in monthly installments or in a lump sum.

death education   Teaching about death, dying, and the bereavement process as part of an established curriculum. This is often an important element in a suicide prevention program. *See* Betty R. Green and Donald P. Irish, eds., *Death Education:*

Preparation for Living (Cambridge, Mass.: Schenkman Publishing, 1971); and R.G. Stevenson and H.L. Powers, "How to Handle Death in the Schools," *Educational Digest* (May 1987).

debate   *See* FORENSICS.

debenture   A corporation's or school district's obligation to pay money (usually in the form of a note or a bond) that is not secured (backed up) by any specific property. The common use of the word includes only long-term bonds. *See also* BOND and LIABILITIES.

debits and credits   The basic entries in a double entry accounting system. Each transaction is entered in two places; each debit and its matching credit(s) should equal zero. If they do not, the accounting system is out of balance. A debit usually is abbreviated "DR" and a credit "CR."

All accounts are categorized as either assets, liabilities, fund balances, income, or expenses. Each category of accounts is defined as carrying a debit or a credit balance. Each accounting transaction changes an account balance. *See also:*
ACCOUNTING CYCLE
ACCOUNTING SYSTEM
ASSETS
BOOKKEEPING
LIABILITIES

debt, amortization of   *See* AMORTIZATION.

debt, bonded   *See* BONDED DEBT.

debt, floating   *See* FUNDED DEBT.

debt, general obligation   Long-term debt backed by the full-faith-and-credit of the issuing jurisdiction.

debt, nonguaranteed   Long-term debt payable solely from pledged specific sources. Includes only debt that does not constitute an obligation against any other resources if the pledged sources are insufficient.

debt financing   Paying for government programs or capital improvements by borrowing.

debt fund   A fund that is used to finance the payment of principal and interest of debt.

debt limit   The maximum amount of gross or net debt legally permitted.

debt service   Or debt servicing; regular payments of principal, interest, and other costs (such as insurance) made to pay off a financial obligation.

debt service fund   An account for the payment of interest and principal on all general obligation debt.

debt-equity ratio   An accounting ratio obtained by dividing total debt by total equity or fund balances.

decertification   *See* CERTIFICATION.

decision algorithm   *See* ALGORITHM.

decision package   A technique used in zero-base budgeting to look at the effects of programmatic resource requirements, products, and levels of performance of alternative levels of funding. *See also* ZERO-BASED BUDGETING.

decision rule   Any directive established to make decisions, particularly decisions in the face of uncertainty. For example, a payroll office might be given a decision rule to deduct one hour's pay from employees' wages for each lateness that exceeds 10 minutes but is less than one hour. *See also* ALGORITHM.

decision theory   A body of knowledge concerned with the nature and process of decision-making. Decision theory abstracts given situations into a more structured problem so that the decisionmaker can deal with the situation by an objective judgment. Frequently dependent upon quantitative analysis, decision theory is also called statistical decision theory and Bayesian decision theory. Bayesian refers to Thomas Bayes (1702-1761), who provided a mathematical basis for probability inference.

decision tree   Graphic method of presenting various decisional alternatives so that the various risks, information needs, and courses of action are visibly available to the decision maker. The various decisional alternatives are displayed in the form of a tree with nodes and branches. Each branch represents an alternative course of action or decision, which leads to a node that represents an event. Thus, a decision tree shows both the different courses of action available as well as their possible outcomes (with estimated probabilities).

See John F. Magee, "Decision Trees for Decision-Making," *Harvard Business Review* (July-August 1964).

deductible   1. The amount of loss or expense that must be incurred by an insured or otherwise covered individual or organization before an insurer will assume any liability for all or part of the remaining cost of covered services or losses. Deductibles may be either fixed-dollar amounts or the value of specified services (such as two days of hospital care or one physician visit). 2. Amounts that can be subtracted from income for calculating taxes owed.

deductible charitable contribution   A contribution or gift to a tax-exempt organization that, under tax laws and IRS rules, can be subtracted from income when calculating taxes owed. Under current law and rules, deductions for contributions are limited to a percentage of Adjusted Gross Income (AGI).

deduction   Any amount that for any reason is withheld from an employee's pay and credited toward a legitimate purpose, such as taxes, insurance, loan repayment, or the United Way.

deduction, tax   See DEDUCTIBLE and DEDUCTIBLE CHARITABLE CONTRIBUTION.

defalcation   The failure of a person to account for money trusted to his or her care. There is the assumption that the money was misused.

deferred annuity   An annuity that does not start until after a specified period or until the annuitant reaches a specified age.

deferred giving program   A planned development program for encouraging deferred giving, usually for the purpose of increasing an organization's endowment. Deferred giving programs range from relatively simple attempts to secure bequests to more polished and complex programs involving, for example, living trusts. See also:
    BEQUEST
    ENDOWMENT FUND
    TRUST

deferred graded vesting   A pension plan which provides that an employee acquires a right to a specified percentage of accrued benefits if and when he or she meets the participation requirements stipulated by the plan.

deferred life annuity   An annuity that becomes effective at a specified future date. If death occurs before the specified date, no benefits are paid.

Once the annuity has started, it continues only for the life of the insured.

deferred wage increase   A negotiated pay increase that does not become effective until a specified future date.

deficit   Amount by which an organization's expenditures exceed its revenues.

deficit financing   A situation in which a government's excess of outlays over receipts for a given period is financed primarily by borrowing from the public.

defined benefit plan   A pension plan that includes a formula for calculating retirement benefits (such as a specified percent of earnings or flat dollar amount per year of service) and obligates the employer to provide the benefits so determined. Therefore, employer contributions are not fixed but are whatever is needed, together with earnings of pension fund investments, to finance the required benefits.

defined contribution plan   A pension plan that obligates the employer to contribute money to a pension fund according to a formula (such as a specified percent of earnings). Benefits are not fixed, but depend on the amount of employer contributions and the earnings of pension fund investments.

DeFunis v. Odegaard 416 U.S. 312 (1974)   The U.S. Supreme Court case concerning a white male who was denied admission to law school at the same time minority applicants with lesser academic credentials were accepted. DeFunis challenged the school's action on the grounds that it denied him equal protection of the laws in violation of the 14th Amendment. He was successful in state court and was admitted. On appeal, the school won a reversal. Nevertheless, DeFunis remained in school pending further action by the Supreme Court. As the nation awaited a definitive resolution of the issue of reverse discrimination in school admissions, the Supreme Court sought to avoid the problem. Since DeFunis had completed all but his last quarter of law school and was not in danger of being denied his diploma, a majority of the justices seized upon this fact and declared that the case was consequently "moot"—that it was beyond the court's power to render decisions on hypothetical matters of only potential constitutional substance. *See* Larry M. Lavinsky, "*DeFunis v. Odegaard*: The 'Non-Decision' With a Message," *Columbia Law Review* (April 1975); and Allan P. Sindler, *Bakke, DeFunis, and Minority Admissions: The Quest for Equal Opportunity* (New York: Longman, 1978). *See also*:

> REGENTS OF THE UNIVERSITY OF
>   CALIFORNIA V. ALLEN BAKKE
> REVERSE DISCRIMINATION
> UNITED STEELWORKERS OF AMERICA V.
>   WEBER, ET AL.

degree   A title conferred by a college or university as official recognition for the completion of a program of studies or for other attainment.

degree mill   1. A derogatory reference to organizations that grant (or sell) phony or non-rigorous higher education degrees. 2. A slang term for any higher education institution that, while accredited and legitimate, is thought to be insufficiently prestigious or demanding in its educational requirements.

degree requirements   The minimum courses and other work in a curriculum that a student must complete to earn a particular degree.

deinstitutionalization   1. A movement away from placing individuals into institutions and, instead, providing the supports and services they need to live in typical community settings. 2. Developing alternative community living options for persons who had previously lived in institutions.

delegation   The designating or appointing of a person with the power to act as one's representative or agent in specified matters. A delegation of authority in an organizational sense may be implied in statements of responsibility for functional entities or group endeavors but can also be documented by other methods. Certain delegations that are granted to a single individual may be restricted as to further re-delegations. Delegation of authority begins at the board of directors or executive level and filters down through an organization to people who must have enough authority to make decisions called for in their daily tasks.

deliberate speed   The pace of school integration. The Supreme Court held in *Brown v. Board of Education*, 349 U.S. 294 (1955) that school integration should proceed "with all deliberate speed." This is a good example of the Court's use of a vague word in order to avoid dealing head on with a difficult policy problem. *See* John H. McCord, ed., *With All Deliberate Speed: Civil Rights Theory and Reality* (Urbana: University of Illinois Press, 1967).

delinquent behavior   1. The behavior of a juvenile who is habitually wayward, disobedient, truant, or acting in such a manner as to impair or endanger the morals or health of self or others. 2. The behavior of a minor that would, in the case of an adult, constitute criminal conduct. If a juvenile violates a law or ordinance and is convicted in a court of law as a juvenile, he or she is sometimes considered a juvenile delinquent, depending on the severity of the violation. Some jurisdictions use a term other than "conviction" in juvenile cases.

delinquent taxes   Taxes remaining unpaid on and after the date on which they become delinquent by statute.

delphi method   Or delphi technique; a procedure for forecasting specific technological and social events, or selecting organizational or program goals. Experts are asked to write their best judgment as to the probability of a specific event occurring and the implications of occurrence or nonoccurrence. The results are collated and then returned to the original experts for their perusal along with an opportunity to revise their own predictions. Revised estimates with supporting arguments are then recorded and recirculated again and again. In theory, the feedback always narrows the range of predictions. In the end, a group prophecy will have been arrived at without the possibility of distortion from face-to-face contact, leadership influences, or the pressures of group dynamics. For an application of the method, *see* Frances Shords and Reuven R. Levary, "Weighting the Importance of Various Teacher Behaviors by Use of the Delphi Method," *Education* (Winter 1986).

Delta Kappa Gamma   An honorary fraternal organization in education of 163,000 members.

Delta Kappa Gamma
P.O. Box 1589
Austin, TX 78767
(512) 478-5748

democratic teaching   An approach to classroom management where the students are expected to assume some of the responsibility for their own learning. Decisions are shared among teacher and students about instructional content and methodology.

demographics   1. Statistics showing an area's population characteristics such as age, race, income, and education. 2. Basic information about an individual, including such characteristics as age, place of residence, and marital status.

demonstration teaching   The modeling of effective instructional strategies by a supervisor, professor, or experienced teacher for other teachers or teachers-in-training.

demotion   1. The assignment of an employee to a job of lower status, responsibility, and pay. There are three basic kinds of demotion: (a) *voluntary demotion*, usually the result of a reduction in force; (b) *involuntary demotion* results from a worker's inability to perform adequately on the job; (c) *disciplinary demotion* usually takes place after an employee has been repeatedly warned to stop some kind of misconduct or disruptive behavior. 2. A change of a student's grade-level placement from a higher to a lower grade; the opposite of promotion. *See also* PROMOTION.

density index   A quotient that is determined by dividing the total number of pupils transported by the total number of miles of public roads in the district.

density of information   From programmed instruction, indicates the amount of new information that is presented before the learner has an opportunity to respond.

dental plan   Also called dental insurance. Group insurance program, either contributory or noncontributory, that pays for some portion of dental services for an employee and his or her family. *See also* SUPPLEMENTAL MEDICAL INSURANCE.

Denver Developmental Screening Test (DDST) An individually-administered norm-referenced screening instrument that quickly assesses a wide range of developmental skills in order to identify children who may be at risk for developmental or behavioral problems. It is intended for children between the ages of birth and six years. It is published by:

Ladoca Project and Publishing Company
East 51st Avenue and Lincoln St.
Denver, CO 80216

department An administrative subdivision with a teaching staff responsible for instruction in a particular subject-matter area or field of study.

department head (or chair) A staff member performing assigned activities in directing and managing a designated division of the instructional program in a school.

Department of Defense Overseas Dependents School An elementary or secondary school operated for dependents of active duty military and civilian personnel of the U.S. Department of Defense who are stationed overseas.

Department of Education *See* EDUCATION, DEPARTMENT OF.

departmental seniority Also called unit seniority. Seniority based on years of service in a particular subsection of a larger organization as opposed to seniority based simply on total years of service in the larger organization.

departmentalized organization The organization of instruction in such a way that each teacher specializes in one or two subject-matter areas and gives instruction in these areas to several classes. Under the departmentalized organization, pupils or teachers move from room to room for different classes during the school day.

dependent An organization or person who relies on another for a significant portion of support; sometimes used to mean a dependent blood relative.

dependent variable A factor in an experimental relationship, which has or shows variation that is hypothesized to be caused by another independent factor or variable.

deposits Funds deposited as a prerequisite to receiving services and/or goods.

deposits payable Liability for deposits received as a prerequisite to providing or receiving services and/or goods.

depreciation The cost of wear and tear on assets that are expected to last more than one year (fixed assets), such as buildings, vehicles, and equipment. Depreciation is not an out-of-pocket cost; rather, it is shown only in financial records. However, depreciation expenses are very important, even to tax-exempt organizations, because they reflect the cost of services provided and, if there is a surplus, they provide the "source of funds" to replace worn out or obsolete fixed assets (in other words, non-spent monies, because they are non-cash expenses). For accounting purposes, fixed assets should be depreciated even if the organization did not pay for them—if they will need to be replaced in the future.

Straight line depreciation is computed by: (a) subtracting the amount that may reasonably be expected to be realized from sale of the item at the end of its useful life (that is, its trade-in value, scrap value, or salvage value) from its purchase price, and (b) dividing the difference by the number of years or annual units (for example, miles driven) of its useful life.

Accelerated depreciation methods are used primarily by for-profit corporations for tax-deduction/rapid capital accumulation purposes. Assets are depreciated more rapidly during the early years of their useful life and more slowly during their later years.

deprogramming   An effort by parents to reverse the effects of purported brainwashing by religious cults of their teenage and young adult sons and daughters.

derived score   A test score that has been converted to an index of rank, scale, position, or other classification as differentiated from raw score, which is the number of correct answers on the test.

deschooling   A philosophical notion that nontraditional or alternative modes of education may make students more independent both socially and in their thinking. Advocates of deschooling resent the fact that schools basically teach students to work well in institutions as opposed to working well as human beings. *See* Ivan Illich, *Deschooling Society* (New York: Harper, 1974).

descriptive course title   In a departmentalized organization, the descriptive title by which a course is identified (e.g., American History, English III); in a self-contained class, any portion of the instruction for which a mark is assigned or a report is made (e.g., reading, composition, or spelling).

descriptive heading   A heading under which items that are similar in terms of a given reference are shown and are in part described by the heading.

descriptive research   A form of scientific investigation that is undertaken to answer the question "what is." The investigator describes and interprets conditions or relationships that exist, beliefs that are held, effects that are observed, or trends that are developing. Examples of descriptive research include case studies, surveys, follow-up studies, trend analyses, and correlational studies.

desegregation   1. Refers to the movement of students from racially separate public school facilities to a more balanced mix of black (or other minority) and white students in the same schools. For a collection of scholarly reviews of theoretical and methodological research, *see* Jeffrey Prager, Douglas Longshore, and Melvin Seeman, eds., *School Desegregation Research* (New York: Plenum, 1986). *See also* Charles V. Willie, *School Desegregation Plans That Work* (Westport: Greenwood Press, 1984). *See* BROWN V. BOARD OF EDUCATION and SEGREGATION.
2. Also refers to the movement of students who are handicapped from separate, "handicapped-only" schools to regular public school buildings with non-handicapped students.

designated fund   A fund used to continue support to particular charitable organizations after a person dies. Designated funds are often found in and managed by community foundations that send donations to the designated recipient organizations. *See also* COMMUNITY FOUNDATION.

desk audit   Also called JOB AUDIT; review of the duties and responsibilities of a position through an interview with the incumbent and/or the incumbent's supervisor made at the employee's desk or regular place of work. *See also* POSITION CLASSIFICATION.

detention   1. The disciplinary technique of requiring students to remain after school for a stated time period under teacher supervision. Depending on the school's policy students may or may not be allowed to read and/or do homework while sitting in a detention room. 2. The temporary confinement of a person by a public authority. In a case of child abuse or neglect, a child may be detained pending a trial when a detention hearing indicates that it is unsafe for the child to remain in his/her own home. This is often called protective custody or emergency custody. The child may be detained in a foster home, group home, hospital, or other facility.

Detroit Plan   The ABILITY GROUPING of elementary school children in three groups (X, Y, and Z) according to their scores on intelligence or achievement tests; first used in the Detroit public school system in 1919.

Detroit Tests of Learning Aptitudes   An individually administered test that measures several aspects of mental processing. It is standardized for ages four through adult and any of its 19 sub-tests may be given and scored independently to assess particular learning attributes (such as auditory memory or visual-motor processing). It is available through:

Bobbs-Merrill Company, Inc.
4300 W. 62nd Street
Indianapolis, IN 46206

development   1. Activities concerned with the evolving process of utilizing the products of research and considered judgment in the deliberate improvement of educational programs. 2. The planned promotion of understanding, participation, and support among potential donors. Usually, *development* is used broadly and is considered to consist of three major, distinct groups of activities that need to be coordinated if development is to be effective: planning, public relations, and fundraising. 3. The typical human growth that occurs—physically, intellectually, socially, and emotionally—as a function of age and experience.

development director   A person who manages a development (fundraising) program. In larger organizations, the development director position may be filled by a full-time person with a supporting staff; in smaller organizations, the functions typically are performed on a part-time basis by, for example, the executive director.

Developmental Indicators for the Assessment of Learning (DIAL)   A commonly-used preschool screening instrument that is designed to identify children with potential learning problems at the pre-kindergarten level. It is individually administered to children between the ages of 2 1/2 and 5 1/2 years and assesses four developmental skills areas: gross motor, fine motor, concepts, and communication. It is published by:

DIAL, Inc.
Box 911
Highland Park, IL 60035

developmental supervision   A model for supervision described by Carl D. Glickman that recognizes various stages that teachers go through as they gain maturity and experience. A different mode of supervision is suggested for each stage.

Developmental Test of Visual Motor Integration (VMI)   A group-administered test to assess visual preception and motor coordination in children ages two to 15 years. The test involves 24 geometric designs to be copied. It is published by:

Follett Publishing Company
1010 West Washington Boulevard
Chicago, IL 60607

Developmental Test of Visual Perception (Frostig) A commonly used test that can be administered individually or in groups to measure perceptual skills: eye-hand coordination, figure ground, form constancy, position in space, and spatial relations. The test is norm-referenced for children between the ages of four and eight years. It is published by:

Consulting Psychologists Press, Inc.
577 College Avenue
Palo Alto, CA 94306

deviation Amount by which a score differs from a reference value such as the mean or the norm.

Dewey Decimal System The most commonly used system for cataloging non-fiction books in a library. It is a numerically based system in which the number series (000-900) are associated with broad subject areas and the numerical breakdown within each series relates to more specific topics within each subject area. The system was developed by Melvil Dewey.

Dewey, John B. (1859-1952) A 19th and early 20th century educational reformer who contended that learning and schooling should focus on the individual and should include all life experiences rather than focusing narrowly on academic subject matter. Dewey was thought to be one of the primary forces behind the Progressive Movement in education.

For a comprehensive biography, *see* George Dykhuizen, *The Life and Mind of John Dewey* (Carbondale: Southern Illinois University Press, 1973).

Dewey, Melvil (1851-1931) The librarian who invented the Dewey Decimal Classification system for books. For a biography, *see* Fremont Rider, *Melvil Dewey* (Chicago: American Library Association, 1944).

dexterity test Also called PSYCHOMOTOR TEST. Any testing device that seeks to determine the motor/mechanical skills of an individual.

DHHS *See* HEALTH AND HUMAN SERVICES, DEPARTMENT OF.

diagnostic reading test An examination giving in-depth information about specific weaknesses in a person's reading skills that must be remedied before the person can be expected to make normal progress in his or her schoolwork.

diagnostic teacher A teacher possessing special training and skills in diagnosing the learning problems of individuals and in planning and providing therapeutic educational programs based on such diagnoses.

diagnostic teaching An approach to individualized educational assessment that utilizes a variety of instructional strategies to identify specific learning problems and to determine the most effective method for teaching a particular student.

diagnostic test 1. Any testing device that is primarily designed to identify and specify the nature and source of an individual's health problems or other physical, psychological, developmental, or emotional problems. 2. Personality tests given by school counselors or psychologists are often referred to as diagnostic tests.

See Theodore S. Fremont, David M. Seifert, John H. Wilson, *Informal Diagnostic Assessment of Children* (Springfield, Ill.: Charles C. Thomas, 1977); and Philip H. Mann et al., *Handbook in Diagnostic-Prescriptive Teaching*, 2nd ed. (Boston: Allyn and Bacon, 1979).

DIAL   *See* DEVELOPMENTAL IN-
DICATORS FOR THE ASSESSMENT OF LEARN-
ING.

dialectic method   A Socratic
means of teaching which emphasizes
dealing with ideas through logical
arguments and discussion. Complex
theories are clarified by the teacher
through a constant questioning of their
logic and the introduction of con-
tradictory concepts.

See Nicholas Rescher *Dialectics: A
Controversy-Oriented Approach to the
Theory of Knowledge* (Albany: State
University of New York Press, 1977).

Diana v. State Board of Education
C-70, 37 RFP (N.D. Calif. 1970)   A
case challenging the placement of
Mexican-American students in special
classes for children with mental retardation on the basis of inappropriate testing. It was argued that so-called "intelligence" tests standardized on white,
middle-class, English-speaking children
were biased against children from different ethnic cultures, and the court
determined that children could not be
placed in special classes solely on the
basis of such testing. This case was the
first of several during the early 1970s
that dealt with standards and practices
used in classifying children as handicapped, especially as related to the
overrepresentation of minority populations in special education classes.

dichotomy   Refers to the classification of phenomena into two mutually
exclusive groups; the differentiation of
ideas by kind rather than by degree.

dicta   In the context of arbitration,
any opinion or recommendation an
arbitrator expresses in making an award
that is not essential to the resolution of
the dispute. Compare to OBITER DICTUM.

*Dictionary of Occupational Titles
(DOT)*   A comprehensive body of
standardized occupational information

for purposes of job placement, employment counseling, and occupational
career guidance. The DOT includes
standardized and comprehensive
descriptions of job duties and related information for 20,000 occupations;
covers nearly all jobs in the U.S.
economy; groups occupations into a
systematic occupational classification
structure based on interrelationships of
job tasks and requirements; and is
designed as a job placement tool to
facilitate matching job requirements and
worker skills. *See* Employment and
Training Administration, U.S. Department of Labor, *Dictionary of Occupational Titles* (Washington, D.C.: U.S.
Government Printing Office, "latest edition").

didactic teaching   A lecture-
based approach to teaching that is fairly
rigid and that emphasizes compliant behavior on the part of the student while
the teacher dispenses information.

Dienes multi-base apparatus
Wooden blocks that are used to teach
basic math concepts to elementary
school students.

dietitian   A staff member performing assigned activities concerned with
planning menus and special diets.

Differential Aptitude Test (DAT)
A widely used test that may be
administered individually or in groups
and is designed to predict future success
in various career fields. The test is intended for students in grades eight to
12. It is published by:
The Psychological Corporation
757 Third Avenue
New York, NY 10017

differential user charge   Any
user charge scaled to meet the requirements of different kinds of customers,
levels of usage, time or season of use, or
other differentiating characteristics.

differential validation   Also called differential prediction. The underlying assumption of differential validation/prediction holds that different tests or test scores might predict differently for different groups. Some social groups, because of a variety of sociological factors, tend to score lower (higher) than other groups on the same test.

differentiated curriculum   A program of educational offerings designed to meet the unique needs of pupils comprising special target populations; for example, students who are disadvantaged, gifted, or handicapped.

differentiated diplomas   1. Diplomas that reflect a specific course of study or deviation from the traditional secondary curriculum, for example, vocational education. 2. A diploma that may be granted to handicapped students who are unable to satisfy typical graduation requirements, i.e., a certificate of attendance.

differentiated staffing   Team teaching using a mix of instructional personnel; for example, a master teacher, a regular teacher, a student teacher, and a teacher's aide may all compose one instructional team with varying responsibilities. See Richard A. Dempsey and Rodney P. Smith, Jr., *Differentiated Staffing* (Englewood Cliffs, N.J.: Prentice-Hall, 1972).

differentiation   1. An instructional plan that makes provision for the individualized needs of the various pupils by enrichment or other modification of a common basic program. 2. In psychology, an individual's ability to see significant differences, as opposed to only amorphous wholes, in life experiences.

difficulty index   Any of a variety of indexes used to indicate the difficulty of

a test question. The percent of some specified group, such as students of a given age or grade, who answer an item correctly is an example of such an index.

diploma   A formal certificate of educational achievement. A high school student normally receives a diploma as certification of graduation. A college graduate earns a degree but the degree paper itself (traditionally parchment or sheepskin) is called the diploma.

diploma mill   1. An institution with slight reputation where one can earn a degree with little real academic effort. 2. A virtually nonexistent institution that awards essentially fraudulent degrees to anyone who pays for them.

direct cost   See COST, DIRECT.

direct labor   Also indirect labor. Work performed on a product or to deliver a service that is a specific contribution to its completion. Indirect labor consists of all overhead and support activities that do not contribute directly to the completion of a product or delivery of a service.

direct mail campaign   A form of fund-raising that involves mailing large numbers of letters to potential donors asking for financial support. Most development officers contend that direct mail campaigns should be ongoing efforts rather than one-time appeals. See also DEVELOPMENT and FUNDRAISING.

direct services   1. Activities identifiable with a specific program; those activities concerned with the teaching-learning process are considered to be direct services for instruction. 2. Activities that involve direct instructor-student contact as contrasted with consultation.

direct solicitation (of funds)   A form of fund-raising which involves asking individuals, businesses, fraternal organizations, and other groups directly for contributions to support an organization. *See also* FUNDRAISING.

direct student-teacher interaction   Instruction by one or more teachers who are physically present.

directed interview   Also NON-DIRECTIVE INTERVIEW. The directed interview has the interviewer in full control on the interview content, typically soliciting answers to a variety of specific questions. In the nondirective interview, by contrast, it is more the responsibility of the interviewee to determine the subjects to be discussed.

directive   1. An order, whether oral or written, issued by one civilian government official commanding action from lower rank officials who might be affected. 2. Any direct assignment from a superordinate to a subordinate.

director   1. A staff member performing assigned activities having the purpose of expediting and directing the operation of the school system for which policy and program plans have been broadly established. 2. One member of a board of directors, the body which—under an organization's constitution and bylaws— controls and governs the affairs of the organization. Many charitable organizations use *trustee* and *board of trustees* rather than director and board of directors. In this context, there is no meaningful difference between the two. *See also*:
> BOARD OF DIRECTORS
> BOARD OF TRUSTEES
> TRUSTEE

directorates, interlocking   Organizations with substantial overlapping membership on their boards of directors.

directors, board of   *See* BOARD OF DIRECTORS.

disability compensation   Compensation made to employees who become disabled due to job-related incidents.

disability insurance   Insurance designed to compensate individuals who lose wages because of the incurrence of a long-term illness or injuries.

disability retirement   Retirement caused by a physical or mental inability to perform on the job.

disabled veteran   Veteran of the armed services who has a service-connected disability and is rated 10 percent or more disabled by the Veterans Administration. *See also* VETERANS PREFERENCE.

disadvantaged persons   Unless defined differently for specific educational programs (e.g., vocational education, consumer, and homemaking programs), persons who have academic, socioeconomic, cultural, or other handicaps that prevent them from succeeding in educational programs designed for persons without such handicaps; and who, for that reason, require specially designed educational programs and related services. The term includes persons whose needs for such programs or services result from poverty, neglect, delinquency, or cultural, racial, or linguistic isolation from the community at large. The term does not include physically or mentally handicapped persons except where such persons also are subject to the other handicaps and conditions referred to in this paragraph. *See also* HANDICAPPED CHILDREN.

disbursements   Payments. *Gross disbursements* represent the amount of checks issued, cash or other payments made, less refunds received. *Net disbursements* represent gross disbursements less income collected and credited to the appropriate account, such as amounts received for goods and services provided.

discharge   *See* DISMISSAL.

discharge warning   A formal notice to an employee that he or she will be discharged if unsatisfactory work or behavior continues.

disciplinary action   1. Any action short of dismissal taken by an employer against an employee for violation of policy. 2. Any action taken by school officials against a student for the infraction of accepted rules.

disciplinary demotion   *See* DEMOTION.

disciplinary fine   A fine that a union or professional association may levy against a member for violating a provision of its bylaws.

disciplinary layoff   Suspension of an employee as punishment for violating some rule or policy.

discipline   1. A broad, logically organized body of subject matter that is distinguished by its scholarly prestige. 2. Punishment for infractions of school rules. 3. The maintenance of order in the classroom. 4. Authoritative control over students. 5. An internalized system for controlling one's own impulses or behavior.

George F. Will wrote in a 1987 *Newsweek* column (January 5): "In the 1940s a survey listed the top seven discipline problems in public schools: talking, chewing gum, making noise, running in the halls, getting out of turn in line, wearing improper clothes, not putting paper in wastebaskets. A 1980s survey lists these top seven: drug abuse, alcohol abuse, pregnancy, suicide, rape, robbery, assault."

See William Bagley, *School Discipline* (New York: Macmillan, 1976); Naomi F. Faust, *Discipline and the Classroom Teacher* (Port Washington, N.Y.: Kennikat Press, 1977); Laurel N. Tanner, *Classroom Discipline* (New York: Holt, Rinehart and Winston, 1978); and Elizabeth H. Weiner, *Discipline in the Classroom*, 2nd ed. (Washington, D.C.: National Education Association, 1980); and Meryl E. Englander, *Strategies for Classroom Discipline* (New York: Praeger, 1987).
See also:
ADMONITION
ADVERSE ACTION
DISCIPLINARY ACTION
PREVENTIVE DISCIPLINE
PROGRESSIVE DISCIPLINE
REPRIMAND

discipline clause   A provision of a collective bargaining agreement that stipulates the means for disciplining workers who violate management or union rules.

discovery learning   1. A teaching method whereby students are presented with ambiguous materials and are given the opportunity to organize them conceptually or draw their own conclusions about the materials. 2. Inductive learning. Contrast with EXPOSITORY LEARNING.

See John D.W. Andrews, "Discovery and Expository Learning Compared: Their Effects on Independent and Dependent Students," *Journal of Educational Research* (November/December 1984).

discovery method   A teaching technique designed to allow a student to "discover" a concept or principle. Jerome S. Bruner in "The Act of Discovery" *Harvard Educational Review* (Winter 1961) defined it as "rearranging or transforming evidence in such a way that one is enabled to go beyond the

The Differences Between Discipline and Punishment

Discipline is often confused with punishment, particularly by abusive parents who resort to corporal punishment. Although interpretations of both "discipline" and "punishment" tend to be vague and often overlapping, there is some consensus that discipline has positive connotations and punishment is considered negatively. Some general comparisons between the terms are:

a) Discipline can occur before, during, and/or after an event; punishment occurs only after an event.

b) Discipline is based on respect for a child and his/her capabilities; punishment is based on behavior or events precipitating behavior.

c) Discipline implies that there is an authority figure; punishment implies power and dominance vs. submissiveness.

d) The purpose of discipline is educational and rational; the purpose of punishment is to inflict pain, often in an attempt to vent frustration or anger.

e) Discipline focuses on deterring future behavior by encouraging development of internal controls; punishment is a method of external control that may or may not alter future behavior.

f) Discipline can lead to extrapolation and generalized learning patterns; punishment may relate only to a specific event.

g) Discipline can strengthen interpersonal bonds and recognizes individual means and worth; punishment usually causes deterioration of relationships and is usually a dehumanizing experience.

h) Both discipline and punishment behavior patterns may be transmitted to the next generation.

According to legal definitions applying to most schools and school districts, to accomplish the purposes of education, a schoolteacher stands in the place of a parent and may exercise powers of control, restraint, discipline, and correction as necessary, provided that the discipline is reasonable. The Supreme Court has ruled that under certain circumstances, the schools may also employ CORPORAL PUNISHMENT.

Source: U.S. Department of Health and Human Services, *Interdisciplinary Glossary on Child Abuse and Neglect* (Washington, D.C.: U.S. Government Printing Office, DHHS Publication No. [OHDS] 80-30137), p. 14.

---

evidence so reassembled to additional new insights." *See* John Foster, *Discovery Learning in the Primary School* (London and Boston: Routledge and Kegan Paul, 1972).

discrepancy evaluation   A type of program evaluation in which actual performance is compared against a predetermined standard and the difference between the two, or the "discrepancy," is measured. The findings may lead to a change in the program or the standard, or both. For a descriptive manual, *see* Diane Kyler Yavorsky, *Discrepancy Evaluation: A Practitioner's Guide*, 7th ptg. (Charlottesville: University of Virginia, Evaluation Research Center, 1984).

discrimination   1. In the context of employment, the failure to treat equals equally. Whether deliberate or unintentional, any action that has the effect of limiting employment and advancement opportunities because of an individual's sex, race, color, age, national origin, religion, handicap, or other irrelevant criterion is discrimination. Because of the EEO and civil rights legislation of recent years, individuals aggrieved by unlawful discrimination now have a variety of administrative and judicial remedies open to them. Employment discrimination has its origins in the less genteel concept of bigotry. For the standard history, *see* Gustavus Myers, *History of Bigotry in the United States*, edited and revised by Henry M. Christman (New York: Capricorn Books, 1943, 1960).

Also see Frank P. Samford, III, "Toward a Constitutional Definition of Racial Discrimination," *Emory Law Journal* (Summer 1976); and William P. Murphy, Julius G. Getman, and James E. Jones, Jr., *Discrimination in Employment*, 4th ed. (Washington, D.C.: Bureau of National Affairs, Inc., 1979).

See also:
CIVIL RIGHTS ACT OF 1964
EQUAL EMPLOYMENT OPPORTUNITY
EQUAL EMPLOYMENT OPPORTUNITY ACT OF 1972
REVERSE DISCRIMINATION
RIGHTFUL PLACE

2. The ability of a test to truly differentiate among the skills of those who take it.

discrimination index   Any of a variety of statistical indexes used to indicate the extent to which a test item differentiates among examinees with respect to some criterion (such as the test as a whole).

disinhibition effect   From social learning theory, the notion that if negatively sanctioned behavior is not penalized when it occurs, the likelihood of observers imitating the behavior increases.

dismissal   Also called DISCHARGE. 1. Management's removal of an employee from employment. 2. The last part of a class, period, or school day.

dismissal pay   *See* SEVERANCE PAY.

dispatcher   A staff member performing the activities of assigning vehicles and drivers to perform specific services and recording such information concerning vehicle movement as the school system may require.

district   Subdivision of many different types of areas (such as countries, states, or counties) for judicial, political, or administrative purposes. *Districting* is the process of drawing a legislative district's boundary lines for purposes of APPORTIONMENT.

district, school   *See* SCHOOL DISTRICT.

district council   A level of labor organization below the national union but above the locals. The district council is composed of local unions in a particular industry within a limited geographic area. The district councils of local government employee unions are often major influences in municipal affairs.

See Edward Handman and Norman Adler, "District Council 37 (AFSCME) and the Community," *Social Policy* (Spring 1983); and Bernard Bellush and Jewel Bellush, "Participation in Local Politics: District Council 37 in New York," *National Civic Review* (May 1985).

dock   Deduct a part of an employee's wages as a penalty for tardiness, absenteeism, breakage, or other infringement upon the organization.

doctor's degree   An earned degree carrying the title of doctor. The doctor of philosophy degree (Ph.D.) is the highest academic degree, and requires mastery within a field of knowledge and demonstrated ability to perform scholarly research. Other doctorates are awarded for fulfilling specialized requirements in professional fields, such as education (Ed.D.), musical arts (D.M.A.), business administration (D.B.A.), and engineering (D.Eng. or D.E.S.). Many doctor's degrees in both academic and professional fields require an earned master's degree as a prerequisite. Professional (as opposed to academic) degrees, such as M.D., J.D., and D.D.S., are counted separately and are not included under this heading.

DOE   See EDUCATION, DEPARTMENT OF.

DOL   See LABOR, DEPARTMENT OF.

Dolch word list   A list of words most commonly used in children's reading material that may provide the basis for an early program of reading instruction. See KEY WORDS and WORD LISTS. See also Edward L. Dolch, *Methods in Reading* (Champaign, Ill.: Garrard, 1955).

domains   A system for categorizing instructional objectives or curricular content. There are several such systems. Traditional categorization was in three basic domain areas: cognitive, affective, and psychomotor. More specific domains that are frequently used for individualized planning in special education include cognitive, educational, physical, communicative, and social/emotional. A more recent trend is to categorize curriculum according to more functional, adult-referenced domains: domestic, vocational, recreation/leisure, and general community.

Doman-Delacato Method   See PATTERNING.

domicile   An individual's permanent legal residence. While an individual can legally have many residences, he or she can have only one domicile. Some government jurisdictions have residency requirements that require employees to be domiciled within the bounds of the jurisdiction.

See Stephen L. Hayford, "Local Government Residency Requirements and Labor Relations: Implications and Choices for Public Administrators," *Public Administration Review* (September/October 1978). See also *MCCARTHY V. PHILADELPHIA CIVIL SERVICE COMMISSION*.

donated services   Those contributed services that, if not contributed, would have to be paid for in order to operate a program. Thus, donated services are distinguished from other volunteered services such as service on boards of directors and committees. Compare to CONTRIBUTED SERVICES.

D1, D2, D3...   Symbols used to identify students who discontinue or drop out of school, according to reason, as follows:

D1 - Physical Illness
D2 - Physical or Sensory Disability
D3 - Emotional Disturbance
D4 - Mental Retardation
D5 - Behavioral Difficulty
D6 - Academic Difficulty
D7 - Lack of Appropriate Curriculum
D8 - Poor Student-Staff Relationships
D9 - Poor Relationships with Fellow Students
D10 - Dislike of School Experiences
D11 - Parental Influence
D12 - Need at Home
D13 - Economic Reasons
D14 - Employment
D15 - Marriage
D16 - Pregnancy
D17 - Religion
D18 - Other Known Reason

D19 - Reason Unknown
D20 - New Residence, School
Status Unknown

dormitory   1. A residence hall for students who may or may not share rooms. 2. A room that a group of students share as sleeping quarters.

double entry   Method of bookkeeping that shows each transaction as both a debit and a credit by using both horizontal rows and vertical columns of numbers. The totals of the rows and columns should always be the same. This makes it easier to find out where mistakes are than if the records were kept with only one entry for each item. *See also* DEBITS AND CREDITS.

double indemnity   *See* ACCIDENTAL DEATH BENEFIT.

double period   Two consecutive class periods denoted in the same subject.

double sessions   A school day consisting of separate sessions for two groups of pupils in the same instructional space, e.g., one room used by one fourth-grade class in the morning and by another fourth-grade class in the afternoon; or one school building used by high school juniors and seniors during a morning session and by freshmen and sophomores during an afternoon session.

double time   Penalty or premium rate of pay for overtime work, usually for holiday or Sunday work, amounting to twice the employee's regular hourly wage.

Down Syndrome   Also known as Down's Syndrome; a genetic disorder caused by chromosomal abnormalities that typically results in some degree of mental retardation, from mild to severe, and a wide array of health problems, including congenital heart defects and chronic ear infections. Children with Down Syndrome share a number of similar physical characteristics: a short stature, distinctive facial features (flat nose, large tongue, thick folds in the corners of the eyes), and broad hands with short fingers. Research has consistently shown that the incidence of children with Down Syndrome increases as the age of the mother increases and more recent evidence suggests there may be a similar correlation with the father's age. *See* Siegfried M. Pueschel and John E. Rynders, eds., *Down Syndrome: Advances in Biomedicine and the Behavioral Sciences* (Cambridge, Mass.: Ware Press, 1982); Siegfried M. Pueschel, *The Young Child with Down Syndrome* (New York: Sciences Press, 1984).

downgrading   Reassignment of an employee to a position having a lower rate of pay and/or lesser responsibilities.

Draw-A-Person Test   A projective test that uses a person's drawings of self and others to assess personality characteristics. This test is to be differentiated from the GOODENOUGH-HARRIS DRAWING TEST that uses drawings to measure cognitive development in children. It is published by:
Charles C. Thomas Publisher
301-327 E. Lawrence Avenue
Springfield, IL 62717

dress code   A written policy on how students (and sometimes faculty) should dress during regular school sessions. A dress code might also cover grooming issues such as makeup and beards.

dropout   A student who leaves a school, for any reason except death, before graduation or completion of a program of studies and without transferring to another school. The term ''dropout'' is used most often to designate an elementary or secondary school student who has been in membership during the regular school term and who withdraws from membership before graduating from secondary school (grade 12) or before completing an equivalent program of studies. Such an individual is considered a dropout whether the individual's dropping out occurs during or between regular school terms, whether the individual's dropping out occurs before or after the individual has passed the compulsory school attendance age, and, where applicable, whether or not the individual has completed a minimum required amount of schoolwork. The term "dropout" is used synonymously with the term "discontinuer."

For a series of essays examining the issues regarding students who leave school, see Gary Natriello, ed., *School Dropouts: Patterns and Policies* (New York: Teachers College Press, 1986, 1987). *See also* Andrew Hahn, "Reaching Out to America's Dropouts," *Phi Delta Kappan* (December 1987); Larry W. Barber and Mary C. McClellan, "Looking at America's Dropouts," *Phi Delta Kappan* (December 1987).

dropping out   Leaving a school, for any reason except death, before graduation or completion of a program of studies and without transferring to another school. For a nationwide research analysis and extensive bibliography, see Russell W. Rumberger, "Dropping Out of High School: The Influence of Race, Sex and Family Background," *American Educational Research Journal* (Summer 1983).

drug addiction   Also drug abuse; any habitual use of a substance that leads to psychological and/or physiological dependence. *Drug abuse* consists of using drugs to one's physical, emotional, and/or social detriment without necessarily being addicted.

dual enrollment   An arrangement whereby a student regularly and concurrently attends two schools that share direction and control of his or her studies. For example, the student attends a public school part-time and a nonpublic school part-time, pursuing part of the elementary or secondary studies under the direction and control of the public school and the remaining part under the direction and control of the nonpublic school; or, he or she attends a public secondary school part-time and an area vocational school part-time with the direction and control of studies similarly shared by the two institutions.

dual grading system   A grading policy that calls for giving a student's efforts two grades: one relative to the work of other students, and one relative to the individual student's ability.

dual processing hypothesis   A controversial theory that material which is concrete and pictorial is processed by the brain differently from abstract, linguistic material.

dual progress plan   An experimental program developed to departmentalize curriculum in the elementary school and to introduce specialist teaching and non-graded advancement. The plan was conceived by George D. Stoddard in 1956 and implemented in two New York school systems. The dual progress plan separates curriculum into two tracks: cultural imperatives, which are seen as essential for ultimate effective functioning in our culture, and cultural electives, which are all other subject matter determined to be less essential. Language arts and social studies comprise the imperative track. One noteworthy feature of the program is that it allows for students to progress slowly or rapidly depending on their abilities. *See* George D. Stoddard, *The*

Dual Progress Plan (New York: Harper and Row, 1961).

dual school system   A racially segregated school system. Such systems if de jure would be illegal in the United States. However, some segregated systems exist de facto.

dual unionism   Situation where two rival unions claim the right to organize workers in a particular locality.

due process   The constitutional requirement that "no person shall be deprived of life, liberty, or property without due process of law." While the specific requirements of due process vary with new Supreme Court decisions, the essence of the idea is that individuals must be given adequate notice and a fair opportunity to present their side in a legal dispute and that no law or government procedure should be arbitrary or unfair.

See Deborah D. Goldman, "Due Process and Public Personnel Management," *Review of Public Personnel Administration* (Fall 1981); David L. Kirp and Donald N. Jensen, "What Does Due Process Do?" *Public Interest* (Fall 1983); and J.S. Fuerst and Roy Petty, "Due Process—How Much is Enough?" *Public Interest* (Spring 1985). See also MATHEWS V. ELDRIDGE.

due process, procedural   The legal process and machinery thatshould work to ensure due process is afforded all citizens. Daniel Webster gave the classic description of due process as that "which hears before it condemns, which proceeds upon inquiry, and renders judgment only after trial." Procedural due process thus requires the legal system to follow the rules that exist. Substantive due process, in contrast, allows people to challenge the rules.

due process, substantive   1. The constitutional guarantee that no person

shall be arbitrarily deprived of life, liberty, or property. The essense of substantive due process is a notion of fundamental fairness that protects against arbitrary and unreasonable action on the part of the government. 2. The formal legal requirement that due process requirements be observed by government or its agents.

due process of law   A right guaranteed by the Fifth, Sixth, and 14th Amendments and generally understood to mean that legal proceedings will follow rules and forms that have been established for the protection of private rights. The 14th Amendment's provision that "no person shall be deprived of life, liberty, or property without due process of law" is considered to be a powerful restraint on the procedures by which governments in the U.S. limit the rights or property interests of their citizens. However, the concept raises considerable questions regarding both the procedures deemed "fair" and the kinds of rights and interests protected by it. For the most part, these two elements are related in that the more fundamental the right or interest, the greater the procedural protections afforded the citizen when the state seeks to abridge it. The degree of protection ranges from a jury trial and appellate processes to a hearing of some sort, perhaps including a right to counsel, confrontation, and cross-examination of adverse witnesses before an impartial examiner. Of course, there are instances in which citizens are adversely affected by administrative decisions but nevertheless have no right or opportunity to be heard.

In recent years the most interesting developments in this area of constitutional law have been: (1) the extension of the procedural safeguards afforded citizens at the hearing stage and (2) the extension of the right to have a hearing to situations previously not deemed sufficiently important to warrant such protections. Consider the procedural protections afforded public employees in dismissals. It has now been found that where constitutionally protected rights and interests are at stake, there may be a right to an open hearing including counsel, confrontation, and cross-examination.

See M.A. McGhehey, "The Overextension of Due Process," *Education and Urban Society* (February 1982); and Jerry L. Mashaw, *Due Process in the Administrative State* (New Haven, Conn.: Yale University Press, 1985).

dues   1. Fees that must be periodically paid by association and union members in order for them to remain in good standing. The dues are used to finance activities. 2. Fees assessed by school clubs and organizations of their memberships to support activities.

dues checkoff   *See* CHECKOFF.

dunce   An academic failure. The classic cartoon of a dunce has a child standing in a corner wearing a dunce's cap, which is shaped like a pointed, inverted funnel. A pejorative term of questionable taste.

Durrell Analysis of Reading Difficulty   An individually-administered diagnostic reading test that assesses oral reading, silent reading, listening comprehension, and word recognition and analysis in children from the preprimer through all grade levels. The test is designed to pinpoint specific areas of strength and weakness. It is published by:

The Psychological Corporation
555 Academic Court
San Antonio, TX 78204

duty of fair representation   Obligation of a labor union to represent all of the members in a bargaining unit fairly and without discrimination.

See Jean T. McKelvey, ed., *The Duty of Fair Representation* (Ithaca: New York State School of Industrial and Labor Relations, Cornell University, 1977); George W. Bohlander, "Fair Representation: Not Just a Union Problem," *The Personnel Administrator* (March 1980); and Stanley J. Schwartz, "Different Views of the Duty of Representation," *Labor Law Journal* (July 1983).

duty to bargain   Positive obligation under various state and federal laws that employers and employees bargain with each other in good faith. Section 8(d) of the Labor-Management Relations (Taft-Hartley) Act of 1947 holds that the duty to bargain collectively is the performance of the mutual obligation of the employer and the representative of the employees to meet at reasonable times and confer in good faith with respect to wages, hours, and other terms and conditions of any employment, or the negotiation of an agreement, or any question arising thereunder, and the execution of a written contract incorporating any agreement reached if requested by either party, but such obligation does not compel either party to agree to a proposal or require the making of a concession.

For legal analyses, *see* Archibald Cox, "The Duty to Bargain in Good Faith," *Harvard Law Review* (June 1958); and Stanley A. Gacek, "The Employer's Duty to Bargain on Termination of Unit Work," *Labor Law Journal* (October 1981).

dyslexia   A general term that refers to the condition of children who have difficulty learning to read in the absence of any other obvious handicaps. Though a great deal has been written about dyslexia and the disorder has been categorized and sub-categorized in a number of ways, there remains considerable controversy about its definition, etiology, and prevalence, and whether dyslexia exists at all as a specific, identifiable condition. For a comprehensive review of the literature, *see* Martha M. Evans, *Dyslexia: An Annotated Bibliography* (Westport, Conn.,: Greenwood Press, 1982). For an interesting summary (and extensive bibliography) of the physiology of dyslexia and other reading disorders, *see* Drake D. Duane, "Neurobiological Correlates of Reading Disorders," *Journal of Education Research* (September/October 1983).

E

EAP *See* EMPLOYEE ASSISTANCE PROGRAM.

early childhood education Generally connotes education at the prekindergarten level but also refers to any educational experiences provided by a school at the preprimary and primary levels. *Also see* PRESCHOOL PROGRAM. *See* Marjorie L. Hipple, *Early Childhood Education* (Pacific Palisades, Calif.: Goodyear, 1975).

For a discussion of the benefits of early childhood education *see* J.R. Berrcuta-Clement et al., *Changed Lives: The Effects of the Perry Preschool Program on Youths Through Age 19* (Ypsilanti, Mich.: The High Scope Press, 1984).

early departure Also called early dismissal; leaving school before the official close of the school's daily session.

early intervention 1. Educational and related services for preschool-aged children who may have, or be at risk for, handicapping conditions. There is considerable research and literature in support of early intervention services as effective in reducing the impact of handicaps on children and their families. It has been shown that children who attend preschool are more likely to graduate from high school, are less likely to repeat grades, and are either less likely to need special education services, or they require less intense services, in elementary and secondary school. They are more likely to hold down jobs when they finish school, and they are less likely to get into trouble with the law. Families of handicapped children who receive early intervention services experience less stress and feel less socially isolated. There are numerous models for early intervention

services, some of which are home-based and include parent training, particularly when the students are below the age of three. Many early intervention models were developed through federally funded demonstration projects. Contact the High Scope Foundation, Ypsilanti, MI 48197, for long-term (over 20 years at this writing) longitudinal follow-up data on graduates of early intervention programs.

See Brian McNulty, David Smith and Elizabeth Soper, *Effectiveness of Early Education* (Denver: Colorado Department of Education, 1983).

2. Programs and services focusing on prevention by relieving family stress before child abuse and neglect occur; for example, help-lines, Head Start, home health visitors, and other family-oriented programs.

Eastex, Inc. v. National Labor Relations Board 437 U.S. 556 (1978) The Supreme Court case that affirmed a National Labor Relations Board ruling that union members have the right to distribute, on their employer's property, leaflets containing articles pertaining to political issues (such as right-to-work laws and minimum wages) as well as those directly connected to the union-employer relationship.

echolalia A type of abnormal speech pattern that is characterized by the assumedly meaningless repetition of words, phrases, or sentences that have been heard.

ECIA *See* EDUCATION CONSOLIDATION AND IMPROVEMENT ACT OF 1981.

eclectic reading method An approach to the teaching of reading that incorporates a variety of materials, usually supplementary to a basal reader. The term eclectic can be applied to any instructional program that draws from a number of different sources in developing the content and procedures for instruction.

ecological inventory　A technique used by special education teachers for identifying skills that may be needed by students who are handicapped in order for them to function successfully in typical community environments. The strategy involves the observation of non-handicapped persons in those environments in order to specify the activities they typically accomplish in places like stores, restaurants, buses, and parks, and the skills they use in doing so. *See* COMMUNITY-BASED TRAINING OR COMMUNITY-REFERENCED TRAINING.

ecological validity　In educational research, the extent to which the results of an experiment can be generalized, from the specific environment and conditions created by the researcher, to other environments.

economies of scale　Cost savings resulting from aggregation of resources and/or mass production. In particular, it refers to decreases in average costs when all factors of production are expanded proportionately. For example, costs for a unit of service are generally less in a school of 3,000 students than in one of 300.

economy and efficiency audits　Audits that seek to determine: (a) whether an organizational entity is managing and utilizing its resources (such as personnel, property, and space) economically and efficiently; (b) the causes of inefficiencies or uneconomical practices; and (c) whether the entity has complied with laws and regulations concerning matters of economy and efficiency.

EDGAR　*See* EDUCATION DEPARTMENT GENERAL ADMINISTRATIVE REGULATIONS.

educable mental retardation　A somewhat outdated term generally synonymous with mild mental retardation.

education　1. In broad terms, the life-long process of acquiring new knowledge and skills through both formal and informal exposure to information, ideas, and experiences. 2. In narrow terms, systematic planned instruction that takes place in school.

Education　A quarterly journal that prints articles concerned with all aspects of teacher education.
　Editorial Address:
　Education
　1362 Santa Cruz Court
　Chula Vista, CA 92010
Printed and circulated by:
　Peterson Press, Inc.
　Appleton, WI 54912

education, adult　*See* ADULT EDUCATION PROGRAM.

education, adult basic　*See* ADULT BASIC EDUCATION.

education, adult/continuing　*See* ADULT/CONTINUING EDUCATION.

education, basic　*See* BASIC EDUCATION.

education, board of　*See* BOARD OF EDUCATION.

education, community　*See* COMMUNITY EDUCATION.

education, continuing　*See* ADULT/CONTINUING EDUCATION.

education, cooperative　*See* COOPERATIVE EDUCATION.

education, cooperative extension *See* COOPERATIVE EXTENSION EDUCATION.

Education, Department of (DOE) Or U.S. Department of Education. The cabinet-level department that establishes policy for, administers, and coordinates most federal assistance to education. Created on October 17, 1979, by the Department of Education Organization Act, when the Department of Health, Education, and Welfare was divided in two. The Reagan administration came into office pledging to eliminate DOE, but has bowed to political pressures and retained it as a platform for the administration's stands on education policy. The Department of Education currently administers almost all programs of an educational nature that are included under federal statute. For a series of articles relating to the U.S. Department of Education and public schools in America, *see* "A Special Issue: Rethinking the Federal Role in Education," *Harvard Educational Review* (November 1982).

See also David Stephens, "President Carter, the Congress, and NEA: Creating the Department of Education," *Political Science Quarterly* (Winter 1983-84); and Beryl A. Radin and Willis D. Hawley, *The Politics of Federal Reorganization: Creating the Department of Education* (Elmsford, N.Y.: Pergamon Press, 1987).

U.S. Department of Education
400 Maryland Ave., S. W.
Washington, DC 20202
(202) 245-3192

education, early childhood *See* EARLY CHILDHOOD EDUCATION.

education, federal aid for *See* FEDERAL AID FOR EDUCATION.

education, Indian, also Native American education *See* INDIAN EDUCATION.

education, migrant *See* MIGRANT EDUCATION.

education, outdoor *See* OUTDOOR EDUCATION.

education, postsecondary *See* POSTSECONDARY EDUCATION.

education, prevocational *See* PREVOCATIONAL EDUCATION.

education, public adult *See* PUBLIC ADULT EDUCATION.

education, public board of *See* PUBLIC BOARD OF EDUCATION.

education, special *See* SPECIAL EDUCATION.

education, state board *See* STATE BOARD OF EDUCATION.

education, state department of *See* STATE DEPARTMENT OF EDUCATION.

education, state system of *See* STATE SYSTEM OF EDUCATION.

education, technical *See* TECHNICAL EDUCATION.

education, vocational-technical *See* VOCATIONAL-TECHNICAL EDUCATION.

Education Commission of the States A national clearinghouse, forum, and resource for information on state education policies and practices. The commission serves as the operating arm and governing board of the Interstate Compact for Education, an organization of the governors or other representatives from participating states that is specifically concerned with public education.

Education Commission of the States
300 Lincoln Tower Building
1860 Lincoln Street
Denver, CO 80295
(303) 830-3600

Education Index　A cumulative index of authors and subjects in selected (English-language) educational periodicals. The *Index* has been published since 1929 and includes the following subject areas: administration and supervision; pre-school, elementary, secondary, higher and adult education; teacher education, vocational education; counseling and personnel service; teaching methods and curriculum. Subject fields indexed include the arts, audiovisual education, comparative and international education, computers in education, English language arts, health and physical education, languages and linguistics, library and information science, multi-cultural/ethnic education, psychology and mental health, religious education, science and mathematics, social studies, special education and rehabilitation, and educational research relative to areas and fields indexed.

> The H.W. Wilson Company
> 930 University Avenue
> Bronx, NY 10452

education major　An undergraduate student whose program of studies gives primary emphasis to subject matter in the area of education and who, according to his/her institutional requirements, concentrates a minimum number of courses or semester hours of college credit in the specialty of education.

Education of the Handicapped Act of 1983 (P.L. 98-199)　This act reaffirmed the original intent of Congress with regard to federal involvement in special education when it passed P.L. 94-142, the Education for All Handicapped Children Act. These amendments, passed eight years after enactment of the original law, primarily emphasized services that had been most difficult to implement, such as those at the preschool and the secondary/postsecondary age levels. Major features included the restoration of a national advisory committee, permission to use federal funds for children under the age of three, establishing state grants to develop comprehensive early childhood education services, expanding postsecondary programs in the areas of vocational, technical, and continuing education, establishing grants for parent training, and emphasizing federal research on improving teaching methodology and curriculum.

Education of the Handicapped Act of 1986 (P.L. 99-457)　This act constituted the second major revision of P.L. 94-142, the original Education for All Handicapped Children Act of 1975, and contained amendments that significantly expanded the role of the federal government in education for preschool-aged children with handicaps. Although the law contained other provisions, such as personnel training and research, the major focus is on preschool education for three- to five-year-olds and early intervention services for children from birth to two years of age.

Educational Administration Quarterly　A printed forum for empirical research and theoretical reviews related to the administration of educational organizations. Published quarterly under the sponsorship of the University Council for Educational Administration.

> Editorial Address:
> University of Utah
> 225 Milton Bennion Hall
> Salt Lake City, UT 84112
> Subscription Address:
> Sage Publications, Inc.
> 2111 West Hillcrest Drive
> Newbury Park, CA 91320

educational anarchism　The educational ideology that supports minimizing institutional restraints on personal behavior, de-institutionalizing school systems, and emphasizing personal responsibility and a radically simplified world. This ideology would view the elimination of the current system of schools as a movement toward humanistic reform.

educational assistance programs 1. An employee benefit that allows the employee time off from work to attend courses or to take advantage of other continuing education opportunities with or without financial assistance. 2. Federal or state government grant programs to financially assist local school districts.

educational attainment (years of school completed) The highest grade of regular school attended and completed.

educational community That body of persons, usually considered to be nationwide, that is actively engaged in the educational enterprise.

educational conservatism The educational ideology that espouses adherence to existing cultural institutions and a respect for law and order. Under this ideology the central goal of the school is seen as being the preservation and transmission of established social patterns and traditions.

educational counseling A one-to-one process between a student and a school staff person, usually a counselor, in which the student is assisted in planning and preparing for immediate and future educational programs.

educational expenses 1. Employee expenses that are required to gain skills for a current job or to meet an employer's educational requirements. 2. Any expenses involved in furthering one's education.

educational fundamentalism The educational ideology that is essentially anti-intellectual in the sense that it espouses an uncritical acceptance of "fundamental truths" and established social consensus. Under this ideology the goal of school is to restore conventional standards of belief and behavior and thus avoid the otherwise imminent moral collapse of contemporary society.

educational gerontology The study of learning in the later years of life. See Ronald H. Sherron and D. Barry Lumsden, eds., *Introduction to Educational Gerontology* (Washington, D.C.: Hemisphere, 1978); and Victor M. Agruso, *Learning in the Later Years: Principles of Educational Gerontology* (New York: Academic Press, 1978).

educational ideologies The application of underlying moral, social, and political positions to the nature and conduct of schooling. There are six basic social systems applied to education as ideologies. Three are called conservative ideologies (educational fundamentalism, educational intellectualism, educational conservatism) and three are called liberal ideologies (EDUCATIONAL LIBERALISM, EDUCATIONAL LIBERATIONISM, EDUCATIONAL ANARCHISM).

educational indicators The elements of a method of evaluation of educational practices that assesses desired outcomes or describes core features of the system. Appropriate indicators should provide information that is feasible to gather and that is valid and useful for making policy decisions. For a series of articles pertaining to educational indicators, see *Phi Delta Kappan* (March 1988).

educational institution Any organization whose primary purpose is the provision of instruction.

ORGANIZATIONAL CHART U.S. DEPARTMENT OF EDUCATION

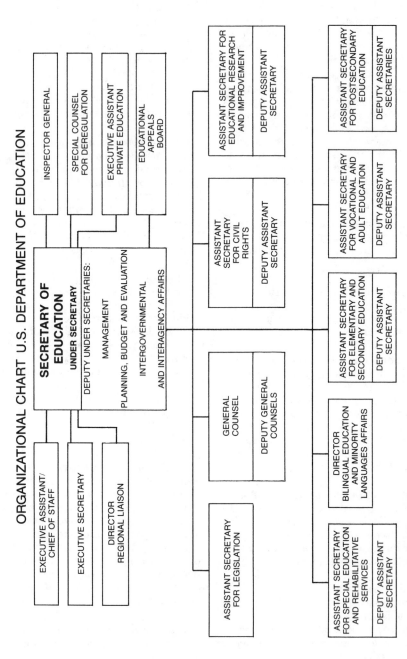

SOURCE: U.S. GOVERNMENT MANUAL

Education Consolidation and Improvement Act of 1981 (ECIA)
(P.L. 89-313)   A reauthorization of the Elementary and Secondary Education Act of 1965 that consolidated a number of separate educational aid programs into major block grants. The act was divided into two sections: Chapter 1, which essentially replaced Title 1 of ESEA in the provision of programs for low-income, disadvantaged youth, and Chapter 2, which consolidated approximately 28 additional discretionary programs. *See*:

BLOCK GRANT
CHAPTER 1
CHAPTER 2

Education Department General Administrative Regulations (EDGAR)   Replaced the U.S. Department of Education's "Part 74, Administration of Federal Grants" in 1981, as the administrative guidelines for nonprofit organizations' expenditures of federal education funds.

Education For All Handicapped Children Act   (P.L. 94-142) Landmark legislation passed by the United States Congress in 1975 that allowed for the provision of a free appropriate public education for all children regardless of handicapping conditions. The law was derived from section 504 of the 1973 Rehabilitation Act (P.L. 93-112), which prohibited discrimination on the basis of handicap. The law provides federal funds for special education and related services, requiring that states meet all provisions of the statute, guaranteeing services and due process protections to all handicapped children ages three to 21 years (with allowable exclusions for three- to five-year-olds and 18- to 21-year-olds) in order to receive these funds. Up until 1985 all states except one (New Mexico) participated in the implementation of P.L. 94-142. In 1985 New Mexico chose to join the other 49 states,

as well as the District of Columbia and a number of the United States Trust Territories, in implementing the law.

The central component of the law is the "Grants to States" program that provides funding for mandated services to school-age children. Other provisions of the law fund discretionary programs such as personnel preparation, research, model demonstrations, technical assistance, and services to particular populations (e.g., deaf-blind and preschool).

P.L. 94-142 has been amended significantly on two occasions. In 1983 P.L. 98-199 was passed and in 1986 P.L. 99-457 was passed. Both of these amendments substantially expanded the role of the federal Department of Education with regard to preschool services and secondary and post secondary education as well as expanding other portions of the law. Attempts were made during 1982-83 to change the regulations pertaining to the law in response to the 1981 Executive Order of the President to "reduce the burden and costs of existing and future regulations." The notice of proposed rulemaking, published in the *Federal Register* in August 1982, and the subsequent public hearings met with unprecedented public reaction and opposition. Thus the regulations, which are considered by many special education professionals to be cumbersome, have remained consistent since they were first authorized and adopted.

For a thorough explanation written for the regular educator, *see* Roberta Weiner, *P.L. 94-142: Impact on Schools* (Arlington, Va.: Capitol Publications, 1985). For a study of the implementation of this law over a period of several years in five diverse school districts across the country *see* Judith D. Singer and John A. Butler, "The Education for All Handicapped Children Act: Schools As Agents for Social Reform," *Harvard Educational Review* (May 1987).

educational intellectualism
The educational ideology, based upon a closed and authoritarian philosophical system of thought, that sees the goal of school as changing existing educational practices to conform more closely to some established intellectual or spiritual ideal.

Educational Leadership A popular educational journal produced in magazine format by the Association for Supervision and Curriculum Development and intended for leaders in elementary and secondary education. It is distributed eight times per year, monthly September to May, with a bimonthly December-January issue, to ASCD members. Subscription address:
Association for Supervision and Curriculum Development
125 N. West St.
Alexandria, VA 22314

educational leave   *See* LEAVE WITHOUT PAY.

educational liberalism   The educational ideology that supports the preservation and improvement of the existing social order by teaching students to deal more effectively with their own life problems. Under this ideology the goal of school is to provide students with the information and skills they need to learn effectively for themselves and to solve problems.

educational liberationism   The educational ideology that supports the reconstruction of society along humanistic lines that emphasize the development of each person's unique potentialities. Under this ideology the goal of school is to provide students with information and skills necessary to learn for themselves, to solve problems, and to recognize the need for constructive social reform.

educational media   Any device, content material, method, or ex-perience used for teaching and learning purposes. These include printed and nonprinted sensory materials. *See also* AUDIOVISUAL AIDS.

educational media services   Activities concerned with the use of all teaching and learning resources, including hardware and content materials. *See* Robert Heinich, Michael Molenda, and James D. Russell, *Instructional Media and the New Technologies of Instruction*, 2nd ed. (New York: Wiley, 1985).

educational park   A reasonably large tract of land (80-100 acres) containing schools serving kindergarten through high school-aged students and, perhaps, a community college, which is generally located in the inner ring of suburbs or just inside a central city boundary. It is designed to serve a portion of the metropolitan area and may enroll 12,000 to 15,000 public school students of various ethnic groups. The concentration of facilities makes possible large-scale or special facilities such as swimming pools, auditoriums, and theaters. A campus-like atmosphere for adults and children includes family recreational and educational facilities. The educational park is designed to provide a school in the community that improves the aesthetic environment of both the school and the surrounding urban area.

educational psychology   1. The academic discipline that combines education and psychology and studies how knowledge of the individual applies to learning situations. 2. The application of psychological theories, concepts, and practices to educational processes.
See Steven Owen et al., *Educational Psychology: An Introduction*, 2nd ed. (Boston: Little, Brown, 1981); Richard E. Mayer, *Educational Psychology* (Boston: Little, Brown, 1987).

educational reform   A general term for proposed or recommended changes in the content and/or structure of traditional American schools. *See* Ralph W. Tyler, "Making Education Reform Work," *Phi Delta Kappan* (December 1987); also, National Commission on Excellence in Education, *A Nation at Risk: The Imperative for Educational Reform* (Washington, D.C.: Department of Education, 1983).

Educational Research Information Center   *See* ERIC.

Educational Research Quarterly A research journal published by the University of Southern California School of Education that includes both empirical research reports and articles, reviews, commentaries, and position papers.
> Editorial Address:
> *Educational Research Quarterly*
> School of Education, WPH-703D
> University of Southern California
> Los Angeles, CA 90089-0031

educational specialist   An individual with advanced training, experience, or skill in some aspect of education or in an educationally related field. There is a formal program of postgraduate university training that leads to an educational specialist degree (Ed.S.).

educational specifications development services   Activities concerned with preparing and interpreting to architects and engineers descriptions of specific space requirements for the various learning experiences of pupils to be accommodated in a building. These specifications are interpreted to the architects and engineers in the early stages of blueprint development.

educational technology   1. The media that are products of the application of science to educational problems. 2. A systematic approach to solving the problems of instruction that includes the development of instructional systems, identification of resources, and the delivery of those resources to students.

educational television services Activities concerned with planning, programming, writing, and presenting educational programs or segments of programs by way of closed circuit or broadcast television.

Educational Testing Service (ETS)   A widely utilized private, nonprofit, test publisher that provides tests and related services for schools, colleges, government agencies, and the professions. This is the largest testing and assessment service in the world. *See* Allan Nairn et al., *The Reign of ETS: The Corporation that Makes Up Minds* (Washington, D.C.: Learning Research Projects, 1980).
> Educational Testing Service
> Rosedale Road
> Princeton, NJ 08541
> (609) 921-9000

educational TV   1. An instructional process that utilizes television programs as a part of the educational program of a school; it includes writing, programming, and directing educational television programs. 2. Viewer supported noncommercial public television.

educationally deprived children As defined for federal compensatory education programs, those children who have need for special assistance in order that their level of educational attainment may be raised to that appropriate for children of their age. The term includes children who are handicapped or whose needs for such special educational assistance result from poverty, neglect, delinquency, or cultural or linguistic isolation from the community at large.

Edwards Personal Preference Schedule (EPPS)   An inventory widely used in personal counseling and personality research that is designed to measure the relative importance of 15 "key needs" or motives (i.e., achievement, deference, order, exhibition, autonomy, affiliation, intraception, succorance, dominance, abasement, nurturance, change, endurance, heterosexuality, and aggression). Published by:

Psychological Corporation
555 Academic Court
San Antonio, TX 78701
See Janet E. Helms, *A Practioner's Guide to the Edwards Personnel Preference Schedule* (Springfield, Ill.: Charles C. Thomas, 1983).

Edwards v. Aguillard 96 L.Ed. 2d 510 (1987)   The 1987 U.S. Supreme Court decision that ruled against a Louisiana law (the Balanced Treatment Act) that required the teaching of the theory of creationism in all public schools where the theory of evolution was taught. The Court upheld lower court rulings that the act violated the establishment clause of the First Amendment of the U.S. Constitution regarding separation of church and state.

EEO Officer   *See* EQUAL EMPLOYMENT OPPORTUNITY OFFICER.

EEO-1   The annual report of the sex and minority status of various work force categories that is required of all employers with 100 or more employees. The report must be filed with the Joint Reporting Committee of the Equal Employment Opportunity Commission and the Office of Federal Contract Compliance.

EEOC   *See* EQUAL EMPLOYMENT OPPORTUNITY COMMISSION.

Efbrandt v. Russell 384 U.S. 11 (1966)   The Supreme Court case holding an Arizona loyalty oath unconstitutional—in violation of freedom of

association since, coupled with a perjury statute, the oath had proscribed membership in any organization having, for only one of its purposes, the overthrow of the government of the State of Arizona. The Court reasoned that one might join such an organization without supporting its illegal purposes. *See also* LOYALTY OATH.

effective schools   An important educational concept of the 1980s that mushroomed in response to growing concerns that public schools in America were not adequately preparing students for higher education or for life. Specifically, it was stated that high school graduates were scoring lower on standardized achievement tests, that they were failing to develop the ability to think critically or to adapt to a changing environment, and that they lacked the skills to work cooperatively in a complex society. The effective school was conceptualized as an avenue to increase students' achievement scores, increase motivation for learning, instill self-discipline and responsibility, and teach skills relevant to in-depth and critical thinking about complex issues.

For some of the major literature in this growing body of knowledge, *see* John Goodlad, *A Place Called School: Prospects for the Future* (New York: McGraw-Hill, 1984); Theodore Sizer, *Horace's Compromise: The Dilemma of the American High School* (Boston: Houghton-Mifflin, 1984); E.L. Boyer, *High School: A Report on Secondary Education in America* (New York: Harper, 1983); and National Commission on Excellence in Education, *A Nation at Risk: The Imperative for Educational Reform* (Washington, D.C.: Department of Education, 1983).

For a research study of school factors related to student achievement, *see* Delwyn L. Harnisch, "Characteristics Associated with Effective Public High Schools," *Journal of Educational Research* (March/April 1987).

effective schools research   A phenomenon beginning in the late 1970s in an effort to improve student academic performance through an analysis of those components in schools that seem to be related to high test scores. The initial impetus is traced back to the 1966 COLEMAN REPORT. For a review of research articles, see Stewart Purkey and Marshall Smith, "Effective Schools—A Review," *Elementary School Journal*, 83:(1983).

See also Larry Cuban, "Transforming the Frog into a Prince: Effective Schools Research, Policy and Practice at the District Level," *Harvard Educational Review* (May 1984).

efficiency   Also efficiency ratio. Measure generally determined by seeking the ratio of outputs to inputs, which is called the *efficiency ratio*. Generally speaking, efficiency refers to the promotion of administrative methods that produce the largest store of results for a given objective at the least cost; the reduction of materiel and personnel costs while maximizing precision, speed, and simplicity in administration.

elective course   A non-required course usually at the secondary or postsecondary level that a student choses to take, usually based on interest or future plans, and for which academic credit is earned.

eleemosynary   Related to charity or charitable donations; dependent on or supported by charity.

elementary programs   Learning experiences concerned with the knowledge, skills, appreciations, attitudes, and behavioral characteristics that are considered to be needed by all pupils in terms of their awareness of life within our culture and the world of work and that normally may be achieved during the elementary school years as defined by applicable state laws and regulations.

elementary school   A school classified as elementary by state and local practice and composed of any span of grades not above grade eight. A preschool or kindergarten school is included under this heading only if it is an integral part of an elementary school or a regularly established school system. See Kenneth H. Hoover and Paul M. Hollingsworth, *A Handbook for Elementary School Teachers*, 2nd ed. (Boston: Allyn and Bacon, 1978).

Elementary Science Study (ESS) A collection of science materials (or kits) that were developed for study in grades kindergarten to eight and that are distributed by the Webster Division of McGraw-Hill.

McGraw-Hill Publishers
1221 Avenue of the Americas
New York, NY 10020
(212) 512-2000

Elementary and Secondary Education Act of 1965 (ESEA) The passage of this act in 1965 signaled the first major breakthrough of federal involvement in local education and set forth principles concerning the interaction among levels of government in the delivery of education services. This act was a part of President Lyndon Johnson's proclaimed "war on poverty," with a focus on mechanisms to supplement local educational practices in response to social concern about poverty. The law contained eight significant components that had an impact on later educational legislation, such as the Education for All Handicapped Children Act of 1975. These were: a focus on a disadvantaged population, a focus on individual needs, a focus on systems planning, a focus on consumer participation, a focus on personnel development, a focus on public/nonpublic cooperation, a focus on supplementing regular school services, and a focus on evaluation and accountability. In 1967 the act was amended to extend provisions for the coverage of services for handicapped students. In 1981 the Education Consolidation and Improvement Act (ECIA) was passed in place of reauthorization of ESEA. ECIA consolidated many of the separate discretionary programs that had been authorized under ESEA into block grants to the states. See EDUCATION CONSOLIDATION AND IMPROVEMENT ACT and EDUCATION FOR ALL HANDICAPPED CHILDREN ACT.

eligibility   Criteria for determining which organizations (e.g., Indian tribes, medical schools, or nonprofit organizations) and individuals are entitled to be recipients of grant or assistance programs.

emancipated minor   A minor who is free (emancipated) from parental control and may be exempted from the provisions of compulsory school attendance.

emergency management   Public-private cooperative activities that are concerned with reducing the risk to life and property posed by natural and man-made hazardous events.

eminent domain   A government's right to take private property for the public's use. The Fifth Amendment requires that, whenever a government takes an individual's property, the property acquired must be taken for public use, and the full value thereof paid to the owner. Thus, a government cannot take property from one person simply to give it to another. However, the Supreme Court has held that it is permissible to take private property for such purposes as urban renewal, even though ultimately the property taken will be returned to private ownership, since the taking is really for the benefit of the community as a whole. Property does not have to be physically taken from the owner to acquire Fifth Amendment protection. If governmental action leads to a lower value of private property, that may also constitute a "taking" and therefore require payment of compensation. Thus, the Supreme Court has held that the disturbance of the egg-laying habits of chickens on a man's poultry farm caused by the noise of low-level flights by military aircraft from a nearby airbase, lessens the value of that farm and that, accordingly, the landowner is entitled to receive compensation equal to his loss.

See James Geoffrey Durham, "Efficient Just Compensation as a Limit on Eminent Domain," *Minnesota Law Review* (June 1985).

emolument   Any monetary gain or other advantage achieved from employment; a more comprehensive term than wages and/or salaries.

emotional handicap   An impairment or deficiency of an individual's emotional responses to situations that may adversely affect the stability and/or performance of the individual.

emotionally disturbed   See SERIOUSLY EMOTIONALLY DISTURBED.

empirical   Findings or conclusions derived from direct and repeated observations of a phenomenon under study.

empirical validity   Validity of a test according to how well the test actually measures what it was designed to measure.

employee assistance program (EAP)   Formal program designed to assist employees with personal problems through both (a) internal counseling and aid and (b) a referral service to outside counseling or treatment resources. The thrust of such programs is to increase productivity by correcting or ameliorating distracting personal problems.

See Harvey Shore, "Employee Assistance Programs—Reaping the Benefits," *Sloan Management Review* (Spring 1984); and Dale A. Masi, *Designing Employee Assistance Programs* (New York: AMACOM, 1984).

employee benefits   Compensation, in addition to regular salary, provided to an employee. This may include such benefits as health insurance, life insurance, annual leave, sick leave, retirement, and social security. *See also* FRINGE BENEFITS.

Employee Retirement Income Security Act of 1974 (ERISA) Popularly known as PENSION REFORM ACT OF 1974—the federal statute enacted to protect "the interest of participants in employee benefit plans and their beneficiaries . . . by establishing standards of conduct, responsibility and obligations for fiduciaries of employee benefit plans, and by providing for appropriate remedies, sanctions, and ready access to the Federal courts." The basic intent of ERISA is to ensure that employees will eventually gain appropriate benefits from the pension plans in which they participate.

Employer Identification Number   A number issued to all employers by the Internal Revenue Service. Applications are filed with the IRS on Form SS-4.

employer unit   Any bargaining unit that holds all of the eligible employees of a single employer.

employment contract   Generally, a promise or set of promises for which the law offers a remedy if the promise(s) is breached. An employment contract is the agreed-upon work (and other contributions) and total compensation (monetary and nonmonetary) commitments between an employer and an employee. Employment contracts are legally enforceable.

employment manager   Job title sometimes given to managers who function as personnel directors.

employment parity   *See* PARITY.

employment permit   A type of legal certificate, sometimes called a "work permit," authorizing youths to engage in certain types of work before they have reached the age of unrestricted employment.

employment relations   General term for all relationships that occur in a worker-manager context. While used synonymously with labor relations and industrial relations, it is often applied in nonunion situations in order to emphasize "nonunion."

Employment Standards Administration (ESA)   Agency of the Department of Labor that administers laws and regulations setting employment standards, providing workers' compensation to those injured on their jobs, and requiring federal contractors to provide equal employment opportunity. Its major divisions include the Wage and Hour Division, the Office of Federal Contract Compliance, and the Office of Workers' Compensation.
Employee Standards Administration
U.S. Department of Labor
200 Constitution Avenue, N.W.
Washington, DC 20210
(202) 523-8165

employment status   The circumstances under which the staff member serves the school system (e.g., probationary status, tenure status, or other status).

employment taxes   Also called PAYROLL TAXES. Any of a variety of taxes levied by governments on an employer's payroll. The most common employment tax is the employer's contribution to social security, known as FICA taxes (after the Federal Insurance Contribution Act). There are also FUTA taxes (after the Federal Unemployment Tax Act) and sometimes other unemployment insurance contributions are required by state law.

enabling act   Legislation permitting cities and/or special districts to engage in particular programs. Such enabling acts prescribe some of the administrative details of implementation. As substate jurisdictions are the creatures of their state, their ability to participate in particular types of programs, especially those of the national government, depends upon state laws.

enabling instruments   See ARTICLES OF ORGANIZATION and BYLAWS.

encumbrance   A claim, charge, or security interest on property, such as a lien or mortgage, that lowers the property's value.

encumbrances   Purchase orders, contracts, and salary or other commitments that are chargeable to an appropriation and for which a part of the appropriation is reserved. They cease to be encumbrances when paid.

endowment fund   A restricted fund, the contents of which must be invested to generate income; the income may be expended, but the principal must usually remain intact. Many foundations make grants only from their endowment income, but this is not necessarily true of smaller corporate foundations which often receive annual contributions from the corporation. See also ENDOWMENT INCOME.

endowment income   Income generated from the resources in a restricted endowment fund.

endowment (insurance)   An insurance policy that pays a set amount at a set time or, if the person insured dies, pays the money to a beneficiary.

end-testing   Examining individuals who have just completed a course of training on the subject in which they were trained in order to measure each individual's attainments and/or the effectiveness of the training.

Engell v. Vitale 370 U.S. 421 (1962) The Supreme Court case based on a New York State law that ruled that state encouragement of the regular recitation of prayer in the public schools was unconstitutional.

engineered classroom   A highly structured, behaviorally-oriented classroom model for students who are labeled emotionally disturbed.

English, sociocultural dialect
A variation of the English language spoken in the United States by many members of a distinct sociocultural group, such as Afro-Americans, Chicanos, Puerto Ricans, and Appalachian mountaineers. Such variations of English—generally denoted as nonstandard—differ from regional standard variations (and from each other) in regard to grammar as well as pronunciation and idiomatic usage.
    See William Labov, *Language in the Inner City: Studies in the Black Vernacular* (Philadelphia: University of Pennsylvania Press, 1972).

English, standard American
The English language as spoken in such mainstream institutions of the United States as governmental bodies, schools, churches, and communications media. While there are regional variations of standard American English (e.g., Southern standard and New England standard), the grammar of these regional variations is similar, and the differences among them are predom-

inantly those of pronunciation and idiomatic usage.

enrichment program   Supplementary instructional experiences provided students according to their special needs, abilities, and interests. For preschool or preprimary, culturally deprived children, this refers to experiences designed to aid in their transition from a home to a school environment; the emphasis is on language development in preparation for reading instruction, and frequently such programs are supplemented by counseling with parents and with home visits by school staff members. For other students, such as the gifted, talented, or college bound, this term refers to special instructional experiences provided in addition to instructions generally provided most pupils.

enrollment   The total number of original entries (students) in a given school unity. In a given state, this is the total number of original entries in public schools plus the total number of original entries in nonpublic schools. In 1986 total public school enrollment in the U.S. was about 40 million.

enrollment information   Information relative to the entrance of students into schools and classes, their membership (including attendance, absence, and tardiness), and their withdrawals (including completion of schoolwork, transfer, dropout, and death).

entitlement authority   Legislation that requires the payment of benefits to any person or government meeting the requirements established by such law (such as social security benefits and veterans' pensions). Section 401 of the Congressional Budget and Impoundment Control Act of 1974 places certain restrictions on the enactment of new entitlement authority. *See also* AUTHORITY, BACKDOOR.

entitlement program   Any government program that pays benefits to individuals, organizations, or other governments who meet eligibility requirements set by law. Social security is the largest federal entitlement program for individuals. Others include farm price supports, Medicare, Medicaid, unemployment insurance, special education for handicapped students, and food stamps. Entitlement programs have great budgetary significance in that they "lock in" such a great percentage of the total federal budget each and every year that changes in the budget can only be made at the margin.

See Eleanor Chelimsky, "Reducing Fraud and Abuse in Entitlement Programs: An Evaluative Perspective," *The GAO Review* (Summer 1981); and Edward J. Green, "Equilibrium and Efficiency under Pure Entitlement Systems," *Public Choice* 39:1(1982).

entry behavior   A psychological term used to describe the knowledge and skills that a student possesses in a particular area of study at the time of beginning formal instruction in that area.

environmental education   The study of an individual's relationship with his or her natural surroundings, with a focus on environmental issues such as pollution, resource allocation, natural resource depletion, and population impact.

Environmental Education Act of 1970   The federal law (P.L. 91-516) which authorized support of the development of school curricula related to environmental quality, model education programs, training for teachers, community education, and other programs designed to promote an enhancement of the country's environmental and ecological balance.

Epperson v. Arkansas 393 U.S. 97 (1968)   The Supreme Court case which ruled that state laws forbidding the teaching of Darwin's theory of evolution were unconstitutional.

equal employment opportunity (EEO)   A concept that applies to a set of employment procedures and practices that effectively prevent any individual from being adversely excluded from employment opportunities on the basis of race, color, sex, religion, age, national origin, or other factors that cannot lawfully be used in employment efforts. While the ideal of EEO is an employment system that is devoid of both intentional and unintentional discrimination, achieving this ideal may be a political impossibility because of the problem of definition. One man's equal opportunity may be seen by another as tainted with institutional racism or by a woman as institutional sexism. Because of this problem of definition, only the courts have been able to say if, when, and where EEO exists.

For the law of EEO, see Charles A. Sullivan, Michael J. Zimmer, and Richard F. Richards, *Federal Statutory Law of Employment Discrimination* (Indianapolis: Michie Bobbs-Merrill, 1980); Arthur B. Smith, Jr., "The Law and Equal Employment Opportunity: What's Past Should Not be Prologue," *Industrial and Labor Relations Review* (July 1980); and Barbara Lindemann Schlei and Paul Frossman, *Employment Discrimination Law* 2nd ed. (Washington, D.C.: Bureau of National Affairs, Inc. 1983).

For the history of EEO in the federal government, see David H. Rosenbloom, *Federal Equal Employment Opportunity: Politics and Public Personnel Administration* (New York: Praeger, 1977).

See also:
ADVERSE EFFECT
ADVERSE IMPACT
AFFECTED CLASS
AFFIRMATIVE ACTION
CHILLING
DISCRIMINATION
FAIR EMPLOYMENT PRACTICE
  COMMISSION
GOALS
MAKE WHOLE
REASONABLE ACCOMMODATION
REPRESENTATIVE BUREAUCRACY
REVERSE DISCRIMINATION
RIGHTFUL PLACE
TITLE VII
TOKENISM

Equal Employment Opportunity Act of 1972   An amendment to Title VII of the 1964 Civil Rights Act that strengthened the authority of the Equal Employment Opportunity Commission and extended anti-discrimination provisions to state and local governments and labor organizations with 15 or more employees; and to public and private employment agencies.

See William Brown III, "The Equal Employment Opportunity Act of 1972—The Light at the Top of the Stairs," *Personnel Administration* (June 1972); and Harry Grossman, "The Equal Employment Opportunity Act of 1972, Its Implications for the State and Local Government Manager," *Public Personnel Management* (September/October 1973).

Equal Employment Opportunity Commission (EEOC)   Created by Title VII of the Civil Rights Act of 1964, the EEOC is composed of five members (one designated chair) appointed for five-year terms by the President, subject to the advice and consent of the Senate. The EEOC's mission is to end discrimination based on race, color, religion, sex, or national origin in hiring, promotion, firing, wages, testing, training, apprenticeship, and all other conditions of employment and to promote voluntary action programs by employers, unions, and community organizations to make equal employment opportunity an actuality.

See William A. Webb, "The Mission of the Equal Employment Opportunity Commission," *Labor Law Journal* (July 1983); Frank J. Thompson, "Deregulation at the EEOC: Prospects and Implications," *Review of Public Personnel Administration* (Summer 1984); and Donald W. Crowley, "Selection Tests and Equal Opportunity: The Court and the EEOC," *Administration and Society* (November 1985).

> Equal Employment Opportunity Commission
> 2401 E Street, N.W.
> Washington, DC 20507
> (202) 634-6922
> (800) USA-EEOC (toll free)

Equal Employment Opportunity Commission v. Wyoming 75 L.Ed. 2d 18 (1983)   The Supreme Court case that upheld the federal government's 1974 extension of the Age Discrimination in Employment Act to cover state and local government workers.

equal employment opportunity officer   The official within an organization who is designated responsible for monitoring EEO programs and assuring that both organizational and national EEO policies are being implemented.

Equal Pay Act of 1963   An amendment to the Fair Labor Standards Act of 1938, the Equal Pay Act of 1963 (Public Law 88-38) prohibits pay discrimination because of sex and provides that men and women working in the same establishment under similar conditions must receive the same pay if jobs require equal or similar skill, effort, and responsibility. *See also* COMPARABLE WORTH.

equality   *See* EQUITY.

equalization   Refers to state-level funding formulas for educational financing that attempt to eliminate differentials in the level of local public support to education between school districts. State supplements are provided to poorer local districts in order to achieve a minimal per-pupil support level.

equalized funding state   Formulas for financial assistance to local school districts that attempt to adjust for variations in the local tax base in order to provide greater funding equity among school districts.

equated scores   Scores from different tests of the same variable which are reduced by weighting in order to have a common basis for comparison.

equating   Process of adjusting the raw statistics obtained from a particular sample to corresponding statistics obtained for a base group or reference population.

equipercentile equating   Process that treats as equivalent those raw scores that fall at the same percentile in different samples although the raw scores themselves may be different.

equity   1. The mathematical excess of assets over liabilities. Generally this excess is called FUND BALANCE. 2. Also EQUALITY. Equal and fair treatment of all people, especially minorities and females, in matters of education and employment. For a discussion of equity in educational administration, *see* Carol Yeakey, Gladys Johnston, and Judith Adkinson, "In Pursuit of Equity: A Review of Research on Minorities and Women in Educational Administration," *Educational Administration Quarterly* (Summer 1986).
    See also Ann Bastain et al., *Choosing Equality: The Case for Democratic Schooling* (Philadelphia: Temple University Press, 1986).

equivalency examination   *See* HIGH SCHOOL EQUIVALENCY EXAMINATION.

ERIC   Educational Research Information Center. A readily accessible, comprehensive collection of educational publications that is supported by the National Institute of Education, a unit of the U.S. DEPARTMENT OF EDUCATION. The center, which includes several decentralized clearing houses, fulfills a variety of functions: collecting and disseminating reports, preparing topical reviews and bibliographies, and providing copies of educational materials at nominal cost. Each of the regionally based clearing houses has distinct responsibilities for specific subject areas. ERIC also publishes its own reference documents, including a dictionary of frequently used ERIC terms, a monthly abstract of research reports, an index of educational journals and a directory of its microfiche collection. See table for a listing of the ERIC clearing houses.

ERIC Clearinghouse on Adult, Career, and Vocational Education (CE)
Ohio State University
National Center for Research in Vocational Education
1960 Kenny Rd.
Columbus, OH 43210
(614) 486-3655 or (800) 848-4815

ERIC Clearinghouse on Counseling and Personnel Services (CG)
University of Michigan
School of Education, Room 2108
610 E. University St.
Ann Arbor, MI 48109
(313) 764-9492

ERIC Clearinghouse on Educational Management (EA)
University of Oregon
1787 Agate St.
Eugene, OR 97403
(503) 686-5043

ERIC Clearinghouse on Elementary and Early Childhood Education (PS)
University of Illinios
College of Education
805 W. Pennsylvania Ave.
Urbana, IL 61801
(217) 333-1386

ERIC Clearinghouse on Handicapped and Gifted Children (EC)
Council for Exceptional Children
1920 Association Dr.
Reston, VA 22091
(703) 620-3660

ERIC Clearinghouse on Higher Education (HE)
George Washington University
One Dupont Circle, NW, Suite 630
Washington, DC 20036
(202) 296-2597

ERIC Clearinghouse on Information Resources (IR)
Syracuse University
School of Education
Huntington Hall, Room 030
150 Marshall St.
Syracuse, NY 13210

ERIC Clearinghouse for Junior Colleges (JC)
University of California at Los Angeles (UCLA)
Mathematical Sciences Building, Room 8118
405 Hilgard Ave.
Los Angeles, CA 90024
(213) 825-3931

ERIC Clearinghouse on Languages and Linguistics (FL)
Center for Applied Linguistics
1118 22nd St. NW
Washington, DC 20037
(202) 429-9551

ERIC Clearinghouse on Reading
and Communication Skills (CS)
National Council of Teachers of
English
1111 Kenyon Rd.
Urbana, IL 61801
(217) 328-3870

ERIC Clearinghouse on Rural
Education and Small Schools
(RC)
New Mexico State University
Computer Center (Room 218)
Stewart St.
Box 3AP
Las Cruces, NM 88003
(505) 646-2623

ERIC Clearinghouse for Science,
Mathematics and Environmental
Education (SE)
Ohio State University
1200 Chambers Rd., Room 310
Columbus, OH 43212
(614) 422-6717

ERIC Clearinghouse for Social
Studies/Social Science Education
(SO)
Indiana University
Social Studies Development Center
2805 East 10th St.
Bloomington, IN 47405

ERIC Clearinghouse on Teacher
Education (SP)
American Association of Colleges for
Teacher Education
One Dupont Circle, NW, Suite 610
Washington, DC 20036
(202) 293-2450

ERIC Clearinghouse on Tests,
Measurements and Evaluation
(TM)
Educational Testing Service
Rosedale Rd.
Princeton, NJ 08541
(609) 734-5176

ERIC Clearinghouse on Urban
Education (UD)
Teachers College, Columbia University
Institute for Urban and Minority
Education
Box 40
525 W. 120th St.
New York, NY 10027
(212) 678-3433

Other ERIC Addresses:

Educational Resources Information
Center (Central ERIC)
U.S. Dept. of Education
Office of Educational Research and
Improvement (OERI)
Washington, DC 20208
(202) 254-5500

ERIC Processing & Reference
Facility
ORI, Inc., Information Systems
4833 Rugby Ave., Suite 301
Bethesda, MD 20814
(301) 656-9723

ERIC Document Reproduction
Service (EDRS)
Computer Microfilm Corporation
(CMC)
3900 Wheeler Ave.
Alexandria, VA 22304
(703) 823-0500 or (800) 227-3742

ERISA   See EMPLOYEE RETIREMENT
INCOME SECURITY ACT OF 1974.

ESA   See EMPLOYMENT STANDARDS
ADMINISTRATION.

escalator clause   Also called cost-of-living escalator provision of a wage agreement, which allows for periodic adjustments in response to changes in the cost of living, usually as determined by the Consumer Price Index of the Bureau of Labor Statistics.

escape clause A contract provision that allows a party to avoid doing something or to avoid liability if certain things happen. For example, in a maintenance-of-membership shop, a union contract may provide for a period of time during which union members may withdraw (escape) from the union without affecting their employment.

escrow Money, property, or documents that belong to organization A that are held by organization B until organization A takes care of an obligation to organization C. For example, a mortgage company may require a nursing home with a mortgage on a building to make monthly payments into an escrow account to take care of a future balloon payment when it comes due.

ESL English as a Second Language, or Teaching English to Speakers of Other Languages. A variety of techniques and approaches for teaching English to students whose primary language is not English. Typically, the non-English-speaking student is immersed in an English-speaking-only environment while in school as a method for encouraging (forcing) the acquisition of English-speaking skills. For a broad resource of methodologies, see J. Donald Bowen, Harold Madsen, and Ann Hilferty, *TESOL: Techniques and Procedures* (Rowley, Mass.: Newbury House, 1985). Contrast with BILINGUAL EDUCATION.

essentialism An educational theory that espouses mastery of basic academics, discipline, and high achievement standards as the core of the educational process.

estate planning Making plans for a person's property to be passed on at his or her death (for example, to a charitable organization) and gaining maximum legal benefit from that property by best using the laws of wills, trusts, insurance, property, and taxes.

estimated revenue On an accrual basis, the amount of revenue estimated to accrue during a given period regardless of whether or not it is all to be collected during the period; on a cash basis, the amount of revenues estimated to be collected during a given period.

estimated uncollectible tax liens That portion of tax liens receivable that it is estimated will never be collected. The account is shown as a deduction from the Tax Liens Receivable account on the balance sheet in order to arrive at the net amount of tax liens receivable.

estimated uncollectible taxes A provision of tax revenues for that portion of taxes receivable which it is estimated will not be collected. The account is shown on the balance sheet as a deduction from the Taxes Receivable account in order to arrive at the net taxes receivable. Separate accounts may be maintained on the basis of tax roll year and/or delinquent taxes.

ethnic group A group with a common cultural tradition and a sense of identity that exists as a subgroup of a larger society.

Ethnic Heritage Program A federal program authorized in 1972 (under P.L. 92-318) that provides grants to educational organizations to promote, through teaching and the development of curricular materials, an understanding of the contributions of different ethnic groups to the national heritage of the United States.

ethnic origin The ethnic origin of various pupil groups, according to state or local classification and definition, e.g., Mexican-American, Japanese-American, Puerto Rican-American, etc. *See also* RACE CATEGORIES.

ethnography A type of anthropology that involves an in-depth analysis and description of a particular population or culture. A qualitative research approach that uses naturalistic, field-based, participant-observer techniques. *See* Perry Gilmore and Allan Glatthorn, *Children In and Out of School: Ethnography and Education* (Washington, D.C.: Center for Applied Linguistics, 1982); and Lawrence Angus, "Developments in Ethnographic Research in Education: From Interpretive to Critical Ethnography," *Journal of Research and Development in Education* (Fall 1986).

For an extensive bibliography of ethnographic research related to education *see* John H. Chilcott, "Where Are You Coming From and Where Are You Going? The Reporting of Ethnographic Research," *American Educational Research Journal* (Summer 1987). For a specific ethnographic study of school culture *see* Stuart B. Palonsky, *900 Shows A Year: A Look at Teaching from the Teacher's Side of the Desk* (New York: Random House, 1986).

evaluation   The use of research techniques to measure the degree to which identified objectives have been achieved in a program—in particular, a program's use of its resources and its operations, and/or its impact on the conditions it seeks to change. Evaluation is conducted for the purpose of determining if changes in a program will improve its effectiveness. There are three major types of evaluation: outcome (or impact), process (or performance) and input (or administrative).

See Richard M. Wolf, *Evaluation in Education: Foundations of Competency Assessment and Program Review* (New York: Holt, Rinehart and Winston, 1979); Ernest R. House, ed., *New Directions in Educational Evaluation* (Philadelphia: Falmer Press, 1986).

evaluation, administrative   Also STRUCTURAL EVALUATION and INPUT EVALUATION. One form of evaluation which measures resources utilized in relation to outcome achieved. One example of an administrative evaluation might be whether or not an organization successfully recruited and trained staff to conduct a new program in a reasonable period of time after receiving a grant. *See also* EVALUATION and HIERARCHY OF OBJECTIVES.

evaluation, adversary   A mode of evaluation that parallels the adversary system in law; two evaluators (or teams of evaluators) defend or attack a program before an impartial arbiter who makes the final decision on the merits of the program. *See* Marilyn Kourilsky, "An Adversary Model For Educational Evaluation," *Evaluation Comment* (June 1973); and Blaine R. Worthen and W. Todd Rogers, "Pitfalls and Potential of Adversary Evaluation," *Educational Leadership* (April 1980).

evaluation, process   *See* PROCESS EVALUATION.

evaluation, program   *See* PROGRAM EVALUATION.

evaluation, teacher   The appraisal of a teacher's performance in order to assist in professional growth when appropriate or to make administrative decisions regarding placement and retention. *See* Ben M. Harris, *Developmental Teacher Evaluation* (New York: Allyn and Bacon, 1986).

evaluation criterion   A standard for judging relative success or failure; a standard for measuring the degree of effectiveness or efficiency with which program or organizational objectives have been met. There are three major types of evaluation criteria: costable, quantifiable, and qualifiable. *See* Donald C. Manlove, ed., *K-12 School Evaluative Criteria* (Falls Church, Va: National Study of School Evaluation, 1983).

evaluation design   A statement of an evaluation's (1) purposes, objectives, and probable limitations; (2) conceptual approach and evaluation technique; (3) data collection, analysis, and interpretative methods; (4) work plan, including tasks and activities to be accomplished, schedule, and milestones; (5) interim reports (written and oral) and final report. Sometimes anticipated costs also are included. *See also* EVALUATION TECHNIQUE.

evaluation research   An organized analysis of specific policy or program options by conducting experiments, assessing their outcomes, and recommending whether the new concept should be broadly applied. *See* Carol H. Weiss, *Evaluation Research* (Englewood Cliffs, N.J.: Prentice-Hall, 1972); and William W. Cooley et al., *Evaluation Research in Education* (New York: John Wiley and Sons, 1976).

evaluation technique   One element in an evaluation design, usually used to mean the basic evaluation research approach that is to be used. For example, a two-group before-and-after comparison, or a single-group time series. *See also* EVALUATION DESIGN.

evaluation-level thinking   From Bloom's Taxonomy, a thinking or learning process involving the ability to make judgments on the basis of identified criteria. Contrast with KNOWLEDGE-LEVEL, COMPREHENSION-LEVEL, APPLICA-TION-LEVEL, ANALYSIS-LEVEL, SYNTHESIS-LEVEL. *See* BLOOM'S TAXONOMY.

evening college   The division of an institution offering a program of college-level study in late afternoon or evening, intended primarily for adults who are working (but also servicing daytime students) and usually under a separate administrative unit.

evening student   A student who attends the majority of his classes during the evening hours, as defined by the institution.

evergreen contract   An agreement that automatically renews itself annually unless one side gives advance notice to the other side that it will end.

ex officio   Latin phrase, "by virtue of his office." Many individuals hold positions on boards, commissions, advisory groups, or councils because of an office that they currently occupy. For example, the mayor of a city may be an *ex officio* member of the board of directors of a mental health center in his or her city.

exceptional children   Children who, because of certain atypical characteristics, have been identified by professionally qualified personnel as requiring special educational planning and services, whether or not such services are available. In general, the term "exceptional children" considers exceptionality on the basis of: (a) physical, health, or sensory handicap; (b) emotional handicap or behavioral problem; and (c) observable exceptionality in mental ability, i.e., mentally gifted and mentally retarded. Some exceptional children have more than one type of exceptionality.
   See Phillip S. Strain et al., *Teaching Exceptional Children: Assessing and Modifying Social Behavior* (New York: Academic Press, 1976); and Daniel P. Hallahan and James M. Kauffman, *Exceptional Children: Introduction to Special Education* (Englewood Cliffs, N.J.: Prentice-Hall, 1978).

exceptional students   Exceptional children, and adults identified as exceptional, receiving instruction in a program of special education. *See also* SPECIAL EDUCATION.

exceptionality   A physical, health, sensory, mental, psychological, or proficiency characteristic by which qualified professional personnel identify individuals as differing significantly from others in their age group.

excess cost   An educational financing term that refers to those actual and direct costs for an education program that exceed the standard funding base.

excess membership in public schools   Commonly referred to as "overcrowding." Membership in excess of the normal student capacity of accessible, publicly-owned school plants in use. This includes any public school students housed in nonpublicly-owned quarters or makeshift or improvised facilities as well as those who are in excess of the normal capacity in permanent, publicly-owned school plants.

excess policy   Insurance that pays only for losses greater than those covered by another policy.

exchange student   A student who completes a portion of his or her formal education enrolled in a program of study at a school in another country and earns credit at the "home" school.

exchange teacher   A teacher who spends a period of time at an educational institution in another country or in another setting under a formal program that involves teaching, study, or research. Frequently, two or more countries enter into agreements for actual "exchange" of teaching personnel. *See* Richard W. Breslin and Paul Pederson, *Cross-Cultural Orientation Programs* (New York: Gardner Press, 1976).

executive   1. Any of the highest managers in an organization. 2. That branch of government concerned with the implementation of the policies and laws created by a legislature.

executive administration services   Activities associated with the overall general administrative or executive responsibility of, for example, an entire local education agency.

executive committee   A standing committee of a board of directors, usually comprised of the board's elected officers. The functions and authority of executive committees vary widely among organizations. Some executive committees serve the function of the board of directors between board meetings; they have full authority to make binding decisions for the board on a broad range of issues. Some executive committees serve as the president or executive director's "kitchen cabinet." Other executive committees are restricted to quasi-housekeeping functions like creating board meeting agendas and recommending committee appointments. *See also* COMMITTEE.

Executive Educator, The   A monthly magazine published and distributed nationwide by the National School Board Association. It offers articles and reports of general interest to school administrators. Subscription and editorial address:

> *The Executive Educator*
> 1680 Duke Street
> Alexandria, VA 22314

executive officer   A staff member assigned to manage and direct an administrative program of the school system, and who has also been delegated administrative authority to direct the work of other staff members in the administrative program.

executive order   Any rule, regulation, or directive issued by a chief executive authority.

executive oversight   The total of the processes by which an executive attempts to exercise control and direction of the organization and to hold individual managers responsible for the implementation of their programs.

executive session Any meeting of a board, commission, or legislative group or subgroup, specifically called, that is not open to the public.

exempt Not included; not obligated to pay taxes on. For example, exempt income.

exempt activities Activities of a tax-exempt organization that will not jeopardize its tax-exempt status.

exempt employees Employees who, because of their administrative, professional, or executive status, are not covered by the overtime provisions of the Fair Labor Standards Act. In consequence, their employing organizations are not legally required to pay them for overtime work.

exempt organization A general term for an organization that is not required to pay federal income tax. Typically, an organization that is exempt under federal law is also exempt under state and local laws.

exempted child A child of compulsory school attendance age who is not required to attend school for any reason other than there being no program that meets his or her special educational need.

exemption from school activities See RESTRICTION ON SCHOOL ACTIVITIES.

expectancy level A level of anticipated achievement or performance that educators frequently assume or establish for an individual student or group of students.

expedited arbitration Because conventional arbitration is frequently so time-consuming and expensive, this new streamlined process is being increasingly incorporated into union contracts in an effort to cut down the backlog of grievance cases. In 1971, in response to the concern of parties over rising costs and delays in grievance arbitration, the Labor-Management Committee of the American Arbitration Association recommended the establishment of expedited procedures, under which cases could be scheduled promptly and awards rendered no later than five days after the hearings. In return for giving up certain features of traditional labor arbitration (such as transcripts, briefs, and extensive opinions), the parties utilizing simplified procedures can get quick decisions and realize certain cost savings. While the term "expedited arbitration" can be applied to any "fast" method of resolving disputes through the use of an arbitrator, it is usually characterized by on-site hearings and the minimal involvement of the hierarchies of both union and management. For details of the technique, see Lawrence Stessin, "Expedited Arbitration: Less Grief Over Grievances," *Harvard Business Review* (January-February 1977).

expenditures The actual spending of money as distinguished from the appropriation of it. Expenditures are made by the disbursing officers of a government; appropriations are made only by a legislature. The two are rarely identical; in any fiscal year expenditures may represent money appropriated one, two, or more years previously.

expense account The advance or reimbursement of monies to an employee or a volunteer who incurs expenses in the ordinary course of the organization's operations.

expense center See COST CENTER.

experience charts A method that is sometimes used to assist or augment

AVERAGE ESTIMATED EXPENDITURE BY STATES ON TEACHERS AND PUPILS (1986-1987)

State	Per Pupil	Salaries	State	Per Pupil	Salaries
Alabama	$2,610	$23,500	Montana	4,070	23,206
Alaska	8,842	43,970	Nebraska	3,437	23,063
Arizona	2,784	26,280	Nevada	3,768	26,030
Arkansas	2,795	19,951	New Hampshire	3,386	21,869
California	3,751	31,170	New Jersey	6,120	28,927
Colorado	4,129	27,388	New Mexico	3,537	23,977
Connecticut	5,552	28,902	New York	6,299	32,620
Delaware	4,776	27,467	North Carolina	3,473	23,775
Dist. of Columbia	5,349	33,797	North Dakota	3,209	21,848
Florida	4,056	23,785	Ohio	3,769	26,317
Georgia	3,167	24,200	Oklahoma	2,701	22,060
Hawaii	4,372	26,815	Oregon	4,236	26,800
Idaho	2,555	21,469	Pennsylvania	4,752	27,429
Illinois	3,980	28,430	Rhode Island	4,574	31,079
Indiana	3,379	25,684	South Carolina	3,005	23,039
Iowa	3,740	22,603	South Dakota	3,190	18,781
Kansas	4,137	23,550	Tennessee	2,842	22,720
Kentucky	3,107	22,612	Texas	3,584	25,308
Louisiana	3,237	21,280	Utah	2,455	23,374
Maine	3,650	21,257	Vermont	4,459	21,835
Maryland	4,659	28,700	Virginia	3,809	25,473
Massachusetts	4,856	28,410	Washington	3,808	27,527
Michigan	3,954	31,500	West Virginia	2,959	21,446
Minnesota	4,241	29,140	Wisconsin	4,701	28,206
Mississippi	2,534	19,575	Wyoming	6,229	27,708
Missouri	3,345	23,468	U.S. average	3,970	26,704

Source: National Education Association

reading instruction at the elementary level whereby the teacher records in an easily displayed chart format the dictated stories or experiences of students in the class.

experience rating   Insurance term that refers to a review of a previous year's group claims experience in order to establish premium rates for the following year.

experiment   In educational research, a situation in which one or more factors are systematically varied according to some pre-conceived plan in order to determine the effects of the variation.

Experiment in International Living
A cultural exchange program through which an individual or groups of students from the United States travel to a foreign country (or foreign students travel to the United States) where each student lives for up to a semester with a host family and participates in intensive cultural and language study.

Experiment in International Living
Kipling Road
Brattleboro, VT 05301
(802) 257-7751

experimental group   A group in a research design that is exposed to the treatment or manipulation called for in that design. *See* John Joseph Kennedy, *An Introduction to the Design and Analysis of Experiments in Education and Psychology* (Washington, D.C.: University Press of America, 1978).

experimental research   A form of scientific investigation undertaken to answer the question "what might be." The investigator manipulates and controls one or more variables (the independent variables) and observes other variables (the dependent variables) to see if there are changes concomitant to the manipulations of the independent variables.

expiration date   Time established in a contract or by a collective bargaining agreement for the agreement to terminate.

exploitation of children   1. Involving a child in illegal or immoral activities for the benefit of a parent or caretaker. This could include child pornography, child prostitution, sexual abuse, or forcing a child to steal. 2. Forcing workloads on a child in or outside the home so as to interfere with the health, education, and well-being of the child.

exploratory vocational education courses   Vocational courses that provide an introduction to, or overview of, a particular subject area. For example, Typing I is often considered an exploratory course while Typing II is classified as an occupational course.

expository learning   1. A teaching approach that starts with the presentation of a concept and then allows students to apply the concept to specific situations. 2. Deductive learning. Contrast with DISCOVERY LEARNING. *See* John D.W. Andrews, "Discovery and Expository Learning Compared: Their Effects on Independent and Dependent Students," *Journal of Educational Research* (November/December 1984).

expulsion   The action, taken by school authorities, compelling a student to withdraw from school for reasons such as extreme misbehavior, incorrigibility, or unsatisfactory achievement or progress in school work. *See also* SUSPENSION.

extended school day   The part of the calendar day, either preceeding or following the daily session, when school-related activities and recreation are provided pupils by the school.

extended school year   The provision of educational programs beyond the minimum number of school days mandated by school law. An extended school year is often referred to as "summer school." If a school district chooses to provide extended year programs for non-handicapped students, it must not deny such services for handicapped students. Furthermore, according to the federal courts' interpretation, in *Yaris v. Special School District of St. Louis County* (550 F. Supp. 545, E.D. Mo. 1983) of the Education for All Handicapped Children Act of 1975 (P.L. 94-142), schools are required to provide extended school year services for students who need them. Need is established on an individual basis according to the degree of regression, over the summer months, that a handicapped student may experience without the provision of services. States and local school districts may develop their own criteria for establishing need. While they are not mandated to provide extended year programs, they must not have policies that preclude such an option.

extended secondary school
See COMMUNITY COLLEGE.

extended-day session   A school day with separate times for different groups of pupils to start and end their sessions in the same school plant. For example, high school juniors and seniors begin their session at 7:30 a.m. and the freshmen and sophomores begin their session at 8:30 a.m., the session for juniors and seniors ending one hour prior to the time the session ends for the freshmen and sophomores.

extension agent   An individual who represents a college, university, or government agency and demonstrates operational techniques, teaches groups about valuable information, or trains individuals or groups in new skills. Historically, extension agents became best known through their use by the U.S. Department of Agriculture.

extension work   Generally, instructional activities other than those connected with the instruction of pupils on the campus. Extension work includes correspondence study, classes for part-time pupils off the campus or at unusual hours on the campus, and similar instructional arrangements.

external audit   See AUDIT.

external equity   Also internal equity. A measure of the justice of an employee's wages when the compensation for his/her position is compared to the labor market as a whole within a region, profession, or industry. *Internal equity* is a measure of the justice of an employee's wages when the compensation for his/her position is compared to similar positions within the same organization.

external evaluation   An evaluation conducted by individuals who are not directly involved in the process, procedure, or program being evaluated.

external services   Services provided to any agency, institution, organization, or individual by a state education agency.

externalities   See SPILLOVER EFFECTS/EXTERNALITIES.

extinction   In behavioral terminology, the process of eliminating a behavior by ignoring it; the reduction in the frequency of a behavior by removing whatever reinforcing contingencies are maintaining it.

extinction burst   A phenomenon that occurs in behavior modification when an attempt is made to eliminate a behavior by ignoring it (*see* EXTINCTION). Initially the frequency or intensity of the behavior may increase markedly as the individual attempts to elicit the reinforcer that previously maintained the behavior.

extraclass activities   Also called extracurricular or COCURRICULAR ACTIVITIES. Activities that are planned by the school and are a part of the sanctioned school program but that are separate from traditional classroom coursework. Examples include musical groups, drama clubs, athletic teams, school government, and publications.

extrinsic motivation   Motivation that comes from rewards external to oneself; the desire to learn or accomplish a task due to something other than inner satisfaction derived from the worthiness of the task itself. Contrast with INTRINSIC MOTIVATION.

F

face amount   In life insurance, the amount stated on the front of the policy that is payable upon the death of the insured. The actual amount payable to the beneficiary may differ according to the policy's specific provisions, such as double indemnity or subsequent riders.

face validity   Also called FAITH VALIDITY. Measure of the degree to which a test appears to be valid. While this is the most superficial kind of validity, it may contribute significantly to the legitimacy of the test in the eyes of the candidates (an important consideration in avoiding legal challenges).

face value   As applied to securities, the amount of the liability stated in the security document.

facilitator   An individual who serves as a catalyst or informal mediator, usually in an organizational or program development effort, in order to improve or maximize the interactions and interpersonal relationships of a group.

facility   1. A piece of land, a building site, a building, or part of a building. 2. In general usage, something designed, built, or installed to serve a specific function affording a convenience or service. In practice, *facility* usually means working space in a building. A leased facility often is an allowable grant cost, and the effective lease costs of facilities usually are allowable for calculating in-kind match. *See also* COSTS, ALLOWABLE and GRANT.

facsimile   Exact copy; for example, facsimile signatures are signatures mechanically imprinted on checks, stock certificates, and bonds. These signatures can be imprinted on checks with checkwriting machines.

fact sheet   Informational piece used in media relations and development. A fact sheet provides a concise statement (not more than one typed page) about an organization or a project. For example, a fact sheet might include statements of purpose, students or clientele served, uniqueness, key staff members and board members, and contact person(s). *See also*:
DEVELOPMENT
MEDIA RELATIONS
PUBLIC RELATIONS

factfinding   In labor relations, an impartial review of the issues in a dispute by a specially appointed third party, whether it be a single individual, panel, or board. The factfinder holds formal or informal hearings and submits a report to the parties involved. The factfinder's report, usually considered advisory, may contain specific recommendations.

factor analysis   Any of several methods of analyzing the inter-correlations among test scores or other sets of variables.

faculty   1. The teaching staff of a school. 2. The ability, capacity, or skill to do something. 3. The subdivision of a teaching staff in a high school or college; for example, the social studies faculty, the business faculty, or the English faculty.

faculty meeting   1. An official gathering of the teaching staff of a building or of any subdivision of the school district, usually for administrative purposes. 2. A formal meeting of the faculty from a given department (e.g., English, mathematics, or home economics).

failing grade   A letter grade or numerical evaluation of work in a course

190

that is below the minimum grade needed for the course credits to be counted toward graduation.

failure rate   The percentage of students who do not achieve a set criterion for passing on an examination or who do not satisfactorily complete a course or program of study.

Fair Employment Practice Commission (FEPC)   A generic term for any state or local government agency responsible for administering and enforcing laws prohibiting employment discrimination because of race, color, sex, religion, national origin, or other factors.

fair employment practice laws All government requirements designed to prohibit discrimination in the various aspects of employment. *See* James S. Russell, "A Review of Fair Employment Cases in the Field of Training," *Personnel Psychology* (Summer 1984).

Fair Labor Standards Act (FLSA) Also called Wages and Hours Act; federal statute of 1938 that, as amended, establishes minimum wage, overtime pay, equal pay, recordkeeping, and child labor standards affecting more than 50,000,000 full-time and part-time workers. *See also GARCIA V. SAN ANTONIO METROPOLITAN TRANSIT AUTHORITY.*

fair representation   *See* DUTY OF FAIR REPRESENTATION.

fair use   Using copyrighted material in such a way as not to infringe upon the copyright holder's rights to payment for use of the material. The concept of fair use allows for quoting small excerpts from and photocopying small portions of copyrighted works. It is definitely not fair use to make multiple copies of copyrighted materials for classroom use. Permission should be sought from the publisher.

fair-share agreement   An arrangement whereby both the employer and the union agree that employees are not obligated to join the union, but that all employees must pay the union a prorated share of bargaining costs as a condition of employment.

false negative   Any incidence whereby an individual, who is in fact qualified or identifiable, is excluded or *not* identified by a test or some other screening criteria.

false positive   Any incidence whereby an individual, who is in fact unqualified or who does not meet some identification criteria, is selected or identified inappropriately by a test or some other screening criteria.

family   1. A unit consisting of a head of household and one or more additional individuals who are related in some manner (most often by genetic connection). 2. A group of people who share common ancestry. *See* NUCLEAR FAMILY.

Family Educational Rights and Privacy Act   *See* BUCKLEY AMENDMENT.

family foundation   Foundation established by, controlled by, and usually supported by one family. Most family foundations are small and target their funds on local charitable organizations that deal with favored causes. *See also* FOUNDATION and PRIVATE FOUNDATION.

family resource education   A part of a home economics curriculum, usually at the secondary level, that focuses on all aspects of home and family management, including consumerism, parenthood, financial planning, and housekeeping. *See* Ruth E. Deacon and Francille M. Firebaugh, *Family Resource Management: Principles and Applications* (Boston: Allyn and Bacon, 1980).

family-expense policy   Health insurance policy that insures both the individual policyholder and his or her immediate dependents (usually spouse and children).

family-life education   A term that is often used in schools for what is more commonly referred to as sex education; a euphemism for sex education.

FAPE   See FREE APPROPRIATE PUBLIC EDUCATION.

farsightedness   Hyperopia or poor vision at close range. In young school children a common symptom is fatigue.

FASB   See FINANCIAL ACCOUNTING STANDARDS BOARD.

feasibility study   A preliminary project that is undertaken to determine whether a new system or program is practical and/or likely to be successful.

federal aid for education   Any grant made by the federal government for the support of education. See also PUBLIC GRANT.

federal assistance programs Any of the large variety of federal programs available to state and local governments, including counties, cities, metropolitan and regional governments; schools, colleges, and universities; health care institutions; nonprofit and for-profit organizations; and individuals and families. Current federal assistance programs are listed in the annual Catalogue of Federal Domestic Assistance.

federal control   The usurping of local and state decision-making authority by the federal government because of the provision of financial assistance and the rules and regulations that accompany it. This tendency is feared and resisted in education because of the constitutional vesting of authority for education at the state level and the tradition of local control of school functions.

Federal Emergency Management Agency (FEMA)   The agency, established by Reorganization Plan No. 3 of 1978, that plans for and coordinates emergency preparedness and response for all levels of government and for all kinds of emergencies—natural, man-made, and nuclear. This is the organization that decides what the various governments should be doing after a nuclear war or after a major flood. See Peter J. May, "FEMA's Role in Emergency Management: Examining Recent Experience," Public Administration Review (January 1985).

FEMA
500 C Street, N.W.
Washington, DC 20472
(202) 646-4600

Federal Management Circulars (FMC)   And OFFICE OF MANAGEMENT AND BUDGET CIRCULARS (OMB). Two extremely important series of management guidelines that define federal government requirements for grantees and contractors. FMCs are issued by the Office of Federal Management Policy and the OMB circulars, obviously, by the Office of Management and Budget. Each FMC and OMB circular addresses a specific topical area, for example, Cost Sharing of Federal Research or Coordinating Indirect Cost Rates.

Federal Mediation and Conciliation Service (FMCS)   Body created by the Labor-Management Relations (Taft-Hartley) Act of 1947 as an independent agency of the federal government. FMCS helps prevent disruptions in the flow of interstate commerce caused by labor-management disputes by providing mediators to assist disputing parties in the resolution of their differences. FMCS can intervene on its own motion or by invitation of either side in a dispute. Mediators have no law enforcement authority and rely wholly on persuasive techniques. FMCS also helps provide qualified third-party neutrals as factfinders or arbitrators.

Federal Mediation and Conciliation
    Service
2100 K Street, N.W.
Washington, DC 20427
(202) 653-5290

Federal Register   A daily publication that is the medium for making available to the public federal agency regulations and other legal documents of the executive branch. These documents cover a wide range of government activities—education, environmental protection, consumer product safety, food and drug standards, occupational health and safety, and many more areas of concern to the public. Perhaps more important, the *Federal Register* includes proposed changes in regulated areas. Each proposed change published carries an invitation for any citizen or group to participate in the consideration of the proposed regulation through the submission of written data, views, or arguments, and sometimes by oral presentations. The *Federal Register* also publishes requests for proposals and applications outlining the procedures by which agencies and organizations can apply for federal assistance under specified priorities.

federal revenue   Revenue provided by the federal government. Expenditures made with this revenue should be identifiable as federally supported expenditures.

fee   A payment, charge, or compensation for services (other than instruction), for privileges, or for the use of equipment, books, or other goods.

feedback   Information provided by another person or by the environment in response to a particular set of behaviors that helps to shape future behavior or actions. In education, grading systems are a common form of feedback.

feedback learning   An important underlying concept of behaviorism that holds that an individual learns as a result of experiencing the consequences of his or her behavior.

feedback loop   A part of a program planning and evaluation design that includes procedures for a continuous flow of information about the consequences or results of steps in implementation. This information is used to correct or redesign the plan in process.

feeder account   Those budgeted accounts whose resources are available only for transfer to other specified accounts.

feeder group   In larger school districts, the elementary schools and middle or junior high schools that are included in the geographic attendance area of one of the high schools.

Feinberg law   A law passed in New York in 1949 that allowed schools to disqualify members of ''subversive organizations'' from teaching in the public schools. The law was upheld in the U.S. Supreme Court in 1952 in *ADLER V. BOARD OF EDUCATION*, 342 U.S. 485, but was later reversed by the same court in *KEYISHIAN V. BOARD OF REGENTS*, 385 U.S. 589 (1967).

Feingold diet   A restrictive diet popularized by Dr. Ben F. Feingold, a California allergist, for the treatment of hyperactivity in children. The diet eliminates all artificial food colorings and flavorings and limits the use of other natural food substances, such as sugar and salicylates. *See* Ben F. Feingold, *Why Your Child Is Hyperactive* (New York: Random House, 1975).

fellow servant doctrine　The common-law concept that an employer should not be held responsible for an accident to an employee if the accident resulted from the negligence of another employee.

fellowship　A financial award, usually on the basis of merit rather than need, made to support the educational expenses of a student, primarily at the graduate level.

FEMA　*See* FEDERAL EMERGENCY MANAGEMENT AGENCY.

FEPC　*See* FAIR EMPLOYMENT PRACTICE COMMISSION.

Fernald method　A multisensory approach to remedial reading instruction that includes techniques such as tracing words, speaking aloud while tracing or copying, and the utilization of high-interest, learner generated vocabulary. For an early description of this method which has since been widely used and adapted, *see* Grace Fernald, *Remedial Techniques in Basic School Subjects* (New York: McGraw-Hill, 1943).

fidelity bond　Insurance on a person against that person's dishonesty; a form of bonding, similar to insurance protection or against embezzlement. Fidelity bonding has two primary advantages: the organization is able to recover (up to) the amount of money embezzled; and fidelity bonding serves as a preventive measure against embezzlement by employees and volunteers.

fiduciary　A person who manages money or property for others. Anyone

who has discretionary authority or responsibility for the administration of a pension plan is a fiduciary. *See* Tamar Frankel, "Fiduciary Law," *California Law Review* (May 1983).

field building　An athletic facility used primarily for housing dressing rooms, shower, and toilet facilities. It may contain additional facilities, such as sleeping quarters for visiting teams.

field day　A planned school activity where students come together from one or more schools for the purpose of competing in outdoor athletic events, usually track and field.

field experience education　A part of a student's formal educational program that occurs off school grounds and that may or may not be directly supervised by school personnel. *See* John Duley, ed., *Implementing Field Experience Education* (San Francisco: Jossey-Bass, 1974).

field house　A school facility that provides a large, unobstructed, indoor space suitable for a variety of sports and other activities.

field test　Preliminary utilization of new materials or a new methodology in a small area, that is supposedly representative of the larger intended population, in order to assess effectiveness prior to full implementation.

field trip　An excursion by a group of school children under the direction of school staff that is usually related to some unit of study.

final mark　A grade, given to a pupil upon the completion of study in a course or subject-matter area of a self-contained class, that represents an evaluation of the work done for the entire course or area and is entered upon the permanent records of the pupil. *See also* MARK.

final offer arbitration   Also called last offer arbitration. Negotiating stratagem that has an arbitrator choose from among the disputing parties' final or last offers. Peter Feuille, in *Final Offer Arbitration: Concepts, Development, Techniques* (Chicago: International Personnel Management Association, 1975), describes its intended role in the collective bargaining process:

> Since the arbitrator will not be free to compromise between the parties' positions, the parties will be induced to develop ever more reasonable positions prior to the arbitrator's decision in the hope of winning the award. And, the theory goes, these mutual attempts to win neutral approval should result in the parties being so close together that they will create their own settlement. In other words, the final offer procedure was purposefully designed to contain the seeds of its own destruction.

For a case study, *see* Gary Long and Peter Feuille, "Final Offer Arbitration: 'Sudden Death' in Eugene," *Industrial and Labor Relations Review* (January 1974). *Also see* Angelo S. DeNisi and James B. Dworking, "Final-Offer Arbitration and the Naive Negotiator," *Industrial and Labor Relations Review* (October 1981).

finals   Examinations taken at the end of a term.

finance   1. The manipulation of money and credit; the fields of banking, taxes, insurance, and the money, foreign exchange, and investment markets. It is an integral part of management in all three sectors of the economy. 2. The art or science of obtaining and managing funds.

finance committee   A standing committee that is usually assigned responsibility for overseeing an organization's financial operations and status. The finance committee usually reviews financial statements with the staff prior to board of directors meetings; compares expenditures with budgets; questions certain expenditures and bookkeeping decisions; and advises the board to take (or not take) financially-related actions. Some finance committees are responsible for drafting and/or presenting budgets, whereas other organizations have separate budget committees. *See also* COMMITTEE.

financial ability   1. A measure of the capacity of a local school district to support public education based on a comparison of the total assessed valuation of the district to its Average Daily Membership (ADM). 2. An estimate of a state's capacity to support public education, derived by relating the personal income of state residents to the number of school-aged children in the state. 3. The personal income and resources of a family in order to determine its capacity to support the cost of educational or other services that may be partially or wholly subsidized by public programs or assistance.

financial accounting   The recording and reporting of activities and events affecting the money of an administrative unit and its program. Specifically, it is concerned: (1) with determining what accounting records are to be maintained, how they will be maintained, and the procedures, methods, and forms to be used; (2) with recording, classifying, and summarizing activities or events; (3) with analyzing and interpreting recorded data; and (4) with preparing and initialing reports and statements that reflect conditions as of a given date, the results of operations for a specific period, and the evaluation of the status and results of operations in terms of established objectives.

financial accounting services
Activities concerned with maintaining records of the financial operations and transactions of a school district, including such activities as accounting and interpreting financial transactions and account records.

Financial Accounting Standards Board (FASB)   A private organization that sets standards for financial accounting and reporting and promulgates generally accepted accounting principles. Its pronouncements are officially recognized as authoritative by the American Institute of Certified Public Accountants and the Securities and Exchange Commission.

financial administration
Activities involving the management of finances. Includes accounting, auditing, and budgeting; the supervision of finances; collection, custody, and disbursement of funds; administration of employee-retirement systems; debt and investment administration; and the like.

financial aid   See STUDENT FINANCIAL AID.

financial analysis   The process of extracting and studying information in financial statements for use in management decision-making.

financial audit   Determination of: (1) whether financial operations are properly conducted, (2) whether the financial reports of an audited entity are presented fairly, and (3) whether the entity has complied with applicable laws and regulations.

financial core member   Someone who pays a union's initiation fees and monthly dues, but does not actually join. Such employees are entitled to fair representation in collective bargaining and grievances by the union, but they have no right to political participation in its affairs. By the same token, however, the union has no disciplinary authority over them.

financial effort   A measure of the extent to which a local school district (or a state) expends money to support public education.

financial ratio   See RATIO and RATIO, ACCOUNTING.

financial statement, comparative
A financial statement that presents comparable information for more than one time period, to allow comparisons; for example, this year and last year, or this month and last month.

financial statements   Also financial reports. The two most common types of financial statements are the balance sheet and the operating statement (or profit-and-loss statement or activity statement). The operating statement or activity statement is a nonprofit organization's equivalent of a for-profit corporation's profit-and-loss statement. See also BALANCE SHEET and OPERATING STATEMENT.

fine arts   A general term for any works that provide for creative expression and aesthetic enjoyment. The fine arts curriculum of a school might include instruction in painting, sculpture, dance, or music. The distinctive feature of fine arts is the emphasis on aesthetic as opposed to practical value.

finger play   A form of creative drama that can be used as a teaching technique with young children. Finger movements are used to act out stories and feelings as well as to practice number and language concepts.

finger spelling   A form of communication, used primarily by individuals who are deaf, whereby words are spelled out using a different hand configuration for each letter of the alphabet.

finishing schools   A 19th-century phenomenon, somewhat offensive to educated 20th-century idealists, that endeavored to provide young women of the era (especially those of limited intellectual ambition) with the skills and accomplishments considered necessary to make them suitable marriage partners.

Fire Fighters Local Union No. 1784 v. Stotts 81 L.Ed. 483 (1984) The Supreme Court case that held that courts may not interfere with bona fide seniority systems to protect newly hired black employees from layoff. Writing for the majority, Justice Byron R. White said that the law permits remedies only for individuals who can prove they are "actual victims" of job discrimination, rather than groups of disadvantaged minorities who may not have suffered specific wrongs in a specific job situation. To back this holding, he cited a 1964 memorandum issued by sponsors of Title VII, which said "Title VII does not permit the ordering of racial quotas in business or unions." Justice White also said that it is "inappropriate to deny an innocent employee the benefit of seniority."

See Louis P. Britt, III, "Affirmative Action: Is There Life After Stotts?" *Personnel Administrator* (September 1984); and Robert N. Roberts, "The Public Law Litigation Model and *Memphis v. Stotts," Public Administration Review* (July-August 1985).

first-dollar coverage   Coverage under an insurance policy that begins with the first dollar of expense incurred by the insured for the covered benefits. Contrast with DEDUCTIBLE.

first-dollar responsibility   In the area of public human services, when a particular service may fall under the purview of more than one agency or organization, the entity that is held to have the primary obligation for providing or paying for the service to the extent of its liability. For example, under the Education for All Handicapped Children Act, schools have the first-dollar responsibility for providing any services that are identified as necessary and related to the education of a student who has been determined to be handicapped. Contrast with LAST DOLLAR RESPONSIBILITY.

first-professional degree   A degree that signifies completion of the academic requirements for beginning practice in a given profession, and is based on a program requiring at least two years of college work prior to entrance and a total of at least six academic years of college work to complete the degree program itself. First-professional degrees are awarded in fields such as dentistry (D.D.S. or D.M.D.), medicine (M.D.), optometry (O.D.), osteopathic medicine (D.O.), podiatry (Pod.D. or D.P.) or podiatric medicine (D.P.M.), veterinary medicine (D.V.M.), general law (LL.B. or J.D.), and general theological professions (B.D., M.Div., Rabbi, or other first-professional degree).

fiscal agent   A person or organization that serves as another's financial agent.

fiscal independence   Refers to a school district's complete and total authority over its business and financial affairs.

fiscal period   Any period at the end of which an agency determines its financial condition and the results of its operations and closes its books. It is usually a year, though not necessarily a calendar year. The most common fiscal period is from July 1 through June 30.

fiscal services   Activities involved with managing and conducting the fiscal operations of a school district. This service area includes budgeting, receiving and disbursing, financial accounting, payroll, internal auditing, and purchasing.

fiscal stress   *See* MANAGEMENT, CUTBACK.

fiscal year   A financial year. A fiscal year consists of 12 consecutive months that may start and end anytime during the calendar year. Some organizations select fiscal years to coincide with their program years and others with the time when officers take office. Many others use the calendar year as their fiscal year. The fiscal year should be established and formally incorporated in the organization's bylaws. The fiscal year is designated by the calendar year in which it ends (e.g., fiscal year 1987 is the fiscal year ending, for example, September 30, 1987).

five- or six-year high school   A secondary school served by one faculty organized under one principal, which includes more than four grades, is not divided on a junior and senior basis, and is not preceded by a junior high school in the same school system; sometimes called an "undivided high school."

five point scale   A commonly used procedure for rating level of performance in academic work beginning with a top grade of A and moving downward through B, C, D, and, ultimately, F, which signifies failure to live up to minimum expectations.

fixation   1. A strong attachment to a particular person, object, belief, or behavior pattern. 2. Maintaining a visual focus on an image, as in reading. 3. Getting "stuck" at a point in development, often psychosexually related.

fixed annuity   An annuity that provides constant, periodic dollar payments for its entire length.

fixed assets   *see* ASSETS.

fixed charges   Charges of a generally recurrent nature that are not readily allocated to other expenditure categories. They consist of such charges as: school board contributions to employee retirement, insurance and judgments, rental of land and building, and interest on current loans. They do not include payments to public school housing authorities or similar agencies.

fixed costs   *See* COST, FIXED.

fixed-benefit retirement plan   A retirement plan whose benefits consist of a fixed amount or fixed percentage.

Flanagan, Edward J. (1886-1948) The Catholic priest who founded Boys Town, an internationally known home and school for abandoned or neglected boys in Omaha, Nebraska. *See* BOYS TOWN.

Flanders Interaction Analysis A method of recording and analyzing teacher behavior in the classroom.

flannel board   A board covered with felt or other cloth that teachers use for displaying instructional materials, usually at the primary level.

flashcards   A commonly used aid for drill practice in word recognition or number facts. Each of a set of cards is imprinted with a single word or a single math computation (e.g., $3 + 5 = ?$) and the student is expected to respond to each card in turn either independently or with the assistance of a teacher.

Flast v. Cohen 392 U.S. 83 (1968) The Supreme Court case concerning the expenditure of federal funds for instructional purposes in religious schools under the Elementary and Secondary Education Act of 1965. The Court found that parties had standing to challenge these expenditures if they could show that: (1) they were taxpayers, and (2) the challenged enactment exceeded specific constitutional limitations imposed on the exercise of the congressional power to tax and spend.

See Boris I. Bittker, "The Case of the Fictitious Taxpayer: The Federal Taxpayer's Suit Twenty Years After *Flast v. Cohen,*" *University of Chicago Law Review* (Winter 1969).

flat grants   A means for distributing state funds to local school districts on the basis of a per unit (i.e., per pupil or per teacher) allocation.

flat organization   One whose structure has comparatively few levels. In contrast, a tall organization is one whose structure has many levels.

flat-benefit plan   Pension plan whose benefits are unrelated to earnings. Such a plan might provide a stipulated amount per month per year of service.

flexible rate mortgage   *See* ADJUSTABLE RATE MORTGAGE.

flexible scheduling   An organization for instruction allowing for varying class sizes within and among courses, and providing for instructional groups that meet at varying frequencies and for varying lengths of time and at varying times of the year. Compare to MODULAR SCHEDULING and YEAR-ROUND SCHOOL.

flexible working hours   *See* FLEX-TIME.

flex-time   Flexible work schedule in which workers can, within a prescribed band of time in the morning

and afternoon, start and finish work at their discretion as long as they complete the total number of hours required for a given period, usually a month. That is, the work day can vary from day to day in its length as well as in the time that it begins and ends. The morning and evening bands of time are often designated as "quiet time." Telephone calls and staff meetings are confined to "core time," which generally runs from midmorning to midafternoon. Time clocks or other mechanical controls for keeping track of the hours worked are usually a part of flex-time systems.

flip chart   A pad of very large sheets of paper (e.g., 2' x 3') that is typically hung on an easel and written upon as a visual aid during group instruction or brainstorming.

floating debt   Liabilities (except bonds) payable on demand or at an early date; for example, accounts payable, bank loans, notes, or warrants. *See also* CURRENT LIABILITIES.

floating holiday   A type of flexible work scheduling that can allow an employee to take time off for a holiday on a day of his or her choosing rather than on an officially designated date.

flowchart   Graphic representation of an analysis of, or solution to, a problem that uses symbols to indicate various operations, equipment, and data flow. *See also* PRECEDENCE DIAGRAM and PROJECT CONTROL CHART.

flow-through budget   A plan of financial operation for the handling of those funds that constitute neither a receipt nor an expenditure by a state department of education. Rather, such funds are distributed by the department (to local school districts) as an intermediary. Federal and state support funds are the most common examples of flow-through money.

FLSA   *See* FAIR LABOR STANDARDS ACT.

flunk   A term that is used to signify: (a) failure to meet minimum standards on an examination or in a course of study, or (b) flunking out, failing to maintain sufficient academic achievement to continue to be enrolled in a higher education institution.

FMCS   *See* FEDERAL MEDIATION AND CONCILIATION SERVICE.

Follow-through Program   A federal program developed primarily as an extension of Head Start programs to provide support for needy students in grades kindergarten through three.

follow-up study   Also longitudinal study. A study made of the experiences or status of former pupils, either for the purpose of assisting them in further adjustment or for securing information to help improve instruction or guidance for those still in school. In vocational education, this term refers to a research activity designed to determine what occupations are pursued by graduates and/or other former pupils in occupational programs, and how effective was their preparation in relationship to job requirements.

foods and nutrition   That part of a home economics curriculum that focuses on the use, preparation, availability, and value of various foods.

force field analysis   A method, based on the work of KURT LEWIN, for analyzing individual or organizational change. The model attributes human behavior to interaction with the environment and identifies two environmental forces that operate to keep an organism (or organization) in a state of equilibrium: *driving forces*, which promote change, and *restraining forces*, which resist change.

forced-choice instrument   A type of rating form that is made up of individual items, each of which requires a choice to be made of one out of several descriptors of the subject being rated.

Ford Foundation   A private philanthropic institution founded in 1936 that supports research and other activities often related to education.
Ford Foundation
320 E. 43rd St.
New York, NY 10017
(212) 573-5000

forensics   1. Public speaking or debating. 2. The study of formal debate. 3. The application of expert knowledge in a field to courtroom testimony (e.g., forensic medicine).

Form W-2   Also called W-2 Form and Wage and Tax Statement. Statement that must be provided to employees by their employers by the end of January of each year. Form W-2 shows earnings for the preceding year and various deductions. Employees must file one copy of their Form W-2 with their federal income tax returns and, in most states, with their state income tax returns.

Form W-4   A federal statement completed by an employee to declare a number of dependents for the purpose of determining the level of income tax to be withheld from regular wage earnings.

formal operational or formal operations   The final stage of cognitive development in children, postulated by Jean Piaget. This stage occurs between the ages of 11 years and 16 years and characterizes adult thought. Rational logic can be applied to all categories of problems, abstract as well as concrete, and children can think beyond phenomena or evidence that is readily perceived.

formal organization A social group whose structure and activities have been rationally organized and standardized, with definitely prescribed group rules, goals, and leaders.

formative evaluation Assessing a program or a product during its developmental or implementation stages. Contrast with SUMMATIVE EVALUATION.

former migratory child As defined for federal compensatory education programs, a child who, with the concurrence of his or her parents, is deemed to be a migratory child on the basis that he or she has been an interstate or intrastate migratory child but has ceased to migrate within the last five years and currently resides in an area where interstate and/or intrastate migratory children will be served. *See also* INTERSTATE MIGRATORY CHILD and INTRASTATE MIGRATORY CHILD.

forms control A set of procedures or a program for improving the use, work flow, storage, and disposition of forms.

formula funding Allocation of financial assistance to a school district on the basis of some predetermined criteria, such as number of students enrolled or census counts.

forty-five/fifteen plan A schedule for year-round schooling where students attend school for 45 days and are then on vacation for 15 days.

forum A public meeting at which topics are discussed by leaders and the audience. The original "forum" was the public meeting place of ancient Rome.

forward funding The practice of obligating funds in one fiscal year for programs that are to operate in a subsequent year.

foster grandparents Retired persons or senior citizens who provide nurturance or support on a paid or voluntary basis for children to whom they are not related. Schools often support a foster grandparent program during school hours for students who have special needs because of family neglect, a paucity of family resources, or handicapping conditions.

foster home A family home, other than the home of a natural parent, into which a child is placed for rearing without adoption. Often this is a temporary placement in which a child lives until he or she is able to return to the natural home.

foundation A general term that includes private and public organizations that have been established for charitable purposes. Foundations serve as important channels through which profits earned by corporations and individuals are distributed for the public benefit. Foundations also serve as informational clearinghouses about sources, needs, and new approaches to problems. The most important forms of foundation include independent foundations, corporate foundations, and community foundations.

F. Emerson Andrews, in his pioneering work, *Philanthropic Foundations* (1956), defined a foundation as "a nonprofit organization, with funds (usually from a single source, either an individual, a family, or a corporation) and program managed by its own trustees or directors, established to maintain or aid social, educational, charitable, religious, or other activities serving the common welfare, primarily through the making of grants."

See also:
COMMUNITY FOUNDATION
CORPORATE (OR COMPANY) FOUNDATION
FAMILY FOUNDATION
PRIVATE FOUNDATION

foundation, community *See* COMMUNITY FOUNDATION.

foundation, private *See* PRIVATE FOUNDATION.

Foundation Center, The An organization that collects, interprets, and reports data and information about foundations and the grants they award. It is not affiliated with any other organization (including foundations), and its information is considered to be highly trustworthy.

The Foundation Center
79 Fifth Avenue
New York, NY 10003
(212) 620-4230

Foundation Center National Data Book A publication of the Foundation Center that provides information (names, addresses, and finances) on all private foundations that are known to be active—large and small.

Foundation Center Source Book Profiles A reference document published by The Foundation Center that provides in-depth information about large foundations, their program preferences, previous grants awarded, and statistical profiles of recent granting histories. *See* FOUNDATION CENTER.

Foundation Directory, The The basic reference on foundations, published by The Foundation Center. It contains information about foundations with more than one million dollars in assets or that make more than $100,000 in annual grants.

Foundation for Exceptional Children An affiliate of the national Council for Exceptional Children (CEC) that was organized to promote research and innovations in special education and that works to protect the legal, educational, and human rights of children who are handicapped. *See* COUNCIL FOR EXCEPTIONAL CHILDREN.

Foundation Grants Index Annual A source of current information about recent grants made by (participating) larger foundations, including the grants' sizes, purposes, and recipients. *The Foundations Grants Index* is published in an annual, a bimonthly journal, and is available through *Comsearch Printouts*. *The Foundation Index* has several versions covering different time periods, ranging from the most recent months (inserted in the bi-monthly *Foundation News*) to the prior six years. Contact:

The Foundation Center
79 Fifth Avenue
New York, NY 10003

foundation program A system whereby state funds are used to supplement local or intermediate district funds in the support of education at the elementary and secondary levels. Such a program usually guarantees a "minimum foundation" of financial support from state funds regardless of the financial ability of the local or intermediate district to support education. The extent to which a foundation program equalizes the educational opportunity of pupils varies among the several states.

foundation school A private Jewish day school that offers a combined academic and religious educational program.

Fourteenth Amendment The basis for due process rights of students in public schools. The 14th Amendment to the U.S. Constitution states that no citizen may be denied the right to "life, liberty or property without due process of law" and the courts have defined public education as a substantial right for all citizens.

four-year high school A four-year secondary school immediately following the elementary school (as in an eight-four plan) or a middle school.

This includes four-year vocational and technical high schools.

Foxfire books A popular book series documenting rural traditions in Southern Appalachia. For the last in the series *see* Eliot Wigginton and Margie Bennett, *Foxfire 9* (Garden City, N.Y.: Anchor/Doubleday, 1986). *See also* Eliot Wigginton, *Sometimes a Shining Moment* (Garden City: Doubleday, 1986).

fraternal organization *See* HONORARY FRATERNAL ORGANIZATIONS IN EDUCATION.

fraternity A social or honorary organization usually associated with higher education. Social fraternities are open only to men and membership is by invitation, generally on the basis of social acceptability rather than academic qualifications. The female equivalent is called a "sorority."

Free Appropriate Public Education (FAPE) A basic provision of the Education for All Handicapped Children Act of 1975 (P.L. 94-142), it is defined in the law to mean "special education and related services which (a) have been provided at public expense, under public supervision and direction, and without charge, (b) meet the standard of the state educational agency, (c) include an appropriate preschool, elementary, or secondary school education in the state involved, and (d) are provided in conformity with the individualized education program."

free bonding capacity At any given time, the total amount of bonds in excess of existing obligations that a school district could issue under any circumstances if it were to reach its debt limit. *See also* BONDED DEBT and DEBT LIMIT.

free exercise clause That portion of the First Amendment to the U.S. Constitution that, together with the establishment clause of the First Amendment, is the basis for separation of church and state.

free rider One who does not belong to an organized group such as a union or a political party, but nevertheless benefits from its activities. For example, a worker in a given organization who does not belong to a union when most of the other workers do will receive all of the wage increases and fringe benefits bargained for by the union, but does not pay dues to the union; thus he or she "rides free."

free schools An alternative school movement that began in California in the late 1960s and that rejected more traditional authoritarian educational models.

Freedom of Information Act of 1966 The law that provides for making information held by federal agencies available to the public unless it comes within one of the specific categories of matters exempt from public disclosure. To locate specific agency regulations pertaining to freedom of information, consult the *Code of Federal Regulations* index under "Information Availability."

free-response test A technique used in psychological testing that places no restriction on the kind of response an individual is to make (so long as it relates to the situation presented).

frequency distribution A distribution of the frequencies with which any set of characteristics appear in a population.

freshman 1. A college student who has earned less than the required number of credit hours for completion of the first year of study. 2. A high school student in grade nine. 3. A college student in his or her first year of post-secondary study.

Freud, Sigmund (1856-1939) The founder of psychoanalysis whose theories have strongly influenced professional views on child development. His daughter, Anna Freud (born in 1895), did much work in the application of psychoanalytic theory to education.

Friend of Education Award   An annual honor bestowed by the National Education Association on an individual who is determined to have contributed significantly to the betterment of education.

fringe benefits   Compensation for work that is provided by an employer in addition to base salary, such as paid leave for sickness or vacations and contributions to retirement accounts or insurance premiums.

Froebel, Friedrich W.A. (1782-1852)   The German educator best known for formulating the concept of kindergarten ("garden of children"). *See* Robert B. Downs, *Friedrich Froebel* (Boston: Twayne, 1978).

frontage assessment   A tax to pay for improvements (such as sidewalks or sewer lines) that is charged in proportion to the frontage (number of feet bordering the road) of each property.

front-loaded   A labor agreement providing for a greater wage increase in its early period; for example, a three-year contract that provides for a 10 percent increase in the first year and four percent in each of the remaining two years. *See also* BACK-LOADED.

Frostig Program for the Development of Visual Perception Techniques developed by Marianne

Frostig for the remediation of eye-hand coordination and other perceptual-motor skills. The program includes primarily paper-pencil activities and materials such as drawing lines from one point to another or following mazes.

Frostig test   A group test of visual-perceptual skills developed by Marianne Frostig and designed to identify specific deficits in visual perception. *See* DEVELOPMENTAL TEST OF VISUAL PERCEPTION.

FTE   *See* FULL TIME EQUIVALENCY.

Fulbright Exchange Program The scholarly exchange program initially created by the Fulbright Act of 1946 and expanded by the Mutual Educational and Cultural Exchange Act of 1961 (the Fulbright-Hays Act, P.L. 87-256), which provides awards to help U.S. citizens, usually college professors, to study or teach in foreign countries. The program conversely provides support for foreign students or educators in the United States.

full coverage   Insurance that pays for every dollar of a loss with no maximum and no deductible amount.

full day of attendance   Attendance during a complete full-day school session or approved curtailed session. Attendance at a state-approved half-day session for kindergarten or prekindergarten also should be counted as a full day of attendance. An excused absence is generally counted as a day of attendance. *See also* SESSION and HALF DAY OF ATTENDANCE.

full funding   Also incremental funding. Providing budgetary resources to cover the total cost of a program or project at the time it is undertaken. Full funding differs from *incremental funding*, where a budget is established or provided for only a portion of total estimated obligations expected to be incurred during a single fiscal year. Full funding is generally discussed in terms of multiyear programs, whether or not obligations for the entire program are made in the first year.

full-day session A school session which contains at least the minimum number of hours recommended by a state education agency for a full day of attendance in a given elementary or secondary grade other than kindergarten or prekindergarten.

Fullilove v. Klutznick 448 U.S. 448 (1980) The Supreme Court case that held that Congress has the authority to use quotas to remedy past discrimination in government public works programs, reasoning that the 14th Amendment's requirement of equal protection means that groups historically denied this right may be given special treatment. *See* SET-ASIDES.

See Peter G. Kilgore, ''Racial Preferences in the Federal Grant Programs: Is There a Basis for Challenge After *Fullilove v. Klutznick?''* *Labor Law Journal* (May 1981).

full-state assumption (FSA) A policy proposal that total financial responsibility for public education be vested at the individual state level in order to reduce financial inequity among local school districts.

full-time equivalency (FTE) The amount of time for a less than full-time activity divided by the amount of time normally required in a corresponding full-time activity. Full-time equivalency usually is expressed as a decimal fraction to the nearest 10th.

full-time equivalency of assignment The amount of employed time normally required of a staff member to perform a less than full-time assignment divided by the amount of time normally required in performing a corresponding full-time assignment. Full-time equivalency of assignment usually is expressed as a decimal fraction to the nearest 10th.

full-time equivalent enrollment The equivalent number of full-time students in a college at an established census date, determined by dividing the assumed normal individual student load of credit hours into the total student credit hours as of that date.

full-time personnel School employees whose positions require them to be on the job on school days throughout the school year, or at least for the number of hours the schools in the district are in session.

full-time staff member A staff member whose total current assignments, regardless of their classification, require his or her services each working day for a number of hours at least equal to the number of hours of a regular working day.

full-time student A student who is carrying a full course load, as determined by a state, a local school system, or an institution. A college student is generally considered to be full-time when he or she carries at least 75 percent of a normal student load.

full-time workers Also part-time workers. According to the Bureau of Labor Statistics, those employed at least 35 hours a week. *Part-time workers* are those who work fewer hours.

full-tuition student A student— usually a nonresident of the geographic area served by a specified school, school system, or institution—for whom maximum allowable tuition is paid.

fully funded pension plan A pension plan whose assets are adequate to meet its obligations into the foreseeable future.

functional classification   A means of presenting budgeted income and expenditure data in terms of the principal purposes that programs are intended to serve. Each account is generally placed in the single function that best represents its major purpose, regardless of who administers the program. Functions are generally subdivided into narrower categories called *sub-functions*.

functional curriculum   An adapted course of study, usually for students who are handicapped, that is referenced to critical, basic skills that are required in adult life. For example, in a functional curriculum students might learn how to purchase food in a grocery store using a calculator, instead of practicing arithmetical computations on worksheets in the classroom.

functional expense reporting *See* BUDGETING, PERFORMANCE.

functional expenses, statement of A financial report that shows the allocation of line-item expenses to each of an organization's functions or programs.

functional skills   In special education, a skill, which is taught to a student, that is relevant to or necessary for general life management. The important question in determining whether a skill to be taught is functional or not is, "if the student does not learn to do this, will someone else have to do it for him or her?"

functionally illiterate   An adult who is unable to read, write, and compute sufficiently well to meet the requirements of adult life. For purposes of many adult/continuing education programs, this is considered to include adults who have not gone beyond the eighth grade or who cannot read, write,

or do arithmetic at or above an eighth grade level of performance. In the United States this term usually is applied also to foreign-born adults having limited ability to use the English language.

functus officio   Latin term that can be applied to an official who has fulfilled the duties of an office that has expired and who, in consequence, has no further formal authority. Arbitrators are said to be *functus officio* concerning a particular case after they have declared their awards on it.

See Israel Ben Scheiber "The Doctrine of Functus Officio with Particular Relation to Labor Arbitration," *Labor Law Journal* (October 1972).

fund   An accounting device established to control the receipt and disbursement of income from sources set aside to support specific activities or attain certain objectives; a sum of money set aside for a particular purpose.

fund, general   *See* GENERAL FUND.

fund, unrestricted   *See* GENERAL FUND.

fund accounting   The traditional accounting approach used by nonprofit and many public organizations. In essence, separate financial records are maintained on restricted funds or groups of restricted funds. The organization's financial statements include mini-financial statements for each. Fund accounting helps to ensure that restricted funds are used for their intended purposes, that grant and other donor restrictions are complied with, etc. *See also* ACCOUNTING CYCLE and FINANCIAL STATEMENTS.

fund accounts   All accounts necessary to set forth the financial operations and financial condition of a fund.

fund balance   The excess of the assets of a fund over its liabilities and reserves except in the case of funds subject to budgetary accounting where, prior to the end of a fiscal period, it represents the excess of the fund's assets and estimated revenues for the period over its liabilities, reserves, and appropriations for the period.

funded debt   Same as BONDED DEBT, which is the preferred term.

funded pension plan   Pension plan that provides for the periodic accumulation of money to meet the pension plan's obligations in future years.

fundraising   All activities that help create support for a nonprofit organization in the form of gifts, grants, contributions, and services. In addition to funds and services from individuals, corporations, groups, fraternal organizations, associations, foundations, and governments, fundraising also includes seeking intangible gifts that inspire confidence and enthusiasm and generate support for the nonprofit organization. Fundraising is the "action" part of development. *See also*:
DEVELOPMENT
DIRECT MAIL CAMPAIGN
DIRECT SOLICITATION
GRANT
SPECIAL EVENT

fundraising committee or development committee   The standing committee responsible for coordinating and controlling an organization's fundraising program, including such activities as its direct solicitations, special events, human resources, fundraising calendar. *See also* COMMITTEE.

fundraising event   *See* SPECIAL EVENT.

fundraising firm   A company that performs contractual fundraising services for nonprofit organizations. Examples of services include planning and organizing fundraising campaigns, developing promotional literature, training volunteers, and soliciting contributions.

fundraising plan   The document for coordinating a fundraising campaign or series of campaigns. A fundraising plan should consist of: (1) the overall fundraising goal; (2) possible sources (that is, potential targeted donors); (3) previous year's actual fundraising experience with the different possible sources; (4) this year's goal for each possible source; (5) the person responsible for each major activity and/or possible source; (6) the specific plan of action; and (7) a specific timetable. A well conceived fundraising plan can be updated relatively easily for use in subsequent years.

funds, current   *see* GENERAL FUND.

fungible   A description for things that are easily substituted for one another. For example, a grant is fungible when the recipient is able to use the grant monies for purposes other than those specified in the grant authorization.

Future Farmers of America (FFA) National organization of high school students who are preparing for future careers in agriculture or agriculturally related occupations. The organization was established in 1928, is headquartered in Alexandria, Virginia, and distributes a bimonthly publication, *The National Future Farmer*.
Future Farmers of America
Box 15160
5632 Mount Vernon Memorial Highway
Alexandria, VA 22309
(703) 360-3600

future funding   The source(s) and method(s) by which a program will be funded after the termination of a supporting grant.

Future Homemakers of America (FHA)   National organization founded in 1945 for high school students enrolled in home economics courses who may, or may not, be interested in pursuing a career in the home economics fields.

Future Homemakers of America
1910 Association Drive
Reston, VA 22305
(703) 476-4900

Future Teachers of America (FTA)
A now-defunct national organization for high school students, which was intended to generate interest in the pursuit of a career in teaching. The FTA was originally established by the National Education Association (NEA) in 1937, was renamed the Student Action for Education (SAE) division of the association in 1974, and relinquished national status in 1975 when its functions were delegated by the national association to state and local educational associations.

G

GAAP   *See* GENERALLY ACCEPTED ACCOUNTING PRINCIPLES.

GAAS   Generally accepted auditing standards, as established by the American Institute of Certified Public Accountants.

gain score   The comparison of pre- and post-test scores in order to measure the extent of benefit from a learning experience.

gainful employment   Employment in a recognized occupation for which persons normally receive a wage, salary, fee, or profit.

Gallaudet, Thomas Hopkins (1787-1851)   A minister from New England who established the first residential "school for the deaf" in the United States in 1817. Gallaudet, while he was a student at Andover Theological Seminary in New Hampshire, was frustrated in his attempts to educate a child with deafness. He traveled to Europe to learn about education for students who were deaf and brought the European techniques back to America. The European approach involved the teaching of manual communication (i.e., sign language and fingerspelling) rather than the oral method that had been used elsewhere in the United States. The school Gallaudet founded was located in Hartford, Connecticut, and is now known as the American School for the Deaf. Gallaudet College, located in Washington, D.C., and the only college in the world specifically for students who are hearing handicapped, was named in his honor.

Gallaudet College   The only liberal arts college in the world that is specifically designed for students who are deaf. It is located in Washington, D.C., and is partially subsidized by the federal government.

game theory   A complex mathematical system for problem-solving that utilizes a format of involving two or more players in a process of identifying, selecting, and testing possible strategies in conflict situations.

gaming simulation   A model of reality with dynamic parts that can be manipulated to teach the manipulator(s) how to better cope with the represented processes in real life.

gang   A colloquial term for a group of students who have established a group identity, including a sense of cohesion and an acknowledged internal hierarchy and set of implicit rules. Often has a negative connotation, as those "gangs" that are most visible in school tend to be those that violate school norms.

Gantt chart   A horizontal bar graph used for comparing planned and completed activities or performance over a period of time.

Garcia v. San Antonio Metropolitan Transit Authority 83 L.Ed. 2nd 1016 (1985)   The Supreme Court case that held that the application of the minimum wage and overtime requirements of the Fair Labor Standards Act to state public employment does not violate any constitutional provision. This reversed *National League of Cities v. Usery*, 426 U. S. 833 (1976), which held that the 10th Amendment prohibited the federal government from establishing wages and hours for state employees. In *Garcia*, the Court held that the states would have to ask Congress for new legislation if they wanted to avoid having federal wage and overtime standards applied to them.

See Martha A. Field, *"Garcia v. San Antonio Metropolitan Transit Authority:* The Demise of a Misguided Doctrine," *Harvard Law Review* (November 1985); and S. Kenneth Howard, "A Message From *Garcia,"* *Public Administration Review* (Special Issue, November 1985).

Gardner v. Broderick 392 U.S. 273 (1968)   And companion case, *Uniformed Sanitation Men's Association v. Commissioner of Sanitation of the City of New York*, 392 U.S. 280 (1968). The Supreme Court decisions holding the dismissals of public employees—for refusing to waive immunity from prosecution or refusing to testify at grand jury hearings—to be unconstitutional.

Garner v. Board of Public Works of Los Angeles 341 U.S. 716 (1951) The Supreme Court case upholding the constitutionality of a municipal loyalty oath requiring employees to disclose whether they were or ever had been members of the Communist Party and to take an oath to the effect that, for five years prior to the effective date of the ordinance, they had not advocated the overthrow of the government by force or belonged to any organization so advocating. *See also* LOYALTY OATH.

garnishment   Any legal or equitable procedure through which the earnings of any individual are required to be withheld for the payment of any debt. Most garnishments are made by court order.

Garrity v. New Jersey 385 U.S. 493 (1967)   The Supreme Court case holding that a New Jersey practice of dismissing public employees who relied upon the 5th Amendment privilege

against self-incrimination was unconstitutional.

Gary Plan   An early example of the PLATOON PLAN.

gatekeeper function   The control of access to certain programs or privileges by the establishment of particular criteria that must be met in order to qualify.

Gates, Arthur (1890-1972)   An educator and a psychologist who is best known for his development of diagnostic tests, particularly in the area of reading, such as the Gates-MacGinitie Reading Test and the Gates-MacGinitie Reading Readiness Test.

Gates-MacGinitie Reading Tests A norm-referenced screening instrument that assesses skill development in reading from grades kindergarten to 12. Vocabulary, comprehension, speed, and accuracy are all assessed. It is published by:

Teachers College Press
1234 Amsterdam Avenue
New York, NY 10027

GED   *See* GENERAL EQUIVALENCY DIPLOMA.

General Accounting Office (GAO)   A support agency created by the Budget and Accounting Act of 1921 to audit federal government expenditures and assist Congress with its legislative oversight responsibilities. The GAO is directed by the Comptroller General of the United States, who is appointed by the President, with the advice and consent of the Senate, for a term of 15 years. While the GAO originally confined itself to auditing financial records to see that funds were properly spent, since the 1960s it has redefined its mission to include overall PROGRAM EVALUATION.

See Erasmus H. Kloman, ed., *Cases in Accountability: The Work of the GAO* (Boulder, Colo.: Westview Press, 1979); and Frederick C. Mosher, *The GAO: The Quest for Accountability* (Boulder, Colo.: Westview Press, 1979).
General Accounting Office
441 G Street, N.W.
Washington, DC 20548
(202) 275-5067

general administration or central administration   The overall responsibilities associated with administering an entire school district.

general aid   Educational support funds provided from a higher governmental level that are not limited to any specific program or purpose but which may be used in financing the general educational program as seen fit by the recipient governing authority.

General Aptitude Test Battery (GATB)   Group of tests designed by the United States Employment Service and used extensively in state employment offices. The series of 12 tests measure nine aptitude areas: intelligence, verbal aptitude, numerical aptitude, spatial aptitude, form perception, clerical perception, motor coordination, finger dexterity, and manual dexterity. Scores from the tests are combined to create measures of individual aptitudes and general intelligence. The GATB has demonstrated impressive validity. *See* Stephen E. Bennis, "Occupational Validity of the General Aptitude Test Battery," *Journal of Applied Psychology* (June 1968).
Published and distributed by:
The U.S. Department of Labor
Government Printing Office
Washington, DC 20016

general continuation class   A part-time class—for persons under 18 years of age who have left full-time instruction to enter the labor force—

providing instruction designed primarily to increase civic intelligence rather than to develop specific occupational competence.

general education   A rather nebulous term for those subjects that all students should study in preparation for whatever else might follow. Typically refers to an elementary school focus on language arts, reading, mathematics, natural science, and social studies.

general educational development program   An instructional program specifically designed to prepare individuals who have discontinued their formal education prior to graduation to take a high school equivalency examination.

General Electric Co. v. Gilbert 429 U.S. 125 (1976)   U.S. Supreme Court case that held that excluding pregnancies from sick leave and disability benefit programs is not "discrimination based on sex" and so is not a violation of Title VII of the Civil Rights Act of 1964. This decision led to a Title VII amendment (the Pregnancy Discrimination Act of 1978) that reversed the court's decision.

General Equivalency Diploma (GED)   *See* CERTIFICATE OF HIGH SCHOOL EQUIVALENCY and TESTS OF GENERAL EDUCATIONAL DEVELOPMENT.

general fund   Also CURRENT FUND. Unrestricted monies and other liquid assets that are available for an organization's general use; a fund consisting of all receipts not earmarked for a specific purpose. It is used for the general operations of an organization.

general ledger   The master accounting sheets that should exist for each account in an organization's chart of accounts. Postings are made to the general ledger from the journals. Information posted should include the transaction date, which journal the transaction was in, the dollar amount, and whether each transaction was a debit or a credit. After posting all journals to the general ledger for the cycle (usually one month), each general ledger account is totaled and the information is "tested" in a trial balance. Information from the general ledger is used to prepare the organization's financial statements. *See also:*

ACCOUNTING CYCLE
CHART OF ACCOUNTS
JOURNAL
POSTING
TRIAL BALANCE

General Schedule   The basic pay system for federal white-collar employees. It is the largest of the civilian pay systems, covering approximately half of the total of three million civilian employees.

general semantics   A theory regarding the nature of language that suggests, among other things, that language is basically arbitrary and that much human conflict emanates from misuse or misunderstanding of language.

General Services Administration   The federal agency, created by the Federal Property and Administrative Services Act of 1949, that establishes policy and provides for the management of the federal government's property and records, including construction and operation of buildings, procurement and distribution of supplies, utilization and disposal of property, transportation, traffic and communications management, stockpiling of strategic materials, and the management of a government-wide automatic data processing resources program.

GSA
General Services Building
18th and F Street, N.W.
Washington, DC 20405
(202) 655-4000

general use room   A term that refers to auditoriums, gymnasiums, cafeterias, libraries, and multipurpose rooms that all students share for specific purposes.

generalist teacher   A teacher who provides instruction in all or most subject areas to a class of students.

generalization   1. The tendency for a response or behavior learned in one situation or under one set of circumstances to be demonstrated in other situations. Compare to TRANSFER OF LEARNING. 2. The application of findings from the study of a limited group of subjects to a larger population.

generally accepted accounting principles (GAAP)   The totality of the conventions, rules, standards, and procedures that collectively define the responsible practice of accounting. Since the 1930s, the Securities and Exchange Commission has had the authority to establish accounting standards, but has never done so. Instead, it has allowed the accounting profession to establish its own guidelines, first through the Committee on Accounting Principles (from 1939 to 1959), and later through the Accounting Principles Board (from 1959 to 1973), both of the American Institute of Certified Public Accountants (AICPA). In 1973, the Accounting Principles Board was superseded by the Financial Accounting Standards Board (FASB).

generation gap   Differences in attitudes, values, and experiences between persons of one generation and those of the generations that immediately precede or follow it, which sometimes impede communication and acceptance among members of the two groups.

Geneva School   A term that is sometimes used to refer to JEAN PIAGET and his colleagues and followers.

genius   1. A person of exceptionally high intellectual ability who has made a significant contribution to some field of study or creative endeavor. 2. Anyone who has a measured IQ of 140 or above.

geography   A school subject that is concerned with the study of the earth and the location, structure, and purpose of its various entities. Typically one of several fields of study that comprise a social studies curriculum.

George-Barden/Deen/Ellzey/Reed Acts   A series of federal laws, beginning in 1929, that established early support for programs of vocational education, home economics, and agricultural education. See Calfrey C. Calhoun and Alton V. Finch, *Vocational and Career Education: Concepts and Operations* (Belmont, Calif.: Wadsworth Publishing Company, 1976).

geriatrics   Also GERONTOLOGY and industrial gerontology. That branch of medicine concerned with the special medical problems of older people; the medical science dealing with the diseases, debilities, and care of aging persons. *Gerontology* is that branch of biology which is concerned with the nature of the aging process. *Industrial gerontology* is a comprehensive term that summarizes all of those areas of study concerned with the employment and retirement problems of workers who are middle-aged and beyond.

German measles   *See* RUBELLA.

gerontology   *See* GERIATRICS.

Gesell, Arnold L. (1880-1961) An American physician and psychologist who pioneered significant work in the observation and study of child behavior and development. He assisted in the founding of the Gesell Institute in New Haven, Connecticut, and devel-

oped a scale for the assessment of infant development.

Gesell Developmental Schedules Scales that measure development and maturation in young children in four areas: motor, adaptive, language, and personal. There are two levels of scales: infant, which covers from four weeks to five months, and preschool, which covers from 1 1/2 to six years. It is published by:

The Psychological Corporation
555 Academic Court
San Antonio, TX 78204

Gestalt psychology   A branch of psychology that concentrates on the wholeness or totality of a person. Gestalt learning emphasizes exposure to the whole rather than fragmented parts of an experience.

Gestalt therapy   Psychotherapy technique pioneered by Frederic S. Perls, which emphasizes the treatment of a person as a biological and perceptual whole. "Gestalt" is a German word for a configuration, pattern, or otherwise organized whole whose parts have different qualities than the whole. *See* V. Van de Riet, M.P. Korb, and J.J. Gorrell, *Gestalt Therapy: An Introduction* (New York: Pergamon, 1980).

ghetto   An area or locality that is populated by a group of people representing some particular identity, such as religious, racial, or ethnic.

gifted   A general term used to refer to children who demonstrate especially high abilities in either intellectual functioning or specific areas of performance.

gifted children, also giftedness   As defined in the Gifted and Talented Children's Act of 1978 (P.L. 95-561): "children and, whenever applicable, youth, who are identified at the preschool, elementary, or secondary level as possessing demonstrated or potential abilities that give evidence of high performance capabilities in areas such as intellectual, creative, specific academic, or leadership ability, or in the performing and visual arts, and who by reason thereof, require services or activities not ordinarily provided by the school." There has been criticism of this definition in the professional literature and many authors subscribe to Renzulli's early description of "the gifted" as children who have cognitive or intellectual superiority, creativity, and motivation in combination and of a sufficient magnitude to set them apart from the majority of their age peers and that make it possible for them to contribute something of particular value to society.

See W.B. Barbe and J.S. Renzulli, eds., *Psychology and Education of the Gifted* (New York: Irvinton, 1975); William C. George et al., *Educating the Gifted: Acceleration and Enrichment* (Baltimore: Johns Hopkins University Press, 1979); Byron L. Barrington, "Curriculum-Based Programs for the Gifted," *Education* (Spring 1986); and Robert J. Sternberg and Janet E. Davidson, *Conceptions of Giftedness* (New York: Cambridge University Press, 1986).

Gifted and Talented Children's Act of 1978 (P.L. 95-561)   The federal law that was passed in response to concern about the specialized educational needs of children who are gifted. While there continues to be criticism about how the law defined the gifted population (see the definition for gifted children), the law authorized a number of federal programs that have in general been inadequately implemented, largely due to a lack of clarity regarding how responsibility for the programs would be organized.

Gilbert case   *See* GENERAL ELECTRIC CO. V. GILBERT.

Gillingham method   A remedial reading approach that is based on phonics and that uses a number of multisensory techniques. The method is described in Samuel A. Kirk et al., *Teaching Reading to Slow and Disabled Learners* (Boston: Houghton Mifflin, 1978).

giveback   Any demand by management that a union accept a reduction in its present terms of employment and/or compensation. *See* The Bureau of National Affairs Editorial Staff, "Givebacks Highlight Three Major Bargaining Agreements," *Personnel Administrator* (January 1983); and Scott A. Kruse, "Giveback Bargaining: One Answer to Current Labor Problems," *Personnel Journal* (April 1983).

Givhan v. Western Line Consolidated School District 435 U.S. 950 (1979)   The Supreme Court decision upholding the constitutional right of an employee (here a teacher) to express his or her views privately on matters of public concern to a supervisor (here a principal).

global education, also international education   The study of complex problems and issues of a worldwide nature that emphasizes relatedness rather than differences among the various cultures of the world. The program of study includes topics such as population growth, pollution, and the preservation of natural resources.

globalism   A concept of a one-world government.

goal   A non-quantified, long-range, visionary statement of intent. In contrast, an *objective* is a measurable statement of commitment to attempt to achieve a specific result. Educators are concerned both with goals that relate to changes in learners and goals that relate to changes in the institution of the system. *See also* OBJECTIVE.

goal displacement   An organizational phenomenon that occurs within some (more rigid) bureaucracies (occasionally school systems) when the means that have been established to achieve goals become themselves the overriding goals of the organization.

goal identification   The process of establishing and prioritizing the desired outcomes of an organization or of a particular project.

goal-free evaluation   An approach to program evaluation that measures the "side effects" or unanticipated outcomes of an educational program rather than the stated goals of the program. This approach can be used in conjunction with a more traditional SUMMATIVE EVALUATION model.

goals   Within the context of equal employment opportunity, realistic objectives that an organization endeavors to achieve through affirmative action. A quota, in contrast, restricts employment or development opportunities to members of particular groups by establishing a required number or proportionate representation that managers are obligated to attain without regard to "equal" employment opportunity. To be meaningful, any program of goals or quotas must be associated with a specific timetable—a schedule of when the goals or quotas are to be achieved.

See David H. Rosenbloom, "The Civil Service Commission's Decision to Authorize the Use of Goals and Timetables in the Federal Equal Employment Opportunity Program," *Western Political Quarterly* (June 1973). *See also FULLILOVE V. KLUTZNICK.*

goals, annual   Within the context of special education, the required part of a handicapped student's individualized educational plan (IEP) that addresses the specific areas of learning and skill development that the student is expected to achieve during the academic year.

golden handcuffs   The feeling of being bound to remain in a job because financial benefits would be forfeited upon resignation.

golden handshake   Dismissing an employee while at the same time providing him or her with a large cash bonus.

Goldman-Fristoe Test of Articulation   An individually-administered, criterion-referenced test of the ability to produce consonant sounds in different contexts. The test can be used for ages two and above. It is published by:
American Guidance Service, Inc.
Publisher's Building
Circle Pines, MN 55014

good faith (equal employment opportunity)   The absence of discriminating intent. The "good faith" of an employer is usually considered by the courts in fashioning an appropriate remedy to correct the wrongs of "unintentional" discrimination.

good faith bargaining   Honest negotiation. Section 8(a)(5) of the National Labor Relations Act makes it illegal for an employer to refuse to bargain in good faith about wages, hours, and other conditions of employment with the representative selected by a majority of the employees in a unit appropriate for collective bargaining. A bargaining representative seeking to enforce its right concerning an employer under this section must show that it has been designated by a majority of the employees, that the unit is appropriate, and that there has been both a demand that the employer bargain and a refusal by the employer to do so.

The duty to bargain covers all matters concerning rates of pay, wages, hours of employment, or other conditions of employment. These are called "mandatory" subjects of bargaining, about which the employer, as well as the employees' representative, must bargain in good faith, although the law does not require "either party to agree to a proposal or require the making of a concession." These mandatory subjects of bargaining include, but are not limited to, such matters as pensions for present and retired employees, bonuses, group insurance, grievance procedure, safety practices, seniority, procedures for discharge, layoff, recall, or discipline, and the union shop.

An employer who is required to bargain under this section must, as stated in Section 8(d), "meet at reasonable times and confer in good faith with respect to wages, hours, and other terms of employment, or the negotiation of an agreement, or any question arising thereunder, and the execution of a written contract incorporating any agreement reached if requested by either party."

good standing   Being in compliance. For example, a union member is in "good standing" with his union if he or she meets all of the requirements for membership and his or her dues and other fees are current.

Goodenough Draw-a-Person test A test of intelligence or mental processing that compares a child's drawing of a person (expanded versions include a house and a tree) to established norms for his or her chronological age.

Goodenough-Harris Drawing Test   A scale used to assess intellectual development on the basis of the degree of detail included in students' drawings. It can be administered either individually or in a group and it has normed references from ages three to 15. It is published by:

The Psychological Corporation
555 Academic Court
San Antonio, TX 78204

Goodland, John I. (1920-)   The author of over 20 books related to educational reform; his best known work is *A Place Called School* (1983), one of the most extensive studies of the public schools in recent times. *See* EFFECTIVE SCHOOLS.

Goss v. Lopez 419 U.S. 565 (1975) The Supreme Court decision that established minimal due process requirements for the suspension of students for short periods of time (not to exceed 10 days). The court ruled that schools were required only to give a student notice of charges against him or her and that they did not need to afford the student the right to counsel or to call or cross-examine witnesses. The court also ruled that longer suspensions or expulsions may require more formal procedures.

Gouldner model   A framework that differentiates two basic role identity types working within educational organizations: *locals*, who identify with and maintain loyalty to the organization (school), and *cosmopolitans*, who are more committed to their area of professional specialization and identify with their national counterparts. The model was first developed by Alvin W. Gouldner in "Cosmopolitans and Locals: Toward an Analysis of Latent Social Roles," *Administrative Science Quarterly* (December 1957 and March 1958).

governance   A general term referring to the collective actions of a board of directors or board of trustees in its governing of a tax-exempt organization.

governing authority   A government official, board, or commission, legally authorized by the constitution or by legislation to assume jurisdiction and responsibility in a specific field of government.

governing board   *See* PUBLIC BOARD OF EDUCATION.

governing instrument Document that governs an organization's actions. IRS regulations identify two types of governing instruments: creating documents (for example, articles of organization) and operating documents (for example, bylaws). *See also:*
ARTICLES OF INCORPORATION
ARTICLES OF ORGANIZATION
BYLAWS

grade   1. That portion of a school program that represents the work of one regular school term, identified by a designation such as kindergarten, grade 1, or grade 2. 2. An established level or zone of difficulty. Positions of the same difficulty and responsibility tend to be placed in the same grade even though the content of the work differs greatly. 3. The measure of a student's level of achievement on an examiniation or in a course of study.

grade card or report card   A written or printed record, usually mailed or sent home, that indicates the grades a student earned in each course taken during a given term or academic year.

grade inflation A phenomenon of the late 1970s and 1980s characterized by an artificial rise in average student grades (particularly at the under-graduate level), which has coincided with a decline in national average scores on the Scholastic Aptitude Test. The rise is not believed to reflect an actual increase in student achievement. For a further description and references, *see* L. David Weller, "Attitude Toward Grade Inflation: A Survey of Private and Public Colleges of Education," *Journal of Research and Development in Education* (Fall 1984).

grade points or grade-point values   The numerical equivalents for letter grades that are used for determining grade point average. Generally:
A = 4
B = 3
C = 2
D = 1
F = 0

grade school   Another designation for elementary school.

graded school   A school composed of separate standard grades, or combinations of grades that serve as the basis for assigning pupils to classes. Students are typically grouped according to chronological age and progress from one grade level to the next each year.

grade-equivalent scales or scores   Measures of achievement that are related to average performance on a test by a group of students at a particular grade level. For example, if the average 10th-grader scores 20 points on a test, anyone who scores 20 points on the test receives a grade-equivalency score of 10th grade.

grade-point average (GPA)   A measure of average performance in all courses taken by a student during a grading period, school term, year, or accumulated for several terms or years (such as grade-point average over the entire course of a student's under-graduate study). The grade-point average is obtained by dividing the total grade-point values by total courses or by total hours of instruction.

grading on the curve Determining the distribution of students' grades on a test or in a course based on a normal distribution curve so that most grades fall within the middle range and are assigned an average grade (usually a C), and as many F's are assigned as A's.

gradual pressure strike Concerted effort by employees to influence management by gradually reducing production (slowing down work) until their objectives are met.

graduate An individual who has received formal recognition for the successful completion of a prescribed program of studies.

Graduate Record Examination (GRE) A nationally administered examination that is required as part of the application procedures for many graduate schools. The examination is administered by the EDUCATIONAL TESTING SERVICE.

graduate student A student who has completed the requirements for graduation from a four-year college program and is pursuing further formal study at a college or university that may lead to such graduate degrees as the master's degree or doctor's degree.

graduate study College-level courses of study beyond undergraduate study that may lead to such graduate degrees as the master's degree and doctor's degree.

graduation 1. Formal recognition given to a pupil for the successful completion of a prescribed program of studies. 2. A ceremony where diplomas or degrees are given to students who have earned them.

grammar The rules for the structure of a language and how words relate to each other to express thoughts.

grammar school 1. Yet another name for an elementary school. 2. In England, a previous designation for secondary schools that were oriented toward the preparation of students who had demonstrated their academic potential for higher education. The

English schools have almost totally eliminated their system of separating secondary level students into different (grammar and technical) schools on the basis of academic ability and now educate almost all secondary students through a system of *comprehensive* schools.

grand mal seizure A form of epileptic seizure that causes generalized convulsions of the body.

grandfather clause A colloquial expression for any provision or policy that exempts a category of individuals from meeting new standards. For example, if a school district were to establish a policy that all new teachers had to have a master's degree as of a certain date, it might exempt those teachers without such degrees who were employed prior to that date. This statement of exemption would be a grandfather clause.

grant 1. A form of gift that entails certain obligations on the part of the grantee and expectations on the part of the grantor; for example, grants from a king or a tax-exempt charitable foundation. 2. An intergovernmental transfer of funds (or other assets). Since the New Deal, state and local governments have become increasingly dependent upon federal grants for an almost infinite variety of programs. They have grown from nothing to over 21 percent of all state and local expenditures in 1985. From the era of land grant colleges to the present, a grant by the federal government has been a continuing means of providing states, localities, public (and private) educational or research institutions, and individuals with funds to support projects the national government considered useful for a wide range of purposes. In recent years grants have been made to support the arts as well as the sciences. All such grants are capable of generating debate

over what the public as a whole, acting through the grant-making agencies of the federal government, considers useful and in the national interest.
See Lawrence D. Brown, James W. Fossett, and Kenneth T. Palmer, *The Changing Politics of Federal Grants* (Washington, D.C.: The Brookings Institution, 1984); and Richard P. Nathan and Fred C. Doolittle, "Federal Grants: Giving and Taking Away," *Political Science Quarterly* (Spring 1985).

grant, block   A grant that is distributed in accordance with a statutory formula for use in a variety of activities within a broad functional area largely at the recipient's discretion.

For example, the community development block grant program, administered by the Department of Housing and Urban Development, funds community and economic development programs in cities, counties, Indian tribes, and U.S. territories. The nature of the block grant allows these jurisdictions to allocate the funds to supplement other resources in ways that they choose.
See Richard S. Williamson, "Block Grants—A Federalist Tool," *State Government*, 54:4(1981); and Timothy J. Conlan, "The Politics of Federal Block Grants: From Nixon to Reagan," *Political Science Quarterly* (Summer 1984).

grant, categorical   A grant that can be used only for specific, narrowly defined activities, such as for the construction of interstate highways. Authorizing legislation usually details the parameters of the program and specifies the types of eligible activities, but sometimes these may be determined by administrators. At least 75 percent of all federal aid to states and localities comes in the form of categorical grants.
See Alan L. Saltzstein, "Federal Categorical Aid to Cities; Who Needs It

Versus Who Wants It," *Western Political Quarterly* (September 1977); and George J. Gordon and Irene Fraser Rothenberg, "Regional Coordination of Federal Categorical Grants: Change and Continuity Under the New Federalism," *Journal of the American Planning Association* (Spring 1985).

grant, conditional   A grant that is awarded with limitations (conditions) attached to use of the funds. Both categorical and block grants are conditional, although the categorical grant generally has a greater number and severity of conditions.

grant, discretionary   A grant awarded at the discretion of a federal administrator, subject to conditions specified by legislation. Generally used interchangeably with project grant.

grant, entitlement   A grant provided under a federal program of aid to states under which each state is entitled to a portion of the federal allocation.

grant, formula-project categorical   A project grant for which a formula specified in statutes or regulations is used to determine the amount available for a state area; then, funds are distributed at the discretion of the administrator in response to project applications submitted by substate entities.

grant, general support   A grant made in a particular area of concern to the grantmaking organization (for example, early child development) for its general support, rather than to support a specific project. The logic for general support grants is that the agencies supported are better able to establish program priorities than the grantmaking organization.

grant, open-end reimbursement
Often regarded as a formula grant, but characterized by an arrangement wherein the federal government commits itself to reimbursing a specified portion of state-local program expenditures with no limit on the amount of such expenditures. Examples include Aid to Families With Dependent Children, food stamps, and MEDICAID.

grant, project   A grant that directs funding to a specific project, in contrast to a general support grant.

grant, project categorical Nonformula categorical grants awarded on a competitive basis to recipients who submit specific, individual applications in the form and at the times indicated by the grantor agency.

grant, target A grant that "packages" and coordinates funds for wide-ranging public services directed at a specific clientele group or geographic area. Major examples include the Appalachian Regional Development Program, the Community Action Program, and the Model Cities Program.

grant application   See GRANT PROPOSAL.

grant closeout procedures   The procedures, specified by granting public agencies, that define financial, reporting, and asset retention or protection steps that must be taken at the termination of a grant.

grant proposal Also GRANT REQUEST or GRANT APPLICATION. A document written and submitted to a foundation or government agency requesting grant funds, usually for specific uses. Many foundations and agencies require specific grant proposal inclusions and formats, but most request: (1) title of the project and the submitting organization; (2) a proposal abstract or very short summary; (3) an introduction to the submitting organization (a little about its history, anything unique about it, some of its major accomplishments, its major long-term goals, and support received from other sources); (4) a problem statement (that is, what needs or problems the grant will be used to address); (5) specific project objectives; (6) the project's methods or strategy; (7) an evaluation strategy; (8) a project budget; and (9) appendices containing, for example, documents, resumes, maps, and other information helpful to the proposal reviewers but that would detract from the flow of the proposal's narrative. *See also:*
GRANT
GRANT PROPOSAL ABSTRACT
GRANT PROPOSAL BUDGET
OBJECTIVE
PROJECT CONTROL CHART

grant proposal abstract A very brief summary of a grant proposal's purpose, needs to be addressed, description of the project's approach, and the total amount of grant funds required or requested.

grant proposal budget   The proposed project budget included in a grant proposal submitted to a foundation or government agency. Many granting organizations require grant proposal budgets to be submitted in a specific format, in which most want included: (1) the total project budget (by line item); (2) the amount requested from the granting organization; and (3) the amount to be contributed from other sources.

grant request   *See* GRANT PROPOSAL.

grant-in-aid   Federal transfers of payments to states, or federal or state transfers to local governments for specified purposes, usually subject to a measure of supervision and review by

EXAMPLE OF A GRANT PROPOSAL BUDGET

BUDGET SUMMARY

	Total	Total Requested	Total Pledged By Other Sources
Total This Grant	$10,067.12	$7,836.62	$2,230.50
1. Personnel	$ 7,776.62	$5,847.12	$1,928.50
A. Salaries & Wages	4,995.00	4,320.00	675.00
B. Fringe Benefits	1,214.62	1,047.12	166.50
C. Contract Services	1,566.00	480.00	1,086.00
2. Non-Personnel	1,230.00	990.00	240.00
A. Space Costs	271.00	208.00	63.00
B. Equipment Rental, Lease, or Purchase			
C. Supplies	128.50	128.50	-0-
D. Travel	176.00	176.00	-0-
E. Telephone	350.00	350.00	-0-
F. Other Costs	135.00	135.00	-0-

the granting government or agency in accordance with prescribed standards and requirements. One function of a federal grant-in-aid is to direct state or local funding to a purpose considered nationally useful by providing federal money on condition that the jurisdiction receiving it match a certain percentage of it. Then the federal government actively monitors the grantees' spending of the funds to ensure compliance with the spirit and letter of federal intent. Grants-in-aid have other public policy implications as well because a jurisdiction that accepts federal money must also accept the federal "strings" or guidelines that come with it. For example, all federal grantees must comply with federal standards on equal employment opportunity in the selection of personnel and contractors.

See Charles L. Vehorn, *The Regional Distribution of Federal Grants-in-Aid* (Washington, D.C.: Academy for Contemporary Problems, 1978); and John E. Chubb, "Excessive Regulation: The Case of Federal Aid to Education," *Political Science Quarterly* (Summer 1985).

grants receivable   An asset account in an organizations's chart of accounts and balance sheet. Grants receivable are posted when formal notification of a grant award has been received. *See also:*
BALANCE SHEET
CHART OF ACCOUNTS
FINANCIAL STATEMENTS

grants-in-kind   Donations of surplus property or commodities.

grantsmanship   The art (or science, depending on one's viewpoint) of writing successful grant proposals. *See also* GRANT PROPOSAL.

grapevine   A colloquial term for the informal communication networks that exist within an organization.

grapheme   The smallest meaningful unit of writing, most often a single letter. The written equivalent of a spoken phoneme (see entry).

gratification, delayed   A reinforcing event or object that does not immediately follow the behavior that earns it.

Gray, William S. (1885-1960) An American educator and professor of reading who is best known as the originator of the Dick and Jane books ("see Spot run"), a widely used Scott-Foresman basic reading series.

great books concept An approach to higher education or a specific course of study that emphasizes the study of certain "great" books (of philosophy, literature, history, science, etc.) as the basis for a liberal education. The concept originated at the University of Chicago under Robert Hutchins. For an early description of the concept *see* Robert Hutchins, *Great Books, The Foundation of a Liberal Education* (New York: Simon & Schuster, 1954).

Green v. Connally   A 1971 federal court decision (330 F. Supp. 1150 [D.D.C. 1971], aff'd sub nom. *Coit v. Green*, 404 U.S. 997 [1971]) that held that the I.R.S. Code "does not contemplate the granting of special Federal tax benefits to trusts or organizations . . . (which) contravene Federal public policy." In this instance, federal public policy concerned racial discrimination in private schools. *See also* BOB JONES UNIVERSITY V. SIMON and WRIGHT V. REGAN.

Green v. County School Board 391 U.S. 430 (1968)   The first Supreme Court desegregation decision to establish percentages of black and white students attending a school as a measure of a school district's effectiveness in achieving a non-racially-segregated system.

grievance   Any dissatisfaction felt by an employee in connection with his/her employment. The word generally refers to a formal complaint initiated by an employee, by a union, or by management concerning the interpretation or application of a collective bargaining agreement or established employment practice.

grievance arbitration   Also called RIGHTS ARBITRATION. Arbitration concerned with disputes that arise over the interpretation/application of an existing agreement. The grievance arbitrator interprets the contract for the parties. See INTEREST ARBITRATION.

grievance committee (labor) Those employee, union, and/or management representatives who are formally designated to review grievances left unresolved by lower elements of the grievance machinery.

grievance machinery   Totality of the methods, usually enumerated in an agreement, used to resolve the problems of interpretation arising during the life of an agreement. Grievance machinery is usually designed so that those closest to the dispute have the first opportunity to reach a settlement.

grievance procedure   Specific means by which grievances are channeled for their adjustment through progressively higher levels of authority in an organization. Grievance procedures, while long considered the "heart" of a labor contract, are increasingly found in nonunionized organizations as managers realize the need for a process to appeal the decisions of supervisors that employees consider unjust.

Griggs et al. v. Duke Power Company 401 U.S. 424 (1971)   The most significant single Supreme Court decision concerning the validity of employment examinations. The court

unanimously ruled that Title VII of the Civil Rights Act of 1964 "proscribes not only overt discrimination but also practices that are discriminatory in operation." Thus, if employment practices operating to exclude minorities "cannot be shown to be related to job performance, the practice is prohibited." The ruling dealt a blow to restrictive credentialism, stating that, while diplomas and tests are useful, the "Congress has mandated the common-sense proposition that they are not to become masters of reality." In essence, the court held that the law requires that tests used for employment purposes "must measure the person for the job and not the person in the abstract."

This case is also well known for recognition of the "disparate impact" theory of employment discrimination wherein an employee alleges that a racially neutral test or employment criteria that disproportionately disqualifies a protected class from employment opportunities is not job-related. Under the disparate impact theory, proof of a discriminatory motive is not required; the focus is on consequences, not motive. An employer may use an employment test that has a disparate impact on racial minorities so long as that test is "job-related." See CONNECTICUT V. TEAL, 457 U.S. 440 (1982).

The *Griggs* decision applied only to the private sector, until the Equal Employment Opportunity Act of 1972 extended the provisions of Title VII of the Civil Rights Act of 1964 to cover public as well as private employees. See Herbert N. Bernhardt, "*Griggs v. Duke Power Co.*: The Implications for Private and Public Employers," *Texas Law Review* (May 1972).

gross income   Total personal or organizational revenues prior to the deduction of any expenses.

grounding   A disciplinary measure commonly used by parents that involves confinement at home except for attendance at school or other required activities.

group annuity Any of a variety of pension plans designed by insurance companies for a group of persons to cover all of those qualified under one contract.

group assignment classification A classification of the assigned activities of a school staff member according to whether the activities constitute a professional educational assignment; a professional or technical assignment, other than educational; or other assignment.

group cohesiveness A measure of the degree of unity and solidarity that a group possesses.

group control A method of property control whereby equipment items that are the same with respect to function, material, shape, and size are accounted for as a group rather than as single units. That is, the individual piece of equipment loses its identity as such and is one of a group.

group counseling A professional approach to personal problem-solving in which an interpersonal relationship is established between one (or occasionally two) qualified counselor(s) and a group of 10 or fewer individuals desiring help.

group dynamics It is generally accepted that Kurt Lewin "invented" the field of group dynamics (that is, he was responsible, either directly or indirectly, for most of the pioneering research on group dynamics). Two of Lewin's close associates, Dorwin Cartwright and Alvin Zander, went on to produce what was for many years the standard text on the subject, *Group Dynamics: Research and Theory*, 3rd ed. (New York: Harper & Row, 1968).

They defined "group dynamics" as the field of inquiry dedicated to advancing knowledge about the nature of groups, how they develop, and their relationships to individuals, other groups, and larger institutions.

See Kurt Lewin, "Frontiers in Group Dynamics: Concept, Method and Reality in Social Science," *Human Relations* (June 1947).

group exemption letter An IRS letter granting tax-exemption to a central nonprofit organization and subordinate organizations under its direct control. Group exemption letters must be applied for; they are not granted automatically.

group home 1. A residential program for children who are not able to live in their natural homes because of serious handicaps, emotional/adjustment problems, or family dissolution. These facilities accommodate as few as six or as many as 40 or more children and are staffed on a 24-hour basis. Usually the children who live there will attend public school programs. 2. A facility for six or more adults who generally have some kind of disability and who require supervision and assistance. *See* Ralph J. Wetzel and Ronald L. Hoschover, *Residential Teaching Communities* (Glenview, Ill.: Scott, Foresman, 1984); and Albert L. Shostack, *Group Homes for Teenagers* (New York: Sciences Press, 1987).

group insurance Any insurance plan that covers individuals (and usually their dependents) by means of a single policy issued to the employer or association with which the insured individuals are affiliated. The cost of group insurance is usually significantly lower than the cost for equivalent individual policies. Group insurance policies are written in the name of the employer so that individual employees are covered only as long as they remain with the insuring employer. Sometimes group insurance policies provide that an employee can continue his/her coverage upon resignation by buying an individual policy. The most common kinds of group insurance are *group health insurance, group life insurance,* and *group disability insurance.* Many employers pay a substantial portion or all of the cost of group insurance.

group psychotherapy   Any form of psychological treatment involving more than one individual. Organization development efforts can be considered a form of group psychotherapy.

See Robert R. Dies, "Group Psychotherapy: Reflections on Three Decades of Research," *Journal of Applied Behavioral Science* (July-August-September 1979); and George M. Gazda, *Basic Approaches to Group Psychotherapy and Group Counseling,* 3rd ed. (Springfield, Ill.: Charles C. Thomas, 1982).

group tests   Refers to standardized examinations that can be administered to a number of individuals at the same time. Such tests usually do not require great skill to either administer or score.

group theory   In group dynamics, theories that explain the behavior of the group or subsets of individuals within the group.

groupthink   The psychological drive for consensus at any cost, which tends to suppress both dissent and the appraisal of alternatives in small decision-making groups. Groupthink, because it refers to a deterioration of mental efficiency and moral judgment due to in-group pressures, has an invidious connotation. For the basic work on the subject, *see* Irving L. Janis, *Victims of Groupthink: A Psychological Study of Foreign Policy Decisions and Fiascoes* (Boston: Houghton Mifflin, 1972); and Irving L. Janis, "Groupthink and Group

Dynamics: A Social Psychological Analysis of Defective Policy Decisions," *Policy Studies Journal* (Autumn 1973).

guaranteed student loan program (GSLP)   A form of student financial aid whereby banks or other lending institutions may make long-term low-interest loans available to undergraduate or graduate students with no requirement for repayment until after the student has completed or withdrawn from school. State or federal government may pay the interest costs during the time the student is enrolled.

guardian ad litem   An adult appointed by the court to represent a minor child in a legal proceeding, such as cases of abuse and neglect or divorce.

guidance area   A room or rooms designed, or adapted, for the use of persons, such as counselors, deans, placement counselors, and clerical personnel, who have been assigned specific duties and school time to carry on recognized functions of the guidance program.

guidance counselor   A somewhat redundant and erroneous term that is occasionally used to refer to a "school counselor" or a trained specialist who works within a school or school system to provide GUIDANCE SERVICES.

guidance services   The activities of counselors working with students and parents, providing consultation with other staff members on learning problems, evaluating the abilities of students, assisting students to make their own educational and career plans and choices, assisting students in personal and social development, providing referral assistance, and working with other staff members in planning and conducting guidance programs for students.

guide words   In a dictionary (or other reference book), the first and last entries on each page that are printed at the top of the page to assist the user in finding words rapidly.

gymnasium An indoor instructional space designed, or adapted, specifically for most physical education activities. *See also* INSTRUCTION AREA.

gymnastics Exercises and calisthenics requiring strength, flexibility, coordina- tion, movement, and endurance, which are used as a part of a physical educa- tion program to develop generalized physical fitness and conditioning.

gymnatorium An instructional space designed, or adapted, specifically for the combined functions that might normally be served by a separate gymnasium and a separate auditorium. *See also:*
AUDITORIUM
GYMNASIUM
INSTRUCTION AREA

H

Haeussermann's Developmental Potential for Preschool Children A screening test that is designed to assess cognitive abilities in children aged two to six years who have cerebral palsy. It is published by:

Grune and Stratton, Inc.
111 Fifth Avenue
New York, NY 10003

half day of attendance Attendance for approximately half of a full-day school session or an approved curtailed session. For example, a student who is present a major part of either the morning or afternoon portion of a school session usually is counted as being in attendance for that half session. This usually is the smallest unit of time reported for attendance purposes by an elementary or secondary school during the regular school term.

half-day session A school session that contains the minimum number of hours recommended by many state education agencies for kindergarten or prekindergarten instruction, when the length of this session approximates half the number of hours recommended for a full-day session in other elementary grades. Kindergarten and prekindergarten students attending a half-day session are considered in membership for the full day. However, for purposes of obtaining statistical comparability only, ratios involving these students are usually computed as though they were in membership for a half day.

half-way house A partially protected residence for persons who are in the process of being rehabilitated from conditions such as substance dependency or psychiatric illness and usually are moving from an even more restrictive setting.

Hall, G. Stanley (1844-1924) The early American psychologist, a strong proponent of education, who is credited with developing the modern concept of adolescence.

See G. Stanley Hall, *Aspects of Child Life and Education*, (Boston: Ginn and Company, 1907; Arno Press, 1975); and Dorothy Ross, *G. Stanley Hall* (Chicago: University of Chicago Press, 1972).

halo effect Bias in ratings arising from the tendency of a rater to be influenced in his or her assessment of specific traits by his or her general impression of the person being rated. The concept was first described by Edward L. Thorndike in "A Constant Error in Psychological Ratings," *Journal of Applied Psychology* (March 1920).

Hammer v. Dagenhart 247 U.S. 251 (1918) The Supreme Court case that held unconstitutional a federal statute barring goods made by child labor from interstate commerce. The court would not concede that the federal government could regulate child labor in interstate commerce until 1941, when it upheld the Fair Labor Standards Act of 1938 that put restrictions on the use of child labor. The landmark case was *United States v. Darby Lumber Company*, 312 U.S. 100 (1941).

handicap An atypical physical, health, sensory, mental, or psychological condition that adversely affects the performance of an individual.

handicapped, mildly Refers to a person who has a handicapping condition but who is able to perform all life functions with only slight accommodation. A mildly handicapped student may require some special services but, in the

HANDICAPPED PERCENT OF ENROLLMENT BY STATE FROM HIGH TO LOW

	State	1985 Percent		State	1985 Percent
1.	Delaware	16.4	28.	Florida	10.8
	Massachusetts	16.4		Oregon	10.8
3.	New Jersey	14.8	30.	Utah	10.7
4.	Rhode Island	14.2		Virginia	10.7
5.	Connecticut	14.0		Indiana	10.7
6.	Illinois	13.4	33.	South Dakota	10.5
	Maryland	13.4	34.	Montana	10.3
8.	Maine	13.2		New Mexico	10.3
9.	Missouri	13.0	36.	Kansas	10.2
10.	Alabama	12.5		Louisiana	10.2
11.	West Virginia	12.2	38.	North Dakota	10.1
12.	Tennessee	12.1	39.	New Hampshire	10.0
13.	South Carolina	12.0	40.	Arizona	9.8
14.	Iowa	11.7		Wisconsin	9.8
15.	Pennsylvania	11.6	42.	Texas	9.7
16.	Kentucky	11.5	43.	Georgia	9.6
	Minnesota	11.5	44.	Michigan	9.5
18.	Nebraska	11.4	45.	Nevada	9.3
	Vermont	11.4	46.	Washington	9.2
20.	Mississippi	11.2	47.	California	8.9
21.	Arkansas	11.1	48.	Idaho	8.7
	Ohio	11.1	49.	Colorado	8.6
	United States	11.0	50.	Dist. of Columbia	8.5
23.	North Carolina	11.0	51.	Hawaii	7.6
	Oklahoma	11.0			
25.	Alaska	10.9			
	New York	10.9			
	Wyoming	10.9			

SOURCE: Department of Education, Office of Planning, Budget and Evaluation.

main, will be able to follow a normal educational curriculum.

handicapped children Defined in P.L. 94-142, the Education for All Handicapped Children Act of 1975, as meaning "mentally handicapped, seriously emotionally disturbed, orthopedically impaired, or other health impaired children, or children with specific learning disabilities, who by reason thereof require special education and related services." This definition refers to those children who are eligible for free appropriate public education (special education) services according to the statutory requirements of P.L. 94-142. An interesting aspect of the definition is that it limits the definition of handicapped children to only those children with handicaps who require special education. A student who might have a disabling condition (for example, an orthopedic impairment or a health impairment) that did not affect his or her educational functioning would not be considered handicapped according to the law. See Joseph N. Murray and Caven S. McLoughlin, eds., *Childhood Disorders* (Springfield, Ill.: Charles C. Thomas, 1984).

handicapped person Also qualified handicapped person. Any person who: (a) has a physical or mental impairment that substantially limits one or more of such person's major life activities; (b) has a record of such an impairment; or (c) is regarded as having such an impairment. A *qualified handicapped individual*, with respect to employment, is one who with reasonable accommodation can perform the essential functions of a job in question. According to the Vocational Rehabilitation Act of 1973 (as amended), federal contractors and subcontractors are required to take affirmative action to seek out qualified handicapped individuals for employment.

hard funding Money obtained from an organization's regular sources of operating funds that is budgeted for activities. In contrast, *soft funding* implies that the money comes from a grant or other source that will not continue indefinitely.

Harlow v. Fitzgerald 457 U.S. 800 (1982) The Supreme Court decision that created new standards for the immunity of public employees from civil suits for damages. The Court held that government officials performing discretionary functions generally are shielded from liability for civil damages insofar as their conduct does not violate clearly established statutory or constitutional rights of which a reasonable person would have known. The test is one of objective reasonableness and not a subjective one.

Harvard Educational Review A journal of opinion and research in the field of education that is highly regarded by academicians and practitioners alike. Published quarterly by Harvard University with articles reviewed and selected by a board of graduate students in the School of Education.

Editorial and subscription address:
Harvard Educational Review
Longfellow Hall
13 Appian Way
Cambridge, MA 02138-3752

Hawthorne effect Any production increase or performance improvement due to known presence of benign observers. Elton Mayo and his associates, while conducting their famous Hawthorne Studies, discovered that the researchers' concerns for and attention to the workers led to increases in production. Similarly, teachers or students who know they are a part of a research study will probably improve their performance solely on the basis of their knowledge of said involvement. For Mayo's account, *see* Elton Mayo,

The Human Problems of an Industrial Civilization (New York: Viking Press, 1933, 1960).

Hazelwood School District v. Kuhlmeier 108 S.Ct. 562 (1988) Supreme Court decision on student rights that represented a rather narrow interpretation of the constitutional rights of students in school matters. The decision of a high school principal to prevent the publication of two pages of a school newspaper, which contained articles on student pregnancy and the effects of divorce on young people, was upheld. The Court decision appears to be placing greater reliance on the judgment of school administrators using "reasonableness" as its standard of scrutiny rather than "probable cause" or "substantial basis." *See* Perry A. Zirkel, "De Jure: Narrowing the Spectrum of Student Expression," *Phi Delta Kappan* (April 1988). For an analysis of several similar cases, *see* Lowell C. Rose, "'Reasonableness—the High Court's New Standard for Cases Involving Student Rights," *Phi Delta Kappan* (April 1988).

Hazelwood School District v. United States 433 U.S. 299 (1977) U.S. Supreme Court case, which held that a public employer did not violate Title VII of the Civil Rights Acts of 1964 if, from March 24, 1972 (when Title VII became effective for public employers), all of its employment decisions were made in a "non-discriminatory way," even if it had "formerly maintained an all-white workforce by purposefully excluding Negroes."

Head Start   A federal program designed to provide early education opportunities for children from poverty environments prior to kindergarten. Head Start centers exist nationwide and offer not only preacademic instruction but also health, social, nutritional, and psychological services. At least 10 percent of Head Start students must be handicapped and these students receive special individualized programs to meet their special needs. The program was begun in 1965 under the federal Office of Economic Opportunity and continues to be recognized as an effective social investment. It was one of the significant programs retained in President Reagan's "SAFETY NET" of the early 1980s when support for many other national programs of social significance were cut or reduced.

For a description of the effectiveness of Head Start programs, *see* Ruth H. McKey et al., *The Impact of Head Start on Children, Families and Communities*, DHHS Publication Number OHDS 85-31193 (Washington, D.C.: U.S. Government Printing Office, 1985).

Head Start is currently administered by the Administration for Children Youth and Families (ACYF), Department of Health and Human Services (HHS), 200 Independence Avenue, S.W., Washington, DC 20201; (202) 245-6296.

head teacher   A somewhat dated reference to a school employee, usually at the elementary school level, who has both full-time teaching responsibilities and administrative duties.

headmaster   1. A term used in private non-sectarian schools to refer to the academic and administrative leader. 2. In England, a school principal.

health education   1. Instruction in matters of health, such as care of the body, illness prevention, drug, alcohol, and tobacco awareness, and sex education. 2. In some contexts refers generally to health instruction, specialized medical services, and maintenance of a healthy school environment. 3. A close relative of physical education but without the rigorous exercise demands on the body. *See* P.M. Lazes, L.H.

Kaplan, and K.A. Gordon, eds., *The Handbook of Health Education*, 2nd ed. (Rockville, Mo.: Aspen, 1987).

Health Education and Welfare, Department of (HEW)   A former cabinet-level department of the federal government. Created in 1953, HEW was reorganized into the Department of Education and the Department of Health and Human Services in 1979. *See also* EDUCATION, DEPARTMENT OF, and HEALTH AND HUMAN SERVICES, DEPARTMENT OF.

Health and Human Services, Department of (DHHS)   The cabinet-level department of the federal government most concerned with health, welfare and income security plans, policies, and programs. Its largest single agency is the Social Security Administration. It was created on October 17, 1979, when the Department of Education Organization Act divided the Department of Health, Education, and Welfare in two.

DHHS
200 Independence Avenue, N.W.
Washington, DC 20201
(202) 245-6296

health insurance, group   *See* GROUP INSURANCE.

health maintenance organization (HMO)   An organized system for prepaid health care in a geographic area that delivers an agreed-upon set of basic and supplemental health maintenance and treatment services to a voluntarily enrolled group of people. The HMO is reimbursed for these services through a predetermined, fixed, periodic prepayment made by or on behalf of each person or family unit enrolled in the HMO, without regard to the amount of services provided or received. The HMO then hires or contracts with health care providers. A federal law (the Health Maintenance Organization Act of 1973)

requires that employers of 25 or more, who currently offer a medical benefit plan, also offer the option of joining a qualified HMO, if one exists in the area.

Participating health care providers are paid a fixed fee for their services. HMO's may qualify for tax exemption as either social welfare or charitable organizations.

health service area   A room or rooms designed, or adapted, for the use of persons in the field of physical and mental health—such as physicians, psychiatrists, nurses, dentists, dental hygienists, psychiatric social workers, and therapists—in providing health services to the student body.

health services   1. Activities concerned with medical, dental, and nurse services provided for local education agency employees. Included are physical examinations, referrals, and emergency care. 2. Physical and mental health services, provided to students, that are not part of direct instruction.

hearing officer   A judge or other duly appointed individual who presides at a legal proceeding. The hearing officer may also be designated as referee or commissioner. In educational due process procedures a hearing before a hearing officer may be required in case of disagreement between a local school district and a student or the student's parent or legal guardian.

Hegge-Kirk-Kirk Method   A highly structured phonic approach to remedial reading instruction that emphasizes drill and practice. *See* Samuel A. Kirk et al., *Teaching Reading to Slow and Disabled Learners* (Boston: Houghton Mifflin, 1978).

helper   A school staff member performing a variety of assigned activities, often under the direction of a skilled worker. A helper may thus learn a trade or acquire the competencies necessary to perform assignments requiring skill, but unlike an apprentice, does not work under an agreement with his employer that such is the purpose of his assignment. 2. A parent or student volunteer who performs specific tasks that assist in the operation of the school or educational program.

helping teacher   A staff member performing assigned professional activities that are directed primarily to assisting the teacher in the classroom to improve teaching techniques. (The term "helping teacher" is not used to denote a teacher aide.)

helping relationship   1. Generally refers to the relationship between a professional employed in the so-called "helping" professions (most commonly social work, psychology, or counseling but also any human service field) and the people that he or she serves. 2. Any humanistically oriented connection between two people in which one person's role is to be of assistance to the other.

See Arthur W. Combs, Donald L. Avila, and William W. Purkey, *Helping Relationships: Basic Concepts For the Helping Professions,* 2nd ed. (Boston: Allyn and Bacon, 1978); Lawrence Martin Brammer, *The Helping Relationship: Process and Skills,* 2nd ed. (Englewood Cliffs, N.J.: Prentice-Hall, 1979); and David L. Avila and Arthur W. Combs, eds., *Perspectives on Helping Relationships and the Helping Professions: Past, Present and Future* (Boston: Allyn and Bacon, 1985).

helping-teacher services   An activity of one or more professional staff members directed primarily toward assisting various teachers in their classrooms to improve their teaching techniques.

Hendrick Hudson School District v. Rowley 50 U.S.L.W. 4925, 4932 (U.S. June 28, 1982)   The first education case concerning students with handicaps and the first interpretation of P.L. 94-142 to reach the U.S. Supreme Court. In this case the question was about the extent and type of services that a school district was required to provide for a handicapped student. Amy Rowley was a deaf student who was progressing satisfactorily in school, with support services being provided by the school district. Her parents argued for a sign language interpreter to allow her to achieve greater than normal progress since she had greater than average intelligence. The Supreme Court reversed a lower court decision and ruled that P.L. 94-142 statutory requirements had been satisfied by providing Amy with sufficient services to make normal progress. This ruling was consistent with many others where the courts have refrained from judging the merit of particular educational methods or approaches.

Herbart, Johann E. (1776-1841) The German philosopher and teacher who is considered the "father of the scientific study of education." His followers founded the National Society for the Study of Education in America.

heterogeneous group   Students with a broad range of abilities, interests, achievement levels, and backgrounds who join together for formal learning experiences. Contrast with HOMOGENEOUS GROUP.

heuristic   Instructional methods that encourage self-discovery and independent problem solving.

hierarchy of needs   *See* MASLOW'S HIERARCHY OF NEEDS.

high match   *See* MATCHING SHARE.

high school   *See* SECONDARY SCHOOL.

high school completion   1. Satisfactory completion of a recognized secondary school curriculum (usually four years) leading to a diploma. 2. Any satisfactory combination of day and night center high school courses that fulfills the time/activity requirements set by a state or local board of education for a four-year high school diploma.

high school diploma   A formal document certifying the successful completion of a prescribed secondary school program of studies. In some states or communities, high school diplomas are differentiated by type such as an academic diploma, a general diploma, or a vocational diploma. In other localities a single diploma is awarded for the completion of whatever course of study the student had undertaken.

high school equivalency diploma   *See* CERTIFICATE OF HIGH SCHOOL EQUIVALENCY.

high school equivalency examination   An examination, approved by a state department of education or other authorized agency, intended to provide an appraisal of a student's achievement or performance in the broad subject-matter areas usually required for high school graduation. The tests of General Educational Development (GED) are the most widely recognized high school equivalency examination. *See also* TESTS OF GENERAL EDUCATIONAL DEVELOPMENT (GED) and CERTIFICATE OF HIGH SCHOOL EQUIVALENCY.

high school graduate   A person who has received formal recognition from the school authorities, as by the granting of a diploma, for completing a prescribed course of study in a high school terminating with grade 12 (grade 11 in a few systems).

high school postgraduate   A student who, after graduating from high school (grade 12), enters a secondary school for additional schoolwork.

High Scope Educational Research Foundation   A private, non-profit organization headquartered in Ypsilanti, Michigan, that has collected and published the most convincing nationwide data regarding the value of preschool education for disadvantaged young children. The foundation has conducted longitudinal follow-up studies spanning over 20 years of groups of students who did and did not experience preschool education services prior to kindergarten. The experimental group (those who did receive preschool) excelled the control group in all aspects: better overall achievement, higher percentage of high school graduates, fewer referrals for special education, fewer teen pregnancies, better-paying jobs, fewer encounters with law enforcement officials, etc. High Scope continues to offer nationwide training for professionals in the components of high quality preschool education. The High Scope model was demonstrated in the Perry Preschool Project, the results of which are reported in J.R. Berrcuta-Clement et al., *Changed Lives: The Effects of the Perry Preschool Program on Youths Through Age 19* (Ypsilanti, Mich.: The High Scope Press, 1984).

The High Scope foundation also engages in a broader range of curriculum development, training, and policy recommendations for all educational levels, infant through high school, with an overall goal of developing practical alternatives to traditional approaches to education.

High Scope Educational Research Foundation
600 N. River
Ypsilanti, MI 48197
(313) 485-2000

higher education Education above the instructional level of the secondary school, usually beginning with grade 13, which is provided by colleges, universities, graduate schools, community or junior colleges, professional schools, and other degree granting institutions. *See* Samuel K. Gove and Thomas M. Stauffer, eds., *Policy Controversies in Higher Education* (Westport, Conn.: Greenwood Press, 1986).

highest grade completed The highest grade of school completed or the grade prior to the highest grade attended but not completed.

Hisky-Nebraska Test of Learning Aptitude *See* NEBRASKA TEST OF LEARNING APTITUDE.

HMO *See* HEALTH MAINTENANCE ORGANIZATION.

holdback Amount of money withheld from periodic payments to contractors to assure compliance with contract terms. Usually the amount to be withheld is expressed as a percentage in the contract provisions. The amounts withheld are paid to the contractor after a designated official certifies that the contractor has completed work pursuant to the contract terms.

Holmes Group An organization of the deans of education in approximately 100 institutions of higher education, founded in 1986 to study reform in teacher education and in the teaching profession. The group was named after Henry Holmes, former dean of the Harvard Graduate School of Education. For a report of the group's recommendations, *see* Frank B. Murray, "Goals for the Reform of Teacher Education: An Executive Summary of the Holmes Group Report," *Phi Delta Kappan* (September 1986).

The Holmes Group, Inc.
501 Erickson Hall
East Lansing, MI 48824

home demonstration agent As a part of cooperative extension services, a trained home economist who provides instruction on an outreach basis, usually in rural areas.

home economics A general field of study that includes several areas, all of which are relevant to the management of a home: such as housing, finance and family economics, food and nutrition, clothing and textiles, house maintenance and repair. Instruction is offered at all levels of school curriculum, with the broadest emphasis at the secondary level and with a career focus at the college level. *See* Marjorie East, *Home Economics: Past, Present and Future* (Boston: Allyn and Bacon, 1980).

home economics room A special instructional space, designed or provided with special built-in equipment, for learning activities involving the varied aspects of food, clothing, and shelter, with particular emphasis on consumer education; management of money, time, energy, and human resources; and human relationships, focused on child growth and development, family relationships, and family health.

homebound student A student who is unable to attend classes and for whom instruction is provided at home by a teacher. *See also* INSTRUCTION FOR HOMEBOUND STUDENT.

homebound teacher A teacher who is assigned to instruct students who are forced to be out of school for substantial periods of time due to illness or other factors. Since the advent of mandatory education in public schools for students who are physically and mentally handicapped, the use of homebound teachers has declined.

homemaker services The provision of assistance, support, and relief for parents who may be having difficulty fulfilling parenting functions because of illness or overwhelming circumstances.

homeroom The room or other space where a teacher meets with a group of students for their homeroom period.

homeroom period A portion of a daily session, in a departmentalized or semidepartmentalized instructional organization, during which a teacher and a group of students meet primarily for purposes of checking attendance, making announcements, and attending to other administrative details. The homeroom period may also be utilized for group guidance activities.

home-school counselors *See* VISITING TEACHER.

homework School assignments—in preparation for a given course or subject-matter area—to be completed within a specified time limit and during nonclass time.

homogeneous group Students assigned to be together because of similarities in intelligence, ability, and/or achievement. Contrast with HETEROGENEOUS GROUP.

honor roll A list of names published each grading period, term, or year indicating those students who have achieved a set standard of performance in their schoolwork. In colleges, this frequently is referred to as the "dean's list."

honor society An association that receives into membership students who have achieved high scholarship and, frequently, who also fulfill established requirements for distinction in leadership or citizenship.

honorary board of directors A board established to honor individuals who have contributed substantially (funds or time and effort) to the organization. Membership on most honorary boards is by vote of the board of directors. In addition to their honoring function, honorary boards also are useful for: (a) maintaining a community-wide network of people who have contributed in the past and who can be called upon again; and (b) increasing the organization's credibility through association with community influentials. For example, many organizations print the names of honorary board members on their letterhead, or on the letterhead used in fund-raising.

honorary fraternal organizations in education There are numerous honorary organizations of professional educators that engage in a variety of activities, such as publications, scholarships, award presentations, and philanthropies in order to support and enhance quality education in America. The largest (over 20,000 members each) are:

Alpha Delta Kappa
Delta Kappa Gamma
Kappa Delta Epsilon
Kappa Delta Pi
Phi Delta Kappa
Kappa Phi Kappa

See individual entries for the address of the national office of each organization.

honors program A separate course of generally more in-depth instruction, offered at secondary schools and colleges for high-achieving students.

hornbook The earliest version of our modern "textbook"; it consisted of instructional material (e.g., the letters of the alphabet or religious sayings) written on a piece of paper that was protected by a layer of transparent horn and glued to a wooden paddle. Hornbooks have been traced back as early as 1450. *See* Andrew W. Tuer, *History of the Horn Book* (New York: B. Blum, 1968; reprint of 1897 ed.).

hospital certificate   A certificate issued by a hospital verifying the name and date of birth of a child; a birth certificate.

hospitalization   Group insurance program that pays employees for all or part of their hospital, nursing, surgical, and other hospital-related medical expenses due to injury or illness to them or their dependents.

hot line   A 24-hour statewide or local answering service that is usually staffed by volunteers trained to respond to crisis situations, such as reported child abuse, suicide attempts, rape, or substance abuse.

house organ   Also internal house organ and external house organ. Any publication—magazine, newspaper, newsletter, etc.—produced by an organization to keep its employees, volunteers, patients, and donors informed about the activities of the organization. *Internal house organs* are directed primarily to an organization's volunteers and employees; *external house organs* find a wider distribution as part of the organization's public relations program. *See also* INTERNAL INFORMATION SERVICES *and* PUBLIC RELATIONS.

housekeeping agency   *See* AUXILIARY AGENCY.

House-Tree-Person Technique
A projective test that utilizes a person's drawings of a house, tree, and person to make psychoanalytic interpretations of personality. It is published by:

Western Psychological Services
12031 Wilshire Boulevard
Los Angeles, CA 90025

Hufstedler, Shirley (1925-   )
The first secretary of the U.S. Department of Education, from its creation in 1979 to 1981. It was she who first asserted: "I'm bilingual. I speak English and I speak educationese."

human development   Refers to the total span of the life cycle from birth (or even conception) to death, with the notion that individuals are in a continuous process of growth and change. *See* Grace Craig, *Human Development*, 2nd ed. (Englewood Cliffs, N.J.: Prentice-Hall, 1980).

human factors engineering
Also called ergonomics, design for human use. The objective of human factors engineering, usually called ergonomics in Europe, is to increase the effective use of physical objects and facilities by people at work, while at the same time attending to concerns such as health, safety, and job satisfaction. These objectives are sought by the systematic application of relevant information about human behavior to the design of the things (usually machines) that people use and to the environments in which they work.

human relations   1. A discipline concerned with the application of the behavioral sciences (for example, psychology, social psychology, sociology, and cultural anthropology) to the analysis and understanding of human behavior in organizations. 2. A euphemistic way of referring to the equal employment opportunity and affirmative action programs of a school district.

human resources   Also called MANPOWER. General term for all of the employees in an organization or the workers in a society. It is gradually replacing the sexist term, *manpower.*

human resources administration
Increasingly popular euphemism for the management of social welfare programs. Many jurisdictions that had departments of welfare have replaced them with departments of human resources.

human resources management (HRM)   Also   personnel management. The administration of human resources. Although often used synonymously with personnel management, HRM transcends traditional personnel concerns, taking the most expansive view of the personnel department's mandate. Instead of viewing the personnel function as simply that collection of disparate duties necessary to recruit, pay, and discharge employees, an HRM approach assumes that personnel's appropriate mission is the maximum utilization of its organization's human resources.

human resources requirements analysis   Also called manpower requirements analysis. Analysis and projection of: (a) the personnel movements, and (b) the numbers and kinds of vacancies to be expected during each stage of management's work force plan.

human resources utilization
Also called manpower utilization. General term for the selection, development, and placement of human resources within an economic or organizational system in order to use these resources in the most efficient manner.

human rights   Just claims to the elimination of want or discrimination on any grounds and to equal educational and employment opportunity. *See also* CIVIL RIGHTS. *See* Donald Vandenberg, *Human Rights in Education* (New York: Philosophical Library, 1983).

human services   A general term for programs or activities that seek to improve the quality of people's lives by providing counseling, rehabilitative, nutritional, informational, and related services.

humanist   1. An individual with an intense concern for human dignity and well-being. 2. A person who is involved and concerned with the humanities.

humanistic education   A general term that describes an approach to education that places a strong emphasis on the social-emotional aspects of the individual. A humanistic approach both teaches and demonstrates concepts such as acceptance, respect for others, social action, human relations, and self-actualization.
   See Donald C. Read and Sidney B. Simon, eds., *The Humanistic Education Sourcebook*, with an introduction by Don Hamacheck (Englewood Cliffs, N.J.: Prentice-Hall, 1975).

humanitarian   Someone concerned with, and/or engaged in, activities for improving the health, welfare, and happiness of humankind; a true philanthropist.

humanities   The literature, languages, history, music, art, and philosophy (or any combination of these) employed to acquaint students with their origins and their neighbors, including the thoughts, creations, and actions of their human predecessors through the ages. The humanities are a record of what humankind over the centuries has felt, thought, and done in the search for answers to questions about such human concerns as personal identity, origin, meaning of life, and destiny.

Hunter Model   A model of teaching, described by Madeline Hunter in 1980, that has received considerable attention in academic and educational circles. The model is characterized by the following components:

a) diagnosis—identifying the students' current level of attainment in a particular area.

b) specific objective—select objectives for a lesson.

c) anticipatory set—focus attention and get ready.

d) perceived purpose—explain objective to students.

e) learning opportunities—choose activities to help achieve objectives.

f) modeling—give verbal and visual examples.

g) check for understanding— determine how well objectives are achieved.

h) guided practice—guide and monitor students' practice.

i) independent practice—create opportunities for additional practice.

See Madeline Hunter and D. Russell, *Planning for Effective Instruction* (Los Angeles: University Elementary School, 1980); Madeline Hunter, "What's Wrong with Madeline Hunter," *Educational Leadership* 42:(1985); and John W. Miller, "Differences in Effectiveness Between Elementary and Secondary Teachers Assessed with Hunter Oriented Variables," *Education* (Spring 1987).

hyperactivity/hyperkinesis (Other terms used include impulse disorder, minimal brain dysfunction, attention deficit disorder.) Designations used for children who are excessively active, have a short attention span and poor impulse control, are easily distracted, and frequently have learning difficulties. These children tend to be identified early in school (and before) because their behavior can cause considerable disruption in routine. They benefit from individually prescribed educational intervention. The benefits of treatment via medication or dietary restrictions are controversial. *See also* FEINGOLD DIET and RITALIN.

See Frank P. Alabiso and James C. Hansen, *The Hyperactive Child in the Classroom* (Springfield, Ill.: Charles C. Thomas, 1977); and Dorothea Ross and Sheila Ross, *Hyperactivity: Current Issues, Research and Theory*, 2nd ed. (New York: John Wiley, 1982).

hypothesis   A testable assertion, statement, or proposition about the relationship between two variables that are in some way related to each other. For example, a personnel manager might hypothesize that a specific kind of job performance can be predicted from a particular kind of knowledge about an applicant (such as scores on tests or grades in school) or a teacher might hypothesize that a particular teaching strategy will help students master material more efficiently. Hypotheses of this kind can be tested and proven—one way or another—by validation studies.

I

IEU *See* INTERMEDIATE EDUCATION UNIT.

illegal strike A strike that violates existing law. While most public sector strikes are illegal, so are strikes that violate a contract, that are not properly authorized by the union membership, or that violate a court injunction.

Illich, Ivan *See* DESCHOOLING.

Illinois Test of Psycholinguistic Abilities (ITPA) A widely used, individually-administered, norm-referenced test of the psycholinguistic skills of children between the ages of 2 1/2 and 10. There are 10 subtests that measure understanding, processing, and producing both verbal and non-verbal communication. It is published by:

Publishers Test Service
2500 Garden Road
Monterey, CA 93940

illiteracy The inability to read and write at a level expected by one's culture. *See* David Harman, *Illiteracy: A National Dilemma* (New York: Cambridge Books, 1987). Contrast with LITERACY.

immediate full vesting Pension plan that entitles an employee to all of the retirement income—both his or her contributions as well as those of his or her company—accrued during his or her time of participation in the plan.

immersion course A technique of intensive instruction where the student is required to be so involved in the subject of education that little else can be attended to at the same time (e.g., when a student is thrust into the midst of a foreign culture for the purpose of learning a new language).

impaired articulation Speech-sound substitutions, omissions, and/or distortions involving the speech mechanism (e.g., tongue, lips, or velum) and resulting in defective speech in producing either syllables or connected speech (e.g., "wabbit" for "rabbit," and "sop" for "stop"). Impaired articulation is characterized by patterns of consistently occurring errors and should not be confused with occasional mispronunciations. *See* Raymond G. Daniloff, ed., *Articulation Assessment and Treatment Issues* (San Diego: College-Hill Press, 1983); and P.W. Newman, N.A. Creaghead and Wayne Secord, eds., *Assessment and Remediation of Articulatory and Phonological Disorders* (Columbus, Ohio: Charles E. Merrill, 1985).

impasse A condition that exists during labor-management negotiations when either party feels that no further progress can be made toward reaching a settlement. Impasses are resolved either by strikes or the helpful intervention of neutral third parties.

See Jonathan Brock, *Bargaining Beyond Impasse: Joint Resolution of Public Sector Labor Disputes* (Boston: Auburn House, 1982); and Marian M. Extejt and James R. Chelius, "The Behavioral Impact of Impasse Resolution," *Review of Public Personnel Administration* (Spring 1985).

impedilexac A contrived word used by Robert Aukerman to designate words that typically create reading problems, i.e., non-technical vocabulary that tends not to be known by students. For an extensive list of such

TYPES OF IMPASSE RESOLUTION

	Mediation	Fact-Finding	Arbitration
Process	Intervention by Federal Mediation and Conciliation Service or other appropriate third party at request of negotiating parties or on own proffering of services	A procedure for compelling settlement, frequently a final alternative to arbitration	A terminal procedure alternative to or following fact-finding
Subject Matter	Terms of new agreement being negotiated	Terms of agreement being negotiated	Terms of agreement being negotiated (also final step in grievance procedure)
Setting	Mediator tries to determine basis for agreement and persuade parties to reach agreement	Parties try to persuade fact-finder by arguments	Parties try to persuade arbitrator by arguments (same as fact-finding)
Third Party	Mediator—a federal commissioner of mediation and conciliation or other third party administrator	Fact-finder—a public employee or a private citizen selected by parties or by an agency	Arbitrator—a public employee or a private citizen selected by parties or by an administrative agency
Power Factor	Mediator limited to persuasion and ability to find	Fact-finder may make recommendations for impasse	Arbitrator makes binding decision compromise resolution
Publicity	Confidential process—no public record kept	Quasi-public process with recommendations recorded and reported	Quasi-public process with decisions recorded and reported

words, see Robert C. Aukerman, Reading in the Secondary School Classroom (New York: McGraw-Hill, 1972).

implementation The process of putting into effect something that has proved to be feasible and desirable.

implied consent A procedure used in educational research to avoid contamination of research findings if full disclosure of the experimental process would impact on the subject's behavior during the experiment. Full informed consent is requested of a sample of the potential population. If a substantial majority agree to participate, it is assumed that the larger population would also agree to consent if given the same information.

imprest system A system for handling disbursements whereby a fixed amount of money is set aside for a particular purpose. Disbursements are made from time to time as needed. At certain intervals, a report is rendered of the amount disbursed, and the cash is replenished for the amount of the disbursements, ordinarily by check drawn on the fund or funds from which the items are payable. The total of cash plus unreplenished disbursements must always equal the fixed sum of cash set aside.

improvement of instruction services Activities that are designed primarily to assist instructional staff in planning, developing, and evaluating the process of providing challenging and rewarding learning experiences for pupils. These activities include curriculum development, evaluating techniques of instruction, and staff training.

impulse control The ability to monitor one's immediate reaction to either external or internal stimuli.

impulsivity The characteristic of some students (and also some adults) that is manifested by a tendency to respond quickly to situations or internal stimuli without reflecting on alternative modes of responding or the potential consequences of one's behavior.

in loco parentis Meaning "in the place of parents," a legal principle that grants teachers parental-like authority for students while they are in school (e.g., to make and enforce rules or to act in their behalf). See Edward C. Bolmeier, Legality of Student Disciplinary Practices (Charlottesville, Va.: The Michie Company, 1976).

For a discussion of the interpretation of this concept under case law, see Perry Zirkel and Henry Reichner, "Is In Loco Parentis Dead?" Phi Delta Kappan (February 1987).

incidental learning Learning occurring concomitantly with an activity or experience, but toward which the activity or experience is not specifically directed; for example, learning how to spell the words "equator" and "cyclone" while studying geography.

incomplete high school A secondary school that offers less than four full years of work beyond grade eight in a school system that is organized such that grades K (or one) through eight constitute the elementary grades. These are sometimes called "truncated high schools."

independent American overseas school An elementary or secondary school, located outside the United States and its outlying areas, that: (a) follows a basically U.S.-type curriculum; (b) uses English as the primary language of instruction; and (c) has a large proportion of U.S. citizens in its student body and staff.

independent nonprofit school A private or nonpublic school that is not a part of a school system and is operated with no intention of making a profit. See also PRIVATE OR NONPUBLIC SCHOOL.

independent study 1. In general, the process of acquiring new learning or new information on one's own. 2. In the context of school, a self-directed course of study under the limited guidance of an instructor and with or without earned academic credit.

independent union A union that is not affiliated with the AFL-CIO.

independent variable In experimental research, the aspects of the study that the investigator manipulates or controls in order to observe the effect on the dependent variables.

index number Measure of relative value compared with a base figure for the same series. In a time series in index form, the base period usually is set equal to 100, and data for other periods are expressed as percentages of the value in the base period. Most indexes published by government agencies are presently expressed in terms of a "1967 = 100" base.

Index numbers possess a number of advantages over the raw data from which they are derived. First, they facilitate analysis by their simplicity. Second, they are a more useful basis for comparison of changes in data originally expressed in dissimilar units. Third, they permit comparisons over time with some common starting point—the index base period.

index of agreement A measure, usually expressed as a percentage, showing the extent to which examiners agree on a candidate's scores.

Indian Education Also Native American Education. Refers to all educational programs at all levels that are specifically available for Native American children, youth, and adults.

Indian Education Act of 1972 A federal law (P.L. 92-318, Title IV) that provided funds for programs to improve the educational opportunities for Native American children and adults.

indirect expenses Those elements of cost necessary in the provision of a service that are of such a nature that they cannot be readily or accurately identified with the specific service. For example, the custodial staff may clean corridors in a school building that is used jointly by administrative, instructional, maintenance, and attendance personnel. In this case, a part of custodial salaries is an indirect expense of each service using the corridors. However, it is impossible to determine readily or accurately the amount of the salary to charge each of these services.

indirect services Services for programs that cannot be identified with a specific program. All support service programs such as building maintenance are indirect services to the instruction programs.

individual instruction An arrangement whereby a student receives instruction by him or herself and not as part of a class, i.e., instruction for a single person or a one-to-one teaching situation. Contrast with INDIVIDUALIZED INSTRUCTION.

individual test Testing device designed to be administered (usually by a specially trained person) to only one subject at a time.

individualized education program (IEP) As defined in the Education for All Handicapped Children Act of 1975 (P.L. 94-142), the IEP is:

> a written statement for each handicapped child . . . which shall include (A) a statement of the present levels of educational performance of such child, (B) a statement of annual goals, including short-term instructional objectives, (C) a statement of the specific educational services to be provided to such child, and the extent to which such child will be able to participate in regular educational programs, (D) the projected date for initiation and anticipated duration of such services, and appropriate objective criteria and evaluation procedures and schedules for determining, on at least an annual basis, whether instructional objectives are being achieved.

The intent in the law was that the IEP would ensure the rights of all handicapped children to a free, appropriate public education in the least restrictive environment. The IEP is required for all handicapped students who are determined to be eligible for special education services.

individualized instruction   A teaching program based on a student's specific educational needs. Individualized instruction may occur as part of a group, singly or independently. Contrast with INDIVIDUAL INSTRUCTION. See Carol M. Charles, *Individualizing Instruction*, 2nd ed. (St. Louis, Mo.: D.V. Mosby Co., 1980).

individualized reading   An approach that deemphasizes group instruction and allows students to progress at their own rate of reading skill acquisition, utilizing books that they have selected at an appropriate reading level.

individually guided education (IGE)   An alternative system and structure for elementary school education that addresses individual differences of students through a multiunit non-traditional school organization and a flexible curriculum. This approach was developed at the Wisconsin Research and Development Center for Cognitive Learning.
See Edward J. Nussel et al., *The Teacher and Individually Guided Education* (Reading, Pa.: Addison-Wesley, 1976); and William Wiersma, "Individually Guided Education," *Education* (Winter 1986).

individually prescribed instruction (IPI)   An instructional approach that bases an individual student's program on the results of diagnostic or placement tests and that relies on considerable use of programmed, computer-assisted, and other self-paced learning materials under teacher guidance and direction. Students progress at their own rate of achievement. It was developed at the Learning Research and Development Center, University of Pittsburgh. See Harriet Talmage, *Systems of Individualized Education* (Berkeley, Calif.: McCutchan, 1975).

inductive approach or inductive reasoning   A thinking or problem-solving process that draws general conclusions from a number of specific observations.

industrial arts   Coursework that includes manual training, such as metalwork, woodwork, and technical drawing, which may be offered at the secondary level of education but which is not necessarily vocationally-oriented. See Donald Maley, *The Industrial Arts Teacher's Handbook* (Boston: Allyn and Bacon, 1978).

inequity theory   Also equity theory. Most fully developed by J. Stacy Adams (he premised his work upon Leon Festinger's theory of cognitive dissonance), who holds that inequity exists for Worker A whenever his or her perceived job inputs and outcomes are inconsistent with Worker B's job inputs and outcomes. Inequity would exist if a person perceived that he or she was working much harder than another person who received the same pay. Adams suggests that the presence of inequity creates tension within Person A to reduce the inequity by, for example, increasing (or decreasing) one's efforts, if the efforts are perceived to be low (or high) relative to another's work efforts.

See J. Stacy Adams, "Toward an Understanding of Inequity," *Journal of Abnormal and Social Psychology* (November 1963); and Paul S. Goodman and Abraham Friedman, "An Examination of Adam's Theory of Inequity," *Administrative Science Quarterly* (December 1971).

infant education   The provision of stimulating enrichment experiences for infants and toddlers between the ages of birth and three years. Differs from infant day care in that it focuses on maximizing physical, social, and intellectual growth.

Infant Intelligence Scale   *See* CATTELL INFANT INTELLIGENCE SCALE.

informal education/learning   1. The process of acquiring new knowledge and skills without the benefit of structured teaching. 2. An educational setting that encourages and facilitates self-directed learning. *See* Danny G. Fulks, *Informal Learning in Elementary Schools* (Washington, D.C.: University Press of America, 1978).

information services   1. Activities concerned with the writing, editing, and other preparation necessary to disseminate educational and administrative information to pupils, staff, managers, or to the general public through direct mailing, the various news media, or personal contact. 2. Activities organized for the dis-

semination of educational, occupational, and personal/social information to help acquaint pupils with the curriculum and with educational and vocational opportunities and requirements. Such information might be provided directly to pupils through group or individual guidance, or indirectly through staff members or parents.

informed consent   A procedure for assuring that any student involved in a special program, such as special education or a research project, is given (or his or her parents are given) full information about the nature of the program, the benefits and potential risks for participation, appropriate alternatives, and available procedural safeguards. This information must be provided in language the individual can understand and with sufficient and reasonable opportunity for consideration prior to giving consent to participate.

Ingraham v. Wright 97 S.Ct. 1401 (1977)   The Supreme Court decision that affirmed the right of public schools to inflict reasonable corporal punishment on students.

initial teaching alphabet (ITA)   A phonic approach to teaching beginning or remedial reading that utilizes an expanded alphabet that has a total of 45 characters for each different sound of the English language; somewhat dated and not in common usage.

initialize   To prepare a blank computer data disk to receive data for storage.

initiation fees   1. Payments required by unions of all new members and/or of employees who, having once left the union, wish to return. Initiation fees serve several purposes: (1) they are a source of revenue; (2) they force the new member to pay for the advantages secured by those who built the union;

and (3) when the fees are high enough, they can be used as a device to restrict membership. 2. Fees that may be charged to a student, on joining an organization, to help support the activities of the organization.

injunction   Also called labor injunction. Court order forbidding specific individuals or groups from performing acts the court considers injurious to property or other rights of an employer or community. There are two basic types of injunction: (1) a temporary restraining order, which is issued for a limited time prior to a formal hearing; and (2) a permanent injunction, which is issued after a full formal hearing. Once an injunction is in effect, the court has contempt power to enforce its rulings through fines and/or imprisonment. For an analysis, *see* Richard D. Sibbernsen, "New Developments in the Labor Injunction," *Labor Law Journal* (October 1977).

inner city school   A school usually located in a high density population area of a central city and normally attended by a high proportion of urban disadvantaged students; the attendance area of the school may be characterized by such factors as a significant proportion of substandard dwellings, of low-income housing, of non-white racial or ethnic groups, of non-English speaking populations, or of health and other social problems. *See* ATTENDANCE AREA.

inquiry method   An approach to education that encourages students to discover their own answers to questions provided by the teacher and to learn resourceful problem-solving strategies with guidance rather than by imposition from the teacher.

in-school instruction   Instruction received by a student within the school plant.

in-service education   A program of systematized activities promoted or directed by the education agency, or approved by the education agency, contributing to the professional or occupational growth in competence of staff members during the time of their service to the agency.
    See Louis J. Rubin, ed., *The In-Service Education of Teachers: Trends, Processes, and Prescriptions* (Boston: Allyn and Bacon, 1978); and Ben M. Harris, *Improving Staff Performance Through In-Service Education* (Boston: Allyn and Bacon, 1980).

in-service education services   Activities developed by a school district for training of personnel in all classifications.

in-service training   1. Term used mainly in the public sector to refer to job-related instruction and educational experiences made available to employees. In-service training programs are usually offered during normal working hours. However, some programs, especially those offering college credit, are available to the employee only on his or her own time. 2. Activities designed to improve the knowledge and skills of employees and, consequently, the quality of services, specifically instructional practices, provided. In-service training is directed at those individuals who are already basically qualified and employed by school systems. In-service training can be presented in a variety of formats. Some teachers continue their education by enrolling in university courses. Local school districts and state education agencies may sponsor workshops, courses, or other continuing education activities. Professional organizations offer conferences and workshops. Teachers may travel and visit other programs to expand their professional growth.

See Euan S. Henderson, *The Evaluation of In-Service Teacher Training* (London: Croom Helm, 1978). For a description of different models, *see* Lori Korinck et al., "In-Service Types and Best Practices," *Journal of Research and Development in Education* (Winter 1985); and Lori Korinck et al., "Coordinating Inservice Programs of College Education," *Journal of Research and Development in Education* (Fall 1981).

Institute for the Development of Educational Activities   *See* KETTERING FOUNDATION.

institution for neglected children As defined for federal compensatory education programs, a public or private nonprofit residential facility (other that a foster home) that is operated primarily for the care of, for an indefinite period of time, at least 10 children and/or youth who have been committed to the institution, or voluntarily placed in the institution, and for whom the institution has assumed or been granted custodial responsibility pursuant to applicable state law, because of the abandonment or neglect by, or death of, parents or persons acting in the place of parents.

institutional   Pertaining to an organization having a social, educational, or religious purpose, as a school, church, hospital, or reformatory.

institutional discrimination Practices contrary to EEO policies that occur even though there was no intent to discriminate. Institutional discrimination exists whenever a practice or procedure has the effect of treating one group of employees differently from another.

instruction   1. The activities dealing directly with the teaching of students and/or with improving the quality of teaching. 2. The act of informing or the act of stimulating thinking.

instruction area   A room (or other area) that was specifically designed, or adapted, to accommodate some form of instructional activity and is available for such purposes. Regular classrooms; special classrooms, such as kindergarten rooms, laboratories, shops, home economics rooms, and music rooms; and other areas, such as libraries, study halls, audiovisual rooms, auditoriums, gymnasiums, and multipurpose rooms—are all considered as instruction areas.

instruction building   A building used primarily for housing personnel and equipment engaged in activities dealing with the teaching of students or improving the quality of teaching.

instruction by correspondence Approved instruction, usually received by the pupil outside the school plant, that provides for the systematic exchange between teacher and pupil of materials sent by mail.

instruction and curriculum development services   Activities designed to aid teachers in developing the curriculum, preparing and utilizing special curriculum materials, and understanding and appreciating the various techniques that stimulate and motivate pupils.

instruction for delinquent children As defined for federal compensatory education programs, a public or private nonprofit residential facility that is operated primarily for the care of—for an indefinite period of time or for a period of time other than one of short duration—children and/or youth who have been adjudicated to be delinquent. Such instruction might also take place in an adult correctional institution in which children are placed. *See also* DELINQUENT BEHAVIOR *and* JUVENILE DELINQUENT.

instruction for homebound student Individual instruction by a teacher, usually at the home of a student who is unable to attend classes. In some instances, such instruction is augmented by telephone communication between the classroom and the student or by other means.

instruction programmer A school staff member performing the assigned activities of providing precise sequences of information to pupils through devices such as teaching machines for the purpose of enhancing learning.

instruction room Any room that was originally designed, or later adapted, to accommodate some form of group instruction on a day-by-day basis and that is available for such purposes. "Adapted," as used here, means that the area of the room has been changed through the movement of the fixed walls or partitions of the room, for the purpose of converting it to an instruction room. Areas such as auditoriums, gymnasiums, lunchrooms, libraries, study halls, and multipurpose rooms are generally not considered as instruction rooms, though they may be used for instruction purposes.

instructional leadership One function for school principals that is often contrasted with responsibilities related to the management of school resources, and that relates more specifically to improving the quality of instruction in the classroom. For several articles about the challenges and rewards of this role see the *NASSP Bulletin* (April 1987). *See also*: J.W. Keefe and J.M. Jenkins, eds., *Instructional Leadership Handbook* (Reston, Va.: NASSP, 1984).

instructional level An indication of the general nature and difficulty of instruction, e.g., elementary instructional level, secondary instructional level, or postsecondary instructional level.

instructional materials center (IMC) An instructional space where school library services and audiovisual services are integrated. When such services are limited to one or more specific subject areas, the space may be referred to as "resource center." For inventory purposes, an instructional materials center is considered to be a school library instructional space. *See also* RESOURCE CENTER.

instructional objectives Expected levels of attainment for individual students or groups of students in particular areas of instruction or courses.

instructional organization A school or other organizational arrangement that provides instruction of a given type or types.

instructional personnel Those who render direct and personal services that are in the nature of teaching. Included here are: teachers (including teachers of the homebound), teaching assistants or technicians, teacher aides, substitute teachers, and clerks serving teachers only. Attendance personnel, health personnel, and other clerical personnel are generally not counted as instructional personnel.

instructional program An individually designed strategy that details the content and methods of an educational plan for a student or group of students. *See* Bruce Wayne Tuckman, *Evaluating Instructional Programs* (Boston: Allyn and Bacon, 1979).

instructional staff training services Activities designed to contribute to the professional or occupational growth and competence of members of the instructional staff during the time of their service to a school district. Among these activities are workshops, demonstrations, school visits, courses for college credit, sabbatical leaves, and travel leaves.

instructional strategies (or instructional techniques)   Activities that are systematically arranged and undertaken by a teacher to help students achieve particular objectives.

instructional technology   A systematic utilization of printed and other audiovisual materials for educational purposes and the description and cataloging of such materials. *See* Frederick G. Knirk and Kent L. Gustafson, *Instructional Technology: A Systematic Approach to Education* (New York: Holt, Rinehart and Winston, 1986).

instructional television   An audiovisual mode of teaching whereby an expanded array of educational experiences can be transmitted to a large number of students, generally through closed-circuit programming.

instrumental conditioning   In behaviorism, a form of classical conditioning in which the consequence of a subject's response (i.e., a resulting stimulus) causes that response behavior to either increase or decrease.

insurable value   Current replacement cost of a piece of property less deductions for depreciation and noninsurable items.

insurable value of a building   Current replacement cost less deductions for depreciation and noninsurable items. The replacement cost of a building can be determined in several different ways. One of these methods is

through comparison of the building with a recently erected building of similar quality and facilities for which cost figures are available. Another method is through the application of a cost factor per square foot of floor area or per cubic foot of volume. Another is through the application of building cost indices that make it possible to determine a percentage increase or decrease in building costs over the years, which can be applied in turn to the original cost of a building to derive estimates of replacement cost. Still another method is through a detailed appraisal showing the quantity of materials and of labor, and the total cost of each, needed to replace the building at current prices.

insurance and bond premiums   Expenditures for all types of insurance coverage, such as property, liability, fidelity, and bond premiums, as well as the cost of judgments. Insurance for group health, life, or workmen's compensation are not charged here, but are recorded under Personal Services-Employee Benefits.

integrated therapy   Providing related therapy services, such as speech therapy or physical therapy, as a part of a student's educational program rather than as separate direct interventions. Meeting a variety of student needs, e.g., communication development or motor skill training, within the context of typical classroom activities.

integration   1. The process of combining subject-matter content from various subject-matter areas into one unified course, project, or unit; e.g., interrelating the teaching of history, geography, science, art, music, and English language arts with the study of the Westward Movement. 2. Usually refers to the racial mixing of students in schools but also applies to the placement of students with handicaps into regular public school buildings and regular school programs and classes.

intelligence   1. There is no agreement on any single definition of intelligence, save that it is a hypothetical construct. Generally, it refers to an individual's ability to cope with his or her environment and deal with mental abstractions. 2. The military, as well as some other organizations, use the word "intelligence" in its original Latin sense—as information.

intelligence quotient (IQ)   Measure of an individual's general intellectual capability. IQ tests have come under severe criticism because of their declining relevancy as a measurement tool for individuals past the age of adolescence and because of their inherent cultural bias, which has tended to discriminate against minorities.

See Ashley Montagu, ed., *Race and IQ* (New York: Oxford University Press, 1975); and Brigitte Berger, "A New Interpretation of the I.Q. Controversy," *The Public Interest* (Winter 1978).

intelligence test   Any of a variety of standardized tests that seek to measure a range of mental abilities and social skills. *See* Eleanor Robinson Russell, "Measurement of Intelligence by Means of Children's Drawings," *American Journal of Art Therapy* (July 1979).

interest arbitration   Arbitration of a dispute arising during the course of contract negotiations where the arbitrator must decide what will or will not be contained in the agreement. *See* Betty Southard Murphy, "Interest Arbitration," *Public Personnel Management* (September-October 1977); and Henry S. Farber, "Splitting-the-Difference in Interest Arbitration," *Industrial and Labor Relations Review* (October 1981).

interest group   A group organized to secure certain objectives that the members value or regard as beneficial to themselves. Interest groups, sometimes referred to as special interest groups, frequently represent particular

---

IQ CLASSIFICATIONS

The following table illustrates a traditional classification of IQ's and indicates the percentage of persons in a normal population who would fall into each classification.

Classification	IQ	Percentage of Population
Gifted	140 and above	1
Very Superior	130-139	2.5
Superior	120-129	8
Above Average	110-119	16
Average	90-109	45
Below Average	80-89	16
Borderline	70-79	8
Mild Mental Retardation	60-69	2.5
Moderate/Severe Mental Retardation	59 and under	1

economic interests, for example, organized labor, large manufacturers, small businessmen, farmers, professional organizations. Interest groups also may be organized to secure noneconomic objectives or objectives that are not purely economic. An interest group may, for example, be a religious group, an ethnic or racial group, parents of children with a particular disability, an association concerned with saving historic landmarks, or a rifle association. Interest groups play a particularly important role in a large, representative democracy, where they seek to exert influence over the passage of legislation and the actions of governmental agencies.

interest inventory   1. An examination used to measure a person's likes and dislikes, typically determining the extent to which a person's pattern of likes and dislikes corresponds to that of persons who are known to be successfully engaged in a given vocation, school subject, program of studies, or other activity. 2. Questionnaire designed to measure the intensity of interest that an individual has in various objects and activities. Interest inventories are widely used in vocational guidance.

See Donald G. Zytowski, *Contemporary Approaches to Interest Measurement* (Minneapolis: University of Minnesota Press, 1973).

interest and receivables   Interest received on temporary or permanent investments in United States Treasury bills, notes, bonds, savings accounts, time certificates of deposit, mortgages, or other interest-bearing obligations and dividends received on stocks.

interfund transfers   Money that is taken from one fund under the control of the board of education and added to another fund under the board's control. Interfund transfers are not receipts or expenditures of a school district.

interim agreement   Collective bargaining agreement designed to avoid a strike and/or to maintain the current conditions of employment while the settlement of a dispute or the signing of a final comprehensive contract is pending.

intermediate administrative unit An administrative unit smaller than the state, which exists primarily to provide consultative, advisory, administrative, or statistical services to local, basic administrative units, or to exercise certain regulatory functions over local, basic administrative units. An intermediate unit may operate schools and contract for school services, but it does not exist primarily to render such services. Such units may or may not have taxing and bonding authority. Where there is a supervisory union board, the union is included as an intermediate unit.

intermediate education unit (IEU) An organizational structure involving the regionalization of particular education services and programs among two or more individual school districts. For the direct operation of programs, special education and vocational education have been the most common needs driving the formation of intermediate units. Other functions shared within an IEU include materials, media, and library services. Intermediate units are organized in various ways by the different states. There are three basic types of IEU:

1) *Special District*, a legally constituted unit of educational governance, generally established by the state and local units collaboratively for the benefit of both

2) *Regionalized Agency*, established as a regional branch of the state education agency to provide services to local units

3) *Cooperative Agency,* established by two or more individual school districts to provide common services exclusively for the member districts

The official names for the intermediate units vary among the states; they include:

Cooperative Educational Service Agency (CESA)—Wisconsin, Indiana, and Georgia

Area Education Agency (AEA)—Iowa

Educational Service Unit (ESU)—Nebraska

Intermediate Unit (IU)—Pennsylvania

Educational Service Center (ESC)—Texas

Intermediate School District (ISD)—Washington and Michigan

Regional Educational Service Agency (RESA)—West Virginia

Boards of Cooperative Services (BOCS)—Colorado

Boards of Cooperative Educational Services (BOCES)—New York

Intermediate Education District (IED)—Oregon

intermediate elementary grades
The grades between the primary grades and the upper elementary grades or the junior high school, usually grades four, five, and six.

intermediate elementary level
Education in grades four, five and six, or the equivalent.

intermediate school   One designation, somewhat dated, for a MIDDLE SCHOOL. *See* Leslie Kindred et al., *The Intermediate School* (Englewood Cliffs, N.J.: Prentice-Hall, 1968).

intermediate school district (ISD)
An administrative educational organization between the local education agency and the state education agency, with various forms and functions. Frequently,

intermediate districts are arranged along county lines and maintain responsibility for the monitoring of state standards. Intermediate districts may also be voluntary cooperatives between two or more school districts for the purpose of sharing specialized services that the districts individually would be unable to provide.

intermediate sources of revenue
An intermediate administrative unit or a political subdivision between school districts and the state that collects revenue and distributes it to school districts in amounts different from those that are collected within such systems.

intermediate unit   *See* INTERMEDIATE EDUCATION UNIT.

intern   An apprentice; an educational professional-in-training, teacher or otherwise, who is engaged in the practice of the profession under the direct supervision of another professional as a part of his or her training. *See also* TEACHING INTERN *and* ADMINISTRATIVE INTERN.

internal auditing services   Activities concerned with verifying the account records, including evaluating the adequacy of the internal control system, verifying and safeguarding assets, reviewing the reliability of the accounting and reporting systems, and ascertaining compliance with established policies and procedures.

internal control   A plan of organization under which employees' duties are so arranged and records and procedures so designed as to make it possible to exercise effective accounting control over assets, liabilities, revenues, and expenditures. For example, under such a system, the employees' work is subdivided so that no one employee performs a complete cycle of operations. For instance, an employee handling cash would not post the accounts receivable records. Again, under such a system, the procedures to be followed are definitely laid down and such procedures call for proper authorizations by designated officials for all actions to be taken.

internal evaluation   The process used by personnel responsible for the conduct and operation of a program to determine the degree to which it has fulfilled its stated objectives.

internal information services   Activities concerned with the writing, editing, and communicating of information to pupils and staff.

International Christian Youth Exchange   A cultural and educational exchange program under which individual students from one country live with a family in another country and attend school for one semester, then do volunteer work for a community agency for the second semester. Twenty-six countries are involved in this program, which is headquartered in the United States at 134 W. 26th St., New York, NY 10001.

International Journal of Group Psychotherapy   Official quarterly of the American Group Psychotherapy Association. Devoted to reporting and interpreting research and practice in group psychotherapy in various settings in the United States and in other countries, it reflects the types of group psychotherapy now employed, and helps stimulate the study of validation of practice and results. It also serves as a forum of ideas and experiences, with a view toward clarifying and enlarging the scope of group psychotherapy techniques.

> International Journal of Group
> Psychotherapy
> American Group Psychotherapy
> Association, Inc.
> 1995 Broadway, 14th Floor
> New York, NY 10023

interpersonal competence   Measure of an individual's capability to work well in relationships with people in a variety of situations. To have interpersonal competence while occupying any given position, one would have to be proficient in meeting all of a position's role demands.

See David Moment and Abraham Zaleznik, *Role Development and Interpersonal Competence* (Boston: Harvard University Graduate School of Business Administration, 1963); and Chris Argyris and Roger Harrison, *Interpersonal Competence and Organizational Effectiveness* (Homewood, Ill.: Richard D. Irwin, 1962).

interpolation   Process of estimating intermediate values between two known values.

interrater reliability   Also called interexaminer reliability. Extent to which examiners give the same score to the same candidate or to different candidates who perform comparably. See J.M. Greenwood and W.J. McNamara, "Interrater Reliability in Situational Tests," *Journal of Applied Psychology* (April 1967).

interscholastic athletics   Organized games and athletic activities engaged in by pupils, specifically trained for such purposes, with similarly trained pupils from other schools.

Interstate Compact for Education   See EDUCATION COMMISSION OF THE STATES.

interstate migratory child   As defined for federal compensatory education programs, a child who has moved with a parent or guardian within the past year across state boundaries in order that a parent, guardian, or other member of his immediate family might secure temporary or seasonal employment in an agricultural activity.

intervention   An approach or strategy designed to change or impact upon a specific task or area of growth of a specific problem or area of deficit, for example developmental tasks or skills, substance abuse, truancy, or learning difficulties.

intramural athletics   Organized games and athletic activities engaged in by pupils of a school with other pupils from the same school. The intramural program may be an integral part of the physical education program or a distinctive program of its own; in either case, the program is confined to a single school.

intrastate migratory child   As defined for federal compensatory education programs, a child who has moved with a parent or guardian within the past year across school district boundaries within a state in order that a parent, guardian, or other member of his immediate family might secure temporary or seasonal employment in an agricultural activity.

intrinsic motivation   Motivation that comes from the potential for satisfaction of a deeply felt personal need; the desire to learn or accomplish a task based on internal drives and/or the sense of value or worthiness of the task itself. Contrast with EXTRINSIC MOTIVATION. See MASLOW'S HIERARCHY OF NEEDS.

inventory   1. A detailed list or record showing quantities, descriptions, values, and, frequently, units of measure and unit prices of property on hand at a given time. Also, the cost of supplies and equipment on hand not yet distributed to requisitioning units. 2. Questionnaire designed to obtain nonintellectual information about a subject. Inventories are often used to gain information on an individual's personality traits, interests, or attitudes.

See Robert C. Droege and John Hawk, "Development of a U.S. Employment Service Interest Inventory," *Journal of Employment Counseling* (June 1977).

inventory, interest   See INTEREST INVENTORY.

investment building   A building that has been acquired by the school district for investment purposes and is held to produce revenue for the support of schools.

involuntary separation   The dismissal of an employee resulting from a decision made solely by a school district after appropriate due process procedures are followed.

involuntary transfer   The transfer of a teacher or other staff person from one school building to another within a school district without regard to the preference of the employee.

Iowa Tests of Basic Skills (ITBS)   General achievement tests for grades three through eight which are widely used in elementary schools for measuring student attainment levels in reading, arithmetic, spelling, language, science, and social studies. They are published by:

Houghton Mifflin Company
Test Editorial Offices
P.O. Box 1970
Iowa City, IA 52240

ISD   See INTERMEDIATE SCHOOL DISTRICT.

Itard, Jean Marc Gaspard (1775-1838).   The French physician who is often credited as being the originator of special education techniques and practices that continue to be used today. These practices include ideas such as individualized instruction, behavior modification, and sequenced tasks. In the early 1800s, Itard successfully took on the education of a boy of about 12 years who had been found roaming wild in the forests of France. The boy, called Victor, was described by others as "hopeless." Itard was able to dramatically improve Victor's behavior through patient and systematic instruction. His efforts are described in Itard's own book, *The Wild Boy of Aveyron*, translated by George and Muriel Humphrey (Englewood Cliffs, N.J.: Prentice Hall, 1962). *See also* H. Lane, *The Wild Boy of Aveyron* (Cambridge, Mass.: Harvard University Press, 1976).

ITBS   *See* IOWA TESTS OF BASIC SKILLS.

item analysis   Statistical description of how a particular question functioned when used in a particular test. An item analysis provides information about the difficulty of the question for the sample on which it is based, the relative attractiveness of the options, and how well the question discriminated among the examinees with respect to a chosen criterion. The criterion most frequently used is the total score on the test of which the item is a part. However, the criterion may be the score on a subtest, or on some other test or, in general, on any appropriate measure that ranks the examinee from high to low.

item validity   Extent to which a test item measures what it is supposed to measure.

itinerant teacher   1. A teacher who travels from one school building to another for the purpose of providing direct, individual assistance to students with special needs and/or to provide consultation to classroom teachers. 2. A teacher of an optional, elective subject such as art or music who teaches in two or more school buildings.

IU (Intermediate Unit)   *See* IN- TERMEDIATE EDUCATION UNIT.

J

Jacques-Dalcroze, Emile (1865-1950) The founder of the DALCROZE METHOD of music education.

jar wars President Reagan's antidrug program in which the main weapon is drug testing through urinalysis. It is called jar wars because urine samples are deposited in small jars, because it is a war on drugs, and because the combination rhymes with another favored Reagan program, "star wars" (Strategic Defense Initiative). The jar wars initiative has become controversial because it is asserted that mandatory testing of all of a group of employees might violate the 14th Amendment prohibition against unreasonable searches and seizures. This has yet to be resolved by the courts.

Jarvis-Gann Amendments *See* PROPOSITION 13.

JDRP (Joint Dissemination Review Panel) *See* NATIONAL DIFFUSION NETWORK.

job action A strike or work slowdown, usually by public employees.
See Russell K. Schutt, "Models of Militancy: Support for Strikes and Work Actions Among Public Employees," *Industrial and Labor Relations Review* (April 1982).

job audit *See* DESK AUDIT.

job classification Grouping a number of individual jobs into levels or categories based on comparability of the required skills, experience, knowledge, and the nature of the job itself. All jobs within a given classification will have similar compensation.

Job Corps The federal training program created by the COMPREHENSIVE EMPLOYMENT AND TRAINING ACT OF 1973 that offers social and occupational development for disadvantaged youth through centers with the unique feature of residential facilities for all or most enrollees. Its purpose is to prepare youths for the responsibilities of citizenship and to increase their employability by providing them with education, vocational training, and useful work experience in rural, urban, or inner-city centers. Enrollees may spend a maximum of two years in the Job Corps. However, a period of enrollment from six months to a year is usually sufficient to provide adequate training and education to improve employability to a substantial degree. Job Corps recruiting is accomplished primarily through state employment services.
See Christopher Weeks, *Job Corps: Dollars and Dropouts* (Boston: Little, Brown, 1967); Sar A. Levitan, "Job Corps Experience with Manpower Training," *Monthly Labor Review* (October 1975); and David A. Long, Charles D. Mallar, and Craig V.D. Thornton, "Evaluating the Benefits and Costs of the Job Corps," *Journal of Policy Analysis and Management* (Fall 1981).

job description A written document that outlines the typical duties and responsibilities of a particular position within an organization.

job engineering Altering the duties, responsibilities, or required skills of a job to suit a particular employee; adapting the job to the person (as opposed to training, which adapts the person to the job).

job enrichment Upgrading or expanding the workload, level of responsibility, status, or autonomy of a position for the purpose of upward mobility for the employee and/or increased job satisfaction.

job market   The level of demand for workers in general or for workers in a specific category of employment.

job posting   Any system that allows and encourages employees to apply for other jobs in their organization. Making available information or notices about job openings.

job rotation   Moving workers from one job to another within a limited group of jobs in order to offer broader experiences or to share the burden of some particular tasks. In many elementary schools playground duty and lunchroom duty are examples of job rotation.

job satisfaction   The extent to which a job provides general satisfaction to the worker, meets personal and/or professional needs and goals and is congruent with personal values.

job sharing   The practice of having two persons—each working part-time—sharing the same job.

Job Training Partnership Act (JTPA) of 1982   See COMPREHENSIVE EMPLOYMENT AND TRAINING ACT OF 1973.

jock   A colloquial term for a school athlete. Sometimes used derogatorily in reference to a student who pursues athletic success in school to the exclusion of academic success.

Johari Window   A model for examining and understanding aspects of one's own behavior. The "window" consists of four quadrants into which aspects of oneself are organized: (1) the public self (known to self and others); (2) the blind self (known to others, not known to self); (3) the private self (known to self, not known to others); and (4) the unknown self (unknown to self and others). The model was developed by Joseph Luft and Harry Ingham, hence the name Jo(e)Har(ry)i, and is sometimes used in personal growth training activities for personnel. It is also used as a strategy in counseling and psychotherapy.

John Henry Effect   In educational research, an effect that occurs when a control group performs above its usual average when being measured against an experimental group that is using a new procedure being proposed to replace the control procedure. Compare with HAWTHORNE EFFECT.

Johnson-O'Malley Act of 1934   The first of several pieces of federal legislation enacted to support Native American education.

joint council   A labor-management committee established to resolve disputes arising during the life of a contract.

Joint Council on Economic Education   An independent, nonprofit organization founded in 1949 that provides assistance, support, and materials to school districts to encourage the study of economics.
   Joint Council on Economic Education
   2 Park Avenue
   New York, NY 10016
   (212) 685-5499

Joint Dissemination Review Panel (JDRP)   See NATIONAL DIFFUSION NETWORK.

joint purchasing agreement   A formal agreement among two or more organizations to purchase professional services, equipment, and supplies. The agreements simplify purchasing and result in economies of scale, which

lower costs. *See also* COOPERATIVE VEN-
TURE.

Joplin Plan   A system of reading
instruction that groups children according to reading ability, regardless of age
or grade level; developed in Joplin,
Missouri.

Jordan Left-Right Reversal Test
A test that can be administered individually or in groups to measure letter
and number reversals in children's
visual perceptual functioning. The test
can be used with children between the
ages of five and 12 years. It is published
by:

> Publishers Test Service
> 2500 Garden Road
> Monterey, CA 93940

journal   1. A chronological recording of accounting transactions. After the
journals are balanced at the end of an
accounting cycle (usually a month), they
are posted to the general ledger and to
the subsidiary ledger accounts. For example, a purchases journal is used to
keep track of items ordered and
purchased. It contains information on
the date of the purchases or placing
orders, from whom the purchase was
made, what was purchased, the
purchase order number, the amount,
and which subsidiary and general ledger
accounts will be affected by the
purchase (debited or credited). *See
also*:

> ACCOUNTING CYCLE
> GENERAL LEDGER
> JOURNALIZING

2. Any chronological recording of
events. 3. A general term for a
professionally-oriented periodical or
magazine.

***Journal of Collective Negotiations
in the Public Sector***   A quarterly
publication that emphasizes practical
strategies for resolving impasses and
preventing strikes in the public sector.

Journal of Collective Negotiations in
the Public Sector
Baywood Publishing Company
120-17 Marine Street
P.O. Box D
Farmington, NY 11735

***Journal of Counseling and Devel-
opment***   Monthly journal of the
American Association for Counseling
and Development (AACD) that
publishes articles of common interest to
counselors and personnel workers in
schools, colleges, community agencies,
and government.

> Journal of Counseling and
> Development
> 5999 Stevenson Avenue
> Alexandria, VA 22304

Journal of Education   A periodical, published three times a year by the
Boston University School of Education,
that focuses on pertinent issues in com-
temporary education.

> Journal of Education
> Boston University School of
> Education
> 605 Commonwealth Avenue
> Boston, MA 02215

***Journal of Educational Psychol-
ogy***   A quarterly publication of the
American Psychological Association,
Inc. (APA), that includes original investigations and theoretical papers dealing with learning and cognition, especially as they relate to instruction.
Articles cover all levels of education for
all age groups.

> Editorial Address:
> Robert C. Calfee, Editor
> School of Education
> Stanford University
> Stanford, CA 94305

> Subscription Address:
> Subscription Section, APA
> 1400 N. Uhle St.
> Arlington, VA 22201

Journal of Educational Research
A bimonthly journal which is one of over 40 journals published by Heldref Publications in the fields of education, health care, arts and humanities, sciences, and social sciences.
Editorial Address:
Journal of Educational Research
4000 Albemarle St., N.W.
Washington, DC 20016

Journal of Research and Development in Education   A quarterly journal published by the College of Education, University of Georgia. Prior to 1982 the journal had a thematic format. Currently it is a refereed periodical of original articles of an experimental or theoretical nature as well as research reviews, historical studies, case studies, and content analyses.
Editorial and Subscription Address:
Journal of Research and Development in Education
College of Education
The University of Georgia
Athens, GA 30602

journal voucher   A paper or form on which the financial transactions of a school district are authorized and from which any or all transactions may be entered in the books. By means of the journal voucher, the budget may be put into operation and expenditures made to meet authorized obligations. Journal vouchers are also used to set up revolving funds and petty cash funds, and for authorizing all entries in the bookkeeping system for which no other authorizations, such as deposit slips or invoices, are available. One form of journal voucher is a memorandum in the school board minutes.

journalizing   The initial recording of an accounting transaction in a journal. *See also* ACCOUNTING CYCLE *and* JOURNAL.

JTPA (Job Training Partnership ACT)   *See* COMPREHENSIVE EMPLOYMENT AND TRAINING ACT OF 1973.

judiciary activities (state education agency)   Activities whereby the state education authority or the chief state school officer serves as a tribunal in holding hearings and rendering decisions regarding education-related controversies within the state.

Jung, Carl Gustav (1875-1961)   The Swiss psychoanalyst who studied with Sigmund Freud and subsequently established his own school of analytical psychology and his own broad following. Jung developed the concepts of introverted and extroverted personality types and ascribed to a belief in the "collective unconscious" or shared ancestral memories. *See* Joseph Campbell, ed., *The Portable Jung* (New York: Viking, 1971).

junior   A student in his or her junior (i.e., next to last) year of high school or college. *See* JUNIOR YEAR.

Junior Achievement   A voluntary program of study in economics, primarily for high school students, that provides for experiential learning through the formation, operation, and eventual liquidation of student-run businesses. The organization, which sponsors Junior Achievement, is subsidized by the business community.
Junior Achievement
550 Summer Street
Stamford, CT 06901
(203) 359-2970

junior college   A postsecondary institution which offers the first two years of college instruction, frequently confers an associate degree, and does not confer a bachelor's degree. The term "junior college" is often used interchangeably with the term "community college." *See also* COMMUNITY/JUNIOR COLLEGE.

junior high school   A separately organized and administered secondary school intermediate between the elementary and senior high schools, usually including grades seven, eight, and nine (in a 6-3-3 plan) or occasionally grades seven and eight (in a 6-2-4 plan). Junior high schools are typically structured and function like a senior high school. The primary differences are the age of the students and the course offerings. Contrast with MIDDLE SCHOOL.

junior year   The third year of a four-year high school, i.e., grade 11, or the third year of a four-year college, i.e., grade 15.

junior-senior high school   A secondary school organized on a junior-senior basis and administered under one head as one unit. This includes secondary schools organized on a two-year junior and a four-year senior high school plan, a three-year junior and a three-year senior high school plan, and any other plan based on a junior-senior organization.

jurisdiction   1. Legally granted authority. 2. A geographical area of authority.

just cause   A legitimate basis for terminating the services of an employee or for breaking any contract, including, in this case, the employee's contract.

juvenile   An individual who is under the legal age at which persons are considered responsible adults.

juvenile delinquent   An offender against the laws of society who, because of age, is not considered a criminal. While the term "juvenile delinquent" is often applied to all youthful offenders tried in juvenile court, these children technically are not legally delinquent until adjudged so by the court. *See also* DELINQUENT BEHAVIOR.

K

Kaiser Aluminum & Chemical Corp. v. Weber, et al. *See* UNITED STEELWORKERS OF AMERICA V. WEBER, ET AL.

Kalamazoo case An 1874 court decision that established the legal precedent for publicly supported secondary schools in the United States. See *Stuart v. School District No. 1 of Village of Kalamazoo*, 30 Mich. 69 (1874).

Kanawha County A West Virginia county that attracted national attention in 1974 when fundamentalist church members boycotted the schools in protest over so-called "dirty" textbooks and the teaching of secular humanism and other values contrary to the local culture. See *Mosert v. Hawkins County Board of Education*, 647 F.Supp. 1194 (E.D. Tenn. 1986), rev'd-F2d-(6th Cir. 1987); *Smith v. Board of School Commission of Mobile County*, 655 F.Supp. 939 (S.D. Ala. 1987).

Kappa Delta Epsilon An honorary fraternal organization in education, with 27,000 members.
Kappa Delta Epsilon
2288 Drew Valley Road, N.E.
Atlanta, GA 30319
(404) 634-7107

Kappa Delta Pi An honorary society for educators open to upper-level and graduate students in education who are in the upper 20 percent of their classes. The organization has 50,000 members and publishes two quarterlies, *The Educational Forum* and the *Kappa Delta Pi Record*.
Kappa Delta Pi
Box A
West Lafayette, IN 47906
(317) 743-1705

Kappa Phi Kappa An honorary fraternal organization in education, with 22,000 members.
Kappa Phi Kappa
1920 Southwood Road
Birmingham, AL 35216
(205) 823-1625

Keller, Helen (1880-1968). An American author and lecturer who was deaf and blind from an early age. She lived a successful and productive life, in part due to the dedication of her teacher, Annie Sullivan. Their relationship was immortalized in the play and movie *The Miracle Worker*. For her autobiography, *see The Story of My Life* (New York: Airmont, 1965).

Kellogg Foundation A private philanthropic organization, founded by Will Keith Kellogg of breakfast cereal fame, that supports a wide range of programs in education, agriculture, and health. The foundation's office is in Battle Creek, Michigan.

Kerner Commission The National Advisory Commission on Civil Disorders, chaired by then-Governor Otto Kerner (1908-1976) of Illinois, which reported in 1968 that the "nation is rapidly moving toward two increasingly separate Americas; one black and one white."

ketogenic diet A highly controlled diet that is sometimes successful in the treatment of epileptic seizures. The dietary regime includes a large proportion of fat with smaller amounts of protein and carbohydrate, is barely palatable and, thus, is not widely used.

Kettering Foundation Institute for the Development of Educational Activities; a private philanthropic organization founded by Charles F. Kettering, an inventor and researcher, that supports programs in education, science and technology, international affairs, and urban affairs.

The foundation was originally established to assist the educational community in bridging the gap between research and innovation and actual practice in the schools.

Kettering Foundation
259 Regency Ridge
Dayton, OH 45459
(513) 434-6969

Key Math Diagnostic Arithmetic Test   An individually-administered test of mathematical skill development for students in grades one to six, which assesses three basic areas (content, operations, and applications) and yields a student profile of specific strengths and weaknesses. It is published by:

American Guidance Service, Inc.
Publisher's Building
Circle Pines, MN 55014

key words   Those words that have been determined to occur with greatest frequency in materials written for children and that, therefore, are targeted for early teaching. The Dolch Word List is one example of an aggregate of key words.

Keyes v. School District No. 1, Denver, Colorado 413 U.S. 189 (1973)   The Supreme Court case that ordered district-wide busing of students to eliminate racial segregation. The ruling also required that Hispanic students be counted as minority students along with black students for the purpose of defining a segregated school, since both groups had suffered the same educational inequities when compared to white students.

Keyishian v. Board of Regents 385 U.S. 589 (1967)   The Supreme Court case that held that laws "which make Communist Party membership, as such, prima facie evidence of disqualification for employment in the public school system are overbroad and therefore unconstitutional."

keynote speech   The introductory lecture at a conference or other professional gathering that is usually delivered by someone of prominent reputation and that, in theory, establishes the theme and tone of the meeting.

kibbutzim   An Israeli communal social structure that has drawn wide attention with regard to its ideologies and practices in child-rearing, education, and family systems. Characteristics of kibbutzim life include non-competition, strong peer orientation, and a socialistic, egalitarian, and highly democratic social design.

Kilpatrick, William Heard (1871-1965)   A well-known teacher, educator, and proponent of progressive education who had great influence on curricular changes in American schools through his writings. Major books include: *Foundations of Method* (1925); *Education and the Social Crisis* (1932); and *Philosophy of Education* (1951).

kindergarten   A group or class that is organized to provide educational experiences for children for the year immediately preceding the first grade. A kindergarten class may be organized as a grade of an elementary school or as part of a separate kindergarten school. In some school districts these groups may be called preprimary, junior primary, or primary.

kindergarten room   A special instructional space designed, or provided, with special built-in equipment, for use by a group or class that is organized to provide educational experiences for children for the year or years preceding the first grade.

kindergarten school   An elementary school only for children in their kindergarten year.   *See also* ELEMENTARY SCHOOL.

kinesics   The study of "body language" as a form of nonverbal communication.

kinesiology   The study and science of human motion. *See* Richard Groves and David N. Campaione, *Concepts in Kinesiology*, 2nd ed. (Philadelphia: Saunders, 1982).

kinesthesia   The internal sensation or awareness of one's own muscular movements, positioning, or presence.

knowledge   The accumulated body of facts, information, and beliefs that one acquires through education and experience.

knowledge worker   Peter F. Drucker's term in *The New Society: The Anatomy of Industrial Order* (1949) for the largest and most rapidly growing group in the working population of the developed countries.

It is a group of 'workers' though it will never identify itself with the 'proletariat,' and will always consider itself 'middle-class' if not 'part of management.' And it is an independent group because it owns the one essential resource of production—knowledge. It is this group whose emergence makes ours a 'new' society.

knowledge-level thinking   From Bloom's taxonomy, a thinking or learning process involving the simplest recall of previously learned information. Contrast with COMPREHENSION-LEVEL, APPLICATION-LEVEL, ANALYSIS-LEVEL, SYNTHESIS-LEVEL, EVALUATION-LEVEL. *See* BLOOM'S TAXONOMY.

Kodaly method   An approach to music education, used widely in elementary schools, that is vocal, as opposed to instrumental, and that focuses on helping children understand and appreciate music rather than developing performing skills. The method was developed by Zoltan Kodaly (1882-1967), a Hungarian composer and music educator. *See* Lois Choksy, *The Kodaly Method: Comprehensive Music Education from Infant to Adult* (Englewood Cliffs, N.J.: Prentice-Hall, 1974).

Koh's Block Design Test   A commonly used nonverbal procedure for intelligence testing in which the person is asked to produce patterns out of a number of blocks with different colored sides that replicate pictured examples.

Kuder-Richardson formulas   A method for measuring the internal consistency and reliability of tests.

L

L. Ed.   The abbreviation for the *Lawyer's Edition* of the *U. S. Supreme Court Reports.*

labeling   A practice of assigning a person to a category based on some particular characteristics of the individual and then assuming that the individual has all of the attributes that one may associate with a stereotype of the category, regardless of whether the person demonstrates those attributes or not. For example, a student labelled as mentally retarded may be assumed by many as being incapable of learning due to preconceived stereotypes even though the student may have demonstrated abilities in a number of areas.

Labor, Department of (DOL) The cabinet-level federal agency, created in 1913 to foster, promote, and develop the welfare of the wage earners of the United States, to improve their working conditions, and to advance their opportunities for profitable employment. In carrying out this mission, DOL administers more than 130 federal labor laws guaranteeing workers' rights to safe and healthful working conditions, a minimum hourly wage and overtime pay, unemployment insurance, workers' compensation, and freedom from employment discrimination. DOL also protects workers' pension rights, sponsors job training programs, helps workers find jobs, works to strengthen free collective bargaining, and keeps track of changes in employment, prices, and other national economic measurements.
   Department of Labor
   200 Constitution Avenue, N.W.
   Washington, DC 20210
   (202) 523-8165

labor agreement   The formal results achieved by collective bargaining.

labor cost   That part of the cost of a product or service that is attributable to wages.

labor dispute   Any controversy concerning terms, tenure, or conditions of employment; or concerning the association or representation of persons in negotiating, fixing, maintaining, changing, or seeking to arrange terms or conditions of employment.

labor intensive   Production process requiring a large proportion of human effort relative to capital investment. Teaching is a labor intensive activity.

labor movement   1. An inclusive phrase for the progressive history of United States unionism. Sometimes it is used in a broader sense to encompass the fate of the "workers." Teachers first began to join the labor movement in the 1960s; today they are a major part of it. *See* Susan More Johnson, *Teacher Unions in Schools* (Philadelphia: Temple University Press, 1984).

labor organization   Any organization of any kind, or any agency or employee representation committee or plan, in which employees participate and that exists for the purpose, in whole or part, of dealing with employers concerning grievances, labor disputes, wages, rates of pay, hours of employment, or conditions of work.

labor organizer   *See* ORGANIZER.

labor relations   Totality of the interactions between an organization's

263

management and its organized employees.

Labor Statistics, Bureau of
See BUREAU OF LABOR STATISTICS.

laboratory education   Also called laboratory method. Terms that are used interchangeably for all of the formal means of learning about human behavior through experiencing group activities that have been specially created for such a purpose. According to Clayton P. Alderfer, in "Understanding Laboratory Education: An Overview," *Monthly Labor Review* (December 1970):

the various forms of laboratory education include a number of common elements such as acceptance of experience-based learning technology, recognition of the role of emotions in human relationships, and utilization of the small group (10 to 12 persons) as a central component in training designs.
The learning laboratory usually takes place on a "cultural island." Participants are taken away from their normal day-to-day activities to a setting where the learning experiences occur. Frequently this new setting is naturally beautiful, but at the very least it is different and thereby provides the participant with both safety from former distractions and a setting that does not necessarily reinforce his usual ways of behaving. A second component of the laboratory involves the use of unstructured or semistructured learning tools. The staff usually attempts to design a set of experiences that serve to heighten certain aspects of human behavior and emotions. Participants learn by becoming actively involved in these activities and by developing skills which allow them to observe both themselves and others during

these experiences. A person is asked to engage himself in the unfolding events and later to step back and try to see the patterns in his own and others' behavior. Much of the sense of excitement and high level of emotionality comes from the participant's becoming involved. Experiential learning is based on the assumption that experience precedes intellectual understanding.

laboratory instruction   1. An experiential, "hands-on" method of teaching commonly utilized in science, engineering, foreign languages, and vocational/technical subjects. 2. The use of small group interaction ("laboratories") to produce social/behavioral changes in the individual.

laboratory room   A special instructional space, designed or provided with special built-in equipment, for pupil participation in learning activities involving scientific or applied experimentation; e.g., a laboratory in one of the sciences, mathematics, languages, driver education, or practical or performing arts.

laboratory school   An elementary or secondary school in which part or all of the teaching staff consists of student teachers and the control and operation of the school rests with an institution that prepares teachers. *See* William Van Til, *The Laboratory School: Its Rise and Fall?* (Terre Haute: Indiana State University Press, 1969).

laboratory training   *Also* SENSITIVITY TRAINING *and* T-GROUP. Generic term for those educational/training experiences that are designed: (1) to increase an individual's sensitivity to his or her own motives and behavior; (2) to increase sensitivity to the behavior of others; and (3) to ascertain those elements of interpersonal interactions that either facilitate or impede a group's effectiveness. Particularly during the 1960s and 1970s, laboratory training was a key tool of organization development (OD). While laboratory training and sensitivity training tend to be used interchangeably, sensitivity training is the subordinate term (being the most common method of laboratory training) and the popular name given to almost all experience-based learning exercises. The basic vehicle for the sensitivity training experience is the T-Group (T for training). According to Chris Argyris in "T-Groups for Organizational Effectiveness," *Harvard Business Review* (March-April 1964), the T-Group experience is designed to provide maximum possible opportunity for the individuals to expose their behavior, give and receive feedback, experiment with new behavior, and develop everlasting awareness and acceptance of self and others. The T-group, when effective, also provides individuals with the opportunity to learn the nature of effective group functioning. They are able to learn how to develop a group that achieves specific goals with minimum possible human cost.

See Robert T. Golembiewski and Arthur Blumberg, eds., *Sensitivity Training and the Laboratory Approach*, 3rd ed. (Itasca, Ill.: Peacock, 1977); Henry Clay Smith, *Sensitivity Training: The Scientific Understanding of Individuals* (New York: McGraw-Hill, 1973); and C.L. Cooper and I.L. Mangham, *T-Groups: A Survey of Research* (New York: Wiley, 1971).

Labor-Management Relations Act of 1947/Taft-Hartley Act   The federal statute that modified what the Congress thought was a pro-union bias in the National Labor Relations (Wagner) Act of 1935. Essentially a series of amendments to the National Labor Relations Act, Taft-Hartley provided:

    1. that "National Emergency Strikes" could be put off for an

80-day cooling-off period during which the president might make recommendations to Congress for legislation;

    2. a list of unfair labor practices by unions, which balanced the list of unfair labor practices by employers delineated in the Wagner Act;

    3. that the "closed shop" was illegal (this provision allowed states to pass "right-to-work" laws);

    4. that supervisory employees be excluded from coverage under the act;

    5. that suits against unions for contract violations were allowable (judgments enforceable only against union assets);

    6. that a party seeking to cancel an existing collective bargaining agreement is required to give 60 days' notice;

    7. that employers have the right to seek a representation election if a union claimed recognition as a bargaining agent;

    8. that the National Labor Relations Board be reorganized and enlarged from three to five members; and

    9. that the Federal Mediation and Conciliation Service be created to mediate labor disputes.

The Taft-Hartley Act was passed over the veto of President Truman.

See Anil Baran Ray, "President Truman and Taft-Hartley Act: A Psycho-Political Inquiry," *Journal of Constitution and Parliamentary Studies* (October-December 1980).

Labor-Management Reporting and Disclosure Act of 1959/ Landrum-Griffin Act   The federal statute enacted in response to findings of corruption in the management of some unions. The act provides for the reporting and disclosure of certain financial transactions and administrative practices of labor organizations and employers, and creates standards with respect to the election of officers of labor organizations. Congress determined that certain basic rights should be assured to members of labor unions, and these are listed in Title I of the act as a "Bill of Rights." Existing rights and remedies of union members under other federal or state laws, before any court or tribunal, or under the constitution and bylaws of their unions are not limited by the provisions of Title I. Executive Order 11491 applied these rights to members of unions representing employees of the executive branch of the federal government.

See Doris B. McLaughlin and Anita L.W. Schoomaker, *The Landrum-Griffin Act and Union Democracy* (Ann Arbor: University of Michigan Press, 1978); and Janice R. Bellace and Alan D. Berkowitz, *The Landrum-Griffin Act: Twenty Years of Federal Protection of Union Members' Rights* (Philadelphia: Wharton School, University of Pennsylvania, 1979).

laissez-faire leadership　A "hands-off" administrative style that is distinguished from either an autocratic or democratic approach in that it tends to manifest itself as a "do nothing" style that is disinclined to intervene in any way in the current direction of the organization.

Lakewood Plan　*See* SERVICE CONTRACT.

land grant colleges　Institutions that were originally authorized by the federal Morrill Act of 1862 to promote the study of agriculture and engineering and that, in most cases, have expanded to offer a wide range of studies.

Landrum-Griffin Act　*See* LABOR-MANAGEMENT REPORTING AND DISCLOSURE ACT OF 1959.

language arts　A curricular area that includes subjects such as reading, writing, spelling, and speech. *See* Sidney W. Tiedt and Iris M. Tiedt, *Language Arts Activities for the Classroom* (Boston: Allyn and Bacon, 1978); and Donald C. Cushenbery, *Directing an Effective Language Arts Program for Your Students* (Springfield, Ill.: Charles C. Thomas, 1986).

language experience approach Instruction in the language arts that is based on the learners' own experiences rather than commercially printed materials.

language impairment　A disability in symbolic communication resulting in markedly impaired ability to acquire, use, and comprehend spoken and written language. Persons considered to have a language impairment as a primary disabling condition exhibit a significant discrepancy between their intellectual level of functioning and their level of language performance. In some cases, there may also be present some degree of sensory or motor incapacity, mental retardation, emotional maladjustment, or environmental disadvantage.

language laboratory　A room equipped for language instruction in which tape recorders, projectors, record players, and other devices are used singly or in combination. *See* Julian Dakin, *The Language Laboratory and Language Learning* (London: Longman Group, 1973).

Larry P. v. Riles　343 F. Supp. 1306 (N.D. Calif. 1972)　A case in which the state school system in California was charged with using testing procedures that discriminated against minority students and that resulted in the classification of a disproportionate number of these students as handicapped. This case specifically focused on black students in the San Francisco Unified School District who were placed in special classes at a rate three times their incidence in the general school population. The case was not ruled upon until 1979 when the California schools were finally prohibited from using culturally biased IQ tests as the main criteria for placing students in special education.

last dollar responsibility   A federal funding concept that dictates the use of fiscal resources from a particular source or program only after all other publicly mandated or publicly provided sources have been accessed.

latch-key child   A student who is typically unsupervised after school because of working parents and, therefore, carries a house key to let him or herself into the house upon return from school in the afternoon. Often the student is assumed by school personnel to be deprived of appropriate attention at home. For a report of findings concerning the effects on latch-key children, *see* Cheryl D. Hayes and Sheila B. Kemerman, eds., *Children of Working Parents: Experiences and Outcomes* (Washington, D.C.: National Academy Press, 1983).

late bloomer   A term affectionately applied to students who achieve academic milestones at an age later than most others. *See* Robert Kraus, *Leo the Late Bloomer* (New York: Windmill Books, 1971).

lateral dominance   Also laterality; a preference for using one side of the body rather than the other, e.g., right- vs. left-handedness, which might also apply to a preference for one foot, one leg, or one eye.

Latin grammar school   A dated reference to a secondary school whose purpose was to prepare male students for university studies.

Lau v. Nichols 414 U.S. 563 (1974)   The Supreme Court case that held that public schools receiving federal aid must provide specialized instruction to non-English-speaking students where the language barrier severely restricts their education.

Law-related Education Act of 1978   Federal legislation (P.L. 95-561) that authorized funding to support education programs that promote knowledge of the law, legal processes, and the legal system, and that allow students to be more informed and effective citizens.

laws, right to work   *See* RIGHT-TO-WORK LAWS.

lay readers   Persons, usually college graduates, who are not teachers but who read and help mark English compositions on a part-time basis under the supervision of a fully qualified classroom teacher. Compare to READING ASSISTANT.

lay teacher   A teacher in a parochial school who is not a member of the clergy of that particular religious persuasion.

LEA   *See* LOCAL EDUCATION AGENCY.

leadership   The exercise of authority, whether formal or informal, in directing and coordinating the work of others. The best leaders are those who can simultaneously exercise both kinds of leadership: the formal, based on the authority of rank or office; and the informal, based on the willingness of others to give service to a particular person whose special qualities of authority they admire. It has long been known that those leaders who must rely only upon formal authority are at a disadvantage when compared to others who can also mobilize the informal strength of a classroom, an organization, or a nation.

leadership, transformational
Leadership that strives to change organizational culture and direction, rather than continuing to move along traditional paths. It reflects the ability of a leader to develop a value-based vision for the organization, convert the vision into reality, and maintain it over time. Transformational leadership is a 1980s concept, closely identified with the concepts of symbolic management and organizational culture.

See W.G. Bennis, "Transformative Power and Leadership," in T.J. Sergiovanni and J.E. Corbally, eds., *Leadership and Organizational Culture* (Urbana: University of Illinois Press, 1984); and N.M. Tichy and D.O. Ulrich, "The Leadership Challenge—A Call for the Transformational Leader," *Sloan Management Review* (Fall 1984).

leadership style   An imprecise term that refers to the blending of a person's knowledge of leadership theory and skills, with his or her own personality and values, and under different organizational circumstances, to yield a "style" of leadership behavior. Some people are relatively rigid and can use only one or two styles; others are more flexible and may have many style options available to them. Many authors have proposed typologies, continuums, and matrices of leadership styles, but none have met with general acceptance.

learned helplessness   A motivational term in education that describes an individual who believes he or she cannot achieve success without assistance, usually from a teacher. The behavior results from teacher reinforcement of the student's need for continual assistance.

learned journal or society   Pronounced "learn-ed," not "learned." Refers to a prestigious publication or organization that is assumed to deal with scholarly matters.

learning   Generally, any behavior change occurring because of interaction with the environment. See Winfred F. Hill, *Learning: A Survey of Psychological Interpretations*, 3rd ed. (New York: Harper and Row, 1977).

learning block   Anything physical, psychological, or educational that might prevent or interfere with learning—e.g., physical handicaps, emotional problems, or lack of specific academic skills such as reading.

learning climate   The psychological and interpersonal atmosphere that exists in a classroom or other educational setting, primarily influenced by the teacher's attitudes and behavior.

learning community   A purposefully organized group of people working together to increase their knowledge, skills, and sensitivity.

learning contract   A commitment or agreement between instructor and student specifying expectations for student accomplishment and outcomes. See Neale R. Berte, ed., *Individualizing Education by Learning Contracts* (San Francisco: Jossey-Bass, 1975); and Malcolm Knowles, *Using Learning Contracts* (San Francisco: Jossey-Bass, 1986).

learning curve   1. A graph that depicts the rate of learning over time by an individual or group. 2. A concept in training that describes a learning process in which increases of performance are large at the beginning but become smaller with continued practice. Learning of any new thing eventually levels off as mastery is attained, at which point the curve becomes horizontal.

learning disabilities   *See* SPECIFIC LEARNING DISABILITIES.

learning disabled   Individuals with specific learning disabilities. *See also* CHILDREN WITH SPECIFIC LEARNING DISABILITIES.

learning laboratory   A teaching environment for students with special learning problems that usually contains specialized self-instructional equipment and materials and may have specialized staff.

learning module   A self-contained unit of instruction that is part of a larger curricular program.

learning network   An informal association of people who get together to learn from and to teach each other. *See* Paul Fordham et al., *Learning Networks in Adult Education* (Boston: Routledge and Kegan Paul, 1979).

learning packets   Commercially-produced or teacher-made instructional materials that are designed to be utilized for self-teaching and that include pre-tests, information to be learned, and post-tests. *See* Patricia S. Ward and E. Craig Williams, *Learning Packets: New Approach to Individualizing Instruction* (West Nyack, New York: Parker, 1979).

learning plateau   That flat part of a learning curve that indicates there has been little or no additional learning.

learning resources center   *See* INSTRUCTIONAL MATERIALS CENTER.

learning sets   Groups of similar problem-solving tasks that assist the learner in generalizing a strategy for solving additional problems.

learning style   Also called cognitive style. The way in which an individual receives and processes new information. A categorization of learning styles frequently includes references such as rigid-inhibited, undisciplined, acceptance-anxious, and creative (the most desirable).

learning theory   1. Psychological explanations for how learning takes place. 2. The systematic study of the learning process. 3. One of several popular frameworks to explain the acquisition of new knowledge or behaviors, such as connectionism, classical or operant conditioning, gestalt, functionalism, or developmentalism. *See* John A.R. Wilson et al., *Psychological Foundations of Learning and Teaching*, 2nd ed. (New York: McGraw-Hill, 1974); Glenn E. Snelbecker, *Learning Theory, Instructional Theory and Psychoeducational Design* (New York: McGraw-Hill, 1974); and Joseph D. Novak and D. Bob Gowin, *Learning How to Learn* (New York: Cambridge University Press, 1984).

least restrictive environment (LRE)   The principle that handicapped children who require special education services should, to the extent possible, receive those services in the same classroom and in the same school building that they would have attended if they were not handicapped. This definition was expanded by a United States Court of Appeals in 1983 (*Roncker v. Walter*, 700 F.2nd 1058, 6th Circuit 1983) to state that "to the maximum extent appropriate, handicapped children must be educated with non-handicapped children." Least restrictive environment is frequently used synonomously with "mainstreaming," although there are clear distinctions between the two concepts. Mainstreaming generally refers to the placement of handicapped children into regular education classrooms with or without the provision of specialized services, whereas least restrictive environment refers first to the specialized services, and second to the provision of those services in a physical location that allows maximum participation with the minimum segregation from the regular education mainstream. Least restrictive environment is a value-laden concept that is a key element in P.L. 94-142, the Education for All Handicapped Children Act of 1975.

For an attempt to describe the parameters of LRE *see* H. Rutherford Turnbull, III, ed., *The Least Restrictive Alternative: Principles and Practices* (Washington, D.C.: Task Force on Least Restrictive Environment, Legislative and Social Issues Committee, American Association for Mental Deficiency, 1981).

leave   Any grant of legitimate absence of the staff member from duty assignment that does not affect his employment status.

leave, birth   *See* BIRTH LEAVE.

leave of absence   An extended absence from work for which the individual usually is not paid, though tenure and/or seniority may be maintained.

leave without pay   Like a leave of absence but usually shorter in duration; an absence from work during which time no payment is earned.

lecture method   An approach to instruction that generally involves the teacher communicating a body of information to a large group of students; typically, the students simply listen and take notes.

ledger   A business account book, usually recording the day-to-day transactions, and usually showing debits and credits separately. *See also*:
ACCOUNTING CYCLE
ALLOTMENT LEDGER
APPROPRIATION LEDGER
COST LEDGER
DEBITS AND CREDITS
GENERAL LEDGER
SUBSIDIARY LEDGER

ledger card   A card that holds one subsidiary ledger account, typically on five-inch by eight-inch, heavy-stock paper. *See also* SUBSIDIARY LEDGER.

legal adult   A person who has reached a specified minimum legal age of adulthood. *See also* ADULT.

legal minor   A person who has not reached a specified minimum legal age of adulthood.

legal services   1. Activities pertaining to counseling services provided to the board of education in regard to laws and statutes. 2. Any services that relate to the interpretation of the law and the application of knowledge of the law to adversarial, or potentially adversarial, situations.

Leiter International Performance Scale   An individually administered, nonverbal test of intelligence standardized for ages two years through adult; it has been determined to be a highly reliable scale that correlates well with other verbal and nonverbal measures. The test involves the matching of increasingly complex sets of pictures and other visual symbols. It is available through:
Western Psychological Services
12031 Wilshire Boulevard
Los Angeles, CA 90025

Lemon v. Kurtzman 403 U.S. 602, 612, 1971   One of several U.S.

Supreme Court cases relating to public support of nonpublic (parochial) schools. This case ruled that direct public support for teacher salaries in parochial schools was unconstitutional, even when the salary was specifically earmarked for the teaching of nonreligious subject matter.

length of term in days The number of days school was actually in session during the year, which is used for computing ADA and ADM. Only days on which the school is open and the pupils are under the guidance and direction of teachers in the teaching process are generally considered as days in session. On some days the school plant itself may be closed and the student body as a whole engaged in school activities outside the school plant under the guidance and direction of teachers. Such days are considered as days in session. Days on which school is closed for such reasons as holidays, teachers' institutes, and inclement weather are not considered as days in session.

LEP *See* LIMITED-ENGLISH PROFICIENT.

leptokurtic A frequency distribution or curve that is more peaked, as opposed to flat-topped, than a normal curve.

lesson 1. An individual session or unit of instruction. 2. An experience that leaves the learner with new understanding or knowledge. 3. A reading from the Bible as a part of a religious service. 4. A punishment or reprimand.

lesson plan A written scheme prepared by the teacher that includes the instructional objectives and methods for a particular functional unit or period of instruction. *See* Danny G. Langdon, *The Construct Lesson Plan: Improving Group Instruction* (Englewood Cliffs,

N.J.: Educational Technology Publications, 1978); and Robert R. Carkhuff et al., *The Skills of Teaching: Lesson Planning Skills* (Amherst, Mass.: Human Resource Development Press, 1978).

less-than-full-time assignment Assigned activities within an assignment classification that do not require all of the time of a full-time staff member to perform. *See also* STAFF ASSIGNMENT WORKLOAD.

letter grade An evaluation of a student's performance in a class that is expressed by a letter of the alphabet, usually A, B, C, D, or F.

level annual premium funding method Pension contributions or premiums that are paid into a fund (or to an insurance company) in equal installments during the employee's remaining working life so that upon retirement the pension benefit is fully funded.

level of performance A predetermined level or stage of performance, or degree of proficiency, as designated by a school or school system.

level of significance A statistical term that refers to the amount of confidence in whether or not the difference between two outcomes is significant or due to mere chance.

levy 1. To impose taxes or special assessments. 2. The total of taxes or special assessments imposed by a governmental unit.

Lewin, Kurt (1890-1947) Popularly noted for his assertion that "there is nothing so practical as a good theory," he was an influential experimental psychologist of the 20th century. His research originated the modern concepts of group dynamics, action research, field theory, and sensitivity training. Major works include: *Principles of Topological Psychology* (New York: McGraw-Hill, 1936); *Resolving Social Conflicts: Selected Papers on Group Dynamics* (New York: Harper & Row, 1948); *Field Theory in Social Science: Selected Theoretical Papers*, ed. by Dorwin Cartwright (London: Tavistock, 1963). For a biography, *see* Alfred J. Marrow, *The Practical Theorist: The Life and Work of Kurt Lewin* (New York: Basic Books, 1969).

liabilities Also CURRENT LIABILITIES and LONG-TERM LIABILITIES. The current and long-term debts owed by an enterprise or jurisdiction. *Current liabilities* are due and payable within a year and include such items as accounts payable, wages, and short-term debt. *Long-term liabilities* are payable more than a year hence and include items such as bonds. *See also* CONTINGENT LIABILITIES.

liability insurance Expenditures for insurance coverage of a school district, or its officers, against losses resulting from judgments awarded against the system. Also recorded here are any expenditures (not judgments) made in lieu of liability insurance.

liberal education A broad and general exposure to information, rather than specialized training for a particular purpose. Liberal arts usually refers to the more basic components of the curriculum, including the arts and sciences. Its original intention was to "free the mind and the spirit" from narrow specialization and vocational preparation. *See* Bruce A. Kimball, *Orators and Philosophers: A History of the Idea of Liberal Education* (New York: Teachers College Press, 1986).

librarian A staff member assigned to perform professional library service activities, such as ordering, cataloging,

processing, and circulating books and other materials; planning the use of the library by teachers, pupils, and others; selecting books and materials; participating in faculty planning for the use of books and materials; and guiding teachers, pupils, and others in the use of the library in schools or community service programs.

library books Books purchased for general use and not primarily for use in certain classes, grades, or other particular student groups. They include reference sets and dictionaries, but not textbooks and periodicals.

library books per student The number of volumes of library books in the library(s) of a school or school system, divided by a student unit of measure.

library classification systems Ways to label and arrange materials on library shelves so they can be easily located. *See* DEWEY DECIMAL SYSTEM and LIBRARY OF CONGRESS CLASSIFICATION.

Library of Congress classification A complex system for cataloging and shelving books that is used primarily in large libraries. Compare to DEWEY DECIMAL SYSTEM.

library science 1. The study of the categorization and use of print and nonprint materials, usually undertaken at the postsecondary level. 2. The professional practice of maintaining a library.

library services staff per 1,000 students in average daily attendance The number representing the total full-time equivalency of library service staff assignments in a school or school system during a given period of time, multiplied by 1,000 and divided by the average daily attendance of students during this period.

license   1. A permission granted to an individual or organization by a designated authority, usually public, to engage in a practice, occupation, or activity otherwise unlawful. Licensure is the process by which the license is granted. Since a license is needed to begin lawful practice, it is usually granted on the basis of examination and/or proof of education, rather than measures of performance. License when given is usually permanent but may be conditioned on annual payment of a fee, proof of continuing education, or proof of competence. Common grounds for revocation of a license include incompetence, commission of a crime (whether or not related to the licensed practice), or moral turpitude. 2. The legal document giving authorization from a state (or an agency or an organization authorized by a state) to perform certain specific services in the field of education. (Sometimes used synonymously with "certificate.")

lien   A claim, charge, or liability against property that is allowed by law, rather than one that is part of a contract or agreement. For example, a tax lien is the government's placing of a financial obligation on a piece of property that must be paid because taxes are delinquent.

life adjustment education   A school curriculum popular in the 1950s that was in general designed to prepare students to be competent, self-accepting adults. The concept of functional, life-referenced instruction was resurrected in the 1980s, particularly in reference to students with special learning problems.

life insurance   Insurance that provides for the payment of a specific amount to a designated beneficiary in the event of the death of the insured. *See also*:

ACCIDENTAL DEATH-BENEFIT

GROUP INSURANCE
TERM INSURANCE

lifelong learning   The process by which an adult continues to acquire, in a conscious manner, formal or informal education throughout his or her life span, either to maintain and improve vocational viability or for personal development. *See* Arthur J. Cropley and Ravindra H. Dave, *Lifelong Education: A Psychological Analysis* (Elmsford, N.Y.: Pergamon Press, 1977).

lighthouse district   A term that refers to a school district offering new and exemplary programs.

Likert Scale   Also called Likert-type scale. One of the most widely used scales in social research. Named after Rensis Likert (1903-1981), who first presented it in "A Technique for the Measurement of Attitudes," *Archives of Psychology* (No. 140, 1932), the scale presents a subject with a statement, to which the subject expresses his or her reaction or opinion by selecting one of five (or more) possible responses arranged at (supposedly) equidistant intervals.

Typical Questions on a Likert Scale
1.   The sick-leave policies of this company are not liberal enough.
    (a)   strongly agree
    (b)   agree
    (c)   no opinion
    (d)   disagree
    (e)   strongly disagree
2.   My supervisor is a good leader.
    (a)   strongly agree
    (b)   agree
    (c)   uncertain
    (d)   disagree
    (e)   strongly disagree

limited-English proficient (LEP)   A designation for students of non-English-language background who have sufficient difficulty speaking, writing, reading, and understanding the

English language to be unable to learn successfully in classrooms where English is the language of instruction.

line organization Those segments of a larger organization that perform the major functions of the organization and have the most direct responsibilities for achieving organizational goals. All classroom teachers are part of a school's line organization. Compare to STAFF.

line staff Those staff who perform the functions that carry out directly the major objectives of the organization. In education those staff who have direct contact with students are considered line staff.

linear programming In the context of programmed self-instruction, a format that follows a predetermined order and sequence that is identical for all learners.

linear responsibility chart See ORGANIZATIONAL CHART.

line-item budget See BUDGET, LINE-ITEM.

line-item structure A budgetary format wherein certain estimated receipts and expenditures appear on a given line and must be restricted to one specific purpose; such funds cannot be commingled with others.

linguistics The study of human speech, i.e., the sounds used in oral communication.

linkage Strategy relating two or more issues in negotiations and then using them as tradeoffs or pressure points, much as in a "carrot and stick" technique.

liquid assets Cash and other current assets that can be converted rapidly to cash. See also ASSETS.

liquidity The rapidity and facility with which assets can be converted to cash. See also ASSETS and LIQUID ASSETS.

literacy The ability to read and write at a level expected by one's culture. For several articles addressing this topic see Phi Delta Kappan (November 1987).

literature Printed materials that are judged to have merit based on social or intellectual values and/or specialized interests. Can include books, poems, essays, or other documents.

literature search The process of investigating resources and finding books, articles, reports, or other documents that might be relevant to a particular topic under study.

literature survey Reviewing all available resources on a topic prior to undertaking independent or original research or study on the topic.

little red schoolhouse Refers nostalgically (and probably with unrealistic affection) to the one-room K-6 (or K-12) schools of early America.

LMRA See LABOR-MANAGEMENT RELATIONS ACT OF 1947.

lobby Also Federal Regulation of Lobbying Act of 1946. Any individual, group, or organization that seeks to influence legislation or administrative action. The term arose from the use of lobbies, or corridors, in legislative halls as places to meet with and persuade legislators to vote a certain way.

The Federal Regulation of Lobbying Act of 1946 requires that persons who solicit or accept contributions for lobbying purposes keep accounts, present receipts and statements to the clerk of the House, and register with the clerk of the House and the secretary of the Senate. The information received is published quarterly in the *Congressional Record*. The purpose of this registration is to disclose the sponsorship and sources of funds of lobbyists, but not to curtail the right of persons to act as lobbyists.

Local Affairs, Department of The generic name of a state agency with oversight responsibilities for local government. Sometimes local governments are required to submit audit and budget reports to such an agency, with the exact requirements varying from state to state.

local basic administrative unit An administrative unit at the local level that exists primarily to operate public schools or to contract for public school services. Normally, taxes can be levied by such units for school purposes. These units may or may not have boundaries that coincide with county, city, or town boundaries. This term tends to be used synonymously with the terms "school district" and "local education agency."

local education agency (LEA) An educational agency, governed by a school board and administered by a superintendent and staff at the local level, that exists primarily to operate schools or to contract for educational services. Normally, taxes may be levied by such publicly operated agencies for school purposes. These agencies may or may not have boundaries that coincide with county, city, or town boundaries. This term tends to be used synonymously with the terms "school district," "school system," and "local basic administrative unit." *See also* LOCAL BASIC ADMINISTRATIVE UNIT.

local employees' association According to IRS Code 501(c)(4), local employees' associations are "local associations of employees, the membership of which is limited to . . . person or persons in a particular municipality,

and the net earnings of which are devoted exclusively to charitable, educational or recreational purposes." Local employees' associations may qualify for tax-exempt status under IRS Code 501 (c)(4).

local independent union Local union not affiliated with a national or international union.

local union A regional organization of union members who are part of a national or international union. A local union is chartered by the national or international union with which it is affiliated.

locational skills A term referring to a number of reading abilities that allow an individual to find information in written sources, such as alphabetizing, locating page numbers in a table of contents, using glossaries or reference books, and using library classification systems.

Locke, John (1632-1704) The English physician and philosopher whose writings on the nature of governance had a profound influence on the Founding Fathers. It is often argued that the first part of the Declaration of Independence, which establishes the essential philosophic rationale for the break with England, is Thomas Jefferson's restatement of John Locke's most basic themes.

Locke's *A Letter Concerning Toleration* (1689) anticipated American thought on religious toleration. Locke held that a policy of toleration was only logical because it permitted all of the religious groups to support the state while the alternative of religious persecution and suppression only led to sedition and internal discord.

In *Some Thoughts Concerning Education* (1693) Locke addressed issues in education, specifically in support of rationality, virtue, and practicality.

John Locke, *Some Thoughts Concerning Education* (1695):
Let therefore your rules to your son be as few as possible, and rather fewer than more than seem absolutely necessary—for if you burden him with many rules, one of these two things must necessarily follow; that either he must be very often punished, which will be of ill consequence, by making punishment too frequent and familiar; or else you must let the transgressions of some of your rules go unpunished, whereby they will of course grow contemptible, and your authority become cheap to him. Make but few laws, but see they be well observed when once made.

lockout   Employer's version of a strike; the closing of a business in order to pressure the employees and/or the union to accept the employer's offered terms of employment. This early weapon against the union movement lost much of its effect when locked-out employees became eligible for unemployment compensation. Almost all union contracts with a no-strike clause also contain a similar ban against lockouts.

locus of control   A construct from social learning theory that describes the kinds of explanations that individuals use to account for their behavior or their level of successful performance. An external orientation attributes control to forces outside of oneself or to luck, chance, or fate; an internal orientation assumes that personal abilities, efforts, or other characteristics control performance. For the origins of locus of control theory, *see* J.B. Rotter, "Generalized Expectancies for Internal vs. External Control of Reinforcement," *Psychological Monographs, General and Applied*, 80(1966).

For a more recent review and discussion, *see* Larry B. Autry, "Locus of Control and Self-responsibility for Behavior," *Journal of Educational Research* (November/December 1985).

longitudinal survey   A study of a group of subjects that follows them through time. *See* Herbert S. Parnes, "Longitudinal Surveys: Prospects and Problems," *Monthly Labor Review* (February 1972); and Wesley Mellow, "Unionism and Wages: A Longitudinal Analysis," *The Review of Economics and Statistics* (February 1981).

long-term debt   Debt payable more than one year after date of issue. *See also* LIABILITIES.

long-term debt offsets   Cash and investment assets of sinking funds and other reserve funds, however designated, that are specifically held for redemption of long-term debt.

long-term debt retired   The par value of long-term debt obligations liquidated by repayment or exchange, including debt retired by refunding operations.

long-term liabilities   *See* LIABILITIES.

long-term original issues   All long-term debt issued other than that issued to refund existing long-term debt. Includes long-term debt issued for funding of existing short-term obligations.

Los Angeles Department of Water and Power v. Manhart   *See* CITY OF LOS ANGELES, DEPARTMENT OF WATER & POWER V. MANHART.

lottery, state-sponsored   A source of state revenue in approximately 23 states (as of 1987), with a portion earmarked for education in seven of those states.

STATES WITH LOTTERIES BENEFITING EDUCATION

	Year Began	1986 Gross Sales*	1986 Net Proceeds*	Division of Gross Proceeds
California	1985	$1,765	$693	Education, 34%; prizes, 50%; administration, 8.6%
Illinois	1974	1,316	552	Education 42.9%; prizes 48.5%; administration, 8.6%
Michigan	1972	999	415	Education, 40%; prizes, 49%; administration, 11%
New Hampshire	1964	34	10	Education, 28.3%; prizes 48.1%; administration, 23.6%
New Jersey	1970	990	419	Education, 42%; prizes, 49%; administration, 9%
New York	1967	1,317	616	Two formulas: education, 45%; prizes, 40%; administration, 15%. Or education, 35%; prizes, 50%; administration, 15%
Ohio	1974	943	370	Education, 39.6%; prizes, 49.3%; administration, 11.1%
Florida	1988**	1,190**	—	Education, 35%; prizes, 50%; administration, 15%

*In millions of dollars   **Projected

Source: *The Executive Educator* (August 1987)

low match   *See* MATCHING SHARE.

lower classman   A freshman or sophomore in either high school or college.

loyalty oath   An affirmation of allegiance. Allegiance may be given to a state or to any organization or religious group that may expect special commitment by its members to the interests of the organization or the group. When the interests of such groups are in conflict with one another, individuals who hold membership in both groups may find themselves with, or be considered by others to have, conflicting loyalties; hence they may be thought inherently or potentially disloyal to one or the other. Many public employers may legitimately require their employees to swear or affirm their allegiance to the Constitution of the United States and to that of a particular state. *See* Paul M. Sniderman, *A Question of Loyalty* (Berkeley: University of California Press, 1981).

See also:
COLE V. RICHARDSON
EFBRANDT V. RUSSELL
GARNER V. BOARD OF PUBLIC WORKS OF
  LOS ANGELES
KEYISHIAN V. BOARD OF REGENTS
SHELTON V. TUCKER

lyceum   1. A hall or auditorium where lectures or other presentations to large audiences are held. 2. A late 19th-century adult education movement.

M

MA   Master of arts.

MAEd   Master of arts in education.

magna cum laude   "With great praise"; a degree awarded with distinction that is at a higher level than "cum laude" but less high than "summa cum laude" (see entries).

magnet school   1. A school within the public school system that offers a unique and/or specialized program for the purpose of attracting students voluntarily from throughout the school district who will represent a racial and ethnic mix, i.e., voluntary desegregation. Generally, a magnet school will emphasize either a specific curricular area (e.g., arts or sciences) or a particular educational philosophy (e.g., "open" concept or fundamentalist orientation). 2. More recently the term has been applied to involuntary centralized services within a school district for students who are handicapped.
See Denis P. Doyle and Marsha Levine, "Magnet Schools: Choice and Quality in Education," *Phi Delta Kappan* (December 1984); and Mary Haywood Metz, *Different by Design: The Context and Character of Three Magnet Schools* (New York: Routledge & Kegan Paul, 1986).

mainstreaming   The integration of students with handicaps into programs and classes with their nonhandicapped peers. Mainstreaming has implications beyond the instructional and social mixing of students with handicaps and those without. Other components include educational planning and a clarification of teacher responsibilities. Systematic educational planning includes strategies to influence the attitudes and behaviors of the regular class peers and structuring of the environment to maximize the benefits for both the handicapped and non-handicapped students. Responsibility for the education of the handicapped student in a mainstreamed setting is shared by the regular classroom teacher and the special education teacher, who each define their respective roles.
See Gary W. Nix, ed., *Mainstream Education for Hearing Impaired Children and Youth* (New York: Grune and Stratton, 1976); Ann P. Turnbull and Jane B. Schulz, *Mainstreaming Handicapped Students: A Guide for the Classroom Teacher* (Boston: Allyn and Bacon, 1979); and Colleen Blankenship and Lilly M. Stephen, *Mainstreaming Students with Learning and Behavior Problems: Techniques for the Classroom Teacher* (New York: Holt, Rinehart and Winston, 1981).

maintenance of effort   Requirement that grant recipients maintain the level of program expenditures financed from their own resources prior to receipt of a grant and use the grant funds to supplement expenditures for the aided activities.

maintenance of plant   In school budgets, a category for maintaining, repairing, or replacing property—such as buying new furnaces or painting—and employing the personnel required to do upkeep.

maintenance personnel   Personnel on the school payroll who are primarily engaged in the repairing and upkeep of grounds, buildings, and equipment.

maintenance warehouse   A building used primarily for housing personnel and equipment engaged in activities concerned with the repair and upkeep of grounds, buildings, and equipment, or with the manufacture of equipment. This includes building facilities for carpenters, cabinet makers, machinists, mechanics, painters, plumbers, electricians, and grounds-keepers.

maintenance-of-membership shop   A union security provision found in some collective bargaining agreements, holding that employees who are members of the union at the time the agreement is negotiated, or who voluntarily join the union subsequently, must maintain their membership for the duration of the agreement as a condition of employment.

maintenance-of-standards clause A contract provision that prevents an employer from changing the conditions of employment unless such changes are negotiated with the union.

major   A concentration of semester hours of college credit representing major specialization in a field of study. The number of college credits constituting a major may be specified in state or national accreditation certification requirements.

major-minor system   An educational system at the secondary or postsecondary level under which students must earn a specified amount of credit in both a major and minor area of study in order to fulfill requirements for graduation.

make whole   A legal remedy that provides for an injured party to be placed, as near as may be possible, in the situation he or she would have occupied if the wrong had not been committed. The concept was first put forth by the Supreme Court in the 1867 case of *Wicker v. Hoppock*. In 1975, the Court held, in the case of *Albermarle Paper Company v. Moody*, 422 U.S. 405, that Title VII of the Civil Rights Act of 1964 (as amended) intended a "make whole" remedy for unlawful discrimination.

malapropism   A humorous misuse of a word or phrase, usually a word that sounds like the intended word. Named for Mrs. Malaprop in the play, *The Rivals* (by Sheridan); she used such terms frequently.

malfeasance   The performance of a consciously unlawful act on the part of a public official. Compare to MIS-FEASANCE.

malpractice   The conduct of one's professional duties that is judged to be improper or a breach of professional responsibility.

management, cutback   Phrase that describes the management of organizations in times of fiscal stress.

management, program   See PROJECT MANAGEMENT.

management audit   Any comprehensive examination of the administrative operations and organizational arrangements that uses generally accepted standards of practice for the purpose of evaluation.

management by objectives (MBO) An approach to managing that controls by outputs and/or results rather than by inputs. The approach's hallmark is a mutual setting—by organizational subordinate and superior—of measurable goals to be accomplished by an individual or team over a period of time. One of the major uses—and misuses —of MBO is for formal performance appraisals.

management calendar A working calendar that displays items such as significant events or periods of heavy work load and that is used for planning by staff, committee members, and directors.

management clause *See* MANAGEMENT RIGHTS CLAUSE.

management development Also called executive development. Any conscious effort on the part of an

EXAMPLE OF A MANAGEMENT CALENDAR

MONTH	JAN	FEB	MAR	APR	MAY	JUN	JUL	AUG	SEP	OCT	NOV	DEC
Board Mtgs. & Agenda Items												
Executive Committee												
Medical Staff												
Finance Committee												
Fund-raising Committee												
Personnel Committee												
Policy & Planning Committee												
Public Relations Committee												
Administrator												
Assistant Administrator												
Division Heads												

organization to provide managers with skills needed for future duties, such as rotational assignments or formal educational experience. The semantic difference between training workers and developing managers is significant. A manager is trained so that he or she can be of greater organizational value not only in present but also in future assignments. In such a context, the development investment made by an organization in a junior manager may only pay off when and if that individual grows into a department head.

management games   Also called business games. Any of a variety of simulation exercises used in management development and education.

management information services Activities concerned with writing and editing and with other preparation necessary to disseminate to management, for logical decision-making: (1) information needed about the operation of the school district; and (2) information about the community, state, and nation.

management information system (MIS)   Any formal process in an organization that provides managers with facts that they need for decision-making. Modern management information systems are almost invariably dependent upon computers.

management letter   *See* AUDITOR'S OPINION.

management prerogatives *See* MANAGEMENT RIGHTS.

management rights   Also called management prerogatives and Reserved Rights. Those rights reserved to management that management feels are intrinsic to its ability to manage and,

consequently, are not subject to collective bargaining. *See also* MANAGEMENT RIGHTS CLAUSE.

management rights clause Also called management clause. That portion of a collective bargaining agreement that defines the scope of management rights, functions, and responsibilities—essentially, all those activities that management can undertake without the consent of the union. A typical management rights clause might read: "It is the intention hereof that all of the rights, powers, prerogatives, authorities that management had prior to the signing of this agreement are retained by management except those rights that are specifically abridged, delegated, granted, or modified by the agreement."

mandamus   Also called writ of mandamus. A court order that compels the performance of an act.

mandate   *See* MANDATORY LEGISLATION.

mandatory bargaining items Those collective bargaining items, if introduced by the other party, that each party must bargain over.

mandatory legislation   Laws at either the state or federal level that all school districts must follow.

Manhart decision   *See* CITY OF LOS ANGELES, DEPARTMENT OF WATER & POWER V. MANHART.

Mann, Horace   (1796-1859) An early educational leader and politician in America who espoused such reforms in education as universal education for girls as well as boys, the establishment of state normal schools, improved teacher training, and a practical curriculum. For a definitive history, *see* Jonathan Messerli, *Horace Mann: A Biography* (New York: Alfred K. Knopf, 1972).

manual   A handbook of instructions. *See also* POLICIES AND PROCEDURES MANUAL.

manual alphabet   The representation of each letter of the alphabet by a different configuration of the hand and fingers. *See* finger spelling.

manual dexterity test   An examination of a person's ability to move the hands easily and skillfully. Such a test may be used in the identification of aptitude for certain occupations.

manual training   The forerunner of industrial arts and vocational education, a part of the school program that emphasized handwork and homemaking skills for the purpose of enhancing basic education through practical application and experience.

manualism or manual communication   The use of sign language and/or fingerspelling in place of oral speech.

manuscript writing, or printing   The form of handwriting that is usually first taught in primary grades, where each letter is formed separately, and that most closely corresponds to the type of print used in primary reading books. Contrast with CURSIVE WRITING.

marginal cost   *See* COST, MARGINAL.

mark or grade   A rating of achievement or academic progress assigned on the basis of some predetermined scale; e.g., letters (A, B, C, D, F), numbers (4, 3, 2, 1, 0), words or phrases (outstanding, satisfactory, needs improvement), and percentiles. *See* Norman Edward Gronlund, *Im-*

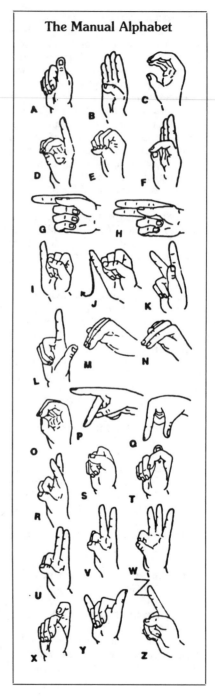

The Manual Alphabet

proving Marking and Reporting in Classroom Instruction (New York: Macmillan, 1974).

mark-point average   *See* GRADE-POINT AVERAGE.

mark-points, or mark point value *See* GRADE POINTS.

martinet   A strict disciplinarian. The word comes from an inspector general in the army of France's Louis XIV, Jean Martinet, who was so despised for his spit-and-polish discipline that he was "accidentally" killed by his own soldiers while leading an assault in 1672.

Maslow, Abraham H. (1908-1970)   Psychologist best known for his theory of human motivation, which was premised upon a "needs hierarchy" within which an individual moved up or down as the needs of each level were satisfied or threatened. Major works include: *Motivation and Personality* (New York: Harper & Row, 1954; 2nd ed., 1970); *Eupsychian Management* (Homewood, Ill.: Richard D. Irwin, 1965). For a biography, *see* Frank G. Goble, *The Third Force: The Psychology of Abraham Maslow* (New York: Grossman Publishers, 1970). *See* NEEDS HIERARCHY.

Maslow's Hierarchy of Needs *See* NEEDS HIERARCHY.

Mason, Lowell (1792-1872) Known as the father of music education in America, he established the Boston Academy of Music in 1833 and advocated the introduction of music teaching into the public schools. *See* Carol A. Pemberton, *Lowell Mason: His Life and Work* (Ann Arbor: UMI Research Press, 1985).

mass picketing   Technique used when a union wants to indicate broad support for a strike. A "mass" of strikers is assembled to picket a place of business in order to discourage nonstrikers from entering the premises.

massed practice   A technique for teaching a new skill through a continuous period of artificial repetitions.

master agreement   Also called master contract. Collective bargaining contract that serves as a model for an entire industry or segment of that industry. While the master agreement serves to standardize the economic benefits of all of the employees covered by it, it is often supplemented by a local contract that deals with the varying circumstances of the various local unions.

master teacher   A teacher who has considerable experience and, perhaps, an advanced level of training, and who is recognized as being especially proficient and capable of providing guidance to other teachers. *See* R.W. Moore, *Master Teachers* (Bloomington, In.: Phi Delta Kappa, 1984).

master's degree   A graduate degree granted upon the completion of graduate work, usually the work of at least one year beyond the bachelor's degree.

mastery learning   An important concept in education that refers to the establishment of minimum expected levels of performance and the provision of the instruction necessary to allow a learner to achieve the stated objective. The underlying theory is that all individuals are capable of learning basic skills and knowledge if the curriculum and instructional methods are appropriately structured.

See James H. Block, ed., *Schools, Society and Mastery Learning* (New York: Holt, Rinehart and Winston, 1974); James H. Block and Lorin W. Anderson, *Mastery Learning in*

Classroom Instruction (New York: Macmillan, 1975); Benjamin S. Bloom, *Human Characteristics and School Learning* (New York: McGraw-Hill, 1976); and Lynn S. Fuchs, Douglas Fuchs, and Gerald Tindal, "Effects of Mastery Learning Procedures on Student Achievement," *Journal of Educational Research* (May/June 1986).

For a step-by-step process of how mastery learning can be used effectively in many subject areas, *see* Thomas R. Guskey, *Implementing Mastery Learning* (Belmont, Calif.: Wadsworth, 1985).

MAT Master of arts in teaching.

matched groups/pairs In experimental research an aspect that attempts to assure that the groups or the individuals that are to be compared in outcome are similar on all variables except for the one that is being tested in the experiment.

matching 1. An accounting concept that holds that expenses should be recognized in the same accounting period that is used to recognize the income they produced. 2. In research, the assurance of like characteristics in groups that are to be compared against specific variables.

matching funds 1. Those funds provided for a specific purpose by one level of government as a condition for receiving additional funds for this same purpose from another level of government. Thus a local government may agree to pay 50 percent of the cost of a capital improvement program if its state provides the other 50 percent. 2. Funds provided by private foundations or government agencies that are contingent upon the donee organization raising equivalent funds from other sources.

matching grant A grant made under the condition that additional funds are raised from other sources. For example, a foundation might make a matching grant to a nursing school up to a certain amount (for example, $10,000), if the remainder of the needed funds for a project (for example, $20,000) is raised from the school's alumni, local hospitals, corporations, and other foundations. Matching grants provide the potential recipient with demonstrable evidence of a foundation's willingness to participate, which is useful in raising funds from other sources.

matching item A test item that asks which one of a group of words, pictures, or other choice matches up with those of another group.

matching share Also HIGH MATCH and LOW MATCH. The contribution that grant recipients are required to make to supplement the grantor's grant money. A *high match* is a recipient's contribution that is 50 percent or greater. A *low match* is a recipient's contribution that is less than 50 percent of the total cost.

match-to-sample A basic technique of instructional technology that involves the use of discrimination skills to match one of a set of items to another that is identical (or similar) in form or configuration.

maternity benefits Insurance coverage for the costs of pregnancy and delivery and, in some cases, family planning, postpartum care, and complications of pregnancy.

maternity leave Leave, in addition to sick leave, allowed a staff member before and after the birth of a child. *See* Meg Wheatly and Marcie Schorr Hirsch, *Managing Your Maternity Leave* (Boston: Houghton Mifflin, 1983). *See also* :
BIRTH LEAVE
CLEVELAND BOARD OF EDUCATION V. LAFLEUR

MONELL V. DEPT. OF SOCIAL SERVICES, NEW YORK CITY
NASHVILLE GAS CO. V. SATTY
PREGNANCY DISCRIMINATION ACT OF 1978

mathematics   Also math or arithmetic. One of the basics of most, if not all, school curricula, along with reading and writing. (The three Rs—reading, 'riting and 'rithmetic.) *See also* NEW MATHEMATICS. For a series of articles concerning the teaching of mathematics in schools, *see* "Some Contemporary Problems in Mathematics Education," *Journal of Research and Development in Education* (Summer 1982).

matriculation   The formal acceptance of a student as eligible to study toward an academic degree.

matrix manager   Any manager who shares formal authority over a subordinate with another manager.

matrix organization   1. Any organization using a multiple command system whereby an employee might be accountable to one superior for overall performance as well as to one or more leaders of particular projects. 2. A generic term that is used to refer to an organizational structure that shows a variety of relationships among tasks and ideas as well as employees. *See also* PROJECT MANAGEMENT.

matron   1. A female staff member performing assigned general housekeeping activities in the school plant. 2. A female guard in a jail or juvenile detention center.

maturation   Physical and psychological growth that occurs during childhood and adolescence as a function of individual internal changes rather than educational or environmental influences.

matured bonds payable   Bonds that have reached or passed their maturity date but that remain unpaid.

matured interest payable   Interest on bonds that have reached their maturity date but that remains unpaid.

maturity   1. The time when a debt or other obligation becomes due or a right becomes enforceable. It is usually the date when the borrower on a loan, note, or bond must pay the full amount of the debt. 2. Reference to the physical, psychological, and social development of an individual to a level of acceptable competence.

maturity, social   A level of social skills and awareness that an individual has achieved relative to particular norms related to an age group. An important component for school success.

maximum class size   The membership of the largest class of a given type as of a given date. Maximum class size is often a major issue of contention between teachers and administrators; it is sometimes decided by collective bargaining.

MBA   Master of business administration degree.

MBO   *See* MANAGEMENT BY OBJECTIVES.

McCarthy v. Philadelphia Civil Service Commission 424 U.S. 645 (1976).   The Supreme Court case that upheld an ordinance requiring that city employees live within city limits.

McCarthy Scales of Children's Abilities   An individually-administered norm-referenced scale of intelligence that is used for children ages 2 1/2 to 8 1/2. It measures six separate areas of cognitive functioning: verbal, perceptual-performance, quantitative, general cognitive, memory, and motor. It is published by:

The Psychological Corporation
757 Third Avenue
New York, NY 10017

McCarthy Screening Test   A screening instrument used to predict a young child's readiness for school work and to identify children at risk for learning problems. It is an individually-administered test for children aged four to 6 1/2 years that draws sample items from the McCarthy Scale of Children's Abilities. It is published by:

The Psychological Corporation
757 Third Avenue
New York, NY 10017

McClelland, David C. (1917-   ) Psychologist widely considered the foremost authority on achievement motivation. The body of McClelland's work asserts that achievement motivation can be developed within individuals, provided that the environment in which they live and work is supportive. Major works include: *The Achievement Motive*, with J.W. Atkinson, R.A. Clark, and E.A. Lowell (New York: Appleton-Century-Crofts, 1953); *The Achieving Society* (Princeton, N.J.: Van Nostrand, 1961); and *Motivating Economic Achievement*, with D.G. Winter (New York: The Free Press, 1969).

McCollum Case   Refers to a 1948 U.S. Supreme Court case, *People of State of Illinois ex. rel. McCollum vs. Board of Education*, 333 U.S. 203, which ruled that students could not be released from public school classes for the purpose of religious instruction. Four years later the Supreme Court took a different stand in ZORACH V. CLAUSON.

McCullough Word Analysis Test A diagnostic reading test that can be administered either individually or in groups and that assesses student reading skills in the areas of word and letter

recognition, discrimination, and interpretation. The test is considered appropriate for all grade levels. It is published by:

Ginn Publishing Company
191 Spring Street
Lexington, MA 02173

McDonnell Douglas Corporation v. Green 411 U.S. 792 (1973). U.S. Supreme Court case that held that an employee could establish a prima facie case of discrimination by showing: (1) that he or she was a member of a racial minority; (2) that he or she applied and was qualified for an opening for which the employer sought applicants; (3) that despite qualifications, he or she was rejected; (4) that after rejection the position remained open and the employer continued to seek applicants.

McGuffey Readers   Also the McGuffey Eclectic Readers. An early and well-known series of elementary reading books which were published during the mid-19th century. The books emphasized moralistic and virtuous themes. See Richard D. Mosier, *Making The American Mind: Social and Moral Ideas in the McGuffey Readers* (New York: Russell and Russell, 1965).

McGuffey, William H. (1800-1873)   Author of the MCGUFFEY READERS, which became the best known textbooks ever published in the United States. See John H. Westerhoff, III, *McGuffey and His Readers: Piety, Morality and Education in Nineteenth Century America* (Nashville: Abingdon, 1978).

McInnis v. Ogilvie 394 U.S. 322 (1969)   The Supreme Court decision that held that state systems for funding public education that rely largely on local property taxes, and thus result in wide variations in per pupil expenditures among districts, are constitutional.

Mead, Margaret (1901-1978) An American anthropologist and prolific writer who is best known, in the field of education, for her comparative studies of adolescence—e.g., *Growing Up in New Guinea* (1930); *Coming of Age in Samoa* (1928); and *Childhood in Contemporary Cultures* (1955). For a description of Margaret Mead's views on education *see* Erna J. Lund, "Margaret Mead and Education: A Visionary Approach," *Education* (Fall 1987).

mean   A simple average of a set of measurements, obtained by summing the measurements and dividing by the number of them. Also called the arithmetic average.

mean deviation   *See* AVERAGE DEVIATION.

means test   Criterion used to determine if someone is eligible for government welfare or other benefits. For example, a family might be allowed certain welfare benefits only if their annual cash income is less than the federal government's definition of poverty for a family of four. The means test would then be income below that level. Means-tested entitlement programs are often compared to non-means-tested programs such as social security, which citizens are entitled to without regard to their private means. It has even been suggested that one way of reducing the nation's social security liability is to means-test future benefits; that is, those otherwise eligible for social security benefits would receive them only if their incomes were below a specified level.

See Alan Lewis, "The Comprehensibility of Government Forms and Pamphlets with Special Reference to Means Tested Benefits," *Policy and Politics* (October 1979).

measure, direct   An evaluation variable that is measured directly—not through an intervening variable or indicator. For example, as vehicle-miles-driven increases, the accident rate probably will change. The change—increase or decrease—is a direct measure of the relationship between accident rate and vehicle-miles-driven.

measure, indirect   Tangential measurement. When a chain of relationships exists among evaluation variables, where variable C depends on variable B, which depends on variable A, then a change in dependent variable C is an indirect measure of the relationship between dependent variable B and independent variable A. For example, if a health advocacy organization initiates a major community anti-drinking and driving campaign (independent variable A), it should have a direct effect on the number of drinking drivers on the roads (dependent variable B). An indirect measure would be the number of convictions or citations issued for drinking while driving (dependent variable C).

measure, quantified   An evaluation or research variable, indicator, or measure that is expressed in numerical terms.

EXAMPLES OF QUANTIFIED MEASURES FOR USE IN AN EVALUATION STUDY

volume amounts	degrees
units of production	phases or stages
time units	percentiles
frequency rates	quartiles
ratios	deciles
index numbers	mean deviations
percentages	ranges
proportions	correlations
number of aggregates	
averages	

measure of dispersion Also called Measure of Variability. Any statistical measure showing the extent to which individual performance scores are concentrated about or spread out from a measure of central tendency.

measurement-driven instruction A strategy for the improvement of education, first proposed in the mid-1980s, that acknowledges the powerful influence that "high-stakes examinations" (i.e., those that are required for promotion from grade to grade or those that are administered on a standardized state-wide basis) have on the planning of instructional programs. For several articles and bibliographic references on the topic, see *Phi Delta Kappan* (May 1987).

mechanical aptitude tests Tests designed to measure how well an individual can learn to perform tasks that involve the understanding and manipulation of mechanical devices. Classified in two subgroups—mechanical reasoning and spatial relations.

med-arb Combination of mediation and arbitration that engages a third-party neutral in both mediation and arbitration. The main idea is to mediate in an effort to resolve the impasse or at least reduce the number of issues going to arbitration. Then, if mediation is unsuccessful, some form of binding arbitration is used.

media 1. Instructional media refers to any type of visual or auditory mode of communication that is used to support formal or informal education. The four main categories of media are: printed, graphic, photographic, and electronic. 2. In the context of public communications it usually refers to the transmittal of information via newspapers, magazines, television, or radio.

media event An activity undertaken as a means of generating publicity from the news media. The defining criteria for a media event is that it would not be done if cameras and reporters were not present. Examples include protest demonstrations that are scheduled for the convenience of the early evening television news programs or a candidate for public office walking through a poor or ethnic neighborhood to demonstrate meaningful (meaning photogenic) concern. See Thomas R. Dye and Harmon Zeigler, *American Politics in the Media Age*, 2nd ed. (Monterey, Calif.: Brooks/Cole, 1986).

media power The power of the visual image (especially television, for school children and adults alike) as a manipulator of human behavior and as an influence on social development.
  See Stephen Brookfield, "Media Power and the Development of Media Literacy: An Adult Educaional Interpretation," *Harvard Educational Review* (May 1986); and D.L. Altheide, *Media Power* (Beverly Hills: Sage Publications, 1985).

media relations A broad, continuing, carefully developed relationship with the media that is necessary for obtaining responsive, accurate, and sometimes friendly media coverage of an organization's programs, drives, and other activities. A sub-function of public information or public relations. Compare to PUBLIC RELATIONS.

median The number that splits a frequency distribution into two equal parts, one above and one below the midpoint.

median age of students For a given group of students, the age that evenly divides the distribution of students when classified by age, i.e., the age such that 50 percent of the students are older and 50 percent are younger.

Mediation Service   Abbreviated name for the Federal Mediation and Conciliation Service or any state agencies performing a similar function.

mediation/conciliation   Any attempt by an impartial third party to help settle disputes. A mediator has no power but that of persuasion. The mediator's suggestions are advisory in nature and may be rejected by both parties. Mediation and conciliation tend to be used interchangeably to denote the entrance of an impartial third party into a dispute. However, there is a distinction. Conciliation is the less active term. It technically refers simply to efforts to bring the parties together so that they may resolve their problems themselves. Mediation, in contrast, is a more active term. It implies that an active effort will be made to help the parties reach agreement by clarifying issues, asking questions, and making specific proposals. However, the usage of the two terms has been so blurred that the only place where it is absolutely necessary to distinguish between them is in a dictionary.

For a bibliography, see Edward Levin and Daniel V. DeSantis, *Mediation: An Annotated Bibliography* (Ithaca: New York State School of Industrial and Labor Relations, Cornell University, 1978). *Also see* Deborah M. Kolb, *The Mediators* (Cambridge, Mass.: M.I.T. Press, 1983); and Arnold M. Zak, *Public Sector Mediation* (Washington, D.C.: Bureau of National Affairs, 1985).

mediator   Individual who acts as an impartial third party in order to help resolve disputes. A mediator's role is to help the parties reach an agreement. *See also* MEDIATION.

Medicaid   A federally-aided, state operated and administered program that provides medical benefits for certain low-income people in need of health and medical care.

medical model   Conceptualizing problems in terms of diagnosis and treatment of identifiable and individual pathology. People in education often apply the medical model to students having problems in school, rather than evaluate the problem within the total context of the school environment.

medical services   Activities concerned with the physical and mental health of pupils, such as health appraisal, including screening for vision, communicable diseases, and hearing deficiencies; screening for psychiatric services; periodic health examinations; emergency injury and illness care; and communications with parents and medical officials.

meditation   An approach to achieving relaxation that is based on either a religious focus of thought or a nonreligious attention to mental neutrality; it is purported to result in such benefits as reduced stress and improved educational performance.

Meek v. Pittenger 421 U.S. 349 (1975)   The Supreme Court case that upheld the principle that public funds can be used for the provision of materials to students in parochial schools (e.g., textbooks) but that direct aid to the school is unconstitutional. *See* CHILD BENEFIT THEORY.

meet-and-confer discussions   A technique, used mostly in the public sector, of determining conditions of employment whereby the representatives of the employer and the employee hold periodic discussions to seek agreement on matters within the scope of representation. Any written agreement is in the form of a nonbinding memorandum of understanding. This technique is often used where formal collective bargaining is not authorized.

megatrends   A concept introduced by John Naisbitt in his popular
book of the same name that analyzes 10
major societal trends, all of which, to a
greater or lesser degree, impact on
education. *See* John Naisbitt,
Megatrends (New York: Warner Books,
1982).

membership   1. A collection of individuals joined together for a common
purpose; the state of belonging to a
group. 2. In the context of school enrollment, the number of pupils on the
current roll of a class or school as of a
given date. A pupil is a member of a
class or school from the date he or she is
first present at school and is placed on
the current roll until he or she
permanently leaves the class or school
for one of the causes recognized as
sufficient by the state. The date of
permanent withdrawal should be the
date on which it is officially known that
the pupil has left school, and not
necessarily the first day after the date of
last attendance. Membership is obtained by adding the total original
entries and the total reentries and
subtracting the total withdrawals; it may
also be obtained by adding the total
number present and the total number
absent. This term is also known as the
"number belonging."

membership, aggregate days
See AGGREGATE DAYS MEMBERSHIP.

membership, average daily
See AVERAGE DAILY MEMBERSHIP.

**membership, date of withdrawal
from**   *See* DATE OF WITHDRAWAL
FROM MEMBERSHIP.

membership, day of   *See* DAY OF
MEMBERSHIP.

membership, percentage in
See PERCENTAGE IN MEMBERSHIP.

membership approval   Agreement by the full membership. The
articles and by-laws of many nonprofit
organizations require the board of
directors to submit certain important
decisions to the membership for
approval. Although the decisions vary
among organizations, typical ones include amending the bylaws, adopting
the annual budget, dissolving the
organization, approving the annual
financial reports, or incurring a substantial debt (for example, to acquire a
building).

membership corporation   Nonprofit, nonstock company created for
social, health, political, charitable, or
other public benefit purposes. In most
membership corporations, the primary
function of the members is to elect
directors or trustees.

**membership in special groupings
and/or special schools**   The
number of students on the current roll in
special programs (e.g., in special
classes, groups, or caseloads) and/or
special schools as of a given date.

membership information   Information indicating the period of time the
student's name is on the current roll of a
class or school, regardless of his being
present or absent. The membership of a
class or school is the number of students
on the current roll as of a given date.
This may be obtained by a simple count
or by adding the total number present
and the total number absent. A student
is a member of a class or school from the
date he or she enters until his or her
name is withdrawn from the rolls. During this period, the student is either
present or absent on each day (or half
day) during which school is in session.
The date of withdrawal from
membership is the first day after the date
of last attendance, if known; otherwise,
the date of withdrawal is considered to

be the date on which it becomes known officially that the student left. Membership usually is terminated after excessive consecutive days of absence, other than for long illness, or upon the completion of schoolwork, transference to another school, discontinuance of school, or death.

membership status, active *See* ACTIVE MEMBERSHIP STATUS.

memorandum accounting An informal record of a school district transaction that cannot be recorded under the regular financial accounts but for which a record is desired.

memory The ability to store and recall information from past experiences.

memory span A psychological term that indicates the amount of information that a person can store and recall fairly immediately after the information has been presented.

Mensa An international organization of over 50,000 persons who share the common trait of scoring highly on tests of intelligence.

Mensa
2626 E. 14th Street
Brooklyn, NY 11235
(718) 934-3700

mental ability test An examination of a person's general ability to make successful and rapid adaptation to new situations and to learn from experience. *See* INTELLIGENCE TEST.

mental age (M.A.) The age level in years and months at which an individual performs on some standardized measure that is supposed to be comparable to the average performance on that particular measure for persons of that chronological age. Inaccurate assumptions are often made about an individual's capabilities on the basis of mental age measurements, especially when one's "mental age" is substantially lower than one's chronological age.

mental disability A difference in mental ability that may impact upon successful participation in the educational program of the school system.

mental handicap An impairment in learning potential that adversely affects the performance of an individual. *See* MENTAL RETARDATION.

mental health personnel *See* PSYCHOLOGICAL PERSONNEL.

mental hygiene A general term referring to all aspects of mental health.

mental retardation Refers to cognitive or intellectual ability that is below the norm for one's age group and that is usually accompanied by deficits in adaptive behavior. Students with mental retardation generally require some modification in their school curriculum, though in recent years they have been more and more successfully integrated with non-handicapped students. Educators frequently categorize students by degree of mental retardation based on IQ level: mild, moderate, severe, and profound. Persons at almost all levels of retardation are capable of learning functional life skills and of being assimilated into normal community life. The large majority can live and work independently as adults. *See* Cecil D. Mercer and Martha E. Snell, *Learning Theory Research in Mental Retardation: Implications for Teaching* (Columbus, Ohio: Merrill, 1977).

mentally gifted Individuals who demonstrate such high potential or such advanced levels of mental development that they have been identified by professionally qualified personnel as needing additional educational opportunities beyond what is provided by the usual school program if they are to be educated to the level of their ability.

mentor   1. Wise counselor. The term has become increasingly important in the context of organizational and political careers as empirical evidence has grown that "mentoring" is a critical aspect of career advancement. The word comes from Homer's *The Odyssey.* When Odysseus set off for the war at Troy, he left his house and wife in the care of a friend named Mentor. When things got rough at home for Odysseus' family, Athena, the goddess of wisdom, assumed the shape of Mentor and provided Telemachus, the son of Odysseus, with some very helpful advice about how to deal with the problems of his most unusual adolescence. 2. A teacher who is especially highly respected by students. 3. In higher education, an instructor who is responsible for guiding a student through a non-traditional degree program.
    See M.M. Fagan and G. Walter, "Mentoring Among Teachers," *Journal of Educational Research*, 76:(1982); N.J. Gehrke and R. S. Kay, "The Socialization of Beginning Teachers Through Mentor-Protégé Relationships," *Journal of Teacher Education*, 35:(1984); Kathy E. Kram, *Mentoring at Work: Developmental Relationships in Organizational Life* (Glenview, Ill.: Scott, Foresman, 1985); Laura L. Vertz, "Women, Occupational Advancement, and Mentoring: An Analysis of One Public organization," *Public Administration Review* (May-June 1985); and Judith W. Busch, "Mentoring in Graduate Schools of Education: Mentors' Perceptions," *American Educational Research Journal* (Summer 1985).

merit pay   A salary differential that is based on a qualitative assessment of the employee's performance. In education the concept is controversial. Supporters believe that merit pay stimulates individual improvement and rewards deserving faculty; critics argue that since performance cannot be objectively measured in teaching, merit pay leads to favoritism and discord among employees. For a critical look at this practice in relation to educational reform, *see* Susan Moore Johnson, "Merit Pay for Teachers: A Poor Prescription for Reform," *Harvard Educational Review* (May 1984). For a series of articles reviewing merit pay schemes, *see Phi Delta Kappan* (October 1985).

merit system   A public sector concept of staffing that was established in the U.S. in the late 1800s in reaction to the previously practiced patronage or "spoils" system that awarded public or governmental positions to supporters of the party or individuals in power. The merit system concept implies that no test of party membership is involved in the selection, promotion, or retention of government employees but that instead a constant effort is made to select the best qualified individuals available for appointment and advancement.

meritocracy   A word coined by Michael Young in his *The Rise of Meritocracy, 1870-2033* (London: Thames & Hudson, 1958; Penguin Books, 1961). It referred to a governing class that was both intelligent and energetic, yet sowed the seeds of its own destruction because of its obsession with test scores and paper qualifications that eventually forced those deemed to have lesser IQs to revolt. A favorite slogan of the revolutionaries was, "Beauty is achievable by all." Today meritocracy is often used to refer to any elitist system of government or education. The grisly connotation of the word's original use has been effectively forgotten. *See* Benjamin B. Ringer, "Affirmative Action, Quotas, and Meritocracy," *Society* (January-February 1976).

Meritor Saving Bank v. Vinson *See* SEX DISCRIMINATION.

Merrill-Palmer Scales of Mental Development A developmental scale used with young children, ages 1 1/2 to six years, that measures cognitive, language, and motor skills. It is published by:
C.H. Stoelting Company
1350 South Kostner
Chicago, IL 60623

meta-analysis A technique for summarizing and analyzing the reported results of multiple educational research studies on the same or similar topics. *See* G.V. Glass, B. McGraw, and M.L. Smith, *Meta-analysis in Social Research* (Beverly Hills: Sage Publications, 1981); and J.E. Hunter, F.L. Schmidt, and G.B. Jackson, *Meta-analysis: Cumulating Research Findings Across Studies* (Beverly Hills: Sage Publications, 1982).

metacognition The ability to think about one's own thinking. A learning concept that received much attention in educational research in the 1980s. For an early description, *see* J.H. Flavell, "Metacognition and Cognitive Monitoring: A New Idea of Cognitive-Developmental Inquiry," *American Psychologist* (1979); and Ralph E. Reynolds and Suzanne E. Wade, "Thinking About Thinking About Thinking: Reflections on Metacognition," *Harvard Educational Review* (August 1986).

metalinguistics The ability to understand the concept of reading. *See* Judith Bowey et al., "Development of Children's Understanding of the Metalinguistic Term *Word*," *Journal of Educational Psychology* (June 1984).

methodology 1. A general term referring to the application of principles, practices, and procedures to any area of concern or interest. 2. Refers to a teaching method or a research approach that may be unique to a particular area of study.

Metric Conversion Act of 1975 An act of the U.S. Congress (P.L. 94-168) that stated that "the policy of the United States shall be to coordinate and plan the increasing use of the metric system in the United States."

metric system A universal system of weights and measurements that uses the base number 10. Multiples of basic units (such as the meter for length and the gram for weight) are expressed by prefixes that represent powers of 10. The metric system, while used in virtually every country in the world, is still secondary in the United States to the more widely used, traditional English system. Schools have stressed the teaching of metrics since 1975 when the Metric Conversion Act was enacted.

METRIC WEIGHTS AND MEASURES

Linear Measure
10 millimeters = 1 centimeter
10 centimeters = 1 decimeter
10 decimeters = 1 meter
10 meters = 1 dekameter
10 dekameters = 1 hectometer
10 hectometers = 1 kilometer

Area measure
100 sq. millimeters = 1 sq. centimeter
10,000 sq. centimeters = 1 sq. meter
100 sq. meters = 1 are
100 ares = 1 hectare
100 hectares = 1 sq. kilometer

Volume Measure
1000 milliliters = 1 liter
100 liters = 1 hectoliter
10 hectoliters = 1 kiloliter

Cubic Measure
1000 cubic millimeters = 1 cubic centimeter
1000 cubic centimeters = 1 cubic decimeter
1000 cubic decimeters = 1 cubic meter
Weight
1000 milligrams = 1 gram
1000 grams = 1 kilogram
1000 kilograms = 1 metric ton

Metropolitan Achievement Tests
A comprehensive system of norm-referenced and criterion-referenced tests of achievement that is group-administered and measures performance in grades K to 12. Tests are provided in the content areas of reading comprehension, mathematics, language, social studies, and science. It is published by:
The Psychological Corporation
555 Academic Court
San Antonio, TX 78204

metropolitanism   A movement toward the centralization of services and activities in metropolitan areas rather than the more traditional division of independent urban vs. suburban units of organization.

Meyer v. Nebraska 262 U.S. 390 (1923)   The U.S. Supreme Court decision that has been widely interpreted as setting limits to the powers of states in the control of private schools. In this case the conviction of a teacher for teaching a foreign language (German) in a private elementary school in violation of state law was set aside by the Supreme Court.

microcomputers   Also personal computers. Small, self-contained, reasonably portable and relatively inexpensive computers, with limited capacity but broad versatility, that are widely used in education. For a series of articles about the application of microcomputer technology in schools, see Colin Terry, ed., *Using Microcomputers in School* (New York: Nichols, 1984).

microcounseling/microteaching
A method for the training of professionals that involves videotaping a short session of counseling or teaching and then critiquing the tape as a means of modifying and improving techniques.

microfiche   A four-inch by six-inch film with 270 pages of print readable, when it is put on a fiche reader. Microfiche is used to store large quantities of printed materials: for example, archives, journals, or newspapers.

microfilm   Filmstrips that contain photographs of printed material that have been reduced to a series of frames, each of which represents a page of text. The film can be read and copied with a specially designed device that enlarges and projects each frame onto a screen.

middle school   A separately organized and administered school, usually beginning with grade five or six, and sometimes seven, with a program designed specifically for the early adolescent learner. The middle school plan for operation is different from that of the traditional secondary school (junior high) design. For example, the middle school tends to organize students and teachers into "teams" that relate to each other within units smaller than the total school population.
See William E. Klingele, *Teaching in Middle Schools* (Boston: Allyn and Bacon, 1979); Larry L. Sale, *Introduction to Middle School Teaching* (Columbus, Ohio: Charles E. Merrill, 1979); Judy Reinhartz and Don M. Beach, *Improving Middle School Instruction: A Research-Based Self Assessment System* (Washington, D.C.: National Education Association, 1983); and William M. Alexander and Paul S. George, *The Exemplary Middle School* (New York: Holt, Rinehart & Winston, 1981).

middle/junior high programs
Learning experiences concerned with the knowledge, skills, appreciations, attitudes, and behavioral characteristics that are considered to be needed by all pupils in terms of understanding themselves and their relationships with society and various career clusters and that normally may be achieved during the middle/junior high school years as defined by applicable state laws and regulations.

migrant education   A program of instruction and services for those children who move periodically with their families from one school district to another in order that a parent or other member of the immediate family may secure seasonal employment.

migratory children   Children whose parents are migratory workers, and who accompany their parents from one temporary residence to another. For school purposes, the term refers to such children within the age limits for which the local school district provides free public education.

migratory children of migratory agricultural workers   Children accompanying a parent whose primary employment is in one or more agricultural activities on a seasonal or other temporary basis and who establishes a temporary residence for the purposes of such employment. For school purposes, the term refers to such children within the age limits for which the local school district provides free public education. Regulations of some states require that such children should be identified according to whether their parents are American citizens or aliens.

migratory worker   An individual whose primary employment is on a seasonal or other temporary basis and who establishes a temporary residence, with or without family, for the purpose of such employment.

milestone   1. Significant event in a work plan or a project control chart. Milestones are used to predict whether or not program or organizational objectives will be accomplished. There are two major types of milestone: *Percent complete milestones* and *significant event milestones. Percent complete milestones* are used to substantiate quantifiable objectives within a given time period (i.e., six months or one year), such as dollars raised by providing services or through pledges, number of visitors to a freestanding emergency center, and number of column inches of an organization's print media coverage.

Significant event milestones are major sub-accomplishments which—if not achieved—probably predict that the objectives will not be accomplished. For example, if an objective is to attract a number of patients to a freestanding center, a significant event milestone might be the successful launching of an advertising/public relations program. *See also* OBJECTIVE and PROJECT CONTROL CHART. 2. In child development, a significant event demonstrating growth and new achievement, e.g., walking, first words, moving around the neighborhood alone, or independently preparing a simple meal.

Mill, John Stuart   (1806-1873) The British political philosopher, social reformer, and educational advocate, who was an early supporter of AFFECTIVE EDUCATION and education for women. *See* F.W. Garforth, *Educative Democracy: John Stuart Mill on Education in Society* (New York: Oxford University Press, 1980).

Miller Analogies Test (MAT)   A test that utilizes 100 verbal analogies to measure scholastic aptitude at the graduate school level and to aid in the selection of individuals for personnel positions. It is primarily a measure of verbal ability that covers a broad range of knowledge. Published by:

Psychological Corporation
555 Academic Court
San Antonio, TX 78701

Milliken v. Bradley 418 U.S. 717 (1974)   The Supreme Court case holding that de facto racial segregation in the Detroit metropolitan area public schools, in which minorities were heavily concentrated in the city as opposed to the suburbs, was not unconstitutional since it did not develop from the specific activities of the suburban school districts or any other public authority. The decision largely foreclosed court-ordered busing between cities and their suburbs.

Mills v. Board of Education of District of Columbia 348 F. Supp. 866 (D.D.C. 1972)   One of the earliest court cases establishing that handicapped children have a right to an education and that it is unconstitutional to deny that right. This case opened the door for a number of subsequent, similar rulings and dealt with several issues concerning special education services. Some of the provisions of this ruling included that the school district must have procedures to guard against indiscriminate suspension or expulsion of handicapped students, that the availability of free public education services must be advertised, and that public funds must be equitably expended for educational programs.

minimum (or minimal) competency testing   A testing program used to measure student achievement in relation to eligibility for grade promotion and/or high school graduation. Minimum standards are established and students must demonstrate the acquisition of skills and/or proficiencies beyond the minimum. Many states have adopted minimal competency testing as a statewide requirement for high school graduation, even though it is a controversial issue. Proponents argue that in the wake of the

back-to-basics movement it will help solve the problem of increasing illiteracy. Critics are concerned that mandatory testing will influence teachers to teach only for the test.

See David A. Gilman, "The Logic of Minimal Competency Testing," *NASSP Bulletin* (September 1978); Peter W. Airasian et al., *Minimal Competency Testing* (Englewood Cliffs, N.J.: Educational Technology Publications, 1979); Rodney Riegle and Ned Lovell, *Minimum Competency Testing* (Bloomington, In.: Phi Delta Kappa Educational Foundation, 1980); R.M. Jaeger and C.K. Tittle, eds., *Minimum Competency Achievement Testing* (Berkeley, Calif.: McCutchan, 1980); C.W. Bracey, "On the Compelling Need to Go Beyond Minimum Competency," *Phi Delta Kappan* (June 1983); and William B. Walstad, "Analyzing Minimal Competency Test Performance," *Journal of Educational Research* (May/June 1984).

minimum path street patterns   In planning for school transportation, the determination of that route that will minimize the total distance to be covered in the redistribution of a group (as of students) from the point of origin (the school) to the set of residences that are the destinations of the members of the group.

minimum permissible class size   The smallest number of students to be assigned to a class of a given type, below which the class may be cancelled.

minimum wage   The smallest hourly rate that may be paid to a worker. While many "minimum wages" are established by union contracts or state laws or organizational pay policies, "the" minimum wage usually refers to the federal minimum wage law—the Fair Labor Standards Act (FLSA). The minimum wage at any given time is

STATES USING MINIMUM-COMPETENCY STUDENT TESTING

In 1984, 23 states used or expected to use minimum competency testing for high-school graduation, and another 16 states used it for other purposes.

Student Minimum-Competency Testing by Grade Levels

States Using Minimum-Competency Testing	Grade Levels Assessed	First Graduating Class Assessed
Alabama	3, 6, 9, 11	1985
Arizona	8, 12	1976
Arkansas	3, 4, 6, 8	
California	4-11, 16 yr. old+	1979
Colorado	9, 12	
Connecticut	4, 6, 8	
Delaware	1-8, 11	1981
Florida	3, 5, 8, 11	1983
Georgia	1-4, 6, 8, 10+	1985
Hawaii	3, 9-12	1983
Idaho	8+	1982
Illinois	local option	
Indiana	3, 6, 8, 10	
Kansas	2, 4, 6, 8, 10	
Louisiana	2, 3, 4, 5, 11	1989
Maryland	3, 5, 7, 8, 9	1982
Massachusetts	local option	
Michigan	4, 7, 10	
Missouri	8-12	
Mississippi	3, 5, 8, 11	1987
Nebraska	5+	
Nevada	3, 6, 9, 11	1982
New Hampshire	4, 8, 12	
New Jersey	9-12	1985
New Mexico	local option, 10-12	1981
New York	3, 5, 6, 8-12	1979
North Carolina	1-3, 6, 9, 11	1980
Ohio	local option	
Oklahoma	3, 6, 9, 12	
Oregon	local option	1978

Pennsylvania	3, 5, 8	
South Carolina	K-3, 6, 8, 11	1990
Tennessee	4-6, 8, 9-12	1982
Texas	1, 3, 5, 7, 9	1986
Utah	local option	1980
Vermont	1-12	1981
Virginia	K-6, 10-12	1981
Wisconsin	1-4, 5-8, 9-10	
Wyoming	local option	

SOURCE: National Center for Education Statistics, *The Condition of Education*, 1985 edition.

established by Congress via FLSA amendments. *See* Peter Linneman, "The Economic Impacts of Minimum Wage Laws: A New Look at an Old Question," *Journal of Political Economy* (June 1982).

ministerial function   A required action. In determining the liability of government agents for the consequences of their actions, courts have created a distinction between ministerial and discretionary functions. Though often blurred in specific cases, the distinction attempted to limit liability to acts done by the agents' volition, hence called discretionary, in comparison to those actions called ministerial, which were viewed as compelled by the constitution, a statute, charter, or other law.

Minnesota Multiphasic Personality Inventory (MMPI)   A 566-item, paper-and-pencil inventory that measures a variety of personality characteristics. Originally designed to reveal pathological tendencies, this test is now widely used by business and industry in personnel selection and counseling procedures. However, proper interpretation of test results requires considerable psychological sophistication. Published by:
   Psychological Corporation
   555 Academic Court
   San Antonio, TX 78701
   See Philip A. Marks, William Seeman, and Deborah L. Haller, *The*

Actuarial Use of the MMPI with Adolescents and Adults (New York: Oxford University Press, 1974); and John R. Graham, *The MMPI: A Practical Guide* (New York: Oxford University Press, 1977).

Minnesota Vocational Interest Inventory (MVII)   A test, designed to ascertain occupational preferences and aptitudes, that consists of forced-choice items that provide occupational and interest patterns. It is designed for those (age 15 years and over) contemplating occupations at the semiskilled and skilled levels (e.g., baker, printer, carpenter/painter, truck driver, sales and office clerk, or electronics worker). Published by:
   The Psychological Corporation
   555 Academic Court
   San Antonio, TX 78701

minor   1. A concentration of semester hours or quarter hours of college credit earned and representing specialization (but not primary specialization) in a field of study. The number of college credits constituting a minor is usually specified in accreditation requirements. 2. A person under legal age for voting, for signing contracts, for marriage, or for any other privileges or requirements assumed for adult citizens.

minor, emancipated   An individual under the usual age of majority who has legally attained the rights of an adult, including the severance of his or her parents' financial obligations.

minority group Any recognizable racial, religious, or ethnic group in a community that suffers some disadvantage due to prejudice or discrimination. As commonly used, this term is not a technical term, and indeed it is often used to refer to categories of people rather than groups, and sometimes to majorities rather than minorities. For example, though women are neither a group (but rather a genetic gender) nor a minority (since they comprise more than 50 percent of the population), some writers call them a minority group because a male-oriented and dominated society discriminates against women. On the other hand, a group that is privileged or not discriminated against but which is a numerical minority (such as wealthy white males) would rarely be called a minority group. Thus, as the term is often used, a minority group need be neither a minority nor a group, so long as it refers to a category of people who can be identified by a sizable segment of the population as objects of prejudice or discrimination. *See* Charles Vert Willie, *Effective Education: A Minority Policy Perspective* (New York: Greenwood Press, 1987).

minority set-asides *See* SET-ASIDES.

mirror reading A visual-perceptual problem that leads to difficulty reading because the student reverses order in letters or words, i.e., perceives images as in a mirror. Examples of mirror reading errors are "b" for "d" or "nap" for "pan."

MIS *See* MANAGEMENT INFORMATION SYSTEM.

miscue A general term used in reading research to describe an error such as substituting one word for another, omitting a word, inserting a word, or failing to identify a word.

misfeasance The unintentionally improper or illegal performance of an otherwise lawful act that may cause harm to someone. This is in contrast to nonfeasance, which is a failure to perform at all, or malfeasance, which implies intentionality.

mission budgeting An end-purpose approach to budgeting. The basic idea is that a mission budget categorizes programs and activities by ultimate outcomes.

mission (organizational) Statement of an organization's macro-level purposes and philosophy.

missionary organization A category of religious organization that carries on religious work, typically evangelizing or proselytizing, in conjunction with operating schools or hospitals, in underdeveloped foreign countries, or in economically depressed areas of this country.

Mitchell, Lucy Sprague (1878-1967) A successful educator who was the first woman dean at the University of California at Berkeley and who was a strong early proponent of progressive education in America. She was associated with the Bureau for Educational Experiments and the Bank Street School, both well-known educational institutions. Her biography was written by Joyce Antler (*Lucy Sprague Mitchell: The Making of a Modern Woman*; New Haven: Yale University Press, 1987).

mixed ability grouping A group of students who demonstrate a wide range of abilities and skills, generally that which would represent the total range of a similar age group. Also called HETEROGENEOUS GROUP. Contrast with TRACKING.

mixed dominance   A lack of consistent preference for one side of the body over the other, or the use of one side for some activities and the other side for others. For example, a person may kick with the left foot but throw with the right hand.

MMEd   Master of music education.

MMPI   See MINNESOTA MULTI-PHASIC PERSONALITY INVENTORY.

mnemonic device   Any aid to remembering complex data; for example, "thirty days hath September . . . ."

mnemonic instruction   1. A technique for learning new vocabulary (or foreign languages) based on the mental construction of interactive visual images. An unfamiliar word may be associated with a familiar, acoustically-similar "keyword," and the two words are paired in a visual image to simplify recall. For example, a new word, "dahlia," meaning flower, is associated with "doll," a known, like-sounding word. The visual image (or concrete picture) of a doll smelling a flower is created. The meaning of the new word can then be recalled through a series of associations: dahlia = doll = doll smelling flower = flower. The essential components of this technique are referred to as: (1) recoding, (2) relating, and (3) retrieving.
   See Debra Veit, Thomas Scruggs, and Margo Mastropieri, "Extended Mnemonic Instruction with Learning Disabled Students," *Journal of Educational Psychology* (August 1986).
   2. More generally, the adding of pictures or illustrations to prose to aid in understanding and recall. *See* Francis

Bellezza, "A Mnemonic Based on Arranging Words on Visual Patterns," *Journal of Educational Psychology* (June 1986); Linnea C. Ehri et al., "Pictorial Mnemonics for Phonics," *Journal of Educational Psychology* (October 1984); and Mark A. McDaniel and Michael Pressley, *Imagery and Related Mnemonics Processes: Theories, Individual Differences, and Applications* (New York: Springer-Verlag, 1987).

mobile classroom   A vehicle that serves as a classroom and that may be moved readily at any time.

mobility training aids   Specific instruction and assistive devices to increase the independence of students with handicaps in moving about from place to place within either the limited environment of a school building or the broader context of the community at large.

mode   A score or value that occurs most frequently in a distribution.

model   1. A simplification of reality or a reduction in time and space that allows for a better understanding of reality. The representation may be expressed in words, numbers, or diagrams. 2. A representation of an ideal implementation of a particular program.

model agreement   Collective bargaining agreement developed by a national or international union to serve as a standard for its locals.

model school   See LABORATORY SCHOOL.

modeling   1. Teaching by example; i.e., the learner observes the teacher's performance with the expectation of subsequent imitation. For a description of this instructional approach in teacher education, see Jill Wilson, "Instructor Modeling in Teacher Education Classes," *Journal of Research and Development in Education* (Spring 1987). 2. The identification of the fixed and variable components in a system, assigning them numerical or economic values, and relating them to each other in a logical fashion to derive optimal solutions to operational problems by manipulating the components of the model. 3. A learning procedure identified in social learning theory.

moderate mental retardation Refers to a degree of mental retardation that is based on an IQ score between 30 and 50. The term has limited relevance for educators. See MENTAL RETARDATION.

modern languages Any language that is still spoken in everyday use; especially refers to those that are commonly taught in school, such as Spanish, German, French, Italian, and Russian. Contrast with CLASSICAL LANGUAGES.

modern mathematics or modern math A movement in education that began in the 1960s to change curriculum in mathematics from mere computation and memorization to a greater emphasis on understanding the underlying concepts and structures of mathematics.

modular scheduling A method of flexible scheduling at the secondary level based on small units of time that can be grouped together to create longer or shorter class sessions, depending on the nature of the class.

Monell v. Department of Social Services, New York City 436 U.S. 658 (1978) The Supreme Court case that held that cities and municipalities may be held liable when their official policies (in this case, a

mandatory maternity leave policy) or customs violate a person's constitutional rights. A local government may not be sued for actions ("injuries") commited by its employees or agents. The government as an entity is responsible only when the execution of a government policy or custom infringes on constitutional rights.

See Eric Schnapper, "Civil Rights Litigation after *Monell*," *Columbia Law Review* (March 1979). *See also Owen v. City of Independence*, 445 U.S. 622 (1980), and *Pembauer v. City of Cincinnati*, 475 U.S. 469 (1986).

money purchase benefit Pension that is entirely dependent on contributions made to an individual's account.

money purchase plan A pension plan in which an employer contributes a fixed amount each year. The ultimate worth of the benefits paid will vary, depending on how much the invested sums earn.

monitor 1. A student assigned specific classroom responsibilities, such as distributing materials or carrying attendance information to the central office. 2. A teacher or other employee who supervises some non-teaching activity that is still essential to school function, such as test-taking, hall-passing, or lunchroom.

monitoring Checking local educational programs for legal compliance with state and/or federal requirements regarding policies and procedures.

monitoring assignment 1. An assignment to perform such activities as helping to keep order on buses and in playgrounds and lunchrooms, and taking attendance. This assignment would include traffic guards for loading buses. 2. Also an assignment to check local adherence/compliance with state and federal regulations.

monitoring system   A set of procedures and programs for a computerized information system that is designed to check recorded or transmitted signals in the process of inputting or retrieving information from data files.

Montessori, Maria (1870-1952)   An Italian physician who was an early expert in the field of cognitive development in young children. She developed schools in Rome, based on particular methods and instructional materials, that were rapidly replicated across Western Europe and the United States. *See* Rita Kramer, *Maria Montessori: A Biography* (New York: Putnam, 1976).

Montessori method   An approach to early childhood education developed by Maria Montessori that emphasizes training of the senses through a variety of experiences, exercises, and materials. The instruction is individualized within the range of available materials. For introductions to the history and application of the method, *see* Paula P. Lillard, *Montessori: A Modern Approach* (New York: Schocken Books, 1972); and Elizabeth G. Hainstock, *The Essential Montessori* (New York: New American Library, 1986).

Monthly Labor Review (MLR)   The journal of the U.S. Bureau of Labor Statistics, published since 1915. Articles deal with labor relations, trends in the labor force, new laws, and court decisions affecting workers. Lists the major labor agreements expiring each month and gives monthly current labor statistics on employment, unemployment, wages and prices, and productivity. Library of Congress Number: HD8051 .A78.

Monthly Labor Review
Superintendent of Documents
Government Printing Office
Washington, DC 20402

Mooney Problem Check List   An instrument to assist individuals in identifying their own perceived "problems" in areas such as health and physical development, home and family, school or occupation, and morals and religion. There are versions of the 210 to 330-item checklist for junior and senior high students as well as college students and adults. It is published by:
The Psychological Corporation
555 Academic Court
San Antonio, TX 78204

moon-ghetto metaphor   The comparison between the great engineering feat of going to the moon and the government's perennial efforts to solve the economic and social problems of the ghetto. It is often posed as a question: If we can go to the moon, why can't we solve the problems of the ghetto? This metaphor has even escaped the confines of the urban ghetto. For example, in 1986 Dr. Ruth Westheimer, in addressing the American Society of Newspaper Editors convention, complained that: "We can send a man to the moon, but we cannot prevent 1.5 million unwanted pregnancies each year."
   See Richard R. Nelson, "Intellectualizing About the Moon-Ghetto Metaphor: A Study of the Current Malaise of Rational Analysis of Social Problems," *Policy Sciences* (December 1974).

moral development   The growth of a child's ability to use moral principles and reasoning as a behavioral determinant. A major, accepted theory of moral development is attributed to Lawrence Kohlberg. See Kohlberg's chapter, "Moral States and Moralization," in Gilbert Geis et al., eds., *Moral Development and Behavior: Theory, Research and Social Issues* (New York: Holt, Rinehart and Winston, 1976). For a collection of essays representing a range of research in moral development theory, *see* Gary L. Sapp, ed., *Handbook of Moral Development* (Birmingham, Alabama: Religious Education Press, 1986).

For an examination of the development of moral character in children, *see* Robert Coles, *The Moral Life of Children* (Boston: Atlantic Monthly Press, 1986).

moral education   Instruction that deals with fundamental rules of society, the nature of good-bad/right-wrong, decision making and values clarification. For various approaches, *see* Richard H. Hersh et al., *Models of Moral Education: An Appraisal* (New York and London: Longman, 1980); Marvin W. Berkowitz and Fritz Oser, eds., *Moral Education: Theory and Application* (Hillsdale, N.J.: Erlbaum, 1985); Barry Chazan, *Contemporary Approaches to Moral Education: Analyzing Alternative Theories* (New York: Teachers College Press, 1985); Robert Carter, *Dimensions of Moral Education* (Toronto: University of Toronto Press, 1984); and Jacques S. Benninga, "An Emerging Synthesis in Moral Education," *Phi Delta Kappan* (February 1988).

Moral Majority   A political organization of fundamentalist Christians founded in 1978 by television evangelist Jerry Falwell (1933-   ). This "majority" tended to support far right Republican candidates, oppose abortion, support efforts to reinstitute mandatory school prayers, oppose gay rights, and generate considerable hostility from the members of the public—perhaps best summarized by a bumper sticker which read "The Moral Majority is Neither." In 1986 Falwell

changed the name of his increasingly attacked Moral Majority to the Liberty Federation. Compare to "People for the American Way."

See John Kater, *Christians on the Right: The Moral Majority in Perspective* (New York: Seabury Press, 1982); Michael Lienesch, "Right-Wing Religion: Christian Conservatism as a Political Movement," *Political Science Quarterly* (Fall 1982); and Emmett H. Buell, Jr., and Lee Sigelman, "An Army That Meets Every Sunday? Popular Support for the Moral Majority in 1980," *Social Science Quarterly* (June 1985).

mores   The customs and beliefs that govern socially acceptable behavior among a specific social group or culture.

morpheme   The smallest structural unit of language that has meaning, usually either a single word or a prefix or suffix attached to a root word.

morphology   1. The study of the form and structure of words in language. 2. In science, the comparison of organisms according to form.

motivation   A psychological term that refers to internal and/or external factors that activate or maintain an individual's behavior. *See* EXTRINSIC MOTIVATION *and* INTRINSIC MOTIVATION.

motivation-hygiene theory   A management theory developed by Frederick Herzberg and applied to education by Thomas Sergiovanni; it identifies two distinct types of factors that influence job satisfaction-dissatisfaction. Hygiene factors (dissatisfiers) are basic to the working environment (e.g., salary, status, physical conditions, interpersonal relationships) and are most significant when they are absent or low, at which time they contribute to dissatisfaction. Motivating factors (satisfiers) go beyond the basic performance of the job and address the employee's need for self-actualization (e.g., recognition, responsibility, achievement) and, when present, contribute to job satisfaction.

See Thomas J. Sergiovanni and Fred D. Carver, *The New School Executive: A Theory of Administration*, 2nd ed. (New York: Harper and Row, 1980).

motor abilities/skills   Any activities that involve physical movement of parts of the body. Fine motor skills relate to small muscle movements, like using the fingers to tie shoelaces. Gross motor skills refer to large muscle movements, like running.

Motor Free Visual Perception Test

An individually-administered multiple-choice test, designed to assess visual perception, that requires the student to point to one of four stimulus choices with no other motor skills required. The test may be used with children between the ages of four and nine years. It is published by:

Publishers Test Service
2500 Garden Road
Monterey, CA 93940

Mott Foundation   A private philanthropic organization that has been a significant contributor to the development of community education programs. The foundation was started by Charles Stewart Mott (1875-1973) of the automotive industry in 1926. For information regarding the background of this philanthropy *see* Clarence H. Young, *Foundation for Living (the Story of Charles Stewart Mott and Flint)* (New York: McGraw-Hill, 1963). For current data *see* Charles S. Mott Foundation, *Facts on Grants* (Flint, Michigan).

Mott Foundation
1200 Mott Foundation Bldg.
Flint, MI 48502
(313) 238-5651

movement education   A type of physical education that emphasizes in-dependent problem-solving in learning the capabilities of the body's movement. *See* Robert E. Gensemer, *Movement Education* (Washington, D.C.: National Education Association, 1979); and Sandra Curtis, *The Joy of Movement in Early Childhood* (New York: Teachers College, Columbia U., 1982).

MPA or MBA   Master of public administration and master of business administration, respectively. These are the leading managerial degrees for general organizational practitioners.

Mt. Healthy Board of Education v. Doyle 429 U.S. 274 (1977)   U.S. Supreme Court case that held that the first amendment does not demand that a discharged employee be placed "in a better position as a result of the exercise of constitutionally protected activity than he would have occupied had he done nothing." This decision allows that an employer not be inhibited from evaluating an employee's performance and "reaching a decision not to rehire on the basis of that record, simply because the protected conduct makes the employer more certain of the correctness of its decision." The case held that where an employment action taken with respect to an employee would be supported apart from the employee's exercise of constitutionally protected conduct, the fact that the exercise of constitutionally protected conduct was a "substantial" factor in the employment decision does not create a constitutional violation.

See William H. DuRoss, III, "Toward Rationality in Discriminatory Cases: The Impact of Mt. Healthy Board of Education v. Doyle Upon the NLRA," *The Georgetown Law Journal* (April 1978).

multibasal reading program
An elementary school reading program that uses several basal readers at each grade level.

multicultural education   A school program designed to teach understanding of and appreciation for the many different cultural, ethnic and social groups in society. Multicultural education grew out of an effort to change the institutions in our society (such as schools) to more accurately reflect society's ideals about equality and the inclusion of racial, ethnic and cultural differences.

See Christine E. Sleeter and Carl Grant, "An Analysis of Multicultural Education in the United States," *Harvard Educational Review* (November 1987); and James A. Banks and James Lynch, eds., *Multicultural Education in Western Societies* (New York: Praeger, 1986).

multidisciplinary   A general term that refers to the involvement of several different professional areas, though not necessarily in an integrated manner.

multidisciplinary assessment An assessment or evaluation by a number of individuals representing a variety of professional disciplines, such as psychology, nursing, social work, education, speech/language, and occupational or physical therapy. Prior to receiving special education services a student undergoes a multidisciplinary assessment to determine whether a handicapping condition exists that prevents the student from benefiting from regular education. The concept of multidisciplinary assessment implies no cooperation among disciplines but, rather, each discipline functioning autonomously to achieve its own objectives.

multiemployer pension plan trust A trust formed to provide funds for multiemployer pension funds. Since passage of the Multiemployer Pension Plan Amendments Act of 1980, multiemployer pension plan trusts may qualify for tax-exempt status under IRS Code 501(c)(22).

multigrade class   A class composed of pupils in two or more grades and having no particular differences in learning experiences due to grade standing of pupils, e.g., a secondary school general science class for freshmen and sophomores.

multigraded class   A class including more than one grade and in which pupils may be identified by grade level, e.g., the single class of a one-teacher school or one-room elementary school. Compare to UNGRADED CLASS.

multihandicapped   Having more than one handicapping condition.

multimedia instruction   A combination of two or more audiovisual presentation modes into a complete materials package for teaching.

multiple-choice test   A test consisting entirely of multiple-choice items, which require the examinee to choose the best or correct answer from several that are given as options. *See* J. Marshall Trieber, "The Use of Multiple-Choice for Testing," *Training and Development Journal* (October 1980).

multipurpose room   An instructional space designed or adapted specifically for combining two or more of the functions—such as assemblies, physical education, lunch, music, clubs, audiovisual work, and library services—that might typically be served by a separate library, separate audiovisual room, separate auditorium, separate gymnasium, or separate cafeteria. Separate gymnatoriums and cafetoriums are not classified as multipurpose rooms.

muscular dystrophy (MD)   A disease that affects all of the voluntary muscles in the body, causing deterioration and physical disability. The disease may begin in childhood or early adolescence and generally results in premature death from related complications.

musicology   The study of musical composition and music history. *See* Joseph Kerman, *Contemplating Music Challenges to Musicology* (Cambridge, Mass.: Harvard University Press, 1985); and James W. Pruett and Thomas P. Slavens, *Research Guide to Musicology* (Chicago: American Library Assoc., 1985).

mutual benefit association   A social organization or corporation for the relief of its members from specified problems or costs (such as the costs of illness or injury). Mutual benefit associations pay losses with assessments on their members for specific losses rather than by fixed premiums payable in advance.

mutual organization   *See* BENEVOLENT ORGANIZATION.

myopia or nearsightedness   A common visual impairment in school-aged children that causes difficulty in seeing distant objects clearly.

mystery box   An activity commonly used by early childhood teachers whereby a child places an object in a closed box and then offers others three clues designed to describe the item. The child is then asked yes/no questions to facilitate guessing. The method involves critical thinking skills, formulation of questions and definitions and the development of cleverness so that clues are not too obvious.

N

NAACP *See* NATIONAL ASSOCIA-
TION FOR THE ADVANCEMENT OF COLORED
PEOPLE.

NABSE *See* NATIONAL ALLIANCE
OF BLACK SCHOOL EDUCATORS, INC.

NACIE *See* NATIONAL ADVISORY
COUNCIL OF INDIAN EDUCATION.

NAEP *See* NATIONAL ASSESSMENT
OF EDUCATIONAL PROGRESS.

NAESP *See* NATIONAL ASSOCIA-
TION OF ELEMENTARY SCHOOL
PRINCIPALS.

NAEYC *See* NATIONAL ASSOCIA-
TION FOR THE EDUCATION OF YOUNG
CHILDREN.

narcotics A category of drugs that
have a powerful effect on the central
nervous system, are addictive and
dangerous to health, and are a
significant problem on secondary school
and college campuses across the
country, which has led to a proliferation
of educational programs on drug abuse
in American schools. Narcotic drugs include morphine, opium, heroin,
codeine, and cocaine.

NASBE *See* NATIONAL ASSOCIA-
TION OF STATE BOARDS OF EDUCATION.

NASDSE *See* NATIONAL ASSOCIA-
TION OF STATE DIRECTORS OF SPECIAL
EDUCATION.

NASE *See* NATIONAL ACADEMY FOR
SCHOOL EXECUTIVES.

Nashville Gas Co. v. Satty 434 U.S.
136 (1977) U.S. Supreme Court
case that held that pregnant women
forced to take maternity leave cannot be
denied their previously accumulated

seniority rights when they return to
work. *See also* PREGNANCY DISCRIMINA-
TION ACT OF 1978.

NASSP *See* NATIONAL ASSOCIA-
TION OF SECONDARY SCHOOL PRINCIPALS.

NASSP Bulletin A journal for
middle and high school administrators
that is published nine times a year,
monthly from September to May, by the
National Association of Secondary
School Principals. Subscriptions are
available only to NASSP members.
Association Address:
NASSP Bulletin
1904 Association Drive
Reston, VA 22091

Nation at Risk A report issued by
the Federal Commission on Excellence
in Education in 1983 that compared
American education with foreign educational systems and strongly criticized the
American system in terms of the level
and quality of student achievement. Because of educational inadequacies the
report warned that the United States
was "at risk" in terms of economic
survival, trade dominance, and national
security. For the full report see National
Commission on Excellence in Education, *A Nation at Risk: The Imperative
for Educational Reform* (Washington,
D.C.: U.S. Government Printing Office,
1983). For an analysis of the controversy sparked by this report *see*
Beatrice and Ronald Gross, eds., *The
Great School Debate* (New York: Simon
and Schuster, 1985). *See also* U.S.
Department of Education, *The Nation
Responds: Recent Efforts to Improve
Education* (Washington, D.C.: U.S.
Department of Education, May 1984).

**National Academy for School Ex-
ecutives (NASE)** A branch of the
American Association of School

307

Administrators that sponsors in-service training opportunities specifically designed to address the needs and interests of educational administrators. *See* AMERICAN ASSOCIATION OF SCHOOL ADMINISTRATORS.

National Advisory Council of Indian Education (NACIE)   A committee appointed by the President of the United States that consists of 15 members all of whom are American or Alaskan natives and that is charged to advise Congress and the Department of Education.

National Alliance of Black School Educators, Inc. (NABSE)   An organization for black teachers and school administrators that was founded in 1970 and that serves as a professional network and conduit of information for black educators. NABSE publishes a quarterly journal, *NABSE Quarterly*, and has headquarters in Washington, D.C.

> NABSE
> 2816 Georgia Avenue, N.W.
> Washington, DC 20001
> (202) 483-1549

National Assessment of Educational Progress (NAEP)   A program that is often referred to as the "Nation's Report Card" and that was established by Congress in 1986 and is administered by the Educational Testing Service to allow for state-by-state comparisons of the performance of elementary and secondary school students in the major academic subjects. *See* Richard M. Wolf, "The NAEP and International Comparisons," *Phi Delta Kappan* (April 1988); and Daniel P. Resnick and Lauren B. Resnick, "Understanding Achievement and Acting to Produce It," *Phi Delta Kappan* (April 1988).

National Association for the Advancement of Colored People (NAACP)   The largest and historically most influential of the black interest groups founded in 1909. The NAACP is much noted for its lobbying for civil rights laws and testing civil rights cases in federal court. Compare to: National Urban League.

> NAACP
> 1733 15th Street, N.W.
> Washington, DC 20005
> (202) 638-2269

National Association for the Education of Young Children (NAEYC)   An organization for professionals who serve young children, primarily in educational settings. It was founded in 1926 as the National Association for Nursery Education and currently has over 30,000 members and over 200 affiliated local and state chapters. The association publishes the journal, *Young Children*.

> NAEYC
> 1834 Connecticut Avenue, N.W.
> Washington, DC 20009
> (202) 232-8777

National Association of Elementary School Principals (NAESP)   The national organization for principals of elementary schools, which has a membership of 22,000.

> NAESP
> 1615 Duke Street
> Alexandria, VA 22314
> (703) 684-3345

National Association of Secondary School Principals (NASSP)   A large, well-established national organization for principals of high schools. Their monthly publication, the *NASSP Bulletin*, is acknowledged as a barometer of current trends in education.

> NASSP
> 1904 Association Dr.
> Reston, VA 20091
> (703) 860-0200

National Association of State Boards of Education (NASBE)   An organization of the boards of education of all states whose purposes are to study issues of mutual interest and concern, to maintain an effective liaison with educational groups and to disseminate information. A monthly magazine, *State Board Connection*, is published as well as special reports and issue papers.

National Association of State Boards
of Education
701 N. Fairfax, Suite 340
Alexandria, VA 22314
(703) 684-4000

National Association of State Directors of Special Education (NASDSE)   The national organization for the directors of state education agency departments of special education.

NASDSE
2021 K Street, N.W.
Suite 315
Washington, DC 20006
(202) 296-1800

National Catholic Education Association (NCEA)   The largest organization for Catholic schools and other religious education centers; it offers training and research and serves as a liaison with government agencies.

National Catholic Education
Association
1077 30th Street, N.W.
Suite 100
Washington, DC 20007
(202) 293-5954

National Children's Book Week Traditionally the third week in November, when American schools, libraries, and bookstores sponsor activities to encourage the reading and enjoyment of children's literature.

National Collegiate Athletic Association (NCAA)   The organization of colleges and universities that governs the standards for intercollegiate competitive activities, sponsors regional and national athletic contests, and compiles and disseminates statistics and records relevant to collegiate athletics. Founded in 1906, the association includes approximately 900 member colleges, universities, and other organizations.

NCAA
P.O. Box 1906
Shawnee Mission, KS 66201
(913) 384-3220

National Congress of Parents and Teachers or National PTA   The national coordinating organization for local parent-teacher associations, with state branches serving as a liaison linking the two. The National PTA's goals are child advocacy, parent education, and service to children, families, and schools.

National Congress of Parents and
Teachers
700 N. Rush St.
Chicago, IL 60611
(312) 787-0977

National Council for the Accreditation of Teacher Education (NCATE)   The only nationally recognized agent that accredits undergraduate and graduate professional education programs.

National Council for the Accreditation of Teacher Education
1919 Pennsylvania Avenue, N.W.
Suite 202
Washington, DC 20006
(202) 466-7496

National Defense Education Act of 1958   Federal legislation (P.L. 85-864) passed in response to the Russian launching of Sputnik I, with the intent of improving the quality of American education, especially in math and science, and thus increasing the status of the United States in the "space race."

National Diffusion Network (NDN)   A nationwide network to assist in the dissemination of exemplary educational programs. The system is supported by the U.S. Department of Education and includes three components: (1) assessment of the quality of programs by a group called the Joint Dissemination Review Panel (this process is known as "JDRP review"); (2) endorsement of a program by the panel ("JDRP endorsement"), after which the program is identified as a "developer/demonstrator"; (3) assistance in replicating endorsed programs through training that is supported by a designated state facilitator. More information about this network can be obtained from NDN, Division of Educational Replication, U.S. Department of Education, Washington, DC 20202.

National Education Association (NEA)

The largest organization for teachers in the nation, with many state and local chapters as well as worldwide affiliates. The organization was founded in 1857 as the National Teachers Association, with a primary focus on quality education. Although the NEA has historically served both teachers and administrators from all levels of education, and previously promoted a philosophy of cooperative team work, since the 1950s the organization has been primarily dominated by teachers and has actively lobbied for teacher rights. Largely prompted by the tactics of the American Federation of Teachers during the early 1960s, the organization currently functions as a trade union for its membership and engages in collective bargaining in many individual school systems. The NEA publishes *Today's Education* and the *NEA Reporter* as well as numerous special reports. *See* Allan M. West, *The National Education Association: The Power Base for Education* (New York: Free Press, 1980).

NEA
1201 16th St., S.W.
Washington, DC 20036
(202) 822-7350

National Foundation on the Arts and the Humanities

An independent federal agency created in 1965 that consists of national endowments for the arts and humanities as well as a Federal Council on the Arts and Humanities.

The activities of the National Endowment for the Arts are designed to foster the growth and development of the arts in the United States. The endowment awards grants to individuals, state and regional arts agencies, and nonprofit organizations representing the highest quality in the fields of architecture and environmental arts, crafts, dance, education, expansion arts, folk arts, literature, museums, music, media arts (film, radio and television), theater, and the visual arts.

National Endowment for the Arts
1100 Pennsylvania Avenue, N.W.
Washington, DC 20506
(202) 682-5400

The activities of the National Endowment for the Humanities are designed to promote and support the production and dissemination of knowledge in the humanities, especially as it relates to the serious study and discussion of contemporary values and public issues. The endowment makes grants to individuals, groups, or institutions— schools, colleges, universities, museums, public television stations, libraries, public agencies, and private nonprofit groups—to increase understanding and appreciation of the humanities. It makes grants in support of research that is productive of humanistic knowledge, with value to the scholarly and general public.

See Francis S. M. Hodsell, "Supporting the Arts in the Eighties: The View from the National Endowment for the Arts," *Annals of the American Academy of Political and Social Science* (January 1984); and James Bovard, "Fast Times at the Arts Endowment," *Policy Review* (Summer 1984).

National Endowment for the Humanities
1100 Pennsylvania Avenue, N.W.
Washington, DC 20506
(202) 786-0438

National Honor Society   A system of local organizations for the acknowledgment of academic achievement and social development by high school students.

National Labor Relations Act of 1935 (NLRA)   Popularly known as the Wagner Act (or the Wagner-Connery Act), this is the nation's principal labor relations law, applying to all private sector interstate commerce except railroad and airline operations (which are governed by the Railway Labor Act). The NLRA seeks to protect the rights of employees and employers, to encourage collective bargaining, and to eliminate certain practices on the part of labor and management that are harmful to the general welfare. It states and defines the rights of employees to organize and to bargain collectively with their employers through representatives of their own choosing. To ensure that employees can freely choose their own representatives for the purpose of collective bargaining, the act establishes a procedure by which they can exercise their choice at a secret ballot election conducted by the National Labor Relations Board. Further, to protect the rights of employees and employers, and to prevent labor disputes that would adversely affect the rights of the public, Congress has defined certain practices of employers and unions as unfair labor practices. The NLRA is administered and enforced principally by the National Labor Relations Board, which was created by the act.

In common usage, the National Labor Relations Act refers not to the act of 1935, but to the act as amended by the Labor-Management Relations (Taft-Hartley) Act of 1947 and the Labor-Management Reporting and Disclosure

(Landrum-Griffin) Act of 1959. The act limits its coverage to those businesses that are engaged in interstate commerce in a substantial way; it was originally intended that its passage would spur the creation of "little" Wagner Acts in the states. The Wagner Act also excluded some forms of labor, most pointedly, household and farm workers.

See Paul Weiler, "Promises to Keep: Securing Workers' Rights to Self-Organization under the NLRA," *Harvard Law Review* (June 1983); Jules Bernstein and Laurence E. Gold, "Mid-Life Crisis: The NLRA at Fifty," *Dissent* (Spring 1985); and Paul C. Weiler, "Milestone or Tombstone: The Wagner Act at Fifty," *Harvard Journal on Legislation* (Winter 1986).

See also:
LABOR-MANAGEMENT RELATIONS ACT OF 1947
LABOR-MANAGEMENT REPORTING AND DISCLOSURE ACT OF 1959
NATIONAL LABOR RELATIONS BOARD.

National Labor Relations Board (NLRB)   The federal agency, created by the National Labor Relations Act of 1935, that administers the nation's laws relating to labor relations in the private and nonprofit sectors. (There are also some public sector organizations under its jurisdiction, most notably the U.S. Postal Service.) The NLRB is vested with the power to safeguard employees' rights to organize, to determine through elections whether workers want unions as their bargaining representatives, and to prevent and remedy unfair labor practices.

National Labor Relations Board
1717 Pennsylvania Avenue, N.W.
Washington, DC 20570
(202) 655-4000

National Labor Relations Board v. Yeshiva University   444 U.S. 672 (1980)   The Supreme Court case that held that private university faculty members who were involved in the governance (management) of their institutions were excluded from the protection and rights offered non-managerial employees by the National Labor Relations Act.

See Joel M. Douglas, "Distinguishing Yeshiva: A Troubling Task for the NLRB," *Labor Law Journal* (February 1983); and Clarence R. Deitsch and David A. Dilts, "*NLRB v. Yeshiva University*: A Positive Perspective," *Monthly Labor Review* (July 1983).

National Merit Scholarships   A program of financial awards given to high school students who demonstrate particular academic talent based on a qualifying examination. The actual level of award is based on need as well as academic ability.

National Middle School Association (NMSA)   An organization formed in 1973 to meet the needs of principals of intermediate level schools, as NASSP does for high school and junior high principals and NAESP does for elementary school principals.

The goal of the association, which has approximately 2,600 members, is to promote the development of the middle school as a distinct and necessary entity in the structure of American education. It publishes a quarterly journal and newsletter.

NMSA
P.O. Box 14882
Columbus, OH 43214
(614) 263-5407

National Organization for Women (NOW)   The leading public interest group for women's issues founded in 1966. NOW is dedicated to using politics (it both endorses and opposes candidates), education, and legal action to improve the political and economic status of American women. Compared to the League of Women Voters, which is nonpartisan, NOW is aggressively partisan.

NOW
425 Thirteenth Street, N.W.
Suite 101
Washington, DC 20004
(202) 347-2279

national origin discrimination   Discrimination based on a person's place of birth. Title VII of the Civil Rights Act of 1964 prohibits disparate treatment, whether overt or covert, of any individual or group of individuals because of their national origin, except when such treatment is necessary because of a bona fide occupational qualification; for example, it might be lawful to require native fluency in Spanish for a position as a patients' rights advocate in a community with a high proportion of Hispanic residents.

National Rehabilitation Association (NRA)   Founded in 1925, a private nonprofit organization of 18,000 people whose purpose is to advance the rehabilitation of all handicapped persons. The organization conducts legislative activities, develops guidelines, provides specialized education programs and publishes a newsletter and quarterly journal.

National Rehabilitation Association
633 S. Washington St.
Alexandria, VA 22314
(703) 836-0850

National Right to Work Committee   An organization founded in 1955 that advocates legislation to prohibit all forms of forced union membership. Its National Right to Work Legal Defense Foundation, Inc., seeks to establish legal precedents protecting workers against compulsory unionism.

National Right to Work Committee
8001 Braddock Road
Springfield, VA 22160
(703) 321-9820

National Safety Council   Chicago-based nonprofit public service organization dedicated to reducing the number and severity of all kinds of accidents by gathering and distributing information about the causes of accidents and ways to prevent them.

National Safety Council
444 N. Michigan Avenue
Chicago, IL 60611
(312) 527-4800

National School Boards Association

A nationwide association representing local public schoool boards that govern the public elementary and secondary school in the United States. Its membership is comprised of the 50 state school board associations and the school boards of the District of Columbia and the U.S. Virgin Islands, plus local school boards. It conducts the largest educational convention in the U.S., publishes the *American School Board Journal*, the *Executive Educator* magazine, and the *School Board News* newspaper, conducts inservice education programs for state associations and local boards and has an extensive federal liaison program.

NSBA
1680 Duke Street
Alexandria, VA 22314
(703) 838-6722

National School Lunch Program

A program whereby the Superintendent of Agriculture assists state education agencies through grants-in-aid and other means to establish, maintain, operate, and expand school lunch programs in all schools making application for assistance and agreeing to operate a nonprofit lunch program in accordance with regulations of the National School Lunch Act, as amended.

National Science Foundation

An entity of the federal government that was established by the National Science Foundation Act of 1950 and that has remained the leading federal supporter

of both education and research in the fields of science.

NSF
1800 G Street, N.W.
Washington, DC 20550
(202) 655-4000

National Teacher of the Year

An annual award program, sponsored by the Council of Chief State School Officers, Encyclopedia Brittanica Companies, and Good Housekeeping Magazine, that recognizes one teacher, out of a group of nominations representing each state, who is determined to be the best teacher for the given year.

National Technical Information Service (NTIS)

The federal agency that was established in 1970 to simplify and improve public access to Department of Commerce publications and to data files and scientific and technical reports sponsored by federal agencies. It is the central point in the United States for the public sale of government-funded research and development reports and other analyses prepared by federal agencies, their contractors, or grantees.

National Technical Information Service
5285 Port Royal Road
Springfield, VA 22161
(703) 487-4600

National Training Laboratories Institute for Applied Behavioral Science (NTL)

Also called NTL Institute. Founded as the National Training Laboratories in 1947 in Bethel, Maine. The early years at Bethel were devoted to the development of human relations laboratories. It was during this period that NTL proved the effectiveness of the new concept of the T Group ("T" for training). NTL's concept of the T Group—in which individuals, working in small groups, develop new insights into self and others—is still an important element in NTL programs and has been widely imitated. During the 1950s and 1960s, major areas for experimentation and development were expanded to include group dynamics, organization development, and community development.

NTL Institute is internationally recognized as a focal agency for experience-based learning programs. It is also known as the institution that has had most to do with developing the new profession of laboratory education, with exploring new means of relating, with new approaches to social change, and with new methods of managing organizations. Interest in laboratory education has grown rapidly, and NTL defines as one of its roles helping to maintain professional standards in a field now popularized and often misunderstood.

National Training Laboratories Institute
1501 Wilson Blvd.
Arlington, VA 22209
(703) 527-1500

national union　Union composed of a variety of widely dispersed, affiliated local unions. The Bureau of Labor Statistics defines a *national union* as one with agreements with different employers in more than one state.

National Urban League　The nonpartisan community service agency, also called the Urban League, that currently has 115 local units and that was founded in 1911 and is devoted to the economic and social concerns of blacks and other minorities. The NAACP and the National Urban League are the two major membership organizations that lobby for the interests of black Americans. While the NAACP has been much concerned with the overall promotion of equal rights by lobbying for civil rights law and testing cases in the federal courts, the National Urban League has tended to con-

centrate its efforts on economic issues. *See* Jesse T. Moore, Jr., *A Search for Equality: The National Urban League: 1910-1961* (University Park: Pennsylvania State University Press, 1981).

National Urban League
425 13th Street, N.W.
Washington, DC 20004
(202) 393-4332

native ability　Actual ability. A test score is usually interpreted to mean that an individual's native ability lies somewhere in a range (plus or minus 10 points, for example) surrounding the score.

Native American, also Indian or American Indian　A racial classification that refers to one whose ancestors resided in the United States prior to population of the area by Europeans.

native language　Refers to the language learned by a person during the stages of early development, usually the language spoken by one's parents.

nativistic theory　The theory that all persons are born with an innate ability to learn and that human knowledge and skill exist in the individual from birth and emerge through experience and teaching.

naturalism　The scientific theory that everything that exists in the physical universe is real and, conversely, that everything that is real can be experienced in physical form.

nature-nurture controversy　Also heredity-environment controversy. An essentially irresolvable difference of opinion as to whether human potential is determined by a person's inherited capacities (nature or heredity) or by experience and learning (nurture or environment).

Naval Reserve Officers Training Corps (NROTC) A college program, including student financial assistance, that combines regular academic study with the study of naval science and that leads to graduation with a bachelor's degree and a commission in either the U.S. Navy or the Marine Corps. Graduates are required to complete three years of active military duty.

NCAA *See* NATIONAL COLLEGIATE ATHLETIC ASSOCIATION.

NCEA *See* NATIONAL CATHOLIC EDUCATION ASSOCIATION.

NDN *See* NATIONAL DIFFUSION NETWORK.

NEA *See* NATIONAL EDUCATION ASSOCIATION.

NEA Today A publication of the National Education Association that is distributed in newspaper format to the association's membership nine times a year. Subscriptions are available only to NEA members. The association's address is:

National Education Association
1201 16th St. N.W.
Washington, DC 20036
See TODAY'S EDUCATION.

nearsightedness *See* MYOPIA.

Nebraska Test of Learning Aptitude An individually-administered test of intelligence that was developed for use with deaf children ages three to 16 years. The test can be administered without verbal instruction and requires no verbal response. It is published by:

Union College Press
Lincoln, NE 68507
A standardized revision is the Hiskey-Nebraska Test of Learning Aptitudes, published by:

Marshall S. Hiskey
5640 Baldwin Street
Lincoln, NE 68507

need 1. The "gap" between an existing status and a desired status. When developing a program or writing a grant, the first step should be to define the need. 2. A student-centered component of designing an individualized education program (as in special education) that defines a requirement that differentiates the student from other students. 3. Sometimes used synonymously with want or desire. *See also* NEEDS ASSESSMENT.

needs analysis Any of a variety of approaches that seek to establish the requirements of a particular situation in order to determine what, if any, program activity should be initiated.

needs assessment 1. The identification of the discrepancy between "what is" and "what ought to be"; the first step in formulating the purposes for a new program or program activities. A needs assessment should be conducted prior to establishing program goals or objectives. 2. Loosely used to refer to any survey method that is used to ask respondents to identify their needs (e.g., for further education or particular services).

needs hierarchy In the July 1943 issue of *Psychological Review*, Abraham H. Maslow published his now classic, "A Theory of Human Motivation," in which he put forth his hierarchical conception of human needs. Maslow asserted that humans had five sets of goals or basic needs, arranged in a hierarchy of prepotency: physiological needs, safety needs, love or affiliation needs, esteem needs, and the need for self-actualization—the desire "to become everything that one is capable of becoming." Once lower needs are satisfied, they cease to be motivators of behavior. Conversely, higher needs cannot motivate until lower needs are satisfied. It is commonly recognized that there are some inescapable incongruities in Maslow's needs hierarchy. Some lower needs in some people, such as security, love, and status, never seem to be satiated. However, this does not take away from the importance of the desire for higher level needs as a motivational force in others. For references, *see* MASLOW, ABRAHAM H.

needs theory   A general term referring to any one of many theoretical constructs that relate human motivation and achievement to basic physical and psychological needs. For examples, *see* Bernard Weiner, *Theories of Motivation* (Chicago: Markham, 1972); and Wallace A. Russell, ed., *Milestones in Motivation* (New York: Appleton-Century-Crofts, 1970).

negative attention   Refers to the inadvertent reinforcement that students may receive from teachers, other school staff, and other students for undesirable or aberrant behavior. The reaction of others, even when theoretically "negative" (or punishing), can serve to increase the frequency of the student's attention-seeking behavior.

negative correlation   In statistics, where a high value on one variable tends to be associated with a low value on another variable.

negative reinforcement   *See* REINFORCEMENT.

negative strike   *See* POSITIVE STRIKE.

negative transfer   *See* TRANSFER OF LEARNING.

neglected child   As defined for federal compensatory education programs, a child residing in a public or private nonprofit residential institution (other than a foster home) that has assumed or been granted custodial responsibility for the child pursuant to state law, because of the abandonment or neglect by, or death of, parents or persons acting in the place of parents. *See also* INSTITUTION FOR NEGLECTED CHILDREN.

negligence   The legal concept that refers to a person's liability for injury to another person because of doing something that a reasonably prudent person would not do or failing to do something that a reasonably prudent person would do.

negotiating assignment   An assignment to perform such activities as resolving labor/management problems and helping to settle disputes and effect compromises. Such an assignment would include representatives of either management or labor (e.g., shop stewards).

negotiating committee, continuous   *See* CONTINUOUS NEGOTIATING COMMITTEE.

negotiation   The process by which representatives of labor and management bargain and directly discuss proposals and counter-proposals, in order to establish the conditions of work, such as wages, hours, benefits, or the machinery for handling grievances. For general theories on the negotiating process, *see* Jeffrey Z. Rubin and Bert R. Brown, *The Social Psychology of Bargaining and Negotiation* (New York: Academic Press, 1975); and Roger Fisher and Wiliam Ury, *Getting to Yes* (Boston: Houghton Mifflin, 1981).

negotiations, collective   *See* COLLECTIVE BARGAINING.

neighborhood   1. A specific geographic area. 2. An informally designated subsection of a city, having distinctive characteristics. 3. A community. While neighborhood and community tend to be used interchangeably, neighborhood has more of a geographic focus—the residents share a common area. Community, in contrast, implies that the population consciously identifies with the community and works together for common ends. See William P. Hojnacki, "What Is a Neighborhood?" *Social Policy* (September-October 1979).

neighborhood agencies and associations   An organized group from a local area, characterized by general community interests and whose purpose it is to solve problems of the neighborhood.

neighborhood association   An organization of residents of a neighborhood. In many American cities, neighbors in a particular area have formally organized into associations. These associations often play important political roles, lobbying local government and protecting neighborhood interests at all levels of government. They often reflect a movement calling for a decentralization of local government. At the extreme are advocates for neighborhood self-sufficiency, seeing both economic and political power possible for poorer neighborhoods only to the extent they can become independent of the dominant urban government.

See Howard W. Hallman, *The Organization of Neighborhood Councils: A Practical Guide* (New York: Praeger, 1977); Richard C. Rich, "The Dynamics of Leadership in Neighborhood Organizations," *Social Science Quarterly* 4 (March 1980); and Anthony Downs, *Neighborhoods and Urban Development* (Washington, D.C.: The Brookings Institution, 1981).

neighborhood school   1. A school within easy walking distance of the pupils' homes. 2. The school that a student is assigned to attend, according to district attendance areas; it may be within walking distance of the student's home or it may require district-supported transportation because of distance or specific circumstances, such as dangerous street intersections.

Neill, A.S. (1884-1973)   The founder of Summerhill school and a leading radical in the development of educational programs for young children. See Ray Hemmings, *Children's Freedom: A.S. Neill and the Evolution of the Summerhill Idea* (New York: Schocken Books, 1973); and Jonathan Croall, *Neill of Summerhill: The Permanent Rebel* (Philadelphia: Temple University Press, 1983).

nepotism   In organizations, the practice of hiring, promoting, or otherwise rewarding one's relatives, in favor over others and on the basis of kinship rather than merit.

net benefit   Also net benefit analysis. A decision criterion that uses the same information and is used for the same basic purposes as a cost-benefit analysis. A net benefit is calculated by subtracting costs from benefits (a cost-benefit analysis divides benefits by costs). If the result of the subtraction is positive, the program is considered to be economically beneficial. See also COST-BENEFIT ANALYSIS.

net expenditure   The actual outlay of money by a school district for some service or object after the deduction of any discounts, rebates, reimbursements, or revenue produced by the service or activity.

net income   The balance remaining to a school district after deducting from the gross revenue for a given period all operating expenses and income deductions during the same period. See also REVENUE.

net social benefit　Social benefits minus the social costs of a proposed program or project.

neurological handicap　A condition of or injury to the central nervous system that may result in disabilities such as cerebral palsy, epilepsy, sensory deficits, or learning disabilities. Neurological handicaps can be the result of pre-natal or birth traumas or can be the consequence of later events, such as encephalitis or meningitis or accidental injury to the brain.

See also:
CHILDREN WITH SPECIFIC LEARNING DISABILITIES.
ORTHOPEDICALLY HANDICAPPED

neurological impress method or impress method　One of many multisensory approaches to remedial reading. This method is distinguished by the technique of teacher and student simultaneously reading aloud from material that is at or above the student's reading level.

neutral　1. Any third party who is actively engaged in negotiations in order to facilitate an agreement and who, theoretically, has an objective, impartial perspective. 2. Any event or consequence that has neither positive nor negative connotations.

New Jersey v. TLO 469 U.S. 325 (1985)　The U.S. Supreme Court decision that upheld the right of a school official to search a student when "there are reasonable grounds for suspecting that the search will turn up evidence that the student has violated or is violating either the law or the rules of the school." This case involved a student whose purse was searched after the student was observed smoking on school premises.

new mathematics　*See* MODERN MATHEMATICS.

new social studies　A term coined by Edwin Fenton and John M. Good in an article in *Social Education*, which supported a social studies curriculum that emphasized inductive teaching and learning, use of inquiry approach, sequential learning methods, and an increased utilization of audiovisual materials. The curriculum was considerably more rigorous than in the past. By the early 1970s the movement had lost momentum for a variety of reasons: (1) those developing classroom materials were by and large university faculty who sought little classroom teacher input; (2) the social equity issues of the 1960s were entirely overlooked by program developers; (3) program designers did not understand or consider constraints of public school systems such as length of class period, financial resources, etc.; and (4) the rigor of the activities planned for students allowed critics to point out that the new social studies made school joyless, heartless and stiffly academic. For an overview of the movement, *see* Edwin Fenton and John M. Good, "Project Social Studies: A Progress Report," *Social Education* (April 1963); John D. Haas, *The Era of the New Social Studies* (Boulder, Colo.: ERIC Clearinghouse for Social Studies, 1977).

Newberry Medal　The annual award that is presented in recognition of the single most outstanding children's book of a given year.

newsprint　The name for large sheets or rolls of inexpensive paper that are commonly used in educational contexts.

night school　The provision of course work and facilities during the evenings for people who are employed during the day and wish to continue their formal education. *See also* ADULT/CONTINUING EDUCATION *and* ADULT BASIC EDUCATION.

NLRA *See* NATIONAL LABOR RELATIONS ACT OF 1935.

NLRB *See* NATIONAL LABOR RELATIONS BOARD.

NMSA *See* NATIONAL MIDDLE SCHOOL ASSOCIATION.

nominal group technique A group procedure commonly used by educational administrators and planners to reach consensus on organizational goals. The technique allows for equal input among participants and provides a structure for setting priorities.

nominating committee A standing committee that prepares an annual slate of candidates for an organization's elected positions. Most nominating committees are responsible for identifying candidates, screening, obtaining assurances of willingness from potential nominees, and formally nominating officers for the board of directors, new members for the board of directors, chairpersons for selected committees, and, in many organizations, successor members of the nominating committee.

noncategorical 1. A term applied to revenue from any or all sources that is not identifiable with specific expenditures, i.e., it is general fund revenue, which loses its identity as it is expended for objects relating to many service areas. 2. A reference to the educational placement of students with handicapping conditions, which is based on criteria (such as specific educational needs or even neighborhood of residence) other than the "category" of handicap.

noncontributory pension plan Pension program that has the employer paying the entire cost.

noncourse activities *See* COCURRICULAR ACTIVITIES.

noncredit course A course for which students do not receive credit applicable toward graduation or completion of a program of studies.

non-directive interview An interview style using open-ended questions in order to elicit spontaneous information from the interviewee.

non-directive teaching An approach to learning where the teacher provides minimal structure but helps the students to define their own goals and determine ways to meet those goals. Usually takes the format of a seminar/discussion class where the teacher's role is to listen and seek clarification from the students but not to lead. This is an outgrowth of Carl Rogers' non-directive therapy techniques.

non-directive therapy An approach to counseling or psychotherapy that allows the individual seeking help to work out his or her own problems with non-judgmental guidance from the professional. This approach is generally attributed to Carl Rogers.
See Carl R. Rogers, *Counseling and Psychotherapy* (Houghton Mifflin, 1942); and Carl R. Rogers et al., *Client-Centered Therapy, Its Current Practice, Implications and Theory* (Houghton Mifflin, 1951).

nongraded class *See* UNGRADED CLASS.

nongraded school *See* UNGRADED SCHOOL.

nonprint materials A library term referring to media for learning that are in a format other than print, e.g., audio or visual tapes, filmstrips, or other holographic slides.

nonprofessional A position that does not require extensive academic training (such as a bachelor's degree) and that is not considered as professional under the laws and regulations established by the state. Examples are school lunch workers, school bus drivers, and school custodians.

nonprofit organization   Also nonprofit association, nonprofit corporation, and NOT-FOR-PROFIT CORPORATION. A broad term—in many respects a concept rather than a specific entity—that can be defined in many different ways. The primary essence of a nonprofit organization, however, is that it is organized and operated for public or societal purposes (such as alleviation of poverty) rather than for private benefit purposes (such as return on shareholders' investments). A second essential element of a nonprofit organization is its reliance on voluntary action for much of its financial and human resources.

Despite common misconceptions to the contrary—and within well defined limitations—nonprofit organizations can realize profits from their activities and programs, and they can engage in commercial-type enterprises. (This is the basis for the historic but no longer valid distinction between *nonprofit organizations* and *not-for-profit corporations*.)

From a (over-simplified) tax-exemption viewpoint, there are two basic types of nonprofit organization: (1) publicly supported charitable organizations, which engage directly in health, religious, educational, or social welfare programs and activities; and (2) private foundations, which tend to support other tax-exempt organizations' programs.

Nonprofit organizations range in size and structure from large international religious denominations and seminational hospital chains to small, local, nonincorporated associations of people with common interests, goals, or concerns. *See also*:

ARTICLES OF ASSOCIATION
ARTICLES OF ORGANIZATION
NOT-FOR-PROFIT ORGANIZATION

non-promotion   The retaining of a pupil in his current grade at the end of the regular school term or at another time when most pupils are promoted.

nonpublic junior college   An independent or church-related junior college not supported by public funds. *See also* JUNIOR COLLEGE.

nonpublic schools   Also private schools. Schools that are operated by entities other than local or state governments and that are generally supported by funds other than public taxation. Nonpublic schools fall into two major categories: church-related and non-church-related. *See* Daniel C. Levy, ed., *Private Education: Studies in Choice and Public Policy* (New York: Oxford University Press, 1986).

nonpublicly-owned property
Any property used by the school district that is not publicly owned. *See also* PUBLICLY-OWNED PROPERTY.

non-pupil contact day   Jargon meaning essentially "no school"; a day on which teachers attend school for meetings or training but students do not attend.

nonrenewal   The failure of a school district to renew a nontenured teacher's contract period, resulting in termination of the teacher's employment with the district.

nonresident student   A student whose legal residence is outside the geographic area served by a specified school, LEA, or institution. *See also* RESIDENT STUDENT.

nonresident student of administrative unit (or school district)   An attending student who resides outside the administrative unit (or school district).

nonresident student of attendance area   A student who resides outside the geographic area normally served by the school he or she attends. *See also* SCHOOL ATTENDANCE AREA.

nonrevenue receipts   Amounts received that either incur an obligation that must be met at some future date or change the form of an asset from property to cash and, therefore, decrease the amount and value of school property. Money received from loans, sale of bonds, sale of property purchased from capital funds, and proceeds from insurance adjustments constitute most of the nonrevenue receipts.

nonschool activities   Activities that are neither sponsored by the school nor under the guidance or supervision of school staff members, but which are considered significant in terms of permanent records about pupils.

nonsense syllables   Meaningless combinations of letters, which have the structure of words but are not words (e.g., gud, pel, atset, das), that are sometimes used on standardized tests to measure memory skills.

nonstandard english   *See* ENGLISH, SOCIO-CULTURAL DIALECT.

non-supplant provision   A frequent provision in grant agreements that does not clearly specify an actual level of spending to be maintained (as in a maintenance of effort provision) but merely stipulates that recipients shall maintain spending from their own resources at the level that would have existed in the absence of the grant. *See also* MAINTENANCE OF EFFORT.

nontraditional education or nonformal education   Education that occurs outside of the context of a formally structured school or educational institution and that may address the teaching of knowledge or skills other than those typically emphasized in school.

non-tuition student   A student for whom no tuition is paid.

nonverbal communication   Gestures, movements, facial expressions, or postures that clearly communicate a message without words or formal symbols.

norm   (1) A standard of performance. (2) The level of achievement or performance of the model group of a population. (3) A rule or standard of expected behavior among any group of people.

norm group   The individuals whose performances are used to establish the norms on a standardized test.

normal capacity   The number of pupils that can be accommodated in the instruction rooms of a given plant for the school day, according to existing state standards and exclusive of multiple sessions.

normal distribution   A frequency distribution that follows the pattern of the normal "bell-shaped" curve, characterized by symmetry about the mean and a standard relationship between width and height of the curve.

normal schools   The early name for professional schools that trained teachers.

normalization   A principle and a philosophical belief that all individuals who may be handicapped (or not) have the right to live as normal a life as possible, regardless of the nature or the severity of the handicap. This principle extends to the educational arena with the belief that all exceptional children should be provided with an education as close to normal as possible and that their education should lead them to increased potential for integration into typical community environments and the larger society.

See Wolf Wolfensberger, *The Principle of Normalization in Human Services* (Toronto: National Institute on Mental Retardation, 1972); and Robert Perske, *New Life in the Neighborhood* (Nashville: Parthenon Press, 1981).

normative Those findings or conclusions that are premised upon morally established norms of right or wrong.

normative standard Standard of performance obtained by examining the relative performances of a group or sample of candidates.

norm-referenced test An examination for which an individual's score indicates the relationship of the individual's performance to that of a specified norm group. *See also* CRITERION-REFERENCED TEST.

norms 1. Average or standard behavior for members of a group. The "norm" is what is "normal." 2. Socially enforced requirements and expectations about basic responsibilities, behavior, and thought patterns of members in their organizational roles. Compare to RECIPROCITY. 3. In psychological testing, tables of scores from a large number of people who have taken a particular test.

not-for-profit organization A tax-exempt nonprofit organization. Although some states' tax laws use the "not-for-profit" terminology, in common usage it tends to be used inter-

changeably with "nonprofit organization." *See also* NONPROFIT ORGANIZATION.

notification of intent (NOI) Usually, a written notification to a granting agency or an area clearinghouse of an organization's intention to submit a grant proposal. Such notifications typically include a brief statement of the proposed project's purpose, rationale, approach, and approximate budget. *See also*:
   CLEARINGHOUSE
   GRANT
   GRANT PROPOSAL

NOW *See* NATIONAL ORGANIZATION FOR WOMEN.

NPO *See* NONPROFIT ORGANIZATION.

NRA *See* NATIONAL REHABILITATION ASSOCIATION.

NSF *See* NATIONAL SCIENCE FOUNDATION.

NTIS *See* NATIONAL TECHNICAL INFORMATION SERVICE.

nuclear education Also peace education. Any school curriculum that focuses on issues concerning the arms race and the threat of nuclear war. For a number of articles addressing examples of such a curriculum, *see* "A Special Issue: Education and the Threat of Nuclear War," *Harvard Educational Review* (August 1984). *See also* Chris Austiff et al., *Decision Making in a Nuclear Age* (Weston, Mass.: Halcyon House, 1983); and Jonathan Schell, *Fate of the Earth* (New York: Knopf, 1982).

nuclear family Generally refers to a single household unit of parent(s) and child(ren). Historically, a nuclear family was defined as two parents and their biological children. As the nature of families has changed over the past generation, the concept of nuclear families has broadened to include single parent and single child households, families with adoptive and foster children, "blended" families (i.e., including stepparents and stepchildren), and families without children. The nuclear family is still differentiated from the extended family, which includes less immediate relatives, such as grandparents, aunts, uncles, and cousins.

null hypothesis A hypothesis used in statistics that asserts there is no difference between two populations that cannot be explained by chance.

number belonging *See* MEMBERSHIP.

number line A commonly used device for teaching basic mathematics. A horizontal line depicts units from one to imagined infinity in one direction and less than (or minus) one to imagined infinity in the opposite direction. Generally, positive numbers are shown to the right of zero while negative numbers are shown to the left.

number skills The ability to understand the value of numbers and use them. Assumed to be a prerequisite for learning mathematical computations.

numerical scale A rating scale that uses numbers to identify an individual performance as compared to some fixed standard (e.g., 1 = poor and 10 = excellent).

nursery The British term for a beginning group or class that is organized to provide educational experiences for children during the year or years preceding kindergarten. A nursery class may be organized as a grade of an elementary school or as a part of a separate nursery school. In the United States nursery generally refers to a place where infants and toddlers are cared for. *See also*:
ELEMENTARY SCHOOL
NURSERY SCHOOL
PRESCHOOL PROGRAM.

nursery school Also preschool. A separately organized and administered elementary school for groups of children during the year or years preceding kindergarten, which provides educational experiences under the direction of professionally qualified teachers. *See* EARLY CHILDHOOD EDUCATION *and* PRESCHOOL PROGRAM.

nurse-teacher A staff member performing assigned teaching activities requiring the technical education and training necessary to qualify the staff member as a nurse as well as a teacher. *See also* TEACHING ASSISTANT.

nursing services Activities generally carried out by qualified nurses that are not instructional, such as health inspection, treatment of minor injuries, and referrals for other health services.

nutritionist A staff member performing assigned technical activities in connection with determining nutritive value of food; measuring vitamin content of foods; measuring amount of proteins, carbohydrates, and minerals in foods; and computing caloric value of foods for diet charts.

O

OASDI   *See* OLD AGE, SURVIVORS, and DISABILITY INSURANCE.

obiter dictum   Latin, meaning "incidental remarks"; those portions of a written court opinion (or arbitrator's decision) that are not germane to the case at hand; in effect, a digression. Consequently, they are not considered binding as precedents, but they do provide clues to a court's rationale and judicial philosophy.

object   The commodity or service obtained from a specific expenditure.

object classification   A category of goods or services purchased.

object lesson   An exemplary demonstration of how to do something.

object permanence   A basic concept learned during Piaget's sensory motor stage of cognitive development (ages birth to two years) that allows a person to acknowledge the existence of an object in the absence of immediate direct sensory contact with the object. This concept is thought to be crucial to all further symbolic development.

objective   A statement of a specific intended accomplishment or result; a commitment to attempt to achieve. An objective should specify three things: the desired performance or behavior, the criteria or standards of quality and/or quantity, and the conditions under which successful performance will be demonstrated. Objectives should be attainable within a specified time frame and measurable or observable. For a programmed instruction book on writing objectives, see Robert Mager's *Preparing Instructional Objectives. See also* EVALUATION *and* MANAGEMENT BY OBJECTIVES.

objective, administrative   Also called input objective and structural objective. A type of objective that is concerned with inputs of resources; for example, to hire three teachers for X program by July 1. The sample objective does not state what the teachers will accomplish; therefore, it is a statement of resource gathering (and, therefore, future resource consumption) rather than a statement of outputs or outcomes.

Administrative objectives are useful during the early, start-up months of a project or organization—while things are "getting organized."

objective, outcome   Also called product objective and impact objective. A type of objective that is concerned with desired changes in the status of a program or an organization's clientele—after the program or organization has delivered its services. For example, at least 60 percent of the sheltered workshop employees who move to regular industry worksites will retain employment with their employer for at least two years. All students who complete the CPR (cardiopulmonary resuscitation) segment of the Emergency Medical Technician course, will demonstrate correct procedures on a recording Resci-Annie.

Note that the service-providing organization does not have control over the accomplishment of the objective. The organization does—and should— influence accomplishment through its service delivery, but "success" is dependent upon subsequent behavior of the people who have been served.

objective, short-term   1. A specific measurable outcome, the achievement of which is anticipated within a definite period of time. 2. In special education, one of those statements of measurable outcomes that define the basis of a student's individualized educational program and against which progress is reviewed on at least an annual basis. Also called Short-term Instructional Objectives.

objective test   Any examining device whose scoring is not dependent upon the discretion of the examiners.

objectivity   An appraisal procedure is objective (that is, it has objectivity) if it elicits observable responses that can be recorded and reported in a precise, specified way. Objectivity seeks to remove personal opinion by reducing the impact of individual judgment.

obligations   Amounts that a school district will be required to pay out of its resources, including both liabilities and encumbrances.

obligatory arbitration   Arbitration requested by one party in a situation where the other party is obligated (for example, by a contract provision) to accept it.

observation   In education, the process by which a person's behavior or performance might be studied by having another individual watch said behavior or performance. *See* Paul Croll, *Systematic Classroom Observation* (Philadelphia: Falmer Press, 1986).

observational techniques   A number of formal or informal procedures for assessing or evaluating either teacher or student behaviors. Observations may be direct or via video recordings, one-way mirrors, or written anecdotal records. They may have a general purpose or may focus on a specific aspect of performance (i.e., a student's language skills as measured by mean sentence length or an analysis of teacher interactional style).

obsession   The persistent repetition of some idea, behavior, or impulse.

obsolescence   The decrease in the value of fixed assets due to curricular, program, economic, social, technical, or legal changes.

occupational certification   Also called CERTIFICATION. The process that permits practitioners in a particular occupation to claim minimum levels of competence. While certification enables some practitioners to claim a competency that others cannot, this type of regulation does not prevent uncertified people from supplying the same services as certified people.

occupational cluster   A grouping of occupations that possess a number of common features, such as types of equipment used, objectives, or processes, but not necessarily implying total uniformity.

occupational education   *See* VOCATIONAL EDUCATION *and* TECHNICAL EDUCATION.

occupational field   A group of recognized occupations having many similarities, including the following characteristics in common: the type of work performed; the basic aptitudes and the acquired knowledge and training required; the tools, machines, instruments, and other equipment used; and the basic materials used.

occupational hazard   Any potential danger related to a person's work or work environment. A common occupational hazard of teaching is BURNOUT.

occupational illness   Also called occupational disease. Any abnormal condition or disorder, other than one resulting from an occupational injury, caused by exposure to environmental factors associated with employment. It includes acute and chronic illnesses or diseases that may be caused, for example, by inhalation, absorption, ingestion, or direct contact.

occupational injury Any injury (such as a cut, fracture, sprain, or amputation) that results from a work accident or from exposure involving a single incident in the work environment.

occupational licensing The requirement that all non-licensed persons be excluded from practicing a particular licensed profession. *See also* CERTIFICATION *and* LICENSE.

occupational program A secondary school, junior college, or adult/continuing education program of studies designed primarily to prepare a student for immediate (i.e., job-entry level) employment or upgrading in an occupation or cluster of occupations.

occupational psychology The study of human behavior in work situations.

occupational therapist A trained and certified professional who provides occupational therapy services.

occupational therapy A broad professional field relating to the treatment of persons who are physically and/ or emotionally handicapped (on either a temporary/transient or an ongoing basis) that typically utilizes purposeful, productive activities for the purpose of rehabilitation of function. In an educational context, occupational therapy tends to focus on specific motor skills that relate to educational or developmental functioning, such as handwriting or using a fork to feed oneself.

OCR *See* OFFICE OF CIVIL RIGHTS.

OCR complaint A complaint registered by a citizen, or organization representing a group of citizens, to the Office of Civil Rights of any governmental agency regarding an alleged infringement upon the civil rights of a constituent, usually based on discrimination. A complaint will precipitate a required *OCR investigation* and will result in an *OCR ruling* which will evaluate the legitimacy of the complaint and recommend corrective actions if necessary.

OD *See* ORGANIZATION DEVELOPMENT *and* OVERDOSE.

Oedipus complex A Freudian concept that refers to the sexual attraction of a child for the parent of the opposite sex, which is a part of the normal psychosexual development of all children. *See* Johanna Krout Tabin, *On the Way to Self: EGO and Early Oedipal Development* (New York: Columbia University Press, 1985).

OFCCP *See* OFFICE OF FEDERAL CONTRACT COMPLIANCE PROGRAMS.

off campus Facilities used or activities offered that are away from the actual buildings or grounds of a school.

office audit *See* AUDIT.

Office of Civil Rights A general reference to several offices within different departments of the federal government that are responsible for enforcing civil rights laws. In the Department of Education, the Office of Civil Rights deals primarily with issues related to education discrimination on the basis of sex, race, religion, color, national origin, or handicapping conditions.

Office of Economic Opportunity (OEO) A federal agency established within the Executive Office of the President by federal legislation in 1964 to plan and coordinate advocacy programs related to the Johnson administration's "war on poverty." The office ceased to function as an independent entity in the mid-1970s, though many of the programs it had begun were continued under the direction of other federal agencies, such as Head Start and Job Corps.

Office of Education   Prior to the establishment of the U.S. Department of Education in 1979, the branch of the Department of Health, Education and Welfare that was concerned with federal education assistance, services, and research.

Office of Federal Contract Compliance Programs (OFCCP) The agency within the Department of Labor delegated with the responsibility for ensuring that there is no employment discrimination by government contractors because of race, religion, color, sex, or national origin, and for ensuring affirmative action efforts in employing Vietnam Era veterans and handicapped workers.

OFCCP
Department of Labor
200 Constitution Avenue, N.W.
Washington, DC 20210
(202) 523-9475

Office of Management and Budget (OMB)   Located within the Executive Office of the President, this is the central budget agency of the U.S. government.

Office of Management and Budget Circulars (OMB Circulars)   A series of regulations issued by the Office of Management and Budget, covering a wide range of requirements and procedures, including requirements for recipients of federal grants and contracts.

Office of Management and Budget (OMB) Circular A-95   A regula-

tion designed to promote maximum coordination of federal programs and projects with state, areawide, and local plans and programs by providing an opportunity to governors, mayors, county elected officials, and other state and local officials, thorugh clearinghouses, to influence federal decisions on proposed projects that may affect their own plans and programs.

The circular sets forth procedures under which applicants for federal grants and other forms of assistance must give state and local governments, through state and areawide clearinghouses, an opportunity to assess the relationship of their proposals to state, areawide, and local plans and programs for the development of their area. Federal agencies are required to consider these assessments in deciding whether or not to proceed with a proposed project. However, clearinghouse recommendations on federal or federally assisted development proposals are advisory only.

OMB
Executive Office Building
Washington, DC 20503
(202) 395-3080

Office of Special Education Programs (OSEP)   Also called SEP, Special Education Programs. The federal office that is responsible for the implementation of the Education for All Handicapped Children's Act of 1975 (P.L. 94-142) and for regulating all federal special education programs. The office is administratively housed in the Office of Special Education and Rehabilitative Services (OSERS) of the U.S. Department of Education.

Office of Special Education and Rehabilitative Services (OSERS) A branch of the U.S. Department of Education that is responsible for regulating all federal special education and rehabilitative programs.

official   An elected or appointed member of a board of education, governing body or administrative structure of a school district, or a state or federal agency governing schools, such as a state or local school board member, a local superintendent, or a state commissioner.

official/administrative   A job classification category that is defined by a grouping of assignments comprising the various skill levels required to perform such management activities as developing broad policies for a school district and executing these policies through direction of staff members at all levels of a school district. Those activities performed directly for policymakers are also included here. The "Official/Administrative" classification does not preclude "Professional-Educational" or "Professional-Other" status.

offset account   An accounting procedure used to balance one set of figures against another to make the books come out even in the end.

off-the-job training   Work-related instruction that takes place somewhere other than the work site.

ogive   A cumulative frequency graph. Also called an S-shaped curve.

Old Age, Survivors, and Disability Insurance (OASDI)   Federal program created by the Social Security Act that taxes both workers and employers to pay benefits to retired and disabled people, their dependents, widows, widowers, and children of deceased workers. *See also* SOCIAL SECURITY.

ombudsman   An individual whose job it is to investigate the complaints of the citizenry concerning public services and assure that such complaints will reach the attention of those officials at levels above the original providers of service. Originally a Swedish word meaning "representative of the King," ombudsmen/ombudswomen are now found in many countries at a variety of jurisdictional levels. Many of the functions of ombudsmen in state and local governments are performed by members of the legislature (and school boards).

See Carolyn Stieber, "Talking Back: States and Ombudsmen," *State Government* 55:2(1982); Larry B. Hill, "The Citizen Participation-Representation Roles of American Ombudsmen," *Administration and Society* (February 1982); and Robert D. Miewald and John C. Comer, "The Complaint Function of Government and the Ombudsman," *State and Local Government Review* (Winter 1984).

ombudsman assignment   An assignment to receive and investigate complaints made by individuals against alleged abuses or capricious acts of administrative school district officials. (The ombudsman usually works for the board of education in a quasi-official status.)

one-teacher school   A school in which one teacher is employed to teach all grades authorized in the school, regardless of the number of rooms in the building. During some years, there may be grades in which no pupils are enrolled.

one-to-one correspondence   A basic mathematical concept that involves matching one member of a set to one member of another set; the underlying notion for counting.

one-trial learning   The accomplishment of a new skill after a single presentation, without the need for practice or repetition.

one-way mirror/window   A specially treated sheet of glass that is transparent from only one direction and that appears as a mirror from the other direction. It is used in schools to allow for observation by an observer, who cannot be seen.

on-the-job supervision   Supervision of the work portion of a course in a work-study program, at the pupil's place of employment and by a supervisor not employed by the school.

on-the-job training   A program of instruction provided to an employed worker by the employer during the normal working hours of the occupation.

opaque projector   A teaching tool that can be used to project natural graphic materials (e.g., books, photographs, printed pages) onto a screen.

open admissions   The policy of some colleges and universities to admit any high school graduate regardless of previous academic standing.

open classroom   1. A large teaching area without permanent partitions that may be used for teaching several classes or groups of students at the same time. 2. Used synonymously with the concept of OPEN EDUCATION.

open education   A concept of classroom structure, usually at the elementary school level, that involves flexible scheduling, small group or individualized instruction, a variety of learning activities taking place simultaneously in the same open classroom space, and some degree of self-direction on the part of the students. See Lillian S. Stephens, *The Teacher's Guide to Open Education* (New York: Holt, Rinehart and Winston, 1974).

open enrollment   1. A period when new subscribers may elect to enroll in a health insurance plan or prepaid group practice. Open enrollment periods may be used in the sale of either group or individual insurance and may be the only period of a year when insurance is available. 2. *See* OPEN ADMISSIONS.

open meetings   *See* SUNSHINE LAWS.

open shop   Any work organization that is not unionized. The term may also apply to organizations that have unions but do not have union membership as a condition of employment. Historically, an *open shop* was the opposite of a union shop, i.e., it rejected unionization.

open space plan   An architectural design for schools that includes few permanent partitions.

open systems   Organizations that interact with their external environments.

open-book test   A test that allows candidates to consult textbooks or other relevant material while the examination is in progress.

open-door policy   A management style that offers employees easy access to supervisory personnel.

open-end agreement   Bargaining agreement providing for a contract that will remain in effect until one of the parties wants to reopen negotiations.

open-end program   1. An entitlement program for which eligibility requirements are determined by law (for example, Medicaid). Actual obligations and resultant outlays are limited only by the number of eligible persons who apply for benefits and the actual benefits received. 2. A program of instruction at the postsecondary instructional level, of an occupational or terminal nature, and designed, often in cooperation with one or more four-year colleges or universities, so that credits earned may be applicable, at least in part, toward the bachelor's degree.

open-ended item/question   A question that is phrased so that more than a single response can be elicited. It is used to facilitate the gathering of a variety of information from the respondent. For example, "tell me what you like about school" rather than "what is your favorite subject?"

operant conditioning   A behavioral term describing the process of shaping behavior through the systematic reinforcement of particular responses. Operant conditioning is most often linked to the work of B.F. SKINNER.

operating expense   Also operating cost. An expense (or cost) incurred in conducting the ordinary activities of an organization, including running its programs, raising funds, and administering the organization.

operating ratio   Operating expenses divided by income from operations.

operating report   *See* OPERATING STATEMENT.

operating statement   Also ACTIVITY STATEMENT. A financial statement showing an organization's revenues and expenses and— preferably for each—budgeted and actual figures and the discrepancy or variance between them in dollars and/or percentages. An *activity statement* is the same basic report used in many nonprofit organizations. *See also* FINANCIAL STATEMENTS.

Operation Head Start   *See* HEAD START.

operation of plant   A school budget category that includes the housekeeping and custodial expenses of the school system.

Operation PUSH   An organization founded in 1971 by the Rev. Jesse Jackson with the goal of building a stronger economic base in the black communities of America through a primary emphasis on black youth who are still enrolled in school. The acronym stands for "People United to Save Humanity."

operational data   A form of secondary evaluation data that is collected and maintained by an organization as an integral part of its ongoing need for information (such as student personnel records). Because operational data are used by an organization for operational purposes, they tend to be more reliable and valid than nonoperational data. Unfortunately, however, operational data often are not maintained in a form that lends itself to evaluation. Also, they tend to be voluminous. *See also:*
> PRIMARY DATA
> SECONDARY DATA
> SOURCES OF DATA

operational personnel   Staff members who are assigned the activities of keeping the physical plant open and ready for use. Included are personnel engaged in cleaning, disinfecting, heating, moving furniture, caring for grounds, operating telephone switchboards, and such other work as is repeated regularly—daily, weekly, monthly, or seasonally.

operational plan   A plan that indicates in detail the objectives to be met, the resources to be applied, and the outputs to be expected in a given fiscal year.

operational unit   A separately budgeted subdivision of a school district established to carry out a major objective or group of objectives, such as an individual school, the transportation unit, or the athletic department.

operational validity   The three basic elements of operational validity are test administration, interpretation, and application. According to William C. Byham and Stephen Temlock, in "Operational Validity—A New Concept in Personnel Testing," *Personnel Journal* (September 1972), "operational validity includes everything that happens with and to a test after test research has been completed. Operational validity can never make invalid tests predictive; it can only assure maximum prediction within the limits of the tests used." According to Dennis M. Groner, in "A Note on 'Operational' Validity," *Personnel Journal* (March 1977), "in the strictest sense of the word, operational validity is not validity at all, but a source of error which reduces the correlation between a predictor and a criterion.

operationalize   To translate a concept or theory into a plan for implementation.

operations services   Activities concerned with scheduling, maintaining, and producing data for statistical reports.

opinion poll   *See* PUBLIC OPINION SURVEY.

opinionnaire   A questionnaire designed to elicit opinions rather than factual information.

opportunity school   Another term for a vocational school.

optimization   1. Any attempt to maximize or minimize a specific quantity, usually called an "objective."

2. A determination of the best mix of inputs to achieve an objective.

oral board   A committee formed for the purpose of interviewing candidates for employment, promotion, or evaluation.

oral committee   A group formed for the purpose of examining a doctoral candidate over the submission of a dissertation or thesis.

oral history   A record of historical events that is obtained via first-hand interviews with persons usually of some prominence. For examples, *see* Alan M. Meckler and Ruth McMullin, *Oral History Collections* (New York: R.R. Bowker, 1975); and Thad Sitton et al., *Oral History: A Guide for Teachers (and others)* (Austin: University of Texas Press, 1983).

oral reading   Reading aloud, usually as an approach to reading instruction. *See* R.L. Allington, "Oral Reading," in P.D. Pearson, ed., *Handbook of Reading Research* (New York: Longman, 1984).

oral test   Any test that has an examiner ask a candidate a set of questions, as opposed to a paper-and-pencil test.

oralism   A philosophy in the field of education for persons who are deaf that all such persons should be taught to speak and lipread.

ordered profile   A graphic (or line) diagram sequentially showing the relative positions of a person or group on each of several measures.

ordinal scale   *See* SCALES OF MEASUREMENT.

ordinance   A local (for example, city or county) law, rule, or regulation.

Orff method   An approach to music instruction that is child-centered and that parallels the historical evolution of music, starting with basic rhythm, then melody, then harmony.

organization, benevolent   *See* BENEVOLENT ORGANIZATION.

organization, date of   *See* DATE OF ORGANIZATION.

organization, labor   *See* LABOR ORGANIZATION.

organization, professional   *See* PROFESSIONAL ORGANIZATION.

organization, social welfare   *See* SOCIAL WELFARE ORGANIZATION.

organization development (OD)   Premised upon the notion that any organization wishing to survive must periodically divest itself of those parts or characteristics that contribute to its malaise, OD is a process for increasing an organization's effectiveness. As a process it has no value bias, yet it is usually associated with the idea that maximum effectiveness is to be found by integrating an individual's desire for personal growth with organizational goals. Wendell L. French and Cecil H. Bell, Jr., in *Organization Development: Behavioral Science Interventions for Organization Improvement* (Englewood Cliffs, N.J.: Prentice-Hall, 1973), provide a formal definition:

> organization development is a long-range effort to improve an organization's problem-solving and renewal processes, particularly through a more effective and collaborative management of organization culture—with special emphasis on the culture of formal work teams—with the assistance of a change agent, or catalyst, and the use of the theory and technology of applied behavioral science, including action research.

Other major texts *include* Warren Bennis, *Organization Development: Its Nature, Origin, and Prospects* (Reading, Mass.: Addison-Wesley, 1969); Chris Argyris, *Management and Organizational Development: The Path From XA to YB* (New York: McGraw-Hill, 1971); and W. Warner Burke, *Organizational Development: Principles and Practices* (Boston: Little, Brown, 1982).

For a practical guide, *see* Richard A. Schmuck and Philip J. Runkel, *The Handbook of Organizational Development in Schools*, 3rd ed. (Palo Alto, Calif.: Mayfield, 1985).

organization plans   A description of how grade patterns within a school district are organized, i.e., how many and what grade levels are assigned to a school at the elementary and secondary levels. Typical patterns are 8-4, 6-3-3, 6-2-4, 5-3-4 and 6-6.

organizational chart   A graphic depiction of members of an organization and how they relate to each other, usually along supervisory lines or functional groupings.

organizational climate   *See* ORGANIZATIONAL CULTURE.

organizational culture   The pattern of fundamental beliefs and attitudes that powerfully affects members' behaviors in and around the organization, persists over extended periods of time, and pervades the organization (to different extents and with varying intensity). The organizational culture is transmitted to new members through socialization (or enculturation) processes; is maintained and transmitted through a network of rituals, rites, myths, communication, and interaction patterns; is enforced and reinforced by group norms and the organization's system of rewards and controls. Organizational cultures vary in intensity, content, and compatibility with the primary pattern of attitudes.

Sources of organizational culture include the attitudes and behaviors of dominant, early organization "shapers" and "heroes"; the nature of the organization's work (or business), including its functions and interactions with the external environment; attitudes, values, and willingness to act of new members. The organizational culture serves useful purposes, including, for example: (1) providing a framework for shared understanding of events; (2) defining behavioral expectations; (3) providing a source of and focus for members' commitments; and (4) functioning as an organizational control system (i.e., through group norms).

Although the concept of organizational culture has similarities to that of organizational climate, the latter typically is limited in use to the "feeling tone" or the "psychological climate." In contrast, organizational culture is typically used more in the traditional anthropological sense. See Edgar H. Schein, Organizational Culture and Leadership (San Francisco: Jossey-Bass, 1985).

organizational development
See ORGANIZATION DEVELOPMENT.

organizational distance   The number of supervisory or authority levels separating two persons in an organization.

organizational iceberg   The concept that the formal or overt aspects of an organization are just the proverbial tip of the iceberg. The greater part of the organization—the feelings, attitudes, and values of its members, for example—remain covert or hidden from obvious view. In short, the formal organization is visible, while the informal is hidden and waiting to sink any ship that ignores it.

organizational identification
The process through which the goals of the individual and the organization become congruent.

organizational   picketing
Picketing an employer in order to encourage union membership. The LANDRUM-GRIFFIN ACT severely limits such picketing.

organizational socialization
The implicit and/or explicit processes used by organizations to prepare or shape members to conform (preferably voluntarily) to the organization's (or suborganization's) values and desired patterns of behavior.

organizational theory   The study of the structure and function of organizations (such as schools) and the behavior of persons within the organizations. See Jay M. Shafritz and J. Steven Ott, eds., Classics of Organization Theory (Chicago: The Dorsey Press, 1987).

organizational unit   A subdivision within any agency, such as a state education agency, established for the purpose of carrying out designated functions or activities.

organized, date   See DATE OF ORGANIZATION.

organized labor   Collective term for members of labor unions.

organizer   Also called LABOR ORGANIZER and union organizer. Individual employed by a union who acts to encourage employees of a particular organization to join the union that the organizer represents.

orientation of staff   A personnel function that is designed to help new staff understand their jobs and their role within the organization or system.

original entry   A student who for the first time in the United States or its outlying areas enters any public or nonpublic elementary or secondary school.

orthography   Refers to the correct or accepted, standard spelling of words in a language.

orthopedically handicapped Individuals with an orthopedic (or physical) condition of a type that might restrict normal opportunity for education or self-support. This term is generally considered to include individuals having impairments caused by congenital anomalies or conditions (e.g., clubfoot, absence of one or more limbs, or cerebral palsy), impairments caused by disease (e.g., poliomyelitis, bone tuberculosis, or muscular dystrophy), and impairments caused by accident (e.g., fractures or burns that cause contractures).

OSEP   *See* OFFICE OF SPECIAL EDUCATION PROGRAMS.

OSERS   *See* OFFICE OF SPECIAL EDUCATION AND REHABILITATIVE SERVICES.

other second-level degree or advanced certificate   A degree (e.g., educational specialist degree), above the master's degree level but below the level of a doctor's degree. Recognition of completed graduate work, such as certificate of advanced graduate study above the master's degree level but below the doctor's degree level, is included here.

outcome   Also IMPACT and PRODUCT. The desired result of an organization's or program's processes. For example, a change in the status or well-being of the clientele, the community, or the environment. For example, counseling (the process) to reduce drug abuse (the outcome); distributing literature (the process) to reduce the incidence of drug-related accidents (the outcome). *See also:*
> EVALUATION
> OBJECTIVE, OUTCOME
> PROGRAM EVALUATION

outcome evaluation   *See* PROGRAM EVALUATION.

outcome objective   *See* OBJECTIVE, OUTCOME.

outdoor education   A means of curriculum enrichment that is experienced in and through the outdoors. In achieving this means of enrichment, instruction is adapted largely to the utilization of resources and activities unique or more appropriate to the outdoor setting, where pupils, instructors, and others may stay for several days. *See* Malcolm D. Swan, ed., *Tips and Tricks in Outdoor Education*, 2nd ed. (Danville, Ill.: Interstate Printers and Publishers, 1978); and David E. Wood and James C. Gillis, Jr., *Adventure Education* (Washington, D.C.: National Education Association, 1979).

outlays   Checks issued, interest accrued, or other payments net of refunds and reimbursements. Total budget outlays consist of the sum of the outlays less offsetting receipts.

out-of-district placement   1. Refers to a student who is placed in a school or facility outside of his or her school district of residence, usually on the basis of an official action by a public agency (e.g., social services) and/or by court order. Such placements are differentiated from out-of-district options that may be chosen by parents. 2. A common phrase in special education that creates concern because of the significant costs involved that become the responsibility of the "home" school district under P.L. 94-142 (the Education of All Handicapped Chidren Act, 1975).

out-of-district student   A student who attends school in a facility outside of the jurisdiction of his or her own school district, usually on a tuition basis.

outplacement   Counseling and career planning services offered to terminated employees to reduce the impact of "being fired," improve job search skills, and ultimately place the "displaced" person in a new job in another organization.

output   End result of any process; in a project management or project control sense, the results of a program's efforts which contribute directly to a desired outcome or impact. For example, immunizations given (output), disease prevented (outcome): clients counseled (output), client behavior changed (outcome). *See also*:
HIERARCHY OF OBJECTIVES
OBJECTIVE, PROCESS
OUTCOME
PROCESS

outreach   1. Process of systematically extending resources and activities to identified populations at risk for the purpose of enhancing their level and quality of participation and their utilization of specified services. 2. Health care or other direct services extended outside of the community already being served. 3. A training process that assists in the development of replications of recognized exemplary programs. 4. Any effort by an institution (such as a college or university) to provide educational, guidance, or other services to those not within immediate proximity of the facility (*e.g.*, campus).

outstationing   The placement of direct service personnel of one organization into another organization's physical facility. However, the service personnel remain accountable to and are paid by their own organization.

Outward Bound   An organization that offers survival training and other educational experiences for youth groups and adults that challenge the individual participant's physical capacities, endurance, and fears, while fostering group trust and interdependence. *See* Robert Godfrey, *Outward Bound: Schools of the Possible* (Garden City, N.Y.: Anchor Press/Doubleday, 1980).
Outward Bound
384 Field Points Road
Greenwich, CT 06830
(203) 661-0797

over compulsory age   A term that refers to any student who has passed the compulsory school attendance age. This information is maintained where required by law or regulation for census or school purposes.

overachievement   Also underachievement. Psychological concepts that describe a discrepancy between predicted and actual achievement/performance. Individuals whose performances exceed or go below expectations are described as overachievers or underachievers. *See* Robert L. Thorndike, *The Concepts of Over and Under Achievers* (New York: Columbia University Press, 1963).

overdose   The ingestion of any substance, but usually a drug or narcotic, at a level that threatens the well-being or life of the individual.

overhead costs   Those elements of cost, necessary in the production of an article or the performance of a service, that are of a nature that the amount applicable to the product or service cannot be determined accurately or readily. Usually they relate to those objects or expenditures that do not become an integral part of the finished product or service, such as rent, heat, light, supplies, management, supervision, and other similar items. *See also* ADMINISTRATIVE COST RATE *and* COST, INDIRECT.

overhead projector   A teaching tool that is used to project images from a sheet of transparent paper onto a screen.

overhead   transparencies
Teaching materials that are used with overhead projectors. Information is written or printed directly onto the transparent paper and then projected on a wall or screen.

P

pacing   1. The rate of presentation or study of learning materials. 2. A counseling procedure that involves "going in tempo" with the counselee.

package settlement   Term that describes the total money value (usually quoted as cents per hour) of an increase in wages and benefits achieved through collective bargaining. For example, a new contract might give employees an increase of 50 cents an hour. However, when the value of increased medical and pension benefits is included, the *package settlement* might come to 74 cents an hour.

Paideia Proposal   A controversial program for "basic schooling" proposed by Mortimer Adler as a means to prepare students for citizenship, to encourage lifelong learning, and to provide the skills necessary to earn a living. The program is a one-track, 12-year required curriculum for all students, emphasizing core didactic instruction, the development of intellectual skills and values, and physical/health education.
     See Mortimer Adler, *The Paideia Proposal* (New York: McMillan, 1982). For a series of articles challenging the proposal, *see* "The Paideia Proposal: A Symposium," *Harvard Educational Review* (November 1983). For additional references, *see* ADLER, MORTIMER.

paired comparisons   A research method, frequently used in educational studies, in which one item of a large group is compared with just one other item at a time until all items can be ranked in order of preference.

Palmer method   A program for teaching good (legible) handwriting skills developed by Austin N. Palmer

(1857-1927) and promulgated by the A.N. Palmer Company through the distribution of commercial materials. For information about available teaching aids, *see Palmer Method Handwriting Catalog* (The A.N. Palmer Company, Schaumburg, IL).

paper   In education, refers to an essay, report, or other written or orally presented evidence of a scholarly endeavor.

paper qualifications   Written or printed documentation of a person's educational and experiential credentials.

paper-and-pencil test   An examination that requires a student to write down answers—rather than respond orally, musically, artistically, or technologically—to questions in order to demonstrate achievement in a subject area.

papier-mâché   An art technique commonly used in schools to create forms from a combination of paper and paste applied over a base structure.

paradigm   A description, sometimes graphic, of the components of a theory or concept.

paradigm shift   A drastic and rather complete change in one's perception of a concept. Described by Marilyn Ferguson in *The Aquarian Conspiracy* (Los Angeles: J.P. Tarcher, distributed by Houghton Mifflin, Boston, 1980).

parallel forms   Two or more forms of a test that are assembled as closely as possible to the same statistical and content specifications so that they will provide the same kind of measurement at different administrations.

paraplegia   A form of physical handicap involving paralysis or dysfunction of the lower body and legs.

paraprofessional   Any individual with credentials different from those standardly accepted for a particular profession, who assists a fully credentialed professional with the more routine aspects of his or her professional work. For example, paralegals assist lawyers, physician assistants assist medical doctors, and teacher's aides assist teachers. *See* Greg H. Firth, *The Role of the Special Education Paraprofessional* (Springfield, Ill.: Charles C. Thomas, 1982).

parapsychology   The study of psychic (i.e., non-physical) phenomena, such as extrasensory perception (ESP), mental telepathy, or out-of-body experiences.

parent cooperative preschool A school for children prior to ordinary age of school attendance that is managed and financed by parents.

parent education   A fairly recent aspect of student education that focuses on teaching parents about child development/child rearing with the goal of making them more competent parents.

parent effectiveness training (PET)   An educational program for parents that focuses on improving communication between parents and children by teaching listening skills and verbal expression techniques. The program was first described by Thomas Gordon in *Parent Effectiveness Training* (New York: Peter H. Wyden, 1970). *See* TEACHER EFFECTIVENESS TRAINING.

Parent Teacher Association (PTA) An organization associated with a particular school (more commonly at the elementary level), the original purpose of which was to foster understanding and shared knowledge between parents and school personnel. The original intent has expanded substantially to include active concern about school accountability and other legal interests. The PTA currently has both a state and national program structure.

Parent Teacher Organization (PTO)   An organizational phenomena in schools that developed with the purpose of offering opportunities for parent involvement and shared activities with school personnel but without (and in response to) the state and/or national costs and constraints associated with PTA affiliation.

Parents Anonymous   A self-help organization founded in 1970 for parents who abuse, or may be at risk for abusing, their children. For additional information about the organization, *see* Patte Wheat and Leonard L. Lieber, *Hope for the Children: A Personal History of Parents Anonymous* (Minneapolis: Winston Press, 1979).
Parents Anonymous
7120 Franklin Avenue
Los Angeles, CA 90046
(800) 426-0353

Parents Without Partners (PWP) A national organization of more than 600,000 members who are both custodial and noncustodial single parents by reason of widowhood, divorce, separation, or other cause. Local affiliates provide support, education, and social activities for members.
Parents Without Partners
7910 Woodmont Avenue, Suite 1000
Bethesda, MD 20814
(301) 654-8850

parent-teacher conference A meeting between a student's teacher and parent(s) for the purpose of reporting on student progress and communicating information about the student that can be useful for both parties.

parity, employment The long-term goal of all affirmative action efforts, which will be achieved after all categories of an organization's employees are proportionately representative of the population in the organization's geographic region. Employment parity exists when the proportion of protected groups in the external labor market is equivalent to their proportion in an organization's total work force, without regard to job classifications.

parity, wage The requirement that the salary level of one occupational classification be the same as for another. The most common example of wage parity is the linkage between the salaries of police and firefighters, but wage parity may also exist among school district employees.

See Paul A. Lafranchise, Sr., and Michael T. Leibig, "Collective Bargaining for Parity in the Public Sector," *Labor Law Journal* (September 1981).

Parker, Francis W. (1837-1902) Often referred to as the father of PROGRESSIVE EDUCATION, he influenced many educational reforms in American schools, such as adapting curriculum to student needs and emphasizing experiential learning.

parliamentarian The official charged with advising the presiding officer of a legislature or deliberative body regarding questions of procedure.

parliamentary inquiry A question about a legislative (or quasi-legislative) body's rules or procedures. Parliamentary inquiries almost always take procedural precedence over any other business of the legislature.

parliamentary procedure The rules by which a deliberative meeting or legislature conducts itself in an orderly fashion according to established precedents. In the United States the most commonly followed parliamentary procedures are *Robert's Rules of Order*. They were originally written, in response to an unruly church meeting, by Henry Martyn Robert (1837-1923), a United States Army officer. First published as the *Pocket Manual of Rules of Order for Deliberative Assemblies* in 1876, it has since been revised many times.

For more comprehensive rules, *see* Lewis Deschler, *Deschler's Rules of Order* (Englewood Cliffs, N.J.: Prentice-Hall, 1976).

parochial schools Full-time schools that are church-related, most commonly to the Roman Catholic Church but also to such Protestant denominations as Lutheran, Quaker, Methodist, Baptist, and Seventh-Day Adventists. Hebrew day schools are also referred to as parochial.

parsimony, law of In educational research, a concept that states that explanations of phenomena should be kept as simple as possible and should be consistent with available data.

partial tuition student A student for whom tuition is paid, but less than the maximum amount.

partially seeing or partially sighted Individuals who have severely impaired vision but have sufficient residual vision (with correction) to include the perception of printed materials as a means of learning.

parts of speech In the study of grammar the classification of words according to function, i.e., nouns, verbs, adjectives, adverbs, prepositions, pronouns, conjunctions, and articles.

part-time personnel   Personnel who occupy positions that require less than full-time service. This includes those employed full-time for part of the school year, part-time for all of the school year, and part-time for part of the school year. *See also* FULL-TIME PERSONNEL.

part-time staff member   A staff member whose total current assignments require less than full-time services. A part-time staff member may be employed full-time for part of the year or part-time for part or all of the year.

part-time student   A student who is carrying less than a full course load, as determined by the state, local school system, or institution.

part-timer general continuation class   In vocational education, a class for persons under 18 who have terminated their full-time education in elementary or secondary school to enter upon employment. Such a class is designed to increase civic intelligence rather than to develop specific occupational competence and is conducted during what would be the usual working hours of the enrollees.

pass rate   The percentage of students passing a qualifying examination or achievement test of some kind.

pass-fail   A grading option, usually exercised at the postsecondary level, which can take the place of the more typical A, B, C, etc., grade system. Also signified by the similar dichotomy of satisfactory/unsatisfactory.

passive learning   Learning that occurs as a result of being "taught at" or lectured to, without active learner participation.

passive vocabulary   Words that one knows by recognition and in context but cannot use spontaneously. Contrast with ACTIVE VOCABULARY.

paternalism   1. In the United States, a derogatory reference to an organization's "fatherly" efforts to better the lot of its employees. Historically, the U.S. labor movement has considered paternalistic efforts to be a false and demeaning charity that inhibited the growth of union membership. 2. A sexist attitude by males towards females; treating grown women as one would treat children. Men who conscientiously provide for the needs of women, but who would at the same time refuse to give women real responsibility or respect them as free-thinking individuals, may be said to be paternalistic. 3. An overconcern by government for the welfare of its citizens. Those who strongly believe in self-reliance would denounce a government's paternalistic interference with their lives.

patronage   The power of elected and appointed officials to make partisan appointments to office or to confer contracts, honors, or other benefits on their political supporters. While subject to frequent attack from reformers, patronage has traditionally been the method by which political leaders assure themselves a loyal support system of individuals who will carry out their policies and organize voters for their continued political control. Patronage has always been one of the major tools by which executives at all levels in all sectors consolidate their power and attempt to control a bureaucracy.

patronage, social   The ability of a chief executive to use the prestige aspects of his or her office to wine and dine and otherwise personally impress critical political forces whose support is desired. Because this depends as much upon force of personality as anything else, some executives, such as Ronald Reagan, have been far more successful at getting political mileage out of social patronage than others.

patterning   A controversial treatment method for brain-injured children developed by Glen Doman and Carl Delacato of the Institute for the Achievement of Human Potential in Philadephia. The treatment involves frequent manipulation of the legs, arms, and body in order to "reprogram" the brain to function more effectively. The method requires the participation of numerous helpers on a "round-the-clock" schedule and is criticized not only for the intensity of effort prescribed but also for the (perhaps) unrealistic promises of success offered.

pauper schools   An early demonstration of the exclusionary practices of American schools whereby separate schools were established for the children of poor people. The concept was not challenged until the late 18th and early 19th century.

Pavlov, Ivan Petrovich (1849-1936)   The Russian physiologist who is best known as an early leader in the field of behavioral psychology. Pavlov's physiological experiments established the basis for differentiating between two types of reflexes: an unconditioned reflex or response, which is an innate reaction to a particular stimulus, and a conditioned or acquired response, which is learned. Pavlov is famous for demonstrating conditioned response with dogs who would salivate in response to a learned stimulus that food would be forthcoming. Compare to CLASSICAL CONDITIONING. *See* B.P. Babkin, *Pavlov: A Biography* (Chicago: University of Chicago Press, 1949, 1971).

pay as you go   1. The automatic withholding of income tax liabilities by means of a payroll deduction. 2. A fiscal policy calling for a BALANCED BUDGET. 3. A pension plan that has employers pay pension benefits to retired employees out of current income.

payable   *See* ACCOUNTS PAYABLE.

paying one's dues   1. The experiences that one must have before being ready for advancement. In effect, "you have to pay your dues" before you can be perceived as a legitimate occupant of a higher position. 2. Past experiences that allow one to be taken seriously by a particular constituency.

payments in lieu of taxes   Payments made out of general revenue by a governmental unit to a school district in lieu of taxes it would have had to pay had its property or other tax base been subject to taxation by the local school district on the same basis as other privately owned property or other tax base. It would include payment made for privately-owned property that is not subject to taxation on the same basis as other privately-owned property due to action by the governmental unit.

payroll   A list of individual employees entitled to pay, with the amounts due to each for personal services rendered. Payments are also made for such payroll-associated costs as federal income tax withholdings, retirement, and Social Security.

payroll deduction and withholding   Amounts deducted from employees' salaries for taxes required to be withheld and for other withholding purposes. Separate liability accounts may be used for each type of deduction.

payroll register   A separate, special form of the cash disbursements journal (or check register) used to record wages and salaries paid, payroll withholding taxes, and other payroll deductions.

The payroll register should contain the date of each payroll check; the name of each person paid (employee or paid volunteer); check number; net amount of the check after withholding taxes and other deductions; details for payroll withholding taxes (for example, Social Security taxes; federal (FWT) and state (SWT) withholding taxes); details for other withholdings (for example, employee contributions to medical insurance); gross pay (before withholding); and which subsidiary and/or general ledger accounts are affected by each transaction.

At the end of each accounting period (for example, each month), all columns in the payroll register are totalled, balanced, and posted to the general ledger. *See also*:

> GENERAL LEDGER
> JOURNAL
> TRIAL BALANCE
> SUBSIDIARY LEDGER

payroll services   Activities concerned with making periodic payments to individuals entitled to remuneration for services rendered. Payments are also made for such payroll-associated costs as federal income tax withholding, retirement, and Social Security.

PBGC   *See* PENSION BENEFIT GUARANTY CORPORATION.

Peabody, Elizabeth P. (1804-1894)   The American educator and writer who established the first public kindergartens in the United States. She was a sister to the wives of Horace Mann and Nathanial Hawthorne, and all three sisters were the subject of *The Peabody Sisters of Salem* by Louise Hall Tharp (Boston: Little, Brown, 1950).

Peabody Individual Achievement Test (PIAT)   A norm-referenced, individually-administered screening measure of academic achievement in reading recognition, mathematics, read-

ing comprehension, spelling, and general information. It can be used for grades kindergarten to 12. It is published by:

> American Guidance Service, Inc.
> Publisher's Building
> Circle Pines, MN 55014

Peabody Picture Vocabulary Test (PPVT)   A commonly used, individually-administered test of receptive vocabulary that is standardized to measure verbal intelligence. It is normed for ages two to adult and requires a picture identification response. There are two forms to the test. It is published by:

> American Guidance Service, Inc.
> Publisher's Building
> Circle Pines, MN 55014

pedagogy   The principles and methods of teaching.

pediatrics   A medical speciality focused on the general health care and treatment of children.

peer counseling   A formal counseling program wherein students help other students learn to better cope with problems by exercising active listening and empathetic skills. *See* Vincent J. D'Andrea and Peter Salovey, *Peer Counseling* (Palo Alto, Calif.: Science and Behavior Books, 1983).

peer group   Associates who are of the same general age group, who have similar interests, and who influence each other in a number of ways.

peer models   A term that refers to the use of same-age, same-sex classmates as demonstrators of appropriate behaviors or effective learning strategies. For a study of the effectiveness of this technique, *see* Dale Schunk and Antoinette Hanson, "Peer Models: Influence on Children's Self-Efficiency and Achievement," *Journal of Educational Psychology* (June 1985).

peer pressure The obligation students feel to conform to the expectations and values of other students as opposed to the expectations and values of their parents and teachers.

peer supervision 1. A type of teacher supervision and method of improving instructional performance that is based on information-sharing between and among teachers. 2. Assigning a new teacher to a more experienced teacher as a resource helper.

peer tutoring The practice of having students of the same or similar age assist with the instruction of other students who may need supplemental aid. This approach is recognized as being equally beneficial to the tutor and the student being tutored. *See* Lilya Wagner, *Peer Teaching* (Westport, Conn.: Greenwood Press, 1982); and Patricia S. Koskinen and Robert M. Wilson, *A Guide for Student Tutors* (New York: Teachers College Press, 1982).

peer tutors A term that refers to the use of same-age classmates as direct instructional aides with students who are handicapped or who otherwise need assistance in learning.

peers Persons generally equal in status, age, and level of attainment.

penalties and interest on taxes Amount collected as penalties for the payment of taxes after the due date or dates, and the interest charged on delinquent taxes from the due date to the date of actual payment. A separate account for penalties and interest on each type of tax may be maintained.

penetration rate Also penetration ratio. In the context of equal employment opportunity, the penetration rate for an organization is the proportion of its workforce belonging to a particular minority group. The penetration ratio is the ratio of an organization's penetration rate to the penetration rate for its geographic region (usually the standard metropolitan statistical area or SMSA). *See also* REPRESENTATIVE BUREAUCRACY.

penmanship or handwriting The practice and accomplishment of the appropriate formation of the letters of the alphabet and spacing between words.

Pennhurst State School v. Halderman 451 U.S. 1 (1981) The Supreme Court case that held that a federal-state grant program, whereby the federal government provided financial assistance to participating states to enable them to create programs to care for and treat the developmentally disabled, did not give rise to any substantive rights in favor of the mentally retarded to "appropriate treatment" in the "least restrictive" environment. This case is known for the proposition that, where Congress enacts legislation pursuant to the Spending Power, which imposes conditions on the grant of federal funds, this legislation is much like a contract: In return for federal funds, the states agree to comply with federally imposed conditions. Conditions imposed by Congress on a grant of federal monies must be unambiguous so that the states may voluntarily and knowingly accept the terms of this "contract."

Pennsylvania Association for Retarded Citizens (PARC) v. Commonwealth of Pennsylvania (343 F. Supp. 279, 302 [E.D. Pa. 1972]) A class action suit filed in 1971 on behalf of all children with mental retardation in Pennsylvania, which requested that all such children be guaranteed a free public education. Although the court did not actually make a ruling on the case, in 1972 a consent agreement was reached whereby the state agreed to guarantee a public education for all children in Pennsylvania and to establish procedural safeguards for families. This case was the first of several similar cases that challenged the constitutionality of children being excluded from school on the basis of handicaps.

pension   Periodic payments to an individual who retires from employment (or simply from a particular organization) because of age, disability, or the completion of a specified period of service. Such payments usually continue for the rest of the recipient's life and sometimes extend to legal survivors.

Pension plans generally have either defined benefits or defined contributions. In *defined benefit plans*, the amount of the benefit is fixed, but not the amount of contribution. These plans usually gear benefits to years of service and earnings or a stated dollar amount. About 60 percent of all pension plan participants are covered by defined benefit plans. In *defined contribution plans*, the amount of contribution is fixed, but the amount of benefit is not. These plans usually involve profit sharing, stock bonus, or money purchase arrangements where the employer contributes an agreed percentage of profits or wages to the worker's individual account. The eventual benefit is determined by the amount of total contributions and investment earnings in the years during which the employee is covered.

Pension Benefit Guaranty Corporation (PBGC)   Federal agency that guarantees basic pension benefits in covered private plans if they terminate with insufficient assets. Title IV of the Employee Retirement Income Security Act of 1974 (ERISA) established the corporation to guarantee payment of insured benefits if covered plans terminate without

sufficient assets to pay such benefits. The PBGC, a self-financing, wholly-owned government corporation, is governed by a board of directors consisting of the Secretaries of Labor, Commerce, and Treasury.

Pension Benefit Guaranty Corporation
2020 K Street, N.W.
Washington, DC 20006
(202) 254-4817

pension fund socialism   Peter F. Drucker's term for the phenomenon that is turning traditional thinking about the "inherent" and historical separation of capital and labor upside down—namely, that the "workers" of the United States are rapidly and literally becoming the owners of the nation's industry through their pension fund investments in diverse common stocks. According to Drucker, pensions funds "own at least 50—if not 60—percent of equity capital." For Drucker's complete analysis, *see: The Unseen Revolution: How Pension Fund Socialism Came to America* (New York: Harper & Row, 1976); and Peter F. Drucker, "Pension Fund 'Socialism,'" *Public Interest* (Winter 1976).

pension plan, fully funded   *See* FULLY FUNDED PENSION PLAN.

pension plan, funded   *See* FUNDED PENSION PLAN.

Pension Reform Act of 1974
See EMPLOYEE RETIREMENT INCOME SECURITY ACT OF 1974.

per capita tax   1. A tax that may be established by a city on all workers working inside the city limit. 2. Tax on each head and the regular payment made on the basis of membership by a local union to its national organization.

per diem   By the day; usually used in relation to payment of subsistence expenses or fees.

per student cost   *See:*
ANNUAL CURRENT EXPENDITURES PER
STUDENT IN ADA
ANNUAL CURRENT EXPENDITURES PER
STUDENT IN ADM
CURRENT EXPENDITURES PER STUDENT
CURRENT EXPENDITURES PER STUDENT
PER DAY (ADA)
CURRENT EXPENDITURES PER STUDENT
PER DAY (ADM)

per student cost of a building
The cost of a building divided by the student capacity of the building.

percentage in membership   *See*
PERCENTAGE OF AGE GROUP IN ALL SCHOOLS *and* PERCENTAGE OF AGE GROUP IN PUBLIC SCHOOLS.

percentage of absence   The average daily absence during a given reporting period divided by the average daily membership for the period, expressed as a percentage; or, the aggregate days absence divided by the aggregate days membership, expressed as a percentage.

percentage of age group in all schools   The number of resident pupils of a given age group (e.g., 14 to 18 years of age) entered in all public and nonpublic schools, divided by the total number of residents within the age group, expressed as a percentage.

percentage of age group in public schools   The number of resident pupils of a given age group (e.g., 14 to 18 years of age) entered in public schools, divided by the total number of residents within the age group, expressed as a percentage.

percentage of attendance   The average daily attendance during a given reporting period divided by the average daily membership for the period, expressed as a percentage; or, the aggregate days attendance divided by the aggregate days membership, expressed as a percentage.

percentage of change in membership from previous year (for a given date)   The change of membership from a given date in one year to a corresponding date the following year, divided by the membership as of the first date, expressed as a percentage.

percentage of change in membership from previous year (for a period of time)   The change in average daily membership from a given period of time in one year to a corresponding period of time the following year, divided by the average daily membership during the first period of time, expressed as a percentage.

percentage of exceptional children in special classes or schools   The number of resident exceptional children entered in special classes or schools, divided by the total number of resident children identified as exceptional, expressed as a percentage.

percentage of high school graduates who completed courses in various subject-matter areas   The number of students in a given high school graduation group who completed courses in each of a number of specific subject-matter areas, divided by the total number of students in the group, expressed as a percentage.

percentage of participation in national school breakfast program   The average daily number of elementary and/or secondary school students participating in the national school breakfast program during a specified month, divided by the average daily attendance for the same month. *See also* AVERAGE DAILY NUMBER OF STUDENTS PARTICIPATING IN NATIONAL

SCHOOL LUNCH AND/OR BREAKFAST PROGRAMS.

percentage of participation in national school lunch program
The average daily number of students participating in the national school lunch program during a specified month, divided by the average daily attendance for the same month. *See also* AVERAGE DAILY NUMBER OF STUDENTS PARTICIPATING IN NATIONAL SCHOOL LUNCH AND/OR BREAKFAST PROGRAMS.

percentage of students in nonpublic schools
The number of students of a given age group or type of instructional organization entered in nonpublic schools, divided by the total number of students in this age group or type of instructional organization entered in all schools, expressed as a percentage.

percentage of students withdrawing, by type of withdrawal
The number of students withdrawing from school during a given regular school term in each of the four principal categories of withdrawal (i.e., transfer, completion of school work, dropout, and death), divided by the total number of students withdrawing, expressed as a percentage.

percentage of school-age population in public (or nonpublic) elementary and secondary schools
The number of resident students of compulsory school attendance age entered in public (or nonpublic) elementary and secondary schools, divided by the total number of residents of compulsory school attendance age, expressed as a percentage.

percentage of students currently members of classes in various subject-matter areas
The number of students in a given school group who are members of classes in each of a number of specific subject-matter areas, divided by the total number of students in the group, expressed as a percentage.

percentage of students making normal progress
The number of students making normal progress during a given reporting period, divided by the membership at the close of the period, expressed as a percentage.

percentage of students not promoted (or retained)
The number of students who, at the close of a given reporting period (usually a regular school term), are reassigned to the same grade, divided by the membership at the close of the period, expressed as a percentage. Students in ungraded classes are not considered "not promoted" unless (and until) they are asked to spend more than the usual amount of time in such classes.

percentage of students participating in various activities
The number of students who, during a given reporting period (e.g., a given regular school term), take part in each of a number of specific activities, divided by the average daily membership of students in the group, expressed as a percentage.

percentage of students promoted
The number of students promoted during or at the close of a given reporting period (usually a regular school term), divided by the membership at the close of the period, expressed as a percentage. For reporting purposes, students in ungraded classes who have made satisfactory progress may be considered separately or they may be considered promoted.

percentage of students transported at public expense
The average daily membership of students transported at public expense, divided by the average daily

membership of the reporting unit, expressed as a percentage.

percentage of time in attendance (for an individual)   The number of days of attendance divided by the number of days of membership, expressed as a percentage.

percentage of time in membership (for an individual)   The number of days in membership divided by the total number of days school was legally in session during a given reporting period, expressed as a percentage.

percentage of total excess public school membership   Total excess membership in public schools divided by the normal student capacity of accessible, publicly-owned school plants in use, expressed as a percentage. *See also* EXCESS MEMBERSHIP IN PUBLIC SCHOOLS *and* STUDENT CAPACITY OF A SCHOOL PLANT.

percentage of total membership being provided appropriate special education   The number of students who have been identified as exceptional by professionally qualified personnel and who are being provided appropriate special education, divided by the total membership, expressed as a percentage. These students may be considered also in smaller groups according to type of exceptionality, e.g., mental retardation, specific learning disabilities, or hearing handicaps.

percentage of transported students riding a given distance   The average daily membership of students who ride a given distance (e.g., five, 10, 15, or 20 miles), divided by the average daily membership of students transported, expressed as a percentage. This percentage may be determined as of a given date or on the basis of averages for a given reporting period.

percentage of transported students riding a given time   The average daily membership of students who ride a given time (e.g., 30 minutes, and one, 1 1/2, and two hours), divided by the average daily membership of students transported, expressed as a percentage. This percentage may be determined as of a given date or on the basis of averages for a given reporting period.

percentile   That point or score in a distribution below which falls the percent of cases indicated by the given percentile. Thus the 15th percentile denotes the score or point below which 15 percent of the scores fall.

percentile band   Interval between percentiles, corresponding to score limits or standard error of measurement above and below an obtained score. The chances are approximately two out of three that the true score of an examinee with a particular obtained score is within these score limits.

percentile rank   Percent of scores in a distribution equal to or lower than a particular obtained score.

perception   The way in which a person views his or her environment based on the senses, past experience, attitudes, current information, and other personal variables.

perceptual disorders   A general term referring to conditions internal to the learner that impact negatively on the ability to take in, recognize, integrate, and interpret new information.

performance bond   A bond that guarantees that a contractor will complete a job correctly and on time.

performance measure   A measurable indicator of performance by an individual, a project, or an organiza-

tion. Performance measures usually are derived from objectives or from generally accepted standards (such as those developed by a national organization). Performance measures may be expressed as absolute numbers, percentages, and ratios. For example: number of new members recruited, average response time following receipt of a call for assistance, percent of eligible clients served, and number of columnar inches of favorable print media coverage per dollar of budgeted public relations monies spent. *See also*:
> ACCOUNTABILITY
> MANAGEMENT BY OBJECTIVES
> OBJECTIVE

performance objectives   *See* IN-STRUCTIONAL OBJECTIVES.

period   In schools, a unit of time allocated for a session of instruction.

periodical   Any publication appearing at regular intervals of less than a year and continuing for an indefinite period.

perks or perquisites   Special benefits that may be made available to employees in an organization. Originally, the term referred only to those unique, tax-exempt privileges conferred upon top management in an organization (for example, company cars or a key to the executive washroom) but in more general usage, "perks" identifies those side-benefits of a particular job beyond basic compensation and benefits.

permanent address   The place that a staff member or student considers to be his or her permanent place of residence; this may or may not be the same as the current address.

permanent arbitrator   Arbitrator who hears all disputes during the life of a contract or other stipulated term.

permanent building   A building designed for its site or placed upon its site and not intended to be moved.

permanent injunction   *See* IN-JUNCTION.

permanent school fund   Money, securities, or land, which have been set aside as an investment for public school purposes, of which the income but not the principal may be expended. These funds have been derived, in most cases, from the sale of state land set aside by the federal and/or state government, from rents and royalties, and from surplus revenue returned to the state by the federal government. In some instances, there may be endowment funds for individual schools. There may be nonexistent funds, also, which are legally recognized as an obligation. *See also* ENDOWMENT FUND.

permanent student record   A student record considered to have permanent or semipermanent value, which remains indefinitely in the files of the school or school system. *See also* STUDENT RECORD *and* CUMULATIVE STUDENT RECORD.

permissive education   1. Teaching situations that place few imposed demands on students. 2. In legal terms, educational programs that may be provided by the local jurisdiction but that are not mandated or required by the state.

perpetual inventory   An inventory system whose accounting is kept current by immediately recording each addition to, or subtraction from, it.

Perry Preschool Project   *See* HIGH SCOPE EDUCATIONAL RESEARCH FOUNDATION.

Perry v. Sinderman 408 U.S. 593 (1972)   U.S. Supreme Court case that held that while a teacher's subjective "expectancy" of tenure is not protected by procedural due process, an allegation that a school had a de facto tenure policy entitles one to an opportunity of proving the legitimacy of a claim to job tenure. Such proof would obligate a school to hold a requested hearing when the teacher could both be informed of the grounds for nonretention and challenge the sufficiency of those grounds.

perseverance The ability of an individual to continue toward completion at a task, regardless of fatigue or boredom.

perseveration Similar to perseverance but with a connotation of lack of control. A tendency to maintain a certain activity beyond the point of usefulness. Difficulty in changing a task, idea, or feeling once a particular direction has been set.

persona A term developed by Carl Jung that refers to the personality or facade that each individual shows to the world. The persona is distinguished from our inner being, because it is adopted and put on like a mask to meet the demands of social life. Persona is the word for the masks that actors wore in ancient Greece.

personal enrichment A type of in-service training that focuses on the development of increased personal effectiveness rather than specific professional skills. Tactics may include self-confrontation, introspection, analysis, values clarification, and interpersonal interactions. The expectation is that as teachers (or other workers) grow personally their commitment and motivation toward their professional responsibilities will be enhanced.

personal leave Leave, either with or without pay, permitted staff members for personal reasons. Many negotiated agreements for teaching staff award a specified number of days per year for personal leave ("no questions asked") *with* pay.

personality 1. A psychological term that refers to the predictable and unique indicators of the way an individual might respond to the environment. 2. A personal reference that usually connotes acceptability and likability.

personality inventory Also called SELF-REPORT INVENTORY. A questionnaire, concerned with personal characteristics and behavior, that an individual answers about himself or herself. Then, the individual's self-report is compared to norms based upon the responses given to the same questionnaire by a large, representative group. *See also* MINNESOTA MULTIPHASIC PERSONALITY INVENTORY.

personality test A test designed to measure any of the non-intellectual aspects of an individual's psychological disposition. It seeks information on a person's motivations and attitudes as opposed to his or her abilities.

personality trait A general aspect of a person that may predispose how he or she reacts to particular situations.

personnel Employees of a school district or any persons under its supervision who are eligible for workmen's compensation, Federal Insurance Contribution Act, and wage or salary tax withholdings. Included are persons who volunteer their services. 2. Collective term for all of the employees of an organization. The word is of military origin—the two basic components of a traditional army being materiel and personnel. Personnel is also commonly used to refer to the personnel management function or the organiza-

350 Personnel Administrator of Massachusetts v. Feeney

tional unit responsible for administering personnel programs.

Personnel Administrator of Massachusetts v. Feeney 442 U.S. 256 (1979)

The Supreme Court case that held that a state law operating to the advantage of males by giving veterans lifetime preference for state employment was not in violation of the equal protection clause of the 14th Amendment. The court found that a veterans preference law's disproportionate impact on women did not prove intentional bias. *See also* VETERANS PREFERENCE.

personnel costs The total cost to the organization of employees' salaries, fringe benefits, and all other direct and indirect components of the total compensation package.

personnel function A service to line management that typically includes assistance in staffing needs, planning, recruiting, selection, training, evaluation, compensation, discipline, and termination. The personnel function also usually includes assistance to management in such areas as labor (or union) relations, affirmative action programs, prevention of discrimination, and complaints processing.

The issue of how the overall personnel function should be organized has been plagued by the attempt to realize several values at once. Foremost among these values have been those of "merit" or neutral competence, executive leadership, managerial flexibility, and representativeness. The main problem of the structure and policy thrusts of personnel units has been that maximizing some of these values requires arrangements ill-suited for the achievement of other values. Thus, achieving neutral competence requires the creation of a relatively independent personnel unit to help insulate employees from the whims and

demands of executives and directors. Yet, the same structural arrangement will tend to frustrate the ability of executives to manage their agencies.

Personnel and Guidance Journal, The

See JOURNAL OF COUNSELING AND DEVELOPMENT (its new name).

PERT Acronym for "program evaluation and review technique," a planning and control process that requires identifying the accomplishments of programs and the time and resources needed to go from one accomplishment to the next. A PERT diagram shows the sequence and inter-relationships of activities from the beginning of a project to the end and uses probabilities for activity start and completion dates. *See also* CRITICAL PATH METHOD *and* PRECEDENCE DIAGRAM.

Peter Doe v. San Francisco Unified School District 60 C.A. 3d 819 (1975)

A California court case that gained national attention when a high school graduate (alias Peter Doe) sued the school district for educational malpractice on the grounds that he was functionally illiterate after 13 years of schooling. A court of appeals found in favor of the school district and the state Supreme Court refused to review the decision.

Peter Principle The principle promulgated by Laurence J. Peter in his worldwide best seller, *The Peter Principle: Why Things Always Go Wrong*, with Raymond Hull (New York: William Morrow, 1969). The "principle" holds that "in a hierarchy every employee tends to rise to his level of incompetence." Corollaries of the Peter Principle hold that "in time, every post tends to be occupied by an employee who is incompetent to carry out its duties." In answer to the logical question of who then does the work that has to be done, Peter asserts that "work is accomplished by those employees who have not yet reached their level of incompetence."

petit mal seizure   The most common type of epileptic seizure seen in schoolchildren; characterized by a momentary (five to 10 seconds) lapse of consciousness that may occur many times during the school day but is so slight that it often goes unnoticed except by experienced observers.

petition   1. Any formal request to a public agency. The First Amendment guarantees the right of citizens to communicate with the government without hindrance. 2. Asking a court to take some specific judicial action. 3. A process usually needed to place a candidate on a ballot, to initiate (or invoke the referendum on) laws, or to seek a recall of an elected official. The petition process usually requires that a certain percentage of a jurisdiction's voters sign the petition document for it to be effective.

See Max Neiman and M. Gottdiener, "The Relevance of the Qualifying Stage of Initiative Politics: The Case of Petition Signing," *Social Science Quarterly* (September 1982).

petty cash   Also petty cash fund; a small revolving cash fund (usually, $20 to $50) usually kept in a cash box and maintained by a secretary or receptionist. The petty cash fund is used to pay for small, unexpected, incidental items, as the need arises, without prior authorization, and without the necessity for writing a check. It is called a "revolving fund," because each time the fund is drawn down to a predetermined minimum level, the vouchers or notes are reconciled with the remaining cash, and the fund is replenished. Compare to IMPREST SYSTEM.

phased testing   Also called progress testing. The testing of those in a training program after specific phases of the program.

Phi Beta Kappa   A national honor society, membership in which signifies the highest academic achievement.

Phi Delta Kappa   A professional fraternal organization of over 130,000 educators that recognizes persons who have demonstrated educational leadership and that promotes quality education. Three publications are sponsored by the organization: *Phi Delta Kappan*, a highly respected monthly journal; *News, Notes and Quotes*, a newsletter; and *Application of Research*, a quarterly research document.

Phi Delta Kappa
P.O. Box 789
Eighth Street and Union Avenue
Bloomington, IN 47402
(812) 339-1156

Phi Delta Kappan   A popular and high-quality monthly (except July and August) magazine, published by Phi Delta Kappa, Inc., that prints articles concerned with issues, trends, and policy in educational research, service, and leadership.

Phi Delta Kappa, Inc.
P.O. Box 789
Bloomington, IN 47402
(812) 339-1156

Phi Epsilon Kappa   A national fraternal organization for professionals in the fields of health, physical education, recreation, and safety. The organization publishes a quarterly journal, *The Physical Educator*, and has a membership of approximately 27,000.

Phi Epsilon Kappa
9030 Log Run Drive N.
Indianapolis, IN 46234
(317) 299-4004

Phi Kappa Phi   A national honor society for college seniors who rank in the upper 10 percent of their classes.

Phi Kappa Phi
P.O. Box 1600
Louisiana State University
Baton Rouge, LA 70893
(504) 388-4917

Phi Theta Kappa   An honorary fraternal organization in education that has 30,000 members.

Phi Theta Kappa
Box 230
PTK Circle
Canton, MS 39046

philanthropy   Donations and gifts of money, property, and time or effort to needy and/or socially desirable purposes. Philanthropy is a broader term than charity in that a return is expected from the donation—in terms of some form of improvement in the public's welfare or general benefit. *See also* BENEVOLENT ORGANIZATION

philology   The study of languages.

philosophy   The general study of values, ethics, logical thinking, and theoretical speculation about the nature of reality and reason. Philosophy of education explores the aims, purposes, and basic concepts of education. *See* S.E. Frost, Jr., *Historical and Philosophical Foundations of Western Education*, 2nd ed. (Columbus, Ohio: Charles E. Merrill, 1973).

phobia   A general term for irrational, persistent, and obsessive fears. *See* SCHOOL PHOBIA.

phoneme   In linguistics, the descriptor for a single speech sound, e.g., the sound "s" as in the words site or cite, must, or place. Phonemes do not always correspond to letters of the alphabet. There are 45 phonemes in the English language.

phonetics   The study of speech sounds (i.e., phonemes).

phonics   An approach to teaching reading that emphasizes "sounding out" words by associating printed letters with their corresponding speech sounds.

physical education (PE)   A standard part of a school curriculum that focuses on developing the body and promoting general fitness through physical activity. *See* ADAPTED PHYSICAL EDUCATION. *See also* Donald R. Hellison, *Goals and Strategies for Teaching Physical Education* (Champaign, Ill.: Human Kinetics Publishers, 1985).

physical handicap   An atypical physical condition that adversely affects the performance of an individual. Individuals with marked physical handicaps may be classified into groups such as those having vision, hearing, speech, or orthopedic handicaps and those having special physical health problems resulting from various diseases and conditions. *See also* HANDICAPPED CHILDREN.

See James L. Bigge and Patrick A. O'Donnell, *Teaching Individuals with Physical and Multiple Disabilities* (Columbus: Charles E. Merrill, 1976); and Harold D. Love and Joe E. Wolthall, *A Handbook of Medical, Educational, and Psychological Information for Teachers of Physically Handicapped Children* (Springfield: Ill.: Charles E. Thomas, 1977).

physical impairment   A physical condition that may adversely affect a student's normal progress in the usual school program.

physical limitation   A physical handicap or other physical condition (e.g., a heart condition, diabetes, or sight defect) that limits the performance of the student or staff member in some activities and must be considered in assignments.

Physical Science Study Committee A group, supported by a grant from the National Science Foundation, that developed, beginning in 1956, a new beginning physics course that emphasized a unified approach to mastering the basic concepts of the science.

physical therapist A staff member performing technical and/or developmental activities for the purpose of assisting students with muscular or motor disabilities to gain optimum functioning. In schools physical therapists generally take a broader, more educationally oriented approach than they do in medical or clinical settings.

physically handicapped Pupils identified by professionally qualified personnel as having one or more PHYSICAL HANDICAPS.

Piaget, Jean (1896-1980) A Swiss psychologist who is best known for his study of the cognitive development of children and his description of the distinct and consistent stages that children go through in the process of intellectual maturation. Piaget's stages, which begin at birth and culminate with adult thinking patterns at about age 16, are sensory motor, preoperational, concrete operational, and formal operational. And each stage has a number of substages. His theories have had a significant impact on educational and instructional methods and programs. Piaget was a prolific writer who published more than 50 books, including *The Psychology of Intelligence* (1947), *The Development of Thought* (1977), and *Behavior and Education* (1978). For insights into Piaget's genius, see Jean Claude Brinquier, *Conversations with Jean Piaget* (Chicago:

University of Chicago Press, 1980); Richard F. Kitchener, *Piaget's Theory of Knowledge: Genetic Epistemology and Scientific Reason* (New Haven: Yale University Press, 1986); S.H. Jacob, *Foundation for Piagetian Education* (Lanham, Md.: University Press of America, 1984); and C.J. Brainerd, *Piaget's Theory of Intelligence* (Englewood Cliffs, N.J.: Prentice-Hall, 1978).

PIAT *See* PEABODY INDIVIDUAL ACHIEVEMENT TEST.

Pickering v. Board of Education 391 U.S. 563 (1968) The U.S. Supreme Court case that held that when a public employee's rights to freedom of speech are in question, the special duties and obligations of public employees cannot be ignored; the proper test is whether the government's interest in limiting a public employee's "opportunities to contribute to public debate is . . . significantly greater than its interest in limiting a similar contribution by any member of the general public." The court identified six elements that would generally enable the state to legitimately abridge a public employee's freedom of expression:

1. The need for maintaining discipline and harmony in the workforce.
2. The need for confidentiality.
3. The possibility that an employee's position is such that his or her statements might be hard to counter due to his or her presumed greater access to factual information.
4. The situation in which an employee's statements impede the proper performance of work.
5. The instance where the statements are so without foundation that the individual's basic capability to perform his or her duties comes into question.

6. The jeopardizing of a close and personal loyalty and confidence.

In addition to the above factors, it has been held that the nature of the remarks or expression, the degree of disruption, and the likelihood that the public will be prone to accepting the statements of an employee because of his or her position, must be weighed. In general, however, only expressions on matters of public concern, as opposed to those primarily of interest to co-workers, are subject to constitutional protection. *See also CONNICK V. MEYERS.*

picketing   1. A political demonstration in which demonstrators walk about a symbolic area (for example, in front of a school or in front of a court) carrying signs with political messages. Picketing of this kind is often done to gain media attention for some issue. 2. An act that occurs when one or more persons are present at an employer's business in order: (a) to publicize a labor dispute; (b) to influence others (both employees and customers) to withhold their services or business; and/or (c) to demonstrate a union's desire to represent the employees of the business being picketed.

The Supreme Court held, in the case of *Thornhill v. Alabama*, 310 U.S. 88 (1940), that the dissemination of information concerning the facts of a labor dispute was within the rights guaranteed by the First Amendment. However, picketing may be lawfully enjoined if it is not peaceful, or if it is for an unlawful purpose or in violation of some specific state or federal law.

picture dictionary   1. A reference book for young children that has an illustration accompanying each entry. 2. A reference book from which a word is looked up from a picture. For example, *see*: Jean-Claude Corbeil, *The Facts On File Visual Dictionary* (New York: Facts On File, 1986).

pie chart   A means of graphically depicting the relative involvement of a number of factors in a total entity. It consists of a circle divided into segments (slices of a pie) representing each factor, with the size of each segment being determined by that factor's relative contribution to the whole.

pigeonholing   The killing of a bill by a legislative committee when it refuses to vote to allow it to go to the entire body for consideration. The committee figuratively puts the bill in a "pigeonhole" and there it stays.

pilot study   A method of testing and validating a survey research instrument by administering it to a small sample of the subject population. According to Sigmund Nosow, in "The Use of the Pilot Study in Behavioral Research," *Personnel Journal* (September 1974), "there is a significant latent use for the pilot study, in a sense somewhat related to feasibility, and that is the creation of a climate of acceptance for such research." For organizations that have not used such research, it is very possible that the acceptance function may be the most important one for a pilot study.

pilot testing   Experimental testing of a newly devised test or proposed project in order to discover any problems before it is put into operational use.

pitch   1. The perceived correlation of the frequency of a sound, i.e., its highness or lowness. 2. Vocal register.

P.L. 89-313   *See* EDUCATION CONSOLIDATION AND IMPROVEMENT ACT.

P.L. 94-142   *See* EDUCATION FOR ALL HANDICAPPED CHILDREN ACT.

place value   In mathematics the value of a digit based on its position in relation to other digits or symbols. For example, the digit "3" has a different and distinct value in each of the following numbers: 3,000, 321, 573, and 18.3.

placebo   In experimental studies, an inert substance that is given to the control group in place of a drug that is being tested in order to compare changes that might occur in either group. Often the control group will experience improvements similar to the experimental group (called a placebo effect) strictly on the basis of thinking they were being given a curative substance.

placement services   Activities organized: (1) to help place pupils in appropriate educational situations and/or in appropriate part-time employment while they are in school, and in appropriate educational and occupational situations after they leave school; and (2) to help pupils in making the transition from one educational experience to another. The latter purpose may include, for example, admissions counseling, referral services, assistance with records, and follow-up communications with employees.

plagiarism   Copying another person's original work and passing it off as one's own.

plan, operational   See OPERATIONAL PLAN.

plan termination insurance Pension insurance available through the Pension Benefit Guarantee Corporation, that provides that, in the event of the financial collapse of a private pension fund wherein the pension fund assets are not sufficient to meet its obligations, the interests of vested employees will be protected.

planning   The formal process of making decisions for the future of in-

dividuals and organizations. There are two basic kinds of planning: strategic and operational.

Strategic planning, also known as long-range, comprehensive, integrated, overall, and managerial planning, has three dimensions: the identification and examination of future opportunities, threats, and consequences; the process of analyzing an organization's environment and developing compatible objectives along with the appropriate strategies and policies capable of achieving those objectives; and the integration of the various elements of planning into an overall structure of plans so that each unit of the organization knows in advance what must be done, when, and by whom.

Operational planning, also known as divisional planning, is concerned with the implementation of the larger goals and strategies that have been determined by strategic planning; it is also concerned with improving current operations and with the allocation of resources through the operating budget. See Roger A. Kaufman, *Educational System Planning* (Englewood Cliffs, N.J.: Prentice Hall, 1972).

planning period   1. That period of time for which active planning is being done. Short-term is usually less than five years, and long-term any period over five years. 2. A class period during which a teacher is not assigned to be with students and thus has time for daily planning.

Planning Programming Budgeting Systems (PPBS)   An elaborate version of program budgeting that requires agency directors to identify program objectives, develop methods of measuring program output, calculate total program costs over the long run, prepare detailed multiyear program and financial plans, and analyze the costs and benefits of alternative program designs. See also BUDGETING.

planning services Activities concerned with: (1) the selection or identification of the overall, long-range goals, priorities, and objectives of an organization or program; and (2) the formulation of various courses of action in terms of identification of needs and relative costs and benefits. Included are decisions on courses of action to be followed in striving to achieve those goals, priorities, and objectives.

plaster of paris A material used in art classes for modeling or casting forms.

plat book A book of maps showing land owned by the school district.

Plato (circa 427-347 B.C.) A Greek philosopher who has had a profound effect on education and the study of philosophy throughout the world. He linked educational theory with political/social beliefs and advocated that appropriate education of the right people could help to assure effective government.

platoon plan, or platoon school A scheduling arrangement for schools that became popular in the early 1900s whereby the student body was divided into two "platoons" that took turns between academic study in the regular classroom and specialized instruction (such as art, music, or physical education) in alternative facilities.

platykurtic A frequency distribution or curve that is more flat-topped, as opposed to peaked, than a normal curve.

play therapy A form of psychological intervention, frequently used with young children, that involves non-directed activities through which the child is allowed to express emotions and grow emotionally. See Thomas D. Yawkey and Anthony D. Pellegrini, eds., *Child's Play and Play Therapy*

(Lancaster, Pa.: Technomic, 1984); and Caroline R. Musselwhite, *Adaptive Play for Special Needs Children* (San Diego: College-Hill Press, 1986).

playground An outside area of a school that is used for recreational activities.

playground building A community services building used primarily in conjunction with a community playground, such as buildings housing playground equipment, restroom and shower facilities, and shelters used during inclement weather.

plenary Refers to a large, general session of a class, conference, or symposium prior to breaking into smaller discussion groups.

plenary power Refers to the concept of holding full or complete power. It is an important term for describing the exclusive power of a board or legislature, for example.

plenary session Any meeting of a legislature, convention, or other group with all members present.

Plessy v. Ferguson 163 U.S. 537 (1896) The Supreme Court case that first established the doctrine of "separate but equal." This case involved railway cars but the doctrine was legally applied to public schools until *BROWN V. BOARD OF EDUCATION* in 1954.

Plowden report A study of English primary schools conducted in 1967 that resulted in recommendations for major educational reforms in England. The report is named after Lady Plowden, the chairperson of the Central Advisory Council for Education, which authorized the report.

plural executive 1. The de facto arrangement of most state governments because most governors share executive authority with other independently elected officers, such as a secretary of state, treasurer, attorney general, or auditor. 2. Any formal arrangement whereby more than one individual or office shares executive power.

pluralism Refers to the coexistence in any one area of multiple social, cultural, ethnic, religious, and racial groups. *See* Donna M. Gollnick and Philip C. Chinn, *Multicultural Education in a Pluralistic Society* (St. Louis: Mosby, 1983).

PNRS *See* PROJECT NOTIFICATION AND REVIEW SYSTEM.

point of order An objection raised by a participant that a formal meeting is departing from rules governing its conduct of business. The objector cites the rule violated, then the chair sustains the objection if correctly made. Order is restored by the chair's suspending proceedings until it conforms to the prescribed "order of business."

policies and procedures manual A manual that is a compendium of an organization's currently operable, formally adopted policies and the supporting methodological procedures. Most policies and procedures manuals are codified. *See also* MANUAL *and* POLICY.

policy A governing principle, plan, or guide for a course of action; a statement of goals that can be translated into a plan or program by specifying the objectives to be obtained. Goals are a far more general statement of aims than are objectives. Goal/objective ambiguity may exist for a variety of reasons. The original sponsors of the policy or program may not have had a precise idea of the end results desired. Formal statements of objectives may be intentionally ambiguous if such vagueness makes it easier to obtain a consensus on action. Value judgments underlying the objectives may not be shared by important groups. Consequently, the end results intended may be perceived by some as implying ill effects for them. So explicit statements of objectives that tend to imply a specific assignment of priorities and commitment of resources may be purposely avoided. Compare to PUBLIC POLICY.

See Eugene J. Meehan, "Policy: Constructing a Definition," *Policy Sciences* (December 1985).

policy analysis A set of techniques that seeks to answer the question of what the probable effects of a policy will be before they actually occur. Policy analysis involves the application of systematic research techniques, drawn largely from the social sciences and based on measurements of program effectiveness, quality, cost, and impact, on the formulation, execution, and evaluation of policy in order to create a more rational or optimal administration.

policy analyst Individual employed to study the effects of a proposed or actual policy.

policy committee A standing committee of a board of directors, usually charged with responsibility for ensuring that the organization is focusing on appropriate needs and clientele, and that its allocation of programs and resources is maximally supportive of its missions and public benefit purposes. The policy committee recommends desirable changes to the board of directors for action. *See also* COMMITTEE *and* POLICY.

policy development The formulation of governing principles, plans, or guides for courses of action.

political appointee A person given a job in government mainly because of political connections (or occasionally because of preeminence in a specific field) as opposed to a person who gains his or her job through the merit system. While a political appointee is any patronage appointment, the phrase tends to be reserved for high-level managerial positions that elected officials use, in their totality, to "take over" the bureaucracy.

See William M. Timmins, "Relations Between Political Appointees and Careerists," *Review of Public Personnel Administration* (Spring 1984).

political executive 1. An individual such as a president, governor, or mayor, whose institutional position makes him or her formally responsible for the governance of a political community. He or she gains this responsibility through election by the people and can have it taken away by not being reelected, by being impeached, or by being recalled. 2. A high-level patronage appointee. 3. The institutions of a government responsible for governing; the totality of the departments, agencies, and bureaus of a government. 4. An elected school board.

political jurisdiction A governmental administrative jurisdiction such as a county, town, township, or special district (such as a school district), which serves as the territorial basis for political representation.

political neutrality The concept that public employees, such as teachers, should not actively participate in partisan politics. The Hatch Acts of 1939 and 1940 restrict the political activities of almost all federal employees and those in state employment having federal financing. Many states have "little" Hatch Acts that further limit the possible political activities of public employees.

population Also called set and universe. A population, set, or universe is composed of all of the cases in a class of things under statistical examination.

portability Characteristic of a pension plan that allows participating employees to have the monetary value of accrued pension benefits transferred to a succeeding pension plan should they leave their present organization.

portable building A building designed and constructed so that it can be transported to another location without major disassembling.

portfolio A collection of student achievements, usually related to an artistic field of study, that is used to demonstrate past accomplishments and future potential. Comparable to an academic vita.

Portland Project A science education curriculum that integrated the study of biology, chemistry, physics, behavioral and environmental science, and mathematics. The development of the project was funded by the National Science Foundation in the early 1960s.

POSDCORB An acronym introduced by Luther Gulick to help students of management and administration remember essential elements of the administrative process: planning, organizing, staffing, directing, coordinating, reporting and budgeting. For a historical perspective, *see* Luther Gulick and L. Urwick, eds., *Papers on the Science of Administration* (New York: Institute of Public Administration, 1937).

position classification The use of formal job descriptions to organize all jobs in a civil service merit system into classes on the basis of duties and responsibilities and for the purposes of delineating authority, establishing chains of command, and providing equitable salary scales. *See* Jay M. Shafritz, *Position Classification: A Behavioral Analysis for the Public Service* (New York: Praeger, 1973).

position paper   Formal statement of opinion on, for example, an organizational, social, or public issue.

positive correlation   In research, a relationship between two variables that signifies that one influences the other in the same direction.

positive reinforcement   Consequences for a behavior that tend to increase the likelihood of a repetition of the same behavior. Frequently equated with a reward. *See* REINFORCEMENT.

positive strike   Also NEGATIVE STRIKE. A strike whose purpose is to gain new benefits. A *negative strike* is one whose purpose is to prevent the loss of present benefits.

posthoc   After-the-fact; in educational research, posthoc analysis (or *ex post facto analysis*) refers to the inference of causes based on observation of effects.

postindustrial society   Term coined by Daniel Bell to describe the new social structures evolving in modern societies in the second half of the 20th century. Bell holds that the "axial principle" of postindustrial society is the centrality of theoretical knowledge as the source of innovation and of policy formation for the society. Hallmarks of postindustrial society include a change from a goods-producing to a service economy, the preeminence of a professional and technical class, and the creation of a new "intellectual" technology.

For the definitive work to date, *see* Daniel Bell, *The Coming of Post-Industrial Society: A Venture in Social Forecasting* (New York: Basic Books, 1973). *See also* John Schmidman,

Unions in Postindustrial Society (University Park: The Pennsylvania State University Press, 1979).

posting   The act of transferring to an account in a ledger the detailed or summarized data contained in the cash receipts book, check register, journal voucher, or similar books or documents of original entry. Compare to JOB POSTING.

postschool performance information   Data about the aspirations and plans of students for postschool vocation, training, and education. Also included is information about employment and other activities of the former student after leaving the school.

postsecondary education   Instructional programs (including curriculum, instruction, and related student services) provided for persons who have completed or otherwise left educational programs in elementary and secondary school.

postsecondary instructional level   The general level of instruction provided for pupils in college programs, usually beginning with grade 13, and any instruction of a comparable nature and difficulty provided for adults and youth beyond the age of compulsory school attendance.

post-test   A test given at the end of a training program to determine if the training objectives have been met.

potential   Abilities that have not yet been realized but which are assumed to be within the capability of a person.

poverty   Defined by the U.S. Bureau of the Census in 1987 as an annual cash income of less than $11,400 for a family of four. This is the subsistence approach, and theoretically is based on the equivalent of three times the amount necessary to provide a nutritionally sound diet. Another way to approach poverty is in terms of relative deprivation, in which the poor are those with less than most others, even if everyone's economic level is well above subsistence level.

Poverty has long been perceived as a natural and a normal condition for some members of a society. The *New Testament* teaches that "ye have the poor always with you" (Matthew 26:11). But in more recent times poverty has come to be thought of as an essentially unnatural or undemocratic condition that measures the weakness of a society that claims equality for all of its citizens.

See N. A. Barr, "Empirical Definitions of the Poverty Line," *Policy and Politics* (January 1981); Sheldon Danziger and Peter Gottschalk, "The Measurement of Poverty: Implications for Antipoverty Policy," *American Behavioral Scientist* (July-August 1983); and Martha S. Hill, "The Changing Nature of Poverty," *Annals of the American Academy of Political and Social Science* (May 1985).

poverty area   An urban or rural geographic area with a high proportion of low income families. Normally, average income is used to define a poverty area, but other indicators, such as housing conditions and incidence of juvenile delinquency, are sometimes added to define geographic areas with poverty conditions.

poverty level   *See* POVERTY.

poverty trap   The dilemma that families on means-tested welfare benefits often face; the welfare system is such that they chance losing benefits if their income rises. Consequently, they are discouraged from seeking employment that pays only marginally better than welfare alone—employment that might have eventually taken them off the welfare rolls.

power test   A test intended to measure level of performance unaffected by speed of response; there is either no time limit or a very generous one.

PPBS   *See* PLANNING PROGRAMMING BUDGETING SYSTEMS.

PPVT   *See* PEABODY PICTURE VOCABULARY TEST.

practical arts   A part of the general school curriculum that is designed to help students be more functional adults in areas of everyday living. Subject areas include industrial arts, home economics, general business, and typing.

practice effect   The influence of previous experience with a test on a later administration of the same test or a similar test; usually an increase in score on the second testing that can be attributed to increased familiarity with the directions, kinds of questions, or content of particular questions. Practice effect is greatest when the interval between testings is small, when the materials in the two tests are very similar, and when the initial test-taking represents a relatively novel experience for the subjects.

pragmatism   A view of the world based on practical outcomes and consequences.

praxis   Practicality as opposed to theory.

precedence diagram   Diagrammatic representation of chronologically sequential activities or steps in a project or toward accomplishment of an objective; a simplified version of a Critical Path Method diagram. *See also:*
CRITICAL PATH METHOD
PERT

precinct An election district of a town, township, county, or other political jurisdiction (such as a school district).

predicting pupil population A procedure for projecting school district enrollment in order to plan for physical plant, personnel, and budget needs.

predictive efficiency A measure of accuracy of a test or other predictive device in terms of the proportion of its predictions that have been shown to be correct.

predictive validity Obtained by giving a test to a group of subjects and then comparing the test results with the job performance of those tested. Predictive validity is the type of validity most strongly advocated by the EEOC, because predictively valid tests are excellent indicators of future performance.

predictor Any test or other employment procedure used to assess applicant characteristics and from which predictions of future performance may be made.

Pregnancy Discrimination Act of 1978 An amendment to Title VII of the Civil Rights Act of 1964; it holds that discrimination on the basis of pregnancy, childbirth, or related medical conditions constitutes unlawful sex discrimination. The amendment was enacted in response to the Supreme Court's ruling in *General Electric Co. v. Gilbert*, 429 U.S. 125 (1976), that an employer's exclusion of pregnancy-related disabilities from its comprehensive disability plan did not violate Title VII.
See Andrew Weissmann, "Sexual Equality under the Pregnancy Discrimination Act," *Columbia Law Review* (April 1983); and Reva B. Siegel, "Employment Equality under the

Pregnancy Discrimination Act of 1978," *Yale Law Journal* (March 1985).

prejudice Either positive or negative internal feelings about a group, or an individual member of a group, based on stereotyped notions of the group rather than specific, first-hand data.

prekindergarten class A group or class organized to provide educational experiences for children during the year or years preceding the kindergarten, which are a part of the elementary school program and are under the direction of a professionally qualified teacher. A prekindergarten class may be organized as a grade of an elementary school or as a part of a separate nursery school. *See* PRESCHOOL PROGRAM *and* EARLY CHILDHOOD EDUCATION.

Premack principle A simple theory of motivation in learning, attributed to David Premack, that involves a reinforcement strategy of alternating less favored activities (e.g., math) with preferred activities (e.g., computer practice). Participation in the preferred activity is contingent upon completion of the less favored activity. Or, "when you finish your math you can work on the computer."
See David Premack, "Reinforcement Theory," in D. Levin, ed., *Nebraska Symposium on Motivation* (Lincoln: University of Nebraska, 1965). For an up-to-date application of the premack principle, *see* David B. Wiley and Andrew J. Heitzman, "Premacking with Micro-computers," *Education* (Winter 1986).

premium 1. The money paid for insurance coverage, usually annually. 2. The amount by which a stock, bond, or other security sells above its par value (face value).

premium on bonds sold That portion of the sales price of bonds in excess of their par value. The premium represents an adjustment of the interest rate.

pre-operational stage One of the stages of cognitive development in children postulated by Jean Piaget. This stage occurs between the ages of two years and seven years and involves the development of language and egocentric precepts about the relationships between events in the environment. See PIAGET.

prepaid expense Any expense or debt paid before it is due; for example, a travel advance to an employee.

prepaid legal services Employee benefit that has the employee and/or employer contribute to a fund that pays for legal services in the same way medical insurance pays for hospitalization. See Guvenc G. Alpander and Jordon I. Kobritz, "Prepaid Legal Services: An Emerging Fringe Benefit," *Industrial and Labor Relations Review* (January 1978).

preparatory postsecondary education programs 1. Learning experiences concerned with the knowledge, skills, appreciations, attitudes, and behavioral characteristics that are considered to be needed by those pupils desiring postsecondary education programs and that normally may be achieved during the secondary school years. 2. Any formal education undertaken after high school and in preparation for college.

preparatory postsecondary employment programs 1. Learning experiences concerned with the knowledge, skills, appreciations, attitudes, and behavioral characteristics that are considered to be needed by those pupils desiring immediate postsecondary employment and that normally may be achieved during the secondary school years. 2. Vocational training that could have been undertaken in high school but is instead taken after leaving high school in preparation for initial employment.

preparatory school (or prep school) A private secondary school that generally prepares students for admission to prestigious colleges and universities. See Peter W. Cookson, Jr., and Caroline H. Persell, *Preparing for Power: America's Elite Boarding Schools* (New York: Basic Books, 1985).

pre-post-testing Administering the same, or equivalent, tests before and after a given intervention in order to measure the effects of the intervention.

preprimary level A distinct organization for classes within an elementary school for groups of children during the year or years preceding the primary level.

preprimary school A separately organized and administered elementary school for pupils in the year or years preceding the first grade. This may include pupils in the prekindergarten and kindergarten years or grades.

preprimers Textbooks that are a part of a basic reading series and that are usually soft-covered and intended for beginning readers. Sequentially in a series, the preprimer follows the "readiness" book and precedes the "primer."

prerequisite 1. A course (completed successfully) or other requirement that is necessary as a preliminary to participation in a given activity or succeeding course. 2. A skill that is purported to be essential to the acquisition of a "higher level" skill. 3. In general, any skill or behavior required for participation in or pursuit of a learning activity.

preschool program   A beginning group or class enrolling children younger than five years of age and organized to provide educational experience under professionally qualified teachers in cooperation with parents during the year or years immediately preceding kindergarten (or prior to entry into elementary school, when there is no kindergarten). There is considerable evidence that good preschool programs have long-lasting, beneficial effects on students who may be at risk for later school problems. For a thorough overview of policy issues regarding preschool and for an extensive bibliography, *see* Lawrence J. Schweinhart et al., "Policy Options for Preschool Programs," *Phi Delta Kappan* (March 1987).

prescriptive teaching   An individualized approach to instruction for students with learning problems that may involve identifying the most effective modality for presenting information, modifying materials or the environment, and using behavioral strategies or specific teaching technologies. For a description of one utilization of this approach *see* Douglas Prillaman, *Educational Diagnosis and Prescriptive Teaching* (Belmont, Calif.: Pitman Learning, 1983).

present   1. A staff member available to perform assigned duties during the hours of the day when such duties are to be performed. 2. A student in attendance.

present   worth   Current replacement cost of a piece of property less the deduction for depreciation.

pre-service training   Professional education that is provided for teachers

and other related professionals prior to professional employment. Contrast with IN-SERVICE TRAINING.

press release   A formal statement made by an organization to representatives of the media in hopes that it will be publicly disseminated (published or broadcast). Press releases are written descriptions of past or upcoming events or activities of significance, or statements about the organization's position on, for example, a controversial public policy. The process of having press releases published or broadcast accurately and with timeliness is a difficult one and requires considerable planning and development of media relations. *See also:*
   MEDIA RELATIONS
   PUBLIC INFORMATION
   PUBLIC RELATIONS

pressure group   1. Any organized group that seeks to influence the policies and practices of government. The difference between a pressure group and a lobby is that a pressure group is a large, often amorphous group, that seeks to influence its fellow citizens as well as the formal political system, while lobbyists are relatively small groups that seek to influence specific policies of government. Lobbies are often the agents of pressure groups, and lobbyists are often professional, full-time entreators. Pressure groups are most often composed of committed amateurs. Lobbyists are often hired by pressure groups to help make their pressure more effective. 2. Less than kind way of referring to legitimate lobbying organizations.

pre-test   Test given before training in order to measure existing levels of proficiency. Such levels are later compared to end-test scores in order to evaluate the quality of the training program as well as the attainments of the individuals being trained. Also a test designed for the purpose of validating new items and obtaining statistics for them before they are used in a final form.

preventive discipline   1. Premised on the notion that knowledge of disciplinary policies tends to inhibit infractions, it seeks to heighten employees' and students' awareness of organizational rules and policies. 2. In the case of students with anticipated behavioral problems, it means studying the environment, situational antecedents, and behavioral precursors that seem to be related to behavioral outbursts and modifying the environment to minimize the likelihood of such occurrences. Asking the question, "What do I do before . . . ?" instead of "What do I do if (when) . . . ?"

preventive mediation   Action taken in order to avoid last-minute crisis bargaining. Negotiating parties sometimes seek preventive mediation—the use of a mediator before an impasse has been reached.

prevocational education   Orientation—to a number of different occupational areas—and counseling designed to assist a person in determining an occupational area(s) for which he or she might best prepare.

primary data   Evaluation data that do not exist prior to initiating an evaluation study. The creation and collection of primary data is accomplished by the evaluator; for example, responses to a questionnaire or public survey. *See also:*
OPERATIONAL DATA
SECONDARY DATA
SOURCES OF DATA

primary grades   The elementary grades preceding the intermediate grades, usually grades one, two, and three.

primary level   A distinct organization within an elementary school for pupils in the primary grades or years, usually grade one through grade three or the equivalent. In some instances, the preprimary and primary levels are combined.

primary school   A separately organized and administered elementary school for pupils at the primary level, usually including grade one through grade three or the equivalent, and sometimes including preprimary years.

primers   1. Textbooks that are a part of a basic reading series designed for young readers. Usually they are the first hard-covered texts in the series and they follow the completion of a number of preprimers. 2. Basic introductory books on a given subject.

Princeton Plan   One attempt to desegregate schools by pairing schools in reasonably close proximity that have opposite racial disbalances (i.e., one predominantly white, one predominantly black) and redistributing the student body between the two schools. Most commonly this is done on the basis of grade; e.g., all kindergarten to third grade students go to one of the schools while all fourth to sixth grade students attend the other. This approach was initiated in Princeton, New Jersey, in 1948.

principal   A staff member who functions as the administrative head of a school (not of a school district) to whom has been delegated the major responsibility for the coordination and direction of the activities of a school. *See* Arthur Blumberg and William Greenfield, *The Effective Principal: Perspective on School Leadership*, 2nd ed. (Newton, Mass.: Allyn and Bacon, 1986); Gerald C. Ubben and Larry W. Hughes, *The Principal: Creative Leadership for Effective Schools* (Newton, Mass.: Allyn and Bacon,

1987); and Thomas J. Sergiovanni, *The Principalship: A Reflective Practice Perspective* (Newton, Mass.: Allyn and Bacon, 1987).

principal of bonds   The face value of bonds. *See also* FACE VALUE.

principals' center   A generic term referring to a nationwide network of approximately 100 independent organizations that developed during the 1980s to provide environments for training, renewal, and collegiality for school principals. For a series of articles by and about a number of principals' centers, see the *NASSP Bulletin* (January 1987).

principal's office   1. A room or rooms, designed, or adapted, for the use of the principal and/or assistant principals in the discharge of their administrative responsibilities, including areas for secretarial and clerical assistants. 2. A place to send students who misbehave.

principle   A comprehensive generalization describing some fundamental process, constant mode of behavior, or property relating to natural phenomena; for example, *see* PETER PRINCIPLE.

prior nonschool employment Nonschool employment before entering into employment with the school system in which currently employed.

prison schools   Educational services offered within prisons, for the benefit of youth and adults who are incarcerated, in an attempt to enhance the rehabilitation aspect of state and federal prison programs.

private foundation   A corporation or trust, of which the endowments are dedicated to philanthropy and proceeds are directed to the public good. Private foundations are controlled by and usually financially supported by a single source, such as an individual, a family, or a corporation. Private foundations were defined statutorily in the Tax Reform Act of 1969. *See also*:

    FOUNDATION
    PHILANTHROPY
    PUBLICLY SUPPORTED ORGANIZATION

private or nonpublic school   A school that is controlled by an individual or by an agency other than a state, a subdivision of a state, or the federal government, and which is usually supported primarily by other than public funds, and the operation of whose program rests with other than publicly elected or appointed officials. *See also* INDEPENDENT NONPROFIT SCHOOL *and* PROPRIETARY SCHOOL.

See Porter E. Sargent, *The Handbook of Private Schools* (Boston: Porter Sargent Publishers, annually since 1914). For a modern history of the private school movement, *see* Patricia M. Lines, "The New Private Schools and Their Historic Purpose," *Phi Delta Kappan* (January 1986).

privatization   The process of returning to the private sector property (such as public lands) or functions (such as trash collection, fire protection, or services to specific categories of people) previously owned or performed by government. The Reagan administration and conservative Republicans in general tend to be in favor of privatizing those government functions that can be performed less expensively or (in their opinion) better by the private sector. In this context privatization and reprivatization tend to be used interchangeably. Some extreme advocates of a wholesale privatization of government functions would even return social security, education, and public health as well as other public service activities over to the private sector.

See E.S. Savas, *Privatizing the Public Sector* (Chatham, N.J.: Chatham

House, 1982); David Heald, "Will the Privatization of Public Enterprises Solve the Problem of Control?" *Public Administration* (Spring 1985); Steve H. Hanke, "Privatization: Theory, Evidence, and Implementation," *Proceedings of the Academy of Political Science* 35:4(1985); and Myron Lieberman, "Privatization and Public Education," *Phi Delta Kappan* (June 1986).

pro bono publico   Latin phrase meaning "for the public good." When abbreviated to *pro bono*, it usually stands for work done by lawyers without pay for some charitable or public purpose; or the representation of low income people by law firms in voluntary legal aid efforts or projects. *See also* PUBLIC INTEREST LAW FIRM.

probability   The chance of an occurrence; the likelihood that an event will occur, expressed as a number from 0 to 1 that can be translated to percentages. Thus, a .25 probability means that there is a 25 percent chance of the event occurring.

probationary promotion   An arrangement whereby a pupil is promoted to the next higher grade on a trial basis in order that his progress and adjustment might be observed; if these prove satisfactory, the pupil is retained in the higher grade.

probationary status   The employment status of the staff member who is employed (subject to discontinuance of employment upon action by, for example, an organizational superior or a governing board) preliminary to being placed on a full employment status upon satisfactory performance over a stipulated period of time.

probationary student   In community/junior colleges, a temporary status for all entering students having

less than a stated academic achievement in their high school graduating class, or who achieve less than a stated score on a standardized test.

problem posing   An approach to mathematics education that teaches students, particularly at the secondary level, to ask questions. For an explanation and exploration of this strategy, *see* Stephen I. Brown and Marion I. Walter, *The Art of Problem Posing* (Philadelphia: Franklin Institute Press, 1984).

problem solving   Strategies that may be used to apply all previously acquired knowledge and experience to new situations and challenges. Education increasingly focuses on the teaching and reinforcement of individual problem-solving skills as a priority area separate from the imparting of accumulated knowledge.

problem-raising method   An instructional approach that uses real or hypothetical issues to guide students into learning about the issues themselves (usually current social issues relevant to the student population) and also about general problem-solving strategies.

process   The procedure used to yield program or organizational outcomes or impacts. For example, counseling (a process) to change students' behaviors (an outcome); distributing literature (a process) to reduce the incidence of drug-related accidents (an outcome). *See also* OUTCOME.

process evaluation   One aspect of evaluation that directs attention to the means that are used to achieve specified performance objectives. In education this will include the monitoring of adherence to system procedures. Contrast with PRODUCT EVALUATION.

process objective *See* OBJECTIVE, PROCESS.

process-centered education
Education where the primary focus is on the learning process, i.e., the teaching of skills such as hypothesizing, deducting, problem solving and summarizing, rather than on the subject matter. Contrast with CONTENT-CENTERED EDUCATION and CHILD-CENTERED EDUCATION.

prodigy An individual who demonstrates phenomenal ability in an activity at an unusually early age. Generally referred to as a "child prodigy."

product *See* IMPACT *and* OUTCOME.

product evaluation One aspect of evaluation that is concerned with the outcome of a particular procedure or program. In education this will generally refer to the measurement of the performance of students on some specified variable.

productivity bargaining Collective bargaining that seeks increases in productivity in exchange for increases in wages and benefits. There are two basic approaches to productivity bargaining—integrative bargaining and pressure bargaining. The latter is the stuff of confrontation and is best illustrated by the adversary model of labor relations, the most commonly adopted model in the United States. Its dysfunctional consequences—strikes and hostility—are well known. The other approach—integrative bargaining—is, in essence, participative management. It is premised upon the notions that a decrease in hostility is mutually advantageous and that management does not have a natural monopoly on brains. The crucial aspect of integrative bargaining is its joint procedure in defining problems, searching for alternatives, and selecting solutions.

profession An occupation requiring specialized knowledge that can only be gained after intensive preparation. Professional occupations tend to possess three features: (1) a body of erudite knowledge that is applied to the service of society; (2) a standard of success measured by accomplishments in serving the needs of society rather than purely serving personal gain; and (3) a system of control over the professional practice, which regulates the education of its new members and maintains both a code of ethics and appropriate sanctions. The primary characteristic that differentiates it from a vocation is its theoretical commitment to rendering a public service.
See Kenneth S. Lynn, ed., *The Professions in America* (Boston: Houghton Mifflin, 1965); Sidney Dorros, *Teaching as a Profession* (Columbus: Charles E. Merrill, 1968); Edgar H. Schein, *Professional Education* (New York: McGraw-Hill, 1972); and Marina Angel, "White-Collar and Professional Unionization," *Labor Law Journal* (February 1982).

professional A term denoting a level of knowledge and skills, possessed by an individual or required of an individual to perform an assignment, that is attained through extensive education and training, usually a minimum of a baccalaureate degree (or its equivalent obtained through special study and/or experience).

professional education courses
Courses (e.g., educational psychology, curriculum, methods, student teaching, and history and principles of education) that are recognized by state certification laws and regulations as courses that distinguish professional education from other professions and occupations.

professional educational staff per 1,000 students in average daily membership The number representing the total full-time equivalency of professional educational assignments in a school system during a given period of time, multiplied by 1,000 and divided by the average daily membership of students during this period.

professional journals Publications, usually in a magazine format, that are distributed on a regular schedule (monthly, bimonthly, quarterly, etc.) and that serve to address the interests of individuals engaged in a particular field of study.

professional leave Leave granted to employees, generally with all or part of their salary paid, for the purpose of professional improvement.

professional organization Also professional association. An organization that promotes a particular profession; for example, a medical society or secondary school principals' association. Professional organizations may qualify for tax-exempt status as business leagues under IRS Code 501(c)(6).

professional and technical services Services of individuals having extensive training in a particular line of work. This includes such services as those provided by architects, auditors, dentists and doctors, consultants, lawyers, tax collectors, data-processing service bureaus, and others.

professionalism A general term for any aspect of one's behavior or appearance that connotes affiliation with a profession.

professionalization Process by which occupations acquire professional status. For example, U.S. police departments are becoming more

professional as increasing numbers of their members gain advanced degrees and take their ethical responsibilities more seriously. This process of professionalization will be complete only when the overwhelming majority of police officers meet the high standards of the present minority.

proficiency test A device to measure the skill or knowledge that a person has acquired.

profile 1. A graph that depicts the relative standing of an individual or group on several different measures as a means of describing the characteristics of the individual or group. 2. A summary of an individual student or teacher's performance over time.

prognosis A prediction about future outcome based on current information.

program 1. Major organizational endeavor, mission-oriented, that is defined in terms of the principle actions required to achieve a significant objective. A program is an organized set of activities designed to produce a particular result or set of results that will have an impact upon a problem or need. 2. An educational program is a group of educational activities or courses that have common objectives or that, together, achieve a singular goal.

program evaluation Also impact evaluation and OUTCOME EVALUATION. 1. Systematic evaluation of any activity or group of activities undertaken to make a determination about their impacts or effects, both short- and long-range. A program evaluation should be distinguished from a management evaluation or an organization evaluation, because these others tend to be limited to a program's internal administrative procedures. While program evaluations may use information such as workload measures, staffing levels, or operational procedural data, the main thrust is necessarily on overall program objectives and impact.

See Jerome T. Murphy, *Getting the Facts: A Fieldwork Guide for Evaluators & Policy Analysts* (Santa Monica, Calif.: Goodyear Publishing Company, 1980); A.C. Hyde and J.M. Shafritz, eds., *Program Evaluation in the Public Sector* (New York: Praeger, 1979); and Daniel Stufflebeam and Wayne Welch, "Review of Research on Program Evaluation in United States School Districts," *Educational Administration Quarterly* (Summer 1986). 2. An assessment by the granting agency of the effectiveness of a program or grant project after it has been completed to determine if its funds were spent effectively, legally, and as expected in the original grant application.

Program Evaluation and Review Technique   *See* PERT.

program management   *See* PROJECT MANAGEMENT.

program of studies   A combination of related courses and/or self-contained classes organized for the attainment of specific educational objectives, e.g., a college preparatory program, an occupational program (in a given occupation or cluster of occupations), or a general education program, or a transfer program.

program results audit   Audits that determine (a) whether the desired results or benefits are being achieved and (b) whether the organization has considered alternatives that might yield desired results at a lower cost.

programmed instruction   Instruction utilizing a workbook, a textbook, or mechanical and/or electronic device, which has been "programmed" to help pupils attain a

specified level of performance by: (a) providing instruction in small steps; (b) asking one or more questions about each step in the instruction and providing instant knowledge of whether each answer is right or wrong; and (c) enabling pupils to progress at their own pace.

programming   1. The preparation of a logical sequence of operations to be performed by a computer in solving a problem or processing data; the preparation of coded instructions and data for such a sequence. 2. Applying a program of individually designed educational objectives and services to a student.

program-oriented budgeting   The preparation of a budget that emphasizes categorization by programs and reflects consideration of present and future costs of these programs. It is more narrow in scope than a planning-programming-budgeting-evaluation system (PPBES) in that it does not include such factors as systematic planning and evaluation procedures and multi-year perspectives.

progress payments   Periodic payments made as work on a contract progresses.

progressive discipline   A concept predicated on the notion that employees and students are both aware of the behavior expected of them and are subject to disciplinary action to the extent that they violate the norms of the organization. A policy of progressive discipline would then invoke penalties appropriate to the specific infraction and its circumstances.

progressive education   An educational reform movement of the late 19th and early 20th centuries that emphasized a more flexible approach to education, including attention to student needs, more democratic participation, and the teaching of problem-solving methods. Individuals closely associated with this movement, which had long-term impact on American education, included John Dewey and Francis W. Parker. *See* Lawrence A. Cremin, *The Transformation of the School: Progressivism in American Education, 1876-1957* (New York: Alfred A. Knopf, 1961).

progressive taxes An economic term referring to a tax rate that increases as the tax base increases, i.e., a tax rate based on ability to pay.

project area As defined for federal educational programs, a school attendance area, or combination of school attendance areas, that, because of a high concentration of children or families of specified characteristics, is thereby designated as an area from which selected children may be served by a particular project. *See also* ATTENDANCE AREA.

project control chart Also FLOWCHART and WORK PLAN CHART. Any one of several alternative diagrammatic approaches for displaying the chronological relationships among a project's or program's tasks, activities and events. *See also*:
 CRITICAL PATH METHOD
 PERT
 PROJECT MANAGEMENT

Project Head Start *See* HEAD START.

project management Also called PROGRAM MANAGEMENT. Management of an organizational unit created to achieve a specific goal. While a project may last from a few months to a few years, it has no further future. Indeed, a primary measure of its success is its dissolution. The project staff necessarily consists of a mix of skills from the larger organization. The success of project management is most dependent upon the unambiguous nature of the project's goal and the larger organization's willingness to delegate sufficient authority and resources to the project manager. Project or program management is an integral part of matrix organizations.

project manager Manager whose task is to achieve a temporary organizational goal using as his or her primary tool the talents of diverse specialists from the larger organization. The authority and responsibility of a project manager vary enormously with differing projects and organizations.

Project Notification and Review System (PNRS) The procedure by which an organization notifies an A-95 clearing house of its intent (NOI: Notification of Intent) to submit a grant proposal—in advance of submittal. PNRS provides the clearinghouse with advance notice of pending grant applications, so it can prepare to review and circulate the grant proposals for review and comment. *See also* GRANT PROPOSAL *and* NOTIFICATION OF INTENT.

Project "Plan" The title is an acronym meaning "Program for Learning in Accordance with Needs"—An individualized instructional program developed in the early 1960s and marketed by the Westinghouse Learning Corporation, which relies heavily on computers for the development of individual programs. For further information on this and other individualized systems, *see* Harriet Talmage, *Systems of Individualized Education* (Berkeley, Calif.: McCutchan, 1975).

projective test Also called projective technique. Any method that seeks to discover an individual's attitudes, motivations, and characteristic traits through responses to unstructured stimuli such as ambiguous pictures or inkblots.

promotion   1. An advancement of a pupil to a higher grade or instructional level. 2. Advancement of an employee to a different and higher-level position.

prompt   In instructional situations, a cue that assists the learner to achieve a correct response.

property tax   *See* TAX, REAL PROPERTY.

proportional taxes   An economic term that refers to tax rates that remain constant regardless of tax base or level of income (e.g., sales taxes).

proposal   *See* GRANT PROPOSAL.

Proposition 13   A 1978 California ballot proposition that was approved by the voters. It limited the revenue-generating (i.e.,taxation) ability of state and local governments and thus had a significant impact on school financing.

proprietary accounts   Those accounts that show actual financial conditions and operations, such as actual assets, liabilities, reserves, surplus, revenues, and expenditures, as distinguished from budgetary accounts. *See also* BUDGETARY ACCOUNTS.

proprietary school   A private or nonpublic school that is operated for business profit. *See also* PRIVATE OR NONPUBLIC SCHOOL.

prorated salary   That portion of a recognized full-time salary that is allocated to a less-than-full-time assignment on the same basis that the full-time equivalency of the assignment is determined.

prorating   1. The allocation of parts of a single expenditure to two or more different accounts. The allocation is made in proportion to the benefits that the expenditure provides for the respective purposes or programs for which the accounts were established. 2. Allocating less than a full entitlement to a school district based on less than a full appropriation being made for a particular function. That is, a school district may be entitled to $1,000,000 for reimbursable transportation costs but receive a prorated distribution of only $750,000 due to a 75 percent appropriation from the legislature.

prospectus   A short document that "advertises" a forthcoming grant proposal. A preview of a grant proposal submitted to a potential grantor to test its potential willingness to consider funding a project—before the submitting organization fully develops or submits a complete grant proposal. *See also* GRANT PROPOSAL.

protected classes/groups   *See* AFFIRMATIVE ACTION GROUPS.

protocols   For standardized tests of intelligence or achievement, the raw data sheets that include all of the examiner's notations of the subject's responses as well as any written or drawn responses completed by the subject. Typically, the information from the protocols is transferred onto a scoring sheet prior to any formal reporting of test results. The protocols are then maintained by the examiner as substantiation of the results in case of any challenge or dispute.

provisional certificate   A temporary teaching or other educational credential issued to an individual who has not yet met the qualifications required for official licensure.

provost In higher education, the administrator in charge of all educational programs, who is generally second-in-command to the college president. Also called vice-president (or chancellor or vice-chancellor) for academic affairs.

proximate cause A legal term that may be used in cases of alleged negligence where the action (or failure to act) of a teacher or other school employee is purported to be the cause of an injury to the plaintiff in the case.

proxy 1. A person authorized to request or complete registration forms or to obtain an absentee ballot on behalf of another person. A proxy may in some cases cast a ballot for another person. 2. Any person who acts for another in a formal proceeding.

psychoanalysis A long-term approach to the resolution of emotional problems, based on the theories of Sigmund Freud who, among other things, attributed current adjustment difficulties to unconscious memories of past experiences.

psycholinguistics A field of study combining psychology and linguistics that is concerned with the intellectual processes related to the use of language. *See* Taylor Insup, *Introduction to Psycholinguistics* (New York: Holt, Rinehart and Winston, 1976).

Psychological Corporation, The A division of Harcourt Brace Jovanovich that publishes and distributes many assessment instruments that are of interest and relevance to educators. Books about the test instruments are also available. A yearly catalog may be ordered.

The Psychological Corporation
555 Academic Court
San Antonio, TX 78204
(800) 228-0752

psychological counseling services Activities that take place between a school psychologist, counselor, or other staff member and one or more pupils (as counselees) and/or their parents, in which the pupils are helped to perceive, clarify, solve, and resolve problems of adjustment and interpersonal relationships.

psychological personnel Also mental health personnel. A general term applied to psychologists and psychometrists that may also apply to psychiatrists, social workers, and psychiatric social workers. The latter categories are sometimes excluded as they are treated as health personnel.

psychological services Activities concerned with administering psychological tests and interpreting the results; gathering and interpreting information about pupil behavior; working with other staff members in planning school programs to meet the special needs of pupils as indicated by psychological tests and behavioral evaluations; and planning and managing a program of psychological services, including psychological counseling for the school or local education agency.

psychological test A general term for any effort (usually a standardized test) that is designed to measure the abilities or personality traits of individuals or groups.

See A. Anastasi, *Psychological Testing*, 4th ed. (New York: Macmillan, 1976); Lewis R. Aiken, *Psychological Testing and Assessment*, 3rd ed. (Boston: Allyn and Bacon, 1979); and J. Lee Cronback, *Essentials of Psychological Testing*, 4th ed. (New York: Harper & Row, 1983).

psychological testing services Activities concerned with administering psychological tests, standardized tests, and inventory assessments of ability, aptitude, achievement, interests, and personality, and the interpretation of these measures for pupils, school personnel, and parents.

psychologist   *See* SCHOOL PSYCHOLOGIST.

psychology   The study of human behavior as it relates to mental processes (i.e., thinking, feeling, reacting).

psychometric data   Psychological data about a student analyzed by the application of mathematical and statistical methods developed for psychological testing.

psychometrician   An individual who is trained to administer and interpret standardized tests of individual abilities and their associated statistical procedures.

psychometrics   That branch of psychology that deals with tests of purported cognitive functioning and their associated statistical procedures. *See* Linda Crocker and James Algina, *Introduction to Classical and Modern Test Theory* (New York: Holt, Rinehart and Winston, 1986).

psychometrist   A staff member assigned to perform professional activities in measuring the intellectual, social, and emotional development of pupils through the administration and interpretation of psychological tests.

psychometry   Measurement and/ or testing of individual abilities or personal characteristics that are assumed to be related to intelligence.

psychomotor domain   The area of behavior that deals with the physical/ muscular functioning of the individual. One of the three general classifications

of behavior described in BLOOM'S TAXONOMY.

psychomotor skills   A broad term referring to any activities that involve coordination between thinking and muscular movements; i.e., the relationship between cognitive processing and physical (motor) output.

psychomotor test   An examination to measure the motor effects of a person's mental or cerebral processes.

psychosis   A severe mental disorder that usually involves the separation of a person's thoughts from reality. In education, psychoses in children are generally referred to as severe emotional disturbances.

psychosomatic   Physical ailments that are caused by psychological stress.

psychotherapy services   Those activities that provide a therapeutic relationship—between a qualified mental health professional and one or more pupils—in which the pupils are helped to perceive, clarify, solve, and resolve emotional problems or disorders.

PTA   *See* PARENT TEACHER ASSOCIATION.

PTO   *See* PARENT TEACHER ORGANIZATION.

puberty   A significant stage in human physical development when secondary sexual characteristics (such as pubic hair, breast growth, vocal changes, change in body build) appear, when reproductive organs become functional, and when hormonal influences on behavior occur.

public administration   1. The executive function in government; the execution of public policy. 2. Organizing and managing people and other resources to achieve the goals of government. 3. The art and science of management applied to the public sector. Public administration is a broader term than public management because it does not limit itself to management, but incorporates all of the political, social, cultural, and legal environments that affect the managing of public institutions.

See Jay M. Shafritz, *The Facts On File Dictionary of Public Administration* (New York: Facts On File, 1985); Jay M. Shafritz and Albert C. Hyde, eds. *Classics of Public Administration*, 2nd ed. (Chicago: Dorsey Press, 1986); and Howard E. McCurdy, *Public Administration: A Bibliographic Guide to the Literature* (New York: Marcel Dekker, 1986).

public adult education   Those organized public educational programs, other than those of regular (full-time and summer) elementary and secondary day schools, community colleges, and college programs, that provide opportunity for adult and out-of-school youth to further their education, regardless of their previous educational attainment. Only those programs that have as their primary purpose the development of skills, knowledge, habits, or attitudes are included. This development may be brought about by formal instruction or by informal group leadership directed toward recognizable learning goals. Activities that are primarily social, recreational, or for the purpose of producing goods, are not included.

public affairs   1. Those aspects of corporate public relations that deal with political and social issues. 2. A more genteel sounding name for a public relations department. 3. The totality of a government agency's public information and community relations activities. 4. An expansive view of the academic field of public administration. Accordingly, a graduate school of public affairs

might include, in addition to degree programs in public administration, programs in police administration, urban studies, etc.

public agency   Any federal, state, or local government organization, or branch thereof. Not to be confused with a public institution or publicly supported institution.

public board of education   The elected or appointed body that has been created according to state law and vested with responsibilities for educational policy-making and other aspects of government in a given geographic area established by the state. Such bodies are sometimes known as school boards, governing boards, boards of directors, school committees, and school trustees. This definition includes state boards of education and the boards of intermediate and local basic administrative units and individual public institutions.

public charge   A person who is supported at public expense.

public domain   1. Land owned by the government. 2. Any property right that is held in common by all citizens; for example, the content of U.S. government publications, expired copyrights, or expired patents. 3. The right of government to take property, with compensation, for a public purpose (see Fifth Amendment).

public goods   Commodities typically provided by a government that cannot, or would not, be separately parceled out to individuals since no one can be excluded from their benefits. Public goods such as national defense, clean air, and public safety are neither divisible nor exclusive.

public grant   A contribution, either money or material goods, made by one governmental unit to another unit and for which the contributing unit expects no repayment. Grants may be for specific or general purposes.

public health administration

That area of public administration generally concerned with preventing disease, prolonging life, and promoting health by means of organized community efforts.

public hearing   A meeting to receive public input—both informational and opinions—on a designated need, issue, problem, or a pending policy or program. Public hearings are held by local, state, and national elected bodies (such as a Senate subcommittee or a local school board), as well as by public agencies (for example, a state department of education).

public information   Information for public consumption through news media about the condition and progress of education in a school district. It consists of such activities as writing news releases, speaking to civic groups or other assemblies, and appearing on local radio and television programs to discuss school district programs.

public interest   This is the universal label in which political actors wrap the policies and programs that they advocate. Would any lobbyist, public manager, legislator, or chief executive ever propose a program that was not "in the public interest?" Because "the public interest" is generally taken to mean a commonly accepted good, the phrase is used both to further policies that are indeed for the common good as well as to obscure policies that may not be so commonly accepted as good. A considerable body of literature has developed about this phrase because it represents an important philosophic point that, if found, could provide considerable guidance for politicians and public administrators alike.

public interest group   An organized pressure group seeking to develop positions and support causes relating to a broader definition of the public good as opposed to any specific social or economic interest. Such groups are often characterized by efforts to obtain a national membership with a high level of participation by members and dissemination of information and authority. Examples of public interest groups are Common Cause, right-to-life groups, the Nader organizations, taxpayers' leagues, the League of Women Voters, the Sierra Club, and Consumer's Union. *See also* INTEREST GROUP.

public interest law   That portion of legal practice devoted to broad societal interests rather than the problems of individual clients.

public interest law firm   A law firm that provides services to advance or protect important public interests in cases that are not economically feasible or desirable for private law firms. Examples of public interests that have been represented by public interest law firms include environmental policy and freedom of information issues. *See also* PRO BONO PUBLICO.

Public Law 89-313   *See* EDUCATION CONSOLIDATION AND IMPROVEMENT ACT OF 1981.

Public Law 94-142   *See* EDUCATION FOR ALL HANDICAPPED CHILDREN ACT OF 1975.

public library   A library operated and directed with public tax dollars by publicly elected or appointed officials and open to the public. Some public libraries are supported and operated wholly or partially by a public school.

public opinion survey   A scientifically designed process to measure public opinion using a statistically sampled cross-section of the population in question. Public opinion polls are used descriptively, for example, to describe public attitudes about crime in America; and predictively, for example, to project voting patterns in a forthcoming election or to gauge public support for a pending bond issue. Compare to SAMPLING.

See Herbert Asher, *Public Opinion Polling* (Washington, D.C.: Congressional Quarterly Press, 1987).

public ownership   Proprietorship by a governmental agency.

public policy   Whatever a government decides to do or not to do. Public policies are made by authoritative "actors" in a political system who are recognized, because of their formal position, as having the responsibility for making binding choices for the society. There are essentially two kinds of literature on public policy. One is process-oriented and attempts to understand and explore the dynamic social and political mechanics and relationships of how policies are made. The other is basically prescriptive and attempts to examine how rational analysis can produce better policy decisions.

public record   A record that by law, regulation, or custom is generally available to the public at large, or to segments of the public having a legitimate reason for reviewing the record.

public relations   A broad, continuing program to promote a reservoir of community goodwill for an organization and/or its programs, which will benefit specific future development campaigns for funding, services, or other purposes. Public relations encompasses, for example, public information and education, and media relations. *See also*:

COMMUNITY RELATIONS

MEDIA RELATIONS
PUBLIC INFORMATION

public relations consultant   Also public relations firm. An individual or organization who provides contracted technical assistance in developing, implementing, and evaluating a public relations program. A public relations firm may or not be associated with an advertising agency.

public school   A school, operated by publicly elected or appointed school officials, in which the program and activities are under the control of these officials and which is supported primarily by public funds.

public support   General term meaning the willingness and potential willingness of people to provide moral, financial, and/or human support to an organization and its programs.

publicly-owned property   1. Land, buildings, and equipment either owned by a school district (or by a unit operating schools) or under its control through a contract to purchase. 2. Land, buildings, and equipment owned by a municipal unit of government (not the unit operating the schools) or by a public school housing authority. 3. Land, buildings, and equipment owned by a state government or the federal government.

publicly-owned quarters   Any public school facility owned by a school administrative unit or under its control through a contract to purchase. Public school facilities designed for school purposes and owned by a county or municipal unit of government, public school housing authority, or similar agency are included.

publicly-owned schoolbus   A schoolbus owned by a school district, a municipal unit of government, a state government, or by the federal government, which is used for the transportation of students, complies with the color and identification requirements set forth by the school system, and has a manufacturer's rated seating capacity of 12 or more. (The designation of schoolbus ownership is based on ownership of the chassis.)

punitive damages   Also EX-EMPLARY DAMAGES. Money awarded by a court to an organization or person who has been harmed in a particularly malicious or willful way by another person or organization. This money is not necessarily related to the actual cost of the injury or harm suffered. Its purpose is to prevent that sort of act from happening again by serving as a warning.

pupil   See STUDENT.

pupil accounting services   Activities concerned with accumulation and maintenance of records on school attendance, location of home, family characteristics, and other census data. Portions of these records become part of the cumulative record, which is maintained for the purposes of counseling and guidance.

pupil activity fund   Financial transactions related to school-sponsored pupil activities and interscholastic activities. These activities are supported in whole or in part by income from pupils, gate receipts, and other fund-raising activities. Support may be provided by local taxation.

pupil appraisal services   Activities having as their purpose an assessment of pupil characteristics, which assessments are used in administration, instruction, and guidance and which assist the pupil in evaluating his purposes and progress in personality and career development.

Test records and materials used for pupil appraisal are usually included in each pupil's cumulative record.

Pupil Behavior Rating Scale   A screening instrument that consists of teacher observations of specific indicators of a student's behavior along three dimensions that relate to school achievement: adaptation to school, emotional states, and interpersonal relations. The scale can be used for students in grades kindergarten to five. It is published by:
Publishers Test Service
2500 Garden Road
Monterey, CA 93940

pupil density   See PUPILS PER SQUARE MILE.

pupil number   See STUDENT NUMBER.

pupil personnel administration The management, coordination, and supervision of the functions included in pupil personnel services in a particular school district. The structure and organization of the administration may vary, from having all functions directed by a single administrative unit to having organizationally separate lines of authority for each of the service functions.   See PUPIL PERSONNEL SERVICES.

pupil personnel services   Sometimes erroneously referred to as "guidance services," pupil personnel encompasses a broad range of services designed to help students get the most out of their school programs. Pupil personnel services are differentiated from both instructional and administrative/management functions, which make up the two other major components of the educational system. According to the bylaws of the National Association of Pupil Personnel Administrators, the following areas are included in pupil personnel programs: guidance and counseling, attendance, psychology, social work, health, speech and hearing, and special education.

The term pupil personnel first appeared in the professional literature and in educational circles after World War II, even though most of the services themselves had been in operation in schools for several years prior to that time. The growth of the concept of pupil personnel in the schools was influenced by the recognition of personnel administration in industry. Just as personnel administration is a factor in production in industry, pupil personnel is thought to be a factor in improving the achievement of students in school.

The introduction of the broad array of "helping" services that comprises pupil personnel programs into the educational setting has not been without problems. The strong push for academic excellence in schools is often in conflict with the notion of meeting individual student needs and differences. The traditional one-on-one clinical model practiced by many of the professionals who provide the services is often not compatible with the demands of the total school environment. And there are frequently unclear boundaries between the roles and responsibilities of instructional functions and pupil personnel functions, creating competition. Another target of competition is the inadequate financial resources that seem to be an ever-present problem in schools.

See Raymond Norris Hatch, *The Organization of Pupil Personnel Programs—Issues and Practices* (East Lansing: Michigan State University Press, 1974); and Howard Lawrence Blanchard, *Organization and Administration of Pupil Personnel Services* (Springfield, Ill.: Charles C. Thomas, 1974).

pupil transportation building   A building used primarily for housing

personnel and equipment engaged in activities that have as their purpose the conveyance of pupils to and from school activities, either between home and school or on trips for curricular or cocurricular activities. This includes building facilities for pupil transportation supervisors, mechanics, and clerks; bus waiting stations; and storage for vehicles and supplies used in the pupil transportation program.

pupil transportation services   Activities concerned with the conveyance of pupils to and from school, as provided by state law. Included are all trips between home and school and trips to school activities.

pupil transportation vehicle   A vehicle owned by the school system, or serving the school system through contractual arrangement, and used for the purpose of conveying pupils to and from school activities, either between home and school or on trips involved in school activities.

pupil unit of measure   A standard of measurement having a pupil-related factor as its unit. Illustrative pupil units of measure for a period of time include average daily membership, average daily attendance, and full-time equivalency of average daily membership or attendance; pupil units of measure as of a given date include membership, attendance, and full-time equivalency of attendance.

pupil-classroom teacher ratio (as of a given date)   The number of pupils in membership, as of a given date, divided by the number representing the total full-time equivalency of classroom teaching assignments serving these pupils on the same date.

pupil-classroom teacher ratio (for a period of time)   The average daily membership of pupils, for a given period of time, divided by the number representing the total full-time equivalency of classroom teaching assignments serving these pupils during the same period.

pupil-counselor ratio (as of a given date)   The number of pupils in membership as of a given date, divided by the number representing the total full-time equivalency of counseling assignments serving these pupils on the same date.

pupil-counselor ratio (for a period of time)   The average daily membership of pupils, for a given period of time, divided by the number representing the total full-time equivalency of counseling assignments serving these pupils during the same period.

pupil-nurse ratio (as of a given date)   The number of pupils in membership, as of a given date, divided by the number representing the total full-time equivalency of nurse assignments serving these pupils on the same date.

pupil-nurse ratio (for a period of time)   The average daily membership of pupils, for a given period of time, divided by the number representing the total full-time equivalency of nurse assignments serving these pupils during the same period.

pupil-principal ratio (as of a given date)   The number of pupils in membership, as of a given date, divided by the number representing the total full-time equivalency of school direction and management assignments serving these pupils as of the same given date.

pupil-principal ratio (for a period of time)   The average daily membership of pupils in the elementary and secondary schools of a school system, for a given period of time, divided by the number representing the total full-time equivalency of school direction and management assignments serving these pupils during the same period.

pupil-professional educational staff ratio (as of a given date)   See STUDENT-PROFESSIONAL EDUCATIONAL STAFF RATIO (AS OF A GIVEN DATE).

pupil-professional educational staff ratio (for a period of time)   See STUDENT-PROFESSIONAL EDUCATIONAL STAFF RATIO (FOR A PERIOD OF TIME).

pupils per square mile   The total number of resident pupils who live in a given attendance area of an administrative unit, divided by the number of square miles in the attendance area or administrative unit.

pupils transported   The average daily attendance of transported pupils.

pupil-school librarian ratio (as of a given date)   The number of pupils in membership, as of a given date, divided by the number representing the total full-time equivalency of all school librarian assignments serving these pupils as of the same given date.

pupil-school librarian ratio (for a period of time)   The average daily membership of pupils, for a given period of time, divided by the number representing the total full-time equivalency of school librarian assignments serving these pupils in school libraries during the same period.

pupil-teacher ratio   The classroom-based proportion of students to teaching personnel, especially in special education programs where student-staff ratios may be regulated by state statute.

purchase order   A written request to a vendor to provide material or services at a price set forth in the order; used as an encumbrance document.

purchased services   Personal services rendered by personnel who are not on the payroll of the school district, and other services that may be purchased by the school district. *See also* CONTRACTED SERVICES.

purchases discount   An allowance made because of either volume purchasing or seasonal purchasing.

purchases journal   The journal used to record items ordered and purchased. It contains information about the date of each item ordered and purchased, what the item is, the purchase order number, the dollar amount of the purchase, and which subsidiary or general ledger account is affected by the purchase (debited or credited).

At the end of each accounting period (usually monthly), all purchases are totaled by account, balanced, and posted to the accounts payable subsidiary ledger and to the general ledger. *See also*:
   DEBITS AND CREDITS

   GENERAL LEDGER
   JOURNAL
   SUBSIDIARY LEDGER
   TRIAL BALANCE

purchasing   Acquiring supplies, equipment, and materials used in school district operation.

purchasing services   Activities concerned with purchasing supplies, furniture, equipment, and materials used in school district operation.

pure tone audiometric test   A test of hearing utilizing tonal stimuli of varying frequencies to measure a student's hearing acuity by both "air conduction" (i.e., into the ear through the ear canal) and "bone conduction" (i.e., into the ear through the bones of the skull).

PWP   *See* PARENTS WITHOUT PARTNERS.

pygmalion effect   In educational research, changes in a student's behavior that might be brought about by an experimenter's expectations. A phenomenon first reported by Robert Rosenthal and Lenore Jacobson in *Pygmalion in the Classroom* (New York: Holt, Rinehart and Winston, 1968).

Q

qualification requirement Education, experience, and other prerequisites to employment or placement in a position.

qualified audit report An opinion of an auditor that cannot be given full credence because the auditor was unable to examine, or has some doubts about, some relevant financial matters.

quality circles 1. Groupings of individuals within organizations, i.e., a "circle of employees" who meet together to discuss those aspects of the organization that hinder or advance the organization's efforts to achieve excellence and high quality production and/or services. 2. Later applied to groups of concerned individuals, usually teachers, parents, community leaders, and taxpayers, who meet voluntarily on a regular basis to identify school problems, suggest solutions, and assist in implementing suggestions. A concept that first developed in industry in Japan after World War II.
See R. Kregorski and B. Scott, *Quality Circles* (Chicago: The Dartness Corporation, 1982); Thomas Haynes and Kathy Allison, "Developing Community-School Involvement via Quality Circles," *Education* (Winter 1986); and E. Paul Torrence, "Education for 'Quality Circles' in Japanese Schools," *Journal of Research and Development in Education* (Winter 1982).

quality points A term used synonymously with the term "grade points." *See also* GRADE POINTS OR GRADE VALUES.

quantified measure *See* MEASURE, QUANTIFIED.

quantitative synthesis A research technique whereby the results of multiple educational research studies of a single topic (or similar topics) can be summarized and analyzed as a whole. For a further description, *see* H.M. Cooper and R. Rosenthal, "A Comparison of Statistical and Traditional Procedures for Summarizing Research," *Evaluation in Education* 4:(1980). For a critical review, *see* P. Hauser-Cram, "Some Cautions in Synthesizing Research Studies," *Educational Evaluation and Policy Analysis,* 5:(1983).

quarter credit hour A unit of measure, frequently used in higher education, denoting class meetings of one hour a week for an academic quarter, generally about 12 weeks time. Satisfactory completion of a course scheduled for three class sections (or the equivalent) per week in an academic quarter earns three quarter credit hours. Three quarter hours is equated with two semester hours.

quartile One of three points that divide the test scores in a distribution into four equal groups.

quasi-judicial agency An agency such as a regulatory commission that may perform many functions ordinarily performed by courts. Its interpretation and enforcement of rules gives it the authority of law. It adjudicates and may bring charges, hold hearings and render judgments. "Quasi" is Latin for "as if" or "almost."

quasi-legislative Having to do with the rule-making authority of administrative agencies. The authority of an administrative agency to make rules gives those rules the authority of law; that is, makes them enforceable as though they had been passed by a legislature.

quick assets   *See* ASSETS.

quid pro quo   Latin meaning "something for something"; initially meaning the substitution of one thing for another. In politics it suggests actions taken because of some action promised in return.

quinmester plan   An alternative school schedule that divides the school year into five 45-day blocks plus one 30-day unscheduled block. Students may attend any four of the five blocks or may choose to attend all five for enrichment or remedial purposes.

quit   Normally, a volunteered resignation, but it can be considered a dismissal for the purposes of arbitral review if evidence suggests that there was not free intent.

quorum   The number of members who must be in attendance to make valid the votes and other actions of a formal group.

R

race 1. A grouping of humans with common characteristics presumed to be transmitted genetically. 2. Human beings in general, as in the human race, to distinguish humans from animals. 3. Ancestry, tribal or national origin. 4. An election or other contest.

race categories The race/ethnic categories that the Equal Employment Opportunity Commission insists be used for EEO reporting purposes are as follows:

White, not of Hispanic Origin Persons having origins in any of the original peoples of Europe, North Africa, or the Middle East.

Black, not of Hispanic Origin Persons having origins in any of the black racial groups of Africa.

Hispanic Persons of Mexican, Puerto Rican, Cuban, Central or South American, or other Spanish culture or origin, regardless of race.

American Indian or Alaskan Native Persons having origins in any of the original peoples of North America and who maintain cultural identification through tribal affiliation or community recognition.

Asian or Pacific Islander Persons having origins in any of the original peoples of the Far East, Southeast Asia, the Indian subcontinent, or the Pacific Islands. This area includes, for example, China, Japan, Korea, the Philippine Islands, and Samoa.

racial balance The proportionate numbers of individuals from different racial groups that make up the population of a school or organization. A school is said to have achieved racial balance when the percentages of students representing different races is reflective of the composition of the community-at-large. That is, if the school district's population is 50 percent white, 30 percent Hispanic and 20 percent Black, then the individual school enrollments should reflect approximately the same percentage ratio.

See Meyer Weinberg, *A Chance to Learn: A History of Race and Education in The United States* (New York: Cambridge University Press, 1977).

racial segregation *See* SEGREGATION.

racism, institutional *See* INSTITUTIONAL DISCRIMINATION.

racist Any person or organization that consciously or unconsciously practices racial discrimination or supports the supremacy of one race over others.

radical acceleration An educational approach to teaching gifted children. This method is described and reported on in *Academic Precocity: Aspects of Its Development*, edited by Camilla Benbou and Julian Stanley (Baltimore: The Johns Hopkins University Press, 1983).

random numbers *See* TABLE OF RANDOM NUMBERS.

random sample A sample of members of a population drawn in such a way that every member of the population has an equal chance of being included in the sample.

range The difference between the lowest and highest scores obtained on a test by some group.

range of class sizes The smallest and largest memberships of classes of a given type as of a given date.

range of motion   Refers to physical therapy exercise that may be a part of an individual student's school program when a handicapped student requires such exercise to maintain muscle function or to prevent muscle contractures in order to benefit from his or her educational program. *See* RELATED SERVICES.

rank and file   A colloquial expression referring to the masses. When used in an organizational context, it refers to those members of the organization who are not part of management; those who are the workers and have no status as officers. Rank and file was originally a military term referring to the enlisted men who had to line up in ranks, side by side, and files, one behind the other. Officers, being gentlemen, were spared such indignities.

ranking test   Any examination used to rank individuals according to their scores so that those with the higher scores have an advantage in gaining employment or promotion.

RAP   *See* RESOURCE ACCESS PROJECT.

rapid reading   *See* SPEED READING.

rapport   The quality of the relationship or interaction between two people such as between a teacher and a student (or students) in his or her class. A positive or good rapport implies mutual respect, liking, and enjoyment from the interaction. In a teaching or instructional relationship the teaching person is assumed to have some responsibility for "establishing good rapport" with the student(s).

rate of pay   The amount of money for a unit of time (e.g., an hour, a day, a week, a month, or a school year) paid a staff member for services to the school system. It is often used to indicate such rates of pay as daily rate for bus drivers, hourly rate for food service workers, and daily rate for substitute teachers.

ratification   In the context of labor relations, formal confirmation by the union membership of a contract that has been signed on their behalf by union representatives.

rating scales   Measures used for the assessment of some trait, characteristic, or attribute based on a predetermined set or criteria. Scales can be numerical (1 to 100), of a general descriptive nature (poor to excellent), or multiple-choice items that are specific to a unique characteristic (e.g., response to criticism).

ratio   A proportional relationship or rate, similar to a percentage. For example, the ratio of minorities to non-minorities served by a program, the ratio of administrative costs to program costs, and the ratio of funds raised to the cost of raising funds. *See also* RATIO, ACCOUNTING.

ratio, accounting   Any ratio used in financial analysis; an account or group of accounts divided by another. Accounting ratios are used as indicators of organizational performance and financial strength. They provide a common denominator for comparing the opinions of one organization (or one chapter) with another. For example, *see*:

    COLLECTION RATE
    LIQUIDITY
    RATIO

ratio, staff-member pupil   *See* STAFF-MEMBER PUPIL RATIO.

ratio, student-administrative staff   *See* STUDENT-ADMINISTRATIVE STAFF RATIO.

ratio, student-counselor   *See* STUDENT-COUNSELOR RATIO.

ratio, student-instructional staff   *See* STUDENT-INSTRUCTIONAL STAFF RATIO.

ratio, student-library services staff   *See* STUDENT-LIBRARY SERVICES STAFF RATIO.

ratio, teacher-instructional supervisor   *See* TEACHER-INSTRUCTIONAL SUPERVISOR RATIO.

rational emotive therapy   A counseling approach applicable to school-aged children (developed by Albert Ellis) that helps individuals to break down irrational belief systems (such as "one should be thoroughly competent, adequate and achieving in all possible respects if one is to consider oneself worthwhile") that can lead to emotional adjustment problems. For Ellis's description of his model, *see* Albert Ellis, *Reason and Emotion in Psychotherapy* (New York: Lyle Stuart, 1967); and Kenneth T. Morris and H. Mike Kanitz, *Rational-Emotive Therapy* (Boston: Houghton-Mifflin, 1975).

Raven Progressive Matrices   A nonverbal individually-administered test of intelligence that has been standardized for ages eight to 65 and that requires the solution of problems resented in abstract figures and designs. It is published by J.C. Raven and distributed by:

The Psychological Corporation
757 Third Avenue
New York, NY 10017

raw score   Also called crude score. The number of items correct on a test, when there is no correction for guessing, or the formula score, when a correction for guessing has been applied.

readability   The ease with which certain material can be read, based on either legibility (i.e., how well the print or handwriting can be deciphered) or the level of difficulty of the content, vocabulary, and structure. For a critical analysis of the validity of several readability formulas, *see* Arthur Olson, "A Question of Readability Validity," *Journal of Research and Development in Education* (Summer 1986).

reading   Instruction designed to develop the skills necessary to perceive and react to patterns of written symbols and to translate them into meaning. The teaching of reading is differentiated according to a number of levels and objectives. The continuous development of reading skills and vocabulary applies to all subject-matter areas, emphasizing selected skills and vocabulary appropriate to pupils' needs in different learning situations.
See R.C. Anderson et al., *Becoming A Nation of Readers: The Report of the Commission on Reading* (Urbana, Ill.: University of Illinois Center for the Study of Reading, 1985); Gerald G. Duffy and Laura R. Roehler, *Improving Classroom Reading Instruction: A Decision-making Approach* (New York: Random House, 1986); and Catherine Wallace, *Learning to Read in a Multicultural Society* (New York: Pergamon Institute of English, 1986).

reading age   Level of reading ability expressed in years.

reading assistant   Someone who reads for a blind employee. Public Law 87-614 of 1962 authorizes the employment of readers for blind federal employees. These reading assistants serve without compensation from the government, but they can be paid by the blind employees, nonprofit organizations, or state offices of vocational rehabilitation. They may also serve on a volunteer basis.

reading comprehension   The ability to infer meaning from printed words. *See* John D. McNeil, *Reading Comprehension: New Directions for*

Classroom Practice, 2nd ed. (Glenview, Ill.: Scott, Foresman, 1987).

reading level A level of achievement attained by readers, generally defined in terms of stages of reading development or grade placement of reading books, e.g., the reading-readiness level and the second-grade level.

reading rate The speed with which one is able to read printed materials.

reading readiness 1. A variety of planned activities designed to develop in children the mental, physical, and emotional maturity prerequisite to instruction in reading. In practice, emphasis is placed on a variety of learning situations, e.g., direct and vicarious experiences involving oral language, such as listening, perceiving speech habits and patterns, developing sequential organization of ideas, developing vocabulary, and gaining experience with books and stories. 2. The level of one's readiness to read. *See* Mary Ann Dzama and Robert Gilstrap, *Ready to Read: A Parents' Guide* (New York: Wiley, 1983).

reading readiness test An examination measuring interrelated factors contributing to a person's readiness for reading, such as linguistic maturity, experiential background, perceptual maturity, and responsiveness to books and storytelling.

reading reversals Perceptual errors in reading where letters, words, or even whole sentences are perceived in some transposed order (e.g., *b* for *d*, *was* for *saw*, *the man told the boy* for *the boy told the man*).

reading textbook A basal reader; a book designed in a particular sequence to teach reading skills, vocabulary, and structure.

real estate tax *See* TAX, REAL-PROPERTY.

real property tax *See* TAX, REAL-PROPERTY.

reality therapy An approach to counseling developed by William Glasser that rejects traditional psychotherapy and the whole concept of mental illness and instead focuses strictly on current behavior. In this approach the therapist confronts the student (or client) with the need to replace irresponsible behaviors with responsible, more acceptable behaviors. The therapy approach is most often applied to delinquent or incarcerated youth but can be applicable to all school children. For Glasser's original description of the approach, *see* William Glasser, *Reality Therapy: A New Approach to Psychiatry* (New York: Harper and Row, 1969).

reappropriation Legislative action to restore or extend the obligational availability, whether for the same or different purposes, of all or part of the unobligated portion of budget authority that otherwise would lapse.

reasonable accommodation Requirement that employers provide a certain level of assistance to employees with handicaps. Once an employee with a handicap is hired, an employer is required to take reasonable steps to accommodate the individual's disability unless such steps would cause the employer undue hardship. Examples of "reasonable accommodations" include providing a reader for a blind employee, an interpreter for a deaf person requiring telephone contacts, or adequate work space for an employee who uses a wheelchair.

rebus approach A method of reading instruction that combines pictures and other symbols with printed words so that a complete sentence contains some words and some pictures. This approach helps the young reader to decode new words by providing the meaning context of the pictures.

recall   1. A procedure that allows citizens to vote officeholders out of office between regularly scheduled elections. A new election requires that a recall petition be presented, with a prescribed percentage of the jurisdiction's voters' signatures. 2. The rehiring of employees from a layoff. 3. The returning of defective products to their manufacturer (often via a retailer) either at the manufacturer's initiative or because of an order from a government regulatory agency enforcing a consumer protection law. 4. One aspect of cognitive processing.

recall item   A test question that requires the examinee to supply the correct answer from memory, in contrast to a recognition item where the examinee need only identify the correct answer.

receivables   *See* ACCOUNTS RECEIVABLE.

receiver   Person appointed by a court to manage the affairs of an organization facing litigation and/or reorganization.

receivership   A court placement of money or property into the management of a *receiver* (a court-appointed, independent manager) to preserve it for the people who ultimately are entitled to it. This is done when the creditors of a business suspect fraud or gross mismanagement and ask the court to step in and watch over the business to protect them.

receiving and disbursing services Activities concerned with taking in money and paying it out, including the current audit of receipts and the preaudit of requisitions or purchase orders to determine: (a) whether the amounts are within the budgetary allowances; and (b) whether such disbursements are lawful school district expenditures.

recertification   1. The renewal of the license required for an educator to perform a particular job. 2. Documentation of the completion of additional training or education beyond that required for the original licensure and within a specified time period.

recertification credit   A unit reflecting a specified amount of time or effort spent engaged in an approved continuing education activity for the purpose of renewing licensure in education or related fields.

recess   1. A play period for pupils in the lower grades. 2. A break in a formal proceeding, such as a trial or hearing, that may last from a few minutes to a few hours. 3. A break in a legislative session. It is distinguished from adjournment in that it does not end a legislative day and so does not interfere with unfinished business. 4. The time between court sessions. For example the U.S. Supreme Court is usually in recess during the summer months.

reciprocity   Interstate agreements that facilitate movement of teachers from one state to another by acknowledging certification or other credentials earned in one state as sufficient evidence for eligibility for certification in another state.

recognition   An employer's official acceptance and designation of a union as the bargaining agent for all of the employees in a particular bargaining unit after a vote of the employees.

recognition item   A test question that calls for the examinee to recognize or select the correct answer from among two or more alternatives.

reconciliation   1. Bringing two accounts into agreement; for example, adjusting the balance in a checking account to agree with the bank's monthly statement. 2. Resolution of conflict between two or more people.

reconstructionism   A theory of education that first emerged in the U.S. in the 1930s and that is based on the tenet that a major purpose of education is to influence social reform.

record   1. A set of related information or facts. For example, an organization's records include its articles of organization, bylaws, and minutes of meetings. 2. In the computer sense of the word, a *record* is a set of related data fields treated as a single unit (for example, a student's academic history).

record, public   A document filed with, or put out by, a government agency and open for public review.

record copy   The copy of a document that is regarded by an organization as the most important or the key official copy.

record cycle   The period of time during which a record is created, used, stored for easy retrieval, transferred to inactive status, and destroyed. *See also* RECORDS MANAGEMENT.

record management   Establishing and maintaining an adequate and efficient system for controlling the records of a school district.

records   A collection of information that is prepared by a person, unit, or organization for the use of that person, unit, or organization.

records maintenance services   Activities organized for the compilation, maintenance, and interpretation of cumulative records of individual pupils, including systematic consideration of factors such as home and family background; physical and medical status; standardized test results; personal and social development; and school performance.

records management   Also information management. The total process of creating, maintaining, storing, and disposing of an organization's records.

recreation   Any voluntary leisure-time activity that provides personal satisfaction and pleasure.

recreational personnel   Personnel employed by a school system for the primary purpose of administering or supervising play activities.

recruitment and placement   Employing and assigning personnel for a school district.

red tape   This somewhat derogatory reference to excessive formality and attention to routine has its origins in the red ribbon with which clerks bound official documents in the last century. The ribbon has disappeared, but the practices it represented linger on.

redemption of principal   Expenditures from current funds to retire serial bonds, long-term loans of more than five years, and short-term loans of less than five years.

reduction in force   *See* RIF.

reductionism   Any attempt to explain complex phenomena in terms of a simple concept. For example, defining all human learning on the basis of the stimulus-response-consequence paradigm.

reemployed annuitant   Employee who, having retired with a pension from an organization, is again employed by that same organization.

reentry A student who enters again any class in the same elementary or secondary school or in any other school in the United States or its outlying areas.

reference 1. A publication or other source referred to in a printed or orally delivered document. 2. A statement regarding a person's qualifications for a job or other position.

reference books Dictionaries, encyclopedias, directories, atlases, and other books that cover many topics more generally rather than one or a few topics more specifically.

reference group The group of individuals that is consciously or unconsciously used as a comparative basis for evaluating or judging the performance of another individual.

referendum A procedure for submitting a proposed law to the voters for ratification and enactment.

referral 1. The act of referring a pupil to a person or agency for study and assistance, whether this person or agency be within or outside the school system. 2. The first step in the legitimate process of obtaining special education services or other individualized attention for a student.

refocusing A skill or technique that teachers use to keep a class discussion from wandering off the subject; making comments that direct group attention to the main topic of interest.

refresher and reorientation training Short, intensive courses for unemployed or potentially unemployed professional persons who are not seeking to qualify for initial employment in a professional occupation but who need to develop their particular professional skills or a new skill so as to maintain their present employment or qualify for new employment within their professions.

refugee An alien who: (a) fled from a given nation or area because of persecution or fear of persecution on account of race, religion, or political opinion; (b) cannot return thereto because of fear of such persecution; and (c) is in urgent need of assistance for the essentials of life.

refund of prior year's expenditures Revenue coming from a refund of an expenditure made to a prior fiscal year's budget. A refund of an expenditure made in the same fiscal year's budget may be recorded in the appropriate expenditure account as a reduction of the expenditure.

refunding 1. Issuance of long-term debt (bonds) in exchange for, or to provide funds for, the retirement of long-term debt already outstanding. 2. A 1980s consumer phenomenon involving cash-back offers from manufacturers for purchases; sometimes used as a fund-raising tactic by schools and other nonprofit organizations.

regents The members of a governing board for a state educational institution or the state-wide system of higher education.

Regents of the University of California v. Allan Bakke 438 U.S. 265 (1978) The Supreme Court case that upheld a white applicant's claim that he had been denied equal protection of the law because he was refused admission to the University of California Medical School at Davis when 16 out of the school's 100 class spaces were set aside for minority applicants. The court ruled that Bakke, whose "objective" qualifications according to the school's admission criteria, were better than some of the minorities, must be admitted to the Davis Medical School as soon as possible, but that the university had the right to take race into account in its admissions criteria. The imprecise nature of taking race into account as one factor among many has created considerable confusion about voluntary affirmative action programs in employment. Nonetheless, Bakke was admitted, did graduate, and is now a practicing physician.

See J. Harvie Wilkinson II, *From Brown to Bakke: The Supreme Court and School Integration 1954-1978* (New York: Oxford University Press, 1979); Cardell K. Jacobson, "The Bakke Decision: White Reactions to the U. S. Supreme Court's Test of Affirmative Action Programs," *Journal of Conflict Resolution* (December 1983); and Timothy J. O'Neill, *Bakke and the Politics of Equality: Friends and Foes in the Classroom of Litigation* (Middletown, Conn.: Wesleyan University Press, 1984).

See also:
DEFUNIS V. ODEGAARD
REVERSE DISCRIMINATION
UNITED STEELWORKERS OF AMERICA V. WEBER, ET AL.

regional district   The consolidation of two separate school districts for the operation of a high school program.

regional laboratories   A nationwide system of independent organizations funded by the federal government for the purpose of research and development in education. These laboratories, as well as the research and development centers (see entry), were established by Congress in the late 1960s.

Directory of Regional Educational Laboratories

Appalachia Educational Laboratory
P.O. Box 1348
Charleston, WV 25325

CEMREL, Inc.
3120 59th St.
St. Louis, MO 63139

Far West Laboratory for Educational Research and Development
1855 Folsom St.
San Francisco, CA 94103

Mid-Continent Regional Educational Laboratory
12500 E. Iliff Ave.
Aurora, CO 80014

The Network, Inc.
290 S. Main St.
Andover, MA 01810

Northwest Regional Educational Laboratory
300 SW Sixth Ave.
Portland, OR 97204

Research for Better Schools
444 N. Third St.
Philadelphia, PA 19123

Southwest Educational Development Laboratory
211 E. 7th St.
Austin, TX 78701

SWRL Educational Research and Development
4665 Lampson Ave.
Los Alamitos, CA 90720

---

register   1. To formally enroll as a student or as a participant in an event or program. 2. Any book of such public facts as births, deaths, and marriages. Other examples of public record books are the register of patents, the register of ships, the register of deeds, and the register of wills. 3. A book of accounts that varies from a one-column to multi-column pages of special design whereon entries are distributed, summarized, and aggregated, usually for convenient posting to summary accounts.

registered warrant   A warrant that is registered by the paying officer for future payment on account of present lack of funds, and that is to be paid in the order of its registration. In some cases, such warrants are registered when issued; in others, when first presented to the paying officer by the holders. *See also* WARRANT.

registrant   A person who has registered for a particular educational program, but who may or may not actually participate in the program.

registration   1. The act of registering; the process of entrance into a school or course; the act of placing the student's name on the rolls of a school or school system. This does not ensure that the student will actually attend and does not constitute entering into membership status. *See also* ACTIVE MEMBERSHIP STATUS. 2. The process whereby a prospective voter is required to establish his or her identity and place of residence prior to an election in order to be declared eligible to vote in a particular jurisdiction. The reason for registration is to prevent election day fraud by making it difficult for one person to vote at more than one location and to ensure that those who do vote have previously established that they are eligible residents. Prior to any major election all political parties make significant efforts to get their potential supporters registered. In recent years many jurisdictions have made major efforts to make it easier for citizens to register by combining registration with driver license application processes and by allowing registration in supermarkets and shopping centers.

See Steven J. Rosenstone and Raymond E. Wolfinger, "The Effect of Registration Laws on Voter Turnout," *American Political Science Review* (March 1978); Robert S. Erikson, "Why Do People Vote? Because They Are Registered," *American Politics Quarterly* (July 1981); and Hulbert James, Maxine Phillips, and Donald Hazen, "The New Voter Registration Strategy," *Social Policy* (Winter 1984).

registry   Also REGISTER. A roster of registered persons.

regression   1. In the context of child development, the temporary lapses or setbacks that occur in the otherwise smooth course of normal development. 2. In the context of learned behaviors or skills, the loss or forgetting of previously learned skills in the absense of opportunities for continued practice. This is an important factor in determining the need for EXTENDED SCHOOL YEAR services for students who are handicapped. 3. A psychological withdrawal to an earlier period of life, which may be manifested by infantile or immature behavior.

regression analysis   Also multiple regression analysis. A method for describing the nature of the relationship between two variables, so that the value of one can be predicted if the value of the other is known. Multiple regression analysis involves more than two variables.

regressive taxes   Taxes, such as sales taxes, that decrease as the tax base increases, therefore imposing a greater burden on those persons who are less able to pay. The same effect is ascribed to proportional taxes, even though the concept is different.

regular class   The general type of class in which most students receive instruction, including most classes other than those that are composed of exceptional students.

regular classroom   An instructional space that is designed, or adapted, in such a manner that it can be used to house any class that does not require special built-in equipment tailored to its specific needs.

regular education   As differentiated from "special education," refers to the education system as it relates to the majority of students, staff, administrators, facilities, materials, instructional methodologies, curricula, etc. The special education community may refer to students in regular education as non-handicapped, non-special education, typical, or normal.

regular four-year high school
See FOUR-YEAR HIGH SCHOOL.

regular programs   1. Instructional activities designed primarily to prepare pupils for experience as citizens, family members, and workers, as contrasted with programs designed to improve or overcome physical, mental, social, and/or emotional handicaps. Regular programs include elementary programs, middle/junior high programs, and high school programs. 2. Those programs, other than the direct operation of schools, that are carried out year after year by a state education agency as a permanent part of its activities. These are programs such as: provision of consultative service to local school districts in administration, curriculum, finance, and transportation; research and statistical services; distribution of state aid; professional licensing; and operation of the state library.

regular salaries   Full-time, part-time, and prorated portions of the gross salary costs for work performed by employees of an educational institution or school district who are considered to be in positions of a permanent nature.

regular school term   That school term that usually begins in the late summer or fall and ends in the spring. A regular school term may be interrupted by one or more vacations. In higher education, this is referred to as the "academic year."

regular student   In community/junior colleges, an unrestricted status for students who meet all the regular admission requirements of the institution.

regulation   The rule-making process of those administrative agencies, such as a state education authority or state board of education, charged with the official interpretation of a statute. These agencies (often independent regulatory commissions), in addition to issuing rules, also tend to administer their implementation and adjudicate interpretative disputes. The Interstate Commerce Commission in 1887 became the prototype of the modern regulatory agency.

rehabilitation   Assisting a person to restore the fullest possible functioning in all areas of life through training and education.

Rehabilitation Act Amendments of 1984   Amendments to the Rehabilitation Act of 1963 (P.L. 98-221) that created expanded services for individuals who are severely handicapped. The amendments mandated cooperation between education agencies and vocational rehabilitation agencies to facilitate the transition of students with severe handicaps from school to work.

Rehabilitation Act Amendments of 1986   Further expansion of the Rehabilitation Act (P.L. 99-506) and its previous amendments to increase opportunities for individuals with severe mental and physical handicaps to be trained to work in competitive employment situations and to be supported in the maintenance of job placement.

Rehabilitation Act of 1973   The federal law (P.L. 93-112) that contains provisions (in Section 504) that prohibit discrimination against the handicapped by the federal government, its contractors and subcontractors, and by any program or activity receiving federal financial assistance. See Judith Welch Wegner, "The Antidiscrimination Model Reconsidered: Ensuring Equal Opportunity without Respect to Hand-

reliability coefficient 393

icap under Section 504 of the Rehabilitation Act of 1973," *Cornell Law Review* (March 1984).

rehabilitation program A program of studies and services designed primarily to restore in whole or in part the ability of disabled individuals to perform biologically, psychologically, or sociologically, just as persons not disabled. This includes rehabilitation center programs and vocational rehabilitation programs for restoring individuals to economic self-sufficiency through education or retraining.

reinforcement Also POSITIVE REINFORCEMENT and NEGATIVE REINFORCEMENT. Inducement to perform in a particular manner. Positive reinforcement occurs when an individual receives a desired reward that is contingent upon some prescribed behavior. Negative reinforcement occurs when an individual works to avoid an undesirable consequence. *See* B.F. Skinner, *Contingencies of Reinforcement: A Theoretical Analysis* (New York: Appleton-Century-Crofts, 1969).

reinforcement schedule A systematic plan for increasing some desired behavior through the provision of reinforcing consequences for the behavior. Types of reinforcement schedules include: (a) fixed ratio (delivering rewards after a certain number of responses); (b) fixed interval (delivering rewards after a predetermined period of time); (c) variable ratio (delivering rewards after a varying number of responses); (d) variable frequency (delivering rewards after varying time intervals). Variable schedules are also called intermittent and tend to be the most effective for maintaining behaviors.

reinstatement 1. Restoration of an employee to his or her previous position without any loss of seniority or other benefits. 2. The readmittance of organization members (such as a student or a union member) who have been suspended; for example, for disruptive behavior or for nonpayment of dues.

related services A term specific to the Education for All Handicapped Children Act of 1975, which means those supportive services "as may be required to assist a handicapped child to benefit from special education." More generally the services primarily referred to under this law, such as speech pathology and audiology, psychological services, physical and occupational therapy, counseling, and transportation, are considered by schools to be related services or support services.

released time An arrangement whereby a school officially and regularly excuses one or more full-time students for part of a session in order to receive religious or other instruction.

reliability Dependability of a testing device, as reflected in the consistency of its scores when repeated measurements are made of the same group. When a test is said to have a high degree of reliability, it means that an individual tested today and tested again at a later time with the same test and under the same conditions will get approximately the same score. In short, a test is reliable if it gives dependable, repeated measures. *See also* INTER-RATER RELIABILITY.

reliability coefficient Numerical index of reliability that is obtained by correlating scores on two forms of a test, from statistical data on individual test items, or by correlating scores on different administrations of the same test. A reliability coefficient can be a perfect 1.00 or a perfectly unreliable -1.00. A reliability of .90 or greater is generally considered a good measure of test reliability. A reliability coefficient can be obtained in comparing any two forms and is not restricted to tests.

religious discrimination   Any act that manifests unfavorable or inequitable treatment toward employees or prospective employees because of their religious convictions. Because of Section 703(a)(1) of the Civil Rights Act of 1964, an individual's religious beliefs or practices cannot be given any consideration in making employment decisions. The argument that a religious practice may place an undue hardship upon an employer—for example, where such practices require special religious holidays and hence absence from work—has been upheld by the courts. However, because of the sensitive nature of discharging or refusing to hire an individual on religious grounds, the burden of proof to show that such a hardship exists is placed upon the employer. *See* AMERICAN BOARD OF EDUCATION V. PHILBROOK, 107 5. Ct. 367 (1986).

religious education   Any teaching that involves religion from dogmatic indoctrination to comparative historical study of the world's religion, the sociology of various belief systems and the nature of moral and ethical behavior. *See* Lawrence Byrnes, *Religion and Public Education* (New York: Harper & Row, 1975).

remedial education   Specialized or additional instruction to correct deficiencies in learner accomplishments or achievements, with the expectation that the student will ultimately master the regular curriculum through regular channels. Contrast with COMPENSATORY METHODOLOGY and ADAPTED EDUCATION.

remedial reading   Planned diagnostic and remedial activities, for individual pupils or groups of pupils, designed to correct and prevent further reading difficulties that interfere with the pupil's expected progress in developing reading skills, understanding, and appreciation.

remedial specialist   A professional employee who performs activities concerned with correcting or improving specific marked deficiencies (such as a deficiency in content previously taught but not learned) that are not due to impairment of mental or physical ability.

removal   1. Separation of an employee for cause or because of continual unacceptable performance. 2. Separation of a student from regular classes because of a continuing pattern of disruptive behavior.

reopener clause   Also wage reopener clause. A provision in a collective bargaining agreement stating the circumstances under which portions of the agreement, usually concerning wages, can be renegotiated before the agreement's normal expiration date. Typically such clauses provide for renegotiation at the end of a specified time period (such as one year) or when the Consumer Price Index increases by an established amount.

reorganization   Changes in the administrative structure or formal procedures of a government or administrative agency that do not require fundamental constitutional change or the creation of new legal entities. Many reorganizations are undertaken—for the purposes of departmental consolidation, executive office expansion, budgetary reform, and personnel administration—primarily to promote bureaucratic responsiveness to central executive control and, secondly, to simplify or professionalize administrative affairs.

replication   1. Repeating an experiment or research study to check the validity of the results. 2. Modeling an educational program after one that has proven to be effective.

report 1. A collection of information that is prepared by a person, unit, or organization for the use of some other person, unit, or organization. 2. A detailed statement describing an event, occurrence, or incident (such as a speech, debate, or meeting). 3. The written result of a study or investigation. 4. An announcement. 5. To give a formal accounting (for example, to report a budget surplus). 6. To notify, for example, organizational superiors, of one's whereabouts. 7. A written description, of a student's performance on individually administered tests, of abilities, aptitudes, or achievement.

report card *See* GRADE CARD.

Report Card on School Reform: The Teachers Speak A 1988 publication of the Carnegie Foundation for the Advancement of Teaching; it reported on a nationwide survey of 13,500 public school teachers regarding their perceptions of school reform and student achievement. Seven out of ten teachers gave school reform a grade of C or less and half felt that teacher morale has declined though student achievement is up. The report was authored by Ernest L. Boyer and published by the Carnegie Foundation, Princeton, New Jersey.

reporting period A period of time for which a report is prepared (e.g., a calendar year, school year, regular school term, summer school term, semester, or marking period).

reporting unit The organizational unit submitting a report (e.g., a state department of education, an intermediate administrative unit, a local basic administrative unit, or a school).

representation election *See* AUTHORIZATION ELECTION.

representative bureaucracy A concept originated by J. Donald Kingsley in *Representative Bureaucracy* (Yellow Springs, Ohio: Antioch Press, 1944); it asserts that all social groups have a right to participation in their governing institutions. In recent years, the concept has developed a normative overlay: that all social groups should occupy bureaucratic positions in direct proportion to their numbers in the general population. A representative bureaucracy is the expressed or implied goal of all affirmative action/equal employment opportunity programs.

For defenses of this normative position, *see* Samuel Krislov, *Representative Bureaucracy* (Englewood Cliffs, N.J.: Prentice-Hall, 1974); Samuel Krislov and David H. Rosenbloom, *Representative Bureaucracy and the American Political System* (New York: Praeger, 1981); and Dennis Daley, "Political and Occupational Barriers to the Implementation of Affirmative Action: Administrative, Executive, and Legislative Attitudes Toward Representative Bureaucracy," *Review of Public Personnel Administration* (Summer 1984).

representative sample Sample that corresponds to or matches the population of which it is a sample with respect to characteristics important for the purposes under investigation. For example, a representative national sample of secondary school students should probably contain students from each state, from large and small schools, and from public and independent schools in approximately the same proportions as these exist in the nation as a whole.

repression A psychological term for the unconscious failure to acknowledge certain feelings, thoughts, or experiences in order to avoid the discomfort associated with them.

reprimand   1. Formal censure for some job-related behavior. A reprimand is less severe than an adverse action, more forceful than an admonition. 2. A mild form of punitive reaction to a student's misbehavior.

repurchase agreement   An agreement by a seller to repurchase something sold to a buyer for a specific price, under certain circumstances or conditions, and usually on a specified date.

request for proposal (RFP)   A formal, printed announcement by a governmental agency or a private foundation of monies available for projects. The RFP includes all of the data needed by potential applicants, such as priority areas that will be considered, time lines, levels of funding, and information required in the application.

required course   A course that all students in a particular program of study must take. Contrast with ELECTIVE COURSE.

requisition   A written request to a purchasing officer for specified articles or services. It is a request from one school official to another school official, whereas a purchase order is from a school official (usually the purchasing officer) to a vendor.

research   Systematic study and investigation in some field of knowledge, undertaken to establish facts or principles. See also BASIC RESEARCH and APPLIED RESEARCH.

research center   Also called research institute. An organization that conducts research as its primary mission. Research centers may be independent or affiliated with other organizations, such as colleges, universities, and hospitals. Funding for research centers may be from combinations of contracts, grants, and public appropriations. Staff members of university-affiliated research centers often carry faculty appointments whose costs are borne in part by the educational institution.

research and development   Activities concerned with systematic studies and investigations in some field of knowledge and with the evolving process of using the products of research to improve educational programs.

research and development centers (R&D Centers)   A number of national centers that have been established by the federal government at major universities for the purpose of bringing scholars together from various disciplines to work on significant educational problems. These centers, as well as the REGIONAL LABORATORIES were established by congress in the late 1960s.

Directory of Research and Development Centers

National Center for Research in Vocational Education
Ohio State University
1960 Kenny Rd.
Columbus, OH 43210

Center for Educational Policy and Management
College of Education
University of Oregon
Eugene, OR 97403

Learning Research and Development Center
University of Pittsburgh
3939 O'Hara St.
Pittsburgh, PA 15260

Research and Development Center for Teacher Education
Education Annex 3.203
The University of Texas
Austin, TX 78712

Center for the Study of Education
UCLA Graduate School of Education
145 Moore Hall
Los Angeles, CA 90024

Wisconsin Center for Educational Research
University of Wisconsin
1025 W. Johnson St.
Madison, WI 53706

Institute for Research on Educational Finance and Governance
CERAS Building
School of Education
Stanford University
Stanford, CA 94305

research services   Activities concerned with the systematic study and investigation of the various aspects of education, undertaken to establish facts and principles.

reserved rights   *See* MANAGEMENT RIGHTS.

residency requirement   1. The requirement that a citizen live in a jurisdiction for a specific length of time before being eligible to vote or hold public office. The Supreme Court has held, in *Dunn v. Blumstein*, 405 U.S. 330 (1972), that a "durational" residency requirement to vote is unconstitutional. However, as a practical matter the court recognizes the necessity of closing voter registration rolls 30 to 50 days before an election. *See* Edward Tynes Hand, "Durational Residence Requirements for Candidates," *University of Chicago Law Review* (Winter 1973).
2. The requirement that an individual be (or become) a resident of a jurisdiction in order to be eligible for employment with the jurisdiction. *See* Peter K. Eisinger, "Municipal Residency Requirements and the Local Economy,"

Social Science Quarterly (March 1983); and Stephen L. Mehay and Kenneth P. Seiden, "Municipal Residency Laws and Local Public Budgets," *Public Choice* (1986).
3. The requirement that an individual be a resident of a jurisdiction for a specific period of time before becoming eligible for welfare benefits. *See* Eugene C. Durman, "The Impact of the Elimination of Residency Laws on Public Assistance Rolls," *Journal of Legal Studies* (January 1975).
4. The requirement in state-supported institutions of higher education that a person be an in-state resident for a given period of time (e.g., one year) to be eligible for differential tuition payment.
5. The requirement imposed by a graduate school of higher education for the period of time that a student must be in full-time attendance (or to satisfy specific credit limits) in order to maintain eligibility for the advanced degree.

resident children per square mile   The total number of resident children, by age, who live in a given attendance area or administrative unit, divided by the number of square miles in the attendance area or administrative unit.

resident student   A student whose legal residence is within the geographic area served by a specified school, school system, or institution. *See also* SCHOOL ATTENDANCE AREA.

resident student of administrative unit (or school district)   A student whose legal residence is within a specified administrative unit (or school district).

resident student of an institution   A student who resides during a school term in an institution (such as a residential school or residential child-caring institution) rather than in a private home.

resident student of school attendance area   A student whose legal residence is within the geographic area served by the school he attends. *See also* SCHOOL ATTENDANCE AREA.

residential school   An educational institution in which students are boarded and lodged as well as taught.

residential school for special education   A residential school providing a program of education for handicapped students.

residual value   The difference between the original worth of an asset (for example, the purchase price or fair market value of a donated automobile) and that portion of it that has been amortized or written off (as a depreciation expense or loss). *See also* AMORTIZATION *and* DEPRECIATION.

resignation   Employee's formal notice that his or her relationship with the employing organization is being terminated.

resolution   A formal statement of an organization's position, stand, or opinion, usually as voted by its board or membership.

Resource Access Project (RAP)   A national network of regionally-based programs funded by the federal government to provide training and technical assistance to the teaching staff of HeadStart centers. The training focus is on services for those HeadStart students who are handicapped.

resource center   An instructional space designed, or adapted, as a place for reading, viewing, listening, and otherwise studying about one or more specific subject-matter areas, and for the custody, circulation, production, and administration of related supplies and equipment for the use of the student body and school staff. For inventory purposes, such a space is considered to be a school library instructional space.

resource room   The space in a school designated for use by students who need specialized instruction from a special education teacher for a portion of their school day and to augment the regular curriculum. *See* Howard Drucker, *The Organization and Management of the Resource Room: A Cookbook Approach* (Springfield, Ill.: Charles C. Thomas, 1976).

resource teacher   A specially trained (special education) teacher who is assigned to work with an individual or with small groups of students who have learning or behavior problems. The resource teacher may also consult with the regular classroom teacher as a means of assisting these students in the regular classroom. *See* J. Lee Wiederholt, *The Resource Teacher: A Guide to Effective Practice* (Boston: Allyn and Bacon, 1978).

resource unit   A written plan or collection of materials including, for a given segment of instruction, a variety of learning experiences, resources, and evaluation techniques from which teachers may select those deemed best suited for each pupil or group of pupils.

resources   Money, materials, personnel, or services that may be available to a local or intermediate basic administrative unit from a variety of sources. Essentially, refers to everything required to manage the needs of a school district or other entity.

response   Any behavior that occurs in reaction to a stimulus or situation.

response rate   1. In survey research, the percentage of those given questionnaires who complete and return them. 2. In fund-raising, the percentage of those to whom an appeal was made who respond (or respond affirmatively). 3. In teaching technology, the frequency with which a student responds to a presented stimulus.

responsibility-oriented budgeting A plan of financial operation expressed in terms of the allocation of each organizational unit within the department. The word "location" is sometimes used to refer to the organizational unit.

restraining order, temporary *See* INJUNCTION.

restricted   grants-in-aid Revenues received as grants by a school district that must be used for a categorical or specific purpose. If such money is not completely used, it usually must be returned to the granting government unit. Separate accounts may be maintained for general source grants-in-aid that are not related to specific revenue sources of the governmental unit.

restriction on school activities The manner in which a pupil's school activities are curtailed because of a physical condition or for any other reason.

restrictive covenant A clause in a group of deeds (for example, in a housing subdivision) that forbids all of the current and future owners from doing certain things. Restrictive covenants have been serious impediments to establishing group homes and halfway houses by social services organizations.

restrictive credentialism A general term for any selection policy adversely affecting disadvantaged groups because such groups lack the

formal qualifications for positions that (in their own opinion) do not truly need such formal qualifications.

resume A written summary of a person's educational and professional history, including job experience and other relevant experiences such as publication or presentation of original materials. Also called a vita or curriculum vitae.

retardation Generally refers to mental retardation, a condition manifested by less than normal intellectual capacity and usually some noticeable deviation in adaptive functioning.

retention For school students, a restriction on activity imposed because of some infraction of the rules. Retention usually involves "staying after school," missing recess, or some similar loss of privilege.

retention period Stated period of time during which records are to be retained. *See also* RETENTION SCHEDULE.

retention preference Or RETENTION STANDING. Relative standing of employees competing in a reduction-in-force (RIF). Their standing is determined by such factors as veterans preference, tenure group, length of service, performance appraisal, and critical skills.

retention schedule A timetable showing how long an organization's records are to be kept. The period of retention for each record is affected by the organization's need for the information (for example, some records may be retained indefinitely for historical purposes), legal requirements and other requirements of the organization. *See also* RECORDS MANAGEMENT.

retention standing   The precise rank among employees competing for a position in the event of a reduction-in-force or layoff. It is determined by tenure groups and subgroups and by length of creditable service.

retention-in-grade   Maintaining a student at the same grade level from one year to the next, rather than promoting to the next grade, generally because the student has not accomplished, to the degree assumed to be satisfactory, the required work at the grade level just completed. For a critical view of this practice see Mary Lee Smith and Lorrie A. Shepard, "What Doesn't Work: Explaining Policies of Retention in the Early Grades," *Phi Delta Kappan* (October 1987).

retirement   1. Voluntary or involuntary termination of employment or voluntary service because of age, disability, illness, or personal choice. 2. Making the final payment owed on a bond or a loan note, and thereby ending its existence and all obligations under it. 3. The removal of fixed assets from service accompanied by adjustments of the accounts containing their costs and accumulated depreciation. It is immaterial whether the retired asset is sold for use or for junk, or just abandoned. *See also* DEPRECIATION.

Retirement Equity Act of 1984 A federal law that amended the Employee Retirement Income Security Act of 1974 and that broadened the conditions under which spouses may receive retirement benefits. Under these amendments, spouses of employees who die after attaining eligibility for pensions are guaranteed a benefit beginning at age 55. Also, the act requires employers to count all service from age 18 in calculating when an employee becomes vested (legally entitled to a pension), permits pension plan members to leave the work force for up to five consecutive years without losing pension credits, and allows plan members to take maternity or paternity leave without loss of service credit.

retirement fund   A fund established and maintained to pay employees following their retirement, under terms specified in the organization's retirement plan. Retirement funds, established in conformity with qualified retirement plans, may be tax-exempt or tax-deferred.

retirement fund system   A plan whereby a fund of money, built up through contributions from participants and other sources, is used to make regular payments to those who retire from service in the educational system by reason of age, disability, or length of service.

retirement plan, fixed-benefit *See* FIXED-BENEFIT RETIREMENT PLAN.

retirement program   The program adopted by a school that formally specifies the benefits that staff members will receive at various ages and lengths of service.

retreat   A method of staff in-service or staff development that involves bringing professional staff together in a relatively isolated, relaxed environment to avoid intrusion by daily routines and problems, to allow concentration on a particular subject or topic, and to achieve group and/or individual renewal.

retroactive seniority   Seniority status that is retroactively awarded back to the date that a woman or minority group member was proven to have been discriminatorily refused employment or promotion. The U.S. Supreme Court has interpreted the "make whole" provision of Title VII of the Civil Rights Act of 1964 to include the award of retroactive seniority to proven discriminatees; however, retroactive seniority cannot be awarded further back than 1964, the date of the act. *See* Hindy Lauer Schachter, "Retroactive Seniority and Agency Retrenchment," *Public Administration Review* (January-February 1983).

revenue   Also gross receipts. Receipts from all sources. Unless otherwise stated, gross receipts represent receipts prior to the deduction of expenses. Revenues constitute additions to assets that do not increase any liability, do not represent the recovery of an expenditure, do not represent the cancellation of certain liabilities without a corresponding increase in other liabilities or a decrease in assets, and do not represent contributions of fund capital in food service and pupil activity funds.

revenue anticipation notes Forms of short-term borrowing used to resolve a cash-flow problem occasioned by a shortage of necessary revenues to cover planned or unplanned expenditures.

revenue ledger   The subsidiary ledger in which the detailed revenue accounts are maintained.

reversal errors   *See* READING REVERSALS.

reverse collective bargaining Activity that occurs when economic conditions force collective bargaining agreements to be renegotiated so that employees end up with a less favorable wage package.

reverse discrimination   A practice generally understood to mean discrimination against white males in conjunction with preferential treatment for women and minorities. The practice has no legal standing. Indeed, Section 703(j) of Title VII of the Civil Rights Act of 1964 holds that nothing in the title shall be interpreted to permit any employer to "grant preferential treatment to any individual or group on the basis of race, color, religion, sex or national origin." Yet affirmative action programs necessarily put some otherwise innocent white males at a disadvantage that they would not otherwise have had. Reverse discrimination is usually most keenly perceived when affirmative action policies conflict with older policies of granting preferments on such bases as seniority or test scores. The whole matter may have been summed up by George Orwell in his 1945 novella, *Animal Farm*, when he observed that "All animals are equal, but some animals are more equal than others."

See Alan H. Goldman, *Justice and Reverse Discrimination* (Princeton, N.J.: Princeton University Press, 1979); Robert K. Fullinwider, *The Reverse Discrimination Controversy: A Moral and Legal Analysis* (Totowa, N.J.: Rowman & Littlefield, 1980); Ralph A. Rossum, *Reverse Discrimination: The Constitutional Debate* (New York: Marcel Dekker, 1980); and R. Kent Greenawalt, *Discrimination and Reverse Discrimination* (New York: Knopf, 1983).

See also:
DEFUNIS V. ODEGAARD
REGENTS OF THE UNIVERSITY OF CALIFORNIA V. ALLAN BAKKE
UNITED STEELWORKERS OF AMERICA V. WEBER, ET AL.

revolving fund   A fund provided to carry out a cycle of operations. The amounts expended from the fund are restored from earnings from operations or by transfers from other funds so that the revolving fund remains intact, either in the form of cash, receivables, inventory, or other assets. These funds are also known as reimbursable funds.

reward or reinforcement   Any consequence a person experiences for a behavior that tends to cause an increase in the frequency of the behavior. Sometimes, consequences that teachers intend to be "punishment" are, in effect, rewards because of the attention value.

reward power   The power an individual has in an organization based on his or her ability to bestow rewards (e.g., promotions, salary increases, other favors).

RFP   *See* REQUEST FOR PROPOSAL.

RIF   1. An acronym for "reduction in force"—the elimination of specific jobs or job categories in organizations due to economic setbacks, such as a decrease in school enrollment. While an employee who has been "riffed" has not been fired, he or she is nevertheless without a job. This acronym has become so common that it is often used as a verb. 2. An acronym for "reading is fundamental," a program to promote literacy.

right to read   The federal program established by Congress in 1974 to promote improvement in the reading skills of all U.S. citizens. The program was broadened in 1978 to include a focus on all "basic skills"—mathematics, reading, and oral and written communication. *See* BASIC SKILLS AND EDUCATIONAL PROFICIENCY PROGRAM.

rightful place   The judicial doctrine that an individual who has been discriminated against should be restored to the job—to his or her "rightful place"—as if there had been no discrimination and given appropriate seniority, merit increases, and promotions. Compare to MAKE WHOLE.

rights arbitration   *See* GRIEVANCE ARBITRATION.

right-to-work laws   State laws that make it illegal for collective bargaining agreements to contain maintenance of membership, preferential hiring, union shop, or any other clauses calling for compulsory union membership. A typical "right-to-work law" might read: "No person may be denied employment and employers may not be denied the right to employ any person because of that person's membership or nonmembership in any labor organization."

It was the Labor-Management Relations (Taft-Hartley) Act of 1947 that authorized right-to-work laws when it provided in section 14(b) that "nothing in this Act shall be construed as authorizing the execution or application of agreements requiring membership in a labor organization as a condition of employment in any State or Territory in which such executioner application is prohibited by State or Territorial law."

The law does not prohibit the union or closed shop; it simply gives each state the option of doing so. Twenty states have done so: Alabama, Arizona, Arkansas, Florida, Georgia, Iowa, Kansas, Louisiana, Mississippi, Nebraska, Nevada, North Carolina, North Dakota, South Carolina, South Dakota, Tennessee, Texas, Utah, Virginia, and Wyoming.

See Ralph D. Elliott, "Do Right to Work Laws Have an Impact on Union Organizing Activities?" *Journal of Social and Political Studies* (Spring 1979); and William J. Moore and Robert J. Newman, "The Effects of Right-to-Work Laws: A Review of the Literature," *Industrial and Labor Relations Review* (July 1985).

risk   1. The specific possible hazard or loss mentioned in an insurance policy. 2. Predictable or measurable uncertainty, as in decision theory. In decision theory, risk is defined as a predictable (for example, a statistical probability) chance (or unknown), whereas uncertainty is an unpredictable or unmeasurable chance or unknown. *See also* AT RISK.

risk management All of an organization's efforts to protect its assets, reputation, and its human resources against loss.

Ritalin A controlled drug often prescribed for the treatment of hyperactivity in children. The drug, which is generally considered a stimulant, tends to have a "paradoxical effect" on some children, i.e., it depresses their hyperactive tendencies. The use and effectiveness of this treatment choice is controversial, especially for very young (under the age of five years) children. Another drug used for the same purpose is Mellaril.

For effects of ritalin and other drugs, *see* Rochelle Simms, "Hyperactivity and Drug Therapy: What the Educator Should Know," *Journal of Research and Development in Education* (Spring 1985).

rite de passage A French term referring to formal rituals and ceremonies that are undertaken to mark the occurrence of a change from one life stage to another, such as GRADUATIONS and CONTINUATIONS.

Robert's Rules of Order The standard reference on issues of parliamentary procedure.

Rochester Method A system for instructing hearing-impaired students that combines finger spelling with speech.

Rodriques v. San Antonio Independent School District 93 S. Ct. 1278 (1973) The Supreme Court decision that upheld the practice of unequal per-pupil expenditures among local school districts in Texas.

Rogers, Carl (1902-1987) The U.S. psychologist who popularized the non-directive (client-centered) approach to therapy and teaching (especially in higher education). For an example of his approach as it relates to education *see* Carl Rogers, "On the Shoulders of Giants: Questions I Would Ask Myself If I Were a Teacher," *The Educational Forum* (Winter 1987). Some of Rogers' other publications include *Client-Centered Therapy* (1951), *On Becoming a Person* (1961) and *Freedom to Learn* (1969).

role Also ROLE PLAYING. In social psychology, the term "role" is used to describe the behavior expected of an individual occupying a particular position. Just as an actor acts out his role on the stage, a teacher, for example, performs a role in real life. Role playing is a very common training technique and is based on the assumption that the process of acting out a role will enable an individual to gain insights concerning the behavior of others that cannot be realized by reading a book or listening to a lecture.

See Fannie R. Shaftel and George Armin Shaftel, *Role Playing for Social Values: Decision-Making in the Social Studies* (Englewood Cliffs, N.J.: Prentice-Hall, 1967); and George Graen, "Role-Making Process Within Complex Organizations," in Marvin D. Dunnette, ed., *Handbook of Industrial and Organizational Psychology* (Chicago: Rand McNally, 1976).

See also STRUCTURED ROLE PLAYING.

role ambiguity Confusion within an organization about what is expected of individual workers (or students).

role conflict When an individual is called upon to perform mutually exclusive acts by parties having legitimate "holds" on him or her, role conflict may be said to exist. For example, a school administrator may not make it to the "big" meeting if he must at that moment rush his child to the hospital for an emergency appendectomy. When such conflicts arise, most individuals invoke a hierarchy of role obligation that gives some roles precedence over others. To most fathers, their child's life would be more important than a meeting—no matter how "big." Real life is not always as unambiguous, however, and role conflict is a common dilemma in the world of work.

See R.H. Miles and W.D. Perreault, Jr., "Organizational Role Conflict: Its Antecedents and Consequences," *Organizational Behavior and Human Performance* (October 1976); James H. Morris, Richard M. Steers, and James L. Koch, "Influence of Organizational Structure on Role Conflict and Ambiguity for Three Occupational Groupings," *Academy of Management Journal* (March 1979); Mary Van Sell, Arthur P. Brief, and Randall S. Schuler, "Role Conflict and Role Ambiguity: Integration of the Literature and Directions for Future Research," *Human Relations* (January 1981); and Robert Kottkamp and John Mansfield, "Role Conflict, Role Ambiguity, Powerlessness and Burnout Among High School Supervisors," *Journal of Research and Development in Education* (Summer 1985).

role perception   Also called role conception. An individual's role perception or role conception delineates the position that the individual occupies in his or her organization and establishes for the individual the minimum and maximum ranges of permissible behavior in "acting out" his or her organizational role.

For empirical studies, see Andrew D. Szilagyi, "An Empirical Test of Causal Inference between Role Perceptions, Satisfaction with Work, Performance and Organizational Level," *Personnel Psychology* (Autumn 1977); and Kevin W. Mossholder, Arthus G. Bedeian, and Achilles A. Armenakis, "Role Perceptions, Satisfaction, and Performance: Moderating Effects of

Self-Esteem and Organizational Level," *Organizational Behavior and Human Performance* (October 1981).

role playing   *See* ROLE.

roll   1. A record of official proceedings. 2. A list of members, as in a payroll. 3. Taxable persons or property, as in the tax rolls. 4. A list of students in a class.

Roncker v. Walter   700 F.2d 1058 (6th Cir. 1983)   A ruling in a U.S. Court of Appeals that "to the maximum extent appropriate" children with handicaps must be educated with nonhandicapped children. The case involved a school district in Ohio that had placed a student with mental retardation in a special county "handicapped only" school instead of in her local school district in a special class. The higher court overruled the district court's determination in favor of the special school setting.

Rorschach inkblot test   One of the earliest and best known of projective tests designed to provide a psychoanalytic interpretation of an individual's personality. The test consists of 10 stimulus cards that resemble inkblots that the subject is asked to describe. There are several categories of interpretive scoring. It is published by:

Grune and Stratton, Inc.
111 Fifth Avenue
New York, NY 10003

ROTC   *See* AIR FORCE RESERVE OFFICER'S TRAINING CORPS, ARMY RESERVE OFFICERS TRAINING CORPS, *and* NAVAL RESERVE OFFICER TRAINING CORPS.

rote counting   The recitation of number names without correspondence to number value.

rote learning or rote memorization   Acquiring information strictly through the process of memorization without necessarily attaching the information to a meaningful context.

Rousseau, Jean J. (1712-1778) The Swiss political philosopher and the developer of the doctrine of NATURALISM who criticized an authoritarian, formal approach to education. *See* Mabel L. Sahakian and William S. Sahakian, *Rousseau as Educator* (New York: Twayne, 1974).

R/REA   *See* RURAL/REGIONAL EDUCATION ASSOCIATION.

Rubella or German measles   A viral infection of mild consequence except when contracted by a pregnant woman during early pregnancy. In that case serious damage may occur to the developing fetus resulting in one or more handicaps at birth, usually deafness, blindness, mental retardation, or heart defects.

rule   1. A regulation made by an administrative agency. 2. A decision of a judge or presiding officer. 3. A standing order governing the conduct of a legislative or deliberative body. 4. An expected norm of behavior in a school or classroom.

rule of three   The practice of certifying to an appointing authority the top three names on an eligible list. The rule of three is intended to give the appointing official an opportunity to weigh intangible factors, such as personality, before making a formal offer of appointment. The rule of one

has only the single highest ranking person on the eligible list certified. The rule of the list gives the appointing authority the opportunity to choose from the entire list of eligibles.

run-off election   When no one person (or union) receives a majority in an election, a second election—the run-off election—is held, and participants choose between the two that received the most votes in the first election.

rural education   The designation for education that takes place in rural communities or small towns, acknowledging the unique problems and concerns that differentiate rural from urban or suburban education—such as low tax base, high teacher turnover, and limited programs and opportunites. For a review of various approaches to education in rural sites, *see* Paul M. Nachtigal, ed., *Rural Education: In Search of a Better Way* (Boulder, Colo.: Westview Press, 1982).

Rural/Regional Education Association (R/REA)   The national organization that works to expand education opportunities in rural settings. The association publishes a quarterly newsletter, *Rural Education News*, and a journal, *Rural Educator*, three times a year.

R/REA
Department of Education
300 Education Building
Colorado State University
Ft. Collins, CO 80523
(303) 491-7022

S

sabbatical Lengthy paid leave for professional, intellectual, or emotional refurbishment. It was an ancient Hebrew tradition to allow fields to lie fallow every seventh year. The words sabbath and sabbatical both come from the Hebrew word shabath, meaning to rest. In modern times, a sabbatical has been a period of paid leave and rejuvenation for teachers, especially at the college and university level. A common practice regarding sabbatical leave is the extension of the privilege—after seven years employment—for either one full year at half regular pay or one-half year at full regular pay.

safety education A course of instruction that stresses accident prevention through improved attitudes, skills, and knowledge of potential hazards in the home, school, workplace, and recreational environment.

safety net President Ronald Reagan's term for the totality of social welfare programs, which, in his opinion, assure at least a subsistence standard of living for all people in the United States. Some programs of particular popular interest, such as HEAD START, were included.

safety patrols A group of "older" students who are assigned to assist other students in street crossings near school buildings. Rules for the operation of safety patrols were developed by the American Automobile Association and other organizations during the 1930s. Such patrols are currently used less frequently in school districts and have largely been replaced by parent volunteers and paid traffic aides.

salary The total amount regularly paid or stipulated to be paid to an individual, before deductions, for personal services rendered while on the payroll of a school district. Payments for sabbatical leave are also considered as salary.

salary differential A difference in salary because of different levels of training or qualifications. For example, a teacher with a master's degree is frequently paid more than a teacher with a bachelor's degree who has the same number of years of experience.

salary increment A predetermined regular increase in pay that is included in a salary schedule for each additional year of experience.

salary schedule A plan for how employees of any system, including school district employees, will be paid, including the increases that are awarded based on years of experience and additional education. Salary schedules may also include provisions for merit pay or extra duty pay.

sale of fixed assets Proceeds from the sale of school property. Separate accounts may be maintained for sale of real property and for sale of equipment.

sales of bonds Proceeds from the sale of bonds, except that if bonds are sold at a premium, only those proceeds representing the par value of the bonds would be included. The proceeds from the sale of bonds constitute a revenue for the capital projects fund but not for the school district as a whole.

sales to adults Money received from adults for sale of food products and services. Regular meals or food products sold to staff can be segregated from special dinners and affairs for special purposes by maintaining separate accounts.

sales to pupils   Money received from pupils for sale of food products and services. Better financial control and analysis and better reporting for federal and state reimbursements can be obtained by maintaining separate accounts by type of sale, such as type of lunch sale, milk program sale, and other sales.

sales and use tax   Taxes imposed upon the sale and consumption of goods and services. It can be imposed either as a general tax on the retail price of all goods and/or services sold within the geographical jurisdiction of a school district with few or limited exemptions, or as a tax upon the sale or consumption of selected goods and services. Separate accounts may be maintained for general sales tax and for selective sales tax.

salutatorian   The student who is the second highest ranking student in the class. Contrast with valedictorian, who is the highest ranking student. Often the salutatorian speaks at the class graduation; for example, he or she may deliver the opening address.

salvage value   The actual or prospective selling price less the cost of removal or disposal of building and equipment that have been retired from service or damaged, but not junked.

sample   Any deliberately chosen portion of a larger population that is representative of that population as a whole. Scientifically selected samples are the foundation of public opinion polling. Selecting interviewees with modern sampling techniques gives every individual in the jurisdiction under study an equal chance of being chosen. *See* Donald P. Warwick and Charles A. Lininger, *The Sample Survey: Theory*

and Practice (New York: McGraw-Hill, 1975).

sampling   Techniques used for selecting the individual members of a sample group. There are several sampling approaches.

Random sampling allows everyone an equal opportunity to be chosen and each selection is independent of the others. *Stratified* (or *representative*) *sampling* selects predetermined numbers of individuals from specific segments of the population so that the composition of the total sample is representative of the population from which it is drawn. *Cluster sampling* divides a larger population into units, selects one or more units randomly, and then includes each individual member of the chosen unit(s) in the sample.

For an overview of this research tool with an emphasis on its application to education, *see* Chester H. McCall, *Sampling and Statistical Handbook for Research* (Ames: Iowa State University Press, 1982).

sampling error   The error caused by generalizing the behavior of a population from a sample of that population that is not totally representative of the population as a whole. For example, it is often reported that a specific survey of public opinion is accurate to plus or minus four percentage points. This eight-point spread represents the sampling error. There would be no sampling error if an entire population (for example, 290 million Americans) were surveyed, instead of a few thousand.

sanction   1. Pressure exerted by organized labor through its membership in an attempt to change what is considered to be poor working conditions or employer practices. Sanctions have been used widely by the National Education Association against school districts where unsatisfactory working conditions exist, by notifying members of the situation, requesting that members not seek or leave the employment of the offending district, and by threatening expulsion of members employed by the district. 2. In general, any threatened or imposed consequence for an offending action or behavior. 3. Permission from an authority that makes an action allowable.

SAT   *See* SCHOLASTIC APTITUDE TEST.

satori   A Japanese concept from Zen Buddhism that refers to a sudden, intuitive insight; an "ah ha!" experience.

Save the Children Federation
A nonprofit agency that was originally organized during the Depression (1932) to assist the children of coal miners in Appalachia. The organization now serves needy children throughout the United States and the world, primarily through efforts at community development. The organization's publications include *Lifeline Magazine* and *Save the Children Reports*.

Save the Children Federation
54 Wilton Road
Westport, CT 06880
(203) 226-7271

save harmless   A legal term relating to the protection of teachers against charges of negligence. In some states local school districts must defend teachers in such cases of litigation and pay any judgments demanded.

scab   An employee who continues to work for an organization while it is being struck by coworkers. Since the 1500s, scab has been used as a term for a rascal or scoundrel. Early in the 1800s, Americans started using it to refer to workers who refused to support organized efforts on behalf of their trade. A scab should be distinguished from a fink or strikebreaker who is brought into an organization only after a strike begins. Samuel Gompers, the first president of the American Federation of Labor, said that "a 'scab' is to his trade what a traitor is to his country. He is the first to take advantage of any benefit secured by united action, and never contributes anything toward its achievement."

scalar chain   Also line of authority. According to Henri Fayol, in *General and Industrial Management* (trans. by Constance Storrs; London: Pitman, 1949):

The scalar chain is the chain of superiors ranging from the ultimate authority to the lowest ranks. The line of authority is the route followed—via every link in the chain—by all communications which start from or go to the ultimate authority. This path is dictated both by the need for some transmission and by the principle of unity of command, but it is not always the swiftest. It is even at times disastrously lengthy in large concerns, notably in governmental ones.

scale   1. A psychological term referring to a standardized reference that allows for the comparison of individual differences in performance. There are many types of scale. A *standard score* has a mean of 0 and a standard deviation of 1.00. A *C scale* is an 11-point scale (0-10) with a mean of 5.0 and a standard deviation of 2.0. A *Stanine scale* is a 9-point scale (1-9) with a mean of 5.0 and a standard deviation of 1.96. 2. In music, notes arranged in a sequence of rising pitch that make up an octave interval. The traditional musical scale is verbally represented as do, re, mi, fa, so, la, ti, do. 3. An instrument for measuring weight.

scaled score   Score on a test when the raw score obtained has been converted to a number or position on a standard reference scale. Test scores reported to examinees and users of tests are usually scaled scores. The purpose of converting scores to a scale is to make reported scores as independent as possible of the particular form of a test an examinee has taken and of the composition of the candidate group at a particular administration. For example, the College Board Achievement tests are all reported on a scale of 200 to 800. A score of 600 on a College Board Achievement test is intended to indicate the same level of ability from year to year.

scales of measurement Different systems for classifying measurement. There are four basic types. *Nominal* scales classify data into categories (e.g., race, nationality). *Ordinal* scales order data on a continuum that has no absolute reference and unequal distances between items on the continuum (e.g., first, second, third; soft, softer, softest). *Interval* scales order data on a continuum that has a fixed and equal distance between each unit but that has no absolute reference (e.g., temperature). *Ratio* scales have both a true zero reference and equal intervals on the continuum (e.g., length).

SCAN team Stands for "suspected child abuse and neglect team," which usually is located in a hospital or medical facility and which generally includes a pediatrician, a social worker, and a psychologist or psychiatrist, who assess a child and family to determine whether or not abuse or neglect has occurred and what treatment might be indicated.

scanning A technique for rapid reading where the reader quickly glances over one or more pages in search of a particular item of information, such as a date, name, or number. This type of reading is often used with a telephone book or catalog.

SCAT (School and College Ability Tests) A battery of tests published by Educational Testing Services to measure the aptitude of students for completing the next higher grade level at school. Available in separate tests for grades four to six, seven to nine, 10 to 12, 13 to 14.

scatter diagram or scatter-gram A display of the relationship between variables using dots on a graph.

schedule 1. A series of items to be handled or of events that will occur at or during a particular period of time; a timetable. 2. Any list; a list attached to a document that explains in detail things mentioned generally in the document. 3. A description of a student's day in school, i.e., what classes he or she attends and at what times.

schedules of reinforcement In behavioral (operant) conditioning the parameters that describe the delivery of reinforcers used to shape behavior, including the timing, sequence, frequency, and intensity of the reinforcement. Some schedules frequently described in the literature are: continuous, intermittent, fixed or variable interval, and fixed or variable ratio. See REINFORCEMENT SCHEDULE.

scheduling cycle The period of time over which a unit of a school schedule extends before it is repeated. Traditional schedules usually have a one-day cycle, while in more flexible schedules the cycle may extend for several days or weeks before it is repeated.

scholarship 1. An award, usually of money or of free or reduced tuition, given to deserving students as recognition of achievement or as encouragement. 2. The achievement of academic excellence.

scholarship fund　Type of fund used to establish scholarships in the name of donors. Scholarship funds are often found in, and managed by, community foundations. *See also* COMMUNITY FOUNDATION.

scholastic aptitude test　1. Any examination of the potential of a person to succeed academically, as measured by tests of performance. 2. An exam administered by the Educational Testing Service, under contract with the College Entrance Examination Board, to high school seniors for the purpose of college admission decisions. Three areas are generally tested: reading comprehension, vocabulary, and mathematics. A practice version, the PSAT (Preliminary Scholastic Aptitude Test) is offered to high school juniors for the consideration of merit scholarships.

For a discussion of the value of the SAT as a selection criterion for college admission, *see* James Crouse, "Does the SAT Help Colleges Make Better Selection Decisions," *Harvard Educational Review* (May 1985); and a reply by George H. Hanford, "Yes, the SAT Does Help Colleges," *Harvard Educational Review* (August 1985).

school　A division of the local school system consisting of students comprising one or more grade groups or other identifiable groups, organized as one unit with one or more teachers to give instruction of a defined type, and housed in a physical plant of one or more buildings. More than one school may be housed in one physical plant, as is the case when the elementary and secondary schools are housed in the same physical plant but are considered separate administrative entities.

school, boarding　*See* BOARDING SCHOOL.

school, business　*See* BUSINESS SCHOOL.

school, community　*See* COMMUNITY SCHOOL.

school, comprehensive high　*See* COMPREHENSIVE HIGH SCHOOL.

school, day　*See* DAY SCHOOL.

school, department of defense overseas dependents　*See* DEPARTMENT OF DEFENSE OVERSEAS DEPENDENTS SCHOOL.

school, elementary　*See* ELEMENTARY SCHOOL.

school, extended secondary　*See* EXTENDED SECONDARY SCHOOL.

school, five- or 6-year high　*See* FIVE -OR 6-YEAR HIGH SCHOOL.

school, four-year high　*See* FOUR-YEAR HIGH SCHOOL.

school, graded　*See* GRADED SCHOOL.

school, incomplete high　*See* INCOMPLETE HIGH SCHOOL.

school, independent American overseas　*See* INDEPENDENT AMERICAN OVERSEAS SCHOOL.

school, independent nonprofit　*See* INDEPENDENT NONPROFIT SCHOOL.

school, junior high　*See* JUNIOR HIGH SCHOOL.

school, junior-senior high　*See* JUNIOR-SENIOR HIGH SCHOOL.

school, kindergarten　*See* KINDERGARTEN SCHOOL.

school, laboratory　*See* LABORATORY SCHOOL.

school, middle   *See* MIDDLE SCHOOL.

school, middle/junior high   *See* MIDDLE/JUNIOR HIGH PROGRAMS.

school, model   *See* MODEL SCHOOL.

school, neighborhood   *See* NEIGHBORHOOD SCHOOL.

school, nongraded   *See* NONGRADED SCHOOL.

school, nonpublic   *See* NONPUBLIC SCHOOLS.

school, nursery   *See* NURSERY SCHOOL.

school, one-teacher   *See* ONE-TEACHER SCHOOL.

school, preprimary   *See* PREPRIMARY SCHOOL.

school, primary   *See* PRIMARY SCHOOL.

school, public   *See* PUBLIC SCHOOL.

school, regular four-year high   *See* REGULAR FOUR-YEAR HIGH SCHOOL.

school, residential   *See* RESIDENTIAL SCHOOL.

school, secondary   *See* SECONDARY SCHOOL.

school, senior high   *See* SENIOR HIGH SCHOOL.

school, summer   *See* SUMMER SCHOOL.

school, technical high   *See* TECHNICAL HIGH SCHOOL.

school, ungraded elementary   *See* UNGRADED ELEMENTARY SCHOOL.

school, ungraded high   *See* UNGRADED HIGH SCHOOL.

school, ungraded   *See* UNGRADED SCHOOL.

school, vocational or trade high   *See* VOCATIONAL OR TRADE HIGH SCHOOL.

school accounting   Maintaining records of a school or school district's financial activities in order to facilitate planning, evaluate programs, report to state and federal agencies, formulate future budgets, and inform the public.

school administration   Those individuals (and the activities under their direction) who have overall responsibility for a single school or a group of schools.

school age   *See* AGE AS OF SEPTEMBER 1 *and* COMPULSORY SCHOOL ATTENDANCE AGE.

school appropriation   Money received out of funds set aside periodically by the appropriating body (district meeting, city council, or other governmental bodies) for school purposes; which funds have not been specifically collected as school taxes.

school architect   A designer of buildings who is especially trained and experienced with school facilities. The architect works closely with educational planners and administrators to assure that building design and construction is consistent with programmatic needs.

school attendance area   The geographic area that is served by a school. It does not necessarily constitute a local taxing unit and likewise does not necessarily have an independent system of administration. Attendance areas for elementary schools may or may not be coterminous with attendance areas for secondary schools.

school board *See* BOARD OF EDUCATION.

School Board News A newspaper published and distributed nationwide by the National School Board Association.
NSBA
1680 Duke Street
Alexandria, VA 22314

school bond A mechanism for financing a district building program or other major capital outlay through the sale of bonds to lenders. There are two general kinds of bond. Term bonds are issued for a fixed period (usually 10 to 30 years) and pay interest only during the term. Serial bonds are repaid on a staggered schedule with low-numbered bonds maturing first. School bonds are typically backed by the commitment of a district's taxpayers to repay according to the stated obligation.

school bond rating A system for ranking bonds on the market according to their safety and other features of appeal to potential lenders. The three major bond-rating firms are Dun and Bradstreet; Moody; and Standard and Poor. Each uses a different rating system based on factors such as the school district's debt history, financial condition, general management, and academic standing, as well as the nature of the proposed project.

school breakfast program A national program whereby the Department of Agriculture assists state education agencies through grants-in-aid and other means to establish, maintain, operate, and expand nonprofit breakfast programs in all schools making application for assistance and agree-

ing to operate a nonprofit breakfast program in accordance with regulations of the Child Nutrition Act, as amended.

school budget A mechanism for planning and managing a school district's activities through financial control. An annual budget, including anticipated income and expenditures, is generally prepared by the district superintendent for consideration and approval by the school board.

school bus A vehicle used for transporting students, with a manufacturer's rated seating capacity of 12 or more. (Seating capacity figures on the basis of at least 13 inches of seat space per pupil.)

school bus accident An accident involving a school bus, when in authorized use, that results in personal injury or property damage, as when a child is injured by the bus or on the bus; or one involving a child immediately before boarding the bus (if the bus is arriving to take on children) or immediately after leaving the bus (before the bus has left the scene).

school bus run The course followed by a school bus during a continuous trip en route to or from school, from the first pickup of students to final unloading at school, at a transfer point, or at the last bus stop.

school business administrator A central office staff person assigned general responsibility for the financial and business aspects of the school district's management, including fiscal planning, accounting, purchasing, auditing, transportation, food service, and building maintenance.

school calendar 1. An instrument for projecting and scheduling dates and events relevant to the school district such as opening and closing dates, district-wide holidays and vacations, athletic events, board meetings, and other activities of general interest. 2. In the context of a typical, traditional district schedule, a span of time beginning sometime around the beginning of September and ending sometime around the beginning of June and including approximately 180 days of school attendance plus weekends, holidays, and vacations.

school census   An enumeration and collection of data, as prescribed by law, to determine the name, age, address, and other pertinent information about children and youth who reside within the geographic boundaries of a local education agency.

school census age   The age span of children and youth included in the school census.

school code   State laws having to do with schools, usually published in a code book.

school colors   Generally associated with secondary schools and institutions of higher education (but more recently extending downward to elementary schools), the colors that signify association and allegiance to one's school of attendance. Usually worn on athletic uniforms and jackets, band and cheerleader uniforms, and displayed on banners and school equipment.

school counselor   A professional staff member who provides counseling and other guidance interventions on behalf of students and significant others impacting on their lives and who engages in consultation with all school staff on behalf of students.

school district   A special district for the provision of local public education for all children in its service area. An elected board, the typical governing body, usually hires a professional superintendent to administer the system. School districts, having their own taxing authority, are administratively, financially, and politically independent of other local government units. There are almost 15,000 independent school districts in the U.S. *See also* LOCAL BASIC ADMINISTRATIVE UNIT.

School District of Abington Township v. Schempp 374 U. S. 203 (1963)   The Supreme Court case that held that school prayers or other religious exercises violated the establishment of religion clause of the First Amendment as applied to the states by the 14th Amendment. *Murray v. Curlett*, 374 U.S. 203 (1963), was decided at the same time on the same grounds. In *Stone v. Graham*, 449 U.S. 39 (1980), the Court forbade posting the Ten Commandments in classrooms; but in *Widmar v. Vincent*, 454 U.S. 263 (1981), the Court allowed on First Amendment grounds that state university classrooms can be used for student religious group meetings.

See H. Frank Way, Jr., "Survey Research on Judicial Decisions: The Prayer and Bible Reading Cases," *Western Political Quarterly* (June 1968); and Albert J. Menendez, *School Prayer and Other Religious Issues in American Public Education: A Bibliography* (New York: Garland, 1985). *See also* ENGELL V. VITALE *and* WALLAS V. JAFFREE.

School District of the City of Grand Rapids v. Ball 473 U.S. 373 (1985)   The U.S. Supreme Court decision that held that public school teachers could not be paid from public funds to teach special programs in religious schools, even when the nature of the program itself is not religious.

school district reorganization   The changing of boundary lines of local or intermediate basic administrative units, the merging of existing districts, and the creation of new districts, under the provisions of state law.

school entrance age   The age of a child, in years and months, when beginning kindergarten or first grade.

school facility   A building or site belonging to or used by a school or school system for school purposes.

school finance   The systems, methods, and procedures whereby funds are provided for the support of education.

school fiscal year   See SCHOOL YEAR.

school for exceptional children A "special" school for children who have been identified by professionally qualified personnel as requiring special education services. While a laudable attempt in theory, such schools have often become "the place" for educating children with exceptional needs. The entire concept of "special schools" has been challenged by professional special educators, by parents, and by the least restrictive environment provision of P.L. 94-142. See EDUCATION FOR ALL HANDICAPPED CHILDREN ACT and LEAST RESTRICTIVE ENVIRONMENT. See also EXCEPTIONAL CHILDREN.

school holiday   A day on which school is not conducted either because of legal provisions or because of designation by the board of education as a holiday. Since such days are not considered as days in session, the students are considered as being neither present nor absent on school holidays.

school improvement   The concept of refining and renovating school practices with the goal of improving the quality of education. For a broad overview as well as a description of the

process, see Bruce R. Joyce et al., *The Structure of School Improvement* (New York: Longman, 1983).

school law   The area of law that studies the legal framework of education, legal concepts in education (such as governmental authority, religious controversies, due process and equal protection), and school-related litigation based on these concepts. For a thorough review of both theoretical background and significant court cases, see Julius Menacker, *School Law: Theoretical and Case Perspectives* (Englewood Cliffs, N.J.: Prentice-Hall, 1987); and see also Richard Gatti and Daniel Gatti, *New Encyclopedic Dictionary of School Law* (Englewood, N.J.: Prentice-Hall, 1987).

school leaver   A term used synonymously with the term "dropout." See DROPOUT.

school leaving age   The youngest age at which school attendance is no longer compulsory. In most states it is age 16.

school librarian   A professional staff member who performs school library service activities such as ordering, cataloging, processing, and circulating books and other materials; planning the use of the library by teachers, pupils, and others; selecting books and materials; participating in faculty planning for the use of books and materials; and guiding teachers, pupils, and others in the use of the library in school programs.

school library   An instructional space designed, or adapted, as a place for study and reading, and for the custody, circulation, and administration of a collection of books, manuscripts, and periodicals kept for the use of the student body and school staff, but not for sale. Study carrels, audiovisual, storage, and other service areas opening into, and serving as adjuncts to, a particular library are considered parts of the library area. When school library services and audiovisual services are located in the same instructional space, this space frequently is referred to as an "instructional materials center."

school library media specialist A professional staff person who is responsible for all types of instructional media including print and nonprint materials and related equipment.

school library services Activities such as selecting, acquiring, preparing, cataloging, and circulating books and other printed materials; planning the use of the library by teachers and other members of the instructional staff; and guiding instructional staff members in their use of library books and materials, whether maintained separately or as a part of an instructional materials center or related work-study area.

school lunch Any lunch served by the school, approximating the minimum nutritional standards of the U.S. Department of Agriculture, regardless of who pays for it. *See also* NATIONAL SCHOOL LUNCH PROGRAM.

"school match" A computer service of the 1980s, developed for use by relocated employees of major corporations in America, that assists families in identifying school districts compatible with their needs and desires in the areas to which they are being relocated.

school mathematics study group (SMSG) A secondary school mathematics curriculum developed in the late 1950s through the support of the National Science Foundation for the purpose of improving the quality of math instruction in the United States.

school media programs Similar to school library services but broadening and changing as modern materials and information technologies rapidly increase. For a number of articles on school media issues, *see* "Critical Issues in School Media Programs," *Journal of Research and Development in Education* (Fall 1982).

school month For school recordkeeping purposes, a period frequently construed to comprise 20 school days, or four weeks of five days each.

school nurse The staff person who has responsibility for managing health services for students in one or more school buildings. The nurse maintains pupil health records, conducts or arranges for screenings and testings, makes referrals, and may render emergency assistance.

school of thought A generally held belief or point of view associated with a professional or academic group.

school personnel or staff All employees of a school or school district that fall into one of three categories: teacher, instructional support, or administration. *See* Ben M. Harris and others, *Personnel Administration in Education*, 2nd ed. (Boston: Allyn and Bacon, 1985).

school phobia An extreme fear of school resulting in a refusal to attend or stay in school, often accompanied by physical symptoms (such as nausea, diarrhea, stomachaches, or headaches). *See* Jack H. Kahn, Jean P. Nursten, and Howard C.M. Carroll, *Unwilling to Go to School: School Phobia or School Refusal, A Psychosocial Problem*, 2nd ed. (New York: Permamon, 1981).

school plant The site, buildings, and equipment constituting the physical facilities used by a single school or by two or more schools sharing the use of common facilities.

school prayer   The recitation of prayer by staff and students as a part of the regular school day routine. *See SCHOOL DISTRICT OF ABINGTON TOWNSHIP V. SCHEMPP.*

school property   Land, site improvements, buildings, and equipment used for public school purposes.

school psychologist   A professional staff member who performs psychological evaluation and analysis of pupils through such activities as measuring and interpreting the pupils' intellectual, emotional, and social development, diagnosing educational disabilities of the pupils, and providing direct mental health counseling services to pupils. The school psychologist may also serve the school system through such activities as collaborating in planning appropriate educational programs, conducting research in the area of pupil adjustment and behavior, and assisting other staff members with specific problems of a psychological nature, and broadening their understanding of the psychological forces with which they deal.
See also EDUCATIONAL PSYCHOLOGY.

school reform   A common reference to any proposal for changes in public school policy and/or operation. School reform has been an ongoing issue in education since shortly after the advent of public school education in America in the early 1800s. For a more contemporary examination of the issue *see* William J. Reese, *Power and the Promise of School Reform* (New York: Methuen, 1986).

school secretary   A staff person who provides direct clerical services for the school principal and who provides support to teachers and other school staff, assists students and families, manages the school office, and helps to maintain community relations.

school security   Programs designed to reduce the risk of crime against both persons and property on school grounds. The need for school security increases with the size of the school, the age of the students and the proximity of urban environments.
See Seymour D. Vestermark, Jr., and Peter D. Blauvelt, *Controlling Crime in the School: A Complete Security Handbook for Administrators* (West Nyack, N.Y.: Parker, 1978); and Peter D. Blauvelt, *Effective Strategies for School Security* (Reston, Va.: National Association of Secondary School Principals, 1981).

school session   *See* SESSION.

school site   The land and all improvements to the site (other than structures), such as grading, drainage, drives, parking areas, walks, plantings, play courts, and play fields.

school social worker   A professional staff person who assists in the prevention and solution of a pupil's personal, social, and emotional problems that involve family, school, and community relationships—when such problems have a bearing upon the quality of the school work of the pupil. The social worker may provide direct assessment and/or intervention services to students and/or the families of students. Intervention may include group or individual counseling or supporting a student's educational achievement. *See also* ATTENDANCE *and* SOCIAL WORK SERVICES.

school spirit   Enthusiastic support by students of their school and particularly of their athletic teams.

school staffing ratios 1. The ratio relationship between the number of teachers (and other professional service providers) and students. 2. The ratio relationship between the number of administrators and staff. *See also* CASELOAD.

school survey A planning term referring to the collection of particular kinds of information in order to assess needs of the school or school district and to establish objectives. Examples include population surveys, financial surveys, comprehensive surveys (covering the total instructional and support programs), and building plant surveys.

school system All the schools and supporting services controlled by a board of education or by any other organization that operates one or more schools. *See also* LOCAL EDUCATION AGENCY.

school term A prescribed span of time (e.g., a number of days, weeks, or months) when school is open and the students are under the guidance and direction of teachers.

school year 1. The 12-month period of time denoting the beginning and ending dates for school accounting purposes, usually from July 1 through June 30. This sometimes is referred to as the "school fiscal year." 2. The nine-month period of time that schools are traditionally in session. Local school districts set their own opening and closing dates and they determine, for the most part, holidays as well as vacation periods within the school year.

State education agencies specify the minimum number of instructional days that districts must have to qualify for state funds. The states may also publish guidelines for holidays and opening and closing dates. Most of America's independent school districts open in late August or early September and conduct classes for approximately 180 days. *See* Charles W. Fisher and David C. Berliner, eds., *Perspectives on Instructional Time* (New York: Longman, 1985).

school-based management Decentralization of administrative responsibility and decision-making authority from the central school district office to the individual building level; the faculty as a whole (usually acting through an elected council) makes virtually all decisions on budget, personnel, and governance. This management technique, which is widely used in Miami-Dade County, is still considered experimental.

school-community relations Efforts to establish and maintain two-way channels of communication between a school, or school district, and the surrounding reighborhood and/or community at large.

schools without walls Also called open space schools. School buildings designed with few interior partitions. Typically, several groups of students and teachers work in different areas of a large open space. This type of arrangement tends to facilitate team teaching and increased teacher-pupil and teacher-teacher interaction.

schools-within-a-school The division, usually at the secondary level, of a school's student body and faculty into a number of administratively distinct units that continue to occupy the same building. Each unit may have its own physical area within the building while some resources and programs are shared. The purpose is to maintain the personal/social advantages of a small school environment while allowing for the diversity of courses and other opportunities of a larger campus.

THE SCHOOL YEAR (1986-1987)

State	Length of School Year
Alabama	175 days
Alaska	180 days
Arizona	175 days
Arkansas	178 days
California	175 days, with additional apportionments for 180 days
Colorado	180 days
Connecticut	180 days
Delaware	180 days for students, 185 days for teachers
District of Columbia	182 days
Florida	180 days for students, 196 days for teachers
Georgia	180 days
Hawaii	varies from 176 to 180 days depending on when certain holidays fall
Idaho	180 days
Illinois	185 days
Indiana	175 days
Iowa	180 days
Kansas	180 days
Kentucky	175 days for students plus 10 days for administration and local holidays
Louisiana	180 days
Maine	180 days
Maryland	180 days
Massachusetts	180 days
Michigan	180 days
Minnesota	170 days for students, 175 days for teachers
Mississippi	175 days
Missouri	174 days

State	
Montana	180 days
Nebraska	1,032 hours of instruction for elementary students, 1,080 hours for high school students
Nevada	180 days
New Hampshire	180 days
New Jersey	180 days
New Mexico	180 days
New York	180 days, including up to 3 superintendent's conference days
North Carolina	180 days
North Dakota	180 days, including 2 days for parent conferences, 2 days for ND Education Assoc. Convention, 3 holidays
Ohio	182 days, which may include up to 2 days for professional meetings, up to 2 days for parent conferences
Oklahoma	180 days
Oregon	178 days for students, 184 days for teachers
Pennsylvania	180 days
Rhode Island	180 days
South Carolina	180 days for students, 190 days for teachers
South Dakota	175 days, which may include 2 days for parent-teacher conferences, 1 day for staff development and 2 days for teachers before school opens
Tennessee	180 days for students, 200 days for teachers
Texas	175 days for students, 183 days for teachers
Utah	180 days
Vermont	175 days for students, 180 days for teachers
Virginia	180 days
Washington	180 days
West Virginia	180 days for students, 200 days for teachers
Wisconsin	180 days, including 5 days for inclement weather that do not have to be made up
Wyoming	175 days

schoolwork Generally refers to homework or other tasks that students are assigned in relation to school.

science The study of natural physical and material phenomena including observations, descriptions, experimentations, and theoretical explanations.

Science Curriculum Improvement Study A kindergarten to sixth grade laboratory-based science curriculum developed at the University of California, Berkeley, in 1961. The curriculum is divided into physical science and life science, with six predominant themes for each area.

See J. David Lockard, ed., *Science and Mathematics Curricular Developments Internationally, 1956-1974* (College Park, Md.: Science Teaching Center, University of Maryland, Joint Project with the Commission on Science Education, American Association for the Advancement of Science, 1974).

science fair A student exhibit of science projects displayed either by individual students or small groups working cooperatively.

science kit A collection of items that can be used for teaching, demonstrating, or experimenting with scientific principles or concepts. May be commercially packaged or prepared by teachers for all age levels and for either general purposes or for specific areas of study.

Science Research Associates (SRA) The educational publishing branch of IBM Corporation that publishes standardized tests and prepackaged materials for individualized instruction. Their achievement series is a norm-referenced and widely-used battery of tests for grades one to nine that measures basic academic accomplishment.

Science Research Associates, Inc.
155 North Wacker Drive
Chicago, IL 60606
(312) 984-7226

Science-A Process Approach (SAPA) A kindergarten to sixth grade science curriculum developed in the early 1960s under the auspices of the American Association for the Advancement of Science that stresses learning the processes of science (e.g., observing, classifying, measuring, inferring, predicting, interpreting, and experimenting) rather than learning specific and discrete content.

scientific management A theory of management that emphasizes efficiency and productivity and that assumes that man's work performance can be precisely defined and that an individual's feelings and personality are irrelevant to the work place. This management approach was espoused by Frederick W. Taylor in 1910, involved detailed descriptions of employees' jobs, and strongly influenced early training programs for school administrators, even though its original application was to factory workers.

scientific method An approach to research that starts with the observation of a phenomenon, then develops an hypothesis about it, and finally tests the hypothesis through experimentation. Then the process or cycle of observation-hypothesis-experimentation begins all over again.

scope of assignment The extent of an identified assignment made to a staff member. The three categories of scope of assignment are: (1) systemwide; (2) more than one school or supporting services facility but less than systemwide; and (3) single school or supporting services.

scope of bargaining Those issues over which management and labor negotiate during the collective bargaining process. *See* Joan Weitzman, *The Scope of Bargaining in Public Employment* (New York: Praeger, 1975); and Stephen A. Woodbury, "The Scope of Bargaining and Bargaining Outcomes in the Public Schools," *Industrial & Labor Relations Review* (January 1985).

scope and sequence A curricular concept that refers to "what" is taught (scope), especially as one subject relates to another, and "when" it is taught (sequence), in relation to longitudinal planning for the introduction of subject matter.

Scopes Trial (or Scopes Monkey Trial) A famous trial, involving a schoolteacher by the name of John Thomas Scopes, that in 1925 challenged a Tennessee law forbidding the teaching of evolution in schools. Part of the trial's fame is due to the participation of two renowned lawyers, William Jennings Bryan and Clarence Darrow. In 1968 the U.S. Supreme Court finally ruled substantively against such anti-evolution laws in *Epperson v. Arkansas*, 393 U.S. 97 (1968). Compare to *EDWARDS V. AGUILLARD*.

See The World's Most Famous Court Trial, State of Tennessee v. John Thomas Scopes (New York: Da Capo Press, 1971).

score 1. An indicator used to report level of performance on a test. 2. To attain a particular level of performance. 3. In an athletic contest, the number of points earned by a given team or participant or the act of earning a point.

score, crude/raw *See* RAW SCORE.

score, scaled *See* SCALED SCORE.

score, standard *See* STANDARD SCORE.

scrap value *See* SALVAGE VALUE.

screening A process of rapidly sifting through the school population to identify students who may be in need of special services. Most commonly, hearing screening and vision screening are provided for all students, though some schools have more extensive screening programs such as developmental screening for all new kindergartners or individualized review of standardized achievement tests.

SEA *See* STATE EDUCATION AGENCY.

sealed bid A potential contractor's offer (bid) to perform work, which is submitted in a closed (sealed) envelope. All sealed bids are opened at the same time, and the "best" bid is selected.

search of students A law enforcement issue that has become of concern to school administrators as a result of student complaints and a series of somewhat ambiguous court decisions. Search of lockers has been ruled permissible on the grounds that lockers are, in fact, school property; however, administrators have been advised to seek student permission in these cases. Search of students' persons, both on and off campus, has been ruled justifiable only in fairly extreme cases. *See* TLO V. N.J., 469 U.S. 325 (1985).

search and seizure A legal term that in schools refers to the examination of a student's locker or other personal property (or his or her person), usually for drugs, stolen property, or weapons. *See* SEARCH OF STUDENTS.

secondary data   Data, maintained by an organization for use in its normal course of operations that can be used for evaluative purposes; evaluation data that already exist prior to initiating an evaluation study; for example, school district statistics on dropouts or on teen pregnancies. *See also:*
OPERATIONAL DATA
PRIMARY DATA
SOURCES OF DATA

secondary instructional level The general level of instruction provided for pupils in secondary schools and any instruction of a comparable nature and difficulty provided for adults and youth beyond the age of compulsory school attendance. *See also* SECONDARY SCHOOL.

secondary school   A school comprising any span of grades beginning with the next grade following an elementary or middle school and ending with or below grade 12.
See Kenneth H. Hoover, *Learning and Teaching in the Secondary School: Improved Instructional Practices,* 3rd ed. (Boston: Allyn and Bacon, 1972); Frederick R. Smith and Benjamin C. Cox, *Secondary Schools in a Changing Society* (New York: Rinehart and Winston, 1976); Kenneth H. Hoover, *The Professional Teacher's Handbook: A Guide for Improving Instruction in Today's Secondary Schools,* abr. ed. (Boston: Allyn and Bacon, 1976); and David G. Armstrong and Thomas V. Savage, *Secondary Education: An Introduction* (New York: Macmillan, 1983).

Secondary School Admissions Test   A standardized test required for admission to many private secondary schools.

secondary school plant   A plant that houses on a permanent basis one school only—a school comprised of any span of grades beginning with the next grade following elementary school and ending with or below grade 12, including junior high schools, the different types of high schools, and vocational or trade high schools.

Secondary School Science Project   A science curriculum called "Time, Space and Matter" that was developed at Princeton University in the early 1960s and that involves a series of investigations and recorded observations through which the student creates an individualized text book.

secondary source   In documenting research, any record that is a reporting of a first-hand account (or primary source).

secretarial school   A postsecondary private institution that offers specific training programs ranging in length from a few weeks to one or two years and geared at teaching skills such as typing, shorthand, word processing, and basic accounting.

sectarian   Referring to a religious sect or denomination. A sectarian school is one associated with a religious organization. Contrast with SECULAR.

Section 504 of the Rehabilitation Act of 1973   A broad federal requirement that ensures, among other things, that all handicapped children receive a free appropriate education. Section 504 was enacted prior to P.L. 94-142, the Education for All Handicapped Children Act of 1975, and is more general in its prohibition of discrimination. Section 504 states: "no otherwise qualified handicapped individual . . . shall, solely by reason of his/her handicap, be excluded from participation in, be denied the benefits of, or be subject to discrimination under any program or activity receiving federal financial assistance." States must comply with Section 504 if they receive any form of financial aid from the federal government. If states discriminate against handicapped children in the provision of a free, appropriate public education, they may lose federal funds beyond those that are specific to special education and to P.L. 94-142.

secular   Pertaining to dimensions other than the spiritual; not related to religion. A secular school is one that has no association with any religious organization. Contrast with SECTARIAN.

secular humanism   A philosophical orientation that emphasizes consideration for the well-being of humankind over religious considerations. Secular humanists believe that man is complete unto himself, without God or a Supreme Being, and that man determines what is right and wrong with no notion of "eternal truths." Many fundamentalist Christians oppose public education on the grounds that public schools are proponents of secular humanism. *See* Paul W. Kurtz, *A Secular Humanist Declaration* (Buffalo, N.Y.: Prometheus Books).

secure test   A test that is made available only during the time of its administration; otherwise its contents are kept completely confidential. Most standardized tests that are used for college or graduate school admissions are secure.

securities   Bonds, notes, mortgages, or other forms of negotiable or nonnegotiable instruments.

securities rating   *See* BOND RATING *and* STANDARD & POOR CORP.

security   1. Property that has been pledged or mortgaged as financial backing for a loan or other obligation. 2. A share of stock, a bond, a note, or other form of document showing a share of ownership in a company or a debt owed.

security services   Activities concerned with maintaining order and safety in school buildings, on the grounds of schools, and in the vicinity of schools. Included are police activities for school functions and traffic control on the grounds and in the vicinity of schools.

seed money   Initial financing to start a project, which is to be supplemented with larger, more permanent funding at a later date.

segregated school   A school where a group of students have been separated from the main student body on the basis of race, housing patterns, or because of other physical differences such as handicapping conditions.

segregation   The separation of people by any particular identifying characteristic. Historically, segregation has been practiced in schools against racial minorities (primarily blacks), women, and persons with obvious handicaps. All local laws calling for racial segregation have been invalidated by federal legislation (see CIVIL RIGHTS ACT OF 1964) and the federal courts (see *BROWN V. BOARD OF EDUCATION*).

Seguin, Edouard (1812-1880) One of the first teachers of children with mental retardation; he successfully challenged the prevailing belief that children with retardation could not be taught anything of significance. Seguin was a student of JEAN ITARD, and his work strongly influenced later educational leaders such as MARIA MONTESSORI. *See* Thomas S. Ball, *Itard, Seguin, and Kephart: Sensory Education—A Learning Interpretation* (Columbus, Ohio: Charles E. Merrill, 1971).

selective admission   The use of criteria or standards in accepting students for admission to a school. Contrast with OPEN ADMISSION and COMPETITIVE ADMISSION. See the report on admission practices by the Carnegie Council on Policy Studies in Higher Education, *Selective Admissions in Higher Education* (San Francisco: Jossey-Bass, 1977).

self esteem   An individual's assessment of his or her own personal worth or competence. For a theoretical and practical discussion of the roles of schools in enhancing self-perception, *see* James A. Beane and Richard P. Lipka, *Self-Concept, Self-Esteem and the Curriculum* (Boston: Allyn and Bacon, 1984).

self-actualization   Apex of Abraham Maslow's needs hierarchy, where an individual theoretically reaches self-fulfillment and becomes all that he or she is capable of becoming. The importance of the concept of self-actualization was established long before Maslow gave it voice. The 19th-century poet, Robert Browning, described its essence when he said, "a man's reach should exceed his grasp, or what's a heaven for?" Maslow's needs hierarchy was originally presented in "A Theory of Human Motivation," *Psychological Review* (July 1943).

For a technique to measure self-actualization, *see* Charles Bonjean and Gary Vance, "A Short Form Measure of Self-Actualization," *Journal of Applied Behavioral Science* (July-August-September 1968). *See also* Harold R. McAlindon, "Education for Self-

Actualization," *Training and Development Journal* (October 1981).

self-concept   1. An individual's perception of self. 2. A psychological construct that is more complex than implied or assumed by most educators. For an in-depth review of the term, *see* Herbert Marsh et al., "Self Concept: Reliability, Stability, Dimensionality, Validity and the Measurement of Change," *Journal of Educational Psychology* (October 1983).

self-contained class   1. A class having the same teacher or team of teachers for all or most of the daily session. 2. In special education, a class where a group of students who all have similar handicapping conditions spend all or most of their school day.

self-contained teacher   1. An individual teacher who is responsible for teaching essentially all subjects to a single group of students for most of the school day. The most common role for an elementary school teacher in the United States. 2. In special education it refers to a teacher who has a small group of students, all of whom are labeled as handicapped, for whom he or she is responsible for the totality of their education throughout most or all of the school day.

self-directed learning   A systematic process in which an individual takes responsibility, in collaboration with others, for diagnosing his or her own learning needs, formulating learning objectives, planning and engaging in a sequence of learning experiences to achieve these objectives, and evaluating progress toward these objectives.

self-fulfilling prophecy   Causing something to happen by believing it will. If a manager or teacher believes that his or her employees or students are or are not capable, they will eventually live up or down to the manager's or teacher's expectations. It can apply to an individual student; if labeled "slow" or "incompetent" from the early school years, the student may, indeed, continue to demonstrate these traits.

See Jere E. Brophy, "Research on the Self-fulfilling Prophecy and Teacher Expectations," *Journal of Educational Research* (October 1983), for an extensive bibliography.

self-insurance   Setting aside a fund of money to pay for possible future losses rather than purchasing an insurance policy.

self-liquidating loan   A loan to buy or produce things that will be sold to obtain cash with which to repay the loan.

self-teaching   The use of materials (self-teaching materials) that are designed so that the student can learn from them independent of a teacher. Examples are programmed instruction and computer-assisted instruction.

semantic differential technique   A method used to measure attitudes about a word or a concept by asking individuals to rate their perception of the concept on a continuous scale between two opposite adjectives. For example, the subject is asked to place an X at the place on the line that most closely reflects his or her feelings:

Theory of Evolution
False _____ True

This technique was developed by Charles E. Osgood and associates in the 1950s in their study of the meanings of words.

See Charles E. Osgood et al., *The Management of Meaning* (Urbana: University of Illinois Press, 1957); and James G. Snider and Charles E. Osgood, eds., *Semantic Differential Technique: A Source Book* (Chicago: Aldine, 1969).

semantics   In linguistics, the study of the meaning of language units.

semester   Half of a regular school year, usually 16 to 18 weeks in duration.

semester credit hour   A unit of measure frequently used in higher education, denoting class meetings for one hour a week for an academic semester, generally about 18 weeks' time. Satisfactory completion of a course scheduled for three class sessions (or the equivalent) per week in an academic semester earns three semester hours.

seminal   In academic jargon, an idea that is believed to contain the roots of further new learning or developments.

seminar method   As contrasted with the lecture method, an instructional technique where the teacher takes less of a leadership role as students meet under the teacher's direction to discuss topics that are generally related to a particular subject. This method is more commonly used at the postsecondary level.

seminary   1. A theological school for the study of religion, usually for people who are preparing for the clergy. 2. An outdated term for a private secondary school for girls.

senior   A student in the last year of study at either a high school (grade 12) or a four-year college.

senior high school   A secondary school offering the final years of high school work necessary for graduation and invariably preceded by a junior high school or middle school.

seniority A social mechanism that gives priority to the individuals who are the most senior—have the longest service—in an organization. Seniority is often used to determine which employees will be promoted, subjected to layoff, or given/denied other employment advantages.

sensitivity analysis A complex analytical procedure for assessing the cost, benefit, output, effectiveness, and other desirable and undesirable impacts of alternative decisions resulting from changes in the underlying assumptions. The steps in a sensitivity analysis include:

1. Construct cost-benefit and/or cost-effectiveness models.
2. Identify the important factors in the models. There is an almost infinite variety of things that can affect the results of a proposed alternative, but there are only a few that should have a significant effect on the result.
3. Determine the range of quantitative values or possible states that could occur. For the important factors, determine the range that could reasonably be expected to occur. For example, the cost of a piece of equipment could range between $150 and $200. Estimate the chances of the cost being outside of that range.
4. Select quantitative and qualitative values or states to use in the sensitivity analysis. In the above example, you might select $150, $175, and $200 for inclusion in the sensitivity analysis. Assess the states of nature, social, psychological, and/or political aspects that might affect the results of the alternatives.
5. Conduct the sensitivity analysis. Run the three (or however many) quantitative values through the original cost/benefit or cost/effectiveness model. Make subjective estimates of the intangible factors that might occur (that is, assess how they might affect the decision we are facing).
6. Arrange the results in a useful format for decisionmaker(s). Only a limited range of alternatives that should bear on the decision should be presented to decisionmakers. Assumptions should be stated explicitly.

See also COST-BENEFIT ANALYSIS.

sensitivity training A group training experience where participants learn, through extensive guided interaction, to better understand themselves and to improve their interpersonal relations with others.

sensory Pertaining to the senses, i.e., sight, hearing, touch, taste, and smell.

sensory education A term used in Montessori schools to refer to the activities that students engage in with materials designed to increase the sensitivity of the senses and, thus, increase the students' sensory discrimination abilities. *See* MONTESSORI METHOD.

sensory motor stage From Piaget, the first stage in a child's cognitive development, covering approximately the first two years of life. During this stage the child develops awareness of the relationship between his or her sensory perceptions and his or her actions. Critical concepts that are learned during this stage are object permanence and cause-effect.

sentence-completion test A test of vocabulary and concepts where the individual is presented with a sentence containing a blank and is expected to fill the blank with the correct word.

separate but equal The doctrine espoused by the Supreme Court in

Plessy v. Ferguson, 163 U.S. 537 (1896), which held that segregated facilities for blacks, facilities that were considered equal in quality to those provided for whites, did not violate the equal protection clause of the 14th Amendment. In BROWN V. BOARD OF EDUCATION, 347 U.S. 483 (1954), the Court nullified this doctrine when it asserted that separate was "inherently unequal."
See David W. Bishop, *Plessy v. Ferguson*: A Reinterpretation," *Journal of Negro History* (April 1977); Stephen J. Riegel, "The Persistent Career of Jim Crow: Lower Federal Courts and the 'Separate but Equal' Doctrine, 1865-1896," *American Journal of Legal History* (January 1984); and Ralph A. Rossum, "*Plessy, Brown*, and the Reverse Discrimination Cases: Consistency and Continuity in Judicial Approach," *American Behavioral Scientist* (July-August 1985).

separation   1. The termination of employment for any reason. 2. SEGREGATION.

sequence   The order of presentation of aspects of the instructional program, as within a grade, a course, or a series of grades or courses.

sequential learning   The presentation of one task after another, each with increased difficulty such that later tasks build on the learning of earlier tasks.

sequential study   A plan for the logical ordering of the presentation of various aspects of content and learning experiences, whether among a series of schools, among a series of grades or courses, or within a grade or course.

serendipity   Benefits that occur unexpectedly in the process of working toward a different goal; for example, striking oil while digging for water.

Occasionally, administrative problem-solving will yield serendipitous results.

serial bonds   Bonds of the same issue, put out at the same time, that have varying dates of maturity, so that the entire debt does not fall due at once. Usually, the group of bonds carrying the longest term (in years) pays a higher rate of interest than bonds with shorter terms. Serial bonds should not be confused with series bonds, which are put out at different times.

seriously emotionally disturbed   Individuals identified by professionally qualified personnel as having an emotional handicap of such a nature and severity as to require one or more special services, whether or not such services are available or whether or not such services are the responsibility of the public schoools. Such services—for schizophrenia and other psychotic conditions—may include, but are not limited to, residential care, other professional treatment or care, and special education services that may or may not involve special class placement.

Serrano v. Priest   A California Supreme Court decision that required the state to develop an equitable school finance formula in order to reduce the discrepancy in quality of education among local school districts (5 Cal. 3d 584, 487 P.2d. 1241, 96 Cal. Rptr. 601, 1971).

service   The activities that provide some support or benefit to another person, agency, or institution.

service club   An organized group of members having as their common purpose working for the benefit of others voluntarily, by request, or to fulfill a social need.

service contract   An agreement between local units of government for one unit (usually larger) to provide a service for another (usually smaller). It is often called the Lakewood Plan because it was first extensively used in the Los Angeles area between the County of Los Angeles and the City of Lakewood. *See* Russell L. Smith and C.W. Kohfeld, "Interlocal Service Cooperation in Metropolitan Areas: The Impact of Councils of Governments," *Midwest Review of Public Administration* (June 1980); and Martin J. Schiesl, "The Politics of Contracting: Los Angeles County and the Lakewood Plan, 1954-1962," *Huntington Library Quarterly* (Summer 1982).

service fee   1. User charges for government services not fully paid for by general taxation. Examples include water fees from municipal governments and fees to be admitted to national parks or other facilities. 2. The equivalent of union dues that nonunion members of an agency shop pay the union for negotiating and administering the collective bargaining agreement. *See ABOOD V. DETROIT BOARD OF EDUCATION.*

Servicemen's Opportunity Colleges   A network of institutions of higher education providing programs to meet the needs of service personnel and veterans. Partially supported by the Department of Defense.

services, budgeting   *See* BUDGETING SERVICES.

services, community   *See* COMMUNITY SERVICES.

services, contracted   *See* CONTRACTED SERVICES.

services, contributed   *See* CONTRIBUTED SERVICES.

services, educational media   *See* EDUCATIONAL MEDIA SERVICES.

services, educational television   *See* EDUCATIONAL TELEVISION SERVICES.

services, executive administration   *See* EXECUTIVE ADMINISTRATION SERVICES.

services, external   *See* EXTERNAL SERVICES.

services, financial accounting   *See* FINANCIAL ACCOUNTING SERVICES.

services, fiscal   *See* FISCAL SERVICES.

services, guidance   *See* GUIDANCE SERVICES.

services, helping-teacher   *See* HELPING-TEACHER SERVICES.

services, improvement of instruction   *See* IMPROVEMENT OF INSTRUCTION SERVICES.

services, information   *See* INFORMATION SERVICES.

services, instructional staff training   *See* INSTRUCTIONAL STAFF TRAINING SERVICES.

services, instruction and curriculum development   *See* INSTRUCTION AND CURRICULUM DEVELOPMENT SERVICES.

services, internal auditing   *See* INTERNAL AUDITING SERVICES.

services, internal information   *See* INTERNAL INFORMATION SERVICES.

services, placement   *See* PLACEMENT SERVICES.

services, planning   *See* PLANNING SERVICES.

services, psychological   *See* PSYCHOLOGICAL SERVICES.

services, psychological counseling   *See* PSYCHOLOGICAL COUNSELING SERVICES.

services, psychological testing   *See* PSYCHOLOGICAL TESTING SERVICES.

services, psychotherapy   *See* PSYCHOTHERAPY SERVICES.

services, pupil accounting   *See* PUPIL ACCOUNTING SERVICES.

services, pupil appraisal   *See* PUPIL APPRAISAL SERVICES.

services, pupil personnel   *See* PUPIL PERSONNEL SERVICES.

services, pupil transportation   *See* PUPIL TRANSPORTATION SERVICES.

services, purchased   *See* PURCHASED SERVICES.

services, purchasing   *See* PURCHASING SERVICES.

services, receiving and disbursing   *See* RECEIVING AND DISBURSING SERVICES.

services, research   *See* RESEARCH SERVICES.

services, school library   *See* SCHOOL LIBRARY SERVICES.

services, security   *See* SECURITY SERVICES.

services, shared   *See* SHARED SERVICES.

services, social work   *See* SOCIAL WORK SERVICES.

services, speech pathology   *See* SPEECH PATHOLOGY SERVICES.

services, staff   *See* STAFF SERVICES.

services, state and federal relations   *See* STATE AND FEDERAL RELATIONS SERVICES.

services, statistical   *See* STATISTICAL SERVICES.

services, statistical analysis   *See* STATISTICAL ANALYSIS SERVICES.

SES   *See* SOCIAL ECONOMIC STATUS.

session   1. The period of time during the schoolday when a given group of students is under the guidance and direction of teachers. *See also* FULL-DAY SESSION *and* HALF-DAY SESSION. 2. An academic term during which classes are offered.

set-asides   Government purchasing and contracting provisions that "set-aside" or allocate a certain percentage of business for minority-owned companies. The use of set-asides was upheld by the Supreme Court in *Fullilove v. Klutznick*, 448 U.S. 448 (1980). *See* Felicity Hardee, *"Fullilove* and the Minority Set Aside: In Search of an Affirmative Action Rationale," *Emory Law Journal* (Fall 1980).

Seton, Elizabeth Ann Bayley (1774-1821)   Credited with being the founder of Roman Catholic parochial education in America.

sets   In mathematics, a defined category of items or individuals. The items that make up a set are called elements. A set with no elements is called a null set. Sets may have subsets; for example, history books are a subset of all books.

severance pay   A single final payment made to a person whose employment has been terminated.

severe mental retardation   A term applied to individuals who learn more slowly than 99 percent of the population and will acquire fewer and less complex skills. In general a person with severe mental retardation has a measurable IQ of below 25.

sex discrimination Any disparate or unfavorable treatment of an individual in an employment or educational situation because of his or her sex. The Civil Rights Act of 1964 (as amended by the Equal Employment Opportunity Act of 1972) makes sex discrimination illegal in most employment except where a bona fide occupational qualification is involved.

In 1980, after the federal courts had decided that sexual harassment was sex discrimination in a variety of cases, the Equal Employment Opportunity Commission issued legally binding rules clearly stating than an employer has a responsibility to provide a place of work that is free from sexual harassment or intimidation. In 1986 the Supreme Court reaffirmed this when, in the case of *Meritor Saving Bank v. Vinson*, 91 L.Ed. 2d 49, it held that sexual harassment creating a hostile or abusive work environment, even without economic loss on the part of the person being harassed, was in violation of Title VIII of the Civil Rights Act of 1964.

See Dail Ann Neugarten and Jay M. Shafritz, eds. *Sexuality in Organizations* (Oak Park, Ill.: Moore, 1980); Mary Coeli Meyer et al., *Sexual Harassment* (New York: Petrocelli, 1981); and Patrice D. Horn and Jack C. Horn, *Sex in the Office: Power and Passion in the Workplace* (Reading, Mass.: Addison-Wesley, 1982).

sex education A course of study covering a broad range of information concerning the physical, psychological, social, and sexual development of individuals. A major focus of many sex education programs is to assist upper elementary and secondary age students to understand and to make responsible choices about their own sexuality. Compare to SIECUS. For a number of articles related to sex education in the schools, *see* "Sex and Education," *Journal of Research and Development in Education* (Winter 1983).

sex equity Refers to the equal treatment of students and/or employers regardless of whether they are male or female.

Sex Information and Education Council of the United States *See* SIECUS.

sexism 1. Stereotyping individual roles and behavior on the basis of gender. 2. Treating or depicting females as if they were inherently inferior to males. For a perspective on the shaping of teacher attitudes, *see* Myra Pollack Sadker and David Miller Sadker, "Sexism in Teacher Education Texts," *Harvard Educational Review* (February 1980). For a number of articles discussing sexism in the schools, *see Phi Delta Kappan* (March 1986).

sexual harassment Action of an individual, in a position to control or influence another's job, career, or grade, who uses his or her power to gain sexual favors or punish the refusal of such favors. Sexual harassment on the job or in the classroom varies from inappropriate sexual innuendo to coerced sexual relations. *See* SEX DISCRIMINATION.

See Billie Wright Dziech and Linda Weiner, *The Lecherous Professor: Sexual Harassment on Campus* (Boston: Beacon Press, 1984); and Frances L. Hoffman, "Sexual Harassment in Academia: Feminist Theory and Institutional Practice," *Harvard Educational Review* (May 1986).

Shane, Harold (1914-   ) A widely-read contemporary educator who authored over 120 books, including *The Elementary School in the United States* (with Alvin Toffler et al., 1973), *Educating for a New Millennium* (1981), and *Teaching and Learning in a Micro-electronic Age* (1986).

Shanker, Albert (1928-   ) Became president of the United Federation of Teachers in New York City in 1964 and president of the American Federation of Teachers in 1974.

shared facilities   Public school buildings, sites, or equipment regularly used without rental fee by nonpublic school pupils who are under the immediate supervision and control of nonpublic school officials; or nonpublic school buildings, sites, or equipment regularly used without rental fee by public school pupils who are under the immediate supervision and control of public school officials.

shared revenue   Revenue that is levied by one governmental unit but shared, usually in proportion to the amount collected, with another unit of government or class of government.

shared services   An arrangement whereby services provided by one school or school system are made available without charge to another school or school system. To illustrate, the health services or school library services of a given public school might be made available without charge to pupils of a neighboring public or nonpublic school on a set schedule or as required, with persons providing such services being staff members of the public school, regardless of the location at which the services are provided.

shared tax   *See* SHARED REVENUE.

shared time   *See* DUAL ENROLLMENT.

sheltered   workshop   An enterprise, usually nonprofit, providing employment (usually at extreme subminimum wage) and/or rehabilitative activity under supervision and direction for workers having one or more handicapping conditions—physical, mental, or emotional. *See* SUPPORTED WORK.

Shelton v. Tucker 364 U.S. 479 (1960)   The Supreme Court case that dealt with the question of whether public employees could have membership in subversive organizations, organizations with illegal objectives, and unions. Their right to join the latter was upheld. With regard to the former, it was held that there could be no general answer. Rather, each case has to be judged on the basis of whether a public employee actually supports an organization's illegal aims.

shop room   A special instructional space designed or provided with special built-in equipment, for developing manipulative and related skills. The type of shop room should be specified.

short-answer test   A variety of test type where only brief responses are required of the students. For example, true-false, multiple choice, sentence completion, and matching tests are all short-answer.

shorthand   A method of rapidly taking notes or transcription through the use of symbols and abbreviations to represent words or phrases. There are many different systems of shorthand. Also called stenography.

short-term loans   A loan payable in five years or less, but usually not before the end of the current fiscal year. *See also* CURRENT LOANS.

show and tell   An activity typically practiced in lower elementary level classes where students bring an item or a piece of information from home and stand up in front of the class to tell the rest of the students about it.

shower room   A room designed as such and equipped with individual shower stalls or group showers. It may also contain drying areas, towel storage and issue areas, dressing and locker areas, lavatory areas, and service toilet areas.

sibling rivalry   A common developmental phenomenon occurring between brothers and/or sisters usually in competition for the attention of their parents. *See* Judy Dunn, *Sisters and Brothers* (Cambridge, Mass.: Harvard University Press, 1985).

siblings   Brothers and/or sisters who have the same parents.

sick leave   Leave permitted staff members for illness and sometimes to care for dependents who are ill.

sickle-cell anemia   An inherited blood disorder that is seen almost exclusively among the black population. Sickle-cell trait is a much more common condition (occurs in approximately 10 percent of black Americans) where a defective gene is present, but the disease itself (which occurs at a rate of one in 400 black Americans) is not manifested. Sickle-cell anemia causes pain, swollen joints, fatigue, and usually a shortened life span.

SIECUS   The Sex Information and Education Council of the United States, a nonprofit organization founded in 1964 that provides information, resources, and services for parents and professionals in the area of sex education. Publishes a bimonthly newsletter, *SIECUS Report.*
SIECUS
80 Fifth Avenue, Suite 801
New York, NY 10011
(212) 929-2300

sight reading   In music, being able to sing or play a piece of music by following the printed score prior to practicing the score.

sight vocabulary   The words that a student is able to read and understand without the aid of reference material.

sight word   A word that a student is able to recognize and read without needing to sound out its individual components.

sign language   A method of communication that utilizes configurations and movements of the fingers and hands to represent letters, words, and complete thoughts. Although sign language has been used primarily by individuals who are deaf, it has more recently been accepted as an alternative system for teaching communication to others who have difficulty learning spoken language (such as children who have mental retardation). Compare to AMERICAN SIGN LANGUAGE.

significance   Also called STATISTICAL SIGNIFICANCE. The degree to which one can be confident in the reliability of a statistical measure. For example, a confidence level of .05 means that the statistical finding would occur by chance in only one sample out of every 20.

silent reading   Reading to oneself without speaking aloud. Contrast with oral reading.

silk screen   A method of stencil printing utilizing an open weave cloth; frequently used in art classes.

simulation   A method of instruction that allows students to experience a situation almost like one they will need to cope with outside of the instructional setting. Simulation may involve technological devices, such as simulated flight training, or role-playing for the practice of interpersonal interactions.

Simulations are considered an effective teaching method because: (1) they allow the student to use a variety of problem-solving techniques simultaneously; (2) decisions are essentially risk-free, allowing participants the opportunity of creative thinking; (3) students are able to see the interrelated nature of problems so that they can begin to predict how one element in the activity leads to the next; and (4) debriefing/evaluation sessions allow students a reflexive opportunity for learning.

single fund accounting   A budgeting and accounting procedure, for a state department of education or other agency or organization, through which all receipts and expenditures are handled in a single fund.

single parent family   A family where only one parent, most often the mother, is present in the household. In the 1980s there were over 6,000,000 single parent families in the United States.

single salary schedule   A pay scale that allows no deviation for merit or for specific assignment but where all members of a job class (e.g., teachers) are remunerated equally, based on education and years of experience.

single subject design   A commonly used methodology in educational research where the sample of subjects is one. This type of design is particularly well suited to research on behavior modification. For a comprehensive discussion of this methodology, see Michael Hersen and David Barlow, *Single Case Experimental Designs* (New York: Pergamon Press, 1976).

single-concept film   A type of audiovisual instruction that uses short, 8mm film strips that a student can view independently to provide repetitive drill on some unit of the curriculum.

sinistral   Referring to the left side of the body. Left-handedness is considered sinistrality.

sinking fund   Money or other assets put aside for a special purpose, such as to pay off bonds as they come due or to replace worn-out or outdated machinery or buildings.

situation audit   A strategic planning technique for assessing an organization's performance. Major aspects of a situation audit include a capability profile and a WOTS-UP ANALYSIS. *See also* PLANNING.

Sizer, Theodore R. (1932-   )
A contemporary advocate for educational reform, particularly at the high school level. Sizer is the author of *Horace's Compromise: The Dilemma of the American High School* (1984), an important study of secondary education in America.

skewness   Also skewed distribution. The tendency of a distribution to depart from symmetry or balance around the mean. If the scores tend to cluster at the lower end of the distribution, the distribution is said to be positively skewed; if they tend to cluster at the upper end of the distribution, the distribution is said to be negatively skewed.

skill analysis   A type of training needs assessment by which employee skills are assessed in comparison with those skills that are determined to be necessary for the individual job or the entire organization.

skill development   Instruction designed to promote the acquisition or improvement of specific abilities.

skill streaming   An instructional program designed to teach social skills to elementary-aged students.

skills   Mental and/or physical abilities acquired by observation, study, or experience, and basic to the mastery of school work or other activity. Such abilities may include proficiency in planning and investigating, operational techniques, comprehension, organization, execution, remembrance, and application of knowledge to acquire a desired result.

skimming   A system of speed reading where the intent is to obtain just a general idea of the content by sacrificing comprehension for speed. This is the fastest method of speed reading.

Skinner, B.F. (1904-   )   Full name Burrhus Frederic Skinner, one of the most influential of behavior psychologists, inventor of the teaching machine, and generally considered to be the "father" of programmed instruction. Major works include: *Walden Two* (New York: Macmillan, 1948, 1966); *Science and Human Behavior* (New York: Free Press, 1953, 1965); *The Technology of Teaching* (New York: Appleton-Century-Crofts, 1968); *Beyond Freedom and Dignity* (New York: Knopf, 1971).

Skinner box   Refers to the type of box used by B.F. Skinner and his associates for their operant conditioning experiments with pigeons and other animals, where the subjects are trained to respond repetitively to stimuli through the systematic delivery of edible reinforcers. The term has a derogatory connotation when similar teaching procedures are applied to human beings.

slander   False statements made about a person that may damage the person's reputation or cast doubt on his or her character. While teachers and other school officials can be charged with slander, in some circumstances they are protected if potentially slanderous statements are a legitimate part of their duty (for example, reporting a case of suspected child abuse).

slide-rule discipline   Approach to discipline that eliminates supervisory discretion and sets very specific quantitative standards as the consequences of specific violations. For example, a discipline policy based on this concept might hold that any student who is late for school more than four times in a 30-day period would be "automatically" suspended for a day.

Slingerland Screening Tests for Identifying Children with Specific Language Disabilities   A group-administered test for young children that screens for potential language/learning disorders through the assessment of such basic skills as visual memory, visual copying, auditory perception, and auditory memory. It is published by:

Educators Publishing Service, Inc.
75 Moulton Street
Cambridge, MA 02138

Slosson Intelligence Test   An individually-administered screening instrument that has been adapted from the Stanford Binet Intelligence Scale and that measures mental ability in individuals from infants to adults. It is published by:

Publishers Test Service
2500 Garden Road
Monterey, CA 93940

slow learners   Students who display evidence of having difficulty in adjusting to the usual curriculum in one or more academic areas, thus requiring modification of school offerings within the regular classroom in order to attain maximum growth and development. The term is used in referring to the student's capability in specific academic areas rather than to the student's general level of mental ability. *See* SELF-FULFILLING PROPHECY.

See Roy Irwin Brown, *Psychology and Education of Slow Learners* (Boston: Routledge and Kegan Paul, 1978).

Sloyd system   A theory and method of industrial arts education developed in Sweden in the 19th century; it espoused training in manual skills as a part of general education rather than introducing such training only for the purpose of career preparation.

slush fund   1. Money collected by the military in the last century by selling grease and other refuse (the "slush"); the resulting funds would then be used to buy small luxuries for the soldiers and sailors. 2. Discretionary funds appropriated by a legislature for the use of an agency head. 3. Private monies used for campaign expenses. 4. Funds used for bribery. 5. Secret funds. All slush funds because of their lack of formal accountability have an unsavory connotation—even when they are perfectly legal.

small pupil transportation vehicle   Any pupil transportation vehicles with a manufacturer's rated seating capacity of less than 12. (Seating capacity figured on the basis of at least 13 inches of seat space per pupil.)

Smith v. Wade 461 U.S. 30 (1983) The Supreme Court case that held that punitive damages can be awarded against public employees for reckless indifference to an individual's constitutional rights, as well as when the conduct was motivated by evil motive or intent. It is not necessary for the plaintiff to prove actual malicious intent. The decision expanded the liability of public administrators to punitive damages.

Smith-Hughes Act   This act was passed during World War I with regard to vocational education services, and it had the first direct federal impact on elementary and secondary education.

Smith-Lever Act   A 1914 federal law with regard to cooperative extension programs that facilitated the dissemination of information about agriculture and home economics through land grant colleges.

Snellen Chart   A device commonly used to measure visual acuity. The chart is made up of lines of letters (though E symbols and pictures are sometimes substituted for young children), which become progressively smaller.

snow day   A day on which school would normally be in session but is cancelled due to inclement weather. Also called school closing.

social alienation   A concept developed to describe the separation of an individual or group of individuals from a social system either by choice or as a result of rejection by the system.

social economic status (SES)   An indicator of an individual or family's social ranking based on such factors as level of education, income, neighborhood of residence, or type of occupation. This term is widely used by sociologists, though it has no precise definition.

social engineering   Attempts to effect substantial social change that are systematic and directed toward specific goals; descriptive of many of the programs of the "Great Society" of the 1960s.

social equity   A normative standard holding that equity, rather than efficiency, is the major criterion for evaluating the desirability of a policy or program. *See* H. George Frederickson, symposium editor, "Social Equity and Public Administration," *Public Administration Review* (January-February 1974).

social handicap   An abnormality or variation in interpersonal relationships that adversely affects the social adjustment of an individual.

social indicators   Statistical measures that aid in the description of conditions in the social environment (e.g., measures of income distribution, poverty, health, and physical environment).
See Raymond Bauer, *Social Indicators* (Cambridge, Mass.: M.I.T. Press, 1967); and Robert Parke and David Seidman, "Social Indicators and Social Reporting," *Annals of the American Academy of Political and Social Science* (January 1978).

social insurance   Any benefit program that a state makes available to the members of its society in time of need and as a matter of right.

social intelligence or social competence   The ability to understand the feelings, thoughts, and behaviors of persons in social/interpersonal situations and to act appropriately based on that understanding. *See* Herbert A. Marlow, "Social Intelligence: Evidence for Multidimensionality and Construct Independence," *Journal of Educational Psychology* (February 1986), for an expanded, more complex attempt at definition.

social maturity   A measure of the developmental competence of an individual with regard to interpersonal relations, behavioral appropriateness, social problem-solving, and judgment.

social mobility   The changing of social status or position by, for example,

educational attainment or occupational promotion.

social promotion   Moving from one grade level to the next highest grade on some basis other than academic achievement.

social psychology   The study of human behavior in the context of society.

social security number   The number assigned to a person by the Social Security Administration.

social service organization   General label for nonprofit organizations that work to preserve and improve nonmembers' physical and/or mental health or general well-being; for example, accident prevention, treatment of illness, and the provision of rehabilitation services. *See also* SOCIAL WELFARE ORGANIZATION.

social stratification   The relative positions of groups of individuals based on such social differences as educational level, income, occupational categories, or inheritance.

social studies   A general field of instruction with the overall purpose of teaching students about society. May include history, geography, politics, civics, economics, and psychology. Also called social sciences. ("Social sciences" more specifically refers to the higher-level academic disciplines, while "social studies" is used in reference to study of these disciplines at the elementary or secondary levels.) More recently the social studies curriculum has become the ''dumping ground'' for state requirements such as law-related education, drug and alcohol problems etc. The discipline has inherited the title ''Social Stew.'' Many educational reformers, including past Secretary of Education Bennett, propose teaching only history, geography, and political science in the social studies. The argument is that "social stew" has no deeply rooted philosophical base and therefore is ineffective. *See* David G. Armstrong, *Social Studies in Secondary Education* (New York: Macmillan, 1980); Hazel Whitman Hertzberg, *Social Studies Reform 1880-1980* (Boulder, Colo.: Social Science Education Consortium, 1981).

social studies, new   *see* NEW SOCIAL STUDIES.

social system   An organization that is made up of individuals carrying out separate but related functions and that has a singular identity. A school can be an example of a social system.

social welfare, promotion of Promotion of social welfare is the least well defined of the tax-exempt charitable purposes. In general, the test of whether an activity is for the promotion of the social welfare turns on whether the specific purpose appears to be reasonably in the community's social interest. IRS regulations define general types of promotion of social welfare as including lessening neighborhood tensions, eliminating prejudice and discrimination, defending human and civil rights, and fighting community deterioration and juvenile delinquency.

social welfare organization Category of tax-exempt entities that are organized and operated to promote the social welfare of specific groupings of people; for example, providing for the general welfare of nonmembers who face problems because of their social situation. Social welfare organizations focus on particular groups of people who have special needs, problems, or requirements. Social welfare organizations may qualify for tax-exempt status under IRS Code 501(c)(4).

social work   Activities concerned with the prevention of, or solution to, those personal, social, and emotional problems of individuals that generally involve relationships such as those with the family, school, and community. *See* Betsy L. Hancock, *School Social Work* (Englewood Cliffs, N.J.: Prentice-Hall, 1982).

social work services   Activities such as investigation and assessment of pupil problems arising from the home, school, or community; casework and group work services (including counseling) for pupils and families; interpreting the problems of pupils for other staff members; and promoting change in the circumstances surrounding the individual pupil, when the circumstances are related to specific problems. *See* Wendy G. Winters and Freda Easton, *The Practice of Social Work in Schools* (New York: Free Press, 1983).

social worker   A professional who performs services in assisting in the prevention of, or solution to, the personal, social, and emotional problems of individuals, which involve family and community relationships. When such problems have a bearing upon the quality of the schoolwork of a student, a school SOCIAL WORKER may provide such services.

socialization, organizational *See* ORGANIZATIONAL SOCIALIZATION.

socially and/or emotionally handicapped   Pupils identified by professionally qualified personnel as having a social and/or emotional handicap, e.g., emotionally disturbed and delinquency prone, and who may be eligible for special education services.

socially maladjusted   Students identified by professionally qualified personnel as having unusual difficulty or unacceptable behavior in interpersonal relationships, to an extent as to require special services.

sociodrama   A form of creative dramatics where students act out a problem that one or more of them may have in order to better understand the problem.

socioeconomic status   See SO-CIAL ECONOMIC STATUS.

sociogram   A way of visually depicting the various relationships among the individual members of a group.

sociolinguistics   The study of the relationship between language and social structure.

sociology   The field of study concerned with group behaviors and human interactions and societies.

sociometrics   Approaches for measuring and analyzing various aspects of social groups. Sociometrics typically involve observation, opinion surveys, and/or questionnaires.

Socrates (470 B.C.-399 B.C.)   A great teacher and philosopher of ancient Athens who is credited with the Socratic method of teaching. Because of his teaching style, which involved the questioning of assumptions, Socrates was tried and convicted of corrupting youth, and he was executed by being ordered to drink hemlock. Rather than escape, which he easily could have, he chose to uphold the law by accepting the sentence. Plato wrote extensively about Socrates.

Socratic method   A method of teaching whereby the instructor asks questions and leads the students, through a shaping of their responses and subsequent discussion, to an understanding of the information being taught. This method was made famous by the ancient Greek philosopher, Socrates.

soft money   1. Funds given by national political parties to their state and local parties for "nonfederal" uses, such as voter-registration drives. The money is "soft" because its use is not watched carefully by the states, and its collection by the national party is often unreported because of its "nonfederal" character. 2. Funds for a program that are not received on a recurring basis from a steady source. For example, grant or gift funds on a one-time or even a several-year basis are "soft" in comparison to the "hard" funds that come each year from a legislative appropriation.

software   All materials that are required to operate computer programs, with the exception of the computer and its associated components (the hardware). The software includes the programs, manuals, diagrams, and instructions that allow the user access to the capacity of the computer.

sokols   Gymnastic organizations that originated in Czechoslovakia and that encouraged participation by gymnasts of all ages.

somatopsychology   The study of the relationship between physical symptoms or handicaps and behavior.

S-1 v. Turlington 635 F 2nd (CA 5, 1981)   A U.S. Circuit Court of Appeals ruling that handicapped students cannot be expelled from school without the utilization of all procedural safeguards that apply to placement in special education. The court ruled that expulsion from school for disciplinary reasons constituted a change in educational placement for a student who had been determined to be handicapped. In order for the student to be expelled persons who are properly qualified must determine that the behavior leading to the expulsion is not a result of the handicapping condition. This requirement is to assure that arbitrary and unilateral decisions to expel will not be made by school administrators. *See also Honing v. Doe,* 793 F. 2nd 1470 (9th Cir. 1986), *cert. granted,* Feb. 23, 1987.

sophism Reasoning that is deliberately intended to mislead; that which seems valid but is not.

sophomore 1. In college, a student who has completed more than the required number of credit hours for completion of the first year of study, but has not completed the requirements for the second year. 2. A high school student in grade 10. 3. Colloquially, the term sophomoric, or like a sophomore, means immature and overly confident.

source of funds The agency, governmental or otherwise, that appropriates the money used by a local school district.

sources of data The three most basic types of sources of data for use in evaluation research are: primary data, secondary data, and operational data. In reality, operational data are one form of secondary data but are sufficiently important to warrant separate consideration. *See also:*
EVALUATION DESIGN
OPERATIONAL DATA
PRIMARY DATA
SECONDARY DATA.

Spalding Method *See* UNIFIED PHONICS METHOD.

span of control The extent of an administrator's responsibility. The span of control has usually been expressed as the number of subordinates that a manager should supervise. Sir Ian Hamilton, in *The Soul and Body of an Army* (London: Edward Arnold & Co., 1921), is generally credited with having first asserted that the "average human brain finds its effective scope in handling from three to six other brains." A.V. Graicunas took a mathematical approach to the concept and demonstrated, in "Relationship in Organization," in Luther Gulick and Lyndall Urwick's *Papers on the Science of Administration* (New York: Institute of Public Administration, 1937), that as the number of subordinates reporting to a manager increases arithmetically, the number of possible interpersonal interactions increases geometrically. Building upon Graicunas' work, Lyndall F. Urwick boldly asserts, in "The Manager's Span of Control," *Harvard Business Review* (May-June 1956), that "no superior can supervise directly the work of more than five or, at the most, six subordinates whose work interlocks." Studies on the concept of span of control abound, but there is no consensus on an "ideal" span.

See also William G. Ouchi and James B. Dowling, "Defining the Span Control," *Administrative Science Quarterly* (September 1974).

Spartan education Education or training that is highly oriented toward military training, with an emphasis on physical strength, courage, endurance, and obedience. In the ancient Greek city of Sparta boys received intensive military education between the ages of seven and 18 while girls stayed home and learned domestic skills.

spasticity A term referring to an individual's difficulty in managing motor movements or physical coordination because of increased muscle tone or uncontrolled muscle spasms; a common manifestation of cerebral palsy.

spatial imagery 1. A mental image of the form of an object. 2. The ability to visualize with one's imagination the relationship in space between various images.

Spearman rank difference correlation coefficient   Comparing an individual student's rank order on one measure (e.g., intelligence score) with another measure (e.g., reading score) in order to determine the relationship between the two measures (i.e., reading aptitude to intelligence).

Spearman-Brown formula   A statistical technique used to measure the reliability of a test.

special assessment   A real estate tax on certain landowners to pay for improvements that will, at least in theory, benefit them all; for example, a paved street.

special district   A unit of government typically performing a single function and overlapping traditional political boundaries. Examples include transportation districts, water districts, and sewer districts. School districts are the most common instance of a special district.

See John C. Bollens, *Special District Governments in the United States* (Berkeley: University of California Press, 1957); Neil D. McFeeley, "Special District Governments: The 'New Dark Continent' Twenty Years Later," *Midwest Review of Public Administration* (December 1978); and Susan A. MacManus, "Special District Governments: A Note on Their Use as Property Tax Relief Mechanisms in the 1970s," *Journal of Politics* (November 1981).

special education   Includes those direct and consultative instructional activities that are designed primarily to deal with such pupil exceptionalities as: (1) physical handicaps; (2) emotional disturbances; (3) cultural differences (including compensatory education); (4)

mental retardation; and (5) mental gifts and talents. Special education instruction is individually designed and may include modified curricular content and adapted methodologies and materials. Special education is differentiated from "regular" education in two major respects: first, special education specifically refers to educational services for students who have been determined to be handicapped or otherwise in need of differentiated services; and second, special education implies adapted, modified, or alternative curricula and/or instructional strategies that are designed to meet the identified individual needs of the student.

See Jay G. Chambers and William T. Hartman, eds., *Special Education Policies: Their History, Implementation, and Finance* (Philadelphia: Temple University Press, 1982). For practical information about special education laws, *see* Kenneth Shore, *The Special Education Handbook: A Comprehensive Guide for Parents and Educators* (New York: Teachers College Press, 1986).

For a review of public special education since the passage and implementation of P.L. 94-142 (THE EDUCATION FOR ALL HANDICAPPED CHILDREN ACT OF 1975) and an extensive bibliography, *see* Alan Gartner and Dorothy Kerzner Lipsky, "Beyond Special Education: Toward A Quality System for All Students," *Harvard Educational Review* (November 1987).

special education, noncategorical   Grouping students who are in need of special education services, because of handicapping conditions, on the basis of their needs or skills rather than on their handicapping condition. Traditionally, schools have grouped such special education students by category, i.e., learning disabled, mentally retarded, emotionally disturbed, deaf, blind, etc. The rationale for non-categorical grouping are: that exceptional children from all categories have much in common regarding educational needs and do not need separate classrooms for each of their disability areas; and that the teaching methods and approaches used for most areas of exceptionality are so similar as to be essentially indistinguishable. Some educators contend that students with handicaps should not be organized into groups of any kind for the purpose of education but that their individual needs should be addressed within the context of regular education.

special event   Fund-raising event usually involving entertainment or recreational activities and requiring a purchased ticket or a fixed donation to attend. Food, beverages, and/or souvenirs (e.g., T-shirts, pins, bumper stickers) and chances (such as lottery tickets) may be sold at a special event to increase income. Types of special event are as varied as the sponsoring organization's members' imaginations. Some examples of a special event include community carnivals, races/marathons, garage sales, swap meets, auctions, barbecues/steak fries, dances, raffles, bake sales, wine tasting parties, baseball or football games, rodeos, dances, concerts, flea markets, and Trivial Pursuit parties.

If the publicity is handled well, special events increase an organization's (or its projects') visibility in its community. They may stimulate or renew interest of staff and volunteers, and they may involve volunteers who do not like to solicit contributions directly.

On the negative side, special events may produce smaller than expected profits, consume considerable amounts of volunteer and staff time and energy, and often distract nonprofit organizations and potential donors from other, more fruitful fund-raising efforts. *See also* FUND-RAISING.

special fund   Any fund other than the general fund.

special instructional spaces Instructional spaces, designed or provided with special built-in equipment, for specialized learning activities, e.g., kindergarten rooms, laboratories, and shops.

special interest group   A group that has common interests, such as consumers, parents of people with developmental disabilities, or people concerned about environmental conservancy. Special interest groups attempt to influence how legislators pass laws and how government administrators interpret and administer laws.

special physical health problems A term referring to pupils identified by professionally qualified personnel as having less than the usual amount of strength, energy, and endurance and hence as needing appropriate modifications in their educational program. Such a condition might result from chronic illness, emotional disturbance, or environmental causes—for example, diabetes, cardiac disease, grief reaction, epilepsy, and lead poisoning. *See also* PHYSICAL HANDICAP.

special programs   Instructional activities primarily designed to deal with pupil exceptionalities. The special program service area includes preprimary, elementary, and secondary services for students who are: (1) gifted and talented; (2) mentally retarded; (3) physically handicapped; (4) socially and/or emotionally handicapped; (5) culturally disadvantaged; and (6) learning disabled.

special purpose district   An area designated by a state or local government to develop and operate facilities and services for a particular need or activity. Examples of special purpose districts are those for parks, water, fire prevention, soil conservation, or vocational education.

special purpose groups　*See* SPE-
CIAL INTEREST GROUP.

special revenue fund　A fund
used to account for money appropriated
or granted for special purposes. Uses
and limitations are specified by the legal
authority establishing the fund; generally, the resources of this fund cannot be
diverted to other uses.

special school　*See* SCHOOL FOR
EXCEPTIONAL CHILDREN.

special student　A status assigned
to a student at a college or university,
allowing him or her to take courses for
credit when they have not enrolled in a
degree program.

special student services record
Confidential information originating as
reports written by personnel employed
by the local education agency for the express use of other professionals within
the agency, including systematically
gathered teacher or counselor observations, verified reports of serious or
recurrent behavior problems, and
selected health data. (Normally, special
student services records are maintained
separately from the cumulative student
record.) *See also* CUMULATIVE STUDENT
RECORD *and* CONFIDENTIAL REPORTS
FROM OUTSIDE AGENCIES.

special youth project　1. A
generic term to identify any project
designed to meet the exceptional needs
of any category of youth. 2. A project
providing guidance, counseling, testing,
basic education, basic work skills, social
adjustment, occupational training, or
other appropriate instruction or services
to meet the special or unique needs of
youths, 16 years of age or older. One
category of youth is those who, because
of inadequate educational background
and work preparation, are unable to
qualify for and obtain employment
without such training or education.

specialized school　Usually a
secondary school that offers a particular
type of curriculum or program, such as a
fine arts school or vocational school.
See David A. Sabatino and August J.
Mauser, *Specialized Education in
Today's Secondary Schools* (Boston:
Allyn and Bacon, 1978).

specific learning disabilities
Defined in P.L. 94-142, the Education
for All Handicapped Children Act of
1975, as children

> who have a disorder in one or more
> of the basic psychological processes
> involved in understanding or in using
> language, spoken or written, which
> disorder may manifest itself in im-
> perfect ability to listen, think, speak,
> read, write, spell or do mathematical
> calculations. Such disorders include
> such conditions as perceptual hand-
> icaps, brain injury, minimal brain
> dysfunction, dyslexia, and de-
> velopmental aphasia. Such term
> does not include children who have
> learning problems which are primari-
> ly the result of visual, hearing, or
> motor handicaps, of mental retarda-
> tion, of emotional disturbance, or of
> environmental, cultural or economic
> disadvantage.

This handicapping condition is
defined in the law with much greater
specificity than any other of the conditions included in the definition of
"handicapped children" because of the
relative ambiguity of the concept and
because of concern by the writers of the
legislation about distortion of the legislative intent.
See Daniel P. Hallahan and William
M. Cruickshank, *Psychoeducational
Foundations of Learning Disabilities*
(Englewood Cliffs, N.J.: Prentice Hall,
1973); S.A. Kirk and W.D. Kirk,
*Psycholinguistic Learning Disabilities:
Diagnosis and Remediation* (Urbana:
University of Illinois Press, 1971); and

Daniel P. Hallahan, James M. Kaufmann, and John W. Lloyd, *Introduction to Learning Disabilities*, 2nd ed. (Englewood Cliffs, N.J.: Prentice-Hall, 1985).

speech discrimination test   A standardized test to measure ability to discriminate among speech sounds, with (or without) the use of hearing aids.

speech and hearing specialist A professional staff member performing such specialized activities as assisting in the identification of speech and hearing handicaps of children; planning and conducting special programs and services for speech and hearing handicapped children (exclusive of students who are deaf); counseling school personnel, parents, and children concerning problems related to speech and hearing impairment; and cooperating with persons in related disciplines and community services.

speech impaired   Individuals with an impairment in speech and/or language (including impaired articulation, stuttering, voice impairment, and a receptive or expressive verbal language handicap). In order to qualify for special education services under P.L. 94-142 in the category of "speech impaired," the impairment must be sufficiently severe to adversely affect the individual's performance in the usual school program. Where used for reporting purposes, the term "speech impaired" often encompasses both the speech handicapped and the language handicapped. *See also* COMMUNICATION DISORDER.

speech pathologist   A specialist in communicative disorders, including the scientific study and management of speech, hearing, and language disabilities. The typical responsibilities of the speech pathologist are of a clinical nature, which involves diagnostic,

evaluative, and therapeutic activities in the area of speech disabilities. In a school setting the speech pathologist may consult with classroom teachers or may provide direct instructional or therapeutic services to students in areas related to communication.

speech pathology and audiology services   Activities that have as their purpose the identification, assessment, and treatment of pupils with impairments in speech, hearing, and language.

speech pathology services Activities organized for the identification of pupils with speech and language disorders; diagnosis and appraisal of specific speech and language disorders; referral for medical or other professional attention necessary to the habilitation of speech and language disorders; provision of required speech habilitation services; and counseling and guidance of pupils, parents, and teachers, as appropriate.

speech reading   Also lipreading. 1. The reception and comprehension of spoken language by careful observation of the movements of the speaker's lips, tongue, and other muscles around the mouth. 2. A method of receptive language comprehension used by deaf and hard-of-hearing students who are taught by an oral approach. 3. A technique used by hearing impaired individuals to assist them in understanding spoken language.

speech reception threshold The lowest intensity level at which an individual can understand familiar and easily discernible words. Used in a typical battery of hearing tests.

speed reading   Gaining meaning from written material at a rate of up to four times the average reading rate (up to 1,000 to 1,200 words per minute as compared to an average rate of 250 to 300 words per minute). Almost all students can increase their reading rate to some degree with the benefit of specific reading exercises.

speed test　A term loosely applied to any test that few can complete within the allotted time or, more technically, a test consisting of a large number of relatively easy items so that a high score depends on how fast an examinee can work within a time limit.

speededness　The appropriateness of a test in terms of the length of time allotted. For most purposes, a good test will make full use of the examination period but not be so speeded that an examinee's rate of work will have an undue influence on the score received.

spelling　Also ORTHOGRAPHY. Instruction designed to teach students to write words using the correct letters in the appropriate sequence. The first publication to reference standardized spelling in the United States was Noah Webster's *An American Dictionary of the English Language*, in 1828.

spelling bee　A school contest where students compete in their ability to spell words aloud. Words are presented in increasing difficulty, with contestants being eliminated whenever a word is misspelled, until only one student, the winner, remains.

spelling demons　Refers to words that are difficult to learn to spell correctly because of silent letters, phonemic irregularities, and exceptionalities to general spelling rules. Approximately three percent of English words are said to be spelling demons.

spillover effects/externalities Benefits or costs that accrue to parties other than the buyer of a good or service. For the most part, the benefits of private goods and services devolve

exclusively upon the buyer (for example, new clothes or a television set). In the case of public goods, however, the benefit or cost usually spills over onto third parties. A new public school, for example, not only benefits its users but also spills over onto the population at large, in both positive and negative ways. Benefits might include a rise in residential property values and the attraction of new businesses, while costs might include noise pollution and traffic congestion.

See E.J. Mishan, "The Postwar Literature on Externalities: An Interpretive Essay," *Journal of Economic Literature* (March 1971).

spina bifida　A congenital disorder, involving damage to the spinal cord and nervous system, that results in some degree of physical paralysis and that may affect learning.

spiral curriculum　A concept credited to Jerome S. Bruner that involves the presentation of the same curricular content, repeatedly and at increasing levels of complexity, as a student progresses longitudinally through school and rises to an ever-expanding level of mastery by building on ideas previously learned.

See Jerome S. Bruner, *The Process of Education* (Cambridge, Mass.: Harvard University Press, 1962).

spiral-omnibus test　A test in which the various kinds of tasks are distributed throughout the test (instead of being grouped together) and are in cycles of increasing difficulty. There is only one timing and one score for such a test.

spirit duplication　A previously popular method for producing multiple copies of materials in schools using a master copy imprinted with a dye that can be transferred to other sheets of paper. Commonly, and incorrectly, called "Ditto," which is a brand name for spirit duplicating materials.

split-half reliability/correlation A measure of the reliability of a test obtained by correlating scores on one half of a test with scores on the other half and correcting for the reduced size.

Spock, Benjamin (1903-1987) A widely-read U.S. pediatrician whose books on baby care and child rearing had a marked influence on child raising practices throughout the mid-20th century. Spock is largely credited (or blamed) for the so-called permissive trend in disciplining children.

sponsor (for overseas dependents' schools of the U.S. Department of Defense) The member of the U.S. Department of Defense (military or civilian) having parental or guardianship responsibility for the student, or having assumed legal responsibility for the student while in the dependents' school.

Sputnik I The first man-made satellite to orbit the Earth. It was launched by the Russians in 1957 and created a strong proliferation of new projects and curricula in the maths and sciences in the U.S. as Americans became concerned that they were falling behind in the "space race." Sputnik I is often credited for the passage of the National Defense Education Act (NDEA) in 1958.

SQ3R Survey, question, read, recite, and review—a study technique to facilitate memorization of written material.

stabilized bond A bond that has its principal or interest adjusted to reflect changes in inflation or deflation as indicated by an index.

stadium A permanent structure consisting of one or more units with tiers of seats for spectators at athletic contests.

staff Those non-teaching employees of a school or school district whose responsibilities and authority are generally limited to their area of specialization.

staff, chief of 1. The military title for the officer who supervises the work of all of the other officers on a commander's staff. 2. A civilian supervisor of an overall management team who reports directly to the chief executive officer.

staff, personal Those members of an organization who report directly to an executive rather than through an intermediary, such as a chief of staff. Personal staff members could be relatively low-level, such as secretaries or chauffeurs, or high-level technical experts.

staff assignment workload Data about the factors used in measuring a staff member's efforts in fulfilling an assignment, including the type of activity, the unit of work, and the time involved in the task. These data elements are used in making decisions regarding the number of staff members needed for a particular task or job; e.g., the number of counselors needed for elementary pupils, the number of teacher aides needed for elementary pupils, the number of teacher aides needed in a particular program area, or the number of painters needed to keep facilities protected from weather.

staff balance 1. The achievement of representativeness on staff with regard to race, sex, age, and ethnicity. 2. Attention to equity in work load among staff. 3. Balancing areas of strength/weakness, competence/incompetence among staff to reduce or eliminate major areas of deficiency within the organization.

staff development   Any activity that promotes the personal and/or professional growth of teachers or other instructional staff. For a review of several approaches to staff development, *see Staff Development*, edited by Gary S. Griffin (Chicago: University of Chicago Press, 1983).

staff member   A person whose relationship with the local education agency meets the following criteria: (a) he or she performs activities or provides services for the local education agency (LEA) that are under the direction or control of the agency's governing authority; (b) he or she is compensated for such services by the LEA and is considered an employee for the purpose of workmen's compensation coverage, the Federal Insurance Contribution Act (FICA), and wage or salary tax withholdings. (Or the person performs such services on a volunteer, uncompensated basis. The LEA should collect the same data—depending upon the assignment—about every employee, whether paid or unpaid.)

staff member-student ratio   A fraction obtained by dividing the number of students in membership by the number representing the full-time equivalency of staff members involved in any particular activity or group of activities as of a particular date.

staff principle   The principle of administration that states that the executive should be assisted by officers who are not in the line of operation but are essentially extensions of the personality of the executive and whose duties consist primarily of assisting the executive in controlling and coordinating the organization and, secondarily, of offering advice.

staff relations and negotiation services   Activities concerned with staff relations system-wide and the responsibilities for contractual negotiations with both instructional and noninstructional personnel.

staff retention rate   The rate, expressed as a percentage, at which employees of a school district remain employed from one period of time to the next, such as from year to year.

staff separation rate   The rate, expressed as a percentage, at which employees leave the employment of a school district during a period of time, usually a year.

staff services   The activities concerned with recruiting, accounting, placing, transferring, and training staff employed by a school district.

staffing   1. This term can specifically refer to requirements under the Education for All Handicapped Children Act of 1975 (P.L. 94-142) as a significant part of the process for developing a handicapped student's Individual Educational Program (IEP). The staffing is a meeting attended by (according to the law) "a representative of the local educational agency or intermediate educational unit . . . qualified to provide, or supervise the provision of, specially designed instruction to meet the unique needs of handicapped children, the teacher, the parents or guardian of such child, and, whenever appropriate, such child" plus any professionals who have participated in the evaluation of the student and who have important information to contribute to the development of the student's IEP. 2. In personnel administration, the recruiting, selecting, and hiring of staff.

staggered sessions   See EX-TENDED DAY SESSION.

standard American English
The written and spoken English that is predominantly used by well-educated persons in the United States without obvious regional or sociological dialects. Includes many details of correct grammar, pronunciation, and syntax.

standard deviation   A measure of the variability of a distribution about its mean or average. In distributions of test scores, for example, a small standard deviation would indicate a tendency of scores to cluster about the mean; a large standard deviation would indicate a wide variation in scores. In a normal distribution, approximately 68 percent of the cases lie between $+1$ S.D. and -1 S.D. from the mean and approximately 96 percent of the cases between $+2$ S.D. and -2 S.D. from the mean.

standard error of the mean   A statistical term referring to the standard deviation of the means of a number of sample sets.

standard error of measurement
Number expressed in score units that serves as another index of test reliability. It can be interpreted as indicating the probability that if an error in measurement of a test is 20 points, there are approximately two chances out of three that an individual's "true score" will be within ± 20 points of his or her "obtained score" on the test. Similarly, the chances are approximately 96 out of 100 that his or her "true score" will be within $+$ or $-$ 40 points of his or her "obtained score."

standard metropolitan statistical area (SMSA)   A term used by the Bureau of the Census to designate large urban areas. The primary criteria include: (a) a county containing a central city of 50,000 or more people or twin cities with a combined population in excess of 50,000; (b) the possible inclusion of additional contiguous counties, if they are functionally integrated with the central county. Such counties may be across state lines from the state containing the central county.

Standard & Poor Corporation
Major publisher of financial information that is best known for its ratings of bonds and other securities.

standard routing patterns
School bus routes established on the basis of student residence distribution and the street pattern for regular schoolday pick-up and return.

standard score   A score that is adjusted to be expressed relative to standard deviations from an arbitrarily established mean. Standard scores are used in psychological testing so that a performance on one test can be compared to another. The most commonly used standard score has a mean of 50 and a standard deviation of 10.

standardization   The specification of consistent procedures to be followed in administering, scoring, and interpreting tests.

standardized test   A test composed of a systematic sampling of behavior, having data on reliability and validity, and administered and scored according to specific instructions, and capable of being interpreted in terms of adequate norms for a given population.

standing committee   A relatively permanent group of individuals with a specified purpose who meet on a regular basis year after year.

Stanford Achievement Tests   A norm-referenced and criterion-referenced test that measures skill development in vocabulary, reading comprehension, mathematics, spelling, language, social studies, and science.

There are six levels, which cover grades one to nine. It is published by:

The Psychological Corporation
555 Academic Court
San Antonio, TX 78204

Stanford Diagnostic Mathematics Test and Stanford Diagnostic Reading Test   Diagnostic tests that measure specific skill development, strengths, and weaknesses in mathematics and reading for all grade levels. The tests are published by:

The Psychological Corporation
555 Academic Court
San Antonio, TX 78204

Stanford-Binet Intelligence Scale   A commonly used, individually-administered test of general intelligence that has been standardized for individuals from age two years to adult. Performance on the test is highly dependent on verbal and language abilities. It is published by:

Houghton Mifflin Company
Test Editorial Offices
P.O. Box 1970
Iowa City, IA 52240

stanine   A normal distribution curve divided into nine intervals and resulting in a standard score measurement. Stanine is a derivation of "standard nine."

state aid for education   1. Any grant made by a state government for the support of local public education. 2. General financing provided by states to local school districts for the support of public education.

state board of education   The legally constituted body having the major responsibility for the general supervision of elementary and secondary education in a state. This board is usually responsible for the state department of education and may also have total or partial responsibility for the supervision of higher education.

state department of education   A governmental agency, composed of the chief executive officer (chief state school officer) and staff, that exists to conduct the work delegated to it by law. The department is usually under the supervision of the state board of education.

state education agency (SEA)   The organization established by law for the primary purpose of carrying out at least a part of the educational responsibilities of the state. It is characterized by having statewide jurisdiction and may be composed of a state board, chief executive officer, and staff. Some state education agencies may lack one or two of these elements, but in any case there must be either a board or a chief executive officer. The term "commission" is sometimes used synonymously with "board." The chief state school officer may be designated as "commissioner" or "superintendent" or have another title.

state education authority   An organized and officially constituted group of individuals or an individual responsible for policy decisions related to constitutional and legislative provisions pertinent to education in the state.

state and federal relations services   Activities associated with developing and maintaining good relationships with state and federal officials.

state operated   A term applying to any program, school, or other facility or institution operated by a state agency.

state plan   A written document, prepared by the state education agency for the U.S. Department of Education, that describes how the state intends to distribute federal funds that are allocated for educational programs.

state superintendent   *See* CHIEF STATE SCHOOL OFFICER.

state system of education   The system that encompasses all educational activities within a state.

state vocational education plan   A written description of a state's vocational education programs submitted to and approved by the U.S. Department of Education as a condition for the allotment of federal funds. It sets forth the state's authority under state law for its administration of such programs and includes the policies to be followed by the state in maintaining, extending, and improving existing vocational education programs, and in developing new programs.

statements, financial   *See* FINANCIAL STATEMENTS.

static equilibrium   A term from systems theory that refers to an organization that tends to remain constant despite changes in its environmental context.

statistical analysis services   Activities concerned with determining the nature and relationships of data elements in order to arrive at conclusions and recommendations. This data element includes institutional, management, and program studies on such topics as cost/effectiveness, space utilization, and teaching load.

statistical inference   The use of information observed in a sample to make predictions about a larger population.

statistical quality control   Also called process quality control. The use of statistical and other mathematical problem-solving techniques to maintain the quality of an operation; for example, screening applications for services or benefit eligibility or ensuring that clients are receiving adequate services. Statistical quality control uses acceptance sampling to determine whether a batch of finished products (i.e., services rendered or things made) meets pre-established quality standards. Using statistical techniques, a random sample is taken from the batch, and the sample is inspected. From this analysis, an inference is made about the quality of the entire batch. *See* Ellis R. Ott, *Process Quality Control* (New York: McGraw-Hill, 1975).

statistical services   Services concerned with collecting, organizing, summarizing, analyzing, and disseminating educational data pertinent to various educational interests, including pupils, staff, instruction, facilities, and finance.

statistical significance   *See* SIGNIFICANCE.

statistical validation   Also called criterion related validation. Validation that involves definition of what is to be measured (the thing being measured is called the criterion) by some systematic method based upon observations of the job behavior of individuals. Possible measures of the knowledge, skills, abilities, and other employee characteristics are then obtained for individuals. Through statistical means, the strength of the relationship between the criterion and the measures is evaluated (validity).

If the criterion has been defined rationally through a careful empirical analysis of job duties, the job-relatedness of the appraisal procedure is considered to be present. If the criterion has not been defined in this way, job-relatedness is inferred but is not assured. *See also* VALIDATION *and* VALIDITY.

statistician   A professional staff member employed in the area of statistical services; an expert or specialist in statistics; a person who assembles, classifies, and tabulates statistical data.

statistics   1. Any gathered numerical data and any of the processes of analyzing and of making inferences from the data. While there are innumerable works on the collection and interpretation of statistics, the classic work on statistical presentation is Darrely Huff's *How to Lie With Statistics* (New York: W.W. Norton, 1954). This work is valuable for those who would lie, those who would not, and those who would not like to be lied to. 2. Colloquially, any numbers that support one's beliefs.

status   One's position in an organization or social structure, which influences relationships, credibility, and power within the system.

status leader   The official leader of an organization or group, whose leadership is associated with an assigned role, such as building principal or school superintendent, rather than a natural tendency to attract followers.

Steiner, Rudolph (1861-1925) The Austrian philosopher who developed an educational approach, called the Waldorf Method, that has been adopted in many private schools in Western Europe and the U.S. The method emphasizes affective and values education in addition to traditional academics. *See* Mary Caroline Richards, *Towards Wholeness: Rudolph Steiner Education in America* (Middletown, Conn.: Wesleyan University Press, 1980).

stenography   *See* SHORTHAND.

stereoscope   A device for measuring visual acuity, stereopsis, visual fusion, color vision, and other kinds of visual functioning.

steward   Also called shop steward and union steward. A local union's most immediate representative in a plant or department. Usually elected by fellow employees (but sometimes appointed by the union leadership), the shop steward handles grievances, collects dues, solicits new members, etc. A shop steward usually continues to work at his or her regular job and handles union matters on a part-time basis, frequently on the employer's time.
   See Allan N. Nash, *The Union Steward: Duties, Rights, and Status*, 2nd ed. (Ithaca: New York State School of Industrial and Labor Relations, Cornell University, 1983).

stimulus   Any event that occurs from outside or inside the organism and elicits a response.

stimulus discrimination   From behavioral theory, being able to distinguish between two different, though similar, stimuli so that a behavior learned in response to one stimulus does not occur in the presence of the other. For example, a student responds to a routine class-changing bell differently than he or she responds to a fire alarm.

stimulus generalization   From behavioral theory, responding to a new stimulus in the same way that one has learned to respond to a different but similar stimulus. For example, a student of driver education will respond to all stop signs in the same way even though they may be at different locations and of slightly different configurations.

stimulus-response theory   A concept central to the field of behavioral psychology that assumes that all behaviors occur in response to specific stimuli and that all learning occurs as a function of a basic stimulus-response paradigm.

stipend   Financial assistance for living expenses provided to a college student.

store front schools   *See* STREET ACADEMICS.

stores   1. Refers to a central warehouse that maintains routine supplies and materials that can be requisitioned by authorized school personnel. 2. In computer terminology the receiving and retention of data by the computer.

story telling   1. The spoken recitation of stories by a teacher or librarian as a part of a language arts curriculum in school. 2. The art of narrating stories. *See* Nancy E. Briggs and Joseph A. Wagner, *Children's Literature Through Storytelling and Drama*, 2nd ed. (Dubuque, Iowa: Wm. C. Brown, 1979).

strategic planning   Long-range, comprehensive, integrated, overall organizational planning that has three dimensions: the identification and examination of future opportunities, threats, and consequences; the process of analyzing an organization's environment (including the internal as well as external environments) and developing compatible objectives along with strategies and policies capable of achieving those objectives; and the integration of the various elements of organizational planning into an overall structure of plans so that each unit of the organization knows in advance what must be done, when, and by whom. *See also* PLANNING.

For a discussion of strategic planning in relation to schools and for extensive bibliographic references, *see* David Crandall, Jeffrey Eiseman, and Karen Louis, "Strategic Planning Issues That Bear on the Success of School Improvement Plans," *Educational Administration Quarterly* (Summer 1986).

strategy   A planned means to achieve change.

streaming   Also TRACKING; grouping students according to ability levels.

street academics   Private, alternative, community-based schools that developed in the 1960s to address the needs of inner-city youth who had dropped out of traditional schools. These schools were primarily college preparatory in nature and were the forerunners of many alternative education programs that have subsequently been offered by public school systems. Also called STORE FRONT SCHOOLS.

strephosymbolia   Jargon for a problem in visual perception that creates difficulty in reading. Specifically it refers to difficulty in distinguishing letters that are similar in configuration or which are "mirror images" of each other (e.g., b and d). Literally, "twisted symbols."

stress   A psychological and/or physiological response to threatening or overly demanding situations. Compare to TEACHER BURN-OUT. *See* James H. Humphrey and Joy N. Humphrey, *Controlling Stress in Children* (Springfield, Ill.: Charles C. Thomas, 1985).

strike   A mutual agreement among workers (whether members of a union or not) to a temporary work stoppage in order to obtain or resist a change in their working conditions. The term is thought to have nautical origins, because sailors would stop work by striking or taking down their sails. A strike or potential strike is considered an essential element of the collective bargaining process. Many labor leaders would claim that collective bargaining can never be more than a charade without the right to strike. Major strikes have been declining in frequency in recent years as unions in both the public and private sectors have, respectively, lost a large measure of economic clout and political support.

strike authorization   Also called STRIKE VOTE. A formal vote by union members that (if passed) invests the union leadership with the right to call a strike without additional consultation with the union membership.

stroke   In transactional analysis, any behavior that gives positive recognition to another person.

Strong Vocational Interest Blank Or Strong-Campbell Interest Inventory. A paper and pencil test that surveys potential aptitude for a number of occupations (a total of 124) by comparing the test taker's general interests with those of people employed in the various occupations. The test is intended for students in grades 11 and 12. It is published by:

Consulting Psychologists Press, Inc.
577 College Avenue
Palo Alto, CA 94306

structural analysis   In linguistics, the study of the meaning of words by examining their various components, such as root, suffix, word family, or derivation.

structural grammar   A method of studying grammar that focuses on its observable form.

structured role playing   Role-play exercise or simulation in which the players receive oral or written instruction giving them cues as to their roles.

student   An individual for whom instruction is provided in an educational program under the jurisdiction of a school, school system, or other educational institution. Properly used, "pupil"

refers to a student at the elementary level; the term "student" is used to include individuals at all instructional levels. A student may receive instruction in a school facility or in another location, such as at home, in a residential facility, or in a hospital. Instruction may be provided by direct student-teacher interaction or by some other approved medium such as television, radio, telephone, or correspondence.

student accounting   A system for collecting, computing, and reporting information about students.

student activity fund   An account for financial transactions related to student body activities, such as organization membership fees or admission fees for special events.

student body activities   Cocurricular activities for students—such as entertainment, publications, and clubs—that are managed or operated by students under the guidance or supervision of staff members. See also COCURRICULAR ACTIVITIES.

student capacity of a school plant The membership that can be accommodated in the classrooms and other instruction areas of a given school plant for the school day according to existing state-approved standards, exclusive of multiple sessions.

student code   Rules and regulations regarding student behavior. Also called code of behavior or CODE OF ETHICS.

student commons area   An area designed or adapted for use by students, for activities such as relaxation, lounging, unsupervised reading, and purchasing of supplies and refreshments.

student council   An elected body of students, usually in secondary schools, who represent the student body as a whole in participating, in an advisory capacity, with the administration of the school.

student descriptive form A standard form published by the National Association of Secondary School Principals that can be used by secondary school teachers to rate students on such factors as class participation, independent study, questioning skills, and responsibility.

student descriptive questionnaire A questionnaire provided as an optional part of the College Board Admissions Testing Programs; it offers additional personal and demographic information to colleges about applicants for admission.

student development programs The integration of a number of student services offered on postsecondary campuses to enhance the total educational experience of the students. Components include counseling, health services, student activities and government, housing, and social opportunites.

student financial aid A general term that refers to programs offered by institutions of higher education to help students to meet educational expenses. Includes grants, loans, work-study programs, scholarships, fellowships, and stipends. For a perspective on student aid, *see* Joseph M. Cronin, "Student Financial Aid: An International Perspective," *Phi Delta Kappan* (May 1986).

student handbook A manual that gives information about the school to new students. Some state boards of education require that every student be issued a student handbook as a type of contract of expectation between the school and the student.

student I.D. card An identification card issued to students by the school to prove that an individual is officially enrolled in the school and therefore eligible for privileges offered to students, such as borrowing from the library collection, or receiving discounts on meals, special events etc. I.D. cards commonly include the student's full name, student number, and a photograph of the student.

Student NEA The student affiliate of the National Education Association; it provides organizational opportunities for teachers-in-training at colleges and universities.

student number The number assigned to a student for identification and recordkeeping purposes. Normally only one number need be used for identification.

student organization 1. An organized group of students who, by virtue of having completed a designated number of grades or school years, pursues common goals and objectives. Such organizations include the senior, junior, sophomore, and freshman classes, and the elementary school grades. They are managed and operated by students under the guidance or supervision of appropriate staff members. 2. An organized group of students having as its main objective the furtherance of a common interest. Such organizations include social, hobby, instructional, recreational, athletic, honor, dramatic, musical, and similar clubs and societies, which, with the approval of appropriate school authorities, are managed and operated by the students under the guidance or supervision of qualified adults. 3. A group of students organized into a single body for the purpose of pursuing common goals and objectives.

student personnel services *See* PUPIL PERSONNEL SERVICES.

student record   Information about one or more students that is kept on file for a period of time in a classroom, school office, system office, or other approved location. A student record usually is intended for the use of the person or office that maintains the record. *See also* CUMULATIVE STUDENT RECORD *and* PERMANENT STUDENT RECORD.

student rights   A legal phrase referring to the constitutional rights of students enrolled in public or private educational institutions at the elementary, secondary, and postsecondary levels. *See* Eve Cary, *What Every Teacher Should Know About Student Rights* (Washington, D.C.: National Education Association, 1975).

students per acre   The average daily membership of a school divided by the total number of developed and undeveloped acres in the school site.

student teaching   Teaching under the supervision of a certified teacher as part of a formalized higher education program of teacher preparation. *See* Carol K. Tittle, *Student Teaching: Attitude and Research Bases for Change in School and University* (Metuchen, N.J.: Scarecrow Press, 1974).

student-administrative staff ratio (as of a given date)   The number of students in membership, as of a given date, divided by the number representing the total full-time equivalency of principal assignments, assistant principal assignments, central administrative staff assignments (including area administrators and their staffs), and assignments for supervising, managing, and directing academic departments in the schools serving these students on the same date.

student-counselor ratio (as of a given date)   The number of students in membership, as of a given date, divided by the number representing the total full-time equivalency of counseling assignments serving these students on the same date.

student-counselor ratio (for a period of time)   The average daily membership of students, for a given period of time, divided by the number representing the total full-time equivalency of counseling assignments serving these students during the same period.

student-instructional staff ratio (for a period of time)   The average daily membership of students, for a given period of time, divided by the number representing the total full-time equivalency of teaching assignments, teaching assistant assignments, teaching intern assignments, teacher aide assignments, and student teaching assignments serving these students during the same period. *See also* STUDENT-PROFESSIONAL EDUCATIONAL STAFF RATIO *and* STUDENT-TEACHER RATIO.

student-library services staff ratio (as of a given date)   The number of students in membership, as of a given date, divided by the number representing the total full-time equivalency of library services staff assignments serving these students on the same date.

student-professional educational staff ratio (as of a given date)   The number of students in membership in a school system, as of a given date, divided by the number representing the total full-time equivalency of all professional educational assignments in the school system on the same date.

student-professional educational staff ratio (for a period of time)   The average daily membership of students, for a given period of time, divided by the number representing the total full-time equivalency of all professional educational assignments in the school system during the same period.

student-psychologist ratio (as of a given date)   The number of students in membership in a school system, as of a given date, divided by the number representing the total full-time equivalency of psychologist assignments serving these students on the same date.

student-psychologist ratio (for a period of time)   The average daily membership of students for a given period time, divided by the number representing the total full-time equivalency of psychologist assignments serving these students during the same period.

student-school administrator ratio (as of a given date)   The number of students in membership, as of a given date, divided by the number representing the total full-time equivalency of principal assignments, assistant principal assignments, and assignments for supervising, managing, and directing academic departments in the school(s) serving these students on the same date.

student-school administrator ratio (for a period of time)   The average daily membership of students, for a period of time, divided by the number representing the total full-time equivalency of principal assignments, assistant principal assignments, and assignments for supervising, managing, and directing academic departments in the school(s) serving these students during the same period.

student-social worker ratio (as of a given date)   The number of students in membership in a school system, as of a given date, divided by the number representing the total full-time equivalency of social worker assignments serving these students on the same date.

student-social worker ratio (for a period of time)   The average daily membership of students, for a period of time, divided by the number representing the total full-time equivalency of social worker assignments serving these students during the same period.

student-teacher ratio (as of a given date)   The number of students in membership, as of a given date, divided by the number representing the total full-time equivalency of teaching assignments serving these students on the same date.

student-teacher ratio (for a period of time)   The average daily membership of students, for a given period of time, divided by the number representing the total full-time equivalency of teaching assignments serving these students during the same period.

student-total staff ratio (as of a given date)   The number of students in membership in a school system, as of a given date, divided by the number representing the total full-time equivalency of all staff assignments in the school system on the same date.

student-total staff ratio (for a period of time)   The average daily membership of students in a school system, for a given period of time, divided by the number representing the total full-time equivalency of all staff assignments in the school system during the same period.

study abroad programs   Any of a variety of programs that offer the opportunity for students to travel to a foreign country for the purpose of studying for a period of time and earning credit at the American college or university where they are enrolled.

study hall An instruction area designed or adapted for housing a group of students engaged in individual, informal study of the lessons or assignments received in regular or special classrooms.

study skills Specific skills that students can be taught to assist them in learning curricular content, such as note taking, organization, test taking, or library use.

study tours Short-term, educationally oriented trips to other areas of the country or world; involving groups of students under the supervision of an instructor.

stuttering Speech often characterized by unusual strain or tension, and by one or more of the following: repetition, blocking, injection of superfluous speech elements, and/or prolongation of sounds or syllables. ("Stuttering" generally is used synonymously with "stammering," except by some specialists who designate speech repetitions as stuttering and speech blocks or stoppages as stammering.)

subject 1. An organized body of knowledge that may be more comprehensive than a course but is less comprehensive than a subject-matter area. 2. An individual involved (from a recipient's perspective) in an experimental design, research study, or other evaluative process.

subject matter A body of facts, understandings, processes, skills, values, and appreciations related to a specific aspect of human activity and experience. Subject matter includes the accumulated knowledge, skills, appreciations, and attitudes comprising the substance of any subject-matter area.

subject-centered curriculum A traditional approach to organizing curriculum around the content of subject areas (e.g., math, science, or georgraphy) without specific regard for the educational/learning process or the priorities of the students.

subjective test A test that is graded on the basis of professional judgment. Contrast with OBJECTIVE TEST.

subject-matter area A grouping of related subjects or units of subject matter under a heading such as English (language arts), foreign languages, art, music, natural sciences, industrial arts, home economics, agriculture, business, physical education, and trades and industrial occupations.

subsidiary accounts Related accounts that support in detail the summaries recorded in a controlling account.

subsidiary journal A journal in which are recorded transactions of like nature. For example, a cash journal is a commonly used journal; in it are recorded all cash transactions. *See also* JOURNAL.

subsidiary ledger A ledger used when more detail is needed on accounts than can be provided in a general ledger. For example, an accounts receivable subsidiary ledger would show each individual who owes money to the organization. In contrast, a general ledger accounts receivable total would include only the total of the accounts receivable subsidiary accounts—or the total amount owed by all individuals. *See also* ACCOUNTING CYCLE *and* GENERAL LEDGER.

substitute   A general term used in reference to an individual who is assigned to take the place of a staff member who is temporarily absent. It is usually used in a more specific manner to indicate such individuals as substitute teacher, substitute bus driver, and substitute custodian.

subvocalization   In silent reading, when words are formed by the lips (or possibly whispered) without actually speaking the words out loud, as in oral reading.

summa cum laude   "With the greatest praise." Graduating with the highest honors that can be awarded with a degree. Compare to CUM LAUDE and MAGNA CUM LAUDE.

summary account   An account that is used to consolidate items of a broad category.

summative evaluation   Assessing the overall impact or outcome of a program after the program has been fully developed and implemented. In reference to personnel evaluation, an approach that emphasizes the outcome or tangible products of an employee's efforts rather than the efforts themselves. Contrast with FORMATIVE EVALUATION.

summer school   The name usually applied to the school session carried on during the period between the end of the regular school term and the beginning of the next regular school term. Summer school is generally offered in order to provide either enhanced or remedial learning opportunities rather than continuing the regular school curriculum. Contrast with EXTENDED SCHOOL YEAR. See John W. Dougherty, Summer School: A New Look (Bloomington, Ind.: Phi Delta Kappa Educational Foundation, 1981).

summer school tuition   Money received as tuition for students attending summer school classes. Separate accounts may be maintained for tuition received for residents, and for tuition received for nonresidents.

Summerhill   One of the earliest nontraditional school programs, established privately shortly after World War I in England for the education of children with a variety of educational and social problems. The Summerhill program is child-centered and emphasizes the affective aspects of child development. For the founder's description of the program, see A.S. Neill, Summerhill: A Radical Approach to Child Rearing (New York: Pocket Books, 1977).

sunk cost   See COST, SUNK.

sunset legislation   A law that includes a provision to automatically terminate the legislation after a specified period of time.

sunshine bargaining   Also called goldfish-bowl bargaining. Collective bargaining sessions open to the press and public. This process is more likely to be used in public sector negotiations (in response to the assertion that since the spending of public funds is the essence of the negotiations, the negotiating process should be open to public scrutiny).

sunshine laws   Laws that require public agencies, including boards of education and schools, to open their official meetings to the general public and to announce such meetings in advance.

superannuation   A pension.

superintendent assignment   An assignment to a staff member (e.g., chief executive of schools or chancellor) to perform the highest level, systemwide executive management functions of a school district.

superintendent of schools The staff member who is the chief executive officer of a school district or administrative unit.

supervising assignment Directing assignments to staff members and managing a function, a program, or a supporting service. Examples include chairs of academic departments, supervisors of purchasing, directors and managers of psychological services, or area supervisors of instructional services.

supervising principal A school building administrator whose primary role is to perform supervisory and/or administrative tasks. Compare to PRINCIPAL.

supervision 1. Assisting teachers and other professional staff to perform to the best of their abilities through observation, feedback interviews, and general staff development activities. 2. A role of educational leaders to ensure quality services by overseeing the performance of personnel. Supervision in schools can be provided by building principals, district-wide program area specialists, central office personnel, and sometimes the superintendent of schools or assistant superintendent. Supervision generally involves interviewing, hiring, and orientation of staff; staff development; curriculum development; program and staff evaluation; and the acquisition of instructional materials and equipment.

For a practical and positive approach to supervision in education, see Ronald C. Doll, *Supervision for Staff Development: Ideas and Application* (Boston: Allyn and Bacon, 1983).

supervisors of instruction School personnel who have been delegated the responsibility of assisting teachers in improving the learning situation and instructional methods.

Supplemental Educational Opportunity Grants (SEOG) Federal grants intended to help exceptionally needy students complete their undergraduate education.

supplemental readers Books and other reading materials that may be used to augment basic instructional programs in any subject area.

supplementary program 1. Any program or activity that is provided to add to or enhance a basic program. For example, a field trip to the state capital is supplemental to the basic civics curriculum. 2. In vocational education this term refers specifically to a program offered as additional training to persons already employed.

supplies An accounting term that refers to materials that are consumable, expendable, and relatively inexpensive.

support services In general, those activities that provide administrative, technical, and logistical support to a program. "Support services" exist to sustain and enhance the fulfillment of the objectives of other major functions.

support services (business administration) Activities concerned with purchasing, paying, transporting, exchanging, and maintaining goods and services for the school district. The services included, for operating all schools, are fiscal, acquisition of facilities, operation and maintenance, and internal.

support services (central administration) Activities, other than general administration, that support each of the other instructional and support services programs. These activities include planning, research, development, evaluation, information, staff, statistical, and data processing services.

support services (general administration)   Activities concerned with establishing policy, operating schools, and providing the essential facilities and services for the staff and students.

support services (instructional staff)   Activities associated with assisting the instructional staff in the content and process of providing learning experiences for students.

support services (pupils)   Activities that are designed to assess and improve the well-being of pupils and to supplement the teaching process.

support services (school administration)   Activities concerned with overall administrative responsibility for a single school or a group of schools.

supported work or supported employment   A system for placing workers with substantial handicaps into the competitive labor market by providing training, habilitation and rehabilitation services, and necessary assistance at the actual work site. A way of redirecting the use of public dollars, previously spent to maintain sheltered work enterprises and environments, to develop and maintain productive, tax-paying workers within regular work settings. See Robinson G. Hollister, Jr. et al., eds., *The National Supported Work Demonstration* (Madison: University of Wisconsin Press, 1984).

supporting services facility   A piece of land, a building, or part of a building that serves more than one school plant, or is not a part of any given school plant.

Supreme Court Decisions   *See* UNITED STATES REPORTS.

surety   A company or person who insures or guarantees that another person's debt will be paid by accepting liability (responsibility) for the debt when it is made.

surety bond   A written promise to pay damages or to indemnify against losses caused by the party or parties named in the document, through nonperformance or through defalcation; for example, a surety bond given by a contractor or by an official handling cash or securities.

surplus   The excess of the assets of a fund over its liabilities; or, if the fund also has other resources and obligations, the excess of resources over obligations. The term is usually used with a descriptive adjective unless its meaning is apparent from the context.

surplus property   Items, usually equipment, that are no longer required by an organization.

surrogate parent   1. An adult who is appointed to represent the interests of a child in nonlegal proceedings, such as school placement staffings, when the natural parent or legal guardian is unavailable. 2. An adult who provides nurturance and other parental functions to a child on a self-selected or assigned basis when the natural parent is incapable of fulfilling these functions. 3. A woman who specifically conceives and gives birth to a child that others will raise. See Amy Z. Overvold, *Surrogate Parenting* (New York: Pharos, 1988).

surtax   An additional tax, a surcharge, on what has already been taxed; that is, a tax on a tax. For example, if you must pay a $1,000 tax on a $10,000 income (10 percent), a 10 percent surtax would be an additional $100.

survey   *See* PUBLIC OPINION SURVEY.

survey course An introductory course in a subject area that offers a broad overview of the area of study.

survey method Obtaining information for research purposes through interviews, questionnaires, opinion polls, and/or observations of a given population of people.

survival skills Those skills that a person needs in order to function as an adult in natural community environments, including home, work, and recreational and general community facilities.

suspension Temporary dismissal of a student from school by duly authorized school personnel in accordance with established regulations.

Suzuki method An approach to teaching instrumental music to very young children. Originally applied only to violin instruction, the method involves listening, playing, and memorizing music prior to learning sight reading. For additional information contact:
Suzuki Association of the Americas
P.O. Box 354
Muscatine, IA 52761
(319) 263-3071

Swann v. Charlotte-Mecklenburg Board of Education 402 U.S. 1 (1971) The first Supreme Court desegregation decision that required cross-district busing of students to achieve racial balance. *See* Bernard Schwartz, *Swann's Way: The School Busing Case and the Supreme Court* (New York: Oxford University Press, 1986).

sweep-check test An initial-hearing screening test that measures whether an individual can hear a predetermined level of sound at various pitches.

syllabication The division of a word into its component syllables.

syllabus An outline of an academic course that generally includes the main topics to be covered, the required readings, the optional readings, and sometimes a schedule of which topics will be covered in what sequence.

symbolic speech Nonverbal behavior, such as hand movements, facial expressions, wearing certain items of clothing, or body postures that convey meaning. Symbolic speech, as opposed to symbolic actions that may be disruptive or destructive, is generally protected by the First Amendment. For example, the Supreme Court held in *Tinker v. Des Moines School District*, 393 U.S. 503 (1969), that students who wore black armbands to protest the Vietnam War could not be punished because this was a symbolic "silent, passive expression of opinion" that was not disruptive.

symposium An educational opportunity that involves the participation of a number of experts in a particular field of study, each of whom gives a lecture about some aspect of a specific topic.

syndrome A consistent and identifiable combination of symptoms and/or characteristics that signify a specific diagnosable condition.

synergogy An educational approach that involves members of small teams learning from one another as a part of a structured, interactive process; peer-oriented rather than authority-oriented learning. Generally applied to adult education but also used in elementary and secondary schools. For a description and examples of application, *see* Jane Mouton and Robert Blake, *Synergogy* (San Francisco: Jossey-Bass, 1984).

synergy   The effects of the combined efforts of a group endeavor.

syntax   Rules of grammar that have to do with sentence structure and word order.

synthesis   Combining separate ideas or items of information into a single concept or conclusion.

synthesis-level thinking   From BLOOM'S TAXONOMY, a thinking or learning process involving the ability to take a number of pieces of previously learned information and to combine them to create knowledge that is new to the learner. Contrast with KNOWLEDGE-LEVEL, COMPREHENSION-LEVEL, APPLICATION-LEVEL, ANALYSIS-LEVEL, EVALUATION-LEVEL.

system   1. Any organized collection of parts that is united by prescribed interactions and designed for the accomplishment of a specific goal or general purpose. 2. The political process in general. 3. The establishment; the power that equates with governance; the domain of a ruling elite. 4. The BUREAUCRACY.

systems analysis   The methodologically rigorous collection, manipulation, and evaluation of data on social units to determine the best way to improve their functioning and to aid a decisionmaker in selecting a preferred choice among alternatives. The systems school or systems approach views social units as complex sets of dynamically intertwined and interconnected elements, including inputs, processes, outputs, feedback loops, and the environments in which they operate. A change in any element of the system inevitably causes changes in its other elements. The interconnections tend to be complex, dynamic, and often unknown. Norbert Wiener's (1894-1964) classic model of an adaptive system, from his 1948 book *Cybernetics*, epitomizes the basic theoretical perspectives of the systems school. *Cybernetics*, derived from the Greek and meaning steersman, was used by Wiener to mean the multidisciplinary study of the structures and functions of control and information processing systems in animals and machines. The basic concept behind cybernetics is self-regulation— biological, social, or technological systems that can identify problems, do something about them, and then receive feedback to adjust themselves automatically. Wiener, a mathematician, developed the concept of cybernetics while working on anti-aircraft systems during World War II.

See E.S. Quade and W.I. Boucher, eds., *Systems Analysis and Policy Planning* (New York: American Elsevier, 1968); Ida R. Hoos, *Systems Analysis in Public Policy: A Critique* (Berkeley: University of California Press, 1972); and Hugh J. Miser and Edward S. Quade, eds., *Handbook of Systems Analysis* (New York: Elsevier Science Publishing, 1985).

systems theory   A view of organizations that considers the organization as the totality of the individuals that make up the system and their interaction with each other and with the whole. *See* J.G. Miller, *Living Systems* (New York: McGraw-Hill, 1976); and G. Egan and M.A. Cowan, *People in Systems* (Monterey, Calif.: Brooks/Cole, 1979).

systemwide   Activities that extend or apply to all of the schools in a school district or to all of the schools where the activities apply.

systemwide assignment   A full-time or less-than-full-time assignment given to a staff member and consisting of activities that extend or apply to all of the schools in the school system or to all of the schools in the school system at one instructional level where the activities apply.

T

TA *See* TRANSACTIONAL ANALYSIS *and* TECHNICAL ASSISTANCE.

table A legislative or procedural motion to suspend the consideration of a proposal.

table of random numbers A statistical chart of numbers that is used in research to aid in selecting a random sample of subjects.

tabula rasa The theory that the human mind begins at birth as a blank slate on which all subsequent experiences are inscribed; from the Latin.

tachistoscope A device that can be used for reading instruction; it allows for the exposure of single words, letters, or phrases for a limited period of time.

tactile learning Learning through the sense of touch.

talented Individuals identified by professionally qualified personnel as being capable of high performance in one or more areas of special competence. Among these areas of special competence are creativity; leadership ability and social adeptness; and facility in the productive and performing arts.

talking books Books that are recorded for use by persons who are blind. Available from the Library of Congress and from Recordings for the Blind, 20 Rozel Road, Princeton, NJ 08540.

tardiness 1. Absence of a student at the time a given class and/or half-day of attendance begins, provided that the student is in attendance before the close of that class or half-day. 2. Reporting to work or school later than the scheduled time.

target group A group in the population at which programs are aimed or on which programs have a significant impact. *See also* DIFFERENTIATED CURRICULUM.

target population A group of learners for whom a particular instructional program is designed.

TASH *See* ASSOCIATION FOR PERSONS WITH SEVERE HANDICAPS.

task analysis Breaking down a task into its discrete component parts for the purpose of designing an instructional program to teach the task.

task force 1. A temporary grouping of disparate military forces under a single commander to undertake a specific mission. 2. By analogy, a temporary interdisciplinary team within a larger organization charged with accomplishing a specific goal. Task forces are typically used in government when a problem crosses departmental lines. 3. A temporary government commission charged with investigating and reporting upon a problem. 4. Any group or committee organized on a short-term basis for the purpose of accomplishing a particular objective.

TAT *See* THEMATIC APPERCEPTION TEST.

tautology In discourse, a reiterated statement that is equivalent in content to the original statement; for example, "he is a senior in his last year of high school."

tax A compulsory contribution exacted by a government for public purposes. This does not include employee and employer assessments for retirement and social insurance purposes, which are classified as insurance trust revenue.

While it was Benjamin Franklin who in 1789 wrote that "in this world nothing is certain but death and taxes," and Oliver Wendell Holmes who in 1927 wrote that "taxes are what we pay for civilized society," it remained for Margaret Mitchell in *Gone With the Wind* (1936) to observe: "Death and taxes and childbirth! There's never any convenient time for any of them!"

tax, real-property   Any tax on land and its improvements; usually referred to simply as "property tax." This is the mainstay of most local governments (involving school districts); it provides nearly half of the revenues that local governments get from their own sources. To administer a property tax, the tax base must first be defined, i.e., housing and land, automobiles, other assets, whatever. Then an evaluation of the worth of the tax base must be made; this is the assessment. Finally, a tax rate, usually an amount to be paid per $100 value of the tax base, is levied. Since the value of the tax base will appreciate or depreciate substantially over time, continuing assessments must be made.

Arguments for the property tax resemble a good news/bad news joke. The good news is that the property tax provides a stable revenue source and has a good track record as a strong revenue raiser. The bad news is that its stability can also be considered inflexibility, as it does not keep pace with income growth. The good news is that since property is generally unmovable, it is hard to miss and therefore provides a good visible tax base for "relatively unskilled" local tax offices to administer. The bad news is that the administration and assessment of property tax is at best erratic and at worst a horrendous mess. The result is that the property tax base tends to erode over time; that most errors are made undervaluing the property of the wealthy or the politically

influential; that there are higher taxes on new residents; and that older residents are being increasingly pressed to meet property tax burdens.

See David Lowery, "Tax Equity Under Conditions of Fiscal Stress: The Case of the Property Tax," *Publius* (Spring 1984); and Dennis Hale, "The Evolution of the Property Tax: A Study of the Relation between Public Finance and Political Theory," *Journal of Politics* (May 1985).

tax, wage   Any tax on wages and salaries levied by a government. Many cities have wage taxes that have the indirect benefit of forcing suburban commuters to help pay for the services provided to the region by the central city.

tax, withholding   Sums of money that an employer takes out of an employee's pay and turns over to a government as prepayment of the employee's federal, state, or local tax obligations. Compare to forced savings.

tax abatement/tax remission
The relinquishment of a tax that would ordinarily be due. For example, local government might temporarily abate certain property taxes in order to encourage the renovation of substandard housing.

tax anticipation notes   Notes (sometimes called "warrants") issued in anticipation of collection of taxes, usually retirable only from tax collections and frequently only from the tax collections anticipated with their issuance. The proceeds of tax anticipation notes or warrants are treated as current loans if paid back from the tax collections anticipated with the issuance of the notes.

tax assessment and collection
Activities concerned with assigning and recording equitable values to real and personal property, assigning a millage

rate (dollars yield per thousand dollars), and receiving yield in a central office.

tax base   The thing or value on which taxes are levied. Some of the more common tax bases include: individual income, corporate income, real property, wealth, motor vehicles, sales of commodities and services, utilities, events, imports, estates, and gifts. The rate of a tax to be imposed against a given tax base may be either specific or ad valorem. Specific taxes, for example, raise a specific, non-variable amount of revenue from each unit of the tax base (for example, 10 cents per gallon of gasoline). Ad valorem taxes, on the other hand, are expressed as a percentage and the revenue yield varies according to the value of the tax base (for example, a mill levy against real property).

tax exemption   Immunity from taxation by the jurisdiction granting the exemption. This is sometimes temporary, such as a 10-year exemption to encourage new housing in a particular area, or permanent, as in the exemptions enjoyed by most schools and churches. *See* John M. Quigley and Roger W. Schmenner, "Property Tax Exemption and Public Policy," *Public Policy* (Summer 1975).

tax exempts   1. Land, buildings, or businesses that do not pay taxes because of legal exemptions. 2. Investments such as municipal bonds that are tax free. 3. Nonprofit organizations that meet legal requirements for tax exemption.
    See Douglas Laycock, "Tax Exemptions for Racially Discriminatory Religious Schools," *Texas Law Review* (February 1982); and Dean M. Kelley, "The Supreme Court Redefines Tax Exemption," *Society* (May-June 1984).

tax and expenditure limitations
A legally binding limitation imposed by state government for controlling increases in property taxes and school district expenditures.

tax lien   Legally executed charges on a property because of unpaid taxes. It can result in a foreclosure and tax sale; that is, the property can be forcibly sold to pay the back taxes due.

tax liens receivable   Legal claims against property that have been exercised because of nonpayment of delinquent taxes, interest, and penalties receivable up to the date the lien becomes effective (plus the cost of holding the sale).

tax revolt   A nationwide grassroots movement, heralded by California Proposition 13 in 1978, to decrease or limit the rate of increase possible on property taxes. In a sense this was a revolt by the middle class against the rising cost of government services. The "revolt" created a period of fiscal stress for state and local government. The tax revolt, it is important to note, was not over the unfairness or uneven distribution of the tax burden, but over the levels of taxation, especially on real estate, which were increasing dramatically in a period of double-digit inflation. By 1980 the tax revolt movement forced 38 states to reduce or at least stabilize tax rates.
    See David Lowery and Lee Sigelman, "Understanding the Tax Revolt: Eight Explanations," *American Political Science Review* (December 1981); and Lee Sigelman, David Lowery, and Roland Smith, "The Tax Revolt: A Comparative State Analysis," *Western Political Quarterly* (March 1983).

tax yield   The amount of tax that could potentially be collected. Tax collections are the portion of the tax yield that is actually collected.

tax-deferred annuity   An annuity with employee contributions not subject to taxes at the time that the contributions are made. Contributions are taxed later as they are paid out after retirement when the annuitant presumably is in a lower tax bracket.

taxes receivable   The uncollected portion of taxes that a school district or other governmental unit has levied and that has become due, including any interest or penalties that may be accrued. Separate accounts may be maintained on the basis of tax roll year and/or current and delinquent taxes.

tax-exempt status   A determination or ruling granted to an organization that frees it from obligation(s) to pay taxes and also permits donors to deduct contributions made to it. Most usually, tax-exempt status refers to a determination by the federal Internal Revenue Service, but the term also is applicable to tax-exempt status as determined by state and local government units (although they usually follow the IRS's lead).

taxonomy   A type of classification system used in many academic fields, including education. *See*, for example, BLOOM'S TAXONOMY.

Taylor Law   In full, Public Employees' Fair Employment Act. New York State's law governing the unionization of state, county, and municipal employees. It grants all public employees the right to organize and be recognized, provides for a Public Employment Relations Board for the resolution of impasses, prohibits strikes, and provides a schedule of penalties for both striking individuals and their unions. The Taylor Law owes its name to George W. Taylor, a University of Pennsylvania-Wharton School professor, who chaired the Governor's Committee on Public Employee Relations that recommended the enacting legislation in 1966.

teachable moment   An optimal time for learning in terms of student readiness and environmental conditions.

teacher   A person who instructs students. There are presently about 2.5 million elementary and secondary teachers in U.S. public schools. *See* Shirley F. Heck and C. Ray Williams, *The Complex Roles of the Teacher* (New York: Teachers College Press, 1984).

teacher accountability   The assumption that educators (teachers) have some direct responsibility for what students learn in school; a highly controversial topic. *See* David S. Seely, "Reducing the Confrontation over Teacher Accountability," *Phi Delta Kappan* (December 1979). *See* ACCOUNTABILITY.

teacher aide   A person who assists a teacher with routine activities associated with teaching, generally those activities that require minor decisions regarding students, such as monitoring, conducting rote exercises, operating equipment, and clerking. In some situations, especially special education, where the ratio of teacher aides is considerably higher than in regular education, teacher aides may perform more complex, direct instructional activities with students under the direction of the teachers. *See also* TEACHING ASSISTANT.

teacher aide assignment   An assignment to a staff member to perform activities which are not classified as professional educational teaching assignments.

teacher assistance team   A type of BUILDING LEVEL TEAM that focuses on the needs of a teacher who is confronted by a problem student rather than focusing on the needs of the student. The role of the team is to counsel the teacher regarding the environmental management of the classroom and to suggest modifications that will allow the teacher to meet the special needs of the student.

teacher burn-out   A stress reaction to the pressures and routines of a teacher's assignment. May be manifested by physical (fatigue, sleeplessness), psychological (moodiness, irritability), and attitudinal (decreased caring for people) symptoms. For the study of a comprehensive model, *see* Richard L. Schwab et al., "Educator Burnout: Sources and Consequences," *Educational Research Quarterly* 10:3(1986).

See also Deborah Kalekin-Fishman, "Burnout or Alienation? A Context Specific Study of Occupational Fatigue Among Secondary School Teachers," *Journal of Research and Development in Education* (Spring 1986); and Anthony Gary Dworkin, *Teacher Burnout in the Public Schools* (Albany: State University of New York Press, 1987).

teacher centers   Organizations authorized and supported by federal law (P.L. 94-482), that offer ongoing and continuous education programs to meet the needs of the teaching profession. *See* Roy A. Edelfelt, *Teacher Centers and Needs Assessment* (Washington, D.C.: National Foundation for the Improvement of Education, Teacher Center Project, and National Education Association, 1980).

teacher certification   *See* CERTIFICATION.

teacher competency testing   1. Testing designed to measure specific abilities and skills that have been determined to be relevant for educating students. 2. A method of evaluating teacher performance that has been suggested as a means for upgrading the quality of personnel in education and increasing teacher accountability.

In recent years critics of the public school system have claimed that schools are not doing a very good job of educating students, as evidenced by declining test scores and increasing adult illiteracy. One potential solution to this problem, which has been adopted by a number of states, is mandatory teacher competency testing. This means of measuring teacher performance, which underlies the competency-based method, is highly controversial. *See* Susan L. Melnick and Diana Pullin, "Implications of the Use of Teacher Competency Tests," *Educational Policy* 1:2(1987).

teacher corps   A federal program enacted in 1965 (Title V of the Higher Education Act) to promote educational opportunities for children of low income families and to increase the number of minorities in the teaching profession.

teacher education   Coursework and experiences designed to prepare an individual to become a teacher or to improve the teaching skills of those already practicing. Education for teachers prior to employment is termed "pre-service." "In-service" training is for teachers who have obtained a teaching degree and are employed in the profession. *See* Thomas S. Poppewitz, ed., *Critical Studies in Teacher Education: Its Folklore, Theory and Practice* (Philadelphia: Falmer Press, 1987).

teacher education institution   A university, liberal arts college, teachers' college, or other professional school in which one of the major functions is the preparation of students for the teaching profession and that has been approved for teacher education by a state, regional, or national accrediting body.

Teacher Effectiveness Training
A program modeled after the well-known Parent Effectiveness Training, which was developed by Dr. Thomas Gordon and which emphasized assertive discipline. This teacher counterpart teaches techniques for effective classroom management and instruction. For a description of the program, see Thomas Gordon and Noel Burch, *T.E.T., Teacher Effectiveness Training* (New York: Peter H. Weyden, 1974).

teacher of the year An annual award sponsored by (among others) the Council of Chief State School Officers to acknowledge excellent teachers in each of the 50 states.

teacher retention Or, conversely, teacher attrition. A term related to the growing problems of not only attracting individuals to the teaching profession but also keeping good teachers from leaving education. For a discussion of theories regarding this issue, see David W. Chapman, "Teacher Retention: The Test of a Model," *American Educational Research Journal* 31:3(1984); and David W. Chapman and Michael S. Green, "Teacher Retention: A Further Examination," *Journal of Educational Research* (May/June 1986).

teacher strikes Work stoppages by teachers that are generally called to force some concession by the school district in terms of working conditions or pay scale. Usually the last step in a series of collective bargaining tactics.

teacher training institution A college or university recognized by the proper state authorities for the training of teachers.

teacher turnover Movement of teachers out of their current teaching positions either to positions in another school district or out of the profession altogether. For one approach to studying teacher turnover rates, see John Seyfarth and William Bost, "Teacher Turnover and the Quality of Worklife in Schools: An Empirical Study," *Journal of Research and Development in Education* (Fall 1986).

teacher unions Organizations of teachers primarily for the purpose of collective bargaining. The two major organizations in the United States are the AMERICAN FEDERATION OF TEACHERS and the NATIONAL EDUCATION ASSOCIATION. Teacher unions have worked to improve working conditions, such as salary, fringe benefits, and smaller class size, for their members by utilizing strikes and collective bargaining techniques to achieve their goals.

teacherage A building that is used as living quarters for teachers. Individual apartments rented by the school district for teachers are not designated by this term.

teacher-centered approach An approach to teaching whereby the teacher's preference dictates the content and method of instruction. Contrast with CHILD-CENTERED, CONTENT-CENTERED, SUBJECT-CENTERED, PROCESS-CENTERED.

teacher-instructional supervisor ratio The total of the full-time equivalencies of all teaching assignments, as of a given date, divided by the total of the full-time equivalencies of all assignments for supervision of instruction as of the same date.

teacher's contract The formal agreement, represented by a legal, signed document entered into by a teacher and the officials of the school system, stating the salary to be paid the teacher, the term of the agreement, and the general duties to be performed by the teacher. This may be an individual or a union contract.

Teachers Insurance and Annuity Association (TIAA) and College Retirement Equities Fund (CREF) A nonprofit annuity company that provides retirement benefits for employees of colleges and universities and a limited number of other educational institutions. TIAA provides a fixed-dollar annual income to retirees. CREF provides a variable dollar amount on retirement, depending on common stock market prices.
TIAA/CREF
730 Third Avenue
New York, NY 10017

teachers other than classroom teachers per 1,000 pupils in average daily membership The number representing the total full-time equivalency of teaching assignments less the number representing the total full-time equivalency of classroom teaching assignments in a school system during a given period of time, multiplied by 1,000 and divided by the average daily membership of pupils during the period.

teachers per 1,000 students in average daily membership The number representing the total full-time equivalency of teaching assignments in a school system during a given period of time, multiplied by 1,000 and divided by the average daily membership of students during this period.

teachers' room or lounge A room, designed or adapted, for use by teachers and other instructional staff for study, class preparation, and relaxation.

teaching The process of helping pupils acquire knowledge, skills, attitudes, and/or appreciations by means of a systematic method of in-

struction. *See* Bruce Joyce and Marsha Weil, *Models of Teaching,* 2nd ed. (Englewood Cliffs, N.J.: Prentice-Hall, 1980).

teaching assistant Also teaching technician. A person who performs the day-to-day activities of teaching students but under the supervision of a teacher. The teaching assistant does not make any diagnostic or long-range evaluative decisions regarding students taught. The person may or may not be certificated but has completed at least two years of formal education preparatory for teaching, or the equivalent in experience or training. *See also* TEACHER AIDE (these terms are often incorrectly used synonymously).

teaching fellow A student in higher education who holds a fellowship that requires some instructional obligations.

teaching field In a departmentalized organization, a major subdivision of the educational program, such as language arts, foreign languages, mathematics, science, music, vocational education, and physical education. In a nondepartmentalized situation, or in assignments to self-contained classroom duties, the general teaching level, such as elementary or secondary, may be the most accurate designation of teaching field.

teaching intern A person who instructs students without having fulfilled all the requirements for a professional in the teaching field. This person usually has a professional level of competence in a field other than education and is allowed to teach while obtaining the necessary knowledge and skills in education and/or educational psychology.

teaching load The workload of a teacher, generally defined by the number of students instructed, the number of periods of classroom instruction (per day or per week), or the number of different courses taught.

teaching machine A device for presenting programmed instruction. *See also* PROGRAMMED INSTRUCTION.

teaching method An approach to instruction that has been systematically described and that can be applicable to a number of subject areas and teachers. Examples include the lecture method, the tutorial method, the Socratic method, and, more recently, such technological approaches as computer-assisted instruction and telecommunication.

teaching order A religious order whose members are committed to instruction in church-run schools.

teaching principal A school building administrator who spends more than half his or her time teaching. Contrast with SUPERVISING PRINCIPAL.

teaching, other than classroom instruction responsibility The area of responsibility for instructing pupils in other than the usual classroom situation. It consists of such activities as teaching the homebound, teaching through correspondence, teaching through radio or television from a studio, providing instruction for exceptional pupils released from regular classes for short periods of time, and instructing pupils in non-course (cocurricular) activities.

team teaching An approach to classroom instruction that involves two or more teachers who are jointly responsible for planning, instructing, and evaluating a given group of pupils at any instructional level or in a selected subject-matter area or combination of subject-matter areas. The team

members may be equal or they may each assume differentiated roles, either according to a hierarchy or according to areas of specialization. A teaching team may or may not include assistants.

See Leslie J. Chamberlin, *Team Teaching: Organization and Administration* (Columbus, Ohio: Charles E. Merrill, 1969).

technical A term denoting a level of knowledge and skills possessed by an individual or required of an individual to perform an assignment. The level of skill is attained through education and training, usually including, at a minimum, an associate degree (or its equivalent obtained through special study and/or experience).

technical assistance A type of staff development activity in which one or more consultants provide direct on-site instruction, related to a specific identified need, to a teacher or group of teachers.

technical education Formal preparation for jobs or occupations that require specific technical skills. The training is frequently postsecondary but does not include the liberal arts orientation of college study. It is, rather, specific to the skills required for a particular job.

technical high school *See* VOCATIONAL AND/OR TECHNICAL SCHOOL.

technical institute An institution, or a division of an institution, offering instruction primarily in one or more of the technologies at the postsecondary instructional level.

technical personnel Personnel working in one or more branches of technology at a level above the skilled trades and below professional status.

technical school A public or private school, other than a normal secondary school program, that offers specific technical skill training for the purpose of job preparation. The training is typically below the level of higher education and does not lead toward a postsecondary degree.

technical staff member   A staff member who possesses the knowledge and skills of a technician (technical level competencies) and performs activities for the school or school system that require this level of expertise for satisfactory completion.

technical staff per 1,000 students in average daily attendance The number representing the total full-time equivalency of technical staff assignments in a school system during a given period of time, multiplied by 1,000 and divided by the average daily attendance of students during this period.

technical staff per 1,000 students in average daily membership The number representing the total full-time equivalency of technical staff assignments in a school system during a given period of time, multiplied by 1,000 and divided by the average daily membership of students during this period.

technology   In education, methods, materials, and devices (including electronics, as in "high tech") that can be utilized to assist in the learning process. For a review of technology in the schools, see NASSP Bulletin (November 1985).

telecommunication   An educational approach that involves both the visual and auditory transmittal of an instructor's presentation to one or more locations that may be at significant geographic distance from the location of origin.

telecourse   A full sequence of lessons offered over closed circuit or broadcast television for credit or auditing purposes. Telecourse instruction may also include written work requirements, reading assignments, and examinations.

telelecture   A simple, inexpensive, instructional application of communications technology involving direct telephone contact, utilizing an amplified speakerphone, between a class of students and an instructor at a different site some distance from the classroom.

temporary salaries   Part-time salaries, and prorated portions of the gross full-time salary costs, for work by employees of a school district who are hired on a temporary or substitute basis to perform work in positions of either a temporary or permanent nature.

tenure   The period of time that one occupies a position. In the academic world and in some government jurisdictions, to have "tenure" means that an individual may continue in his or her position until retirement, subject, of course, to adequate behavior and the continued viability of the organization.

tenure status   The employment status of the staff member whose employment is not subject to discontinuance by the governing authority except in stipulated circumstances. See also EMPLOYMENT STATUS.

term   A prescribed span of time when school is open and the pupils are under the guidance and direction of teachers. Generally a term connotes a quarter, trimester, or semester, depending on how the school year is divided in a particular jurisdiction.

term bonds   Bonds of the same issue, usually maturing all at one time and ordinarily to be retired from sinking funds.

term insurance   Insurance for a fixed period of time.

term paper   A composition that is generally required at the completion of a particular course of study, is longer and more sophisticated than other reports that may be required, and that reflects an in-depth understanding of some aspect of the course.

Terman, Lewis (1877-1956)   The originator of the Stanford-Binet Intelligence Test (he was a professor at Stanford University) and the contributor of the term IQ (intelligence quotient) to the fields of psychology and education. *See* Lewis M. Terman, *The Measurement of Intelligence* (Boston: Houghton Mifflin, 1916).

terminal arbitration   Arbitration that is called for as the final step in a grievance procedure.

terminal contract   A contract agreement setting beginning and ending dates of employment of the staff member, with no legal obligation that the expiration of the contract is to be followed by another contract agreement. *See also* CONTINUING CONTRACT.

terminal degree   The highest degree that can be obtained in a particular field of study, often a PhD or other doctorate degree such as EdD or JD.

terminal letter   A letter from the governing board of the school administrative unit appointing an individual to employment, setting forth beginning and ending dates of such appointment, and serving the staff and

the board much the same as a terminal contract.

terminal program   A unified series of courses that is intended to be complete in itself. At the postsecondary instructional level, this usually refers to a program of instruction that is completed in less than four years and is designed to provide general education or occupational training for individuals who are not planning to enter a bachelor's degree program. Credits earned in such a program normally are creditable toward an associate degree.

termination   *See* SEPARATION.

TESOL   Teaching English to Speakers of Other Languages. *See* ESL.

test   1. Any systematic means of evaluation or assessment. 2. A series of questions or problems designed to determine a level of knowledge, achievement, or aptitude for an individual student. *See* Jon C. Marshall and Loyde W. Hales, *Classroom Test Construction* (Reading, Mass.: Addison-Wesley, 1971); Edward Burns, *The Development, Use and Abuse of Educational Tests* (Springfield, Ill.: Thomas C. Thomas, 1979); and Stanley J. Ahmann and Marvin D. Glock, *Evaluating Pupil Growth: Principles of Tests and Measurement*, 6th ed. (Boston: Allyn and Bacon, 1979).

test anxiety   The nervousness that an examinee experiences before and during the administration of a test. For studies concluding that test anxiety is, except for extremes, inversely correlated with test performance, *see* John Hunsley, "Test Anxiety, Academic Performance and Cognitive Appraisals," *Journal of Educational Psychology* (December 1985); Irwin G. Sarason, ed., *Test Anxiety: Theory, Research and Applications* (Hillsdale,

N.J., Lawrence Erlbaum Associates, 1980); and Ronald Paulman and Kevin Kennelly, "Test Anxiety and Ineffective Test Taking: Different Names, Same Construct?" *Journal of Educational Psychology* (April 1984).

test battery An examination that includes several subtests each of which measures a different area of aptitude or accomplishment.

test bias Aspects of a test that have a discriminatory effect on individuals who may not have been exposed to experiences reflected in the content of the questions on the test. *See* Arthur R. Jensen, *Bias in Mental Testing* (New York: Free Press, 1980); and Cecil R. Reynolds and Robert T. Brown, eds., *Perspectives on Bias in Mental Testing* (New York: Plenum Press, 1984).

Test of English as a Foreign Language (TOEFL) An examination sponsored by the College Entrance Examination Board to assess the English-language proficiency of foreign students applying for admission to U.S. colleges and universities.

test of high school equivalency
An approved examination (e.g., a test of general educational development) on the basis of which a state department of education or other authorized agency may certify that a person has met state requirements for high school equivalency. *See also* HIGH SCHOOL EQUIVALENCY EXAMINATION *and* TESTS OF GENERAL EDUCATIONAL DEVELOPMENT (GED).

Test of Language Development (TOLD) An individually-administered comprehensive test designed to assess language skills in children between the ages of four and eight years. Subtests include picture vocabulary, oral vocabulary, grammati-

cal understanding, sentence imitation, and grammatical completion. It is published by:
Pro-Ed
333 Perry Brooks Building
Austin, TX 78701

test publishers Listed in current edition of O.K. Buros, ed., *The Mental Measurements Yearbook* (Highland Park, N.J.: Gryphon Press) and Richard C. Sweetland, Daniel J. Keyser, and William A. O'Connor, eds., *Tests: A Comprehensive Reference for Assessments in Psychology, Education and Business* (Kansas City, Mo.: Test Corporation of America, 1983).

American Guidance Services, Inc.
Publisher's Building
Circle Pines, MN 55014

Bobbs-Merrill Company, Inc.
4300 West 62nd Street
Indianapolis, IN 46206

California Test Bureau
CTB/McGraw-Hill
Del Monte Research Park
Monterey, CA 94306

Consulting Psychologists Press, Inc.
577 College Avenue
Palo Alto, CA 93904

Educational and Industrial Testing
Service
P.O. Box 7234
San Diego, CA 92107

Follett Educational Corporation
1010 West Washington Blvd.
Chicago, IL 60607

Harcourt, Brace, Jovanovich, Inc.
747 Third Avenue
New York, NY 10017

Houghton Mifflin Company
110 Tremont Street
Boston, MA 02107

Industrial Psychology Inc.
515 Madison Avenue
New York, NY 10022

Institute for Personality and Ability Testing, Inc.
P.O. Box 188
1602 Coronado Drive
Champaign, IL 61820

McCann Associates, Inc.
2763 Philmont Avenue
Huntington Valley, PA 19006

Merit Employment Assessment Services, Inc.
P.O. Box 193
Flossmoor, IL 60422

Psychological Corporation
555 Academic Court
San Antonio, TX 78204

Research Psychologists Press, Inc.
P.O. Box 948
Port Huron, MI 48060

Science Research Associates, Inc.
155 North Wacker Drive
Chicago, IL 60606

Sheridan Psychological Services, Inc.
P.O. Box 6101
Orange, CA 92667

Slosson Educational Publications
P.O. Box 280
East Aurora, NY 14052

Stanford University Press
Stanford, CA 94305

William, Lynde, and Williams
153 East Erie Street
Painesville, OH 44077

Wonderlic, E.F., and Associates
Box 7
Northfield, IL 60093

test sophistication   A particular aptitude in taking tests that comes from experience in test-taking. Also called test wiseness.

tests of general educational development (GED)   A battery of tests taken by individuals, usually over the age of 16, who did not graduate from high school. These tests are intended to measure the extent to which their past experiences (in-school and out-of-school) have contributed to their attaining the knowledge, skills, and understandings ordinarily acquired through a high school education. Certificates of high school equivalency are issued by most state departments of education for the successful completion of the Tests of General Educational Development. See also HIGH SCHOOL EQUIVALENCY EXAMINATION and CERTIFICATE OF HIGH SCHOOL EQUIVALENCY.

Texas Trade School v. Commissioner (30 T.C. 642 (1958), aff'd 272 F. 2d 168, 5th Cir. 1959)   A landmark 1958 United States Tax Court decision in which the Texas Trade School was denied tax-exempt status because officers and past officers of the school were involved in real estate leasing and construction transactions (or schemes) with it. The Court ruled the transactions were for the private inurement of insiders.

textbooks   Books obtained primarily for use in certain classes, grades, or other particular student groups rather than for general school use.

T-Group   Refers to training group, a small-group interactional training technique associated with the National Training Laboratories (NTL), originally of Bethel, Maine. See SENSITIVITY TRAINING.

Thematic Apperception Test (TAT)   A projective test that uses a standard set of pictures and calls for the subject to reveal his or her personality by making up stories about the pictures. Variations of the TAT have been used successfully for vocational counseling and executive selection, as well as for determining attitudes toward labor problems, minority groups, and authority. *See* Leopold Bellak, *The Thematic Apperception Test, The Children's Apperception Test, and the Senior Apperception Technique in Clinical Use*, 4th ed. (Orlando, Fla.: Grune & Stratton, 1986). The test is published by:

> The Psychological Corporation
> 555 Academic Court
> San Antonio, TX 78204

thematic teaching   An instructional approach that organizes curricular content around a specific theme and that generally integrates two or more subject areas. *See* Sylvia Spann and Mary Beth Culp, *Thematic Units in Teaching English and the Humanities* (Urbana, Ill.: National Council of Teachers of English, 1977).

theme   1. A written composition. 2. A unified thread of content or a central idea.

theological school   *See* SEMINARY.

theorem   In mathematics, a statement of a principle to be proved or a previously proven principle that can be applied to other contexts.

theoretical   1. Lacking in proof; not necessarily applicable to practical situations. 2. Referring to general concepts under which particular situations can be better understood.

theory   1. The general principles of a field of study. 2. A hypothesis related to observable phenomena. 3. Abstract reasoning.

Theory X and Theory Y   Opposing theories of personnel motivation in organizations. Theory X holds that employees dislike work and need to be controlled and directed. Theory Y, conversely, holds that individuals find pleasure and satisfaction in work and will exercise self-direction and responsibility, if committed to the organization. *See* Douglas M. McGregor, *The Human Side of Enterprise* (New York: McGraw-Hill, 1960).

Theory Z   A management theory that originated in Japanese industry and more recently has been applied to American schools. Theory Z attempts to combine effective technology and the scientific approach with greater concern for human factors. For a description of its application to education, *see* Paul S. George, *The Theory Z School: Beyond Effectiveness* (Columbus, Ohio: National Middle School Association, 1983). For a briefer summary, *see* Paul S. George, "Theory Z and Schools," *NASSP Bulletin* (May 1984).

therapy   Any treatment procedure that is designed to correct and/or improve mental or physical functioning.

thesis   A scholarly paper written to fulfill academic requirements, usually at the level of a master's degree.

think tank   A colloquial reference to an independent institution where high-level scholars are employed to carry out commissioned studies of major social issues or to pursue independent research.

thinking   A somewhat colloquial term for higher-level mental processes that may involve memory, imagination, problem solving, etc. Attempts to describe this complex concept include Jerome S. Bruner, Jacqueline J. Goodnow, and George Austin, *A Study of Thinking* (New Brunswick, N.J.: Transaction Books, 1986) and Joan Boykoff Baron and Robert J. Sternberg, *Teaching Thinking Skills: Theory and Practice* (New York: Freeman, 1987). *See also* COGNITION.

third party payment Payment by a health insurance company or the government for health services provided to a patient by, for example, a doctor, a hospital, or an ambulance company.

third sector All those organizations that fit neither in the public sector (government) nor the private sector (business). A generic phrase for the collectivity of nonprofit organizations. *See also* NONPROFIT ORGANIZATION.

Thorndike, Edward (1874-1949) A renowned educator of the first half of the 20th century and a prolific writer, best known for his studies of intelligence testing and his widely-used dictionaries, *Thorndike Century Junior Dictionary* (1935) and *Thorndike Century Senior Dictionary* (1941). *See* Geraldine Joncich, *The Sane Positivist: A Biography of Edward L. Thorndike* (Middleton, Conn.: Wesleyan University Press, 1968).

three Rs Traditional reference to the basic elementary school academics: reading, (w)riting, and (a)rithmetic.

Thurstone Scale Attitude scale created by Louis L. Thurstone that has judges rate the favorability of statements, then has subjects select those statements with which they agree. *See* L.L. Thurstone and E.J. Chave, *The Management of Attitude* (Chicago: University of Chicago Press, 1929).

TIAA-CREF *See* TEACHERS INSURANCE AND ANNUITY ASSOCIATION.

time sampling A research or data recording technique in which individual behavior is recorded at fixed intervals, e.g., *every minute or every 10 minutes.*

time series analysis A technique used in forecasting and program evaluations. When used for program evaluation purposes, historical trend data are plotted and projected into the future. Subsequently, the projected data points are compared with actual data, and the distance between them is used as a measure of program impact. For example, an American Heart Association chapter might create a time series showing the historical and projected trend in the number of people who survive certain types of heart attack (for example, ventricular fibrillation) in a city. Then, a massive citizen cardiopulmonary resuscitation (CPR) education program is conducted. Six months later, the actual number of survivors is compared with the projected number. The difference between the two numbers is the measure of the program's success or lack of success. *See also*:

EVALUATION
EVALUATION DESIGN
EVALUATION TECHNIQUE

timed test An examination that must be completed within a certain period of time.

time-on-task 1. The amount of time per day, usually expressed in minutes, that a student is actively engaged in learning activities. 2. The amount of sustained, uninterrupted time that a student spends on productive learning activities.

Tinker v. Des Moines Independent Community School District 393 U.S. 503 (1969) One of the earliest Supreme Court decisions upholding a student's First Amendment rights. In this case three public school students wore black armbands to class in protest of United States involvement in the Vietnam War. Their right to do so was upheld in that no substantial interference with the school routine could be demonstrated. A long series of First Amendment decisions regarding students followed in the 1970s.

Title I   An abbreviated reference to Title I of the Elementary and Secondary Education Act of 1965, which provided aid for educational programs for low-income students. This program was replaced under the Education Consolidation and Improvement Act of 1981 by Chapter I of the Act. See CHAPTER 1 and ELEMENTARY AND SECONDARY EDUCATION ACT OF 1965.

Title VII   In the context of equal employment opportunity, this almost invariably refers to Title VII of the Civil Rights Act of 1964 (as amended), the backbone of the nation's EEO effort. It prohibits employment discrimination because of race, color, religion, sex, or national origin and created the Equal Employment Opportunity Commission as its enforcement vehicle. The federal courts have relied heavily upon Title VII in mandating remedial action on the part of employers.
See George Rutherglen, "Title VII Class Actions," *University of Chicago Law Review* (Summer 1980); David G. Karro, "The Importance of Being Earnest: Pleading and Maintaining a Title VII Class Action for the Purpose of Resolving the Claims of Class Members," *Fordham Law Review* (May 1981); Nestor Cruz, "Abuse of Rights in Title VII Cases: The Emerging Doctrine," *Labor Law Journal* (May 1981); and Elizabeth Bartholet, "Application of Title VII to Jobs in High Places," *Harvard Law Review* (March 1982).
See also:
CITY OF LOS ANGELES, DEPARTMENT OF WATER & POWER V. MANHART
MAKE WHOLE
PREGNANCY DISCRIMINATION ACT OF 1978
SEXUAL HARASSMENT

Title IX   Refers to the Education Amendments of 1972 that prohibit discrimination on the basis of sex. See Norma Raffell, *Title IX: How It Affects*

Elementary and Secondary Education (Denver, Colo.: Education Commission of the States, 1976).

Today's Education   A widely read, non-juried publication of the National Education Association, distributed annually to the association's membership. Produced in magazine format, the publication carries articles of general interest to educators. Subscriptions are available only as a part of NEA membership. The association's office address is:
National Education Association
1201 16th St. N.W.
Washington, DC 20036
See NEA TODAY.

TOEFL   See TEST OF ENGLISH AS A FOREIGN LANGUAGE.

token economy   In behavioral technology, a system whereby students can earn tokens for predetermined levels of acceptable behavior. The tokens have no intrinsic value but can be exchanged for something of value to individual students, e.g., free time, money, food, television watching, or other favored activities.

tokenism   In the context of equal employment opportunity, an insincere EEO effort in which a few minority group members are hired in order to satisfy government affirmative action mandates or the demands of pressure groups. See Donald G. Dutton, "Tokenism, Reverse Discrimination, and Egalitarianism in Interracial Behavior," *Journal of Social Issues* 32:2(1976).

TOLD   See TEST OF LANGUAGE DEVELOPMENT.

Torcaso v. Watkins 367 U.S. 488 (1961)   The Supreme Court case that held that a state requirement of a declaration of a belief in God as a qualification for office was unconstitutional because it invades one's freedom of belief and religion guaranteed by the First Amendment and protected by the 14th Amendment from infringement by the states.

tort   A legal term that refers to the potential liability of an individual for injury to a person or property that results from intentional wrongdoing or negligence.

total communication   A method of teaching deaf or hearing-impaired students that combines both oral (spoken) and manual (sign language) approaches.

total compensation comparability Major means of incorporating fringe benefits into overall pay policy. The comparability principle, which holds that public and nonprofit employees should be paid wages comparable to those of similar workers in the private sector, has not kept pace with changing conditions. Consequently, in some cases, while actual wages and salaries may be comparable to or lower than those of private sector counterparts, the total package of pay plus fringe benefits plus time-off, often gives the public sector (and, in some cases, the third sector) employee a greater total return than that gained by a private sector counterpart.

See Pierre Martel, "A Model of Total Compensation in a Market-Comparability Framework," *Public Personnel Management* (Summer 1982); and Bruce R. Eillig, "Total Compensation Design: Elements and Issues," *Personnel* (January-February 1984).

Toughlove   A ''get-tough'' approach to managing particularly unruly and uncontrollable adolescents that is augmented by a nationwide network of parent support groups and that

emphasizes the need for teenagers to learn and practice responsibility. This movement became popularized and familiar to secondary school counselors and administrators in the 1980s through books such as Phyllis York, David York, and Ted Wachtel's, *Toughlove* (New York: Doubleday, 1982).

Toughlove (for parents)
P.O. Box 1069
Doylestown, PA 18901
(215) 348-7090

town and gown   A term that is used in reference to the sometimes hostile relationship between a general community population and the population of university students and faculty that may reside in the same community environment.

tracking   Also called STREAMING. Grouping students on the basis of assumed or demonstrated ability. There is much controversy about the efficacy of grouping students according to this approach. For one side of the issue *see* Jeannie Oakes, *Keeping Track: How Schools Structure Inequality* (New Haven, Conn.: Yale University Press, 1986). For an alternative viewpoint *see* Charles Nevi, "In Defense of Tracking," *Educational Leadership* (March 1987).

trade school   Dated reference to a technical school, a vocational school that teaches specific technical skills relevant to job preparation.

traditional orthography   The traditional system of writing spoken sounds using the 26-letter English alphabet. Other methods have been introduced, most notably the INITIAL TEACHING ALPHABET (ITA).

trainable mental retardation   A somewhat outdated term that refers to individuals who have a degree of retardation such that they will probably be unable to achieve success with traditional, basic academics. Also called moderate retardation, this term generally applies to individuals with a measurable IQ between 25 and 50.

training A planned and systematic sequence of instruction under competent supervision, designed to impact predetermined skills, knowledge, or abilities with respect to designated occupational objectives and in addition to occupational training; may include to the extent necessary, adult basic education, prevocational training, and refresher and reorientation training for professionals.

training, on-the-job Supervision and instruction provided at an actual job site and focused on teaching the specific skills needed to perform a particular job. May be directed at a beginning employee who is being paid or at a potential employee who is not paid but is, rather, still enrolled in a formal educational program.

transactional analysis (TA) An approach to psychotherapy first developed by Eric Berne. Transactional analysis defines the basic unit of social intercourse as a "transaction." There are three "ego states" from which transactions emanate: those of a "parent," an "adult," or a "child." The transactions between individuals can be classified as complementary, crossed, simple, or ulterior, based upon the response that an individual receives to a "transactional stimulus"—any action that consciously or unconsciously acknowledges the presence of other individuals. The transactional analysis framework has become a popular means of helping managers to assess the nature and effectiveness of their interpersonal behavior. By striving for more adult-to-adult transactions, managers may eliminate many of the "games people play."

For the first published account, *see* Eric Berne, "Transactional Analysis: A

New and Effective Method of Group Therapy," *American Journal of Psychotherapy* (October 1958). For the best seller that made transactional analysis a household term, *see* Eric Berne, *Games People Play: The Psychology of Human Relationships* (New York: Grove Press, 1964). For a general treatment, *see* Thomas A Harris, *I'm OK—You're OK* (New York: Harper & Row, 1969).

transcript An official record of student performance, showing all schoolwork completed at a given school and the final grade or other evaluation received in each portion of the instruction. Transcripts often include an explanation of the grading scale used by the school.

transfer 1. A student who leaves one school or school district and moves to another. 2. The movement of a teacher from one school to another within the same school district.

transfer from other funds Money received unconditionally from another fund without expectation of repayment. Such monies are revenues of the receiving fund, but not of the local educational agency as a whole. Separate accounts may be maintained for specific funds.

transfer of learning The theory that knowledge or abilities acquired in one area aid the acquisition of knowledge or abilities in other areas. When prior learning is helpful, it is called positive transfer. When prior learning inhibits new learning, it is called negative transfer. Also called GENERALIZATION.

transfer program A program of studies, at the postsecondary instructional level, designed primarily to yield credits that are chiefly creditable by four-year colleges and universities toward a bachelor's degree.

transfer voucher   A voucher authorizing posting adjustments and transfers of cash or other resources between funds of accounts.

transferring   Moving from one school or school district to another.

transfers   In the financial accounting sense, money that is taken from one fund under the control of a state department of education and added to another fund under the department's control. Such transfers are not receipts or expenditures of the department.

transition   A term that refers primarily to the movement of students from public school environments to post-school environments (usually the "world-of-work") but also applies to the movements from preschool to kindergarten, elementary school to middle or junior high school, and middle or junior high school to high school. That is, any significant change in schooling environments.

transparency   A type of acetate paper that is used with overhead projectors on which information to accompany lectures or presentations is drawn, written, or printed.

transportation   A significant issue and expense for contemporary public school systems that involves getting students, especially in large population or large area school districts, from home to school and back home again. For a series of articles regarding some of the issues in school bus transportation, see The American School Board Journal (November 1987).

transported student   A pupil who is transported to and from school at public expense.

travel expenses   Costs for transportation, meals, hotel, and other expenses associated with traveling on business or for any legitimate purpose related to one's employment. Payments for per diem in lieu of reimbursements for subsistence (room and board) also are charged here.

traveling teachers   See ITINERANT TEACHER.

trend analysis   The result of repeated assessments of public opinion on certain basic issues over a period of time, which makes possible comparisons between baseline data and subsequent changes.

trial balance   A list of the balances of the accounts in a ledger kept by double entry, with the debit and credit balances shown in separate columns. If the totals of the debit and credit columns are equal or their net balance agrees with a controlling account, the ledger from which the figures are taken is said to be "in balance."

trial and error learning   A term that is broadly used in reference to learning that occurs through experience and without specific instruction.

triennial review   A formal evaluation after the third year of a program. The regulations for the administration of P.L. 94-142, the Education for All Handicapped Children Act of 1975, require that a student's eligibility for special education services be reevaluated at least once every three years. This means that a complete multidisciplinary, multifaceted assessment must be administered to determine whether the student is able to benefit from regular education and whether a handicapping condition exists. The requirements for the triennial review are essentially identical with those established for an initial staffing and development of the Individualized Education Program (IEP). See STAFFING and INDIVIDUALIZED EDUCATION PROGRAM.

trimester   One part of a school year that is divided into three parts rather than the more traditional two parts (semesters). A trimester calendar is more commonly used at the college level.

trivium and quadrivium   An educational distinction of the Middle Ages, dating back to 400 A.D. in Rome. The trivium represented the "lower level" of a liberal arts curriculum (grammar, logic, and rhetoric), and the quadrivium represented the "upper level" (astronomy, music, arithmetic, and geography).

truancy   The failure of a child to attend school regularly as required by law, without reasonable excuse for his or her absence. *See* Roger White, *Absent With Cause: Lessons of Truancy* (Boston: Routledge and Kegan Paul, 1980).

true score   A score entirely free of measurement errors. True scores are hypothetical values, never obtained in actual testing, that always involve some measurement error. A true score is sometimes defined as the average score that would result from an infinite series of measurements with the same or exactly equivalent tests, assuming no practice or change in the examinee during the testings.

true-false test   A type of short-answer test where each item is a declarative statement that is either true or false.

trust   Legal fiduciary relationship in which one organization or person (the trustee) holds the title and accepts responsibility for managing property (such as a trust estate) for the benefit of another or others (the beneficiaries). *See also* BENEFICIARY *and* FIDUCIARY.

trust account   Account with a trust company established by a depositor or trustee. The depositor or trustee controls the trust account during his or her lifetime. After the donor's death, the balance of the trust account is payable to the beneficiary(ies).

trust and agency funds   Funds used to account for money and property held in trust by a school district for individuals, government entities, or nonpublic organizations. A trust fund is usually in existence over a longer period of time than an agency fund. Primarily, agency funds function as a clearing mechanism for cash resources collected, held for a short period, and then disbursed to authorized recipients.

trust certificate   Document showing that property is held in trust as security for a debt based on money used to buy property.

trust company   Corporation established and operated to perform the functions of a trustee. Most trust companies also engage in other banking and/or financial business.

trust fund   Money or property set aside in a trust or set aside for a special purpose. *See also* TRUST.

trust indenture   The creating document for a trust. A trust indenture is to a trust as articles of incorporation are to a corporation.

trustee   1. The role that elected representatives adopt when they vote according to their conscience and best judgment rather than according to the narrow interests of their immediate constituents. 2. One who has a fiduciary responsibility.

truth in testing   A requirement established under New York law in 1980, and practiced elsewhere, that the results (including answer sheets identifying questions and correct answers) of standardized admissions tests for college and graduate school be made available to the students who took them.

tryout   A trial contest to determine the relative ability of a student to participate in an activity requiring some specific skill, e.g., on athletic teams, in musical groups, theatrical presentations, or debating teams.

T-scores   A type of STANDARD SCORE.

T-test   A statistical measure used in educational research to determine whether differences between the mean performance of two groups occurred by chance.

tuition   A payment or charge for instruction. *See also* FEE.

tuition expended   Expenditures to reimburse other educational agencies for services rendered to students residing in (or whose parents reside in) the legal boundaries described for a paying school district.

tuition received   Money received from pupils, their parents, welfare agencies, or other schools for education provided.

tuition student   A student for whom tuition is paid.

Turner v. Fouche 396 U.S. 346 (1970)   A Supreme Court decision dealing with charges of racial discrimination in the selection of school board members in a Georgia county. The court held that land ownership could not be a requirement for school board eligibility nor could other arbitrary

standards be applied that, in effect, discriminated against blacks.

tutorial   A method of teaching most common in Great Britain where a teacher meets individually with a student for an intensive discussion of some topic, often based on material that the student has prepared prior to the meeting.

tutoring   A one-on-one method of instruction.

two-year branch college   A division of an institution of higher education, that offers the first two years of college instruction and that is located in a community different from that of its parent institution and beyond a reasonable commuting distance from the main campus of the parent institution.

two-year technical institute   An institution offering instruction primarily in one or more of the technologies at the postsecondary instructional level.

Type A lunch   A lunch which meets the meal requirements prescribed by the Department of Agriculture under the National School Lunch Act of 1946, as amended. Such a lunch is designed to provide one-third of the recommended daily dietary allowance for a 10- to 12-year-old child.

type of exceptionality   A general characteristic by which individuals are identified as being exceptional. *See also* EXCEPTIONALITY.

Type I and Type II errors   In research a Type I error is the rejection of a true hypothesis, while a Type II error is the acceptance of a false hypothesis.

U

unamortized discounts on bonds sold That portion of the excess of the face value of bonds that is over the amount received from their sale and that remains to be written off periodically over the life of the bonds.

unamortized discounts on investments The excess of the face value of securities over the amount paid for them, which excess has not yet been written off.

unamortized premiums on bonds sold An account that represents that portion of the excess of bond proceeds over par value and that remains to be amortized over the remaining life of such bonds.

unappropriated surplus That portion of the surplus of a given fund that is not segregated for specific purposes.

unclassified pupil A school pupil who is not classified according to grade.

unconditioned response/reflex In behavioral theory, an automatic response of the organism to some external stimulus.

uncontrollable expenses Also called uncontrollable spending. Obligations wherein an organization has granted long-term contracts and, therefore, is unable to control the associated expenses.

under compulsory age A term describing a child who has not yet reached the compulsory school attendance age. This information is maintained where required by law or regulation for school census or other purposes.

underachievers Students who score consistently and significantly below their expected performance levels on standardized achievement tests. Their expected performance levels are determined by using scores on standardized tests of ability to predict performance on standardized tests of achievement.

For a discussion of the impact of sex differences in academic underachievement, *see* Jean Stockard and J. Walter Wood, "The Myth of Female Underachievement: A Re-examination of Sex Differences in Academic Underachievement," *American Educational Research Journal* (Winter 1984). "Underachievement" may also connote SPECIFIC LEARNING DISABILITIES.

underclassman/underclasswoman Generally refers to a student, male or female, in the first or second (freshman or sophomore) year of college.

underemployed person An individual whose skills/qualifications are greater than those required for the position he or she presently occupies.

undergraduate A student who is enrolled in a college program leading to a bachelor's degree.

undergraduate study College level-courses of study that may lead to the customary bachelor of arts or bachelor of science degree.

underground press Newspapers and magazines that offer alternative and often radical opinions and visions of society. Sometimes produced by students without the official approval of a school's administration.

underprivileged   Refers to students who lack typical material benefits in life.

underwrite   To insure; to guarantee to purchase any stock or bonds that remain unsold after a public sale.

undivided high school   See FIVE-OR SIX-YEAR HIGH SCHOOL.

unencumbered balance of appropriation or allotment   That portion of an appropriation or allotment not yet expended or encumbered; the balance remaining after deducting from the appropriation or allotment the accumulated expenditures and outstanding encumbrances.

UNESCO   See UNITED NATIONS EDUCATIONAL, SCIENTIFIC AND CULTURAL ORGANIZATION.

unexpended balance of appropriation or allotment   That portion of an appropriation or allotment that has not been expended; the balance remaining after deducting from the appropriation or allotment the accumulated expenditures.

ungraded class   A class that is not organized on the basis of grade and has no standard grade designation. This includes regular classes that have no grade designations, special classes for exceptional students that have no grade designations, and many adult/continuing education classes. Such a class is likely to contain students of different ages who are frequently identified according to level of performance in one or more areas of instruction rather than according to grade level or age level. Ungraded classes are sometimes referred to as "nongraded." See also REGULAR CLASS and GRADE.

ungraded elementary classes   Elementary classes in which children are not grouped according to standard grade classification.

ungraded elementary school   An elementary school that is not organized on a grade basis, but offers work on the elementary instructional level.

ungraded high school   A secondary school that is not organized on a grade basis, but offers work on the secondary instructional level.

ungraded primary unit   An organization, for all or a portion of the primary years of school, that has no grade designations or grade-level standards.

ungraded school   A school that has no grade designations or grade level standards. In such a school pupils are reclassified frequently according to individual progress. Aspects of subject matter taught are designed for the various abilities of individual pupils. Frequently, provision is made for independent study and research by pupils as well as for permissive self-selection of problems and materials. Achievement standards vary with the rate of learning for different pupils, and pupil advancement can occur at any time.

UNICEF   See UNITED NATIONS INTERNATIONAL CHILDREN'S EMERGENCY FUND.

unified phonics method   Also called the Spalding Method. A highly structured approach to teaching reading at the primary level. See Ronalda B. Spalding and Walter T. Spalding, *The Writing Road to Reading* (New York: William Morrow, 1969).

Uniform Guidelines on Employee Selection   Guidelines adopted in

1978 by the four federal agencies most concerned with employee selection processes: the Equal Employment Opportunity Commission, the Civil Service Commission, the Department of Justice, and the Department of Labor. The guidelines are designed to assist employers, labor organizations, employment agencies, and licensing and certification boards to comply with requirements of federal law prohibiting employment practices that discriminate on grounds of race, color, religion, sex, or national origin.

unincorporated   Not a corporation; articles of organization have not been filed with the appropriate state office.

unincorporated area   An urban area that has not become a municipality and has no local governmental structure of its own other than its county.

union security   Generally, any agreement between an employer and a union that requires every employee in the bargaining unit, as a condition of employment, to be a member of the union or to pay a specified sum to the union for its bargaining services. *See* Patricia N. Blair, "Union Security Agreement in Public Employment," *Cornell University Law Review* (January 1975).

union shop   A union-security provision found in some collective bargaining agreements that requires all employees to become members of the union within a specified time (usually 30 days) after being hired (or after the provision is negotiated) and to remain members of the union as a condition of employment.

union-security clause   Provision in a collective bargaining agreement that seeks to protect the union by providing for a constant flow of funds by

any of a variety of means. Union-security clauses typically provide for such things as the checkoff, the closed shop, the union shop, the agency shop, or preferential hiring.

See Thomas R. Haggard, *Compulsory Unionism, the NLRB, and the Courts: A Legal Analysis of Union Security Agreements* (Philadelphia: The Wharton School, University of Pennsylvania, 1977); and Glenn A. Zipp, "Rights and Responsibilities of Parties to a Union-Security Agreement," *Labor Law Review* (April 1982).

unit control   A method of property control whereby a piece of equipment is accounted for as a single unit or entity in itself so that it retains its separate identity in the records, on either an individual record card or form, or as a line item in a ledger.

unit cost   Expenditures for a function, activity, or service divided by the total number of units for which the function, activity, or service was provided.

unit of instruction   A major subdivision of instruction within a course or within an aspect of subject-matter content provided for a class of pupils. Generally composed of several topics, a unit of instruction includes content and learning experiences developed around a central focus, such as a limited scope of subject matter, a central problem, one or more related concepts, one or more related skills, or a combination of these.

unit of measure   A combination of statistical elements in education usually expressed in ratios, such as pupils per teacher, square feet per pupil, cost per pupil, or cost effectiveness ratio.

unit of work   The number or amount of objects serviced or recipients served by a staff member's efforts.

United Nations Educational, Scientific and Cultural Organization (UNESCO) An agency of the United Nations, formed in 1946, that has focused on general educational issues including—particularly—illiteracy and teacher preparation in the underdeveloped countries of the Third World. The United States National UNESCO Commission serves as a liaison between the U.S. government, UNESCO, and the American people.

U.S. National UNESCO Commission
1750 K Street, N.W.
Suite 1200
Washington, DC 20006
(202) 785-0055

United Nations International Children's Emergency Fund (UNICEF) An agency of the United Nations that functions somewhat autonomously with the purpose of helping developing nations to improve conditions for children through special projects focused on nutrition, education, and community development, among other efforts. The United States UNICEF committee is a national liaison that serves to inform the citizens of the United States about the activities of UNICEF.

U.S. UNICEF Committee
331 E. 38th Street
New York, NY 10016
(212) 686-5522

United States Department of Education *See* EDUCATION, DEPARTMENT OF.

United States Department of Health, Education and Welfare (HEW) *See* HEALTH, EDUCATION AND WELFARE, DEPARTMENT OF.

United States Reports The official record of cases decided by the U.S. Supreme Court. When cases are cited, *United States Reports* is abbreviated to

"U.S." For example, the legal citation for the case of *Pickering v. Board of Education* is 391 U.S. 563 (1968). This means that the case will be found on page 563 of volume 391 of the *United States Reports*, and that it was decided in 1968.

United Steelworkers of America v. Weber, et al 443 U.S. 193 (1979) Decided together with *Kaiser Aluminum & Chemical Corporation v. Weber, et al.* This was the Supreme Court decision that upheld an affirmative action program giving blacks preference in the selection of employees for a training program. Justice Brennan, in delivering the majority opinion of the Court, stated that "the only question before us is the narrow statutory issue of whether Title VII forbids private employers and unions from voluntarily agreeing upon bona fide affirmative action plans that accord racial preferences." The Court concluded that "Congress did not intend to limit traditional business freedom to such a degree as to prohibit all voluntary, race conscious affirmative action." Brennan went on to add that because Kaiser's preferential scheme was legal, it was unnecessary to "define in detail the line of demarcation between permissible and impermissible affirmative action plans."

See David H. Rosenbloom, *"Kaiser vs. Weber: Perspective From the Public Sector," Public Personnel Management* (November-December 1979); Bernard D. Meltzer, "The *Weber* Case: The Judicial Abrogation of the Antidiscrimination Standard in Employment," *University of Chicago Law Review* (Spring 1980); and Jerome L. Epstein, "Walking a Tightrope Without a Net: Voluntary Affirmative Action Plans After *Weber*," *University of Pennsylvania Law Review* (January 1986).

See also:
AFFIRMATIVE ACTION
CIVIL RIGHTS ACT OF 1964

REGENTS OF THE UNIVERSITY OF CALIFORNIA V. ALLAN BAKKE REVERSE DISCRIMINATION TITLE VII

United Way   Also United Way of America. An umbrella organization that raises and distributes funds to a wide variety of community agencies. United Way has established a network of approximately 2,300 autonomous United Way organizations, each with its own approach to improving the quality of life in the communities it serves. Local United Way organizations are dues-paying affiliates, each retaining its own autonomy. Most United Way organizations raise funds for participating charitable organizations, conduct community needs assessments, develop plans for meeting human care needs, engage in community problem-solving, and assist in recruiting and placing volunteers. Most United Ways receive approximately 30 percent of their funds from corporate contributions and about 70 percent from employee workplace contributions. United Way of America is an umbrella association for the United Way organizations, located at 701 North Fairfax Street, Alexandria, VA 22314; (703) 836-7100.

unity of command   The concept that each individual in an organization should be accountable to only a single superior. See N. Takahasi, "On the Principle of Unity of Command: Application of a Model and Empirical Research," *Behavioral Science* (January 1986).

universal birth number   An identification number assigned to an individual by the Bureau of Vital Statistics of a state, using a combination of digits representing area code, birth registration number, and year of birth.

university   A postsecondary institution that typically comprises one or more colleges and one or more graduate professional schools and that emphasizes research as well as teaching. See also COLLEGE.

university press   A publishing company, owned and operated by a university, that primarily produces scholarly academic works.

University Press of America   A publishing company that specializes in the publication and distribution of books and other printed materials "by academics for academics." Established in 1975 the UPA distributes classic reprints as well as soliciting and publishing new manuscripts that are of particular interest to educators.
University Press of America, Inc.
4720 Boston Way
Lanham, MD 20706
(301) 459-3366

university school   A demonstration elementary or secondary school that is associated with a teacher-training department of a university.

unobtrusive measures   Measures taken without the subject being aware that he or she is being observed. Also used in reference to teaching procedures (especially those directed to changing maladaptive student behaviors) that would not be obvious or offensive to the general public. See Eugene J. Webb et al., *Unobtrusive Measures: Nonreactive Research in the Social Sciences* (Chicago: Rand McNally, 1966).

unrestricted grants-in-aid   Revenues, received as grants by a school district, that can be used without restriction for any legal purpose.

upgrading in current occupation programs   Learning experiences concerned with skills and knowledge designed primarily to extend or update workers' competencies for occupations in which they are already employed.

upper elementary grades   The elementary grades following the intermediate elementary grades, usually grades seven and eight in an 8-4 organizational pattern or grades four to six in a 6-3-3 (or 6-2-4) pattern.

upperclassman/upperclasswoman   Generally refers to a student, male or female, in the junior or senior years of college.

Upward Bound   A federally supported program, originally enacted in 1965 as a part of the Higher Education Act (P.L. 89-329), that is intended to assist students from lower socioeconomic families in accessing higher education.

urban education   All education that occurs in an urban environment and that tends to be impacted by a number of factors, including: (1) a large population of low-income families; (2) a low tax/funding base; (3) a broad range of racial/ethnic/social and otherwise different students; (4) large student populations;(5) antiquated facilities; and (6) high teacher turnover.
See Herbert J. Walberg and Andrew T. Kopan, eds., *Rethinking Urban Education* (San Francisco: Jossey-Bass, 1972). For a number of articles on urban education, see also *NASSP Bulletin* (December 1983).

U.S. Public School Directory   A nationwide directory, updated annually, that provides a variety of information on public schools throughout the United States, including a listing of all public schools with names and addresses. Available on data base in the Lockheed DIALOG information retrieval system, which can be accessed through terminals in many university or other major libraries.

U.S. Reports   Or U.S., as abbreviated. See UNITED STATES REPORTS.

useful life   The normal expected operating life of a fixed asset for a particular organization. For example, the useful life of a school bus (which may differ between two school districts). Determination of an asset's useful life is necessary for determining depreciation expense. See also:
ASSETS
DEPRECIATION
SALVAGE VALUE

user charges/user fees   Specific sums that users or consumers of a government service pay in order to receive that service. For example, a homeowner's water bill, if based upon usage, would be a user charge.
See Bruce A. Weber, "User Charges, Property Taxes, and Population Growth: The Distributional Implications of Alternative Municipal Financing Strategies," *State and Local Government Review* (January 1981).

V

vaccination program A program to require the immunization of all schoolchildren to control the spread of certain communicable diseases, most commonly, smallpox, diphtheria, pertussis (whooping cough), tetanus, rubella, and polio.

valedictorian A student who ranks highest in a high school graduating class and who frequently is asked to give a speech at graduation exercises. Compare to SALUTATORIAN.

validation The process of investigation by which the validity of the use of a particular type of test is estimated. What is important here is to identify an ambiguity in the term "to validate" that is responsible for much confusion in the area of employment testing. To validate in ordinary language may mean to mark with an indication of official approval; in this sense, it is also possible to "invalidate" or to indicate official disapproval. In the technical vocabulary of employment testing, to validate is to investigate, to conduct research. Thus, in validating a test (more properly, in validating a use of a test), one is conducting an inquiry. In this context, the term "invalidating" has no meaning at all.

See Douglas D. Baker and David E. Terpstra, "Employee Selection: Must Every Job Test Be Validated?" *Personnel Journal* (August 1982).

validity The extent to which a device measures what it purports to measure.

validity coefficient 1. A correlation coefficient that estimates the relationship between scores on a test (or test battery) and the criterion. 2. A correlation coefficient that estimates the relation between any measurement device and the criterion.

***Valley Forge Christian College v. Americans United for Separation of Church and State* 70 L.Ed. 2nd 700 (1982)** The Supreme Court case that held that a taxpayers' organization dedicated to separation of church and state was without standing to challenge "no-cost transfer of surplus" U.S. property to religious educational institutions.

valuation The process of reducing measurements that are made on different scales to a common base (for example, dollars). Valuation involves establishing and making trade-offs among multiple objectives. The valuation of benefits should not be confused with the quantitative estimates of benefits. For example, it is one thing to estimate the number of lives saved by a program, but it is another matter to place a dollar value on lives saved—and then make a funding value judgment among several programs, all of which save lives.

value 1. The act of describing anything in terms of money. 2. The measure of a thing in terms of money.

values clarification A process that may be used in schools to help students learn to make choices from alternative options based on individual belief systems and consideration of the consequences of choosing particular options. *See* Leon J. Petty, *Reducing Racial Tension in the Schools Through Values Clarification* (Silver Spring, Md.: Universal Ministries, 1981).

values education A variety of school curricula that focuses on basic human values such as making choices, self-respect and personal/cultural dignity. There has been considerable societal controversy and backlash regarding this perceived practice of teaching "morals" in school. *See* Rod Farmer, "Values Education: An Argument for the Defense," *The Educational Forum* (Fall 1987).

vandalism Destruction of or damage to school property or other public or private property. *See* Michael D. Casserly, Scott A. Bass, and John R. Garrett, *School Vandalism: Strategies for Prevention* (Lexington, Mass.: Lexington Books, 1980).

variable In educational research, any entity that can vary. An "independent" variable is one that the researcher manipulates, e.g., a type of instructional program. A "dependent" variable is one that changes in consequence with changes in the independent variable— e.g., and continuing as above, outcome performance on the skill being taught.

variable annuity Also called variable insurance policy. Annuity (or insurance policy) with payments that depend on the income generated by particular investments. *See also* ANNUITY.

variance A statistical measure of the variability of a set of scores, from the mean, computed for the set.

VCR Video cassette recorder. *See* VIDEO RECORDING.

verbotonal method An approach to teaching deaf or hearing-impaired students that emphasizes the use of whatever specific residual hearing the student has to assist the student in learning to understand and produce spoken language.

vesting Granting an employee the right to a pension at normal retirement age even if the employee leaves the organization before the age of normal retirement. Accumulated benefits are "vested" when employees have the nonforfeitable right to receive benefits at retirement, even if they should leave the job before retirement age. Benefits may be partially or fully vested.

veteran A person who served on active duty as a member of the active Armed Forces of the United States and was discharged or released therefrom under conditions other than dishonorable. (National Guard personnel and reservists called to active duty for a limited period—for civil disturbances, disasters, or training—are not considered veterans under this definition.)

veterans' dependents' educational assistance program Provisions (in chapter 35, title 38, U.S. Code) for education and other benefits for spouses, widows, widowers, and children of veterans who died or are totally disabled because of service-connected disabilities, or who are prisoners of war or missing in action for more than 90 days.

veterans preference The concept that dates from 1865, when Congress, toward the end of the Civil War, affirmed that "persons honorably discharged from the military or naval service by reason of disability resulting from wounds or sickness incurred in the line of duty, shall be preferred for appointments to civil offices, provided they are found to possess the business capacity necessary for the proper discharge of the duties of such offices." The 1865 law was superseded in 1919, when preference was extended to all "honorably discharged" veterans, their widows, and wives of disabled veterans. The Veterans Preference Act of 1944 expanded the scope of veterans preference by providing for a five-point bonus on federal examination scores for all honorably separated veterans (except for those with a service-connected disability, who are entitled to a 10-point bonus). Veterans also receive other advantages in federal employment (such as protection against arbitrary dismissal and preference in the event of a reduction-in-force).

All states and many other jurisdictions have veterans preference laws of varying intensity. New Jersey, an extreme example, offers veterans absolute preference; if a veteran passes an entrance examination, he or she must be hired (no matter what the score) before nonveterans can be hired. Veterans competing with each other are rank ordered, and all disabled veterans receive preference over other veterans. Veterans preference laws have been criticized because they have allegedly made it difficult for government agencies to hire and promote more women and minorities.

See Charles E. Davis, "A Survey of Veterans' Preference Legislation in the States," *State Government* (Autumn 1980); Charles E. Davis, "Veterans' Preference and Civil Service Employment: Issues and Policy Implications," *Review of Public Personnel Administration* (Fall 1982); and Gregory B. Lewis and Mark A. Emmert, "Who Pays for Veterans' Preference?" *Administration and Society* (November 1984).

See also PERSONNEL ADMINISTRATOR OF MASSACHUSETTS V. FEENEY.

veterans' vocational rehabilitation program   Provisions (in chapter 31, title 38, U.S. Code) for vocational rehabilitation for service-disabled veterans who served in the U.S. Armed Forces, were discharged under conditions other than dishonorable, and are in need of such rehabilitation because of the handicap of their service-connected disabilities.

vicarious learning   Learning through the experiences of others.

video recording   The recording of both a visual image and sound on magnetic tape, more recently in cassette format. Video recording and playback are media frequently used in education, both as a means to disseminate information and as a self-teaching tool for teachers to allow them to observe their own teaching interactions in retrospect.

Vineland Social Maturity Scale   A commonly used test that is administered by interview, usually with a parent or other third party, to assess an individual's social competence in areas of self-help skills, communication, locomotion and socialization. The scale is referenced for ages birth to adult. It is published by:
American Guidance, Inc.
Publisher's Building
Circle Pines, MN 55014

visiting teacher   A person who visits pupils and parents in the home, assisting the school and the home in solving the personal adjustment problems of pupils. *See also* SOCIAL WORK.

VISTA   *See* VOLUNTEERS IN SERVICE TO AMERICA.

visual discrimination   Essential to successfully learning to read, the ability to recognize differences among such forms as letters and words. Visual discrimination exercises are frequently used as a part of "pre-reading" instruction, and visual discrimination difficulties are sometimes cited as a contributing factor in student reading failure.

visual handicap   An impairment in vision that is sufficiently severe to adversely affect an individual's performance. A person identified as having a visual handicap may be referred to as partially seeing or blind, according to the nature and severity of his handicap. *See* Berthold Lowenfeld, ed., *The Visually Handicapped Child in School* (New York: John Day, 1973); and Kenneth A. Hanninen, *Teaching the Visually Handicapped* (Columbus, Ohio: Charles E. Merrill, 1975).

VMI (Visual-Motor Integration) *See* DEVELOPMENTAL TEST OF VISUAL-MOTOR INTEGRATION.

vocational clusters   1. A group or family of jobs or occupations with rather closely related requirements for employment. 2. The organization of vocational education courses so that the students in the program can be made employable in a number of related jobs and industries.

vocational counseling   Any professional assistance given to an individual preparing to enter the workforce concerning the choice of occupation. For an historical and classic treatise, *see* John M. Brewer et al., *History of Vocational Guidance: Origins and Early Development* (New York: Harper, 1942).

vocational course   A course approved under state plan requirements for vocational and technical education.

vocational education   Curriculum designed to prepare students for employability in an occupation that does not require a college degree. *See* Gordon G. McMahon, *Curriculum Development in Trade and Industrial and Technical Education* (Columbus, Ohio: Charles E. Merrill, 1972); and John F. Thompson, *Foundations of Vocational Education: Societal and Philosophical Concepts* (Englewood Cliffs, N.J.: Prentice-Hall, 1973).

Vocational Education Act Amendments of 1984   *See* CARL D. PERKINS VOCATIONAL EDUCATION ACT.

Vocational Education Act of 1963   The federal statute that authorized federal grants to states to assist them to maintain, extend, and improve existing programs of vocational education; to develop new programs of vocational education; and to provide part-time employment for youths who need the earnings from such employment to continue their vocational training on a full-time basis. *See also* SMITH-HUGHES ACT.

vocational habilitation   The development of people with handicaps to the fullest physical, mental, social, vocational, and economic usefulness of which they are capable. *See also* VOCATIONAL REHABILITATION.

vocational maturity   A term premised upon the belief that vocational behavior is a developmental process, which implies a comparison of an individual's chronological and vocational ages. For a model of vocational maturity, *see* John O. Crites, "Career Development Processes: A Model of Vocational Maturity," in Edwin Herr, ed., *Vocational Guidance and Human Development* (Boston: Houghton Mifflin, 1974).

vocational maturity quotient   Ratio of vocational maturity to chronological age.

vocational or trade high school   A secondary school that is separately organized, under a principal, for the purpose of offering training in one or more skilled or semiskilled trades or occupations—whether such a school is federally aided or not. Departments of other types of high schools, which offer commercial, agricultural, home economics, industrial arts, and other applied art courses, would not be considered as separately organized under the direction and management of an administrator (such as a principal).

vocational psychology   Scientific study of vocational behavior and development that grew out of the practice of vocational guidance.

vocational rehabilitation   The restoration of people with handicaps to the fullest physical, mental, social, vocational, and economic usefulness of which they are capable. See also VOCATIONAL HABILITATION.

vocational and/or technical school   A school that is separately organized under the direction and management of an administrator (such as a principal) for the primary purpose of offering education and training in one or more semiskilled, skilled, or technical occupations.

vocational training   Formal preparation for a particular business or trade. See Manuel Zymelman, *The Economic Evaluation of Vocational Training Programs* (Baltimore: Johns Hopkins University Press, 1976).

vocational-technical education   Education in one or more semiskilled, skilled, or technical occupations, provided by a school that is separately organized under the direction and management of an administrator (such as a principal). For a critical analysis of the history and outcomes of vocational education, see Harvey Kantor and David B. Tyack, eds., *Work, Youth and Schooling: Historical Perspective on Vocationalism in American Education* (Stanford: Stanford University Press, 1982).

voluntary arbitration   Arbitration agreed to by two parties in the absence of any legal or contractual requirement.

voluntary bargaining items   Those items over which collective bargaining is neither mandatory nor legal.

voluntary employees' beneficiary association   Voluntary association of employees that pays life, sickness, accident, or other benefits to its members or their beneficiaries. Voluntary employees' beneficiary associations may qualify for tax-exempt status under IRS Code 501(c)(9).

voluntary organization   An organization that depends upon voluntary actions and contributions to support its operations.

voluntary sector   The "third sector," with the public and private sectors as the first two. The voluntary sector is generally considered to consist of nonprofit organizations which pursue social welfare goals. See also NONPROFIT ORGANIZATION and THIRD SECTOR.

voluntary termination   The situation existing when a staff member, acting on his or her own initiative, elects to separate from employment with the school system.

voluntary transfer   The transfer of a teacher or other staff person from one school building to another within the same school district, at the request, or with the cooperation, of the employee.

volunteer   Person who provides a service without compulsion or requirement and, typically, without compensation. However, with the growth of the voluntary sector the definition of a volunteer appears to be changing. For example, most volunteer ambulance services now pay volunteers for their standby time and/or for making runs. These paid persons still are called volunteers or paid volunteers so long as their work with the ambulance service is not their primary source of income.

volunteered services   Services provided to a school without compensation to the provider.

Volunteers in Service to America

Or VISTA, "the domestic Peace Corps." A federal program, administered by ACTION, that deploys volunteers into low-income areas to teach self-improvement and self-help skills.

VISTA
806 Connecticut Avenue, N.W.
Washington, DC 20525
(202) 634-9445

voting   The exercise of the right of suffrage. This is the only means by which most citizens can participate in political decision-making. See Stanley Kelley, Jr., and Thad W. Mirer, "The Simple Act of Voting," *American Political Science Review* (June 1974); and Elizabeth Sanders, "On the Costs, Utilities, and Simple Joys of Voting," *Journal of Politics* (August 1980).

voting residence   A voter's domicile, generally. However, the voting residence of an American who is voting pursuant to the Overseas Citizens Voting Rights Act, and no longer domiciled in the United States, will be the place where the voter was last domiciled immediately prior to departure from the United States.

Voting Rights Act of 1965

The law that extended the elective franchise to millions of once-excluded minority group individuals, arguably the most important civil rights legislation *ever* passed (with the possible exception of the Civil Rights Act of 1964). At the heart of the Voting Rights Act is the Section 4 triggering formula, providing for automatic coverage of jurisdictions with low minority electoral participation, and the section 5 requirement of preclearance of all voting law changes (by such jurisdictions) with the Attorney General or the Federal District Court for the District of Columbia. Additionally, other sections authorize the appointment of federal examiners to enforce the right to vote guaranteed by the 15th Amendment, and permit federal observers to attend elections in order to monitor the election process. The act, which was amended in 1970, 1975, and 1982, also incorporates a permanent ban on the use of literacy tests and imposes bilingual election requirements on many covered jurisdictions. The constitutionality of the act was upheld by the Supreme Court in *South Carolina v. Katzenbach*, 383 U.S. 301 (1966).

See Howard D. Neighbor, "The Voting Rights Act Old and New: A Forecast of Political Maturity," *National Civic Review* (October 1983); Alan Howard and Bruce Howard, "The Dilemma of the Voting Rights Act—Recognizing the Emerging Political Equality Norm," *Columbia Law Review* (November 1983); and Lorn S. Foster, ed., *The Voting Rights Act: Consequences and Implications* (New York: Praeger, 1985).

voucher system   1. A government program that issues redeemable vouchers to eligible citizens so that they can use them to purchase services on the open market. For example, housing vouchers have been suggested as an alternative to public housing and education vouchers have been suggested as a means of encouraging the further development of private, precollegiate education.

See R. Freeman Butts, "Educational Vouchers: The Private Pursuit of the Public Purse," *Phi Delta Kappan* (September 1979); and Shawn Timothy

Newman, "Education Vouchers and Tuition Tax Credits: In Search of Viable Public Aid to Private Education," *Journal of Legislation* (Winter 1983).

2. A bookkeeping system that calls for the preparation of vouchers for transactions involving payments and for the recording of such vouchers in a special book or original entry known as a voucher register in the order in which payment is approved.

vouchers payable   Liabilities for goods and services received as evidenced by vouchers that have been preaudited and approved for payment but that have not been paid.

W

WAIS *See* WECHSLER ADULT IN-TELLIGENCE SCALE.

Waldorf Education *See* STEINER, RUDOLPH.

Wallas v. Jaffree 472 U.S. 38 (1985) The Supreme Court decision that reaffirmed the separation of church and state and the unconstitutionality of prayer in school by striking down an Alabama law that authorized a daily "moment of silence" in public schools for "meditation or voluntary prayer."

ward 1. A subdivision of a city often used as a legislative district for city council elections, as an administrative division for public services, or as a unit for the organization of political parties. Wards are often further divided into precincts. 2. A minor who is placed under the jurisdiction of a guardian or of a court.

warrant 1. In criminal proceedings a writ issued by a judge that directs a law enforcement officer to do something; for example, a search warrant or an arrest warrant. Warrants are required because of the Fourth Amendment's assertion that the people be free from unreasonable searches and seizures. Compare to probable cause. 2. A short-term obligation issued by a government in anticipation of revenue. The instrument (a draft much like a check), when presented to a disbursing officer, such as a bank, is payable only upon acceptance by the issuing jurisdiction (such as a school district). Warrants may be made payable on demand or at some time in the future. Local governments, in particular, have used delayed payment of warrants as a way to protect cash flow.

warrant interest Interest paid on registered warrants. *See also* REGISTERED WARRANT.

warrants payable Warrants issued by the school board but not yet signed by the treasurer.

Washington, Booker T. (1856-1915) The preeminent American black educator of his time. While born into slavery, he would later found and head Tuskegee Institute. *See* Booker T. Washington, *Up From Slavery: An Autobiography* (Cambridge, Mass.: Houghton Mifflin, 1901); and Louis R. Harlan, *Booker T. Washington: The Making of a Black Leader, 1856-1901* (New York: Oxford University Press, 1972).

Watson, John B. (1878-1958) One of the founders of the field of behaviorism. Unlike B.F. Skinner, some of his research involved children, especially with regard to their acquisition of emotions (from a behavioral perspective).

Webster, Noah (1728-1843) The author of the first substantial dictionary published in the United States, *An American Dictionary of the English Language* (first published in 1828). Webster's dictionary is largely responsible for the standardization of American spelling.
See Harry R. Warfel, *Noah Webster: Schoolmaster to America* (New York: Macmillan, 1936); and John S. Morgan, *Noah Webster* (New York: Mason, Charter, 1975).

Wechsler Adult Intelligence Scale (WAIS) An individually administered test of intelligence that has been

standardized for individuals above the age of 16. This grouping of tests yields either a verbal IQ, a performance IQ, or a full-scale IQ score. It is published by:
The Psychological Corporation
555 Academic Court
San Antonio, TX 78204

Wechsler Bellevue Intelligence Scale
The forerunner of the Wechsler Adult Intelligence Scale (WAIS) and the Wechsler Intelligence Scale for Children (WISC), first published in 1939 to assess the intelligence of adults. David Wechsler was the developer of the test, which was meant to be used at New York's Bellevue Hospital.
See David Wechsler, *The Measuring of Adult Intelligence*, 3rd ed. (Baltimore: Williams and Wilkins, 1944); and Joseph D. Matarazzo, *Wechsler's Measurement and Appraisal of Adult Intelligence* (Baltimore: Williams and Wilkins, 1972).

Wechsler Intelligence Scale for Children-Revised (WISC-R)
The most commonly used, individually-administered test standardized for children ages six to 17 years. The scale has 10 sub-tests that are divided into verbal items and performance items, which yield a verbal IQ, a performance IQ, and a full-scale IQ. It is published by:
The Psychological Corporation
555 Academic Court
San Antonio, TX 78204
See A.S. Kaufman, *Intelligent Testing With The WISC-R* (New York: John Wiley, 1979).

Wechsler Preschool and Primary Scale of Intelligence (WPPSI)
An individually-administered test of intelligence standardized for children ages four to 6 1/2 years. It was developed in 1967 as a downward revision of the Wechsler Intelligence Scale for Children (WISC). It is published by:

The Psychological Corporation
555 Academic Court
San Antonio, TX 78204

welfare　The system for providing goods and/or services to financially indigent or physically incapacitated persons or other families, for the purpose of sustaining a minimal lifestyle for an indeterminate period. Eligibility requirements are established by law or ordinance at the funding source, which may be either local, state, or federal.

welfare activities　1. Providing for personal needs of indigent persons. 2. Providing services in connection with disaster relief.

welfare agencies　Governmental or private organizations having the purpose of aiding poor and disadvantaged individuals.

white academies　1. Racially segregated, white-only private schools that proliferated in Southern states following the 1954 *Brown v. Board of Education* Supreme Court decision requiring racial integration in public schools. 2. Any private elementary or secondary school that has no (or only token) minority representation in its student body.

white flight　1. A common response to public school busing to achieve school racial integration; white citizens, if they can afford it, tend to move out of the central city into the suburbs so that their children can attend neighborhood schools. White flight most often occurs when it is perceived that the schools are turning overwhelmingly minority and when bus rides are deemed excessively long.
See Diane Ravitch, "Social Science and Social Policy: The 'White Flight' Controversy," *Public Interest* (Spring

1978); and William H. Frey, "Central City White Flight: Racial and Nonracial Causes," *American Sociological Review* (June 1979).

2. More recently, as in the case of Miami, there has been a backlash from English-speaking citizens as they move away from an area that has become increasingly Hispanic in language and culture.

whole language   A generic term for a number of approaches to teaching language—primarily reading and writing—that frame the instruction in a social, communicative context. For a highly readable introduction to the whole language movement, *see* Ken Goodman, *What's Whole in Whole Language* (Portsmouth, N.H.: Heinemann, 1986). For specific curricular planning, *see* Judith M. Newman, ed., *Whole Language: Theory in Use* (Portsmouth, N.H.: Heinemann, 1986).

whole life insurance   Also called straight life insurance and ordinary life insurance. Insurance policy that provides protection for the insured person's entire life, usually for a flat yearly premium. While the face value of a whole life policy will be paid only at death, a "cash surrender value" builds up, and the insured person may borrow against it at very favorable rates.

Wide Range Achievement Test (WRAT)   An individually-administered, norm-referenced test of academic achievement that measures performance in reading, spelling, and arithmetic at two levels, below 12 years of age and over age 12. It is published by:

Jastak Associates, Inc.
1526 Gilpin Avenue
Wilmington, Delaware 19806

wildcat strike   Also called unauthorized strike and outlaw strike. A work stoppage not sanctioned by union leadership and usually contrary to an existing labor contract. Unless it can be shown that unfair employer practices were the direct cause of the wildcat strike, the union could be liable for damages in a breach of contract suit by management.

Willard, Emma (1787-1870)   An early, active proponent of improved and equal education for women. *See* Alma Lutz, *Emma Willard: Pioneer Educator of American Women* (Boston: Beacon Press, 1964).

Winnetka Plan   A divided elementary curriculum, first implemented in the Winnetka, Illinois, schools in 1919, that differentiated basic skills instruction, taught on an individualized basis, from cultural and creative learning, which were taught in a larger group setting. *See* Carleton Washburn and Sidney P. Marland, Jr., *Winnetka: The History and Significance of an Educational Experiment* (Englewood, N.J.: Prentice-Hall, 1963).

WISC-R   *See* WECHSLER INTELLIGENCE SCALE FOR CHILDREN-REVISED.

withdrawal   1. An individual who has withdrawn from membership in a class, grade, or school by transferring, by completing school work, by dropping out, or because of death. 2. The psychophysiological experience upon ceasing the use of addictive drugs.

withdrawing   Leaving a class, grade, or school by transferring, by completing school work, by dropping out, or because of death. The date of withdrawal from membership is the first day after the date of the last day of membership, if known; otherwise, the date of withdrawal is considered to be the date on which it becomes known officially that the pupil has left.

withholding The process of deducting from an individual's salary or wage payment an amount, specified by law or regulation and representing the estimated federal or state income tax of the individual, that the employer must pay to the taxing authority.

women's liberation movement The contemporary social, economic, and political efforts of women to achieve equality with men in all aspects of life. The movement was the major force behind the futile effort to get the Equal Rights Amendment ratified. The origins of the American women's liberation movement are often traced back to a letter that Abigail Adams (1744-1818) wrote in 1776 to her husband, the future president, John Adams, about American independence:

> I long to hear that you have declared an independency. And in the new code of laws which I suppose it will be necessary for you to make, I desire you would remember the ladies, and be more generous and favorable to them than your ancestors . . . If particular care and attention is not paid to the ladies, we are determined to foment a rebellion and will not hold ourselves bound by any laws in which we have no voice or representation.

See Jo Freeman, "The Origins of the Women's Liberation Movement," *The American Journal of Sociology* (January 1973); Barbara Deckard Sinclair, *The Women's Movement*, 3rd ed. (New York: Harper & Row, 1983); and Sylvia Ann Hewlett, *A Lesser Life: The Myth of Women's Liberation in America* (New York: Morrow, 1986).

women's studies Courses that emphasize the contributions to society (economic, cultural, and academic) made by women.

Wood v. Strickland 420 U.S. 308 (1975) The Supreme Court ruling creating new standards for the immunity of public employees from civil suits for damages. The Court held that a school board member (and by implication other public employees) is not immune from liability for damages "if he knew or reasonably should have known that the action he took within his sphere of official responsibility would violate the constitutional rights of the students affected, or if he took the action with the malicious intention to cause a deprivation of constitutional rights or other injury to the student."

See David H. Rosenbloom, "Public Administrators' Official Immunity and the Supreme Court: Developments During the 1970s," *Public Administration Review* (March-April 1980). For a more recent interpretation, *see* HARLOW V. FITZGERALD.

Woodcock Reading Mastery Tests An individually-administered battery of tests that measure specific skill development in five areas of reading: letter identification, word attack, word identification, word comprehension, and passage comprehension. The tests are appropriate for students in grades kindergarten to 12. It is published by:

American Guidance Service, Inc.
Publisher's Building
Circle Pines, MN 55015

Woodcock-Johnson Psychoeducational Battery A commonly used, individually-administered, comprehensive diagnostic and evaluation instrument that has 27 subtests divided into three areas: (1) tests of cognitive ability; (2) tests of achievement; and (3) tests of interest level. It is published by:

Teaching Resources Corporation
100 Boylston Street
Boston, MA 02116

word lists Vocabulary lists, such as Thorndike's, Gates', or Dolch's, that have been used to direct reading instruction programs. Though originally published generations ago, these lists continue to influence elementary reading programs.

See Edward L. Thorndike, *A Teacher's Workbook of 20,000 Words* (New York: Bureau of Publications, Teacher's College, Columbia University, 1926); Arthur I. Gates, *A Reading Vocabulary for the Primary Grades* (New York: Bureau of Publications, Teachers College, Columbia University, 1935); and Edward L. Dolch, *Methods in Reading* (Champaign, Ill.: Garrard, 1955).

word-association   A psychological testing procedure that requires the subject to respond to a stimulus word with another word that seems to be associated with the stimulus.

word-attack skills   Methods that students can be taught to use to assist them in deciphering and understanding new and unfamiliar words. Specific methods may include structural analysis, phonic analysis or, content analysis.

work alienation   A sense of powerlessness in one's job, manifested by an absence of initiative and a feeling of not having much influence on the way the organization is run. *See also* TEACHER BURNOUT. For a discussion of this concept in relation to teachers, *see* Norman Benson and Patricia Malone, "Teachers' Beliefs about Shared Decision Making and Work Alienation," *Education* (Spring 1987).

work in progress   A term limited to a building that is under contract for construction but has not been finally accepted by the school district. A building under construction by school district employees, but which has not been completed, is also classified as work in progress.

work order   A written order authorizing and directing the performance of a certain task, issued to the person who is to direct the work. Among the information shown on the order are the nature and location of the job, specifications of the work to be performed, and a job number that is referred to in reporting the amount of labor, material, and equipment used.

work plan chart   See PROJECT CONTROL CHART.

work to rule   A work slowdown in which all of the formal work rules are so scrupulously obeyed that productivity suffers considerably. Those working to rule seek to place pressure on management without losing pay by going on strike. Work-to-rule protests are particularly popular in the public sector where most formal strikes are illegal.

workbook   An exercise book used to provide students with extra practice in a subject.

workers' compensation   Industrial accident insurance (also known as workmen's compensation) designed to provide cash benefits and medical care when a worker is injured on the job and monetary payments to survivors if a worker is killed on the job. This was the first form of social insurance to develop widely in the United States. There are now 54 different workers' compensation programs in operation. Each of the 50 states and Puerto Rico has its own program. In addition, there are three federal workers' compensation programs, covering federal government and private employees in the District of Columbia, and longshoremen and harbor workers throughout the country.

Before the passage of workmens' compensation laws, an injured employee ordinarily had to file suit against his or her employer and prove that the injury was due to the employer's negligence in order to recover damages. The enactment of the first workmens' compensation laws early in this century introduced the principle that a worker incurring an occupational injury would be compensated regardless of fault or blame in the accident and with a minimum of delay and legal formality. In turn, the employer's liability was limited, because workmens' compensation benefits became the exclusive remedy for work-related injuries.

See Joel A. Thompson, "Outputs and Outcomes of State Workmen's Compensation Laws," *Journal of Politics* (November 1981); and James R. Chelius, "The Influence of Workers' Compensation on Safety Incentives," *Industrial and Labor Relations Review* (January 1982).

workload   A measure denoting the work performed by school employees during the regular school hours.

worksheet   An activity or exercise page given to students for drill purposes or extra practice in a subject. Some educational reformers claim that primary students are expected to do too many worksheets and too little thinking.

workshop   1. A form of educational endeavor designed to bring people with common interests and concerns together for a short period of time to learn new knowledge and skills. 2. A space in an educational setting that is specially equipped for technical teaching.

work-study program   A school program designed to provide employment for students who can not continue in school without the financial support provided through a job. The employment may or may not be curriculum related. (Cooperative programs provide work experiences specifically related to the student's instructional program. The student's on-the-job training is an integral part of his total school curriculum.)

world language   1. An existing language that is spoken and understood by persons throughout the world; examples include English, Spanish, and French. 2. An artificial language specially created so that all individuals can use it. The most commonly known of these is Esperanto.

WOTS-UP analysis   Acronym for weakness, opportunities, threats, and strengths analysis; an analysis that seeks to determine how an organization should best cope with its environment. A WOTS-UP analysis usually is prepared as part of a strategic plan. *See also* PLANNING.

WPPSI   *See* WECHSLER PRESCHOOL AND PRIMARY SCALE OF INTELLIGENCE.

Wright v. Regan (49 A.F.T.R. 2d 82-757 [D.C. Cir. 1982])   Landmark 1982 decision by the U.S. Circuit Court of Appeals for Washington, D.C., that prohibited the United States government from granting tax-exempt status to any private schools that practice racial discrimination. The case involved Bob Jones University and the Goldsboro Christian School. The case was appealed to and upheld by the U.S. Supreme Court. *See also* BOB JONES UNIVERSITY V. SIMON *and* GREEN V. CONNALLY.

Wygant v. Jackson Board of Education 90 L. Ed. 2nd 260 (1986)   The Supreme Court case that held that white teachers could not be laid off in order to preserve the jobs of minority group members. The Court held that while "societal discrimination" was not sufficient reason for racially discriminatory lay offs, such lay offs might be permissible if they were a part of a "narrowly tailored" remedy for past patterns of discrimination by the employer. The Court was careful to distinguish between racially based layoffs and racially conscious hiring. The former imposes a greater burden on the individual excluded. *See also*:

Local 28 of the Sheet Metal Workers v. EEOC, 418 U.S. 106 S.CT. 3019 (1986).

Local 93, International Association of Firefighters v. City of Cleveland, 478 U.S. 106 S.CT., 3063 (1986).

United States v. Paradise, 480 U.S. 107 S.CT., 1053 (1987).

Johnson v. Transportation Agency v. Santa Clara County, California, 480 U.S. 107 S.CT. 1442 (1987).

Y

Yarris v. Special School District of St. Louis County 558 F.Supp. 545 (E.D. Mo. 1983)   A case that established precedent for the provision of extended school year services for students who are handicapped. The court ruled that an appropriate education program necessitates the provision of extended year services when a severely handicapped student will regress significantly over the summer months. While this ruling does not mandate summer programs, it requires that school districts do not have policies that would preclude such services.

yearbook   Commonly refers to an annual student publication that includes student portraits, both individual and group, and that records photographically events of the given academic year. Some schools are using video yearbooks in addition to printed ones.

See N.S. Patterson, *Yearbook Planning, Editing, and Production* (Ames: Iowa State University Press, 1976).

year-round school   A school program that operates on a 12-month basis but that divides the year into time blocks so that students continue to attend the same number of total days. Adopted by many schools and school districts for economic reasons to ensure maximum utilization of school facilities, especially when the student body attends at staggered intervals. For example, students may attend school for nine weeks and then be on vacation for three weeks and alternate this schedule throughout the year. *See* Doris M. Ross, *A Legislator's Guide to the Year Round School* (Boulder, Colo.: Education Commission of the States, 1975).

Z

ZBB   *See* ZERO-BASED BUDGETING.

zero reject   The concept that *no* person, specifically handicapped children, will be denied access to public education.

zero based budgeting (ZBB)   A budgeting process that is first and foremost a rejection of the incremental decision-making model of budgeting. It demands a rejustification of the entire budget submission (i.e., from ground zero) rather than accepting previous budgeting decisions and focusing on the margin of change from year-to-year.

See Peter A. Phyrr, "The Zero-Based Approach to Government Budgeting," *Public Administration Review* (January/February 1977); and Charles E. Hill, "Zero-Based Budgeting: A Practical Application," *Governmental Finance* (March 1983).

Zorach v. Clauson 343 U.S. 306 (1952)   A Supreme Court case that upheld a New York law that allowed public schools to release students for religious instruction that took place outside of public school facilities and required no public financial support. Contrast with the MCCOLLUM CASE in Illinois, four years earlier.